D1200599

HANDBOOK OF AGRICULTURAL ECONOMICS
VOLUME 2A

HANDBOOKS IN ECONOMICS

18

Series Editors

KENNETH J. ARROW
MICHAEL D. INTRILIGATOR

ELSEVIER

AMSTERDAM · BOSTON · LONDON · NEW YORK · OXFORD · PARIS
SAN DIEGO · SAN FRANCISCO · SINGAPORE · SYDNEY · TOKYO

HANDBOOK OF AGRICULTURAL ECONOMICS

VOLUME 2A
AGRICULTURE
AND ITS EXTERNAL LINKAGES

Edited by

BRUCE L. GARDNER
University of Maryland, College Park

and

GORDON C. RAUSSER
University of California, Berkeley

N·H

2002

ELSEVIER

AMSTERDAM · BOSTON · LONDON · NEW YORK · OXFORD · PARIS
SAN DIEGO · SAN FRANCISCO · SINGAPORE · SYDNEY · TOKYO

ELSEVIER SCIENCE B.V.
Sara Burgerhartstraat 25
P.O. Box 211, 1000 AE Amsterdam, The Netherlands

© 2002 Elsevier Science B.V. All rights reserved

This work is protected under copyright by Elsevier Science, and the following terms and conditions apply to its use:

Photocopying
Single photocopies of single chapters may be made for personal use as allowed by national copyright laws. Permission of the Publisher and payment of a fee is required for all other photocopying, including multiple or systematic copying, copying for advertising or promotional purposes, resale, and all forms of document delivery. Special rates are available for educational institutions that wish to make photocopies for non-profit educational classroom use.

Permissions may be sought directly from Elsevier Science via their homepage (http://www.elsevier.com) by selecting 'Customer support' and then 'Permissions'. Alternatively you can send an e-mail to: permissions@elsevier.com, or fax to: (+44) 1865 853333.

In the USA, users may clear permissions and make payments through the Copyright Clearance Center, Inc., 222 Rosewood Drive, Danvers, MA 01923, USA; phone: (+1) (978) 7508400, fax: (+1) (978) 7504744, and in the UK through the Copyright Licensing Agency Rapid Clearance Service (CLARCS), 90 Tottenham Court Road, London W1P 0LP, UK; phone: (+44) 207 631 5555; fax: (+44) 207 631 5500. Other countries may have a local reprographic rights agency for payments.

Derivative Works
Tables of contents may be reproduced for internal circulation, but permission of Elsevier Science is required for external resale or distribution of such material.
Permission of the Publisher is required for all other derivative works, including compilations and translations.

Electronic Storage or Usage
Permission of the Publisher is required to store or use electronically any material contained in this work, including any chapter or part of a chapter.

Except as outlined above, no part of this work may be reproduced, stored in a retrieval system or transmitted in any form or by any means, electronic, mechanical, photocopying, recording or otherwise, without prior written permission of the Publisher.
Address permissions requests to: Elsevier Science Global Rights Department, at the mail, fax and e-mail addresses noted above.

Notice
No responsibility is assumed by the Publisher for any injury and/or damage to persons or property as a matter of products liability, negligence or otherwise, or from any use or operation of any methods, products, instructions or ideas contained in the material herein. Because of rapid advances in the medical sciences, in particular, independent verification of diagnoses and drug dosages should be made.

First edition 2002

Library of Congress Cataloging in Publication Data
A catalog record from the Library of Congress has been applied for.

British Library Cataloguing in Publication Data
A catalogue record from the British Library has been applied for.

ISBN: 0-444-51081-8 (set, comprising vols. 2A & 2B)
ISBN: 0-444-51080-X (vol. 2A)
ISBN: 0-444-51079-6 (vol. 2B)
ISSN: 0169-7218 (Handbooks in Economics Series)

⊗ The paper used in this publication meets the requirements of ANSI/NISO Z39.48-1992 (Permanence of Paper).
Printed in The Netherlands.

INTRODUCTION TO THE SERIES

The aim of the *Handbooks in Economics* series is to produce Handbooks for various branches of economics, each of which is a definitive source, reference, and teaching supplement for use by professional researchers and advanced graduate students. Each Handbook provides self-contained surveys of the current state of a branch of economics in the form of chapters prepared by leading specialists on various aspects of this branch of economics. These surveys summarize not only received results but also newer developments, from recent journal articles and discussion papers. Some original material is also included, but the main goal is to provide comprehensive and accessible surveys. The Handbooks are intended to provide not only useful reference volumes for professional collections but also possible supplementary readings for advanced courses for graduate students in economics.

KENNETH J. ARROW and MICHAEL D. INTRILIGATOR

PUBLISHER'S NOTE

For a complete overview of the Handbooks in Economics Series, please refer to the listing at the end of this volume.

CONTENTS OF THE HANDBOOK

VOLUME 1A

PART 1 – AGRICULTURAL PRODUCTION

VOLUME 2A

VOLUME 2B

PART 5 – AGRICULTURAL AND FOOD POLICY

INTRODUCTION

The subject matter of agricultural economics has both broadened and deepened in recent years, and the chapters of this Handbook present the most exciting and innovative work being done today. The field originated early in the twentieth century with a focus on farm management and commodity markets, but has since moved far into analysis of issues in food, resources, international trade, and linkages between agriculture and the rest of the economy. In the process agricultural economists have been pioneering users of developments in economic theory and econometrics. Moreover, in the process of intense focus on problems of economic science that are central to agriculture – market expectations, behavior under uncertainty, multimarket relationships for both products and factors, the economics of research and technology adoption, and public goods and property issues associated with issues like nonpoint pollution and innovations in biotechnology – agricultural economists have developed methods of empirical investigation that have been taken up in other fields.

The chapters are organized into five parts, contained in two volumes. Volume 1 contains Part 1, "Agricultural Production", and Part 2, "Marketing, Distribution and Consumers". These two parts include much of the traditional scope of agricultural economics, emphasizing advances in both theory and empirical application of recent years. Volume 2 consists of three parts: "Agriculture, Natural Resources and the Environment", "Agriculture in the Macroeconomy", and "Agricultural and Food Policy". Although agricultural economists have always paid attention to these topics, research devoted to them has increased substantially in scope as well as depth in recent years.

A large-scale effort to review and assess the state of knowledge in agricultural economics was previously undertaken by the American Agricultural Economics Association (AAEA), with publication in four volumes from 1977 to 1992.[1] Those earlier survey volumes have strikingly different subject-matter content from that of the present Handbook, especially considering that they described the same field only 20 years ago. The AAEA volumes have extensive coverage of farm management issues, costs of production in agriculture, and estimates of efficiency of marketing firms. In our judgment little in any fundamental way has been added to our knowledge in these areas, and applications have become routine rather than imaginative research. The largest AAEA volume was devoted entirely to agriculture in economic development. This remains a

---

[1] *A Survey of Economics Literature*, Lee Martin, ed., Minneapolis: University of Minnesota Press. Volume 1, Traditional Field of Agricultural Economics (1977); Volume 2, Quantitative Methods in Agricultural Economics (1977); Volume 3, Economics of Welfare, Rural Development, and Natural Resources (1981); Volume 4, Agriculture in Economic Development (1992).

most important topic, but we cover it in only one complete chapter and parts of several others. This reflects in part the integration of work on developing countries with mainstream applied work. For example, our chapters on production economics, expectations, and risk management also encompass applications to agriculture in developing economies.

That integration points to another gradual but notable change in agricultural economists' research. The AAEA surveys had most of the chapters of one volume devoted to quantitative methods. We do not have any separate methodological chapters. In contrast, we have several chapters with substantial development of economic theory. This reflects an evolution in the research priorities of leading agricultural economists who, following the earlier work of Nerlove on supply and Griliches on technological change, are working at the theoretical frontiers and simultaneously undertaking empirical work – not just purveying new theories to their more "applied" colleagues.

As its title indicates, the AAEA volumes were surveys of literature, and aimed at completeness of coverage within their subject matter. We asked our authors to be selective, to focus on what they saw as the main contributions to the area they covered, and to assess the state of knowledge and what remains to be learned. This approach has left some gaps in our coverage, and has given us some chapters that are perhaps more idiosyncratic than is usual for a survey chapter. In order to pull things together at a higher level of aggregation, we commissioned five "synthesis" chapters, one for each of the five parts of the Handbook. And, to provide our own even broader overview, the editors have written closing syntheses of each volume. Because these syntheses provide capsule summaries of each Handbook chapter, we will not present further description of content here.

Although advances in research in agricultural economics are increasingly being made in many countries, our authors and coverage of applied topics is heavily U.S.-weighted (only six authors work outside of the U.S.: two in Europe, two in Australia, one in Canada, and one in Israel). Of those in the U.S., however, six are economists at the World Bank, an international rather than American institution. Probably in another twenty years or so one will have to become more international to capture the most interesting and exciting developments in the field, but that day has not arrived yet.

Among the many debts we have accrued in the preparation of this Handbook, the most important was Rachael Goodhue. She not only assessed the substance of many chapters, but she persuaded many reviewers and authors alike to complete their assigned responsibilities. Other critical contributors include the dedicated staff who provided support at the University of California, Berkeley, and at the University of Maryland. At Maryland, Liesl Koch served as copy editor and guided the authors' final revisions and preparation of the manuscript with sure judgment and a firm but diplomatic hand, a job best likened to driving a herd of cats. Coordination of correspondence with authors and reviewers was organized and carried out at Berkeley with exemplary efficiency and organizational skill by Jef Samp, Jessica Berkson, and Jennifer Michael, under the direction of Nancy Lewis.

We also want to recognize the comments and suggestions received from 45 reviewers of chapter drafts: Julian Alston, Jock Anderson, Richard Barichello, Eran Beinenbaum, Michael Boehlje, Dan Bromley, Steve Buccola, Allan Buckwell, David Bullock, Michael Caputo, Jean-Paul Chavas, John Connor, Klaus Deininger, Jeffrey Dorfman, Marcel Fafchamps, Gershon Feder, Joe Glauber, Dan Gilligan, Rachael Goodhue, Tom Grennes, Zvi Griliches, Geoff Heal, Eithan Hochman, Matt Holt, Wallace Huffman, D. Gale Johnson, Zvi Lerman, Erik Lichtenberg, Ethan Ligon, Alan Love, Jill McCluskey, Mario Miranda, Arie Oskam, Dick Perrin, Mark Rosegrant, Vern Ruttan, Ed Schuh, Kathleen Segerson, Larry Sjaastad, Spiro Stefanou, Jo Swinnen, Frans van der Zee, Finis Welch, Abner Womack, and Jacob Yaron.

BRUCE GARDNER
GORDON RAUSSER

CONTENTS OF VOLUME 2A

PART 4 – AGRICULTURE IN THE MACROECONOMY

Chapter 26
Applied General Equilibrium Analysis of Agricultural and Resource Policies
THOMAS W. HERTEL

PART 3

AGRICULTURE, NATURAL RESOURCES
AND THE ENVIRONMENT

Chapter 22

THE ECONOMICS OF AGRICULTURE IN DEVELOPING COUNTRIES: THE ROLE OF THE ENVIRONMENT

RAMÓN LÓPEZ

Department of Agricultural and Resource Economics, University of Maryland, College Park, MD

Contents

Handbook of Agricultural Economics, Volume 2, Edited by B. Gardner and G. Rausser
© *2002 Elsevier Science B.V.   All rights reserved*

Abstract

This chapter is concerned with agricultural supply responses in developing countries. Its main emphasis is in explicitly considering the dynamics of the natural resource base (e.g., soil quality, water, etc.) of agriculture as well as the endogenous evolution of rural environmental institutions (e.g., property rights) that may impinge upon agricultural productivity over the long run. The endogenous nature of the natural resource and institutional dynamics is particularly relevant for poor tropical areas where the agricultural and natural resource base is fragile and the rural institutions are both heterogeneous and in process of change. Under those conditions certain government policies can easily have unexpected adverse effects on agricultural productivity and farmers' income.

Keywords

natural resource dynamics, institutions, policies, economic growth

JEL classification: O13

Agricultural production in most developing areas is subject to peculiarities that require significant adaptation of conventional production theory. Considerable progress has been made in this adaptation, particularly over the last two decades. A new paradigm is in the making by incorporating into the analysis at least four features essential to understanding the economics of agriculture in developing countries.

(i) *Factor market interlocking*. The interlocking of factor markets in rural areas is one of the first features to have been recognized in the literature. Though not exclusive to developing countries, it is much more predominant in these countries than in the developed areas [Johnson (1950), Stiglitz (1974), Newbery (1977)].

(ii) *The farm-household*. The view of the farm-household as an entity where production and consumption decisions may be interdependent is not new and goes back to the classical writings of Chayanov (1966). But incorporating this insight into a formal neoclassical framework that yields empirically functional models is relatively new [López (1981, 1984, 1985), Singh, Squire and Strauss (1985), de Janvry, Fafchamps and Sadoulet (1991), Benjamin (1992), Caillavet, Guyomard and Lifren (1994)].

The interdependence of production and consumption decisions (instead of simple recursiveness from production or income to consumption) arises mostly because of incomplete, missing or imperfect markets, a dominant feature of rural areas in less developed countries (LDCs). Incomplete markets and, sometimes, imperfect local markets generate large transaction costs and rationing of certain goods and services, including off-farm work by household members. This, in turn, causes endogenous (shadow) prices for products or factors of production that the household has to provide itself. These endogenous shadow prices become the primary source of interdependence of production and consumption decisions of the farm-household.

The key implication of endogeneity of shadow prices is that to understand farm-households' production responses in LDCs it is essential to consider household wealth and preferences for goods and leisure in addition to the production technology and production behavioral assumptions. Poor and rich households or large and small households do not respond in the same way to price incentives and other sectoral or economy-wide policies.

(iii) *Endogenous and evolving institutions*. Institutions are usually not static anywhere in the world, but they tend to be much more fragile and, in many cases, subject to a more rapid process of change in developing countries than in industrialized countries. While, in analyzing supply responses, assuming a fixed institutional framework for developed countries might be a good approximation, doing the same for developing countries might provide misleading results. Unlike in the case of developed countries, property rights institutions in LDCs are usually not static and rather are in a process of evolution which can be easily and unintentionally affected by agricultural policies [Bardhan (1991)].[1] Similarly, labor, credit, and commodity markets in rural areas are

---

[1] In many areas of sub-Saharan Africa, Latin America, and parts of Asia, private land property coexists with transitional forms reflecting a spontaneous process of privatization, common property, and land under open access [Baland and Platteau (1996)].

still being developed, and policies that could be effective in promoting productivity in a context of complete markets may have little effect or even be inimical, particularly for poor rural households, in a context of institutional fragility.

In analyzing agriculture in LDCs one needs to explicitly consider the specific institutional framework, which, unlike in the case of developed countries, tends to exhibit great heterogeneity across countries and even across regions within a country. Moreover, agricultural policies (and economy-wide policies that indirectly affect the sector) may affect the nature of the process of institutional adjustment which, in turn, could have important effects on agricultural productivity and farm-household income, both through the institutional transitional period and even in the new institutional steady state.

(iv) *The dynamics of the environmental base of agriculture.* Most LDCs are located in tropical or sub-tropical areas of the world where the ecological conditions that support farm-household incomes are more fragile (e.g., soils are chemically poor, physically unstable prone to erosion, and less able to retain nutrients) than those prevailing in temperate areas, where most developed countries are located [Sanchez (1976), Webster and Wilson (1980)]. This fragility imposes restrictions on the pace of intensification and may require major investments to improve the stability and resilience of tropical soils and other natural resources.

Tropical soils are not only fragile but they are also subject to threshold effects [Sanchez (1976)]. That is, if degradation reaches a certain point, the process accelerates and becomes irreversible. At that time the land could be abandoned as farmers decide to search for and deforest other lands. Notice, however, that if farmers are aware of the threshold of irreversible degradation, their investment patterns can be quite peculiar. They may either implement the relatively large investments required at a minimum to prevent triggering such threshold effects, or do nothing at all if uncertainty about property rights is great enough that the return of such an investment is expected to be unprofitable.

Agricultural intensification without such protective investments can induce short-run gains at the cost of rapid degradation of soils, which may lead to great income losses in the long run. The inherent fragility of soils and other natural resources of tropical and sub-tropical regions, combined with the institutional weakness of LDCs discussed above, may cause large inefficiencies in resource allocation in agriculture, with detrimental effects for both the environment and the income of the rural communities. Vast amounts of rural resources are in public lands, but de facto are open access due to lack of enforcement of public property rights. Another important segment of natural resources is those held in common property with very diverse degrees of controls on their use by communities, ranging from effective open access to complete exclusion of potential external users and tight controls on their use by community members. Even many land and water resources subject to individual rights are affected by tenure insecurity due to institutional limitations in registration and enforcement of such rights [Feder (1987), López (1996)]. Moreover, vast amounts of public and communal land resources are in a process of spontaneous privatization at various stages, from squatting to long-term usufruct where farmers are seeking legal recognition.

In a context like this with fragile resources, weak and evolving property right institutions, and market imperfections, the potential for serious environmental externalities is high. Moreover, policies to promote agricultural development may have unintended environmental effects that could render them ineffective and even counterproductive for farm productivity and incomes.

The traditional approach to environmental economics has been one of partial equilibrium focused mostly on microeconomic instruments needed to correct environmental externalities [see, for example, the recent survey on environmental economics by Cropper and Oates (1992)]. The reality of LDCs, however, is that first-best micro policies (including both market-based instruments and command and control regulations) are extremely hard to implement, in part due to the institutional weakness discussed above and in part due to poverty itself. This has led to the recognition that economy-wide policy reforms should not be implemented under the assumption that any nasty environmental impacts of such policies can be dealt with via first-best sectoral or micro environmental policies and/or regulations. Thus the emergence of a literature that emphasizes the use of general equilibrium analysis to evaluate economy-wide policies with explicit recognition of their environmental implications. Most of this new literature focuses on the welfare and environmental effects of increased international trade and/or unilateral trade liberalization.[2] Recently, the literature has extended this approach by considering other economy-wide policies, including exchange rate and macroeconomic adjustment programs.[3]

In general it appears that economic globalization imposes increased demands on natural resources in countries that have comparative advantages in natural resource based industries, including agriculture, while it reduces environmental pressures in countries that have comparative advantages in labor-intensive industries. This suggests a rough geographic distinction between Latin America and sub-Saharan Africa that generally falls within the first group, on the one hand, and the most populated areas of Asia that tend to fall in the second group, on the other.

Additionally, it can be argued that soil degradation is likely to be magnified by globalization in extremely poor areas where market failure is more generalized and discount rates tend to be high, while it may be improved in less poor areas where capital/credit markets are more accessible to producers. The reason for this is that in the latter cases land property rights are usually well defined, while in poor areas even

---

[2] López and Niklitscheck (1991) was one of the first theoretical analyses of the impact of unilateral trade liberalization on the environment and welfare for a small open economy that is heavily dependent on agriculture. Brander and Taylor (1997) also look at the small open economy case, while Chichilnisky (1994) and Copeland and Taylor (1995) provide analyses of the implications of increased North–South trade on welfare and the environment in the South.

[3] See, for example, Warford, Munasinghe and Cruz (1997).

if they are well defined, high discount rates combined with lack of access to credit may conspire against investment in soil conservation.

Attempts to improve our understanding of LDCs' agriculture traditionally have focused on (i) and (ii) above; consideration of the issues in (iii) and (iv) – the integration of the institutional and environmental dynamics in the agricultural production model – is much more recent. Despite the proliferation of theoretical and, to a lesser extent, empirical research, relatively limited progress has been made.

The objective of this chapter is to take stock of the state of knowledge in these areas and to extend the analysis towards a more satisfactory conceptual synthesis. We first consider the issue of the responsiveness of agriculture to policies under various extreme institutional conditions in a context of resource fragility. That is, first we consider how supply responses and farm-household income are affected by policies in a context of endogenous environmental dynamics for given institutions. The second part of the chapter provides some insights concerning a much more difficult problem: the endogenous interactions of the environmental and institutional dynamics. That is, instead of taking institutions as given, we try here to consider agriculture responses when both the environmental resource and the institutions are endogenous.

The environmental focus of the analysis is primarily on the interface of agriculture and other natural resource dependent industries, deforestation, and soil degradation. The central question is how government policies, particularly policies that affect the domestic prices of agricultural output and factors of production, may affect agricultural income once various environmental degradation mechanisms such as soil degradation and deforestation are explicitly considered. Another issue that we will consider is the role of economic growth and the consequent agricultural intensification process in a context of evolving institutions and fragile natural resources.

1. Agriculture and the environment with fixed institutions

Agriculture in tropical and sub-tropical zones, where most developing countries are located, is extremely dependent on natural resources. This is due to at least two reasons: First, soils are generally able to retain nutrients only for short periods once in cultivation, and they tend to be relatively thin and unstable. This implies that, unless significant and usually expensive investments in soil conservation are implemented, continuous cultivation quickly leads to serious degradation and loss of productivity. For these reasons, traditional farming systems in the tropics have usually involved discontinuous rotational cultivation, the so-called "shifting cultivation" or "slash-and-burn", to allow the natural vegetation to replenish soil fertility during the fallow periods and to preserve the physical properties of the soils. Additionally, the potential for externalities is very significant because most cultivation, particularly in the poorest areas, takes place on steep lands where the impact of forest-clearing to cultivate a plot of land or for other purposes can have negative consequences for farmers cultivating nearby plots due to increased risks of soil erosion and landslides.

The second reason is that modern inputs such as fertilizers and new improved seed varieties are usually less effective in tropical and sub-tropical areas than in temperate zones. Substitution of natural soil fertility by chemical fertilizers is much less successful in tropical than in temperate areas of the world. Fertilizers are much more prone to be quickly lost through run-off, due to heavy and highly concentrated rainfall in conjunction with a reduced ability of tropical soils to retain fertilizers. The elasticity of substitution between natural capital and man-made capital is, in general, smaller in tropical and sub-tropical zones than in temperate zones of the world.[4]

We sequentially consider three alternative extreme institutional situations:

   (i) Agriculture takes place in public land, where property rights are not enforced, effectively implying open access to land resources;

  (ii) Property rights are communal rather than individual and communities are able to exclude outsiders from the use of the communal lands, but land allocations within the communities may not necessarily be socially optimal;

 (iii) Fully enforced private land rights, of two distinct sub-cases, namely, commercial farm operations and subsistence agriculture.

1.1. Open access agriculture

Open access agriculture is found most often in frontier forest areas, where the land is formally owned by the government but where there is little enforcement of land ownership.[5] Moreover, land in these areas is often "up for grabs", as governments may legitimize occupation by eventually recognizing land ownership. The best way of obtaining land rights recognition is by "developing" the land, which usually involves deforestation and more intensive agricultural uses of the land. In this context the land may be exploited as much as a speculative vehicle for eventually obtaining a capital gain associated with rights recognition as for agriculture production itself.

Farmers who occupy these lands have considerable uncertainty regarding whether and when their land rights will be recognized. A minimum requirement for this is to clear the land, but farmers are likely to underinvest in land-attached capital because of the eviction risks. Most land-protective investments are attached to the land, e.g., terracing, diversion canals, agroforestry, etc. Another reason why farmers may not invest enough in maintaining the productive capacity of the land is the plentiful availability of public forested lands that can be converted to agriculture if their existing lands become degraded beyond repair. Thus, deforestation followed by land cultivation and extensive livestock activities without the required land-

---

[4] Indirect evidence of this is the large elasticity of natural biomass as a factor of agricultural production, empirically shown by López (1993, 1997) for Côte d'Ivoire and Ghana, respectively, and by agronomic studies such as Ellis and Mellor (1995).

[5] Most of the Amazon region in South America, vast areas in South East Asia, particularly the Outer Islands of Indonesia, and areas in sub-Saharan Africa are the most prominent regions of agriculture taking place in a context of open access to forested lands.

protective investments in a context of land fragility is likely to cause land degradation.

Infrastructure and government budgets.   The limits to agriculture expansion into open access forest lands are given in large part by the availability of infrastructure (mainly roads, and other public services) and distance to markets [Jones (1990), Andersen et al. (1996), Rudel and Roper (1997)]. Governments' budgetary restrictions, which have reduced their ability to extend the public infrastructure system into frontier lands, have been a key factor in preventing even faster rates of forest-clearing for agriculture and other activities. Structural adjustments policies have considerably improved public finances by allowing for greater tax collections, reduced government bureaucracies, and the privatization of money-losing state enterprises. This has, in turn, made it possible for governments to generate greater resources to be used in one of government's "proper" roles – to build public infrastructure, including extending the public services to frontier areas. This has considerably increased the attractiveness of frontier lands for agricultural expansion.[6]

Effects of prices and expectations.   Improvement of agricultural prices under open access conditions is likely to increase pressure by commercial farmers to develop more land. As agriculture prices move up, it becomes more profitable to expand the agriculture frontier, even if lack of recognition of property rights implies simply mining the land for its nutrients. That is, rising agriculture farm prices will increase deforestation as agriculture land is a normal factor of production.

Increased deforestation occurs whether the price improvement is expected to be permanent or only temporary. In fact, if prices are expected to increase in the short run but return to lower levels in the long run (if, for example, the policy reform that induces better terms of trade for agriculture is not credible), the deforestation effect is likely to be even more intensive.

The extent of degradation of the already exploited or occupied frontier agricultural lands, however, certainly depends on price expectations. If the price increase is judged only temporary, the mining of the land resources under insecure ownership will increase and, thus, land degradation will accelerate. If the price improvement is considered permanent, incentives to implement land protection investments increase. That is, even if rights are not secured, the expected marginal benefits of certain land-attached investments increase with prices. If this effect is strong enough, it could cause some of these investments to be implemented, thereby reducing land degradation.

Thus, improvement of the terms of trade of agriculture will unambiguously increase deforestation, but may reduce degradation of frontier land already used in agriculture (but still subject to insecure property rights) if the price change is expected to be permanent, or worsen degradation if this is not the case.

---

[6] Wunder (1997), for example, finds that in periods of strong macroeconomic performance, forest-clearing has increased in Ecuador.

Agricultural extension. Public agriculture extension programs that promote increased productivity in already developed lands are likely to cause greater demands for deforestation from commercial farmers if the new techniques promoted can also be used in the newly deforested lands. That is, agriculture intensification programs would increase the marginal profitability of forested lands converted to agricultural use. This, contrary to conventional wisdom, raises the incentives for commercial farmers to push further the agriculture frontier, causing greater forest losses. For subsistence farmers, however, these programs may be effective in reducing their incentives to further expand into frontier areas and, thus, may contribute to reducing deforestation caused by subsistence farmers [Angelsen (1997)].

1.2. Common property with restricted access[7]

A vast amount of land resources in developing countries is owned or controlled by local communities rather than by individuals. These communities are typically quite large, up to several hundred households or more. It is estimated that between 240 and 300 million people in developing countries depend directly on shifting cultivation as their primary system of production [FAO (Food and Agriculture Organization of the United Nations) (1986)]. Most cultivation takes place in communal lands, although agricultural production on individually owned plots is in some cases also very significant. Shifting cultivation, or "slash and burn", is a rotational system that combines cultivation periods with fallow periods, each with lengths of from 1 or 2 years up to 8 to 10 years. Additionally, common lands (typically wooded areas and pastures) provide other vital services to poor farmers, including fuelwood, grazing lands, fodder, water, and other services.

Most of the lands under shifting cultivation as well as wooded areas that are never cultivated are not privately owned. Private usufruct rights exist mostly while the land is being cultivated, but while fallow the land reverts to the community. The system of allocation of fallow lands for cultivation varies quite significantly across communities, from tight communal controls to completely decentralized systems. Similarly, controls on the extraction of resources from common wooded and grazing lands also vary significantly. That is, community controls on the use of the land resources are quite heterogeneous. If community controls fail, the usual inefficiencies related to the "tragedy of the commons" may arise. This, in turn, leads to overexploitation of the land by reducing the fallow periods to sub-optimal levels (and, hence, by increasing the proportion of the total land that is cultivated to excessive levels) and by the excessive and unsustainable extraction of fodder and fuelwood from common lands, with the consequent loss of agricultural productivity and community income in the long run.

The fallow periods in these systems are an integral component of the productive system. The natural fertility and desirable physical properties of the soil are replenished

---

[7] The Technical Appendix provides a formalization of many of the results described in Sections 1.2, 1.3, and 1.4 in a context of a two-sector endogenous growth model.

during the fallow periods. The ashes left from the burning of the natural vegetation provide vital nutrients, while the root systems of the natural vegetation give a degree of stability to the soils that may last for one or a few years of cultivation. Both the nutrient replenishment and the temporary soil stability induced by the fallows are particularly important for the fragile tropical soils, especially when soil slopes are relatively steep. Given the fragility of tropical soils, agriculture intensification associated with reductions of fallow periods needs to be accompanied by using large volumes of fertilizers and significant investments to prevent soil erosion and degradation. These investments can be quite demanding in labor and other resources, but if intensification proceeds without them and without greatly increasing the use of fertilizers, it can lead to significant reductions of agricultural productivity.

Given the costs of fallow substitutes (chemical fertilizers and soil protection investments), and given output and factor prices and discount rates, there is a socially optimal land allocation between cultivation and fallow. Or, equivalently, given a fixed total amount of community land, there is an optimal portion of the land that should be cultivated. If more land is cultivated, farm production increases in the short run, but at a cost of productivity losses in the intermediate and long run that offset the short-run gains. That is, if more than the optimal level of land is cultivated, the present value of all present and future agriculture income falls for the community as a whole [López and Niklitscheck (1991)]. Similarly, there is an optimal level of extraction of fuelwood, water, fodder, and other resources from common uncultivable areas which if surpassed leads to soil degradation and unsustainable deforestation of wooded areas.

Imperfect allocation of communal resources. It appears that most traditional communities were in the past able to implement controls on the use of communal natural resources including land as well as fuelwood, water, and other resources, that led to their efficient allocation and to a degree of sustainability. As population grows and as communities are increasingly more integrated to markets and more exposed to Western values, however, communal controls on the use of common property resources seem to have weakened.[8] In fact, a handful of recent empirical studies have shown that while communal resource allocation is different from open access allocation, it is not socially optimal either [López (1993, 1997), Ahuja (forthcoming)]. That is, the allocation of communal resources is imperfect and there is a clear tendency to overexploit these resources by individual members. The effect of this has been biomass losses and soil degradation that cause significant income losses for the rural communities.

Price effects. Given these allocative imperfections, what is the impact of a change in the terms of trade of agriculture on farm output and income? The short-run effect of

---

[8] The existence of solid hierarchical relations in traditional communities is a vital instrument in promoting an efficient allocation of land and other resources held in common property. Increased Westernization of cultural values seemed to have helped to deteriorate the acceptance of such relationships within the villages, thus increasing the difficulties of enforcement of community rules that prevented overuse of communal resources.

improved agriculture profitability is an increase in the area cultivated, which, in turn, induces an expansion of output. The price improvement may also induce greater use of fertilizers and, if this improvement is considered permanent, could also lead to more investments in soil protection. But as long as individual land tenure is uncertain and as long as plenty of community land is still available, the main source of supply response is likely to be the expansion of area cultivated. In fact, empirical studies in western Africa have shown that this is exactly what happens [López (1993)]. Higher agriculture prices induce an expansion of cultivated land with the consequent fallow reduction and loss of biomass and with little change in the use of other inputs.

Thus, the short-run effect of agricultural price increases is to expand output primarily via increases in cultivated area and fallow reduction. This, however, causes a fall in productivity of cultivated land in the intermediate or long run. This is due to the restricted possibility of replenishing the chemical and physical properties of the cultivated land due to the reduced fallow periods, which is not compensated for by greater use of chemical fertilizers and soil conservation investment. Agricultural output eventually falls with respect to the levels reached in the short run after the price increase, and could be even lower than its pre-price-increase levels because soils become more degraded and may not fully recover to their pre-price-increase levels. (The possibility of a negative long-run supply response is more plausible when the initial intensification due to the price increase causes irreversible soil losses.) In any case, the long-run supply response to price is necessarily weaker than the short-run response: the le Chatellier principle upside down!

Whether or not the new level of agriculture output in the long run is higher than the pre-price-increase level of output, the net wealth of the communities (e.g., the present value of future net agriculture income) may fall: The improved agricultural prices exacerbate the original distortion associated with the fact that community controls were inefficient in the first place. Too much land was already cultivated (and too little land was in fallow) before the price increase. When prices go up, even more land is cultivated, thus increasing the wedge between the actual level of cultivated land and the optimal. The net wealth of the communities may fall if these increased efficiency losses more than offset the increased community revenues due to the higher agricultural prices. That is, the increased natural resource degradation induced by the price rise may cause a fall of income that is greater than the income rise due to higher prices.

The above analysis assumes that all agricultural output prices rise by about the same proportion. If they do not, we need to be concerned with the land intensity of the various outputs. If the overall agriculture price improvement is accompanied by changes in relative prices that favor land-intensive agricultural commodities (say, cereals or livestock) vis-à-vis labor-intensive commodities (say, tubers and perhaps tree crops), then the previous analysis is reinforced. If, however, relative agriculture prices change against the land-intensive commodities, the net effect on the extent of land cultivation and on fallow periods is in general ambiguous. Ambiguity arises if the improvement of average agriculture price occurs by increases of the prices of labor-intensive outputs and decreases of the prices of land-intensive commodities [López and Niklitschek (1991)].

Prices and the privatization of common property resources.   An additional effect of improved profitability of agriculture due to better terms of trade is related to the institutional dynamics. Greater farm profitability increases the value of the communal land at least in the short run. This could increase pressures for privatization of communal lands.[9] In fact, a gradual process of spontaneous privatization of communal lands has been observed in many places. One way of acquiring recognition of individual rights is by a more continuous cultivation of the land. (Another way consists in investing in land-attached capital, but given the uncertainties about the eventual outcome of the privatization process, this is not likely to be the preferred mechanism to induce private ownership.) Thus, better agriculture prices may accelerate the spontaneous process of privatization but at the cost of even more continuous land cultivation.

In areas where soils are more resilient with little risk of reaching the threshold levels of irreversible deterioration, the increased agriculture prices may induce only a temporary worsening of land productivity. But by accelerating the process of privatization it can in the intermediate run increase the incentive for investments in soil protection and increase the use of other adequate substitutes for the reduced fallows.

Under conditions of greater resource fragility, however, it is possible that the very mechanisms used to privatize communal lands could result in an irreversible spiral of resource degradation and productivity losses, which eventually may lead to the complete destruction and abandonment of large land areas and to entire communities disappearing.

1.3. Private property

If producers internalize the full productive value of natural resources then permanent increases in the profitability of agriculture and other activities that depend on them would lead to an improvement of such resources. The best way of seeing this is by assuming homothetic production technology where output is a function of man-made capital and natural capital. Producers can invest in man-made capital and natural capital. For given prices and other exogenous variables, in competitive long-run equilibrium producers will choose an optimal combination of each form of capital by equalizing their net marginal value products. Moreover, the homothetic nature of the production technology plus certain regularity conditions imply that there is a unique optimal man-made to natural capital ratio. That is, in competitive equilibrium we have that, for given factor and output prices, man-made and natural capital are in the long run used in fixed proportions despite the fact that the production technology is entirely neoclassical. Even if man-made and natural capital are technically substitutes, the behavioral implication of competitive equilibrium in the long run is one of complementarity. Any price incentive to expand investment in man-made capital will also be an incentive to

---

[9] See Demsetz (1967) for an interesting illustration of this in the context of territorial rights among Canadian Indians as fur prices increased during colonial times.

increase investment in natural capital. The main reason is that as man-made capital increases, the marginal productivity of natural capital will also generally increase under weak technological assumptions.[10] Greater (permanent) profitability of agriculture is an incentive to improve the natural resources that are held in private property with full tenure security.

Intuitively, perhaps the best way of explaining this is by using an example borrowed from a problem that agricultural economists nicely solved some time ago: the dynamics of the cow-calf cycle [Yver (1972), Jarvis (1974)]. When beef prices increase, cattle farmers who believe such an increase is permanent react by withholding more calves, thus reducing their supply of beef in the short run. The reason why they do this is because they expect that the higher prices will persist into the future, e.g., that the long-run profitability of the industry has increased. Higher expected long-run profits prompt farmers to increase their herd capital, and they do this by retaining more calves to increase their stocks of cows (and bulls). That is, they invest more by conserving more animals. Two key facts determine this response: One is that farmers have complete and secure rights on their herd, and the other is that they expect prices to remain high in the long run. If they did not have secure rights on the herd, farmers would be reluctant to expand it, and if they believed that the price increase was purely temporary, they would probably find that the temporary price bonanza was a good time to dispose of a large part of the herd.

The analogy with natural resources is complete. Higher permanent prices for activities that depend on natural resources, such as agriculture, under conditions of secure rights on them would induce farmers to invest in expanding and/or improving the stock of natural resources for the same reasons that farmers increase their herd stocks if they expect increased long-run profitability of the beef industry. Thus, permanently higher agricultural profits stimulate greater investments in both man-made and natural capital.[11] If, however, the price increase is expected to be only temporary, "unsustainable" exploitation of securely owned land may become profitable.

---

[10] In fact, it will be an incentive to increase both factors proportionally if (i) the (marginal) cost of factor accumulation is identical for both factors in the long run. Note, however, that in a general equilibrium context this assumption is not as restrictive as it may seem. The cost of factor accumulation is equal to the marginal utility of foregone consumption needed to save, which does not need to be affected by the choice of the factors that are accumulated. And, if (ii) we neglect the fact that some of the capital goods may be specific. But factor specificity is likely to be less relevant in the long run.

[11] See technical appendix for a formal derivation of this result. Much recent literature has concluded that agriculture prices play an ambiguous role in soil conservation [Barrett (1991), LaFrance (1992), Grepperud (1997)]. One reason for this ambiguity is that these authors use partial equilibrium analysis with a strictly concave production function and, more importantly, investment in natural capital is not allowed by their models. The model in the technical appendix uses a two-sector endogenous general equilibrium model assuming constant returns to scale production technologies (although homotheticity is sufficient to remove the ambiguities). The assumption of constant returns to scale is consistent with empirical production functions estimated for agriculture in many countries [López and Valdés (2000)]. López (1994), using a neoclassical economic growth model, also shows that under constant returns to scale technologies the relationship between agricultural prices and the stock of natural capital is unambiguously positive.

Price increases caused by policies that lack credibility, for example, may cause greater degradation even if resources are privately owned.

An important caveat: Natural resources usually have values over and above their direct production values, but even if they are subject to fully secured private rights, they may not be fully internalized due to lack of or highly imperfect markets for services provided by natural resources that are not directly productive. These may include, for example, values associated with biodiversity, carbon retention services of forest habitats, etc. If there are no markets for these services, farmers are unlikely to take these additional values of natural resources into consideration. A higher profitability of natural resource based industries may lead to, for example, greater investments in soil conservation and more planting of trees, while at the same time more deforestation. When natural forests are replaced with plantation forests, the biodiversity value of the natural habitat can be lost very rapidly.

Moreover, in areas where private ownership of resources coexists with common resources with a degree of open access, increased profitability of resource-based industries could lead to a complete destruction of the common resources before investments in expanding the stocks of private natural resources take place. Consider, for example, the effect of increased profitability of fishing in an open access lake: fishermen will not make major investments in aquaculture until the common resource is more or less exhausted. But after this the resource will be replenished only in its directly productive component, while the natural habitat of the lake will not be restored.

Subsistence farmers. The price responsiveness of subsistence farmers who do not participate in the labor market or whose off-farm work is subject to rationing due to labor market imperfections can be quite different from that of commercial farmers. Increases of farm prices or technological improvements due to, for example, greater technical assistance may in these conditions lead to reductions of the land cultivated by subsistence farmers [López (1992), Angelsen (1997)]. That is, higher farm prices could be an instrument in this case to increase land fallows and to reduce deforestation. In fact, the conventional wisdom among development practitioners is that a way to reduce deforestation is to increase technical assistance to farmers and improve their prices so that they will not continue clearing forest land for agriculture [Bandy et al. (1993), Tomich and van Noordwijk (1995)].

The closer to a minimum subsistence level of consumption farm-households are, the more likely it is that such an anomalous response to price incentives (e.g., lower demand for land) may occur [Angelsen (1997)]. Also, it can be shown that for subsistence farmers who use few inputs other than labor and land, a reduction of cultivated land implies a *negative* output supply response as well. In general, if the cost share of inputs other than labor and land is small, a negative land cultivated response to higher output prices is likely to be accompanied by a negative output response as well. That is, if the presumptions of development practitioners were correct, e.g., if higher agricultural prices brought about less deforestation, then peasants who use little of other inputs would also reduce agricultural production![12]

A more plausible story among development practitioners is that increasing agricultural productivity or prices may reduce pressures on common property resources that *cannot* be used for agriculture because of communal controls that impede it and/or because they are in areas that do not permit even a minimum of cultivation. The most common case is communal wooded areas, usually located in very steep lands, devoted to fuelwood extraction and other purposes. Agriculture and the natural resource extraction activities do not compete for land, but they do compete for the use of other factors of production, mainly labor, that can be used either in agricultural production on private lots or in the extraction of resources (fuelwood, construction wood, etc.) from common lands. In this case, the higher agricultural prices do not increase cultivation of the wooded areas and they may instead induce less pressure on the resource by subsistence farmers. Higher agricultural prices or productivity may cause a reallocation of labor away from fuelwood gathering in favor of work on the agricultural land.[13]

1.4. Economic growth and natural capital with fixed institutions

What are the interactions between the evolution of natural capital and economic growth? In the technical appendix we show that given exogenous parameters of the economy such as prices, institutions, discount rates, resilience of natural capital and others, the economy may be able to achieve sustainable long-run growth with positive and constant growth of natural capital and man-made capital. An initially resource rich economy (e.g., an economy characterized by a "low" man-made to natural capital ratio) will grow by expanding man-made capital and degrading natural capital *regardless of the nature of the institutions that regulate the use of natural capital.* That is, a resource-rich economy characterized by private exclusive resource ownership will not deplete natural resources less than an economy where natural resources are subject to open access.

The key difference between the two economies is that the economy with efficient institutions will stop natural resource degradation earlier and is more likely to achieve balanced long-run growth (where both natural and man-made capital grow at the same rate) than the economy characterized by inefficient institutions. That is, economies with perfect institutions will stop degrading the natural resource at a man-made/natural capital ratio that is lower than that of the economy with imperfect institutions. This increases the likelihood that the marginal value product of man-made capital compared to the marginal cost of capital is greater in the institutionally efficient economy than

---

[12] Recent empirical studies, however, have shown that even poor farmers, in areas where land is still available, respond to price incentives by expanding their cultivated area [López (1993, 1997), Ahuja (forthcoming)]. In fact, the main source of supply response is by adjusting the cultivated area.

[13] López (1998) has shown that this is true if increased prices or technical assistance benefit labor-intensive crops. If they benefit land-intensive activities, however, pressure on non-agriculture common lands increases rather than falls.

in the inefficient one. This implies that the former has a greater likelihood of having positive long-run growth where the man-made/natural capital ratio is preserved. In this case an environmental Kuznets process is likely to emerge where natural capital falls with income until the desired man-made/natural capital ratio is achieved, at which point natural capital starts growing at a rate similar to man-made capital.

In Technical Appendix we show that there is a critical degree of institutional inefficiency that still allows positive balanced growth in the long run. If institutions are more inefficient than this critical level, long-run economic stagnation will take place, where the natural capital is never recovered.

2. Endogenous institutions

Theories of institutional change focus mostly on the motivations for discarding old institutions and replacing them with new, usually more efficient ones, but they have little to say about the mechanics of institutional reform [Bardhan (1991)]. The mere fact that an institution is inefficient does not necessarily mean that a collection of rational individuals will discard it and replace it with socially desirable new institutions. More important, even if a new institution is potentially more efficient than the old one, the efficiency of the new institutional steady state may depend critically on the adjustment path followed to transform the old institution. The new institutional steady state may even be inferior to the old one, depending on the mechanism of adjustment followed.

In this section we provide some insights about the mechanics of institutional change and the impact of alternative paths of change on economic efficiency, agricultural responses, and environmental resources. We focus on two institutions that crucially affect economic outcomes: (i) institutions for the management of common property resources, and (ii) privatization of open access and common property resources.

Engines of institutional change.   Increased scarcity of land and other natural resources has been considered to be the prime motivation for institutional change affecting the management of common property resources and for privatization. This increased scarcity may be triggered by population growth [Boserup (1965, 1981)]. Increased population would induce progressive intensification in the use of land resources and higher food prices. This, in turn, would cause higher potential rents that would motivate increased tightness of the controls to access and management of resources that remain in common property and/or their privatization.

Alternatively, resource scarcity can be generated by increased integration into national and international markets even if local population does not expand very rapidly. This latter source of resource scarcity and institutional change is more important for our purposes than population growth because it is more directly related to economic policies. Trade policies, price policies, and public investment in infrastructure are likely to play a great role in affecting the degree of integration of rural areas into national and international markets. In resource-abundant economies (as are most countries in

Latin America and sub-Saharan Africa) increased market integration may dramatically enhance the potential rents of land and other natural resources, which, in turn, may rapidly increase demands for institutions entailing communal or individual exclusive rights over the resources.

Additionally, while the population-institutional mechanism may be quite gradual even if population grows fast, the market integration-institutional change mechanism can be much more rapid and even explosive, as shown by recent case study evidence for Central America, South Asia, and the Amazon region [Browder (1988), Collins (1987), Kates and Haarmann (1992)]. This gives greater relevance to the market integration factor than population in affecting the interdependency of supply responses and institutional change.

2.1. Market incentives and communal institutions

Increased agricultural prices and market integration leads to a more intensive utilization of common resources. As indicated in Section 1.2, in a context of resource fragility (as in most poor tropical zones), intensification requires significant investments and usually more demanding methods of cultivation to avoid excessive resource degradation. To achieve this, however, common property institutions have to evolve to permit much more elaborate forms of cooperation. Traditional common property management, which emphasizes exclusion of outsiders and reduced risks of conflicts among community members for access to the common resources [Baland and Platteau (1996)], becomes no longer sufficient to prevent the overuse of common resources. As economic incentives for more intensive use of communal resources increase (resulting in shorter fallows, increased livestock in community pastures, etc.), cooperation needs to be directed much more toward planning and implementing large investments in communal areas that require significant contributions of individual members, particularly their manpower.

Unfortunately, the vast case study literature overwhelmingly suggests that the institutions that would enable this superior form of cooperation do not spontaneously emerge as intensification of resource use develops [Baland and Platteau (1996), Ahuja (1996), Anderson (1987), Garcia-Barrios and Garcia-Barrios (1990), Kates and Haarmann (1992)]. Indeed, the evolution of cooperation into increasingly more elaborate forms seems to require a number of conditions that are not always present in rural communities.

Understanding certain key relationships such as the resource-flow relationships and the causal linkages between patterns of exploitation and the evolution of the natural resource stocks seems to be rarely present in most agricultural communities [Baland and Platteau (1996)]. Additionally, cultural norms developed throughout history for essentially autarkic conditions cease to be efficient when communities become increasingly integrated into national and international markets. Finally, rising in- and out-migration that economic integration brings about reduces the cohesiveness of traditional communities and decreases the incentives for cooperation, particularly by individuals contemplating out-migration.

All of this constitutes a formidable obstacle to institutional evolution towards the superior forms of cooperation needed because of increased scarcity of natural resources. At the very least it delays the development of new institutions for cooperation in many traditional communities. But such delay, in conditions of environmental fragility, may lead to the degradation of the common resources, thus decreasing their economic value. The reduction of the economic value of common resources may, in turn, decrease the incentives of the communities to implement the necessary norms for implementing the conservation investments. That is, increasing market integration initially may raise the value of the common resources, causing their more intensive use and, in principle, increasing the incentives for improving the institutions that rule their management. But if institutions do not evolve in a relatively short period of time, intensification causes degradation of the natural resources which, in turn, gradually reduces the incentives for institutional reform. Thus a vicious cycle of resource degradation and falling incentives for expending community efforts in improving institutions emerges.

If communal institutions do not swiftly adapt to the new conditions, agriculture response to the increased economic incentives that market integration brings about may be positive in the short run but could become smaller and even negative in the intermediate run as communal resources degrade. If resource degradation reaches a certain threshold, the process may become irreversible and eventually the communal resources may cease to be productive. If, on the other hand, institutions do evolve rapidly, intensification may take place in a context of increasing productivity of the natural resources.

Success and failure of this process in different areas of the world have been extensively documented in the literature [Tiffen, Mortimore and Gichuki (1994), World Bank (1992), Baland and Platteau (1996), Kates and Haarmann (1992)]. The development of the Machakos district in Kenya is a good illustration of a virtuous cycle where positive institutional change, natural resource investments, investment in physical capital and technology, and increased agricultural productivity have had mutually reinforcing effects. Tiffen et al. (1994) show how over the period 1930–1990 soil productivity recovered, large areas previously barren were planted with trees, water supply improved due to better management of watersheds, investment in capital increased, and per capita income dramatically increased despite a fivefold rise in population. For several illustrations of the opposite phenomenon, a vicious cycle of natural resource degradation, institutional erosion, disinvestment, and increased poverty, see, for example, Kates and Haarman (1992).

It appears that some of the factors that determine success or failure of the intensification process are the following:

(i) *Population density*. The larger the size of the communities, the more difficult is institutional evolution as the costs of monitoring increase and cheating and free-riding become easier.

(ii) *Education*. Communities with higher levels of education are more likely to be able to understand the basic relations between agricultural intensification and resource degradation and, therefore, are also more likely to generate norms for preserving efficiency in the use of natural resources.

(iii) *The abruptness of market integration.* A gradual process of market integration allows more time for the institutions of cooperation to evolve than when market integration and agriculture price increase occurs more explosively.

(iv) *The formal legal framework.* In countries where communal ownership is legally recognized and the legitimacy of communal authorities is formally sanctioned by law, the institutional evolution for cooperation may be more rapid than in countries where this is not the case. Thus, the risks of unsustainable agricultural responsiveness are greater in the latter than in the former countries.

(v) *Other external influences.* Judicious interventions by NGOs and government agencies can have dramatic effects in creating the ground rules for the new institutional set-up that permits increased contribution of the community members to the improvement and maintenance of the productive capacity of common resources [Chopra and Gulati (1996), Intal (1991)].

In summary, increasing market integration and globalization provides incentives for intensifying the use of common resources, which could trigger either a vicious cycle of resource degradation, output reduction, and poverty, or, alternatively, a virtuous process of increased intensification and natural resource improvement if communal institutions rapidly evolve to permit superior forms of cooperation. Which of these paths is followed depends on a number of conditions already existing in the communities, the speed of market integration, and certain external influences such as the overall legal framework and the extent that cooperation is promoted by NGOs or governments.

2.2. Privatization

The increased potential profitability of agriculture that market integration usually brings about normally leads to greater pressure for the privatization of both public lands and part of the common property resources. In most cases documented in the literature this process is spontaneous, taking place in the absence of any transparent macrolegal framework. The privatization process is just one more, but essential, component of the supply response of agriculture to economic liberalization policies.

In the absence of a clear legal framework that is fully enforced, producers (and speculators) usually embark themselves on what has been called a "race for property rights" [Anderson and Hill (1990)]. The process starts by producers occupying public or communal lands in the hope of eventually receiving recognition in the form of individual private ownership. A key mechanism of legitimizing ownership of land and avoiding having recently acquired land claimed by others is to "develop" the land, which typically means to clear it and to intensify its exploitation.[14]

---

[14] Land-clearing and deforestation is thus an investment for receiving land ownership recognition. Interestingly, deforestation apparently tends to increase when the prospects of land tenure security is higher.

It is important, however, to realize that intensification goes beyond what would be required to optimize the use of the land as a factor of production. Land use intensification is more a means to capture the rents associated with acquiring permanent land rights than to achieve socially optimal resource allocation. That is, although market integration naturally induces more intensive land utilization, the fact that it also triggers a race for property rights implies that land intensification goes beyond what it would otherwise be.[15] This process of rent dissipation is of course socially inefficient by causing efficiency losses related to socially necessary expenditure in land intensification.

While in a context of solid and resilient natural environments, as in many temperate zones, this rent seeking process may cause temporary efficiency losses that disappear once the process of privatization is completed, in environmentally fragile areas these losses can become permanent, persisting after the privatization process has been completed. The reason for this is clear: the investments in soil improvement (terracing, drainage, agroforestry, etc.) that are necessary for sustainable intensification in fragile areas are generally not implemented by farmers who do not have secured rights [López (1996), Feder (1987)]. Given the uncertainties that individual farmers face regarding the final outcome of the process, they will try to obtain recognition for land rights using means that involve investments that are not attached to the land because, otherwise, they would lose them if evicted.

Profit maximization of farmers implies that the preferred land "developments" in seeking land rights are activities that also give some immediate returns without requiring tying the farmers' capital to the land. This includes cutting trees that can be used for fuel or sold as timber, more continuous cultivation of the land, avoiding fallows – which is when the land becomes most vulnerable to expropriation or reversion to the community – and increasing livestock. All these activities imply dramatic increases in the pressures on the natural resources, normally resulting in degradation of them, particularly in the most fragile areas.[16] If degradation goes beyond certain thresholds, the soil damage becomes irreversible.

The reason is that the rate of return to the investment in deforestation rises when the prospect in land tenure security increases. This leads to expansion of such investment [Angelsen (1997)]. In fact, Kaimowitz (1995) claims that recent land titling programs in Central America to provide more secure land rights to occupants have fueled speculative demand for (forested) lands. Similar findings are reported by Mahar and Schneider (1994) for the Amazon region.

[15] An interesting natural experiment is provided by what is perhaps the largest land privatization process in history, the privatization of over one billion acres in the United States between 1790 and 1920. Anderson and Hill (1990) showed that privatization to the highest bidder without any conditions resulted in a much slower and less intensive process of land development than privatization through preemption (squatting) or homesteading.

[16] André and Platteau (1998) illustrate how the impressive evolution toward privatization through a spontaneous de facto process in Rwanda over the 1970s and 1980s resulted in a vicious cycle of poverty and resource degradation.

In summary, in conditions where private land ownership coexists with vast amounts of public and communal land resources, as is the case in most tropical and sub-tropical areas in Latin America and Africa, agricultural supply responses to economic liberalization and market integration (especially when the latter includes significant investment in infrastructure) are likely to be significant and the process of spontaneous resource privatization through rent seeking is accelerated. However, this process usually brings about increased deforestation and soil degradation, which cause social efficiency losses both during the process and even in the new private property steady state. The losses are projected into the steady state particularly when the short-run resource degradation is deep enough to prevent or make very expensive the repair of the productive capacities of the natural resources. Private property rights, the "sacred cow" of neoclassical institutions, do not necessarily bring economic efficiency because the dynamic path of their own emergence may leave permanent scars on the steady state. An obvious role for the state is to develop policies and programs that prevent such destructive races for property rights.

3. Conclusion

This chapter argues that the economics of agriculture in developing countries is quite different and more complex than that in developed countries. The reason is that the overall agricultural system is much less stable in the former than the latter. Several factors that are largely a "given" in developed countries are, in LDCs, very sensitive to sectoral and macroeconomic policies. An integral part of the responsiveness of agriculture to exogenous factors, including policies, is formed not only by the microeconomic and sectoral behavioral relationships directly affecting the production conditions of agriculture, but also by the evolution of the relatively unstable natural resource base of agriculture and by changes of the also unstable institutions, particularly those governing property rights.

Our understanding of developing country agriculture can be greatly increased by incorporating natural resource and institutional dynamics explicitly in our models. This is, of course, a major challenge both theoretically and empirically. Our analysis shows that considerable progress has been made in understanding the farm-household as a unit and in allowing for natural capital to explicitly enter into the agricultural production function. Additionally, our understanding of how policies may affect natural capital and, thence, agricultural production in this context is gradually increasing.

Much more progress, however, is needed in developing a conceptual paradigm for the mechanics of institutional change and the interactions between the environmental and the institutional dynamics. No formal conceptual framework that integrates these interactions is, to our knowledge, available. Additionally, more efforts are needed to empirically analyze these interactions in the context of dramatic structural adjustment policies that many LDCs have instituted over the 1980s and early 1990s.

Several LDCs appear to have initiated a process of rapid economic growth. This growth is largely associated with a dramatic process of structural adjustment (which includes eliminating price distortions, privatization of state enterprises, increased roles for markets, deregulation, etc.) and globalization encompassing both increased international trade and increased international capital mobility. It appears that this revival of growth has been spurred mostly by an accelerated rate of accumulation in physical capital and to a lesser extent human capital improvement. Natural capital, however, has not been a priority, and new evidence points rather to a rapid degradation of it [World Bank (1999)]. According to the conceptual framework developed in this chapter, such an unbalanced growth pattern with continuous increases in the physical/natural capital gap is likely to render economic growth unsustainable as the rate of return to physical capital falls. The fall in the rate of return of physical capital is likely to be more severe in countries that are more natural resource dependent, in which case this fall may lead to economic stagnation. Thus, for countries that have comparative statics in natural resource intensive sectors such as (tropical) agriculture, the final outcome of globalization of trade and increased capital mobility could be not only one of greater environmental problems, but also of rapid decline in economic growth if measures are not taken to stimulate a more balanced growth that allows natural capital to recover in conjunction with rapid accumulation of physical capital. This may require rapid institutional development, which may not automatically arise.

Technical Appendix. Two-sector endogenous growth model of a small open economy

The economy is assumed to be comprised of two sectors, a natural resource based sector ("agriculture") and a sector that uses natural resources less intensively ("manufacturing"). The two sectors use two factors of production, natural resources, θ, and man-made capital that includes physical and human capital, K. Agriculture uses a third factor that is sector-specific. The resource-based sector production function is

$$q_A = F(K_A, x; \theta_A), \tag{1}$$

where q_A is output of the resource-based sector, K_A is capital used by this sector, x is a sector-specific factor, and θ_A is the stock of the natural resources used by agriculture.

Interpreting (1) as the production function of agriculture, x could be regarded as the cultivated area covered by agriculture in the context of shifting cultivation or rotational systems, and θ_A the quality of the fallow land that is periodically incorporated into production [López and Niklitscheck (1991)]. In general, x can be interpreted as a factor specific to agriculture (θ could be more generally interpreted too as biomass energy that could be used in agriculture or in the other sector). The function $F(\cdot)$ is assumed increasing and homogeneous of degree one.

The non-agricultural sector production function is assumed to also be characterized by constant returns to scale, e.g., the production function is linearly homogeneous,

$$q_N = G(K_N, \theta_N), \tag{2}$$

where K_N is capital used by the non-agricultural sector and θ_N is natural resource used by the non-agricultural sector. $G(\cdot)$ is assumed strictly increasing in each factor of production.[17]

A gross domestic product or GDP function for the economy can be defined as

$$\widetilde{R}(p_A, p_N; K, x, \theta) \equiv \max_{K_A, K_N, \theta_N, \theta_A} \{ p_A F(K_A, x; \theta_A) + p_N G(K_N, \theta_N) :$$

$$K_A + K_N = K, \theta_A + \theta_N = \theta \}, \tag{3}$$

where K is the total stock of capital in the economy, θ is the total stock of natural resources, and p_A and p_N are the prices of the agriculture good and non-agriculture good, respectively. The function $R(\cdot)$ is increasing and linearly homogeneous in p_A, p_N, and, given the properties of the underlying production functions, it is also increasing and linearly homogeneous in K, x and θ [Diewert (1973), Kohli (1991)]. Moreover, given that agriculture is the more intensive user of natural capital, the Stolper–Samuelson conditions imply

$$\widetilde{R}_{14} \equiv \frac{\partial^2 R}{\partial p_A \partial x} > 0; \qquad \widetilde{R}_{15} \equiv \frac{\partial^2 R}{\partial p_A \partial \theta} > 0; \qquad \widetilde{R}_{13} < 0;$$

$$\widetilde{R}_{23} > 0; \qquad \widetilde{R}_{24} < 0; \qquad \widetilde{R}_{25} < 0.$$

That is, agricultural output expands as θ or x increase and contracts as K rises, while the non-agricultural sector contracts if θ and/or x increase and expand with K. Note that by Hotelling's lemma the first partial derivation of R with respect to the price corresponds to the output supplies, e.g., $R_1 = q_A$ and $R_2 = q_N$, where q_A and q_N are the outputs of the agricultural and non-agricultural sectors, respectively. We also make the reasonable assumption that all factors of production are gross complements, e.g., $\widetilde{R}_{34} > 0$, $\widetilde{R}_{35} > 0$, $\widetilde{R}_{45} > 0$.

---

[17] We could also include an extraction activity in the $G(\cdot)$ function as well. But for simplicity we ignore this component of $G(\cdot)$ to emphasize the key distinction between resource-extractive sectors such as agriculture, fishery, forestry, etc., and sectors that use natural resources but extract much less of the resource. This is generally valid for natural resources but not for air pollution and other mostly urban contaminants, which are greatly affected by non-agricultural activities. A good illustration is tourism versus agriculture. Tourism uses natural resources (beaches, forests, mountains, etc.) but, though it does induce some extraction of the resource (by somehow degrading it), this is much smaller compared to the resources extracted by agriculture in terms of forest-clearing and soil nutrients. At the same time, agriculture and tourism compete for the use of natural resources, and the use of them in either activity more or less precludes their use by the other activity.

The consumption sector of the economy is modeled using the representative consumer assumption. Preferences are represented by the indirect utility function,

$$u = \tilde{u}(p_A, p_N, \tilde{y}), \tag{4}$$

where $\tilde{y}$ is total consumption expenditures of the representative consumer. The indirect utility function $\tilde{u}(\cdot)$ is homogeneous of degree zero in its arguments. Also, it is decreasing in p_A and p_N and increasing in y [Diewert (1974)]. Moreover, we assume that it is strictly concave in y.

Given the zero homogeneity property of $\tilde{u}(\cdot)$, we can represent preferences in a normalized form,

$$u = u(p, y), \tag{5}$$

where $p \equiv p_A/p_N$ is the relative price of the agricultural good and $y \equiv \tilde{y}/p_N$ is consumer expenditures in units of the non-agricultural good.

The total income of the economy $(\tilde{R})$ can be either consumed or invested. There are two types of investments, namely, the economy can invest in expanding K or in improving the natural resource base θ. That is, we have I_K and I_θ as investments in increasing the man-made capital and improving the natural capital stock, respectively. I_θ may correspond, for example, to terracing, or expenditures in soil conservation technologies such as contour cultivation, intercropping, etc. These types of investments contribute to improving the quality of the soil or other natural resources by mitigating the impact of agriculture on them. We assume that both I_K and I_θ consist of non-agricultural goods and, therefore, their unit price is p_N. The budget constraint of this economy is, therefore,

$$\tilde{y} = \tilde{R}(p_A, p_N; K, x, \theta) - p_N I_K - p_N I_\theta. \tag{6}$$

Notice that since this is a small open economy, the fact that all investments consist of one type of good only (the manufacturing good) does not require disaggregating the budget constraint. If the use of the manufactured good for investments subtracts from desired expenditures of the manufactured good, the economy would import more of this good (or export less). We can now normalize (6) by p_N. Recalling that $y \equiv \tilde{y}/p_N$ and $p \equiv p_A/p_N$, we have

$$y = R(p; K, x, \theta) - I_K - I_\theta, \tag{7}$$

where $R(p; K, x, \theta) \equiv \tilde{R}/p_N = \tilde{R}(p_A/p_N, 1; K, x, \theta)$. We note that $R(\cdot)$ has the same properties as $\tilde{R}(\cdot)$ in K, x, θ and, also, it can be shown that $R_{13} < 0$, $R_{14} > 0$, $R_{15} > 0$ and, finally, by Hotelling's lemma, $R_1(\cdot) = q_A$.

The motion of the stock of man-made capital is given by the usual capital accumulation equation,

$$\dot{K} = I_K - \delta K, \tag{8}$$

where δ is the rate of depreciation of K. The change through time of the stock of natural resources depends on the natural rate of reposition α on the investment in natural capital and on the rate of extraction of the natural resource,

$$\dot\theta = \alpha\theta - (\beta - I_\theta/x)x, \tag{9}$$

where we choose units of θ in a way that the contribution of one unit of investment I_θ to the improvement of the natural capital is equal to one, and $\beta > 0$ is a coefficient indicating the gross impact of x on changes in θ. The net impact of x on $\dot\theta$, however, can be mitigated by investing in soil conservation activities. That is, the net impact of x on $\dot\theta$ can be less than β, equal to $(\beta - I_\theta/x)$, if producers invest in soil conservation.

The representative consumer is assumed to maximize the discounted present value of welfare,

$$\max_{y,x,I_K,I_\theta} \int_0^\infty u(p,y)\,e^{-rt}\,dt, \tag{10}$$

subject to Equations (7), (8) and (9), and to given initial conditions $K(0) = \overline{K}_0$ and $\theta(0) = \bar\theta_0$. Additionally, we include non-negativity constraints $I_K \geqslant 0$ and $I_\theta \geqslant 0$. R is the discount rate. The Hamiltonian associated with this problem is

$$H = u(p,y) + \lambda\big[R(p; K, x, \theta) - I_K - I_\theta - y\big]$$
$$+ \gamma(I_K - \gamma K) + \eta\big(\alpha\theta - (\beta - I_\theta/x)x\big), \tag{11}$$

where λ is the Lagrangian multiplier of the budget constraint, γ is the costate variable of the man-made capital stock, and η is the co-estate variable associated with natural capital.

The usual first order necessary conditions include

$$
\begin{aligned}
&\text{(i)} \quad u_2(p,y) = \lambda, \\
&\text{(ii)} \quad \lambda R_3(p; K, x, \theta) = \eta\beta, \\
&\text{(iii)} \quad (\gamma - \lambda)I_K = 0, \quad I_K \geqslant 0, \\
&\text{(iv)} \quad (\eta - \lambda)I_\theta = 0, \quad I_\theta \geqslant 0, \\
&\text{(v)} \quad \dot\gamma = (r + \delta)\gamma - \lambda R_2(p; K, x, \theta), \\
&\text{(vi)} \quad \dot\eta = (r - \alpha)\eta - \lambda R_4(p; K, x, \theta), \\
&\text{(vii)} \quad \dot K = I_K - \delta K, \\
&\text{(viii)} \quad \dot\theta = \alpha\theta - (\beta - I_\theta/x)x,
\end{aligned}
\tag{12}
$$

where $R_3 \equiv \partial R/\partial x$, $R_2 \equiv \partial R/\partial K$, $R_4 \equiv \partial R/\partial\theta$, and $u_2(\cdot) \equiv \partial u/\partial y$. In order to have a meaningful solution of (12), the restriction $r - \alpha > 0$ is required.

First we want to determine the long-run equilibrium solution to system (12). To do this we note that if both $I_K > 0$ and $I_\theta > 0$,[18] then

$$\lambda = \gamma = \eta. \tag{13}$$

This also implies that $\dot{\gamma} = \dot{\eta}$. Using this and (13) in (12.v) and (12.vi), we obtain

$$R_2(p; K, x, \theta) - \delta = R_4(p; K, x, \theta) + \alpha. \tag{14}$$

Condition (14) states that in long-run equilibrium the net marginal contribution of man-made capital to income should be equal to the net marginal contribution of natural capital.[19] Linear homogeneity of $R(\cdot)$ in K, x, and θ implies that R_2, R_3, and R_4 are homogeneous of degree zero in K, x, and θ. This allows us to express the marginal value products of K, x, and θ solely as functions of the factor ratios. Then, we can rewrite Equations (12.ii) and (14) in this form. Recalling that $\lambda = \eta$, we have from (12.ii),

$$R_3\left(p; \frac{K}{\theta}, \frac{x}{\theta}, 1\right) = \beta, \tag{15}$$

and

$$R_2\left(p; \frac{K}{\theta}, \frac{x}{\theta}, 1\right) - \delta = R_4\left(p; \frac{K}{\theta}, \frac{x}{\theta}, 1\right) + \alpha. \tag{16}$$

Thus, we have that (15) and (16) govern the long-run equilibrium. We can solve this system for the relevant long-run factor ratios as

$$\text{(i)} \quad \left(\frac{K}{\theta}\right)^* = \phi(\alpha + \delta, \beta, p),$$

$$\text{(ii)} \quad \left(\frac{x}{\theta}\right)^* = \varphi(\alpha + \delta, \beta, p). \tag{17}$$

An implication of (17) is that in long-run equilibrium, man-made capital and natural capital grow at the same rate as long as p, β, and $\alpha + \delta$ are constant. That is, though the production technology specified assumes substitution between natural and man-made capital, the long-run behavioral implication of the model is one of perfect complementarity.

---

[18] Equivalently, the long-run equilibrium can be regarded as the solution of the system if we did not impose the non-negativity constraints for I_K and I_θ. It is the total investment $I_K + I_\theta$ that is limited in the short run (given the strict concavity of u in y) but not necessarily the individual investments.

[19] See Barro and Sala-i-Martin (1995) for a similar long-run condition in the context of a one-sector model with two stocks of capital.

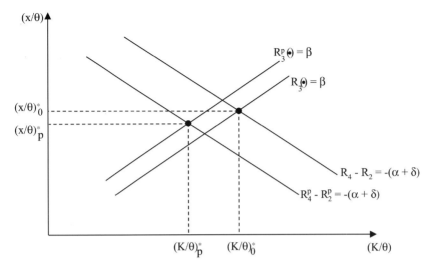

Figure 1. The effect of an increase of the terms-of-trade of the natural resource-intensive sector (agriculture).

Given the assumptions about the $R(\cdot)$ function, it can be shown that

$$\frac{\partial (K/\theta)^*}{\partial p} < 0.$$

Figure 1 shows this result. Given the properties of $R(\cdot)$, we have that the schedule $R_3(\cdot) = \beta$ (Equation (15)) should be upward-sloping in the x/θ and K/θ space. Similarly, the schedule $R_2(\cdot) - \delta = R_4(\cdot) + \alpha$ (Equation (16)) should be downward-sloping. The long-run equilibrium at the initial level of p is given by $(K/\theta)^*_o$ and $(x/\theta)^*_o$ in Figure 1.[20] A permanent increase in p causes an upward shift of the schedule $R_3(\cdot) = \beta$ and a downward shift of schedule $R_2 - \delta = R_4 + \alpha$. To see this, differentiate (15) with respect to p and x/θ, keeping K/θ constant, and differentiate (16) with respect to p and K/θ, keeping x/θ constant. The fact that $R_{41} > 0$, $R_{21} < 0$, $R_{42} > 0$, and $R_{22} < 0$ is sufficient for the schedule $R_2 - \delta = R_4 + \delta$ to shift downwards. Similarly $R_{31} > 0$ and $R_{33} < 0$ is sufficient for the schedule $R_3(\cdot) = \beta$ to shift upwards. Thus, the new long-run equilibrium $(K/\theta)^*_p$ and $(x/\theta)^*_p$ necessarily implies a fall of K/θ after a permanent increase in the relative price of the agricultural good. That is, an improvement in the terms of trade for agriculture induces a fall in the long-run man-made to natural capital ratio. The intuition behind this is clear: Since agriculture is more intensive in natural

---

[20] We are abstracting here from the various patterns of specialization that may arise: First, an economy that is resource-rich specializes only in agriculture (e.g., the resource-intensive industry), then it enters into a phase of diversification as the K/θ ratio increases, and it can eventually end up specialized in the manufacturing sector if the terms of trade or other exogenous factors do not change [see López (1999)].

capital than is manufacturing, an increase in the relative price of agriculture will induce an increase in the demand for natural capital relative to man-made capital.

What happens with growth in the long run? Differentiating (12.i) with respect to time using $\dot{\gamma} = \dot{\lambda}$ and (12.v) we have

$$\frac{\dot{y}}{y} = \frac{1}{a}\left[R_2\big(p; (K/\theta)^*, (x/\theta)^*, 1\big) - (r + \delta)\right], \tag{18}$$

where $a \equiv -(u_{22}/u_2)y > 0$ is the Frish coefficient of the indirect utility function which is positive given the strict concavity assumption. Since $(K/\theta)^*$ and $(x/\theta)^*$ are constants for given exogenous variables, we have that $R_2(\cdot)$ does not change through time. Given that the cost of capital, $r + \delta$, is also constant, the gap between the marginal value product of capital and its opportunity cost is never closed in the long run. If the productivity of the system is such that $R_2(p; (K/\theta)^*, (x/\theta)^*, 1) > r + \delta$, then we have permanent growth with K, θ and x growing at the same rate as real consumption expenditures, y, if the coefficient a is constant, as is usually assumed by most studies that postulate a Cobb–Douglas utility function. In general, a is a function of p and y. The effect $\partial a(p, y)/\partial y$ is likely to be positive under relatively weak conditions [López (1994)]. If this is the case, the rate of growth of consumption would be declining through time but always positive. This declining rate happens despite the fact that the rate of growth of K is equal to the rate of growth of θ (and x). When $\partial a/\partial y > 0$, the total rate of savings declines through time, causing the common rate of growth of K and θ (and, consequently, of x) to fall through time, but still being always positive.

If the parameters $p, \beta, \alpha + \delta$, and r are such that the term in square brackets in (18) is less than or equal to zero, then there will be no positive economic growth in the long run. A zero growth steady state would be reached and condition (16) may not hold.

What happens in the short run? In the short run one of the non-negativity constraints $(I_K \geqslant 0$ or $I_\theta \geqslant 0)$ is likely to be binding. If initially $K/\theta < (K/\theta)^*$, then $I_\theta = 0, \eta = 0$, and $I_K = R(\cdot) - y$, i.e., the country reduces θ as fast as it can and uses all savings to increase K. That is, a resource-abundant country will tend to accumulate K fast and to let θ fall. The increase of K causes x at first to increase as $R_3(\cdot)$ goes up. The higher x eventually causes $\dot{\theta} < 0$.

In the short run, when natural capital is abundant relative to man-made capital (e.g., when $(K/\theta) < (K/\theta)^*$), we have that $\eta = 0$, and hence (12.ii) becomes

$$R_3(p; K/\theta, x/\theta, 1) = 0. \tag{19}$$

Also $\gamma > 0$ and $\lambda = \gamma$, implying from (12.v) that

$$\dot{\gamma} = (r + \delta)\gamma - \gamma R_2(p; K/\theta, x/\theta, 1). \tag{20}$$

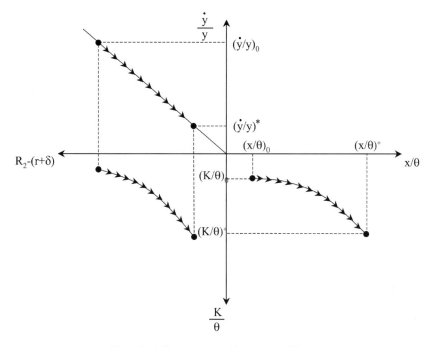

Figure 2. Adjustment toward long-run equilibrium.

Economic growth then is given by

$$\dot{y}/y = \frac{1}{a}\big[R_2(p, K/\theta, x/\theta, 1) - (r+\delta)\big].\qquad (21)$$

In the movement from the initial natural resource abundant equilibrium to the long-run balanced equilibrium, three trends take place:

(1) K/θ is initially lower than in long-run equilibrium and, therefore, increases towards $(K/\theta)^*$;

(2) x/θ is initially lower than $(x/\theta)^*$ and increases toward this level; and

(3) economic growth is faster initially than in the long run and gradually falls toward its long-run level.

Using (19) it is clear that as K/θ increases x/θ should also rise because by strict concavity R_3 is decreasing in x/θ and by gross complementarity it is increasing in K/θ. Thus K/θ and x/θ move in the same direction. Also, $R_2(\cdot) - (r+\delta)$ should fall as K/θ and x/θ increase through time. That is, along the path of adjustment toward long-run balanced equilibrium, $R_2(\cdot) - (r+\delta)$ is falling. If a is constant, we have that this implies that $\dot{y}/y$ is also falling through time. Figure 2 depicts the adjustment towards long-run equilibrium just described.

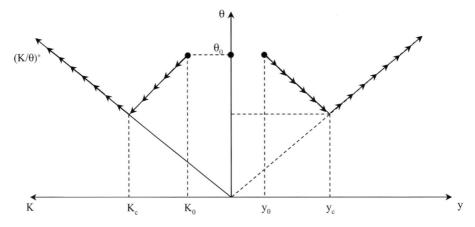

Figure 3. Adjustment and long-run equilibrium growth.

In summary, the natural capital falls and the overall growth rate falls while the rate of extraction of natural capital and man-made capital stock increase during the adjustment process. During the adjustment there is no investment in natural capital: all savings are used to invest in man-made capital. But once the long-run equilibrium is reached, the savings are then distributed between investment in natural capital and man-made capital so that the rates of growth of both stocks become identical, e.g., in long-run equilibrium

$$\frac{\dot{\theta}}{\theta} = \frac{\dot{K}}{K} > 0. \tag{22}$$

Figure 3 provides a view of the complete pattern of evolution of the three key variables, namely, θ, K and y. The predicted relationship between θ and y and θ and K is U-shaped. That is, for a growing economy the model predicts a Kuznets-type relationship through time.

Imperfect internalization of the social value of natural capital. So far we have assumed that producers consider the full social cost of θ in their investment decisions. In reality, institutions in LDCs are very imperfect and at least part of the natural resources are open access and/or common property with highly imperfect social control of their use. We consider here these cases. The easiest way of looking at this is by considering the value of the shadow price of natural resources, η in our model. Imperfections in the market for natural resources will be reflected in the actual value of η that is taken into consideration in resource allocation decisions. That is, imperfect institutions create a wedge between the true and actual value of the price of the natural resource considered in the resource allocation decisions. That is, $\eta^D \leqslant \eta$, where η^D is the actual price of the natural capital used by producers.

First, let us consider the other extreme case, where the internalization of the price of θ, instead of being perfect as in the previous model, is negligible, e.g., $\eta^D = 0$ at all stages. *This will have no effect on the adjustment process. That is, the pattern of adjustment of a natural resource rich economy will not be affected by the institutions governing natural resource exploitation.* In both cases, $\eta = 0$, and in both cases θ will be identical and declining and the pressure on natural resources will be increasing (i.e., x/θ is rising). Also, in both cases economic growth is the same and declining through time.

The key difference is that the economy with adequate natural resource institutions may be able to reach a long-run equilibrium path with positive growth, while in the economy without such institutions, the long-run equilibrium necessarily implies zero growth. That is, in the latter case economic growth is choked after θ reaches a certain critical level at which $R_2(p; K/\theta, x/\theta, 1) = r + \delta$. At this point growth stops – K, θ, x and y become stagnant. There is no recovery of the natural capital.

This can be seen in the mathematical model itself. Assume that $\eta^D = \Omega \eta$, where $0 \leqslant \Omega \leqslant 1$. That is, Ω is a coefficient measuring the degree of institutional efficiency of the economy. From conditions (12) the long-run equilibrium would now imply that $\lambda = \gamma = \Omega \eta$ and, if Ω is constant, that $\dot{\gamma} = \Omega \dot{\eta}$. Thus, using this in (12.v), (12.vi) and (12.ii) gives the long-run equilibrium conditions

$$-(r+\delta)\gamma + \gamma R_2(\cdot) = \Omega\big[(r-\alpha)\eta - \gamma R_4\big], \tag{23}$$

$$R_3(\cdot) = \beta. \tag{24}$$

Thus, if there is complete resource imperfection, $\Omega = 0$, and in long-run equilibrium, $R_2 = r + \delta$. This means that growth comes to a halt in the long run because of the institutional imperfection.

If the resource control failure is only partial we have that $0 < \Omega < 1$. Using (23) and (24) it is easy to show that $(K/\theta)^*$ and $(x/\theta)^*$ both increase with Ω. That is, if $\Omega < 1$ we have that in long-run equilibrium the capital/natural resource ratio is higher than if $\Omega = 1$. Thus, long-run equilibrium will be achieved at a lower θ when $0 < \Omega < 1$, but in the long run θ will recover if at the new long-run levels $R_2(\cdot)$ is still larger than $r + \delta$. If not, growth will disappear in the long run and there will be no resource recovery.

Solving (23) and (24), we find that there is a critical value of Ω, $\widetilde{\Omega}$, which yields $(\widetilde{K/\theta})^D$ and $(\widetilde{x/\theta})^D$ at which long-run growth becomes zero. This is defined by

$$R_2\big[p, \phi(p, \delta+\alpha, \beta; \widetilde{\Omega}), \psi(p, \delta+\alpha, \beta; \widetilde{\Omega}), 1\big] = r + \delta. \tag{25}$$

That is, if the actual $\Omega \leqslant \widetilde{\Omega}$, the economy becomes stagnant in the long-run and there is no recovery of the natural resources.

Thus, institutional inefficiency for a resource-rich economy is of no consequence in the short run for growth or for stock of natural resources. Moreover, if the institutional

inefficiency is corrected along the adjustment towards long-run equilibrium, institutional inefficiencies are of no consequence for the long-run either. If the institutional
inefficiency is not corrected along the adjustment path, then the process of adjustment
lasts longer than in the case of efficient institutions and the long-run rate of growth of
θ (and K) is slower than the optimal one. But as long as the institutional inefficiency is
not too profound (e.g., $\Omega^D > \widetilde{\Omega}$), growth of θ, K and y in the long run is still positive.
The environmental Kuznets curve of Figure 2 would still apply. If, however, the institu-
tional inefficiency is large enough ($\Omega^D < \widetilde{\Omega}$), a significant qualitative change occurs:
Economic growth is smothered in the long run and there is no recovery of the stock of
natural resources. The environmental Kuznets curve does not in this case apply.

The role of prices. First we consider the effect of changes in the terms of trade of
agriculture that originated in changes in world prices. Next we look at changes induced
by distortionary policies that tax agriculture.

The world price change can be analyzed with the model already presented. Consider
first a *permanent* unexpected change in p for a resource-rich economy that is growing
towards its long-run equilibrium level. This will affect long-run equilibrium represented
by Equations (15) and (16). It was shown earlier that, given the properties of $R(\cdot)$,
an increase in p will induce a reduction of $(K/\theta)^*$. Also, given that a resource-rich
economy in the short run does not invest in natural capital ($I_\theta = 0$), we have then to
move towards a lower K/θ ratio, which implies a higher level of θ and lower K, and the
economy has to reduce x/θ in the short run. That is, the rate of resource extraction in the
short run falls in response to a permanent increase of the terms of trade of agriculture.
The wedge between $R_2(\cdot)$ and $(r + \delta)$ deepens and, therefore, the economy will in the
long run be able to grow at a faster rate (assuming the Frish coefficient a is constant).
That is, the adjustment path will stop earlier, at a lower value of K/θ. Thus, the natural
resource will be allowed to depreciate less during the adjustment process and the rate
of recovery of the natural resource along the long-run balanced growth path is faster at
higher levels of p.

If the increase in p is only temporary, then the long-run K/θ^* and x/θ^* ratios remain
unchanged, but in the short run the x/θ ratio jumps (see Equation (19)). This causes an
acceleration of the rate of degradation of the stock of natural resources in the short
run. But as the level of p returns to its original value, K/θ asymptotically returns to its
original path of adjustment, reaching the long run at the same level. What happens is that
producers use the price bonanza to sell more of the agriculture commodity, extracting
more natural capital to exploit the short-run profit opportunities.

References

Ahuja, V. (forthcoming), "Land degradation, agricultural productivity and common property: Evidence from
    Côte d'Ivoire", Environment and Development Economics.

Ahuja, V. (1996), "Efficiency of resource use in common property: A case of land in sub-Saharan Africa", Ph.D. dissertation (Department of Agricultural and Resource Economics, University of Maryland, College Park).

Andersen, E., C. Granger, L. Huang, E. Reis and D. Weinhold (1996), "Report on Amazon deforestation" (Department of Economics, University of California, San Diego).

Anderson, J.N. (1987), "Lands at risk, people at risk: Perspectives on tropical forest transformation in the Philippines", in: P. Little and M. Horowitz, eds., Lands at Risk in the Third World (Westview Press, Boulder, CO).

Anderson, T., and P. Hill (1990), "Race for property rights", Journal of Law and Economics 33:177–197.

André, C., and J.-P. Platteau (1998), "Land relations under unbearable stress: Rwanda caught in the Malthusian trap", Journal of Economic Behavior and Organization 34(1):1–47.

Angelsen, A. (1997), "Deforestation: Population or market driven? Different approaches in modeling agricultural expansion", Mimeo (Michelsen Institute, Bergen, Norway).

Baland, J.-M., and J.-P. Platteau (1996), Halting Degradation of Natural Resources (Clarendon Press, Oxford, UK).

Bandy, D., D. Garrity and P. Sanchez (1993), "The Worldwide problem of slash and burn agriculture", Agroforestry Today 5:2–6.

Bardhan, P. (1991), The Economic Theory of Agrarian Institutions (Clarendon Press, Oxford, UK).

Barrett, S. (1991), "Optimal soil conservation and the reform of agricultural pricing policies", Journal of Development Economics 36:167–187.

Barro, R., and X. Sala-i-Martin (1995), Economic Growth (McGraw-Hill, Inc., New York).

Benjamin, D. (1992), "Household composition and labor demand: A test of rural labor market efficiency", Econometrica 60:287–322.

Boserup, E. (1965), The Conditions of Agricultural Growth: The Economics of Agrarian Change Under Population Pressure (Aldine, New York).

Boserup, E. (1981), Population and Technological Change: A Study of Long-Term Change (University of Chicago Press, Chicago).

Brander, J., and M. Taylor (1997), "International trade and open-access renewable resources: The small open economy case", Canadian Journal of Economics 30(3):526–552.

Browder, J. (1988), "Public policy and deforestation in the Brazilian Amazon", in: R. Repetto and M. Gillis, eds., Public Policies and the Misuse of Forest Resources (Cambridge University Press, Cambridge).

Caillavet, F., H. Guimard and R. LiFran (1994), Agricultural Household Modeling and Family Economics (Elsevier Press, Amsterdam).

Chayanov, V. (1966), The Theory of Peasant Economy (American Economic Association, Illinois).

Chichilnisky, G. (1994), "North–South trade and the global environment", American Economic Review 85:755–787.

Chopra, K., and S. Gulati (1996), "Environmental degradation: Property rights and population movements: Hypotheses and evidence from Rajasthan" (Institute of Economic Growth, New Delhi, India).

Collins, J. (1987), "Labor scarcity and ecological change", in: P. Little and M. Horowitz, eds., Lands at Risk in the Third World (Westview Press, Boulder, CO).

Copeland, B., and M. Taylor (1995), "Trade and transboundary pollution", American Economic Review 85(2):675–740.

Cropper, M., and W. Oates (1992), "Environmental economics: A survey", Journal of Economic Literature 30(2):675–740.

de Janvry, A., M. Fafchamps and E. Sadoulet (1991), "Peasant household behavior with missing markets: Some paradoxes explained", Economic Journal 101:1400–1417.

Demsetz, H. (1967), "Towards a theory of property rights", American Economic Review 57:347–359.

Diewert, W. (1973), "Functional forms for profit and transformation functions", Journal of Economic Theory 9:284–316.

Diewert, W. (1974), "Applications of duality theory", in: M.D. Intriligator and D.A. Kendrick, eds., Frontiers of Quantitative Economics (North-Holland, Amsterdam).

Ellis, S., and A. Mellor (1995), Soils and Environment (Routledge, London).

FAO (Food and Agriculture Organization of the United Nations) (1986), "Efficient fertilizer use in acid upland soils of the humid tropics", Fertilizer and Plant Nutrition Bulletin No. 10 (FAO, Rome, Italy).

Feder, G. (1987), "Land ownership and farm productivity: Evidence from Thailand", Journal of Development Studies 24(1):16–30.

Garcia-Barrios, R., and L. Garcia-Barrios (1990), "Environmental and technological degradation in peasant agriculture: A consequence of development in Mexico", World Development 18:1569–1585.

Grepperud, S. (1997), "Soil conservation as an investment in land", Journal of Development Economics 54:455–467.

Intal, P. (1991), "Commentary on 'Environmental consequences of agricultural growth'", in: R. Vosti, ed., Agricultural Sustainability, Growth and Poverty Alleviation: Issues and Policies, Proceedings of a Conference (Feldafing, Germany).

Jarvis, L. (1974), "Cattle as capital goods and ranchers as portfolio managers: An application to the Argentina cattle sector", Journal of Political Economy 82:489–520.

Johnson, D.G. (1950), "Resource allocation under share contracts", Journal of Political Economy 58:111–123.

Jones, J. (1990), Colonization and Environment. Land Settlement Projects in Latin America (United Nations University, Tokyo).

Kaimowitz, D. (1995), "Livestock and deforestation in Central America in the 1980s and 1990s: A policy perspective" (Center for International Forestry Research, Bogo, Indonesia).

Kates, R., and V. Haarmann (1992), "Where the poor live: Are the assumptions correct?", Environment 34:4–28.

Kohli, U. (1991), Technology, Duality and Foreign Trade: The GNP Approach to Modeling Inputs and Exports (University of Michigan Press, Ann Arbor, MI).

LaFrance, J.T. (1992), "Do increased commodity prices lead to more or less soil degradation?", Australian Journal of Agricultural Economics 1:57–82.

López, R. (1981), "Economic behavior of self-employed households", Ph.D. dissertation (Department of Economics, University of British Columbia, Vancouver, BC, Canada).

López, R. (1984), "Estimating labor supply and production decisions of self-employed farm producers", European Economic Review 24:61–82.

López, R. (1985), "A structural non-recursive model of the farm-household", in: Singh, Squire, and Strauss, eds., Agricultural Household Models: Extensions and Applications (The Johns Hopkins University Press, Baltimore, MD).

López, R. (1992), "Environmental degradation and economic openness in LDCs: The poverty linkage", American Journal of Agricultural Economics 74:1138–1145.

López, R. (1993), "Resource degradation, community controls and agricultural productivity in tropical areas", Mimeo (Department of Agricultural and Resource Economics, University of Maryland, College Park).

López, R. (1994), "The environment as a factor of production: The effects of economic growth and trade liberalization", Journal of Environmental Economics and Management 27:163–184.

López, R. (1996), "Land titles and farm productivity in Honduras" (Department of Agricultural and Resource Economics, University of Maryland, College Park).

López, R. (1997), "Environmental externalities in traditional agriculture and the impact of trade liberalization: The case of Ghana", Journal of Development Economics 53:17–39.

López, R. (1998), "Agricultural intensification, common property resources and the farm-household", Environmental and Resource Economics 11:443–458.

López, R. (1999), "Growth and stagnation in natural resource-rich economies" (Department of Agricultural and Resource Economics, University of Maryland, College Park).

López, R., and M. Niklitscheck (1991), "Dual economic growth in poor tropical areas", Journal of Development Economics 34:329–338.

López, R., and A. Valdés (2000), Rural Poverty in Latin America (MacMillan, UK; St. Martin Press, U.S.).

Mahar, D., and R. Schneider (1994), "Incentives for tropical deforestation: Some examples from Latin America", in: K. Brown and D. Pearce, eds., The Causes of Tropical Deforestation (UCL Press, London).

Newbery, D. (1977), "Risk-sharing, sharecropping, and uncertain labour markets", Review of Economic Studies 44:585–594.

Rudel, T., and J. Roper (1997), "The paths to rainforest deforestation: Cross national patterns of tropical deforestation", World Development 25(1):53–65.

Sanchez, P. (1976), Properties and Management of Soils in the Tropics (Wiley, New York).

Singh, I., L. Squire and J. Strauss (1985), Agricultural Households: Extensions and Applications (The Johns Hopkins University Press, Baltimore, MD).

Stiglitz, J. (1974), "Incentives and risk-sharing in sharecropping", Review of Economic Studies 41:219–255.

Tiffen, M., M. Mortimore and F. Gichuki (1994), More People, Less Erosion: Environmental Recovery in Kenya (J. Wiley, New York).

Tomich, T., and M. Van Noordwijk (1995), "What drives deforestation in Sumatra?", Paper presented at the Regional Symposium on "Montana mainland Asia in transition" (Chiang Mai, Thailand).

Warford, J., M. Munasinghe and W. Cruz (1997), The Greening of Economic Policy Reform (The World Bank, Washington, DC).

Webster, C., and P. Wilson (1980), Agriculture in the Tropics (Longman, London).

World Bank (1992), World Development Report 1992 (Oxford University Press, New York).

World Bank (1999), Revisiting the Lessons of Development (Washington, DC).

Wunder, S. (1997), "From Dutch disease to deforestation: A macroeconomic link" (Centre for Development Research, Copenhagen, Denmark).

Yver, R. (1972), "Investment behavior and the supply response of cattle farmers in Argentina", Ph.D. dissertation (Department of Economics, University of Chicago).

Chapter 23

AGRICULTURE AND THE ENVIRONMENT

ERIK LICHTENBERG

Department of Agricultural and Resource Economics, University of Maryland, College Park, MD

Contents

Handbook of Agricultural Economics, Volume 2, Edited by B. Gardner and G. Rausser
© *2002 Elsevier Science B.V. All rights reserved*

Abstract

The distinctive nature of environmental quality problems in agriculture – an industry based on the extraction of highly variable natural resources under stochastic conditions – has important implications for policy design. First, we examine the source of environmental quality problems and the strength of incentives for resource stewardship that may incidentally induce farmers to protect environmental quality. In turn, we examine environmental policy design under two features that are pervasive in agriculture: (1) heterogeneity caused by resource variability and (2) uncertainty. Next, we examine the effects of interactions between agricultural, environmental, and resource policies. Finally, we review important areas for further research.

Keywords

environmental quality, pesticides, fertilizers, livestock waste, erosion, stewardship, water

JEL classification: Q19

1. Introduction

Agriculture provides a wide variety of environmental amenities and disamenities. On the positive side, farms provide open space and scenery. On the negative side, agriculture is a major contributor to numerous environmental problems. Nitrate and pesticide runoff impair drinking water quality and degrade habitat for aquatic organisms including fish, affecting commercial fisheries and recreational uses of estuaries, lakes, and streams. Bacterial contamination from animal wastes animal wastes impairs drinking water quality and contaminates shellfish. Odor from concentrated livestock facilities worsens the quality of life in nearby residential areas. Erosion-induced sedimentation of waterways increases drinking water treatment costs and accelerates the need for dredging to maintain navigability. Pesticide exposure causes both acute and chronic illness among farmers and farm workers, while pesticide residues on foods may also threaten human health. Ecological damage from agriculture includes kills of fish, birds, animals, and invertebrates from pesticides and, most important, habitat loss from conversion of forests, wetlands, and grasslands. Heavy metals like selenium and arsenic in drainage water have been implicated in wildlife kills and reproductive problems and can pose hazards to human health. Negative externalities also occur within agriculture. Salinization of rivers by irrigation runoff damages crop production in downstream areas. Upslope irrigation may cause drainage problems in downslope areas. Pesticide drift kills bees and thus impairs orchard pollination.

These problems have spawned a large, wide-ranging literature exploring efficient and equitable policy design. This chapter reviews some of the major developments in that literature, concentrating on the portion that addresses the major features distinguishing agriculture from other industries.

We begin by considering the size, scope, and origins of environmental problems in agriculture. Agriculture involves extraction of renewable resources under naturally occurring conditions. Agricultural productivity has traditionally depended on the natural resource base of agriculture, giving farmers economic incentives for conserving that resource base. Protection of environmental quality has historically been a side effect of those conservation efforts. These economic incentives for resource conservation have traditionally been referred to as "stewardship". Section 2 explores the implications of stewardship for environmental policy.

The resource base of agriculture varies substantially both across growing regions and across farms and fields within growing regions. As a result, both agricultural productivity and environmental quality exhibit significant heterogeneity. Section 3 explores the implications of heterogeneity for environmental policy design.

As noted above, agricultural production occurs largely under naturally occurring conditions. Thus, stochastic factors exert significant influence on both agricultural productivity and environmental quality. Section 4 explores the implications of uncertainty for environmental policy design.

For millennia, agriculture has been central to human existence. The irreducible human need for food has led governments in virtually all countries to adopt policies relating specifically to the agricultural sector. Environmental policies aimed at agriculture operate in combination with these farm-sector policies. Section 5 explores interactions between environmental and agricultural policies.

Finally, Section 6 sums up the major lessons of this literature and highlights topics of special interest for further research.

2. Agriculture, stewardship, and the environment

Farming is, at bottom, a resource extraction industry. Both crop and livestock production involve harvesting biota, that is, renewable natural resources produced by biological processes. Both utilize as intermediate inputs a variety of natural resources, such as soils, water, genetic material, non-crop plant life, and naturally occurring fauna that mitigate damage caused by pest species. These natural resources may simultaneously influence environmental spillovers from agricultural production like water pollution, pesticide poisonings, or scenic amenities.

The farm environment has also traditionally been an important source of direct consumption goods for farmers and their families. Hunting and fishing have historically provided significant shares of farmers' diets (and continue to do so in many developing countries). Groundwater and local streams can be major sources of drinking water. Protecting wildlife habitat, water quality, and other aspects of environmental quality at the local level can thus be equivalent to protecting farmers' standard of living.

Until recently, agriculture was considered a clean industry, largely because farmers' well-being depended on the resource base of agriculture and on local environmental quality. Farmers were thought to be stewards of both in their own self-interest. Even today, stewardship is often invoked as a solution to environmental problems in agriculture, and attempts to popularize more environment-friendly farming practices remain the major form of environmental policy in agriculture, at least in developed countries.

In this section, we consider stewardship as a means of dealing with environmental problems. We begin by developing a formal model of the market failures underlying these environmental problems. We then use the model to formalize the notion of stewardship. Finally, we consider the empirical evidence on the strength of these stewardship incentives and discuss the relationship between stewardship and technical change. The section as a whole addresses some of the central questions arising in discussions of sustainable agriculture, e.g., the extent to which farmers have incentives for protecting environmental quality voluntarily and how those incentives are influenced by technical change.

2.1. Agriculture and environment: theory

We begin with two formal models for characterizing the market failures underlying environmental problems in agriculture. The first is an output-oriented model in which the natural resource base enters only implicitly. The second is an input-oriented model that can incorporate those resources explicitly.

Overall, environmental spillovers are perhaps best conceptualized as arising from a multiple-output production system in which agricultural production and environmental quality are produced simultaneously from a given vector of inputs. Let y be a vector of agricultural products, q be a vector of environmental impacts, and x be a vector of inputs. Agricultural technology is then a set $T = \{(y, q, x): x \text{ can produce } (y, q)\}$.

The output-oriented model represents this technology using a joint cost function for agricultural output and environmental quality $C(y, q, w) = \min\{wx: (y, q, x) \in T\}$, where w is a vector of input prices. Let $U(y, q)$ represent society's gross benefit from the consumption of agricultural output and environmental quality. We assume that these benefits are strongly separable from other forms of consumption or, equivalently, that the agricultural sector accounts for a share of the overall economy sufficiently small that income effects are negligible. Optimal joint production of agricultural products and environmental quality is found by choosing (y, q) to maximize net benefits $U(y, q) - C(y, q, w)$. The necessary conditions are

$$U_y(y, q) - C_y(y, q, w) = 0,$$

$$U_q(y, q) - C_q(y, q, w) = 0,$$

i.e., the marginal benefits of agricultural output and environmental quality should be equated to their marginal costs. (Subscripts denote partial derivatives.)

If market (inverse) demands for agricultural output and environmental quality equal $U_y(y, q)$ and $U_q(y, q)$, respectively, then perfectly competitive markets will generate the socially efficient levels of agricultural output and environmental quality in equilibrium. But in most cases, environmental quality problems arise in agriculture because effective market demand for environmental quality in agriculture is incomplete or lacking. For example, farmers are not required to pay for disposal of sediment, nutrients, or pesticides into surface or ground waters. Similarly, farmers cannot charge for the open space, greenery, and scenic views their farms provide for neighboring residents and for passersby. Both the environmental resources farmers provide and those they use are thus subject to open access exploitation. At bottom, the lack of markets for these environmental resources is due to the extreme difficulty – or even downright impossibility – of establishing and enforcing clear property rights. [For a more complete discussion of property rights issues see Bromley (1991).] Most scenic amenities from agriculture, for example, are public goods. The consumption of farm scenery is non-exclusive and non-rival. Moreover, since the marginal cost of providing scenery to an additional consumer is minimal, leaving these scenic amenities unpriced can be efficient at the margin. But leaving such amenities unpriced fails to provide farmers with incentives to forego development of their land, even when doing so is in the public interest. Open access occurs in water pollution from agricultural emissions of nutrients, sediment, or pesticides for a somewhat different reason. Emissions of agricultural pollutants are diffuse and enter water bodies at numerous different points. Furthermore, it is difficult to distinguish agricultural emissions of nutrients and sediments from those that occur naturally. It is impossible to restrict access to these water bodies, and hence impossible to levy charges for access to them.

In the absence of markets for environmental quality, farmers tend to treat it as freely disposable. In an unregulated market, the joint production of agricultural output and environmental quality will thus be characterized by the conditions

$$U_y(y, q) - C_y(y, q, w) = 0,$$

$$C_q(y, q, w) = 0,$$

which imply too much agricultural output and too little environmental quality. In other words, the level of agricultural output generated by competitive markets exceeds the socially optimal level, while the level of environmental quality generated by competitive markets falls short of the socially optimal level.

In many cases, environmental effects of agriculture are associated with the use of one or more specific inputs, such as fertilizers or pesticides in the case of water pollution or farmland in the case of scenic amenities. Let z be the specific input(s) of interest and v be the associated price(s). Let $e(z)$ represent the environmental effects of input use, where $e_z > 0$. Let the agricultural output technology be represented by a revenue function $R(p, w, z) = \max_{x,y}\{py - wx: (y, x, z) \in T\}$. Note that decreasing marginal productivity of z implies increasing marginal income foregone due to reductions in z, so that this formulation is equivalent to one characterized by increasing marginal cost of producing environmental quality. Let $S(p, e(z))$ be the social surplus accruing when the price of agricultural output is p and the level of environmental quality is $e(z)$. Under standard assumptions, $S_p = -y$, that is, the derivative of S with respect to p equals the negative of demand for agricultural output, and $S_{pp} = -\partial y/\partial p > 0$. S_e is negative for adverse environmental effects and positive for beneficial ones.

The socially optimal usage level(s) of z and agricultural output price(s) p in this case maximize net social surplus $S(p, e(z)) + R(p, w, z) - vz$ and is characterized by the necessary conditions

$$S_p(p, e(z)) + R_p(p, w, z) = 0,$$

$$S_e(p, e(z))e_z + R_z(p, w, z) - v = 0.$$

The first condition is the market clearing condition that the quantity of agricultural output demanded $(-S_p)$ equals the quantity supplied (R_p). The second condition says that the value of the marginal product of z (R_z) should equal its unit price (v) plus (minus) the marginal social cost (benefit) of environmental effects arising from use of the input(s). The marginal social cost of z equals the marginal social willingness to pay for environmental quality (S_e) times the marginal amount of environmental quality produced by z (e_z). If markets for environmental quality are lacking, profit-maximizing farmers will equate the value of the marginal product of z with its unit price, leading to overuse of inputs that create negative environmental effects and underuse of inputs that create positive environmental effects.

2.2. Stewardship incentives in agriculture

Even when explicit markets for environmental quality are lacking, implicit linkages between agricultural productivity and environmental quality may give farmers incentives to provide some environmental protection. Policy discussions have traditionally referred to these incentives under the rubric of stewardship. On the production side, these incentives arise via resources that simultaneously improve both agricultural productivity and environmental quality. The canonical example is soil conservation: Preventing erosion simultaneously preserves long-run land productivity and prevents sedimentation and nutrient pollution of waterways. On the consumption side, resources may be significant sources of consumption items for farm families: Wildlife habitat allows for hunting while good water quality provides safe drinking water, fishing, and recreational opportunities.

These examples can be modeled as forms of demand for environmental quality. Using the input-oriented model, divide social surplus from consumption into three components: (1) off-farm surplus from the consumption of agricultural output, $CS(p)$, (2) off-farm damage from use of the input of interest, $D(e(z))$, and (3) on-farm surplus from consumption of agricultural output and goods associated with the resource base of agriculture, $L(p, e(z))$, $L_p > 0$, $L_e < 0$. In the case of soil erosion, for example, z represents the erosion rate, $e(z)$ denotes the long-run reduction in soil depth associated with erosion rate z, and $D(e(z))$ represents off-farm damage from sedimentation and nutrient pollution of waterways. Assuming stationary prices for agricultural output, the value of agricultural productivity in the future can be written as $L(p, e(z))$. When markets for agricultural land are well developed, $L(p, e(z))$ equals the price of farmland [Burt (1981), McConnell (1983)]. In the case of drinking water quality, z might represent fertilizers or pesticides and $e(z)$ the corresponding concentration in well or stream water, while $L(p, e(z))$ represents farm families' surplus from consumption. In the case of pesticides and farmer health, z would represent the toxicity, frequency of application, and/or pesticide application rate, $e(z)$ the corresponding applicator exposure, and $L(p, e(z))$ the farm household's combined demand for agricultural output and health status.

In the absence of explicit markets for environmental quality, the equilibrium is characterized by the conditions

$$CS_p + L_p + R_p = 0,$$
$$L_e e_z + R_z - v = 0.$$

Farmers' unit cost of using the input z, $v - L_e e_z$, exceeds the market price v by an amount equal to the marginal reduction in land value. It is conceivable that these incentives for stewardship are strong enough to replicate the social optimum. The social optimum is characterized by the conditions

$$CS_p + L_p + R_p = 0,$$

$$[L_e - D_e]e_z + R_z - v = 0.$$

The social and private optima coincide if $D_e(e(z)) = 0$ at the profit-maximizing level of z, that is, if profit-maximizing off-farm damage remains below a threshold level [Shortle and Miranowski (1987)].

Alternatively, incentives for stewardship may arise from complementarity between environmental quality and agricultural output in production ($C_{yq} < 0$) or in consumption ($U_{yq} > 0$). If environmental quality and agricultural output are complements in production, farmers will have an incentive to increase environmental quality as a means of lowering the marginal cost of agricultural output. An example is altering pesticide use and other crop management practices to preserve naturally occurring beneficial insects. If demand for agricultural output is greater when environmental quality is greater (environmental quality and agricultural output are complements in consumption), then there will likely exist equilibria in which improvements in environmental quality support increased agricultural production. Organic food is perhaps the most familiar example. In either case, farmers will not treat environmental quality as costless.

2.2.1. Strength of stewardship incentives in modern agriculture

The strength of these stewardship incentives depends on the level of on-farm demand for environmental quality and on the degree of complementarity between agricultural output and environmental quality in production and consumption. These factors vary according to the type of environmental quality problem as well as across nations.

Soil conservation. In theory, well-functioning land markets should provide farmers with sufficient incentives to conserve soil optimally in order to protect farm productivity optimally [Burt (1981), McConnell (1983)], suggesting that stewardship incentives for soil conservation should be strong in developed countries. Empirical evidence from the U.S. and Australia indicates that farm land prices do reflect both past erosion and erosion potential [see, for example, Miranowski and Hammes (1984), Ervin and Mill (1985), Gardner and Barrows (1985), King and Sinden (1988), Palmquist and Danielson (1989)] and that farmers exert greater soil conservation effort on land more vulnerable to erosion [see, for example, Ervin and Ervin (1982), Saliba and Bromley (1986), Norris and Batie (1987), Gould, Saupe and Klemme (1989)]. In the U.S., productivity losses from erosion appear small. For example, the Natural Resource Conservation Service of the U.S. Department of Agriculture estimates that in 1992, only 19 (14) percent of U.S. cropland suffered sheet and rill (wind) erosion at rates high enough to impair productivity in any degree, while only 2 percent suffered severe erosion of either type

[Natural Resource Conservation Service (1994)]. Simulation studies suggest erosion would reduce U.S. agricultural productivity only on the order of 3 to 4 percent over 100 years [Crosson (1986)].

These measures appear insufficient to ensure adequate environmental quality, however. According to the U.S. Environmental Protection Agency, siltation and nutrients from agriculture remain the principal sources of water pollution in the U.S. despite substantial growth in the use of conservation tillage and other soil conservation measures [United States Department of Agriculture, Economic Research Service (ERS) (1997)]. To the best of current knowledge, off-farm damage from sedimentation and associated nutrient pollution in the U.S. is tens or hundreds of times greater than the value of erosion-induced productivity losses [Crosson (1986), Ribaudo (1989)].

About 16 percent of agricultural land in developing countries is estimated to have suffered serious degradation from erosion, waterlogging, and salinization, and soil degradation is believed to have caused significant declines in agricultural productivity in a number of countries [Scherr (1998)]. Poorly operating credit markets and, in some countries, lack of clear property rights in land appear to be major impediments to investment in land, including soil conservation. Stewardship incentives for soil conservation thus appear to play less of a role in environmental protection in these countries than in developed countries. Deininger and Feder (2001) discuss these issues in this Handbook.

Pesticides and farmer/worker safety. Pesticide poisonings from occupational exposures are not uncommon, even in developed countries, although severe cases are relatively rare. In the U.S., for example, the incidence of reported cases of occupational exposure leading to clinically observable symptoms is about 200 per 100,000 workers. Occupational fatalities from pesticides, however, occur on average only once every few years [Levine (1991)]. Farmers' desire to avoid adverse health effects may be one factor in limiting occupational poisoning risk: One would expect informed farmers to take expected adverse health effects into account in making decisions about which pesticides to use, how often to apply those pesticides, pesticide application rates, and application methods. The empirical evidence available to date indicates this motive plays some role. Hedonic studies indicate a negative correlation between acute mammalian toxicity and the prices of pesticides used on corn, cotton, sorghum, and soybeans [Beach and Carlson (1993), Fernandez-Cornejo and Jans (1995)]. U.S. apple growers were less likely to use pesticides with higher acute mammalian toxicity, while those using more toxic pesticides applied them at lower rates [Hubbell and Carlson (1998)]. Corn and soybean growers in the mid-Atlantic with personal experience of adverse health effects from pesticides were more likely to use non-chemical pest control methods [Lichtenberg and Zimmerman (1999a)].

Farmers' incentives for avoiding health effects from pesticide use appear less strong in developing countries. For example, Antle and Pingali (1994) found that the opportunity cost of lost work time from pesticide poisonings among rice farmers in the Philippines exceeded the increased value of rice production due to pesticide use.

Scenic amenities, wetlands preservation, and wildlife habitat. Farmers usually live on or near their farms, making local environmental quality an item of consumption. Farmers frequently engage in outdoor recreational activities like hunting, fishing, and hiking, giving them an incentive to preserve wildlife and scenery in their local area. In these cases, farmers' demand for environmental quality can make up most or all of society's demand for environmental quality, so that farmers' use of inputs that impair environmental quality could coincide with the social optimum.

Several empirical studies have found that farmers who stated greater concern over environmental quality were more likely to use at least some farming practices that reduce runoff and erosion [Napier, Camboni and Thraen (1986), Lynne, Shonkwiler and Rola (1988), Amacher and Feather (1997), Weaver (1996)]. Lichtenberg and Zimmerman (1999b) found that mid-Atlantic farmers were willing to incur substantial extra pesticide costs on average in order to prevent pesticide leaching; concern for overall environmental quality rather than protection of human health appeared to be their principal motivation.

Other empirical findings suggest that farmers' demand for environmental quality may not be very strong. Van Kooten and Schmitz (1992) find that modest payments were insufficient to induce many Canadian farmers to preserve prairie potholes for wildfowl habitat. Weaver (1996) finds that Pennsylvania farmers who had adopted conservation practices in the past because it was the "right thing to do" currently exerted no greater conservation effort than those who had not. Beach and Carlson's (1993) hedonic price study turned up equivocal evidence: Farmers appeared willing to pay more for corn herbicides with shorter half lives and greater soil adsorption, characteristics associated with a lower likelihood of leaching into groundwater, but also for herbicides with greater water solubility, which is associated with a higher likelihood of leaching. Moreover, greater soil adsorption is associated with greater weed control as well as less leaching.

Overall, then, the literature suggests that stewardship incentives do operate in agriculture, but also that they are unlikely to satisfy society's overall demand for environmental quality from agriculture. Measures that protect farm productivity adequately typically fail to suffice for protecting broader environmental quality. Farmers' demand for environmental quality as a consumption good generally makes up only a small share of society's total demand and is thus generally inadequate to ensure attainment of socially desirable levels of environmental quality.

2.2.2. *Technical change, farm structure, and stewardship*

Some have argued that the emergence of agriculture as a source of environmental quality problems is linked to forms of technical change that have attenuated the importance of stewardship incentives [see, for example, Strange (1988)]. For example, the introduction of synthetic chemicals (fertilizers, pesticides) lowered the marginal value of the resource base of agriculture (soil fertility, natural populations of beneficials) and thus stewardship incentives. Moreover, they may have changed the efficient structure of farm enterprises. Strange (1988) and others have argued that, if the costs of environmental damage were fully internalized in farm decision making, smaller-scale joint crop/livestock production would be more profitable than larger-scale, specialized "industrial" farming. This idea is voiced frequently in the sustainable farming advocacy literature but has not been studied rigorously.

It has also been argued that new technologies may be the best means of reducing environmental damage from agriculture. Precision input application methods offer the greatest promise in this regard. A materials balance perspective suggests that matching input application rates more closely to crop uptake rates simultaneously tends to reduce environmental damage from such inputs. As Khanna and Zilberman (1996) point out, in most cases environmental damage is caused only by inputs that are not taken up by the crop or other organisms in the crop ecosystem.

One way to conceptualize improvements in matching application and crop ecosystem uptake rates is to use the distinction between applied and effective input use introduced by Caswell and Zilberman (1986). In their model, effective input use hz is assumed to be proportional to applied input use z. The constant of proportionality h may depend on such factors as water infiltration rates, slope, soil water-holding capacity, or soil nutrient stocks, and may be embodied in a specific delivery technology, e.g., low-pressure irrigation systems. Environmental damage is a function only of residual inputs $[1 - h]z$. Hanemann, Lichtenberg and Zilberman (1989), Caswell, Lichtenberg and Zilberman (1990), and Dinar and Letey (1991) use this conceptualization to investigate the potential for low-volume irrigation methods to mitigate drainage problems in irrigated agriculture. They note that low-volume, pressurized delivery systems like drip can attain efficiencies as high as 95 percent, while gravity-based delivery systems typically are only about 60 percent efficient. Switching from a gravity-based to a low-volume delivery system, then, can decrease effluent production by as much as 87.5 percent. At the same time, improved matching between ecosystem demand and input application rates may result in increased crop productivity. For example, low-volume delivery systems tend to have higher yields because water delivery can be adjusted to match crop uptake rates more closely than is possible with gravity-based delivery systems. Similarly, increased crop productivity has been a major benefit of California's CIMIS evapotranspiration forecasting system [Cohen et al. (1998)].

More generally, assume that crop production is a function of effective input use, which is itself an intermediate output $s(z, h)$ produced by the input application rate z and the application efficiency h. Assume also that agricultural emissions $e(z, h)$ are increasing in the input application rate z but decreasing in application efficiency, i.e., $e_z > 0$, $e_h < 0$. Application efficiency can be increased at a unit cost I. Increased application efficiency will result in reductions in input application rates if the two are complements, $s_{zh} > 0$. When effective input use hz is proportional to applied input use, application efficiency and application rates are complements when the elasticity of the marginal product of the effective input s is greater than one in absolute value [Caswell and Zilberman (1986)]. Socially optimal application efficiency and input application rates are given by

$$pf_s(h, z)s_h(h, z) - I - D_e\big(e(z, h)e_h(z, h)\big) = 0,$$
$$pf_s(h, z)s_z(h, z) - v - D_e\big(e(z, h)e_z(z, h)\big) = 0,$$

while the farmer's profit-maximizing application efficiency and input application rates are given by

$$pf_s(h, z)s_h(h, z) - I = 0,$$
$$pf_s(h, z)s_z(h, z) - v = 0.$$

In the absence of government intervention, farmers will tend to underinvest in application efficiency h and over-apply the input z, so that environmental damage will be greater than socially optimal.

Improvements in efficiency of this kind will tend to mitigate environmental damage on the intensive margin, that is, damage from emissions given existing cultivation patterns. But improvements in efficiency may also have extensive margin effects, e.g., changes in cropping patterns. For example, the principal impact of introducing low-volume irrigation in California was the expansion of fruit and nut cultivation onto hillsides [Caswell and Zilberman (1986), Green et al. (1996)]. Irrigated crop production replaced dry land pasture, so that the introduction of a water-saving technology resulted in increased aggregate water demand. Similarly, the main impact of introducing center-pivot irrigation in the northern High Plains was replacement of pasture by irrigated corn, resulting in increased risk of wind erosion [Lichtenberg (1989)]. Thus, it is by no means certain that improved input application efficiency will improve environmental quality.

2.3. Agriculture and the environment: empirical evidence

Quantitative information about the extent of agriculture's impacts on environmental quality is remarkably scant. Even in developed countries like the U.S., most of this information is anecdotal. In particular, there are few reliable quantitative estimates of how changes in agricultural production or practices affect environmental quality.

Most empirical studies of agriculture's impacts on environmental quality use farm-level simulation models like the Universal Soil Loss Equation (USLE) for erosion and sedimentation [see, for example, Jacobs and Timmons (1974), Taylor and Frohberg (1977), Wade and Heady (1977), Batie and Sappington (1986), Ribaudo (1989), Ribaudo, Osborne and Konyar (1994), Babcock et al. (1996)] or the Erosion/Productivity Impact Calculator (EPIC) for groundwater [see, for example, Johnson, Adams and Perry (1991), Mapp et al. (1994), Teague, Bernardo and Mapp (1995), Helfand and House (1995)]. Inferences from such models are of limited value. One reason is that there is not a simple monotonic relationship between emissions at the level of an individual field and impacts on environmental quality at the ambient scale with which policy is actually concerned. Fate and transport are typically non-linear and depend on space and time in complex ways, making extrapolation of field-level emissions to ambient pollutant concentrations quite complex. Thus, while the USLE may be appropriate for describing movement of sediment from an individual field, it does not address sediment movement across fields into waterways and thus does not capture the relationship between agriculture and ambient pollution. EPIC is similarly designed to model leaching of chemicals through the crop root zone, but addresses neither lateral movement into surface water nor deep percolation into groundwater. The estimated costs of producing environmental quality appear to be quite sensitive to specification of these fate and transport relationships [Braden et al. (1989)]. The relationship between pollutant emissions and environmental quality impacts is similarly complex. The effects of pollutants are mediated by a variety of influences. Environmental effects frequently exhibit thresholds, that is, concentrations of pollutants at or below which there are no environmental effects due to natural degradation and/or detoxification processes. In these cases the relationship between emissions and environmental quality is not monotonic, so that models like EPIC or the USLE are not even appropriate for measuring relative impacts of alternative policies. For example, EPIC simulations may indicate that nitrate leaching from the root zone under one policy regime is twice that under another. But under certain natural conditions (e.g., fields sufficiently far from surface water, intervening forested buffers, sufficiently small percolation), nitrate leached from the root zone may be completely removed before it reaches any body of water, and ambient pollution will be the same under both regimes.

A few studies to date have attempted to estimate agriculture/environment relationships statistically. The most noteworthy come from interdisciplinary efforts to model health effects of pesticide use on rice in the Philippines [Antle and Pingali (1994), Pingali, Marquez and Palis (1994)] and on potatoes in Ecuador [Crissman, Cole and Carpio (1994)]. The Philippines project combined data on production (yield, pesticide use, use of other chemicals, family and hired labor, etc.) with data on health impairments collected by a medical team. Pingali, Marquez and Palis (1994) link health impairments with pesticide usage patterns. Antle and Pingali (1994) develop a health impairment index that they link both to pesticide use and to the cost of rice production. The Ecuador project combined production data with information on the incidence of pesticide poisonings [Crissman, Cole and Carpio (1994)].

A few other studies have attempted to fit statistical relationships characterizing parts of the overall joint agricultural production/environmental quality technology. Anderson, Opaluch and Sullivan (1985) obtained data on use of the insecticide aldicarb on potatoes and on concentrations of aldicarb in water in nearby wells. They were able to use these data to estimate a spatial model of aldicarb leaching into shallow well water, but were unable to obtain information on crop yields that would permit estimation of a link between well water contamination and potato productivity. Huszar (1989) combined household survey data on expenditures attributable to dust with wind erosion rates derived from the Natural Resources Inventory to estimate costs of wind erosion, but did not link wind erosion rates with agricultural production. Lichtenberg and Shapiro (1997) estimated a model linking nitrate concentrations in community water system wells with hydrological characteristics of the pertinent water-bearing formations and indicators of agricultural production (crop acreage and livestock numbers in the counties in which the wells were located) and other nitrate sources such as septic systems.

Other studies of agriculture/environment tradeoffs have used some form of detailed process modeling of agricultural production and environmental impacts, taking into account information from both crop and environmental sciences. Information from these other disciplines in specifying and parameterizing these submodels can yield important qualitative insights for policy formulation. For example, the impacts of pesticide use on farm worker safety are usually conceptualized in terms of the quantities of pesticides applied; that is, health damage from pesticides is typically modeled as a function $H(x)$, where x indicates the total amount of pesticides applied [see, for example, Edwards and Langham (1976)]. A process model developed by Lichtenberg, Spear and Zilberman (1994), however, indicated that the timing of pesticide application relative to harvesting operations is a critical determinant of the risk of acute poisoning from occupational exposure to the insecticide parathion on fruit trees.

3. Heterogeneity

Because of its dependence on natural resources and natural production conditions, agriculture in most countries is heterogeneous. Crop productivity (and thus crop choice), farming practices, and input use patterns vary according to such factors as climate, topography, geology, and pest complexes. Human variability (e.g., differences in human capital across farmers) also affects crop productivity and choice. Environmental effects of agriculture vary in similar ways, partly because of variations in crop choice and cultivation methods and partly because heterogeneity in physical, chemical, and biological characteristics of the environment create differences in environmental fate and transport, exposure, and toxicity.

In this section, we explore the implications of this heterogeneity for efficient policy design. We begin by developing a conceptual model of land allocation/crop choice in land market equilibrium in a heterogeneous industry. We use this model to discuss the efficiency of the four kinds of policies used most frequently to address underprovision of environmental quality in agriculture:

(1) Requiring the use of so-called best management practices;
(2) Imposing restrictions on the use of specific inputs;
(3) Taxing inputs associated with environmental problems; and
(4) Subsidizing environmental quality measures.

We then turn to issues of implementation. We discuss the feasibility of implementing first-best policies for each of the major classes of environmental problems associated with agriculture. We then turn to policy design in cases where heterogeneity is important but regulators either cannot observe it or cannot use the information they have. We extend the basic model to encompass the design of second-best policies under hidden information (adverse selection). We conclude with a discussion of the likely applicability of such second-best policies.

The preceding list of policies has two obvious omissions: (1) taxes imposed on pollutant emissions (nitrogen runoff, pesticide leaching) rather than on inputs, and (2) pollution trading.

Emissions taxes have been used little, if at all, in agriculture. The United States has not used emissions taxes to address pollution problems generally, preferring direct regulation or, more recently, tradable permit systems. Effluent charges have been used more widely in Europe for pollution problems, but appear to have been designed to raise revenue rather than to correct externalities [see, for example, Cropper and Oates (1992)]. Belgium and the Netherlands levy taxes on surplus nutrients from manure and fertilizers, respectively [OECD (1994)], but these levies are based on theoretical rather than measured surpluses and are thus imposed on anticipated average emissions rather than measured actual emissions. Several features of agricultural pollution problems suggest that effluent taxes would be difficult to implement. First, sources of agricultural emissions tend to be numerous, widely dispersed, and difficult to identify. Second, emissions of pollutants like nitrogen or pesticides leached from fields or aerial pesticide drift are not readily observable and can be monitored only by installing expensive devices. Third, heterogeneity of production conditions and biological, physical, and chemical factors influencing the effects of emissions on ambient environmental quality makes it difficult to rely on inferences from models in order to economize on monitoring stations. As a result, monitoring emissions tends to be prohibitively costly, making emissions taxes unattractive in practice.

Pollution trading or purchasing systems have been established formally for nonpoint source nutrient problems affecting a number of watersheds throughout the U.S. Interest in these systems is growing even though few trades have occurred to date. Heterogeneity is, of course, a necessary condition for the desirability of emissions trading – without differences in the cost of pollution reduction, agents cannot realize gains from trade. Pollution trading systems with free initial distribution of permits might be especially attractive in agriculture because such systems help mitigate the distributional effects of regulation, which tend to be pronounced in environmental policies relating to agriculture [Osteen and Kuchler (1987), Lichtenberg, Parker and Zilberman (1988), Zilberman et al. (1991), Sunding (1996)]. The broader environmental economics literature has discussed a variety of issues relating to the design of such systems, including definition of permits and establishing baselines, monitoring and enforcement, market structure (the number of participants), transaction costs, initial distribution of permits, and political-economic acceptability [see Stavins (1998) for an overview, and Letson (1992) or Crutchfield, Letson and Malik (1994) for discussion in the context of point/nonpoint trading]. The infeasibility of monitoring emissions suggests that pollution trades would need to apply to inputs associated with environmental quality. Malik, Letson and Crutchfield (1993) analyze trading between point and nonpoint sources theoretically in situations where nonpoint source emissions are random, but assume that emissions are observable. Overall, the literature lacks analyses of the features that distinguish emissions trading in agricultural situations from other methods of pricing environmental quality such as taxes or subsidies. In what follows, therefore, we treat pollution trading simply as a form of incentive.

3.1. Efficiency of alternative policies in a heterogeneous industry

A version of the input-based model modified along the lines developed by Caswell and Zilberman (1986) and by Lichtenberg (1989) is useful for discussing the relative efficiency of these alternative policy instruments. The basic model was introduced by Hochman and Zilberman (1977) as a tractable means of investigating pollution-production tradeoffs. Moffitt, Just and Zilberman (1978), Hochman, Zilberman and Just (1977a, 1977b), and Lichtenberg and Zilberman (1987) have applied it to problems of dairy waste management in two California river basins. Caswell and Zilberman (1986) and Lichtenberg (1989) used it to study the effects of land quality on irrigation technology choice and on cropping patterns. Caswell, Lichtenberg and Zilberman (1990), Hanemann, Lichtenberg and Zilberman (1989), and Shah, Zilberman and Lichtenberg (1995) have used it to examine drainage problems in the San Joaquin Valley, California. Just and Antle (1990) discuss its use in aggregating micro-level economic and environmental models to estimate aggregate effects. Malik and Shoemaker (1993) use it to discuss targeting of cost-sharing programs for adoption of pollution-reducing agricultural practices.

Let θ represent a source or index of heterogeneity, for example, land quality (soil productivity, slope) or human capital. Let $G(\theta)$ be the cumulative distribution of θ, that is, the number of production units (acres) having at most type θ, and $g(\theta)$ be its density. For convenience, let θ be scaled such that $\theta \in [0, 1]$, $G(0) = 0$, and $G(1) = N$, the total number of production units. In the short run, the number and sizes of production units can be considered fixed. Alternatively, one can assume that both technologies exhibit constant returns to scale and that the potential number of production units is limited by natural conditions such as the amount of potential farmland. In the latter case it is important to bear in mind that not all production units will necessarily be in agricultural production, so that shutdown conditions matter.

Assume also that farmers choose between two activities, which can be two different methods for producing the same crop, as in Caswell and Zilberman (1986), or different crops or crop/technology combinations as in Lichtenberg (1989). Assume that production of each is increasing and neoclassical in θ as well as use of the polluting input z_j, so that each can be represented by a revenue function $R^j(p_j, w, z_j, \theta)$. Let $\delta_1(\theta)$ denote the share of production units of type θ allocated to activity 1 and $\delta_2(\theta)$ denote the share of production units of type θ allocated to activity 2. Assume also for the moment that level of environmental quality is proportional to the use aggregate of z

and is thus invariant with respect to production unit type θ and activity. Environmental quality can thus be written as a function of total use of z:

$$e(z) = \gamma \int_0^1 (\delta_1 z_1 + \delta_2 z_2) g(\theta) \, d\theta.$$

This restriction that environmental quality is invariant with respect to production unit type and activity will be relaxed later. Assume also that social surplus from consumption is additively separable in agricultural output (p_1, p_2) and environmental quality $e(z)$ and that the marginal value of environmental quality is constant. Let c denote the marginal value of environmental quality. It is negative for environmental damage and positive for environmental amenities.

The relevant decision problem is to choose p and z to maximize net social surplus plus agricultural income

$$S(p_1, p_2, e(z)) + \int_0^1 \left[\delta_1 \left(R^1(p_1, w, z_1, \theta) - (v + c\gamma) z_1 \right) \right.$$

$$\left. + \delta_2 \left(R^2(p_2, w, z_2, \theta) - (v + c\gamma) z_2 \right) \right] g(\theta) \, d\theta$$

subject to the constraints that $\delta_1, \delta_2 \leqslant 1$, $\delta_1 + \delta_2 \leqslant 1$, and non-negativity constraints on δ_1 and δ_2. The necessary conditions for a maximum include

$$S_{p_j} + \int_0^1 \delta_j R_p^j(p_j, w, z_j, \theta) g(\theta) \, d\theta = 0, \quad j = 1, 2,$$

$$R_z^j - (v + c\gamma) = 0, \quad j = 1, 2, \ \forall \theta,$$

$$R^j(p_j, w, z_j, \theta) - (v + c\gamma) z_j - \lambda_j - \lambda_0 \leqslant 0,$$

where λ_0 and λ_j are associated with the respective constraints $\delta_1 + \delta_2 \leqslant 1$ and $\delta_j \leqslant 1$. The first set of conditions is again the market-clearing conditions that aggregate demand equal aggregate supply for each activity. The second set of conditions states that the marginal net return from the use of the input z in each activity, $R_z^j - (v + c\gamma)$, should equal marginal social willingness to pay for environmental quality, $S_e e_z$. Note that optimal use of z varies across farm types and activities, since its marginal productivity varies with θ and j. The third set of conditions implies that all of each type of production unit should be allocated to the activity with the greatest social return.

The analysis that follows will be based on one of many possible equilibria. The results obtained under other possibilities are similar, but not identical. Assume that there exists a farm type $\theta_j^* > 0$ such that $R^j(p_j^*, w, z_j^*, \theta_j^*) - [v + c\gamma] z_j^* = 0$, $j = 1, 2$, where p_j^* and z_j^* are the optimal prices and levels of input use z. Assume without loss of generality that $\theta_1^* < \theta_2^*$, so that it is optimal for the lowest type of production unit engaged in agriculture to use activity 1. This assumption implies further that farms of types lower than θ_1^* should not engage in agricultural production, e.g., land of sufficiently low quality should not be farmed. Assume also that $R^2(p_2^*, w, z_2^*, 1) - [v + c\gamma]z_2^* > R^1(p_1^*, w, z_1^*, 1) - [v + c\gamma]z_1^* > 0$ and that $R_\theta^2 > R_\theta^1$ for all θ. These latter assumptions imply the existence of a unique critical type θ_c^* defined by

$$R^1\left(p_1^*, w, z_j^*, \theta_c^*\right) - [v + c\gamma]z_1^* = R^2\left(p_2^*, w, z_2^*, \theta_c^*\right) - [v + c\gamma]z_2^*.$$

All production units of type $\theta_1^* \leqslant \theta < \theta_c^*$ should use activity 1 ($\delta_1 = 1$, $\delta_2 = 0$), while all production units of type $\theta_c^* \leqslant \theta \leqslant 1$ should use activity 2 ($\delta_1 = 0$, $\delta_2 = 1$). Thus, the remaining first-order conditions can be rewritten as

$$S_{p_1} + \int_{\theta_1^*}^{\theta_c^*} R_p^1(p_1, w, z_j, \theta)g(\theta)\,\mathrm{d}\theta = 0,$$

$$S_{p_2} + \int_{\theta_c^*}^{1} R_p^2(p_2, w, z_j, \theta)g(\theta)\,\mathrm{d}\theta = 0,$$

$$R_z^1 - (v + c\gamma) = 0, \qquad \theta_1^* \leqslant \theta < \theta_c^*,$$

$$R_z^2 - (v + c\gamma) = 0, \qquad \theta_c^* \leqslant \theta \leqslant 1.$$

Finally, assume for the sake of convenience that activity 1 has a smaller detrimental (or larger positive) effect on environmental quality than activity 2. If the use of z impairs environmental quality, this assumption implies activity 1 uses the input z less intensively than activity 2, that is $z_2^* > z_1^*$ for any θ. If the use of z enhances environmental quality, the opposite holds.

Without government intervention, farmers will not take environmental quality into account in choosing how intensively to use the input z or how extensively to use activities 1 and 2. If the use of z impairs environmental quality, then farmers of every production type will use too much z in both activities ($z_j^0 > z_j^*$ for all θ). Returns to agricultural production will be higher than socially optimal (see Figure 1). Both the break even production type below which agricultural production will not occur and the critical production type at which activity 2 becomes more profitable than activity 1 will be lower than socially optimal ($\theta_1^0 < \theta_1^*$, $\theta_c^0 < \theta_c^*$). As a result, production units of types $\theta_c^0 < \theta < \theta_c^*$ and $\theta_1^0 \leqslant \theta < \theta_1^*$ will be allocated suboptimally. Output of activity 2 will be higher than socially optimal both because of the increased intensity of use of z and because of the increased extent to which activity 1 is used. The price of the output of activity 2 will consequently be lower than socially optimal. Output of activity 1 may be higher or lower than socially optimal because increases in output due to more intensive use of z and more extensive use of activity 1 on low type production units may be counterbalanced by decreases in output due to the decreased extent to which activity 1 is used on higher type production units.

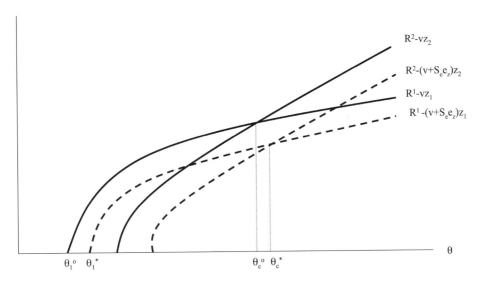

Figure 1. Private versus socially optimal land allocation.

If the use of z enhances environmental quality, as in the case of scenic amenities from farmland, the distortion caused by ignoring environmental quality will involve less intensive use of z and less extensive use of activity 1 ($\theta_1^0 > \theta_1^*$, $\theta_c^0 < \theta_c^*$) than is socially optimal.

3.1.1. Best practice requirements

One approach to remedying the underprovision of environmental quality in agriculture is to mandate the use of practices that are less profitable but provide more environmental quality. For example, storage of animal wastes prevents runoff during storms and permits expanded use of manure as a substitute for chemical fertilizers during the growing season. Requiring installation of manure storage facilities and restrictions on spreading manure have been used to address runoff of animal wastes in Denmark [Dubgaard (1990)] and some localities in the U.S. [Moffitt, Just and Zilberman (1978)]. In Australia, local districts require landowners to carry out specific erosion control measures, while Australia and Japan restrict land clearing [OECD (1994)]. In the U.S. and Europe, leaching of pesticides into groundwater and aerial drift of pesticides have been addressed primarily through restrictions on mixing, loading, and application methods [Lichtenberg (1992), OECD (1994)]. Zoning land for agricultural use, used in the U.S. and other countries, effectively requires landowners to maintain certain forms of open space.

For convenience, consider the case in which the use of z has negative effects on environmental quality while activities 1 and 2 both produce the same kind of output but with different input intensities. Social surplus from the consumption of agricultural output and environmental quality is thus $S(p) + c\gamma e(z)$. Imposition of a best practice requirement corresponds to mandating the use of the less-polluting activity (activity 1) while prohibiting the use of the more polluting activity (activity 2).

Since $R^2 - vz_2^0 > R^1 - vz_1^0$ and $z_2 > z_1$ for production types $\theta \geqslant \theta_c^0$, agricultural output from activity 2 is greater than output from activity 1 for production types $\theta \geqslant \theta_c^0$. Thus, the best practice requirement will result in a reduction of agricultural output and an increase in its price, although neither will necessarily attain its socially optimal level. The minimum production type engaged in agricultural production will remain θ_1^0. Use of the input z will fall in production types $\theta \geqslant \theta_c^0$ due to the shift from activity 2 to activity 1 and will remain the same in production types $\theta_1^0 \leqslant \theta < \theta_c^0$. Environmental quality will improve, although it will not necessarily attain its socially optimal level. Overall, best practice requirements cannot replicate a first-best allocation of resources because they operate only on the extensive margin (altering choice of activity among production types), and then only in a relatively crude way.

3.1.2. Input use restrictions

A second policy approach is placing restrictions on the use of inputs associated with environmental quality degradation or enhancement. Most developed countries prohibit the sale of pesticides for use in situations (i.e., specific crops or locales) where they are thought to have excessive negative environmental or human health effects [OECD (1994)]. The use of sewage sludge as fertilizer may be limited or prohibited in areas where treated fields are thought to breed mosquitoes or be a source of bacterial contamination of water bodies. Fertilizer application may be limited in areas with severe problems of nitrate contamination.

Consider again the case in which the use of the input z has negative effects on environmental quality and uniform restrictions on its use are imposed to attain the socially optimal level of environmental quality. There will exist critical types $\bar{\theta}_1$ and $\bar{\theta}_2$ at which these constraints become binding for activities 1 and 2, respectively. If $R_{z\theta} > 0$, so that optimal use of z is greater on higher-type production units, then the use of z will be unaffected on types below these critical types ($z_1^r = z_1^0$, $\theta_1^r \leqslant \theta < \bar{\theta}_1$ and $z_2^r = z_2^0$, $\theta_c^r \leqslant \theta < \bar{\theta}_2$) and will equal the constrained level on all other types ($z_1^r = \bar{z}_1$, $\bar{\theta}_1 \leqslant \theta < \theta_c^r$ and $z_2^r = \bar{z}_2$, $\bar{\theta}_2 \leqslant \theta \leqslant 1$). The lowest type of production unit engaged in agriculture will remain unchanged ($\theta_1^r = \theta_1^0$). The lowest type of production unit using activity 2 will fall ($\theta_c^r < \theta_c^0$) because the constraint on use of z will be binding for activity 1 but not activity 2 on production unit type θ_c^0, making activity 1 less profitable than activity 2 for units of that type. Agricultural output from both activities will decline and their prices will rise, but neither is likely to attain its socially optimal level.

As is well known, uniform restrictions fail to replicate social optima because they fail to take heterogeneity into account. However, the size of efficiency loss associated with the use of uniform restrictions depends on the degree of heterogeneity. For example, Moffitt, Just and Zilberman (1978) find that the minimum costs of managing dairy waste to meet water quality standards in the Santa Ana River Basin in California were over 20 percent lower than the costs associated with standards requiring the same disposal area per cow for all dairies. Fleming and Adams (1997) find that farmers' returns were about 13 percent higher under a spatially differentiated tax than under a uniform tax when both taxes achieved the same level of groundwater quality. In two of the four soil types considered, there was no difference in farm returns. Lichtenberg, Zilberman and Bogen (1989) find that the cost of meeting uniform standards for the carcinogenic pesticide DBCP in drinking water in all wells of a multiple-well system in California exceeded the minimum cost by only 4 to 6 percent. Helfand and House (1995) find that the welfare cost of meeting nitrogen standards in groundwater in California was only about 2 percent higher under a uniform tax than under taxes differentiated by soil type.

3.1.3.   Linear input taxes and subsidies

Taxes on polluting agricultural inputs have received only limited use for addressing environmental quality problems in agriculture. In the United States, the state of Iowa imposed a relatively small tax on fertilizer whose primary purpose was to fund development and dissemination of best farming practices rather than influence fertilizer consumption. Austria, Germany, Finland, Denmark, Sweden, Spain, and the United Kingdom tax fertilizers and pesticides, although it is not clear whether they set tax rates according to environmental criteria [Oskam, Viftigschild and Graveland (1997)].

Subsidies for inputs thought to enhance environmental quality are more widely used. Sweden, Austria, Switzerland, and the United Kingdom pay farmers to maintain amenities such as wildlife habitat and mountain landscapes. Most developed countries use subsidies to keep land in agriculture. Many national and local governments also provide implicit subsidies by taxing agricultural land at lower rates than land in other uses [OECD (1994)].

It is apparent from the necessary conditions for a social optimum that imposition of a constant per-unit tax (subsidy) equal to $c\gamma$ levied on a polluting (environmental quality enhancing) input z will induce farmers of all types to choose optimally the level of z and the kind of agricultural activity. Thus, when environmental quality is sensitive only to input use z and not to farm type θ, a uniform tax (subsidy) on the polluting (environmental quality enhancing) input will achieve a social optimum even when heterogeneous conditions lead farmers to choose different crops, different farming practices, and different input mixes. The result follows because the tax (subsidy) gives farmers the appropriate incentives on both the intensive and extensive margins.

An alternative to taxing polluting input use (or emissions) is to tax farmers on the basis of observed ambient environmental quality. When environmental quality is sensitive only to input use z and not to farm type θ, a tax c on observed ambient environmental quality $e(z)$ will induce farmers of all types to choose optimally the level of z and the kind of agricultural activity [Griffin and Bromley (1982)].

In contrast, a constant per-unit subsidy on reductions in the use of a polluting input will not achieve a social optimum and may even worsen environmental quality. In the best case, one could subsidize reductions in the use of z from (known) profit-maximizing levels at a rate equal to the marginal value of environmental quality enhancement in the social optimum, in other words, offer a subsidy of the form $c\gamma[z_j(\theta) - z_j^0(\theta)]$. Such a subsidy will lead to socially optimal levels of z on most types of production units, but not all. The subsidy will lower the minimum type of production unit engaged in farming,

$$\frac{\partial \theta_1^0}{\partial t} = -\frac{z_1^0 - z_1^*}{R_\theta^1} < 0,$$

where t is the subsidy rate. The use of z will thus increase on all production units of types $\theta_1^s \leqslant \theta \leqslant \theta_1^0$, where θ_1^s is the minimum type of production unit engaged in agriculture. The subsidy will also change the critical type θ_c^0 by

$$\frac{\partial \theta_c^0}{\partial t} = -\frac{(z_2^0 - z_2^*) - (z_1^0 - z_1^*)}{R_\theta^2 - R_\theta^1}.$$

If the distortion in the use of z is greater for activity 2 than activity 1 ($z_2^0 - z_2^* > z_1^0 - z_1^* > 0$), the subsidy will lower the critical quality, and increase the use of z on all production units of types $\theta_c^s \leqslant \theta \leqslant \theta_c^0$, where θ_c^s is the critical minimum type engaged in activity 2. If the distortion is greater for activity 1 than activity 2, the reverse holds. Since the subsidy increases the use of z for some types of production unit, it may actually lead to increased total use of z and thus decreased environmental quality. This result, of course, corresponds to the well-known result that subsidies for pollution reduction may increase pollution in the long run [see, for example, Cropper and Oates (1992)]. The results and derivation also correspond closely to Caswell and Zilberman's (1986) demonstration that the introduction of a water-saving irrigation technology may not result in aggregate water savings. If activities 1 and 2 produce different crops, then these shifts on the extensive margin will lead to a suboptimal mix of agricultural products as well as excessively low environmental quality.

3.1.4. Best practice subsidies

Subsidies for best practices are used widely to addressing environmental quality problems in agriculture, at least in the United States and Europe. The principal approach taken toward water quality issues in the United States has been to provide subsidies for best management practices thought to reduce erosion and runoff and for maintaining highly erodible land in conservation uses [for surveys of programs see Reichelderfer (1990) or OECD (1994)]. The Conservation Reserve Program (CRP), which features paid retirement of land thought to contribute excessively to environmental problems,

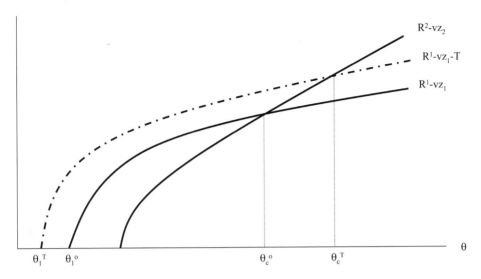

Figure 2. Impact of best practice subsidies on land allocation.

is arguably the most significant environmental initiative in agriculture in the United States. Conceptually, the CRP is a narrowly targeted form of best practice subsidy in which grassland or forestry is the socially optimal use of land. The European Union, New Zealand, Japan, and Turkey have similar programs. Most of these countries also provide subsidies in the form of cost sharing for farmers adopting approved practices, usually for readily observable actions such as installation of structures, establishment of perennial crops, or planting winter cover crops. Free extension service advice regarding such practices, a common component of these programs, can also be considered a form of subsidy.

In the case where use of the input z impairs environmental quality, such best practice subsidies can be modeled as a lump-sum subsidy to farmers choosing to use activity 1. Such a subsidy will not change farmers' incentives to use z on the intensive margin, but it will affect farmers' choices regarding whether to engage in farming and which activity to select. Its effects are shown in Figure 2. Like a subsidy on reductions in the use of z, a lump-sum payment T to users of practice 1 will lower the minimum type of production unit engaged in farming ($\theta_1^T < \theta_1^0$) and raise the critical type choosing activity 2 ($\theta_c^T > \theta_c^0$). The impact on the use of z is thus ambiguous: Farmers switching from activity 2 to activity 1 will use less of z, while those switching to farming from non-agricultural activities will use more.

Land retirement programs like the CRP feature paid diversion of land thought to contribute excessively to environmental problems. An optimal program of this type will pay farmers to retire land that is privately profitable but socially inefficient to farm. Formally, such policies should address types of production units characterized by the conditions

$$R^j - vz_j^0 > 0,$$

$$R^j - (v + c\gamma)z_j^* < 0,$$

which apply to production units of types $\theta_1^0 \leqslant \theta < \theta_1^*$, i.e., an efficiently structured program like the CRP should pay farmers $R^1 - vz_1$ to retire land of types $\theta_1^0 \leqslant \theta < \theta_1^*$. Agricultural production and input use will be socially optimal in units of these types, but will be unaffected in all other types. Thus, a land retirement program like the CRP is capable of generating a full social optimum only if environmental quality is unaffected by input use in production units of other types.

In sum, best practice subsidies are generally incapable of achieving social optima because they affect farmers' decisions only on the extensive margin. Best practice subsidies that reduce the use of polluting inputs sufficiently to achieve a socially optimal level of environmental quality will simultaneously produce socially suboptimal levels of agricultural output and output prices. Moreover, subsidies of this kind tend to be excessively costly due to targeting problems, since the subsidy affects only the decisions of a few types of production units even when offered to all users of a practice. Land retirement programs like the CRP can be structured to generate socially optimal production in production units of types that should not be engaged in agricultural production, but cannot affect input use in units of types remaining in production. They can be efficient within these limits but cannot replicate social optima by themselves. In other words, land retirement programs like the CRP can be efficient only when coupled with other policies that influence input use on the intensive margin.

3.2. Heterogeneity and implementability

It has been assumed so far that the production of environmental quality depends only on the amount of the input z used. But in many cases environmental quality effects depend on both the type of production unit and the agricultural activity. For example, leaching of fertilizers tends to be greater on sandier soils and on irrigated crops. Similarly, some crops have greater fertilizer requirements or take up nutrients less efficiently than others. Erosion and thus sediment damage and nutrient pollution tend to be greater on land with steeper slopes and for row crops. Fish kills from pesticide drift are more common when fields are closer to streams and lakes. Cropland irrigated using drip systems generates less runoff and drainage than cropland irrigated with gravity systems. Farmland located close to urban areas provides more scenic amenities.

Suppose that environmental quality does vary by type of production unit and production activity, so that environmental quality provided by a production unit of type θ in activity j is $e^j(z_j, \theta)$ and total environmental quality is

$$e(z) = \int_0^1 \left[\delta_1 e^1\big(z_1(\theta), \theta\big) + \delta_2 e^2\big(z_2(\theta), \theta\big) \right] g(\theta)\, d\theta.$$

The necessary conditions for a social optimum in this case are

$$S_{p_j} + \int_0^1 \delta_j R_p^j(p_j, w, z_j, \theta) g(\theta)\, d\theta = 0,$$

$$R_z^j - v - ce_z^j = 0 \quad \forall \theta,$$

$$R^j(p_j, w, z_j, \theta) - v - ce^j - \lambda_j - \lambda_0 \leqslant 0.$$

The optimal input tax in the present case is ce_z^1 if activity 1 is more profitable and ce_z^2 if activity 2 is more profitable and thus varies according to both production activity and type of production unit [see also Griffin and Bromley (1982), Segerson (1988)]. In contrast to the results of Section 4.2.3, therefore, the social optimum cannot be implemented by a uniform tax on inputs that impair environmental quality or by a uniform subsidy on inputs that enhance environmental quality. Suppose, for example, that the polluting input is nitrogen fertilizer, that θ indexes land quality, that the two activities using fertilizer are corn and wheat production, and that nitrogen leaching into surface water causes damage from eutrophication. Then a nitrogen tax varying according to land quality and crop produced will induce farmers to apply nitrogen and to allocate their land optimally between corn, wheat, and pasture. If nitrogen leaching is lower on higher quality land (e.g., higher quality land has higher water holding and/or cation exchange capacity), then the optimal nitrogen tax on both corn and wheat should be lower on fields of higher quality. If corn uses nitrogen more efficiently than wheat (e.g., corn takes up a higher percentage of applied nitrogen than wheat), then the nitrogen tax on corn should be less than the nitrogen tax on wheat. Put another way, a tax on nitrogen that is not differentiated according to land quality and crop will be suboptimal on both the intensive and extensive margins: It will fail to induce farmers to apply nitrogen optimally on each crop (the intensive margin) and will also fail to induce farmers to allocate land optimally between corn and wheat (the extensive margin).

The social optimum can be implemented by a uniform tax equal to c levied on emissions e^j, as Griffin and Bromley (1982) note. But monitoring emissions tends to be excessively costly or infeasible. Regulators may therefore be unable (or find it too costly) to observe production unit type, for example, land quality or human capital, either directly or by inference from observed emissions, production practices or yield. For example, the same crop may be grown in a number of different types of land or by farmers with different levels of expertise. Alternatively, the government may observe farmers' types and actions, but may lack the legal authority to impose policies that discriminate among farmers on the basis of either [Chambers (1992)]. The U.S. Department of Agriculture has offices in almost every county in the United States, for example. It has mapped soils extensively. Commodity programs in the past required farmers to report cropping patterns. USDA surveys estimate crop yields and input usage. Data on weather is available from numerous stations located in reasonable proximity to most farms. One would thus expect USDA to have the capacity to monitor the use of inputs affecting environmental quality either directly or by inference. Yet it may still be prevented from implementing differential taxes needed to achieve a social optimum. For example, imposing on fertilizer used on corn and wheat or on water applied with different irrigation methods may be prohibited by law, either specifically by statute or by judicial interpretation of common law. Heterogeneity can thus be a source of regulatory failure, that is, of the inability of regulation to achieve a socially optimal allocation of resources.

3.2.1. Implementability of first-best taxes and subsidies

The extent to which it is feasible to implement a social optimum (or a reasonable approximation thereto) varies according to the type of environmental quality problem.

Fertilizers.   As noted above, environmental damage from fertilizers typically varies according to both cropping pattern and attributes of land quality such as slope and soil texture. Nutrient pollution of surface and ground waters tends to be greater on greater slopes, on land closer to streams, and on sandier soils. Crops differ in efficiency of nutrient uptake and thus in the supply of residual nutrients available for runoff and leaching. Crop rotations featuring winter cereal crops often generate less nutrient pollution because the cereal crops absorb significant shares of residual nutrients.

   Implementing differential taxes on fertilizers would be difficult. Farmers use the same fertilizer formulations on different crops and different types of land, making it infeasible to impose differential taxes at the point of sale. Variations in yield are caused by numerous factors, including ones that are not easily observed like seed variety, pest infestation levels, and microclimate, making it difficult to infer fertilizer application rates from observed yields. One would thus expect it to be difficult to implement first-best taxes on fertilizers.

   The situation may differ in areas suffering from drainage problems. Emissions of leached fertilizers (more generally, of nutrients or heavy metals occurring naturally in soils) in such areas come from water pumped from subsurface drains. In essence, nutrient emissions in such areas come from point sources that can be monitored. The energy required for pumping is proportional to the volume of water pumped. When pumps are powered by electricity, the volume of effluent can be inferred from electricity consumption, so that taxes on effluent can be levied on electricity use. Soil maps can be used to adjust such taxes for differences in emissions due to soil quality or the presence of naturally occurring nutrients or heavy metals. It would be more difficult to make adjustments for cropping patterns, however. Further difficulties are likely to arise in areas in which subsurface drains capture leachate from neighboring farms as well as from the farm on which the drains are located. Such situations are common in areas with perched water tables, such as the west side of the San Joaquin Valley, California [Loehman and Dinar (1994)]. Thus, implementation of first-best taxes is likely to be feasible in areas where drainage flows across farm boundaries are small and where there is little variation in cropping patterns or pollutant emissions across crops.

Livestock wastes. Environmental damage from livestock wastes typically varies according to the location of the livestock operation, the extent to which animals are concentrated, and the type of livestock involved. Nutrient pollution from livestock wastes tends to be greater on land near streams, near feedlots, and on sandier soils. Poultry litter and hog waste have greater concentrations of nutrients than cow manure. Livestock wastes present a mixed case for implementability. In some cases, livestock operations can be treated as point sources and thus regulated differentially. Moffitt, Just and Zilberman (1978), Hochman, Zilberman and Just (1977a, 1977b), and Lichtenberg and Zilberman (1987) investigate cases of surface water pollution from dairy wastes left on pastures or spread on disposal areas that can be treated as point sources. In other situations, livestock wastes are spread on cropland as fertilizer. In such situations, differential taxation of livestock wastes would be characterized by the implementation problems discussed above for fertilizers.

Erosion. Environmental damage from erosion (sedimentation, nutrient pollution) typically varies according to topography, soil characteristics, location (e.g., proximity to streams), crop choice, and farm production practices, all of which should be considered observable by USDA and extension personnel or from soil survey data. (In contrast to variable input use, most farm practices with significant effects on erosion are easily observed.) In principle, then, it should be feasible to levy on farmland first-best taxes that are adjusted for crop type and farming practices. Legal restrictions likely constitute the most significant barrier to doing so.

Pesticides. Environmental damage from pesticides typically varies according to the formulation (and thus application method) used and according to the location of the field to which pesticides are applied. It should be feasible to impose differential taxes on different formulations of any given pesticide active ingredient (e.g., liquid versus granular), although additional measures may be required in some cases to prevent dealers or farmers from evading higher taxes by reformulating pesticides themselves. Similarly, it should be feasible to impose differential taxes on pesticides purchased in different regions, although it may be necessary to simultaneously implement enforcement measures to limit smuggling. Existing pesticide regulation provides precedents for differential treatment of this kind. The U.S. Environmental Protection Agency (EPA) banned all uses of granular formulations of the insecticide carbofuran due to concerns over bird kills but did not take regulatory action against other formulations. EPA has similarly cancelled the registrations of numerous chemicals in specific states or growing regions while permitting legal use to continue in other areas.

Scenic amenities, wetlands preservation, and wildlife habitat. Environmental quality enhancement from farmland preservation or other land use restrictions (wetlands preservation, wildlife habitat, paid conservation set-asides) depends primarily on the location of the farm and secondarily on agricultural production practices. One would expect demand for scenic amenities to be greater for farms closer to urban areas with larger populations. Concentrated livestock operations tend to have negative impacts on environmental quality due to odor. How much the public is willing to pay for the different kinds of scenery associated with different crops has not been investigated. Estimates of public willingness to pay for open space and scenery as functions of farm location and farm characteristics can be used to derive values for the purchase of development rights or agricultural easements or rental of land for wetlands preservation, wildlife habitat, or erosion control. Implementing a first-best thus seems feasible for all of these environmental services. However, lack of information about differences in returns to farming due to human capital or about farmers' subjective assessments of future returns to farming and of the price of their land for development may hinder implementation of first-best policies, especially in programs that are local in scope and thus feature limited numbers of potential participants (e.g., preserving farmland for scenic amenities). Programs aimed at environmental quality problems on a larger scale can exploit competition among potential participants to achieve a first-best. From this perspective, for example, the decision to administer the CRP on a county basis is inconsistent with a goal of minimizing the cost of achieving environmental quality improvements.

3.2.2. Second-best implementation under hidden information

When the government is unable to observe (or use its knowledge about) heterogeneity in the conditions governing the production of agricultural output and environmental quality, it is forced to consider second-best policies. One example of such policies is non-linear taxes on polluting inputs, in which the tax rate varies according to the amount of the input purchased. Other examples include auctions for CRP or wetlands reserve rentals, farmland easement purchases, and sale of development rights, in which the price paid for a unit of land varies according to the size of the parcel offered.

The derivation of such second-best policies is performed under the assumption that the government has perfect information about the structure of the farm economy and of environmental quality but cannot distinguish between individual farmers. In other words, the government knows agricultural production technology and thus $R^j(p_j, w, z_j, \theta)$, emissions and thus $e^j(z_j, \theta)$, and the distribution of types of production units $G(\theta)$, but does not know the type θ of any individual farm operation.

Second-best taxes and subsidies of this kind can be implemented using a revelation mechanism that induces farmers to report their type θ truthfully to the government in return for a payment (positive or negative) that depends on the type reported [for a detailed exposition see Chambers (2002) in this Handbook]. Suppose, for example, that the government wants to maximize social surplus from the consumption of agricultural output and environmental quality $S(p_1, p_2) - ce(z)$ (i.e., the input z has a negative effect on environmental quality) plus revenue from a non-linear tax $t(\tilde{\theta})$, where the tax payment depends on the type reported to the government $\tilde{\theta}$. (If revenue from the tax reduces the need to levy other distortionary taxes, then the social value of each dollar of revenue from the tax on the polluting input may be worth more than a dollar.)

This problem is the same in most respects as the case investigated by Spulber (1988) in which a regulator attempts to maximize surplus from consumption of a product less the social value of pollution damage when the costs of pollution control vary across firms and when the regulator knows the distribution of firm types but cannot observe or infer the type of any individual firm. It differs in two important respects. First, it considers multiple outputs (the two agricultural activities) and thus examines switches among outputs on the extensive margin. Second, it considers the possibility of shutdown, that is, of zero production by some types.

The amount earned by a farmer operating a production unit of type θ who reports type $\tilde{\theta}$ is

$$\delta_1\left[R^1\left(p_1, w, z_1(\tilde{\theta}), \theta\right) - vz_1(\tilde{\theta})\right] + \delta_2\left[R^2\left(p_2, w, z_2(\tilde{\theta}), \theta\right) - vz_2(\tilde{\theta})\right] - t(\tilde{\theta}).$$

If truthful revelation is optimal for the farmer, earnings for a farmer of type θ must be at a maximum when the farmer reports type $\tilde{\theta}$. A necessary condition is thus that

$$\left(\delta_1\left[R_z^1 - v\right] + \delta_2\left[R_z^2 - v\right]\right)z_\theta - t_\theta = 0,$$

which implies that z_θ and t_θ have the same sign. The incentive compatibility condition implies that if optimal use of the polluting input z is higher (lower) on production units of higher (lower) types, then the total tax payment will be higher (lower) as well. Note that this does not imply that the tax rate per unit of input rises as use of the input rises.

This condition will be sufficient for a maximum when

$$\frac{\partial}{\partial\tilde{\theta}}\left\{\left(\delta_1\left[R_z^1 - v\right] + \delta_2\left[R_z^2 - v\right]\right)z_\theta - t_\theta\right\} \leqslant 0.$$

For the first-order condition to hold for every type of production unit θ, it must also be true that

$$\frac{\partial}{\partial\tilde{\theta}}\left\{\left(\delta_1\left[R_z^1 - v\right] + \delta_2\left[R_z^2 - v\right]\right)z_\theta - t_\theta\right\} + \left(\delta_1 R_{z\theta}^1 + \delta_2 R_{z\theta}^2\right)z_\theta \leqslant 0$$

[see, for example, Guesnerie and Laffont (1984) or Fudenberg and Tirole (1991)]. Since the first term is non-positive by assumption, a separating equilibrium is assured if z_θ and $R_{z\theta}^j$ have the same sign. If the marginal product of z is higher on units with higher production types, as has been assumed in the previous section, then a second-best tax should ensure that use of z is higher on higher-type production units. If this monotonicity condition is not met for some types of production unit, then it will be optimal to impose taxes that ensure that all units of those types use the same amount of z; for these types, the second-best tax will achieve a pooling equilibrium.

Under the assumptions of the preceding section, the social optimum has the following characteristics. Activity 1 uses less of the polluting input z than activity 2. It is socially optimal to use activity 1 on lower-type production units. There exist critical types θ_1^* and θ_c^* such that agricultural production should not occur for types $\theta < \theta_1^*$. Activity 1 is socially optimal for types $\theta_1^* \leqslant \theta < \theta_c^*$, and activity 2 is socially optimal for types $\theta \geqslant \theta_c^*$.

Assume there exists minimum production unit type $\theta_1^m > 0$ that earns zero quasirent,

$$R^1\left(p_1, w, z_1, \theta_1^m\right) - vz_1 - t\left(\theta_1^m\right) = 0,$$

when z_1 is chosen to maximize the farmer's earnings. Integrating the incentive compatibility condition implies that

$$t(\theta) = \left(\delta_1\left[R^1(\theta) - vz_1(\theta)\right] + \delta_2\left[R^2(\theta) - vz_2(\theta)\right]\right) - \int_{\theta_1^m}^{\theta} \left[\delta_1 R_\theta^1 + \delta_2 R_\theta^2\right] ds.$$

Note that for types $\theta < \theta_1^m$, the optimal tax is

$$t(\theta) = R^1(\theta) - vz_1(\theta) + \int_\theta^{\theta_1^m} R_\theta^1 \, ds > R^1(\theta) - vz_1(\theta),$$

which implies that the optimal tax will force out of production all units of types less than the socially optimal minimum θ_1^m.

The government implements the second-best program by selling a farmer revealing herself to be type $\tilde{\theta}$ the right to purchase an amount of the polluting input z at the market unit price v in return for a payment $t(\tilde{\theta})$. Its objective is to choose z and t to maximize social surplus from consumption of agricultural output and environmental quality plus tax payments:

$$S(p_1, p_2) - c \int_{\theta_1^*}^1 \left[\delta_1 e^1(z_1) + \delta_2 e^2(z_z)\right] g(\theta) \, d\theta + \int_{\theta_1^*}^1 t(\theta) g(\theta) \, d\theta.$$

(The extension to the case where tax payments displace distortionary taxes is straightforward.) Assuming truth-telling implies that the objective function can be expressed (after integration by parts) as

$$S(p_1, p_2) + \int_{\theta_1^*}^1 \left\{ \delta_1\left[R^1(p_1, w, z_1, \theta) - vz_1 - ce^1(z_1, \theta)\right] \right.$$

$$\left. + \delta_2\left[R^2(p_2, w, z_2, \theta) - vz_2 - ce^2(z_2, \theta)\right] \right\} g(\theta) \, d\theta$$

$$- \int_{\theta_1^*}^1 \left\{ \frac{N - G(\theta)}{g(\theta)} \left[\delta_1 R_\theta^1 + \delta_2 R_\theta^2\right] \right\} g(\theta) \, d\theta.$$

The necessary conditions for a maximum are

$$S_{p1j} + \int_{\theta_1^m}^{\theta_c^m} \left\{ R_p^1 - \frac{N - G(\theta)}{g(\theta)} R_{\theta p}^1 \right\} g(\theta) \, d\theta = 0,$$

$$S_{p2} + \int_{\theta_c^m}^{1} \left\{ R_p^2 - \frac{N - G(\theta)}{g(\theta)} R_{\theta p}^2 \right\} g(\theta) \, d\theta = 0,$$

$$R_z^j - v - ce_z^j - \frac{N - G(\theta)}{g(\theta)} R_{\theta z}^j = 0,$$

where θ_c^m is defined by the equation

$$\left[R^1 \left(\theta_c^m \right) - vz_1 \left(\theta_c^m \right) - ce^1 \left(\theta_c^m \right) \right] - \left[R^2 \left(\theta_c^m \right) - vz_2 \left(\theta_c^m \right) - ce^2 \left(\theta_c^m \right) \right]$$

$$- \frac{N - G(\theta)}{g(\theta)} \left[R_\theta^1 - R_\theta^2 \right] = 0.$$

These conditions are sufficient if the monotonicity condition holds. The monotonicity condition can be checked by differentiating the system first-order conditions with respect to θ and solving for z_θ. As usual, monotonicity of the hazard rate $[N - G(\theta)]/g(\theta)$ is necessary but not sufficient for the second-order condition for truth-telling to hold.

First, note that at θ_c^* the first two terms of the equation defining θ_c^m are equal while the third term is negative, indicating that $\theta_c^* > \theta_c^m$. Thus, the optimal second-best tax will induce production units of types $\theta_c^m \leqslant \theta < \theta_c^*$ to use activity 1 instead of the socially optimal activity 2.

Second, note that the condition defining the minimum quality of land cultivated, θ_1^m, similarly indicates that $\theta_1^m > \theta_1^*$ (since the condition defining θ_1^m is negative at θ_1^* and quasirent is increasing in land quality). Thus, imposing the second best tax will force out of production some types that would be socially optimal to keep in production.

Third, if $R_{z\theta} > 0$, that is, the marginal product of z is greater on higher-type units, then units of types $\theta_1^m \leqslant \theta < \theta_c^m$ and $\theta_c^* \leqslant \theta < 1$ will use less of the input z than is socially optimal. Units of type 1 will use the socially optimal level of z, that is, there is no distortion of input use or production "at the top". (Recall that $G(1) = N$ so that the optimal second-best tax equals the optimal first-best tax for units of type 1.) The use of z on units $\theta_c^m \leqslant \theta < \theta_c^*$ will also be less than socially optimal because activity 2 uses z more intensively than activity 1.

Fourth, the second-best tax will result in less agricultural output from both activities and more environmental quality than is socially optimal on the intensive margin. [Spulber (1988) derives a similar result.] The output of activity 2 will always be less than socially optimal. Environmental quality will be higher than socially optimal because of the reduced use of z on all units remaining in production and because some units that would be producing in the social optimum are forced out of production by the second-best tax. The output of activity 1 may be more or less than socially optimal because the output by production units of types $\theta_c^m \leqslant \theta < \theta_c^*$ will counteract the reduced use of z on types remaining in production and the loss of output by forcing types $\theta_1^m \leqslant \theta < \theta_1^*$ out of production. If both activities 1 and 2 produce the same output, total output will be lower than socially optimal.

3.2.3. Implementability of second-best mechanisms under hidden information

Most discussions of implementability of second-best mechanisms under hidden information focus on the monotonicity condition discussed in the preceding section. But several other conditions are necessary for these second-best mechanisms to be enforceable. Two in particular – compliance monitoring and secondary markets – are crucial but frequently overlooked.

First, the government must be able to observe compliance in some way. If it imposes a tax on the use of a polluting input, it must be able to monitor tax collections to ensure that quantity discounts or premia are actually applied to farmers' purchases. If the second-best tax involves quantity premia, the government must be able to monitor cumulative purchases to ensure that farmers do not simply avoid higher tax rates through multiple purchases of smaller quantities. If the government offers a subsidy for conservation practices or for open space, it must be able to observe whether farmers actually carry out their side of the bargain. If the government offers a payment in return for conservation effort, it must be able to observe that effort (the equivalent of a time sheet for labor) or infer it from observable outcomes.

Second, second-best mechanisms are enforceable only when secondary markets are infeasible, e.g., when the input z cannot be stored or resold or when users of z cannot collude (for example, by forming purchasing cooperatives). Otherwise, if the optimal second-best tax rate featured discounts for larger purchases, farmers using smaller amounts of the input z would find it optimal to purchase larger amounts than would be profitable for a single season and either store the excess for the following season or sell the excess to other users. The formation of purchasing cooperatives would accomplish the same end. Similarly, if the optimal second-best tax rate featured price premia for larger purchases, farmers using larger amounts of z would find it profitable to make multiple purchases of smaller lots.

These considerations suggest that second-best mechanisms will not generally be viable methods of handling environmental problems associated with the use of variable inputs like chemicals (fertilizers, pesticides). Second-best taxes on such would involve extensive reporting to ensure that the appropriate tax be assessed on farmers' cumulative purchases from all dealers. If the second-best tax involved quantity premia, periodic inspections would be needed to limit the use of straw buyers. Even so, secondary markets for chemicals can emerge readily. Chemicals are storable and easily repackaged. Moreover, some farmers already engage in contract chemical application for others, making enforcement more complex. The resulting enforcement problems could well eclipse those traditionally associated with moonshine.

Subsidies for limiting chemical use like the "green payments" program suggested by Wu and Babcock (1995, 1996) are similarly unenforceable without extensive, intrusive government inspection. Monitoring cumulative purchases presents the difficulties noted above. Moreover, because chemicals are storable, their (single-season) use cannot be inferred reliably from purchases. Actual applications can be adjusted on a continuing basis, so compliance monitoring would require virtual continuous observation of farm operations. In the absence of effective monitoring, there is nothing to prevent farmers from accepting payments and then simply applying chemicals at profit-maximizing levels. Furthermore, subsidies for reductions in polluting activities may have undesirable extensive margin effects like crop switching or bringing extra land into cultivation.

Second-best mechanisms are more likely to be enforceable in cases involving the use of durable inputs such as conservation structures (terraces), perennial crops (stripcropping, filter strips, riparian buffers, reforestation), or the maintenance of environmental amenities (open space, scenic amenities, wildlife habitat). In these cases, inspection at relatively infrequent intervals suffices to assess compliance. Smith (1995), for example, considers the design of a bidding system for enrolling land in the CRP in cases where farmers possess private information about the profitability of the land they offer. His model is more applicable to programs that are local in scope, such as those aimed at preserving farmland as open space, since administration of the CRP on a national basis would create sufficient competition among potential participants to allow the government to avoid paying information rents.

Mechanisms involving the use of durables are not necessarily self-enforcing, however. Livestock wastes are a case in which further enforcement is likely necessary. The government can observe at relatively low cost whether farmers build and maintain waste storage structures, but monitoring waste disposal is more costly, because manure can be spread at almost any time. It is possible that farmers will build waste storage structures yet continue to spread manure for disposal rather than use it as a fertilizer substitute [see Dubgaard (1990) for an example from Denmark]. Similarly, the government may be able to require farmers to build waste storage lagoons or holding ponds with sufficient capacity to prevent spills in all but extremely severe weather events but is likely to be unable to ensure that farmers manage waste levels to ensure maintenance of that overflow capacity [Lichtenberg and Zilberman (1987), Innes (2000)].

The preceding discussion suggests that the greatest scope for the application of hidden information models to environmental problems in agriculture lies in design of auctions and other bidding mechanisms for paid diversions, conservation set-asides, land retirement, agricultural easements, purchases of development rights, etc., in cases where these programs deal with problems that are local in scope. Land use can be monitored at low cost and land-use restrictions cannot be sidestepped easily, so land-use contracts are likely to be enforceable. Hidden information is likely to be a problem when the number of potential participants is small enough that competition between them is limited.

4. Uncertainty

Agricultural production and its environmental effects are both subject to considerable uncertainty. Two sources of uncertainty can be distinguished [Braden and Segerson (1993)]: unmeasured heterogeneity and randomness. As noted in the preceding section, both agricultural productivity and environmental effects of agriculture vary according to differences in climate, topography, geology, pest complexes, and other exogenous factors in addition to human variability such as differences in human capital across farmers. When not measured, this heterogeneity constitutes a source of uncertainty. The remaining uncertainty is attributable to randomness, that is, the effects of factors like rainfall that cannot be predicted deterministically.

This section explores three general issues arising due to uncertainty: (1) efficient policy design under uncertainty, (2) regulatory aversion to uncertainty, and (3) the role of information in policy design. We begin by exploring the implications of uncertainty for policy design. We begin by developing a conceptual model of *ex ante* regulation in which government and farmers are risk neutral. We use the model to assess the relative efficiency of incentives (taxes, subsidies, tradable permits) and best practice standards both in general and with respect to specific inputs associated with environmental quality problems. We then turn to implementation in cases where the government is unable to assess emissions of individual farmers. We take up two types of policies: taxes (subsidies) on ambient environmental quality and *ex post* liability for environmental damage. Next, we consider policy design in cases where regulators are averse to uncertainty, either for political reasons or by statutory instruction. Finally, we consider the role of information in policy design. Acquisition of information about states of nature can be considered an input into the production process. It may thus affect the use of inputs that influence environmental quality. Information-intensive farming methods have been widely regarded as opportunities for strengthening stewardship. We discuss briefly their potential effects on environmental quality.

4.1. *Taxes, subsidies, and best practice standards under uncertainty*

We begin with a situation in which government and/or farmers are risk neutral but must act before uncertainty is resolved, so that they know the results of their actions only stochastically. A modified form of the input-oriented model will be useful for exploring policy design in this context. Let output be a function $f(z, \varepsilon)$ of an input affecting environmental quality z and a random factor ε. Without loss of generality, scale ε so that $f_\varepsilon > 0$, higher realizations of ε are associated with greater output. If $f_{z\varepsilon} < 0$, the input z can be said to be risk-reducing because it increases income more in bad states of nature (low ε) than good states (high ε), thereby reducing the variability of income. Similarly, if $f_{z\varepsilon} > 0$, the input z can be said to be risk-increasing because it increases income more in good states of nature than in bad states, thereby increasing the variability of income.

As is well known from the work of Weitzman (1974), under uncertainty, quantity controls like best practice standards may be preferable to price instruments like

Pigouvian taxes, subsidies, or tradable permits. Consider the case where monitoring emissions is excessively costly, so that regulation is applied to inputs associated with environmental quality. Let $\hat{z}$ be the socially optimal usage level of the input z that affects environmental quality and $\tilde{z}$ be the usage level chosen by a farmer facing a price of environmental quality equal to $E\{D_e e_z\}$ that implements the social optimum. Assume that the best practice standard imposes the socially optimal usage level of z, $\hat{z}$. Following Weitzman (1974), the difference between the social net benefits under the price incentive and the best practice standard equals, to a second-order approximation around $(\hat{z}, \bar{\varepsilon})$, where $\bar{\varepsilon} = E\{\varepsilon\}$,

$$\Delta \approx \left[p f_z(\hat{z}, \bar{\varepsilon}) - v - D_e\big(e(\hat{z}), \bar{\varepsilon}\big) e_z(\hat{z}) \right](\tilde{z} - \hat{z})$$

$$+ \frac{1}{2} \left[p f_{zz}(\hat{z}, \bar{\varepsilon}) - D_{ee}\big(e(\hat{z}), \bar{\varepsilon}\big) e_z^2(\hat{z}) - D_e\big(e(\hat{z}), \bar{\varepsilon}\big) e_{zz}(\hat{z}) \right](\tilde{z} - \hat{z})^2$$

$$+ \left[p f_{z\varepsilon}(\hat{z}, \bar{\varepsilon}) - D_{e\varepsilon}\big(e(\hat{z}), \bar{\varepsilon}\big) e_z(\hat{z}) \right](\tilde{z} - \hat{z})(\varepsilon - \bar{\varepsilon}).$$

If the farmer is risk-neutral, the optimal usage level of the input z satisfies

$$E\{ p f_z - v - E\{D_e e_z\} \} = 0.$$

A first-order approximation of this necessary condition around $(\hat{z}, \bar{\varepsilon})$ indicates that

$$\tilde{z} - \hat{z} \approx p f_z(\hat{z}, \bar{\varepsilon}) - v - E\{D_e e_z\} - \frac{f_{z\varepsilon}(\hat{z}, \bar{\varepsilon})}{f_{zz}(\hat{z}, \bar{\varepsilon})}(\varepsilon - \bar{\varepsilon}).$$

Substituting for $(\tilde{z} - \hat{z})$ in Δ and taking expectations gives

$$E\{\Delta\} \approx \sigma^2 \left\{ \frac{D_{z\varepsilon} e_z f_{z\varepsilon}}{f_{zz}} - \frac{f_{z\varepsilon}^2}{2 f_{zz}^2} \left[p f_{zz} + \big(D_{ee} e_z^2 + D_e e_{zz}\big) \right] \right\}.$$

The second term in curly brackets corresponds to Weitzman's main result (p. 484), derived under an assumption of no correlation between the random elements affecting benefits and costs. If environmental damage is more sensitive to random variations than crop productivity, the term in square brackets is positive and the effect on $E\{\Delta\}$ is negative, that is, the social loss from best practice standards is less than the social loss from pricing environmental quality. If crop productivity is more sensitive to randomness than environmental damage, on the other hand, then incentives are likely to be preferable.

The first term in curly brackets represents the effect of correlation between random variations in crop productivity and environmental damage, and corresponds to the finding noted in Weitzman's footnote 1 (p. 485) and in Stavins (1996). Its sign depends on the combined risk effects of z on crop productivity and environmental damage. Recall that ε is scaled so that $f_\varepsilon > 0$, that is, higher values of ε represent better (random) growing conditions. The effect of growing conditions on environmental damage likely depends on the type of damage, although materials balance considerations suggest that environmental damage is likely lower under better growing conditions, that is, $D_\varepsilon < 0$ and $D_{z\varepsilon} < 0$. For example, one would expect crop nutrient uptake to be greater under better growing conditions and nutrient runoff and/or leaching correspondingly less, implying $D_{z\varepsilon} < 0$. Similarly, herbicide uptake by weeds is likely greater (and thus residual herbicide in soils likely less) when growing conditions are better and thus weed densities are greater. If $D_{z\varepsilon} < 0$, the sign of this first term depends on the risk effect of z on crop productivity. If the input z is risk-increasing in terms of crop productivity, then incentives are likely to be preferable. If, on the other hand, the input z is risk-reducing in terms of crop productivity, then best practice standards are likely to be preferable. More generally, incentives are more likely to be preferable when $f_{z\varepsilon}$ and $D_{z\varepsilon}$ have opposite signs, while best practice standards are more likely to be preferable when $f_{z\varepsilon}$ and $D_{z\varepsilon}$ have the same signs.

4.1.1. Incentives versus best practice standards in agriculture

Weitzman's main result is that the choice between incentives and best practice standards depends on the relative sensitivity of crop productivity and environmental damage to uncertainty. The empirical economic literature has not addressed this issue at all. However, when $D_{z\varepsilon} > 0$, as generally expected, Weitzman's argument also suggests that economic incentives are more likely to be preferable under uncertainty for risk-increasing inputs while best practice standards are more likely to be preferable for risk-reducing inputs. In this section, we briefly review the literature on risk effects of the agricultural inputs associated with environmental quality. Additional treatment of this issue can be found in Moschini and Hennessy (2001) in this Handbook.

Fertilizers. Fertilizers are widely believed to be risk-increasing, at least in rain fed agriculture. When soil moisture is low (and thus growing conditions are poor), crop uptake of macronutrients (nitrogen phosphorus, potassium) and thus marginal nutrient productivity are low. Nitrogen in particular may cause crop burn and thus have negative marginal productivity when soil moisture is low. As growing conditions improve, crop uptake and the marginal productivity of nutrients increase. In other words, nutrient productivity and states of nature tend to be positively correlated, $f_{z\varepsilon} > 0$.

Nitrogen has been the most extensively studied macronutrient. Most empirical studies have found it to be risk-increasing. Roumasset et al. (1989) survey the literature on fertilizer and yield variability through the mid-1980s, with an emphasis on developing-country applications. Of the roughly 20 studies they cite, all but two [Farnsworth and Moffitt (1981) and Rosegrant and Roumasset (1985)] found nitrogen to be risk-increasing. In all cases, however, the estimated risk effects of nitrogen were small. The subsequent literature contains a similar pattern of results. Studies using estimated parameters of a conditional beta distribution for Iowa corn yields found that nitrogen increased the variance of yield [Nelson and Preckel (1989), Love and Buccola (1991),

Babcock and Hennessy (1996)]. Horowitz and Lichtenberg (1993) found that corn growers in the U.S. Corn Belt who purchased crop insurance used more nitrogen per acre, indicating that nitrogen is risk-increasing.

There is less evidence about risk effects of other macronutrients. Studies of Iowa corn indicated that phosphorus is risk-increasing while potassium is risk-decreasing [Nelson and Preckel (1989), Love and Buccola (1991)], while Horowitz and Lichtenberg (1993) found that corn growers who purchased crop insurance did not use phosphorus or potassium in significantly different per acre amounts than those who did not, suggesting that whatever risk effects these chemicals have are likely small. Finally, Smith and Goodwin (1996) found that Kansas wheat growers who purchased crop insurance spent less on fertilizers in the aggregate, a category that includes items thought to have risk effects of opposite signs.

Soil erosion. As noted earlier, preserving the value of their land gives farmers an incentive to engage in soil conservation by presenting farmers with a tradeoff between current yield and the future value of their land. Their choice of erosion level (equivalently, soil conservation effort) is simultaneously a choice about investment in land quality. Both current yield and future land prices are subject to uncertainty. Ardila and Innes (1993) note that the effect of increased uncertainty (in the form of a Sandmo-type mean-preserving spread) on optimal soil conservation depends on the relative sizes of yield and land price risks. We are unaware of any empirical studies on the relative sizes of these risks and are thus unable to draw inferences about appropriate policy design.

Pesticides. The literature on risk effects of pesticides is somewhat confusing, in part because it seems to have arisen from a misunderstanding regarding terminology between economists and crop scientists. The latter noted that farmers frequently used pesticides preventively, that is, before the degree of infestation was observed. They argued on that basis that farmers were responding to the risk of infestation rather than actual infestation and thus characterized pesticide use in terms of insurance [van den Bosch and Stern (1962)]. Economists responded to this characterization by developing models in which pesticides reduced the variability of income or output, producing the conventional wisdom that pesticides are risk-reducing. Feder (1979), for example, analyzed pesticides using a Sandmo-type model in which pest damage was assumed to be additively separable from potential output and equal to the product of pest population size, damage per pest, and survivorship from pesticide application. He found that pesticides are risk-reducing when there is uncertainty about pest population size or damage per pest, but risk-increasing when there is uncertainty about the marginal effectiveness of the pesticide.

Farmers' use of preventive treatments is not, of course, in and of itself evidence of risk aversion. Even when pest infestations are observable, preventive treatment may be more profitable on average if rescue treatment is insufficiently effective, if the error in estimating infestation from observed levels is excessive, or if monitoring (scouting) is sufficiently costly. Moreover, correlation between random factors affecting price or potential yield and pest damage may create situations in which pesticides increase rather than decrease yield and income variability [Pannell (1991), Horowitz and Lichtenberg (1994)]. For example, greater early-season soil moisture and solar radiation may promote the growth of all plants, crops and weeds included, while low moisture and solar radiation may lead to poor plant growth. In such situations, the marginal productivity of herbicides is likely to be higher in good states of nature than bad ones, implying that pesticides are risk-increasing. Similarly, insecticides are thought to reduce the stability of crop ecosystems during the growing season by suppressing invertebrate predators and by altering competition among insect, weed, and disease species in ways that create less tractable pest problems [see, for example, Bottrell (1979)].

The empirical evidence available to date suggests that pesticides frequently are risk-increasing. Using a Just–Pope production function, Farnsworth and Moffitt (1981) found that pesticides increased the yield variability of irrigated cotton in California's San Joaquin Valley. A more recent study of the same crop and region by Hurd (1994) using a similar specification of production found that pesticides had no impact on yield variability. Antle (1988), using the moment-based econometric procedure of Antle (1983), found that insecticide use had no statistically significant effect on yield variability of processing tomatoes in California. Gotsch and Regev (1996) and Regev, Gotsch and Rieder (1997), also using the moment-based approach of Antle (1983), found that fungicide use increased the variability of wheat revenue (which captures both quantity and quality effects) in Switzerland. Horowitz and Lichtenberg (1993) found that corn growers in the U.S. Corn Belt who purchased crop insurance applied more herbicides and insecticides and spent more on pesticides, suggesting that pesticides are risk-increasing.

In cases where pesticides are risk-increasing, economic incentives are likely to be preferable to best practice standards. In such cases, shifting to incentive-based pesticide regulation could improve performance with respect to uncertainty as well as with respect to heterogeneity. Overall, however, the risk effects of pesticides have not been studied sufficiently to permit broad generalizations, and it is possible that broad generalizations may never be possible. Herbicides, insecticides, and fungicides may differ in their risk effects, and those risk effects may differ across crops and regions.

4.1.2. Moral hazard

Environmental quality is frequently influenced by inputs that are neither traded in markets nor readily observable. Examples include the observance of setback requirements and similar wellhead protection measures in mixing and loading pesticides; banded application of pesticides; scouting prior to pesticide application; and split application of fertilizers as a means of increasing the share of nutrients taken up by crops. Input taxes and subsidies are ineffective in such cases. When pollution control effort of these kinds can neither be observed directly nor inferred from production, the regulatory problem is characterized by moral hazard, or hidden action.

Nevertheless, a social optimum can be attained provided that ambient environmental quality is observable and that all farmers influencing environmental quality face the same set of random factors. In such cases, observing ambient environmental quality is equivalent to observing each farmer's pollution control effort, and moral hazard is not a factor. Holmstrom (1982) shows that a principal contracting for production of a single output produced collectively by risk-averse agents can induce those agents to exercise first-best effort as long as the reward scheme is not required to be budget-balancing, e.g., as long as total pollution tax revenues are not required to equal the social cost of pollution. Rasmusen (1987) shows that, if agents are risk-averse, it is possible to attain a social optimum with mechanisms that are budget-balancing by random differential treatment of one out of many agents. Segerson (1988) applies Holmstrom's result to a nonpoint-source pollution control problem in which (crop) output is nonrandom while environmental quality is stochastic and influenced by unobservable effort. The optimal mechanism in this context consists of two parts. If actual observed ambient pollution exceeds a pre-specified level, each farmer pays a pollution tax proportional to the difference between actual and that pre-specified level. If actual observed ambient pollution is less than the pre-specified level, each farmer receives a pollution subsidy proportional to the difference between actual and the pre-specified level. The socially optimal level of crop production can be attained in the long run by adding to the pollution tax a lump-sum payment or tax as needed to induce appropriate entry or exit. This result generalizes to the case where both crop output and environmental quality are random and farmers are risk-averse. As long as environmental quality consists of observable ambient pollution from uniformly mixed emissions, a combination of crop insurance and an ambient pollution tax will achieve a first-best allocation of crop output and environmental quality [Chambers and Quiggin (1996)]. We examine interactions between insurance and environmental policy at greater length in Section 5.2 below.

If there are many farmers with differential impacts on ambient environmental quality, ambient pollution taxes can be used to achieve first-best environmental quality on average if the regulator has perfect information about the effects of each farmer's environmental quality effort on the probability distribution of ambient pollution [Segerson (1988)], including fate and transport of pollutants [Cabe and Herriges (1992)]. This information is costly to obtain. Xepapadeas (1995) shows there may be conditions under which farmers can be induced to reveal fully their own environmental quality effort. Farmers must be averse to the riskiness of tax payments (but not crop production or income) and able to reduce their own tax liability under an ambient pollution tax by reporting indicators of environmental quality effort. Participating in integrated pest management (IPM) programs, obtaining conservation plans from government agencies, and applying for cost sharing to install runoff or erosion control facilities might be interpreted as methods of reporting such effort.

Ambient pollution taxes capable of achieving first-best environmental quality may be too high to be acceptable politically. For example, it may be optimal to charge each farmer a tax equal to the marginal damage from all ambient pollution in order to create incentives for first-best environmental quality effort [Segerson (1988)].

4.1.3. Environmental quality and the tort system

A number of authors have argued that *ex post* liability for harm can provide sufficient incentives to ensure that farmers exercise socially optimal precautions against stochastic environmental damage. There has been particular interest in the role of the tort system in mitigating groundwater quality degradation, since well owners can take legal action in the event of impairment of drinking well water quality. Segerson (1990) considers the extent to which farmers and pesticide manufacturers should be held liable for pesticide contamination of drinking water wells. Wetzstein and Centner (1992) examine the potential effects of legislation that would replace strict liability for groundwater contamination by agricultural chemicals with a negligence standard.

Menell (1991) has argued forcefully that the tort system gives polluters few incentives to take action to mitigate environmental damage because of the difficulty of establishing causal links between (1) the actions of any single agent and ambient pollutant concentrations and (2) ambient pollutant concentrations and harm suffered. The source or sources of well water contaminants, for instance, cannot be readily identified. The current state of biomedical knowledge is insufficient to prove to a legal standard that the low concentrations of pesticides or nitrate typically found in drinking water cause long-term health effects or other forms of environmental damage. Most such health effects have multiple causes, making identification of causality difficult, even in the case of acute health effects from direct exposure to pesticides. Moreover, Menell argues, the tort system is extremely costly, time-consuming, and inequitable. Furthermore, inadequate financial resources may prevent those harmed from bringing suit, further weakening incentives for precautionary behavior [see, for example, Shavell (1987)].

Davis, Caswell and Harper (1992) compare tort liability with direct regulation and workers' compensation as means of protecting farm workers from pesticide poisonings. Their simulation analysis indicates that experience-rated workers' compensation is the most cost-effective of these policy instruments. The fact that insurance premiums increase as the number of valid claims filed goes up regardless of the specific cause of those claims gives farmers strong incentives to take precautionary action. Tort liability is less cost-effective because farm workers frequently fail to seek medical care, because doctors frequently fail to attribute observed symptoms to pesticides, and because farm workers lack resources to support legal action, while administrative regulation has high enforcement costs.

4.2. Regulatory aversion to uncertainty

Thus far, the government has been treated as neutral with respect to uncertainty, that is, interested only in environmental quality on average. Indeed, government is typically assumed to be risk-neutral because its large size permits adequate diversification. But this assumption may not be appropriate for environmental issues. Environmental quality tends to be idiosyncratic and thus non-diversifiable. It is difficult, for example, to imagine means of compensating for an increment in premature deaths due to exposure to environmental toxicants or for the destruction of rare ecosystems. Governments are frequently sensitive to the prospect of making mistakes, especially to the possibility that realized environmental damage will turn out to be worse than expected. For example, most environmental legislation in the United States requires regulation to incorporate a margin of safety adequate to protect against uncertainty in meeting environmental quality standards. It is thus reasonable to treat governments as averse to uncertainty about environmental quality.

Lichtenberg and Zilberman (1988) have studied the engineering approach to uncertainty management implicit in the requirement of an adequate margin of safety. They argue that this requirement corresponds to a safety-fixed decision problem in which regulators choose instruments to minimize the social cost of regulation subject to the constraint that a nominal standard not be exceeded with more than a specified frequency. Beavis and Walker (1983) use a similar framework to derive optimal effluent taxes on random discharges from a set of polluters. Bigman (1996) proposes a modification of this criterion that incorporates the size of the deviation from the nominal standard.

In terms of the modified output-based model of the preceding section, optimal regulation in Lichtenberg and Zilberman's (1988) analysis involves choosing inputs x and environmental quality-enhancing effort a to minimize cost $wx + ra$ subject to the technological constraint $(y, q, x, a) \in T$ and the safety-fixed constraint $\Pr\{q > \bar{q}\} \leqslant 1 - \alpha$ (alternatively, $\Pr\{q \leqslant \bar{q}\} \geqslant \alpha$), where α, the frequency with which the nominal standard $\bar{q}$ is met, corresponds to the statutory margin of safety. As Lichtenberg, Zilberman and Bogen (1989) note, this decision problem generates an uncertainty-adjusted cost function $C(y, q, \alpha) = \min\{wx + ra: (y, q, x, a) \in T, \ \Pr\{q \leqslant \bar{q}\} \geqslant \alpha\}$. The margin of safety α can be interpreted as a measure of society's aversion to uncertainty. A higher value of α corresponds to lower tolerance for violations of the nominal standard and thus greater aversion to uncertainty. This interpretation suggests that social benefits, too, should reflect social preferences for uncertainty about environmental quality, so that the social benefit function should be written as $U(y, q, \alpha)$ and maximized by choices of crop output, environmental quality, and margin of safety.

Lichtenberg and Zilberman (1988) examine theoretically the properties of cost-minimizing regulatory decisions in the case where the safety-rule constraint can be represented as a weighted sum of the mean and standard deviation of environmental quality. They show that the optimal regulatory policy consists of a portfolio of instruments of which some have comparative advantage in enhancing environmental quality on average while others have comparative advantage in reducing uncertainty about environmental quality. They show that increased aversion to uncertainty (a higher margin of safety α) leads to a higher total cost of regulation and increased use of instruments with comparative advantage in reducing uncertainty, a class that includes research and data acquisition. The marginal cost of environmental quality will fall, however, and use of instruments with comparative advantage in enhancing environmental quality on average may fall as well. When there is greater background uncertainty about environmental quality, it becomes efficient to increase reliance on instruments with comparative advantage in enhancing environmental quality on average, while the use of instruments with comparative advantage in reducing uncertainty may fall.

Empirical applications of this framework include Lichtenberg, Zilberman and Bogen (1989), who estimate the cost of reducing the risk of cancer from pesticide contamination of drinking water; Lichtenberg and Zilberman (1987), who estimate the cost of mitigating the risk of gastroenteritis from consumption of shellfish contaminated by dairy wastes; Hanemann, Lichtenberg and Zilberman (1989), who estimate the cost of meeting standards for selenium in river water; Harper and Zilberman (1992), who estimate the cost of reducing farm workers' cancer risk from insecticide exposure; and Lichtenberg and Penn (in press), who estimate the cost of meeting nitrate standards in well water. Estimated uncertainty premia (that is, incremental costs due to increases in the margin of safety) range from 1 percent or less in cases of lax standards and low margins of safety to as much as 35 percent for stringent standards and high margins of safety.

4.3. Information acquisition: IPM and precision agriculture

As noted previously, uncertainty springs from two types of sources, randomness and unobserved or unmeasured heterogeneity. Uncertainty from both sources can be reduced or, in some cases, eliminated entirely. Weather forecasts can be used to reduce uncertainty about rainfall, which affects optimal fertilizer application rates [Babcock (1990)], or uncertainty about evapotranspiration demand, which influences optimal irrigation water application rates [Cohen et al. (1998)]. Scouting can reduce uncertainty about crop disease [Carlson (1970)] or insect pressure [Moffitt (1986), Stefanou, Mangel and Wilen (1986)] and thus influence optimal pesticide use. Soil tests can reduce or eliminate uncertainty about soil fertility, water infiltration rates, or other soil characteristics due to unmeasured soil heterogeneity [Babcock and Blackmer (1992), Babcock, Carriquiry and Stern (1996)]. In some cases it may be feasible to wait until random events are realized and act with certainty in accordance with the realization of the random variable. Scouting falls into the latter category if it is sufficiently accurate, since it is generally undertaken with the intent of postponing the use of pesticides or other pest control methods until the extent of infestation has been observed.

Information-intensive technologies are widely cited in policy discussions as potential means of improving environmental quality and farm profitability simultaneously, that is, of enhancing stewardship. This proposition has received relatively little careful economic analysis. The few analyses that have been performed suggest a need for caution in making such inferences.

Reducing uncertainty by acquiring information can affect environmental quality in two major ways. First, it can lead to changes in the use of inputs that impair environmental quality (equivalently, in the use of inputs that enhance environmental quality). Second, it can improve targeting of inputs to improve application efficiency, as was discussed in Section 2.2.2. In what follows, we discuss potential environmental quality effects in both of these cases.

4.3.1. Information, input use, and environmental quality

Reductions in uncertainty due either to measurement of previously unobserved heterogeneity or to more accurate forecasts of random events have been modeled as mean-preserving contractions of the distribution of the unobserved factor or by using explicit Bayesian models. Most studies have examined the acquisition of information using single-input production models, such as the model in which output $y = f(y, \varepsilon)$, used in the preceding sections. In the present case, the random factor ε represents either unobserved but measurable factors of production such as soil nutrient stocks or the water infiltration rate of the soil at a specific location, or random factors such as pest infestation rates. Feder's (1979) study of the risk effects of pesticides, discussed above, is undertaken with scouting explicitly in mind. Babcock and Blackmer (1992) model pre-sidedress nitrogen test information as a mean-preserving contraction in the distribution of the soil nitrogen stock in a model in which nitrogen fertilizer and soil nitrogen are treated as perfect substitutes. Feinerman, Letey and Vaux (1983) use this framework to investigate the effects of uniformity of soil infiltration rates on optimal irrigation water application rates. (See also Moschini and Hennessy (2001) in this Handbook for a more general discussion.)

Reductions in uncertainty influence input use even if farmers are risk-neutral, as can be seen using a second-order approximation of expected profit around the mean of ε:

$$E\{pf(z, \varepsilon) - vz\} \approx p\left[f(z, \bar{\varepsilon}) + \frac{1}{2}f_{\varepsilon\varepsilon}(z, \bar{\varepsilon})\sigma^2 \right] - vz.$$

The term $\frac{1}{2}f_{\varepsilon\varepsilon}\sigma^2$ is what Babcock and Shogren (1995) term production risk. It is negative by the concavity of the production function in ε, i.e., $f_{\varepsilon\varepsilon} < 0$. The first-order condition defining optimal use of the input z is

$$p\left[f_z(z, \bar{\varepsilon}) + \frac{1}{2}f_{\varepsilon\varepsilon z}(z, \bar{\varepsilon})\sigma^2 \right] - v = 0.$$

A reduction in uncertainty (i.e., in σ^2) leads to decreased (increased) use of z if $f_{\varepsilon\varepsilon z} > (<) 0$, that is, if increases in z reduce (increase) the concavity of the production function in ε. Alternatively, a reduction in uncertainty leads to decreased (increased) use of z if increases in ε make the input more (less) risk-increasing, that is, if $\partial f_{\varepsilon z}/\partial \varepsilon > (<) 0$. There is no extant empirical evidence about the sign of this third derivative, however.

Information has value to farmers even if they are risk-neutral. By the envelope theorem, a reduction in σ^2 increases the farmer's expected profit by the amount $\frac{1}{2}pf_{\varepsilon\varepsilon}$. But acquiring information about ε may not increase overall social welfare. If environmental damage is not taken into account in farmers' input use decisions, the social value of information acquisition is

$$\frac{1}{2}[pf_{\varepsilon\varepsilon} - D_{\varepsilon\varepsilon}] - \frac{1}{2}\sigma^2[D_e e_z + D_{\varepsilon\varepsilon z}]\frac{\partial z}{\partial \sigma^2}.$$

The first term in square brackets is negative, but the second term can be positive. In the absence of regulation, then, reductions in uncertainty can decrease social welfare by exacerbating environmental quality problems.

There have been few, if any, studies investigating optimal sampling or testing strategies in an economic context, that is, in the context of improved crop production decisions. Carlson (1970) estimates the impact of peach disease-loss forecasts on the mean and standard deviation of returns from four fungicide use strategies. Stefanou, Mangel, and Wilen (1986) derive scouting-based spraying strategies for lygus bug on cotton and estimate the value of scouting information of varying accuracy. Babcock, Carriquiry and Stern (1996) present a Bayesian model of soil nitrogen testing and an application to Iowa corn production. There have also been discussions of scouting methods in the entomology and weed science literatures, but they have not been combined with economic models of pest management decision making. Grid sample size for soil testing has emerged recently as an important issue given the costliness of sampling [see, for example, National Research Council (1997)]. One issue of interest is whether decreased grid size improves the accuracy of information about important soil characteristics. There is some evidence that variability of soil characteristics may not decrease appreciably at smaller sampling scales [National Research Council (1997)]. If it does not, then soil sampling may have limited effects on environmental quality.

4.3.2. Information and application efficiency

Information can also be used to target input application more precisely, thereby improving environmental quality. For example, scouting may reduce risks to human health and wildlife from pesticide use by reducing pesticide applications on average (although not necessarily in every single year), by permitting the use of narrower-spectrum chemicals with fewer spillover effects, or by permitting spot treatments of areas with high infestation rates. Similarly, soil testing allows farmers to take existing soil nutrient stocks into account in choosing chemical fertilizer application rates, reducing excess applications and thus eventual leaching. Information on expected crop evapotranspiration rates derived from weather forecasts allows farmers to match irrigation application rates with crop demands. In most cases, optimal water use declines, creating the potential to improve in-stream environmental quality by reducing water diversion for irrigation [Cohen et al. (1998)]. However, it is not necessarily true that improved information will reduce the use of inputs that impair environmental quality, even on average and even on only the intensive margin.

The following analysis, adapted from Moffitt (1986, 1988), uses a modified form of the input-oriented model to discuss this point in the context of scouting. Let agricultural output be a function $f(z, \varepsilon)$ of an input affecting environmental quality z and a random factor ε such that $f_\varepsilon > 0$. Let $z^*(\varepsilon)$ be the privately optimal pesticide application rate when pest pressure is ε, defined by

$$pf_z\big(z^*(\varepsilon), \varepsilon\big) - v = 0.$$

Assume also that there exists a threshold level of pest pressure ε^c such that $z^*(\varepsilon) = 0$ for $\varepsilon \leqslant \varepsilon^c$ [Headley (1972), Mumford and Norton (1984), Moffitt (1988)].

The optimal pesticide application rate of a risk-neutral farmer engaging in preventive treatment z^p is defined by

$$\int p f_z(z^p, \varepsilon) \psi(\varepsilon) \, d\varepsilon - v = 0,$$

where $\psi(\varepsilon)$ is the probability density of ε and $\Psi(\varepsilon)$ is the corresponding cumulative distribution. There exists a level of pest pressure ε^p such that

$$p f_z(z^p, \varepsilon^p) - v = \int p f_z(z^p, \varepsilon) \psi(\varepsilon) \, d\varepsilon - v = 0,$$

that is, $z^p = z^*(\varepsilon^p)$. The difference in pesticide use between preventive treatment and the scouting regime is

$$z^p \Psi(\varepsilon^c) + \int_{\varepsilon^c}^{\varepsilon^p} \left[z^p - z^*(\varepsilon) \right] \psi(\varepsilon) \, d\varepsilon + \int_{\varepsilon^p} \left[z^p - z^*(\varepsilon) \right] \psi(\varepsilon) \, d\varepsilon.$$

If $f_{z\varepsilon} > 0$, $z^*(\varepsilon) > (<) z^p$ when $\varepsilon < (>) \varepsilon^p$. The first and third terms of this difference are thus positive, while the second term is negative. If $\Psi(\varepsilon^p) - \Psi(\varepsilon^c)$ is sufficiently large, total pesticide application will be greater with scouting than under a preventive regime. (If $f_{z\varepsilon} < 0$, the inequalities will be reversed but the basic analysis still holds.) In such cases, providing free scouting services could have detrimental effects on environmental quality and social welfare overall.

Constraints on timing of application may be a significant impediment to the use of such information-based application strategies. Feinerman, Choi and Johnson (1990) model split application of nitrogen fertilizer as a form of increased application efficiency. They assume that initial soil nitrogen stocks and pre-plant applications of nitrogen are subject to leaching, runoff, and volatilization losses, while side-dress applications are not. Let z_0 denote the initial stock of soil nitrogen, z_1 the pre-plant application rate, z_2 the side-dress application rate, and $(1 - h)$ denote losses of pre-plant nitrogen, all of which are known with certainty. Effective nitrogen $s(z, h)$ is then $z_2 + h[z_0 + z_1]$. Side-dressing is more efficient, but some pre-plant application may be optimal because of the risk that adverse weather conditions (too much rainfall) will prevent side-dressing. Let ε represent soil moisture, scaled to lie in the unit interval, so that crop production is $f(z_2 + h[z_0 + z_1], \varepsilon)$. Environmental damage is $D(e((1 - h)[z_0 + z_1]), \varepsilon)$. Side-dress application is infeasible when soil is excessively wet, that is, $z_1 = 0$ when $\varepsilon \geqslant \varepsilon^c$, making pre-plant application optimal (thereby creating environmental damage) for both risk-neutral and risk-averse farmers when nitrogen is sufficiently cheap. Lichtenberg, Spear and Zilberman (1994) note that reentry regulation of pesticides may create similar disincentives for using reactive rather than preventive pesticide application. In such cases, even subsidies for information acquisition may be of limited effectiveness.

Matching input application rates with crop ecosystem uptake rates requires knowledge about both natural characteristics affecting production and about the ways in which applied inputs interact with those characteristics, that is, about technological structure. More precise measurement of field conditions has little value without knowledge of the structure of crop production technologies [National Research Council (1997)]. Biological knowledge may be an important source of *a priori* information permitting improved specification of agricultural technology structure.

Modeling crop nutrient response provides one important example. A series of papers by Paris and his colleagues and by others examines the applicability of the von Liebig hypothesis of limitationality to nutrient response modeling. This hypothesis has two major features: (1) limited substitutability between nutrients and (2) yield plateaus, that is, zero marginal productivity of non-limiting nutrients at some levels. Empirical studies on corn provide evidence of this limitationality: Best-fitting models combine yield plateaus and diminishing marginal nutrient productivity [see, for example, Lanzer and Paris (1981), Ackello-Ogutu, Paris and Williams (1985), Grimm, Paris and Williams (1987), Paris and Knapp (1989), Frank, Beatty and Embleton (1990), Cerrato and Blackmer (1990), Paris (1992), Chambers and Lichtenberg (1996)]. Limitationality could have important implications for understanding the effects of policy-induced changes in fertilizer use on nutrient pollution. First, fertilizer recommendations generated from polynomial specifications tend to exceed those from a von Liebig specification. If the von Liebig specification is correct, standard functional forms generate excessive nutrient application rates [Ackello-Ogutu, Paris and Williams (1985)]. Second, policies for enhancing water quality are typically targeted toward the limiting nutrient governing eutrophication (usually either nitrogen or phosphorus). But reductions in application rates of one nutrient could make it limiting in crop production, leading to increased runoff of other nutrients. For example, application of poultry litter to crops has been advocated as a means of reducing nitrogen loadings into the Chesapeake Bay. Application rates are targeted on crop nitrogen requirements, leading to accumulations of excess phosphorus. It now appears possible that excess phosphorus may be leaching from fields, exacerbating the Bay's nutrient pollution problem.

In a similar vein, Lichtenberg and Zilberman (1986a) attempt to introduce crop ecosystem thinking into models of pesticide productivity. They argue that pesticides should be treated differently from normal inputs because they limit damage rather than contribute to potential output. They propose a model in which pesticides (and other inputs) produce an intermediate input called abatement. The fact that abatement cannot exceed potential output implies that the marginal product of pesticides and other damage control inputs declines faster than most first-order approximations such as a log-linear model. Babcock, Lichtenberg and Zilberman's (1992) analysis of apple production found a substantial difference in marginal productivity and thus in profit-maximizing pesticide application rate recommendations. The appropriateness of this damage control model has been the subject of some debate. Several studies have found that some form of abatement function provides a better model fit than a standard log-linear model [Carrasco-Tauber and Moffitt (1992), Babcock, Lichtenberg and Zilberman (1992), Chambers and Lichtenberg (1994), Saha, Shumway and Havenner (1997)], while others have found generic functional forms better fitting [Crissman, Cole and Carpio (1994), Carpentier and Weaver (1997)]. (Carpentier and Weaver's claim is weakened by the fact that they compared a generic specification with fixed farmer effects with a damage control specification without those fixed effects.)

An additional attraction from a policy perspective is the fact that the damage control model permits inference of crop damage, that is, of the percentage of crop lost to pests under any configuration of pest control inputs. The notion that relative crop losses to pests have remained virtually constant at about 30 percent over the past three decades [Pimentel et al. (1991)] has been one of the main arguments used to motivate the need for stricter overall regulation of pesticides. The estimates on which this claim is based are derived from a potpourri of field studies. Chambers and Lichtenberg (1994) used a dual formulation of the damage control model to estimate the share of aggregate U.S. crops lost, and found that losses were much smaller initially and have declined markedly due to pesticide use. They also found no evidence of a "pesticide treadmill" in which ecological damage leads to a spiral of ever-increasing pesticide use.

5. Interactions among agricultural, resource, and environmental policies

Agriculture has been treated thus far as a competitive industry characterized by market failures in the provision of environmental quality. In most countries, however, agricultural markets are also subject to significant distortions, primarily due to government intervention. Virtually all countries have agricultural policies that influence agricultural markets. In developed countries, such policies are typically designed to bolster farm income and/or stabilize the prices of agricultural commodities. In developing countries, such policies are typically designed to reduce food prices in urban areas and transfer income from agriculture to other sectors of the economy [see, for example, Schiff and Valdés (1992)]. Many countries also have policies designed to promote the use of inputs associated with environmental quality such as chemical fertilizers, pesticides, water, and land. Some such policies have survived in developed countries, for example, irrigation water subsidies originally introduced in order to promote economic growth in the western United States.

As a result, it is necessary to design and evaluate environmental policies aimed at agriculture in a second-best context that takes into account the distortions introduced by agricultural and other resource policies [Lichtenberg and Zilberman (1986b)]. These distortions can be substantial. Lichtenberg and Zilberman (1986b), for example, analyze the impacts of a hypothetical marginal output cost-increasing environmental regulation affecting a crop subject to a simple deficiency payment program. The supply price farmers face exceeds the demand price, resulting in excessive output and deadweight efficiency loss. An environmental regulation that increases the marginal cost of production reduces producer and consumer surplus in the affected market but reduces the size of the deadweight loss as well. Back-of-the-envelope calculations using supply and demand elasticities, output levels, market prices, and target prices typical of the mid-1980s indicate that the reduction in deadweight loss largely counteracts reductions in market consumer and producer surplus for crops like cotton and rice. Moreover, estimates of market-level economic costs of regulation calculated under an assumption that markets are perfectly competitive far exceed the true market-level costs.

This section discusses the implications of interactions between environmental and agricultural policies for policy design. We focus on three kinds of agriculture sector policies: (1) those designed to raise average income (price and income support programs), (2) those designed to reduce income variability (price stabilization and crop insurance), and (3) those designed to promote certain kinds of agricultural production technologies by subsidizing key inputs such as water, fertilizers, or pesticides.

5.1. Agricultural price and income policies

Agricultural price and income policies are used widely. In developed countries, the main goal tends to be maintaining the farm sector by increasing farm income. In developing countries, these policies are typically aimed at transferring income from the farm sector to urban consumers and/or industries [Schiff and Valdés (1992)]. These policies typically drive a wedge between the price farmers face and consumers' willingness to pay for agricultural output. In the context of the output-based model introduced earlier, farmers' decision problem in such situations is to choose agricultural output y and environmental quality q to maximize profit $py - C(y, q)$, where p is determined by government agricultural policy. The necessary conditions are

$$p - C_y(y, q) = 0,$$

$$C_q(y, q) = 0.$$

If government policy raises the supply price p above consumers' willingness to pay $U_y(y, q)$, agricultural output exceeds the socially optimal level. If agricultural output and environmental quality are substitutes ($C_{yq} < 0$), such a price support policy exacerbates environmental quality problems. If agricultural output and environmental quality are complements ($C_{yq} > 0$), then price support mitigates environmental quality problems.

Environmental quality and agricultural output are likely to be substitutes in situations where environmental problems are associated with the use of agricultural chemicals (fertilizers, pesticides) or with conversion of land to agricultural uses (deforestation, loss of wetlands, wind erosion from cultivation of virgin prairie). In these cases, price support programs like those used widely in developed countries are likely to worsen environmental quality problems. In developing countries, however, agricultural policies typically depress farm-level prices and are thus likely to mitigate environmental damage.

Environmental quality and agricultural output are clearly complements in cases where agriculture provides environmental quality directly, as in the case of scenic amenities from farming. Price support programs in developed countries thus tend to promote farmland preservation and thus the provision of such amenities, at least to the extent that price support policies apply to the products typically raised near urban areas.

The case of soil erosion is more complex. Price supports increase the return to current production and thus the return to erosion. At the same time, they tend to increase expected future prices and thus the marginal user cost of soil erosion, that is, the expected returns to soil conservation. Consider the input-based model used earlier to discuss soil conservation at the farm level in the case where the price of agricultural output p is determined by government policy. An increase in p above the competitive market equilibrium level changes the soil erosion rate z by

$$\frac{\partial z}{\partial p} = -\frac{R_{pz} + L_{ep}e_z}{R_{zz} + L_{ee}e_z^2 + L_e e_{zz}}.$$

The sign of $\partial z/\partial p$ equals the sign of the numerator. The term R_{pz} represents the effect of an output price increase on current returns to erosion. It is positive if erosion is a normal input. The term $L_{ep}e_z$ represents the change in the future value of the farm $L(p, e(z))$ due to increased soil losses e_z. One would expect an increase in p to increase the marginal value of soil, i.e., $L_{ep} < 0$. Thus, the effect of price support on soil erosion is ambiguous, as LaFrance (1992) discusses in detail. Claims to the contrary depend on specialized assumptions about the tradeoff between present and future income. For example, Barrett's (1991) claim that soil conservation is invariant with respect to price policy depends on the rather unrealistic assumptions of stationary prices and additive separability between soil depth/soil erosion and the use of other variable inputs [LaFrance (1992)]. Clarke (1992) uses a model in which erosion *per se* does not affect crop productivity in deriving the result that price supports unambiguously reduce erosion.

Price support programs are complex. Most require farmers to comply with production controls like acreage set-asides and/or meet eligibility conditions like base acreage requirements in order to limit budgetary exposure. As a result, these programs generate countervailing incentives. Moreover, most environmental quality problems are regional or local in scope and must thus be analyzed on a regional or local scale. Aggregate nationwide assessments are relatively uninformative.

If agriculture is characterized by constant returns to scale, as is widely believed for crop production, price and income support programs may influence the use of inputs that affect environmental quality on both the intensive and extensive margins, as discussed in Section 4. Rausser, Zilberman and Just (1984) discuss the effects of deficiency payment programs with set-asides on land allocations using such a model. They argue that farmers may find it profitable to rent low-quality land in order to meet set-aside requirements, i.e., that set-asides may create a market for "diversion-quality" land. Just and Antle (1990) discuss extensive-margin effects of alternative policy configurations in greater detail.

If agricultural production is not characterized by constant returns to scale, price and income support programs may affect scale of operation as well. This issue has received relatively little attention.

Underwood and Caputo (1996) present a theoretical model of the impacts of deficiency payments, base acreage requirements, and set-asides on farmers' allocation of land between program and non-program crops and of pest control measures between pesticides and alternative knowledge-based pest control methods.

Leathers and Quiggin (1991) present a theoretical model of the impacts of price supports on risk-averse farmers' demand for inputs that may influence environmental quality. They show that a higher output price unambiguously increases demand for a risk-reducing input only if farmers exhibit constant absolute risk aversion, while the effect of a higher output price on demand for a risk-increasing input is indeterminate under any assumption about risk preferences. If one considers only the effects of price and income supports on average output prices, therefore, little can be said qualitatively about the potential effects of these programs on environmental quality.

Beginning in 1985, the United States attempted to reduce potential environmental damage from agriculture by decoupling deficiency payments from current yields. Per-acre deficiency payment rates were thus determined by the difference between the target and market prices and by the amount of land enrolled in the program and thus eligible for payments. Of these two, only acreage is under the farmers' control. Recent research on environmental impacts of commodity programs in the United States has therefore focused on land allocation, that is, on extensive-margin effects. Policy discussions on environmental effects of commodity programs in the United States leading up to the 1995 farm bill focused increasingly on base acreage requirements as impediments to the use of crop rotations for fertility and pest management [see, for example, National Research Council (1989)].

There have been few such empirical studies to date, none of which has examined base acreage requirements. Following Lichtenberg (1989), Wu and Segerson (1995) use county-level data from Wisconsin to estimate a logit model of shares of county farmland allocated to alternative crops as functions of output and input prices, land quality characteristics, and farm program parameters such as the target price of corn and acreage set-asides for corn, oats, and wheat. Their treatment of environmental quality effects is crude. Land quality characteristics are also used to construct an index of leaching vulnerability that classifies soils as having high, moderate, or low leaching potential. Corn and soybeans are classified as "high-polluting", wheat and oats as "low-polluting", and hay as non-polluting. The estimated model is then used to simulate the effects of changes in feed grain program parameters (the target price and set-aside for corn) on crop acreage allocations and thus potential leaching. Plantinga (1996) similarly estimates a logit model of the shares of land in four land capability class groups in southwestern Wisconsin allocated to either dairying or forest as a function of the timber:milk price ratio. Conversion from dairying to forest is assumed to decrease soil erosion by amounts taken from 1987 National Resources Inventory data, and Ribaudo's (1989) estimates are used to value the water quality benefits of decreased erosion.

Stavins and Jaffe (1990) combine U.S. Forest Service data on county-level forest and cropland acreage, average per-acre crop returns derived from the Census of Agriculture, Natural Resource Inventory data on natural flood and drainage conditions, and weather data with parametric assumptions about land quality distributions to estimate conversion of forested wetlands in the southeastern United States. Their model indicates that increases in average crop prices increase deforestation and wetlands loss substantially. Van Kooten (1993) uses data from a survey of Saskatchewan farmers to estimate a cost function for converting wetlands and native pasture to cropland. This cost function is combined with budget data under alternative price scenarios in a dynamic decision framework to estimate the effects of grain price supports on wetlands conversion over an 80-year period. Kramer and Shabman (1993) use budget data to estimate the net returns to conversion of wetlands to cropland under several agricultural policy and tax reform scenarios.

5.2. Price stabilization and crop insurance

Agricultural programs may also be aimed at reducing price or income risk. Most developed countries also have policies aimed at stabilizing the prices of agricultural commodities. For example, in recent years the United States has set crop loan rates sufficiently low that they influence market prices only in exceptional circumstances. As a result, crop loans reduce price risk by giving farmers the equivalent of free put options. As is well known, reductions in price risk tend to increase agricultural production [Sandmo (1971)], exacerbating environmental quality problems in situations where environmental quality and agricultural output are substitutes, and enhancing environmental quality in situations where the two are complements. Many countries also use crop insurance to protect farmers against catastrophic risk, e.g., major crop failure [see Hazell, Pomareda and Valdes (1986) or Hueth and Furtan (1994) for descriptions of these programs; Chambers (2002) discusses issues in the design of agricultural insurance].

As Chambers and Quiggin (1996) point out, when the government is risk-neutral and farmers are risk-averse, optimal environmental policy has two tasks: (1) providing farmers with insurance against income variability and (2) correcting incentives to ensure socially optimal crop choices and input allocations. Crop insurance may affect environmental quality by influencing both crop choice and input use (see Moschini and Hennessy (2001) in this Handbook for a review of theoretical analyses). The little empirical literature available has shown that input use effects can be substantial. Horowitz and Lichtenberg (1993) found that corn growers in the U.S. Corn Belt who purchase crop insurance use significantly more herbicides, insecticides, and nitrogen fertilizer per acre and spend more per acre on pesticides than those who do not purchase crop insurance. Smith and Goodwin (1996) find that Kansas wheat growers who purchased crop insurance spent significantly less on fertilizers and on all agricultural chemicals than those who did not purchase crop insurance. A simulation study by Babcock and Hennessy (1996) suggested that crop insurance reduces optimal nitrogen application rates on corn in Iowa, albeit relatively little. An econometric study by Wu (1999) suggests that crop insurance shifted cropping patterns in the Central Nebraska Basin toward more erosive crops. The impact of crop insurance on total land in cultivation has not been investigated, nor have there been studies of input use effects and crop choice in a broader variety of crops and locations.

5.3. Input subsidies

As noted in Section 3, input subsidies influence environmental quality in two ways. On the intensive margin, they induce farmers to increase the use of the subsidized inputs. On the extensive margin, they induce shifts in output composition toward crops that use the subsidized input more intensively.

In developing countries, subsidies for agricultural chemicals (fertilizers, pesticides) have been blamed for exacerbating environmental quality problems ranging from impairment of human health [see, for example, Levine (1991) and Boardman (1986)] to poisonings of fish and other aquatic wildlife to degradation of water quality [see, for example, Way and Heong (1994)]. Subsidies of this sort have been used widely in order to promote the adoption of Green Revolution hybrid crop varieties. Recent empirical work suggests that the net social benefits of these subsidies may be negative. Antle and Pingali (1994), for instance, find that the value of lost work time due to sickness caused by pesticide exposure in Philippine rice production outweighs the value of damage avoided. Heong, Escalada and Mai (1994) argue that early-season insecticide use on rice does not reduce crop damage and may actually result in increased damage by suppressing invertebrate predators that control later-season insect infestations [see also Bottrell and Weil (1995)]. Grepperud (1995) argues that programs that enhance farm productivity or the productivity of off-farm labor may reduce farmers' soil conservation effort. Overall, however, empirical work on these issues is sparse.

In some cases, however, input subsidies of these kinds may actually enhance environmental quality. López and Niklitscheck (1991) show that in an economy with both a modern agricultural sector and traditional agriculture based on shifting cultivation, subsidization of inputs used in the modern sector can reduce deforestation by attracting labor from the traditional sector. In cases where it is infeasible to control entry into the traditional sector, fertilizer and/or pesticide subsidies may be an effective second-best policy for reducing adverse climate change effects, erosion and sedimentation of rivers, and species loss due to tropical deforestation.

In the United States, subsidies for irrigation water in the arid West have been a major source of environmental quality problems such as increased river salinity, heavy metal (selenium, arsenic) discharges into surface waters and consequent damage to wildlife, wildlife damage caused by reduced in-stream flows, and habitat loss due to conversion of land to agricultural uses. Water price distortions arise from a number of sources, including below-cost pricing of water from federal water projects, use of hydroelectric power revenues to offset the costs of providing irrigation water, exclusion of interest from capital repayment charges, and differential pricing for water delivered with lower reliability. Ultimately, however, these distortions continue to influence water demand primarily because of limitations on water marketing due to legal restrictions on water transfers. If water were freely marketable, farmers would face an opportunity cost of foregone revenue from potential water sales to higher-value users (urban areas, higher-value crops) regardless of the cost of acquiring irrigation water. This opportunity cost of water appears to be on the order of 2–5 times the current price that federal and state irrigation projects charge for irrigation water. Institution of water markets would thus likely increase farmers' opportunity cost of water substantially, leading to reductions in drainage and saline effluent through reductions in water application rates, shifts to less water-using crops, and investment in more efficient irrigation technologies.

When drainage and effluent are increasing functions of water application rates, as is typically the case, an increase in the price of water can function as the equivalent of a Pigouvian tax. Linear programming [Horner (1975), Gardner and Young (1988)] and econometrically based simulation studies [Caswell, Lichtenberg and Zilberman (1990), Dinar and Letey (1991), Weinberg, Kling and Wilen (1993), Weinberg and Kling (1996)] indicate that increases in water prices (and thus institution of water markets) could alleviate drainage and saline effluent problems substantially through shifts in cropping patterns, changes in irrigation technology, and reductions in water application rates for given crops and irrigation technologies. Moore and Dinar (1995), however, argue that water may be quantity-rationed at present in many areas, that is, that farmers presently are willing to purchase more water than is available at current prices. In such situations, increases in water prices can result in smaller than anticipated reductions in on-farm water use. They present econometric evidence indicating that California farmers using water from the Central Valley Project may be quantity-rationed.

Creation of water markets or other institutional reforms that price water at its true value may be effective means of controlling environmental damage in irrigated agriculture caused by other inputs as well. Larson, Helfand and House (1996) note that increases in the price of water will reduce the use of complementary inputs and therefore environmental damage from the use of those inputs. They present simulation results indicating that taxing irrigation water achieves given reductions in nitrate leaching from lettuce at per-acre costs roughly equal to those required under combined water and nitrogen taxes.

Government investment in infrastructure and other public goods may implicitly provide subsidies for agricultural inputs that influence environmental quality. Stavins and Jaffe (1990) argue that federal drainage and flood control projects have played an important role in fostering conversion of forested wetlands to agricultural use in the Mississippi Delta region. By reducing flood risk over broad areas, these projects implicitly lower the cost of land that would otherwise require significant private investment to make cultivation attractive. Their empirical model suggests that close to one-third of conversion of forested wetlands in the Mississippi Delta between 1934 and 1984 could be attributed to projects of this nature.

6. Concluding remarks

As we noted in the introduction, the centrality of agriculture to human existence and the dependence of agricultural productivity on natural conditions give environmental quality problems in agriculture certain distinctive features. Agriculture's dependence on natural conditions creates incentives for resource stewardship that may incidentally induce farmers to protect environmental quality. This dependence also means that heterogeneity and uncertainty are important factors in environmental policy design. The centrality of agriculture to human existence lies behind the presence of agriculture sector policies in virtually all countries. As a result, interactions between agricultural and resource policies play important roles in determining the effects of environmental policies in agriculture.

We began with a discussion of stewardship in order to answer the question of whether environmental regulation is needed in agriculture. If stewardship incentives are sufficiently strong, it is possible that farmers' pursuit of their own self-interest will result in adequate provision of environmental quality. Education and exhortation should suffice to fill any gaps by bringing unnoticed opportunities to farmers' attention. Such a view underlies the bulk of current environmental policy for agriculture in the U.S. The existing literature suggests that stewardship incentives are not sufficiently strong in most countries; the emergence of environmental problems association with agriculture is *prima facie* evidence that they are not. Therefore, there is a need for some form of environmental regulation. The literature also suggests that promotion of more environment-friendly farming methods does not always enhance environmental quality. New precision application technologies that reduce input requirements on the intensive margin may have extensive margin effects that impair environmental quality, so that introduction of a new precision application method may worsen environmental quality overall. Information-intensive technologies may similarly worsen environmental quality by increasing the use of polluting inputs. Even when these technologies do help improve environmental quality, the extent of improvement is likely to be less than anticipated. In general, careful empirical analysis is needed to determine the likely effects of these technologies. Relatively little has been conducted to date, however.

While more traditional forms of regulation (economic incentives, standards) appear to be needed, the empirical basis for setting such standards is generally lacking. The bulk of the empirical literature relies on farm-level simulation models. There is considerable evidence that these models predict ambient environmental quality poorly at scales of interest to policymakers, suggesting that alternative approaches are needed. Approaches involving interdisciplinary collection and analysis of data linking ambient environmental quality and agricultural production seem the most promising.

One interesting sidelight in this discussion was the claim of the sustainable farming advocacy literature that environmental regulation in agriculture might resuscitate traditional family farms in developed countries like the U.S. The formal argument is that once the full social value of environmental quality is taken into account, the joint costs of agricultural output and environmental quality are lower in smaller-scale integrated crop/livestock operations than in larger-scale specialized crop or livestock operations. While this proposition seems to enjoy considerable currency in policy discussions (at least in the U.S.), it has not been analyzed rigorously either theoretically or empirically.

We then turned to the question of the appropriate instruments for environmental regulation in agriculture. Developed countries mainly use a combination of direct regulation (imposition of best practice standards) and subsidies for the adoption of best practice farming methods to deal with both adverse and beneficial environmental effects. Emissions-based regulation tends to be infeasible given the high cost and technical difficulty of monitoring associated with nonpoint source problems like those typical in agriculture. Our analysis of regulation in a heterogeneous industry implied that negative (positive) incentives applied to inputs were preferable for cases involving adverse (beneficial) environmental effects because they gave farmers the proper signals on both the intensive and extensive margins. Our analysis of the choice of policy instruments under uncertainty was inconclusive due to lack of information about the relative sensitivity of crop productivity and environmental damage to uncertainty, although the fact that most of the inputs associated with environmental quality problems are risk-increasing argues for the superiority of incentives. Input taxes (subsidies) differentiated across farm types (e.g., crops, soils, slopes, location) seemed feasible to implement in many cases where inputs have adverse (beneficial) environmental effects. The major exception was fertilizer, which we discuss further below.

We also examined the design of environmental regulation under hidden information (adverse selection) and hidden action (moral hazard). Most studies of problems involving hidden information have neglected issues of contract enforcement such as compliance monitoring and secondary markets. The difficulty of monitoring compliance and the ease with which secondary markets can arise suggests that hidden information is relatively intractable for most environmental quality problems in agriculture. The major exception is land use. Hidden information is likely to be an issue in local-scale land use policies (farmland preservation) but can be avoided when the number of potential participants is sufficiently large (e.g., national land retirement programs). Very few studies have examined environmental policy design in cases involving hidden action. Most have examined cases where emissions were either observable directly or could be inferred from observation of ambient environmental quality and thus have little applicability to nonpoint source problems.

Emissions trading would seem an attractive way to implement incentive-based regulation of environmental quality in agriculture. However, there has been very little research on emissions trading under conditions characteristic of agriculture, namely when monitoring emissions is excessively costly, when the environmental quality effects of alternative farming practices vary across farms, and when there is significant uncertainty about those effects. Further research is clearly indicated given the growth of interest in such programs.

Of the inputs associated with environmental quality problems, fertilizers appear to be the least amenable to regulation. The environmental quality effects of fertilizers vary according to crop type and natural production conditions in ways which first-best taxes or best practice standards cannot take into account. Second-best taxes or best practice standards are unlikely to be enforceable due to the ease of creating secondary markets and the difficulty of monitoring compliance. The empirical literature suggests that nitrogen and phosphorus, the nutrients most commonly associated with pollution problems, are risk-increasing, so that price and income stabilization programs tend to increase their use. This latter finding is troubling because countries like the U.S. tend to keep stabilization and insurance programs in place even while phasing out price and income support programs. Moreover, to the best of current knowledge, nutrient pollution of surface and ground waters tends to be the most widespread environmental quality problem associated with agriculture. These considerations suggest that creative thinking about policy design is especially needed for dealing with nutrient problems.

The importance of understanding interactions between agricultural, natural resource, and environmental policies is well established by now. Careful theoretical analyses show that these interactions are frequently too complex to permit simple unambiguous generalizations, e.g., about the effects of price support or price stabilization programs on environmental quality. As a result, empirical studies of these interactions are especially important for policy design. Unfortunately, sound empirical studies are generally lacking.

One final set of issues generally neglected in the literature to date relates to environmental quality effects of marketing. Most studies of environmental quality problems in agriculture assume a simple, two-sector competitive agricultural economy consisting of price-taking farmers and consumers. In developed countries, at least, processors and marketers (wholesalers, retailers) account for a large share of the food sector. Much of the interaction between farmers and their immediate customers is conducted under some form of vertical coordination, ranging from contracts to integration of operations. In many cases, processors and growers supply some production inputs, so that agricultural output and environmental quality are produced jointly by both sets of agents. Vertical interactions can play an important role in environmental quality problems even in industries without explicit forms of coordination. For example, quality standards, which can arise from informational problems encountered in marketing, can influence inputs such as pesticides [Babcock, Lichtenberg and Zilberman (1992), Starbird (1994), Lichtenberg (1997)]. To date, research on environmental quality problems in agriculture has concentrated on situations involving independent farms, ignoring the possibility that numerous agents jointly produce both environmental quality and agricultural output. Both conceptual and empirical research could help improve environmental policy design in such industries.

Acknowledgements

I am grateful to Jean-Marc Bourgeon, Bob Chambers, Bruce Gardner, and David Zilberman for many illuminating conversations and comments on drafts of this chapter and to Arie Oskam for perspectives on policies in the European Union. Responsibility for any errors, of course, is mine alone.

References

Ackello-Ogutu, C., Q. Paris and W.A. Williams (1985), "Testing a von Liebig crop response function against polynomial specifications", American Journal of Agricultural Economics 67(4):873–880.

Amacher, G.S., and P.M. Feather (1997), "Testing producer perceptions of jointly beneficial best management practices for improved water quality", Applied Economics 29(2):153–159.

Anderson, G.D., J.J. Opaluch and W.M. Sullivan (1985), "Nonpoint agricultural pollution: pesticide contamination of groundwater supplies", American Journal of Agricultural Economics 67(5):1238–1243.

Antle, J.M. (1983), "Testing the stochastic structure of production: a flexible moment-based approach", Journal of Business Economics and Statistics 1:192–201.

Antle, J.M. (1988), Pesticide Policy, Production Risk, and Producer Welfare (Resources for the Future, Washington, DC).

Antle, J.M., and P.L. Pingali (1994), "Pesticides, productivity, and farmer health: a Philippine case study", American Journal of Agricultural Economics 76(3):418–430.

Ardila, S., and R. Innes (1993), "Risk, risk aversion and on-farm soil depletion", Journal of Environmental Economics and Management 25(1):S27–S45.

Babcock, B.A. (1990), "The value of weather information in market equilibrium", American Journal of Agricultural Economics 72(1):63–72.

Babcock, B.A., and A.M. Blackmer (1992), "The value of reducing temporal input nonuniformities", Journal of Agricultural and Resource Economics 17(2):335–347.

Babcock, B.A., A.L. Carriquiry and H.S. Stern (1996), "Evaluation of soil test information in agricultural decision making", Applied Statistics 46(4).

Babcock, B.A., and D.A. Hennessy (1996), "Input demand under yield and revenue insurance", American Journal of Agricultural Economics 78(2):416–427.

Babcock, B.A., P.G. Lakshmirayan, J.-J. Wu and D. Zilberman (1996), "The economics of a public fund for environmental amenities: a study of CRP contracts", American Journal of Agricultural Economics 78(4):961–971.

Babcock, B.A., E. Lichtenberg and D. Zilberman (1992), "Impact of damage control and quality of output: estimating pest control effectiveness", American Journal of Agricultural Economics 74(1):163–172.

Babcock, B.A., and J.F. Shogren (1995), "The cost of agricultural production risk", Agricultural Economics 12(2):141–150.

Barrett, S. (1991), "Optimal soil conservation and the reform of agricultural pricing policies", Journal of Development Economics 36:167–187.

Batie, S.S., and A.G. Sappington (1986), "Cross compliance as a soil conservation strategy", American Journal of Agricultural Economics 68(4):880–885.

Beach, E.D., and G.E. Carlson (1993), "A hedonic analysis of herbicides: do user safety and water quality matter?", American Journal of Agricultural Economics 75(3):612–623.

Beavis, B., and M. Walker (1983), "Achieving environmental standards with stochastic discharges", Journal of Environmental Economics and Management 10:103–111.

Bigman, D. (1996), "Safety-first criteria and their measures of risk", American Journal of Agricultural Economics 78(1):225–235.

Boardman, R. (1986), Pesticides in World Agriculture (Macmillan, London).

Bottrell, D. (1979), Integrated Pest Management (Council on Environmental Quality, Washington, DC).

Bottrell, D.G., and R.R. Weil (1995), "Protecting crops and the environment: striving for durability", in: A.S.R. Juo and R.D. Freed, eds., Agriculture and Environment: Bridging Food Production and Environmental Protection in Developing Countries (American Society of Agronomy, Madison, WI).

Braden, J.B., G.V. Johnson, A. Bouzaher and D. Miltz (1989), "Optimal spatial management of agricultural pollution", American Journal of Agricultural Economics 71(2):404–413.

Braden, J.B., and K. Segerson (1993), "Information problems in the design of nonpoint-source pollution policy", in: C.S. Russell and J.F. Shogren, eds., Theory, Modeling and Experience in the Management of Nonpoint-Source Pollution (Kluwer Academic Publishers, Boston).

Bromley, D.W. (1991), Environment and Economy: Property Rights and Public Policy (Blackwell, Oxford).

Burt, O.R. (1981), "Farm level economics of soil conservation in the Palouse area of the Northwest", American Journal of Agricultural Economics 63:83–92.

Cabe, R., and J.A. Herriges (1992), "The regulation of non-point-source pollution under imperfect and asymmetric information", Journal of Environmental Economics and Management 22(2):134–146.

Carlson, G.E. (1970), "A decision theoretic approach to crop disease prediction and control", American Journal of Agricultural Economics 52(2):216–223.

Carpentier, A., and R.D. Weaver (1997), "Damage control productivity: why econometrics matters", American Journal of Agricultural Economics 79(1):47–61.

Carrasco-Tauber, C., and L.J. Moffitt (1992), "Damage control econometrics: functional specification and pesticide productivity", American Journal of Agricultural Economics 74(1):158–162.

Caswell, M., E. Lichtenberg and D. Zilberman (1990), "The effects of pricing policies on water conservation and drainage", American Journal of Agricultural Economics 72(4):883–890.

Caswell, M.F., and D. Zilberman (1986), "The effects of well depth and land quality on the choice of irrigation technology", American Journal of Agricultural Economics 68(4):798–811.

Cerrato, M.E., and A.M. Blackmer (1990), "Comparison of models for describing corn yield response to nitrogen fertilizer", Agronomy Journal 82(1):138–143.

Chambers, R.G. (1989), "Insurability and moral hazard in agricultural insurance markets", American Journal of Agricultural Economics 71(3):604–616.

Chambers, R.G. (1992), "On the design of agricultural policy mechanisms", American Journal of Agricultural Economics 74(3):646–654.

Chambers, R.G. (2002), "Information, incentives, and the design of agricultural policies", in: B.L. Gardner and G.C. Rausser, eds., Handbook of Agricultural Economics, Vol. 2 (North-Holland, Amsterdam) 1751–1825.

Chambers, R.G., and E. Lichtenberg (1994), "Simple econometrics of pesticide productivity", American Journal of Agricultural Economics 76(3):407–417.

Chambers, R.G., and E. Lichtenberg (1996), "A nonparametric approach to the von Liebig–Paris technology", American Journal of Agricultural Economics 78(2):373–386.

Chambers, R.G., and J. Quiggin (1996), "Non-point-source pollution regulation as a multi-task principal-agent problem", Journal of Public Economics 59:95–116.

Clarke, H.R. (1992), "The supply of non-degraded agricultural land", Australian Journal of Agricultural Economics 36(1):31–56.

Cohen, D.R., D.E. Osgood, D.D. Parker and D. Zilberman (1998), "The California Irrigation Management Information System (CIMIS): intended and unintended impacts of public investment", Choices (third quarter):20–25.

Crissman, C.C., D.C. Cole and F. Carpio (1994), "Pesticide use and farm worker health in Ecuadorian potato production", American Journal of Agricultural Economics 76(3):593–597.

Cropper, M.L., and W.E. Oates (1992), "Environmental economics: a survey", Journal of Economic Literature 30(2):675–740.

Crosson, P.R. (1986), "Soil erosion and policy issues", in: T.T. Phipps, P.R. Crosson and K.A. Price, eds., Agriculture and the Environment (Resources for the Future, Washington, DC).

Crutchfield, S.R., D. Letson and A.S. Malik (1994), "Feasibility of point–nonpoint source trading for managing agricultural pollutant loadings to coastal waters", Water Resources Research 30(10):2825–2836.

Dasgupta, P., P. Hammond and E. Maskin (1980), "On imperfect information and optimal pollution control", Review of Economic Studies 47:857–860.

Davis, J.U., J.A. Caswell and C.R. Harper (1992), "Incentives for protecting farm workers from pesticides", American Journal of Agricultural Economics 74(4):907–917.

Day, R.H. (1945), "Probability distributions for field crop yields", Journal of Farm Economics 47(3):713–741.

Deininger, K., and G. Feder (2001), "Land institutions and land markets", in: B.L. Gardner and G.C. Rausser, eds., Handbook of Agricultural Economics, Vol. 1 (North-Holland, Amsterdam) 287–331.

Dinar, A., and J. Letey (1991), "Agricultural water marketing, allocative efficiency, and drainage reduction", Journal of Environmental Economics and Management 20(3):210–223.

Dubgaard, A. (1990), "Programs to abate nitrate and pesticide pollution in Danish agriculture", in: J.B. Braden and S.B. Lovejoy, eds., Agriculture and Water Quality: International Perspectives (Lynne Rienner, Boulder, CO) 117–130.

Edwards, W.F., and M.R. Langham (1976), "Public welfare in relation to alternative pesticide policies", Journal of Environmental Economics and Management 2:295–308.

Ehrlich, I., and G.S. Becker (1972), "Market insurance, self-insurance, and self-protection", Journal of Political Economy 80:623–648.

Ervin, C.A., and D.E. Ervin (1982), "Factors affecting the use of soil conservation practices: hypotheses, evidence, and implications", Land Economics 58:277–292.

Ervin, D.E., and J.W. Mill (1985), "Agricultural land markets and soil erosion: policy relevance and conceptual issues", American Journal of Agricultural Economics 67:938–942.

Farnsworth, R., and L.J. Moffitt (1981), "Cotton production under risk: an analysis of input effects on yield variability and factor demand", Western Journal of Agricultural Economics 6:155–163.

Feder, G. (1977), "Impact of uncertainty on a class of objective functions", Journal of Economic Theory 16:504–512.

Feder, G. (1979), "Pesticides, information, and pest management under uncertainty", American Journal of Agricultural Economics 61(1):97–103.

Feinerman, E., E. Bresler and G. Dagan (1985), "Optimization of a spatially variable resource: an illustration for irrigated crops", Water Resources Research 21(6):793–800.

Feinerman, E., E.K. Choi and S.R. Johnson (1990), "Uncertainty and split nitrogen applications in corn production", American Journal of Agricultural Economics 72(4):975–984.

Feinerman, E., J. Letey and H.J. Vaux Jr. (1983), "The economics of irrigation with nonuniform infiltration", Water Resources Research 19(6):1410–1414.

Fernandez-Cornejo, J., and S. Jans (1995), "Quality-adjusted price and quantity indices for pesticides", American Journal of Agricultural Economics 77(3):645–659.

Fleming, R.A., and R.M. Adams (1997), "The importance of site-specific information in the design of policies to control pollution", Journal of Environmental Economics and Management 33(2):347–358.

Foster, W.E., and B.A. Babcock (1991), "Producer welfare consequences of regulating chemical residues on agricultural crops: maleic hydrazide and tobacco", American Journal of Agricultural Economics 73(4):1224–1232.

Foster, W.E., L.S. Calvin, G.M. Johns and P. Rottschaeffer (1986), "Distributional welfare implications of an irrigation water subsidy", American Journal of Agricultural Economics 68(4):778–786.

Fox, G., and A. Weersink (1995), "Damage control and increasing returns", American Journal of Agricultural Economics 77(1):33–39.

Frank, M.D., B.R. Beatty and M.E. Embleton (1990), "A comparison of alternative crop response models", American Journal of Agricultural Economics 72(3):597–603.

Fudenberg, D., and J. Tirole (1991), Game Theory (MIT Press, Cambridge, MA).

Gardner, K., and R. Barrows (1985), "The impact of soil conservation investments on land prices", American Journal of Agricultural Economics 5(67):943–947.

Gardner, R.L., and R.A. Young (1988), "Assessing strategies for control of irrigation-induced salinity in the upper Colorado River basin", American Journal of Agricultural Economics 70(1):37–49.

Gotsch, N., and U. Regev (1996), "Fungicide use under risk in Swiss wheat production", Agricultural Economics 14(1):1–9.

Gould, B.W., W.E. Saupe and R.M. Klemme (1989), "Conservation tillage: the role of farm and operator characteristics and the perception of soil erosion", Land Economics 65:167–182.

Green, G., D. Sunding, D. Zilberman and D. Parker (1996), "Explaining irrigation technology choices: a microparameter approach", American Journal of Agricultural Economics 78(4):1064–1072.

Grepperud, S. (1995), "Soil conservation and governmental policies in tropical areas: does aid worsen the incentives for arresting erosion?", Agricultural Economics 12(2):129–140.

Griffin, R.C., and D.W. Bromley (1982), "Agricultural runoff as a nonpoint externality: a theoretical development", American Journal of Agricultural Economics 64(3):547–552.

Grimm, S.S., Q. Paris and W.A. Williams (1987), "A von Liebig model for water and nitrogen crop response", Western Journal of Agricultural Economics 12(2):182–192.

Guesnerie, R., and J.-J. Laffont (1984), "A complete solution to a class of principal-agent problems with an application to the control of a self-managed firm", Journal of Public Economics 25:329–370.

Hanemann, M., E. Lichtenberg and D. Zilberman (1989), "Conservation versus cleanup in agricultural drainage control", Working Paper No. 88-37 (Department of Agricultural and Resource Economics, University of Maryland, College Park).

Harper, C.R., and D. Zilberman (1992), "Pesticides and worker safety", American Journal of Agricultural Economics 74(1):68–78.

Hazell, P., C. Pomareda and A. Valdés (eds.) (1986), Crop Insurance for Agricultural Development: Issues and Experience (Johns Hopkins University Press, Baltimore).

Headley, J.C. (1972), "Defining the economic threshold", in: National Research Council, Pest Control Strategies for the Future (National Academy Press, Washington, DC).

Helfand, G.E., and B.W. House (1995), "Regulating nonpoint source pollution under heterogeneous conditions", American Journal of Agricultural Economics 77(4):1024–1032.

Heong, K.L., M.M. Escalada and V. Mai (1994), "An analysis of insecticide use on rice: case studies in the Philippines and Vietnam", International Journal of Pest Management 40(2):173–178.

Hiebert, L.D. (1983), "Self-insurance, self-protection, and the theory of the competitive firm", Southern Journal of Economics 50:160–168.

Hoag, D.L., and H.A. Holloway (1991), "Farm production decisions under cross- and conservation compliance", American Journal of Agricultural Economics 73(1):194–203.

Hochman, E., and D. Zilberman (1977), "Examination of environmental policies using production and pollution microparameter distributions", Econometrica 46(4):739–759.

Hochman, E., D. Zilberman and R.E. Just (1977a), "Internalization in a stochastic pollution model", Water Resources Research 13:877–881.

Hochman, E., D. Zilberman and R.E. Just (1977b), "Two-goal environmental policy: the case of the Santa Ana River basin", Journal of Environmental Economics and Management 4:25–39.

Holmstrom, B. (1982), "Moral hazard in teams", Bell Journal of Economics 13:324–340.

Horner, G.L. (1975), "Internalizing agricultural nitrogen pollution externalities: a case study", American Journal of Agricultural Economics 57(1):33–39.

Horowitz, J.K., and E. Lichtenberg (1993), "Insurance, moral hazard, and chemical use in agriculture", American Journal of Agricultural Economics 75(4):926–935.

Horowitz, J.K., and E. Lichtenberg (1994), "Risk-reducing and risk-increasing effects of pesticides", Journal of Agricultural Economics 45(1):82–89.

Hubbell, B.J., and G.E. Carlson (1998), "Effects of insecticide attributes on within-season insecticide product and rate choices: the case of U.S. apple growers", American Journal of Agricultural Economics 80(2):382–396.

Hueth, D., and W.H. Furtan (eds.) (1994), Economics of Agricultural Crop Insurance: Theory and Evidence (Kluwer Academic, Boston).

Hurd, B. (1994), "Yield response and production risk: an analysis of integrated pest management in cotton", Journal of Agricultural and Resource Economics 19(2):313–326.

Huszar, P.C. (1989), "Economics of reducing off-site costs of wind erosion", Land Economics 65(4):333–340.

Innes R. (2000), "The economics of livestock waste and its regulation", American Journal of Agricultural Economics 82(1):97–117.

Innes, R., and S. Ardila (1994), "Agricultural insurance and soil depletion in a simple dynamic model", American Journal of Agricultural Economics 76(3):371–384.

Jacobs, J.J., and J.F. Timmons (1974), "An economic analysis of agricultural land use policies to control water quality", American Journal of Agricultural Economics 56(4):791–798.

Johnson, S.L., R.M. Adams and G.M. Perry (1991), "The on-farm costs of reducing groundwater pollution", American Journal of Agricultural Economics 73(4):1063–1073.

Just, R.E., and J.M. Antle (1990), "Interactions between agricultural and environmental policies: a conceptual framework", American Economic Review 80(2):197–202.

Just, R.E., and R.D. Pope (1978), "Stochastic specification of production functions and economic implications", Journal of Econometrics 7(1):67–86.

Just, R.E., and D. Zilberman (1988), "A methodology for evaluating equity implications of environmental policy decisions in agriculture", Land Economics 64(1):37–52.

Khanna, M., and D. Zilberman (1996), "Incentives, precision technology, and environmental protection", Ecological Economics 23(1):25–43.

King, D., and J. Sinden (1988), "Influence of soil conservation on farm land values", Land Economics 64:242–255.

Kramer, R.A., and L. Shabman (1993), "Wetland drainage in the Mississippi delta", Land Economics 69(3):249–262.

Kumm, K.I. (1990), "Incentive policies in Sweden to reduce agricultural water pollution", in: J.B. Braden and S.B. Lovejoy, eds., Agriculture and Water Quality: International Perspectives (Lynne Rienner, Boulder, CO) 105–116.

LaFrance, J.T. (1992), "Do commodity prices lead to more or less soil degradation?", Australian Journal of Agricultural Economics 36(1):57–82.

Lanzer, E.A., and Q. Paris (1981), "A new analytical framework for the fertilization problem", American Journal of Agricultural Economics 63(1):93–103.

Larson, D.M., G.E. Helfand and B.W. House (1996), "Second-best tax policies to reduce nonpoint source pollution", American Journal of Agricultural Economics 78(4):1108–1116.

Leathers, H., and J. Quiggin (1991), "Interactions between agricultural and resource policy: the importance of attitudes toward risk", American Journal of Agricultural Economics 73(3):757–764.

Letson, D. (1992), "Point/nonpoint source pollution reduction trading: an interpretive survey", Natural Resources Journal 32:219–232.

Levine, R. (1991), "Recognized and possible effects of pesticides in humans", in: W.J.J. Hayes and E.R. Laws Jr., eds., Handbook of Pesticide Toxicology, Vol. 1 (Academic Press, San Diego).

Lichtenberg, E. (1989), "Land quality, irrigation development, and cropping patterns in the northern high plains", American Journal of Agricultural Economics 71(1):187–194.

Lichtenberg, E. (1992), "Alternative approaches to pesticide regulation", Northeast Journal of Agricultural and Resource Economics 21(2):83–92.

Lichtenberg, E. (1997), "The economics of cosmetic pesticide use", American Journal of Agricultural Economics 79(1):39–48.

Lichtenberg, E., D.D. Parker and D. Zilberman (1988), "Marginal analysis of welfare costs of environmental policies: the case of pesticide regulation", American Journal of Agricultural Economics 70(4):867–874.

Lichtenberg, E., and T. Penn (in press), "Prevention versus treatment under precautionary regulation: A case study of groundwater contamination under uncertainty", American Journal of Agricultural Economics.

Lichtenberg, E., and L.K. Shapiro (1997), "Agriculture and nitrate concentrations in Maryland community water system wells", Journal of Environmental Quality 26(1):145–153.

Lichtenberg, E., R.C. Spear and D. Zilberman (1994), "The economics of reentry regulation of pesticides", American Journal of Agricultural Economics 75(4):946–958.

Lichtenberg, E., and I.E. Strand Jr. (1997), The On-Farm Value of Soil and Water Conservation Measures: A Revealed Preference Approach (Department of Agricultural and Resource Economics, University of Maryland, College Park).

Lichtenberg, E., and D. Zilberman (1986a), "The econometrics of damage control: why specification matters", American Journal of Agricultural Economics 68(2):261–273.

Lichtenberg, E., and D. Zilberman (1986b), "The welfare economics of price supports in U.S. agriculture", American Economic Review 76:1135–1141.

Lichtenberg, E., and D. Zilberman (1988), "Efficient regulation of environmental health risks", Quarterly Journal of Economics 103(1):167–178.

Lichtenberg, E., and D. Zilberman (1987), "Regulation of marine contamination under environmental uncertainty: shellfish contamination in California", Marine Resource Economics 4(3):211–225.

Lichtenberg, E., D. Zilberman and K.T. Bogen (1989), "Regulating environmental health risks under uncertainty: groundwater contamination in California", Journal of Environmental Economics and Management 17(1):22–34.

Lichtenberg, E., and R. Zimmerman (1999a), "Adverse health effects, environmental attitudes, and pesticide usage behavior of farm operators", Risk Analysis 19(2):283–294.

Lichtenberg, E., and R. Zimmerman (1999b), "Farmers' willingness to pay for ground water protection", Water Resources Research 35:833–841.

Loehman, E., and A. Dinar (1994), "Cooperative solution of local externality problems: a case of mechanism design applied to agriculture", Journal of Environmental Economics and Management 26(3):235–256.

López, R.E., and M. Niklitscheck (1991), "Dual economic growth in poor tropical areas", Journal of Development Economics 36(2):189–211.

Love, H.A., and S. Buccola (1991), "Joint risk preference-technology estimation with a primal system", American Journal of Agricultural Economics 73(3):765–774.

Lynne, G.D., J.S. Shonkwiler and L.R. Rola (1988), "Attitudes and farmer conservation behavior", American Journal of Agricultural Economics 70(1):12–19.

Malik, A.S., D. Letson and S.R. Crutchfield (1993), "Point/nonpoint source trading of pollution abatement: choosing the right trading ratio", American Journal of Agricultural Economics 75:959–967.

Malik, A., and R. Shoemaker (1993), Optimal Cost-Sharing Programs to Reduce Agricultural Pollution (Economic Research Service, U.S. Department of Agriculture, Washington, DC).

Mapp, H.P., D.J. Bernardo, J.G. Sabbagh, S. Geleta and K.B. Watkins (1994), "Economic and environmental impacts of limiting nitrogen use to protect water quality: a stochastic regional analysis", American Journal of Agricultural Economics 76(4):889–903.

McConnell, K.E. (1983), "An economic model of soil conservation", American Journal of Agricultural Economics 65(1):83–89.

Menell, P.S. (1991), "The limitations of legal institutions for addressing environmental risks", Journal of Economic Perspectives 5(3):93–113.

Meyer, J. (1987), "Two-moment decision models and expected utility maximization", American Economic Review 77(3):421–430.

Meyer, J., and M.B. Ormiston (1989), "Deterministic transformations of random variables and the comparative statics of risk", Journal of Risk and Uncertainty 2(2):179–188.

Miranowski, J., and B.D. Hammes (1984), "Implicit prices of soil characteristics for farmland in Iowa", American Journal of Agricultural Economics 66(5):745–749.

Moffitt, L.J. (1988), "Incorporating environmental considerations in pest control advice for farmers", American Journal of Agricultural Economics 70(3):628–634.

Moffitt, L.J. (1986), "Risk-efficient thresholds for pest control decisions", Journal of Agricultural Economics 37:69–75.

Moffitt, L.J., R.E. Just and D. Zilberman (1978), "A 'putty clay' approach to aggregation of production/pollution possibilities: an application to dairy waste control", American Journal of Agricultural Economics 60(3):452–459.

Moore, M.R., and A. Dinar (1995), "Water and land as quantity-rationed inputs in California agriculture: empirical tests and policy implications", Land Economics 71(4):445–461.

Moschini, G., and D.A. Hennessy (2001), "Uncertainty, risk aversion, and risk management for agricultural producers", in: B.L. Gardner and G.C. Rausser, eds., Handbook of Agricultural Economics, Vol. 1 (North-Holland, Amsterdam) 87–153.

Mumford, J.D., and G.A. Norton (1984), "Economics of decision making in pest management", Annual Review of Entomology 29:157–174.

Napier, T.L., S.M. Camboni and C.S. Thraen (1986), "Environmental concern and the adoption of farm technologies", Journal of Soil and Water Conservation 41:109–113.

National Research Council (1989), Alternative Agriculture (National Academy Press, Washington, DC).

National Research Council (1997), Precision Farming (National Academy Press, Washington, DC).

Natural Resource Conservation Service (1994), 1992 National Resources Inventory, National Summary (U.S. Department of Agriculture, Washington, DC).

Nelson, C.H., and P.V. Preckel (1989), "The conditional beta distribution as a stochastic production function", American Journal of Agricultural Economics 71(2):370–378.

Norris, P.E., and S.S. Batie (1987), "Virginia farmers' soil conservation decisions: an application of Tobit analysis", Southern Journal of Agricultural Economics 19:79–90.

Organization for Economic Cooperation and Development (1994), Paris, OECD Environment Monographs No. 89.

Oskam, A.J., R.A.N. Vijftigschild and C. Graveland (1997), Additional EU Policy Instruments for Plant Protection Products (Wageningen Agricultural University).

Osteen, C., and F. Kuchler (1987), "Pesticide regulatory decisions: production efficiency, equity, and interdependence", Agribusiness 3:307–322.

Palmquist, R.B., and L.E. Danielson (1989), "A hedonic study of the effects of erosion control and drainage on farmland values", American Journal of Agricultural Economics 71(1):55–62.

Pannell, D.J. (1991), "Pests and pesticides, risk and risk aversion", Agricultural Economics 5:361–383.

Paris, Q. (1992), "The von Liebig hypothesis", American Journal of Agricultural Economics 74(4):1019–1028.

Paris, Q., and K. Knapp (1989), "Estimation of von Liebig response functions", American Journal of Agricultural Economics 71(1):178–186.

Park, W.M., and L.A. Shabman (1982), "Distributional constraints on acceptance of nonpoint pollution controls", American Journal of Agricultural Economics 64(3):455–462.

Pimentel, D., L. McLaughlin, A. Zepp, B. Lakitan, T. Kraus, P. Kleinman, F. Vancini, W.J. Roach, E. Graap, W.S. Keeton et al. (1991), "Environmental and economic impacts of reducing U.S. pesticide use", in: D. Pimentel, ed., Handbook of Pest Management in Agriculture (CRC Press, Boca Raton, FL).

Pingali, P.L., C.B. Marquez and F.G. Palis (1994), "Pesticides and Philippine rice farmer health: a medical and economic analysis", American Journal of Agricultural Economics 76(3):587–592.

Plantinga, A.J. (1996), "The effects of agricultural policies on land use and environmental quality", American Journal of Agricultural Economics 78(4):1082–1091.

Pope, R.D., and R.E. Just (1991), "On testing the structure of risk preferences in agriculture", American Journal of Agricultural Economics 73(3):743–748.

Pope, R.D., and R.A. Kramer (1979), "Production uncertainty and factor demands for the competitive firm", Southern Economic Journal 46(2):489–501.

Quiggin, J. (1991), "Comparative statics for rank-dependent expected utility theory", Journal of Risk and Uncertainty 4(4):339–350.

Ramaswamy, B. (1993), "Supply response to agricultural insurance: risk reduction and moral hazard effects", American Journal of Agricultural Economics 75(4):914–925.

Rasmusen, E. (1987), "Moral hazard in risk-averse teams", RAND Journal of Economics 18(3):428–435.

Rausser, G.C., D. Zilberman and R.E. Just (1984), "The distributional effects of land controls in agriculture", Western Journal of Agricultural Economics 9:215–232.

Regev, U., N. Gotsch and P. Rieder (1997), "Are fungicides, nitrogen, and plant growth regulators risk-reducing? Empirical evidence from swiss wheat production", Journal of Agricultural Economics 48(2):167–178.

Reichelderfer, K. (1990), "National agroenvironmental incentives programs: the U.S. experience", in: J.B. Braden and S.B. Lovejoy, eds., Agriculture and Water Quality: International Perspectives (Lynne Rienner, Boulder, CO) 131–146.

Reichelderfer, K., and W.G. Boggess (1988), "Government decision making and program performance: the case of the conservation reserve program", American Journal of Agricultural Economics 70(1):1–11.

Ribaudo, M.O. (1989), "Targeting the conservation reserve program to maximize water quality benefits", Land Economics 65(4):320–332.

Ribaudo, M.O., C.T. Osborn and K. Konyar (1994), "Land retirement as a tool for reducing agricultural nonpoint source pollution", Land Economics 70(1):77–87.

Rosegrant, M.W., and J.A. Roumasset (1985), "The effect of fertilizer on risk: a heteroscedastic production function with measurable stochastic inputs", Australian Journal of Agricultural Economics 29(2):107–121.

Roumasset, J.A., M.W. Rosegrant, U.N. Chakravorty and J.R. Anderson (1989), "Fertilizer and crop yield variability: a review", in: J.R. Anderson and P.B.R. Hazell, eds., Variability in Grain Yields: Implications for Agricultural Research and Policy in Developing Countries (Johns Hopkins University Press, Baltimore).

Saha, A., C.R. Shumway and A. Havenner (1997), "The economics and econometrics of damage control", American Journal of Agricultural Economics 79(3):773–785.

Saliba, B.C., and D.W. Bromley (1986), "Soil management decisions – how they should be compared and what factors influence them", North Central Journal of Agricultural Economics 8:305–317.

Sandmo, A. (1971), "On the theory of the competitive firm under uncertainty", American Economic Review 61(1):65–73.

Scherr, S.J. (1998), Productivity-Related Economic Impacts of Soil Degradation in Developing Countries: An Evaluation of the Evidence (Department of Agricultural and Resource Economics, University of Maryland, College Park).

Schiff, M., and A. Valdés (1992), The Political Economy of Agricultural Policy: A Synthesis of the Economics in Developing Countries (Johns Hopkins University Press, Baltimore).

Segerson, K. (1988), "Uncertainty and incentives for nonpoint pollution control", Journal of Environmental Economics and Management 15(1):87–98.

Segerson, K. (1990), "Liability for groundwater contamination from pesticides", Journal of Environmental Economics and Management 19(3):227–243.

Shah F., D. Zilberman and E. Lichtenberg (1995), "Optimal combination of pollution prevention and abatement policies: the case of agricultural drainage", Environmental and Resource Economics 5:29–49.

Sharp, B.M.H., and D.W. Bromley (1979), "Agricultural pollution: the economics of coordination", American Journal of Agricultural Economics 61(4):591–600.

Shavell, S. (1987), Economic Analysis of Accident Law (Harvard University Press, Cambridge).

Shortle, J.S., and J.W. Dunn (1986), "The relative efficiency of agricultural source water pollution control policies", American Journal of Agricultural Economics 68(3):668–677.

Shortle, J.S., and J. Miranowski (1987), "Intertemporal soil resource use: is it socially excessive?", Journal of Environmental Economics and Management 14:99–111.

Smith, J., and G. Umali (1985), "Production risk and optimal fertilizer rates: a random coefficient model", American Journal of Agricultural Economics 67(3):654–659.

Smith, R.A., R.B. Alexander and M.G. Wolman (1987), "Water-quality trends in the nation's rivers", Science 235:1607–1615.

Smith, R.B.W. (1995), "The conservation reserve program as a least-cost land retirement mechanism", American Journal of Agricultural Economics 77(1):93–105.

Smith, R.B.W., and T.D. Tomasi (1995), "Transaction costs and agricultural nonpoint-source water pollution control policies", Journal of Agricultural and Resource Economics 20:277–290.

Smith, V.H., and B.K. Goodwin (1996), "Crop insurance, moral hazard, and agricultural chemical use", American Journal of Agricultural Economics 78(2):428–438.

Spulber, D. (1988), "Optimal environmental regulation under asymmetric information", Journal of Public Economics 35(2):163–181.

Starbird, S.A. (1994), "The effect of quality assurance policies for processing tomatoes on the demand for pesticides", Journal of Agricultural and Resource Economics 19:78–88.

Stavins, R.N. (1996), "Correlated uncertainty and policy instrument choice", Journal of Environmental Economics and Management 30(2):218–232.

Stavins, R.N. (1998), "What can we learn from the grand policy experiment? Lessons from SO_2 allowance trading", Journal of Economic Perspectives 12(3):69–88.

Stavins, R.N., and A.B. Jaffe (1990), "Unintended impacts of public investments on private decisions; the depletion of forested wetlands", American Economic Review 80(3):337–352.

Stefanou, S., M. Mangel and J. Wilen (1986), "Information in agricultural pest control", Journal of Agricultural Economics 37:77–88.

Strange, M. (1988), Family Farming: A New Economic Vision (University of Nebraska Press, Lincoln, NE).

Sunding, D.L. (1996), "Measuring the marginal cost of nonuniform environmental regulations", American Journal of Agricultural Economics 78(4):1098–1107.

Taylor, C.R., and K.K. Frohberg (1977), "The welfare effects of erosion controls, banning pesticides, and limiting fertilizer application in the corn belt", American Journal of Agricultural Economics 59(1):25–36.

Teague, M.L., D.J. Bernardo and H.P. Mapp (1995), "Farm-level economic analysis incorporating stochastic environmental risk assessment", American Journal of Agricultural Economics 77(1):8–32.

Underwood, N.A., and M.R. Caputo (1996), "Environmental and agricultural policy effects on information acquisition and input choice", Journal of Environmental Economics and Management 31(2):198–218.

United States Department of Agriculture, Economic Research Service (ERS) (1997), Agricultural Handbook No. 712 (U.S. Department of Agriculture, Washington, DC).

van den Bosch, R., and V. Stern (1962), "The integration of chemical and biological control of arthropod pests", Annual Review of Entomology 7.

van Kooten, G.C. (1993), "Evaluation of wetlands conversion", Land Economics 69(1):27–38.

van Kooten, G.C., and A. Schmitz (1992), "Preserving waterfowl habitat on Canadian prairies: economic incentives versus moral suasion", American Journal of Agricultural Economics 74(1):79–89.

Wade, J.C., and E.O. Heady (1977), "Controlling nonpoint sediment sources with cropland management: a national economic assessment", American Journal of Agricultural Economics 59(1):13–24.

Way, M.J., and K.L. Heong (1994), "The role of biodiversity in the dynamics and management of insect pests of tropical irrigation rice – a review", Bulletin of Entomological Research 84:567–587.

Weaver, R.D. (1996), "Prosocial behavior, agriculture, and the environment", Land Economics 72(2):231–247.

Weinberg, M., and C.L. Kling (1996), "Uncoordinated agricultural and environmental policy making: an application to irrigated agriculture in the West", American Journal of Agricultural Economics 78(1):65–78.

Weinberg, M., C.L. Kling and J.E. Wilen (1993), "Water markets and water quality", American Journal of Agricultural Economics 75(2):278–291.

Weitzman, M. (1974), "Prices vs. quantities", Quarterly Journal of Economics 41(4):477–491.

Wetzstein, M.E., and T.J. Centner (1992), "Regulating agricultural contamination of groundwater through strict liability and negligence legislation", Journal of Environmental Economics and Management 22(1):1–11.

Wu, J.-J. (1999), "Crop insurance, acreage decisions, and nonpoint-source pollution", American Journal of Agricultural Economics 81(2):305–320.

Wu, J.-J., and B.A. Babcock (1995), "Optimal design of a voluntary green payment program under asymmetric information", Journal of Agricultural and Resource Economics 20(2):316–327.

Wu, J.-J., and B.A. Babcock (1996), "Contract design for the purchase of environmental goods from agriculture", American Journal of Agricultural Economics 78(4):935–945.

Wu, J.-J., and K. Segerson (1995), "The impacts of policies and land characteristics on potential groundwater pollution in Wisconsin", American Journal of Agricultural Economics 77(4):1033–1047.

Xepapadeas, A.P. (1995), "Observability and the choice of instrument mix in the control of externalities", Journal of Public Economics 56:485–498.

Young, D.L., D.J. Walker and P.L. Kanjo (1991), "Cost effectiveness and equity aspects of soil conservation in a highly erodible region", American Journal of Agricultural Economics 73(4):1053–1062.

Zilberman, D., A. Schmitz, G. Casterline, E. Lichtenberg and J.B. Siebert (1991), "The economics of pesticide use and regulation", Science 253:518–522.

Chapter 24

COMMON-POOL RESOURCES AND INSTITUTIONS: TOWARD A REVISED THEORY*

ELINOR OSTROM

*Department of Political Science, Workshop in Political Theory and Policy Analysis,
Center for the Study of Institutions, Population, and Environmental Change, Indiana University*

Contents

*Sections of this chapter draw on "Self-Governance of Common Pool Resources", in P. Newman (ed.), *The New Palgrave Dictionary of Economics and the Law*, Vol. 3 (London: Macmillan Press, 1998, pp. 424–433). Support for the preparation of this entry from the Ford Foundation and the MacArthur Foundation is deeply appreciated. The author received excellent comments on a prior draft by C. Dustin Becker, Ken Bickers, Tomas Koontz, Michael McGinnis, Charles Schweik, James Walker, John Williams, and a careful editing by Patty Zielinski.

Handbook of Agricultural Economics, Volume 2, Edited by B. Gardner and G. Rausser
© 2002 Elsevier Science B.V. All rights reserved

Abstract

In the conventional theory of common-pool resources, participants do not undertake efforts to design their own governance arrangements. Substantial empirical evidence exists, however, that many common-pool resources are self-governed. Thus, in this chapter, I briefly review the conventional theory of common-pool resources. Then, I provide an overview of the empirical studies that test this theory in experimental laboratories. In the third section, I provide an overview of the empirical studies of this theory conducted in field settings. Since research in the lab and in the field both provide evidence that appropriators from common-pool resources do self-organize, the fourth section is devoted to the presentation of an initial theory of self-organization focusing on the benefit-cost calculus of individual appropriators. Two major theoretical puzzles remain, having to do with the effect of the size of a group and its heterogeneity.

Keywords

common-pool resources, institutional analysis, laboratory experiments, comparative case studies, self-organized user groups

JEL classification: Q28

1. Introduction

Common-pool resources are systems that generate finite quantities of resource units so that one person's use subtracts from the quantity of resource units available to others [E. Ostrom, Gardner and Walker (1994)]. Irrigation systems are among the most important types of common-pool resources [E. Ostrom (1992a)]. Most common-pool resources are sufficiently large that multiple actors can simultaneously use the resource system and efforts to exclude potential beneficiaries are costly. When the resource units (e.g., water) are highly valued and many actors benefit from appropriating (harvesting) them for consumption, exchange, or as a factor in a production process, the appropriations made by one individual are likely to create negative externalities for others.

The "tragedy of the commons" will occur in highly valued, open-access commons where those involved and/or external authorities do not establish an effective governance regime [G. Hardin (1968)]. Governance regimes regulate one or more of the following:
- who is allowed to appropriate resource units;
- the timing, quantity, location, and technology of appropriation;
- who is obligated to contribute resources to provide or maintain the resource system itself;
- how appropriation and obligation activities are to be monitored and enforced;
- how conflicts over appropriation and obligation activities are to be resolved; and
- how the rules affecting the above will be changed over time with changes in the performance of the resource system and the strategies of participants.

A self-governed common-pool resource is one where actors, who are major appropriators of the resource, are involved over time in making and adapting rules within collective-choice arenas regarding the inclusion or exclusion of participants, appropriation strategies, obligations of participants, monitoring and sanctioning, and conflict resolution. Some common-pool resources that are located far from centers of governmental authority are governed entirely by appropriators and are not governed at all by external authorities. In most modern political economies, however, it is rare to find any resource systems – including the treasuries of private for-profit corporations – that are governed *entirely* by participants without rules made by local, regional, national, or international authorities also affecting key decisions [V. Ostrom (1991, 1997)]. Thus, in a self-governed system, participants make many, but not necessarily all, rules that affect the sustainability of the resource system and its use.

In the conventional theory of the commons, participants do not undertake efforts to design their own governance arrangements. Substantial empirical evidence exists, however, that many common-pool resources are self-governed. Thus, in this chapter, I first briefly review the conventional theory of common-pool resources. Then, I provide an overview of the empirical studies of this theory conducted in experimental laboratories. In the third section, I provide an overview of the empirical studies of this theory conducted in field settings. Since research in the lab and in the field both provide evidence that appropriators from common-pool resources do self-organize, the fourth section is devoted to the presentation of an initial theory of self-organization focusing on the benefit-cost calculus of individual appropriators. Two major theoretical puzzles remain, which are discussed in the fifth section before the chapter concludes with a brief sixth section.

2. The conventional theory of common-pool resources

Since the important early studies of open-access fisheries by Gordon (1954) and Scott (1955), most theoretical studies by political economists have analyzed simple common-pool resource systems using relatively similar assumptions [Feeny, Hanna and McEvoy (1996)]. In such systems, it is assumed that the resource generates a highly predictable, finite supply of one type of resource unit (one species, for example) in each relevant time period. Appropriators are assumed to be homogeneous in terms of their assets, skills, discount rates, and cultural views. They are also assumed to be short-term, profit-maximizing actors who possess complete information. In this theory, *anyone* can enter the resource and appropriate resource units. Appropriators gain property rights only to what they harvest, which they then sell in an open competitive market. The open access condition is a given. The appropriators make no effort to change it. Appropriators act independently and do not communicate or coordinate their activities in any way.

> In this setting, as the incisive analysis of Gordon and Scott demonstrates, each fisherman will take into account only his own marginal costs and revenues and ignores the fact that increases in his catch affect the returns to fishing effort for other fishermen as well as the health of future fish stocks ... [E]conomic rent is dissipated; economic overfishing, which may also lead to ecological overfishing, is the result [Feeny et al. (1996, p. 189)].

Many textbooks in resource economics and law and economics present this conventional theory of a simple common-pool resource as the only theory needed for understanding common-pool resources more generally [see Dasgupta and Heal (1979); for a different approach, see Baland and Platteau (1996)]. With the growing use of game theory, appropriation from common-pool resources is frequently represented as a one-shot or finitely repeated, Prisoner's Dilemma game [Dawes (1973), Dasgupta and Heal (1979)]. These models formalize the problem differently, but do not change any of the basic theoretical assumptions about the finite and predictable supply of resource units, complete information, homogeneity of users, their maximization of expected profits, and their lack of interaction with one another or capacity to change their institutions.

3. A common-pool resource in the laboratory

The structure of Gordon's time-independent model (1954) has been used as the foundation to create a series of baseline laboratory experiments that examine the empirical generality of the conventional theory [Walker, Gardner and Ostrom (1990)].

In these experiments, eight subjects are similarly endowed with either 10 or 25 tokens in each period of a finitely repeated game. Any or all of these tokens can be invested in a joint activity with the mathematical structure of a quadratic production function (the common-pool resource) or in an alternative activity that generates a fixed return per token (similar to investing time in wage labor). Subjects are privately paid at the end of the experiment based on the total returns obtained during the experiment and earn between $15 to $25 per experiment lasting from 1 to 1.5 hours. In this stark institutional setting, appropriators are not allowed to communicate. Given the payoff parameters, a group investment of 36 tokens yields the optimal level of investment. The noncooperative Nash equilibrium for a finitely repeated game is for each subject to invest 8 tokens in the common-pool resource (regardless of the number of tokens provided as an endowment). Thus, the predicted outcome is for a total group investment of 64 tokens. The outcome reached at the predicted Nash equilibrium is 39 percent of the joint optimum that could be earned.

In these baseline experiments, subjects make investment allocations to the common-pool resource that are well above optimum. Significant rent dissipation occurs as predicted. The Nash equilibrium is the best predictor of the average level of outcomes achieved for low-endowment experiments. In the high-endowment setting, average outcomes are far from Nash in early rounds but approach Nash in later rounds. In this series of experiments, as well as others [see E. Ostrom, Gardner and Walker (1994)], virtually *no* evidence supports the prediction that individual appropriators follow Nash equilibrium strategies. In many experiments, no single subject adopted the Nash equilibrium strategy even though the average outcome approximated that predicted using a Nash equilibrium. A further result that is not predicted by the theory is that the amount of tokens invested by subjects is affected by token endowments. Yields as a percentage of optimum are much lower in the high-endowment (25-token) experiments than in the low-endowment (10-token) experiments.

Overall, the prediction of excessive appropriation from a common-pool resource by appropriators who are constrained not to communicate but unconstrained by prior appropriation rules is supported by evidence from experimental studies. These conditions are roughly analogous to unorganized, large groups of actors appropriating from an international commons. Many common-pool resources, however, are contained within a single country where a smaller number of actors may be able to communicate, coordinate strategies, and even find means to enforce these strategies themselves.

3.1. Communication in the laboratory

While the basic model involved no communication, evidence from the field shows individuals making and keeping contingent promises to one another. Frequently, no external authorities are present to enforce these agreements. Communication has also increased the level of cooperation achieved in many public good experiments [see E. Ostrom and Walker (1997), for citations]. The theoretical role of communication in noncooperative game theory, however, is problematic. Words alone are viewed as frail constraints – or cheap talk – when individuals face settings with dominant strategies to overuse a resource. The inability to make enforceable agreements is a core assumption of noncooperative game theory that has been adopted extensively as the modeling tool of preference in resource economics. Thus, common-pool resource theory has treated the ability to communicate as inessential and unlikely to change results unless the individuals involved can call on external agents to enforce agreements. Consequently, it is important to examine the effect of allowing face-to-face communication in common-pool resource games similar to the baseline experiments briefly described above.

The impact of communication on outcomes has been explored in three experimental designs. In the first, subjects are given an opportunity to communicate only once and then return to make a series of independent decisions. In the second, subjects are given an opportunity to communicate before each decision round. In the third, subjects have to pay in order to communicate, and communication is authorized only when the subjects voluntarily contributed a predetermined sum. In all three conditions, agreements made by subjects are *not* enforced by the experimenters. After communication, each subject subsequently makes his or her own independent and anonymous appropriation decision.

Subjects use their communication opportunities to discuss the number of tokens that gains the most money for the group and to agree on a formula for allocating those tokens to each other so as to achieve their perception of optimality. Subjects in repeated, high-endowment, common-pool resource games, with only one opportunity to communicate, obtain an average percentage of net yield above that obtained in baseline experiments without communication (55 percent compared to 21 percent). Subjects in repeated, high-endowment, common-pool resource games, with *repeated opportunities* to communicate, obtain an average percentage of net yield that is substantially above that obtained in baseline experiments without communication (73 percent compared to 21 percent). In low-endowment games, the average net yield is 99 percent as compared to 34 percent. Repeated communication opportunities in high-endowment games lead to higher joint outcomes (73 percent) than in one-shot communication (55 percent), as well as lower defection rates (13 percent compared to 25 percent) [E. Ostrom, Gardner and Walker (1994)]. In the costly communication experiments, subjects obtained outcomes that averaged around 80 percent of optimum as contrasted to 34 percent. Consequently, the capacity to communicate in these experiments enables subjects to achieve higher levels of return than when no communication is allowed [see also Messick, Allison and Samuelson (1988)]. In low-endowment settings – analogous to a set of farmers cutting trees from a forest with handsaws – repeated opportunities to communicate enable participants to achieve near-optimality. In high-endowment settings – analogous to a setting where the farmers have powerful chain saws – repeated opportunities to communicate enable participants to improve their returns substantially, but the temptation to defeat is greater, and defections occur more often.

Communication in a repeated situation enables subjects to accomplish three potentially important activities. First, it enables those involved to identify the joint strategy that would enable them to get close to an optimal return [Ledyard (1995)]. The first topic normally discussed is what joint strategy obtains the highest return for the group.

Identifying the optimal joint strategy could change the beliefs that each player has about the likely strategies to be adopted by others. If this were all that occurred, communication would involve strictly a coordination role. Second, the capacity to communicate provides an opportunity for the group to come to an overt agreement about what each person should do. Agreeing on a joint strategy and observing that the agreement is followed by most players allows participants to gain trust in one another and to risk a strategy other than that of a Nash equilibrium. Third, in those experiments where communication occurs between every decision round, subjects could exercise a form of sanctioning by verbally chastising the group if there was evidence that defection from an agreement had occurred. While subjects did not know which member of their group had defected from an agreement, they knew the outcomes achieved, and thus whether anyone invested more tokens than their agreement. They could use the opportunity for communication to criticize untrustworthiness and those who took advantage of others.

Moir (1995) explored whether the efficacy of communication was based primarily on the first coordination activity rather than on contracting and gaining trust or using verbal sanctions. Moir clearly told subjects in a common-pool resource game what joint strategy would gain them the highest group outcomes. Telling subjects about the symmetric optimum had no effect on the level of appropriation in the remaining rounds of the experiment, with the exception of the round immediately following this announcement [Moir (1995, p. 36)]. Isaac, McCue and Plott (1985) also overtly told subjects (in a public good experiment) the joint strategy that would maximize their group payoffs and found that this information did not change the level of noncooperation that existed prior to the exogenous provision of this information. Communication facilitates the exchange of information about what strategies lead to optimal outcomes, but it also plays a more crucial role in gaining agreement and trust and in allowing verbal criticisms as a nonmonetary form of generalized sanctions [Orbell, van de Kragt and Dawes (1988)].

3.2. Monitoring and sanctioning in the laboratory

In the field, appropriators not only communicate and "jaw bone" one another, they frequently authorize one another to patrol a resource and ascertain if anyone is appropriating beyond agreed-upon levels. In a game-theoretical model of self-organized monitoring and sanctioning related to irrigation systems, Weissing and Ostrom (1991, 1993) establish that multiple equilibria exist in such games, including some where monitoring is ineffective or counterproductive. There is one set of equilibria, however, where unauthorized behavior – stealing water, in this case – is held in check. To hold cheating in check, however, requires that monitors be sufficiently rewarded for discovering a cheater so as to overcome their costs of monitoring activities. Consequently, self-governed common-pool resources depend upon appropriators gaining rewards – either internal or external – from monitoring and sanctioning one another.

While face-to-face communication in the laboratory substantially increases the joint returns obtained by subjects, the nonbinding aspect of this institution is less effective when the temptation to cheat on an agreement is strong, such as with subjects with high endowments. E. Ostrom, Gardner and Walker (1994) designed a series of experiments to explore whether subjects in a laboratory setting would take costly actions in order to sanction one another overtly. The sanctioning mechanism is added to the baseline appropriation game described above with one additional feature: costless information is provided to subjects about the individual tokens invested during every round. The personal identity of each of the eight subjects is not revealed, since the display only indicates the computer number of a subject that is not related to the order in which subjects sat in the experimental lab. After 10 rounds without a sanctioning mechanism, subjects are given new instructions. These assign them the capability to incur a cost (a fee) after each appropriation decision in order to sanction another subject (who then is charged a fine). Subjects cannot discuss this new institutional rule with one another. The amount of the fines received by an individual is reported in writing to the subject who is being fined (but not the identity of the person(s) punishing them) and subtracted from their payoff for that round. It is possible for a subject to be fined by several others and in multiple rounds. At the end of the experiment, the experimenters subtract the total of all fees and all fines from subjects' total profits.

In experiments where the sanctioning institution is imposed by the experimenter and the subjects have no opportunity to communicate, Ostrom, Gardner and Walker find significantly more sanctioning than predicted. Subjects in these games sanction one another more when the cost of sanctioning is lower – thus exhibiting an economic response to the cost of sanctioning. Sanctioning is primarily directed to heavy investors in the common-pool resource. The average net yield increases from 21 percent with no sanctioning to 37 percent with sanctioning. When the costs of fees and fines are subtracted from average net yield, however, *net* yield drops to 9 percent. Subjects tend to *overuse* the sanctioning mechanism. It would appear that participants obtain a personal reward for sanctioning those who overinvest or whom they suspect have sanctioned them.

In experiments where communication and sanctioning are combined, on the other hand, the results are entirely different. With an imposed sanctioning mechanism and only a single opportunity to communicate, subjects achieve an average net yield of 85 percent. When the costs of fees and fines are subtracted, average net yield is still 67 percent. These represent substantial gains over baseline experiments where net yield averaged 21 percent. When subjects are given an opportunity to meet face-to-face, followed by an opportunity to vote on whether they would adopt a sanctioning mechanism, subjects who adopt a sanctioning mechanism achieve an average net yield of 93 percent. When the costs of fees and fines are subtracted, average net yield is still 90 percent. In addition, the defection rate from agreements is only 4 percent. Thus, subjects who use the opportunity to communicate to agree to a joint strategy and a majority vote for their own sanctioning mechanism achieve close to optimal results based entirely on the promises they make, their own efforts to monitor, and their own investments in sanctioning [see Moir (1995), for further extensions and replications]. This is especially impressive in the high-endowment environment.

In summary, evidence from controlled laboratory experiments of small groups of homogeneous appropriators possessing complete information about their endowments and the results of their actions provides strong support that when appropriators are not allowed to communicate, their behavior is consistent with the conventional theory of common-pool resources. When appropriators are allowed to communicate, however, they achieve substantially higher joint returns than when they cannot communicate. Appropriators given an opportunity to engage in costly monitoring and sanctioning are willing to pay these costs. And, when appropriators overtly discuss and agree on their own appropriation levels and sanctioning systems, they keep cheating on agreements at a very low level and achieve close to optimal results. Consequently, in small, well-specified environments where communication is possible, appropriators are willing to pay the costs involved to arrive at their own rules and actively monitor and enforce their rules, thereby achieving close to optimal results. The conventional theory does not explain behavior in such settings.

4. Common-pool resources in the field

A sufficient number of empirical examples exist where the absence of property rights and the independence of actors captures the essence of the problem facing appropriators that the broad empirical applicability of the conventional theory was not effectively challenged by field research until the mid-1980s. Until the work of the National Academy of Sciences' Panel on Common Property [National Research Council (1986)], the conventional theory of common-pool resources was applied to all common-pool resources regardless of the capacity of appropriators to communicate and coordinate their activities. The growing evidence from many studies of common-pool resources in the field, however, called for a serious re-thinking of the theoretical foundations for the analysis of common-pool resources [see Berkes (1986, 1989), Berkes et al. (1989), Bromley et al. (1992), McCay and Acheson (1987), E. Ostrom (1990)]. The consequence of these empirical studies is not to challenge the empirical validity of the conventional theory where it is relevant but rather its generalizability.

In the field, many common-pool resources are characterized by substantially higher levels of complexity than the base theory of homogeneous appropriators taking one type of resource unit from a resource system that generates a predictable flow of units. The rich case-study literature illustrates a wide diversity of settings in which appropriators dependent upon common-pool resources have organized themselves to achieve much higher outcomes than is predicted by the theory described above [Cordell (1989), Wade (1994), Ruddle and Johannes (1985), Sengupta (1991), Singleton (1998)].

Small- to medium-sized irrigation systems approximate these conditions and are, thus, an appropriate setting in which to examine these patterns of relationships quantitatively [Tang (1992)]. One resource unit – water – is the focus of efforts to organize and coordinate activities. Recent research on small- to medium-sized irrigation systems in Nepal has found a very substantial difference in performance between those systems owned and governed by the farmers themselves as contrasted to those systems owned and operated (but in some cases not governed) by a national governmental agency.

While most farmers in Nepal own land, most own very small parcels of less than 1 hectare. They are relatively homogeneous with similar preferences in regard to obtaining water for rice production during the monsoon and winter seasons and for various crops during the spring. Farmers in Nepal have long had the authority to create their own water associations, construct and maintain their own systems, and monitor and enforce conformance to their rules [see Shivakoti and Ostrom (2002), Lam, Lee and Ostrom (1997)]. The irrigation systems constructed and maintained by farmers tend to rely on low-tech construction techniques including building nonpermanent headworks from mud, trees, and stones. International aid agencies have provided considerable funding to government agencies in an effort to upgrade the engineering standards.

In a detailed analysis of data from 150 farmer-governed and national government irrigation systems in Nepal, Lam (1998) develops three performance measures: (1) the physical condition of irrigation systems, (2) the quantity of water available to farmers at different seasons of the year, and (3) the agricultural productivity of the systems. Using multiple regression analysis techniques so as to control for environmental differences among systems, Lam finds several variables strongly related to these dependent variables. One is the form of governance of the system. Holding other variables constant, irrigation systems governed by the farmers themselves perform significantly better on all three performance measures. This variable has the largest explanatory power of any variable in Lam's analysis, including the physical size of the system, terrain characteristics, and the number of farmers.

Thus, farmers with long-term ownership claims, who can communicate, develop their own agreements, establish the positions of monitors, and sanction those who do not conform to their own rules, are more likely to grow more rice, distribute water more equitably, and keep their systems in better repair than is done on government systems. While there is variance in the performance of these Nepali systems, and also among the 47 farmer-governed systems in the Philippines described by de los Reyes (1980), few perform as poorly as government systems, holding other relevant variables constant. Since many of the government systems rely on high-tech engineering, the capability of farmers to increase agricultural production on their "primitive systems" while they also provide the labor to maintain and operate the system, is particularly noteworthy.

5. On the origin of self-governed common-pool resources

Evidence from the field research thus challenges the generalizability of the conventional theory. While it is generally successful in predicting outcomes in settings where appropriators are alienated from one another or cannot communicate effectively, it does not provide an explanation for settings where appropriators are able to create and sustain agreements to avoid serious problems of overappropriation. Nor does it predict well when government ownership will perform appropriately or how privatization will improve outcomes. A fully articulated, reformulated theory encompassing the conventional theory as a special case does not yet exist. On the other hand, scholars familiar with the results of field research substantially agree on a set of variables that enhance the likelihood of appropriators organizing themselves to avoid the social losses associated with open-access, common-pool resources [McKean (1992, 2000), Wade (1994), Schlager (1990), Tang (1992), E. Ostrom (1990, 1992a, 1992b), Baland and Platteau (1996), E. Ostrom, Gardner and Walker (1994)]. Drawing heavily on Ostrom (1992b, pp. 298–299) and Baland and Platteau (1996, pp. 286–289), considerable consensus exists that the following attributes of resources and of appropriators are conducive to an increased likelihood that self-governing associations will form.

Attributes of the resource:

R1. Feasible improvement: Resource conditions are not at such a point of deterioration that it is useless to organize, or so underutilized that little advantage results from organizing.

R2. Indicators: Reliable and valid indicators of the condition of the resource system are frequently available at a relatively low cost.

R3. Predictability: The flow of resource units is relatively predictable.

R4. Spatial extent: The resource system is sufficiently small, given the transportation and communication technology in use, that appropriators can develop accurate knowledge of external boundaries and internal microenvironments.

Attributes of the appropriators:

A1. Salience: Appropriators are dependent on the resource system for a major portion of their livelihood.

A2. Common understanding: Appropriators have a shared image of how the resource system operates (attributes R1, R2, R3, and R4 above) and how their actions affect each other and the resource system.

A3. Discount rate: Appropriators use a sufficiently low discount rate in relation to future benefits to be achieved from the resource.

A4. Distribution of interests: Appropriators with higher economic and political assets are similarly affected by a lack of coordinated patterns of appropriation and use.

A5. Norms of trust, reciprocity, and punishment: Appropriators trust one another to keep promises and relate to one another with reciprocity.

A6. Autonomy: Appropriators are able to determine access and harvesting rules without external authorities countermanding them.

A7. Local leadership and prior organizational experience: Appropriators have learned at least minimal skills of organization through participation in other local associations or learning about ways that neighboring groups have organized.

Many of these variables are in turn affected by the type of larger regime in which users are embedded. Larger regimes can facilitate local self-organization by providing accurate information about natural resource systems, providing arenas in which participants can engage in discovery and conflict-resolution processes, and providing mechanisms to back up local monitoring and sanctioning efforts. The probability of participants adapting more effective rules in macroregimes that facilitate their efforts over time is higher than in regimes that ignore resource problems entirely or, at the other extreme, presume that all decisions about governance and management need to be made by central authorities.

The key to further theoretical integration is to understand how these attributes interact in complex ways to affect the basic benefit-cost calculations of a set of appropriators (A) using a resource [E. Ostrom (1990, Ch. 6)]. Each appropriator i ($i \in A$) has to compare the expected net benefits of harvesting continuing to use the old rules (BO) to the benefits he or she expects to achieve with a new set of rules (BN). Each appropriator i must ask whether his or her incentive to change (D_i) is positive or negative.

$$D_i = BN_i - BO_i.$$

If D_i is negative for all appropriators, no one has an incentive to change. If D_i is positive for some appropriators, they then need to estimate three types of costs: $C1$ – the up-front costs of time and effort spent devising and agreeing upon new rules; $C2$ – the short-term costs of adopting new appropriation strategies; and $C3$ – the long-term costs of monitoring and maintaining a self-governed system over time (given the norms of the community in which they live). If the sum of these expected costs for each appropriator exceeds the incentive to change, no appropriator will invest the time and resources needed to create new institutions. Thus, if

$$D_i < (C1_i + C2_i + C3_i)$$

for all $i \in A$, no change occurs.

In field settings, everyone is not likely to expect the same costs and benefits from a proposed change. Some may perceive positive benefits after all costs have been taken into account, while others may perceive net losses. Consequently, the collective-choice rules used to change the day-to-day operational rules related to appropriation affect whether an institutional change favored by some and opposed by others will occur. For any collective-choice rule, such as unanimity, majority, ruling elite, or one-person rule, there is a minimum coalition of appropriators, $K \subset A$, that must agree prior to the adoption of new rules. If for any individual k, a member of K,

$$D_k \leqslant (C1_k + C2_k + C3_k),$$

no new rules will be adopted. And if for at least one coalition $K \subset A$, it is such that

$$D_k > (C1_k + C2_k + C3_k),$$

for all members of K, it is feasible for a new set of rules to be adopted. If there are several such coalitions, the question of which coalition will form, and thus which rules will result, is a theoretical issue beyond the scope of this entry. This analysis is applicable to a situation where a group starts with an open access set of rules and contemplates adopting its first set of rules limiting access. It is also relevant to the continuing consideration of changing operational rules over time.

The rule used to change institutional arrangements in field settings varies from reliance on the decisions made by one or a few leaders, to a formal reliance on majority or super-majority vote, to reliance on consensus or near-unanimity. If there are substantial differences in the perceived benefits and costs of appropriators, it is possible that K appropriators will impose a new set of rules on the $A - K$ other appropriators that strongly favors those in the winning coalition and imposes losses or lower benefits on those in the losing coalition [Thompson, Mannix and Bazerman (1988)]. If expected benefits from a change in institutional arrangements are not greater than expected costs for many appropriators, however, the costs of enforcing a change in institutions will be much higher than when most participants expect to benefit from a change in rules over time. Where the enforcement costs are fully borne by the members of K, operational rules that benefit the $A - K$ other appropriators lower the long-term costs of monitoring and sanctioning for a governing coalition. Where external authorities enforce the rules agreed upon by K appropriators, the distribution of costs and benefits is more likely to benefit K and may impose costs on the $A - K$ other appropriators [see Walker et al. (2000)].

The attributes of a resource (listed above) affect both the benefits and costs of institutional change. If resource units are relatively abundant (R1), there are few reasons for appropriators to invest costly time and effort in organizing. If the resource is already substantially destroyed, the high costs of organizing may not generate substantial benefits. Thus, self-organization is likely to occur only after appropriators observe substantial scarcity. The danger here, however, is that exogenous shocks leading to a change in relative abundance of the resource units occur rapidly, and appropriators may not adapt quickly enough to the new circumstances [Libecap and Wiggins (1985)].

The presence of frequently available, reliable indicators about the conditions of a resource (R2) affects the capacity of appropriators to adapt relatively soon to changes that could adversely affect their long-term benefit stream [Moxnes (1996)]. A resource flow that is highly predictable (R3) is much easier to understand and manage than one that is erratic. In the latter case, it is always difficult for appropriators (or, for that matter, for scientists and government officials) to judge whether changes in the resource stock or flow are due to overharvesting or to random exogenous variables [see Feeny, Hanna and McEvoy (1996) for a discussion of these issues related to the collapse of the California sardine industry)]. Unpredictability of resource units in microsettings, such as private pastures, may lead appropriators to create a larger common-property unit to increase the predictability of resource availability somewhere in the larger unit [Netting (1972), Wilson and Thompson (1993)]. The spatial extent of a resource (R4) affects the costs of defining reasonable boundaries and then of monitoring them over time.

The attributes of the appropriators themselves (listed above) also affect their expected benefits and costs. If appropriators do not obtain a major part of their income from a resource (A1), the high costs of organizing and maintaining a self-governing system may not be worth their effort. If appropriators do not share a common understanding of how complex resource systems operate (A2), they will find it extremely difficult to agree on future joint strategies. Given the complexity of many common-pool resources – especially multispecies or multiproduct resources – reasoning about how these systems work may be counterintuitive even for those who make daily contacts with the resource. In resources that are highly variable (R3), it may be particularly difficult to understand and to sort out those outcomes stemming from exogenous factors and those resulting from the actions of appropriators. Of course, this is also a problem facing officials as well as appropriators. Appropriators with many other options, who thus discount the importance of future income from a particular resource (A3), may prefer to "mine" one resource without spending resources to regulate it. They simply move on to other resources once this one is destroyed, assuming there will always be other resources available to them.

Appropriators who possess more substantial economic and political assets may have similar interests to those with fewer assets (A4) or they may differ substantially on multiple attributes. When the more powerful have similar interests, they may greatly enhance the probability of successful organization if they invest their resources in organizing a group and devising rules to govern that group. Those with substantial economic and political assets are more likely to be a member of K and thus have a bigger impact on decisions about institutional changes. Olson (1965) long ago recognized the possibility of a privileged group whereby some members bear a disproportionate share of the costs of organizing to provide public goods (such as the organization of a collectivity). On the other hand, if those with more assets also have low discount rates (A3) related to a particular resource and lower salience (A1), they may simply be unwilling to expend inputs or may actually impede organizational efforts that might lead to their having to cut back on their productive activities.

Appropriators who trust one another (A6) to keep agreements and use reciprocity in their relationships with one another face lower expected costs involved in monitoring and sanctioning one another over time. Appropriators who lack trust at the beginning of a process of organizing may be able to build this form of social capital [Coleman (1988), E. Ostrom (1992a)] if they initially adopt small changes that most appropriators follow before trying to make major institutional changes. Autonomy (A7) tends to lower the costs of organizing. A group that has little autonomy may find that those who disagree with locally developed rules seek contacts with higher-level officials to undo the efforts of appropriators to achieve regulation. [See Libecap (1995) for a discussion of the efforts to use the courts to challenge the validity of *de facto* governance of inshore fisheries in the U.S.; see also Alexander (1982).] With the legal autonomy to make their own rules, appropriators face substantially lower costs in defending their own rules against other authorities. Prior experience with other forms of local organization (A7) greatly enhances the repertoire of rules and strategies known by local participants as potentially useful to achieve various forms of regulation. Further, appropriators are more likely to agree upon rules whose operation they understand from prior experience, than upon rules that are introduced by external actors and are new to their experience. Given the complexity of many field settings, appropriators face a difficult task in evaluating how diverse variables affect expected benefits and costs over a long time horizon. In many cases, it is just as difficult, if not more so, for scientists to make a valid and reliable estimate of total benefits and costs and their distribution.

The growing theoretical consensus does not lead to a conclusion that most appropriators using common-pool resources will undertake self-governed regulation. Many settings exist where the theoretical expectation should be the opposite: appropriators will overuse the resource unless efforts are made to change one or more of the variables affecting perceived costs or benefits. Given the number of variables that affect these costs and benefits, many points of external intervention can enhance or reduce the probability of appropriators agreeing upon and following rules that generate higher social returns. But both social scientists and policymakers have a lot to learn about how these variables operate interactively in field settings and even how to measure them so as to increase the empirical warrantability of the growing theoretical consensus. Many aspects of the macroinstitutional structure surrounding a particular setting affect the perceived costs and benefits. Thus, external authorities can do a lot to enhance the likelihood and performance of self-governing institutions. Their actions can also seriously impede these developments as well. Further, when the activities of one set of appropriators, A, have "spillover effects" on others beyond A, external authorities can either facilitate processes that allow multiple groups to solve conflicts arising from negative spillovers or take a more active role in governing particular resources themselves.

Researchers and public officials need to recognize the multiple manifestation of these theoretical variables in the field. Appropriators may be highly dependent on a resource (A1), for example, because they are in a remote location and few roads exist to enable them to leave. Alternatively, they may be located in a central location, but other opportunities are not open to them due to lack of training or a discriminatory labor market. Appropriators' discount rates (A3) in relation to a particular resource may be low because they have lived for a long time in a particular location and expect that they and their grandchildren will remain in that location, or because they possess a secure and well-defined bundle of property rights to this resource [see Schlager and Ostrom (1992)]. Reliable indicators of the condition of a resource (R2) may result from activities that the appropriators themselves do – such as regularly shearing the wool from sheep [see Gilles and Jamtgaard (1981)] or because of efforts to gather reliable information by appropriators or by external authorities [Blomquist (1992)]. Predictability of resource units (R3) may result from a clear regularity in the natural environment of the resource or because storage has been constructed in order to even out the flow of resource units over both good and bad years. They may have autonomy to make their own rules (A6) because a national government is weak and unable to exert authority over resources that it formally owns, or because national law formally legitimates self-governance – as is the case with Japanese inshore fisheries.

When the benefits of organizing are commonly understood by participants to be very high, appropriators lacking many of the attributes conducive to the development of self-governing institutions may be able to overcome their liabilities and still develop effective agreements. The crucial factor is not whether all attributes are favorable but the relative size of the expected benefits and costs they generate as perceived by participants. While all of these variables affect the expected benefits and costs of appropriators, it is difficult – particularly for outsiders – to estimate their impact on expected benefits and costs given the difficulty of making precise measures of these variables and weighing them on a cumulative scale. Further empirical analysis of these theoretical propositions is, thus, dependent on the conduct of careful comparative over-time studies of a sufficiently large number of field settings using a common set of measurement protocols [see Gibson, McKean and Ostrom (2000)].

6. On the design principles of robust, self-governed common-pool resource institutions

Of course, the performance of self-governed common-pool resource systems varies across systems and time. Some self-governed common-pool resource systems have survived and flourished for centuries, while others falter and fail. As discussed above, some never get organized in the first place. In addition to the consensus concerning the theoretical variables conducive to self-organization, considerable agreement also exists about the characteristics of those self-governing systems that are robust in the sense that they survive for very long periods of time utilizing the same basic rules for adapting to new situations over time [Shepsle (1989)].

The particular rules used in the long-surviving, self-governing systems varied substantially from one another. Consequently, it is not possible to arrive at empirical generalizations about the particular types of rules used to define who is a member of a self-governing community, what rights they have to access a common-pool resource and appropriate resource units, and what particular obligations they face. It is possible, however, to derive a series of design principles that characterize the configuration of rules that are used. By "design principles" I mean an "element or condition that helps to account for the success of these institutions in sustaining the [common-pool resource] and gaining the compliance of generation after generation of appropriators to the rules in use" [E. Ostrom (1990, p. 90)]. Robust, long-term institutions are characterized by most of the design principles listed in Table 1. The farmer-owned irrigation systems in Nepal analyzed by Shivakoti and Ostrom (2002) and Lam (1998), for example, are characterized by most of these design principles. Fragile institutions tend to be characterized by only some of these design principles. Failed institutions are characterized by very few of these principles [see, for example, Schweik, Adhikari and Pandit (1997), Morrow and Hull (1996), Blomqvist (1996)].

These principles work to enhance the shared understanding of participants of the structure of the resource and its appropriators and of the benefits and costs involved in following a set of agreed-upon rules. Design Principle 1 – having rules that clearly define who has rights to use a resource and the boundaries of that resource – ensures

Table 1

Design principles illustrated by long-enduring common-pool resource institutions

---

1. Clearly Defined Boundaries

Individuals or households with rights to withdraw resource units from the common-pool resource and the boundaries of the common-pool resource itself are clearly defined.

2. Congruence

A. The distribution of benefits from appropriation rules is roughly proportionate to the costs imposed by provision rules.

B. Appropriation rules restricting time, place, technology, and/or quantity of resource units are related to local conditions.

3. Collective-Choice Arrangements

Most individuals affected by operational rules can participate in modifying operational rules.

4. Monitoring

Monitors, who actively audit common-pool resource conditions and appropriator behavior, are accountable to the appropriators and/or are the appropriators themselves.

5. Graduated Sanctions

Appropriators who violate operational rules are likely to receive graduated sanctions (depending on the seriousness and context of the offense) from other appropriators, from officials accountable to these appropriators, or from both.

6. Conflict-Resolution Mechanisms

Appropriators and their officials have rapid access to low-cost, local arenas to resolve conflict among appropriators or between appropriators and officials.

7. Minimal Recognition of Rights to Organize

The rights of appropriators to devise their own institutions are not challenged by external governmental authorities.

For common-pool resources that are part of larger systems:

8. Nested Enterprises

Appropriation, provision, monitoring, enforcement, conflict resolution, and governance activities are organized in multiple layers of nested enterprises.

Adapted from: E. Ostrom (1990, p. 90).

that appropriators can clearly identify anyone who does not have rights and take action against them.

Design Principle 2 involves two parts. The first is a congruence between the rules that assign benefits and the rules that assign costs. The crucial thing here is that these rules be considered fair and legitimate by the participants themselves [see McKean (1992)]. In many settings, fair rules are those that keep a relative proportionate relationship between the assignment of benefits and of costs. In irrigation systems, for example, rules that allocate water to different farmers according to the amount of land they own as well as that allocate duties for costs of operation and maintenance using the same formula, are usually considered by farmers to be fair (as well as effective from an agricultural perspective). The second part of this design principle is that both types of rules be well-matched to local conditions such as soils, slope, number of diversions, crops being grown, etc.

Design Principle 3 is concerned with the collective-choice arrangements used to modify the operational rules of regular operation of the resource. If most appropriators are not involved in modifying these rules over time, the information about the benefits and costs as perceived by different participants is not fully taken into account in these efforts to adapt to new conditions and information over time. Appropriators who begin to perceive the costs of their system as being higher than their benefits and who are prevented from making serious proposals for change, may simply begin to cheat whenever they have the opportunity. Once cheating on rules becomes more frequent for some appropriators, others will follow suit. In this case, enforcement costs become very high or the system fails.

No matter how high the level of agreement to an initial agreement is, there are always conditions that tempt some individuals to cheat (even when they perceive the overall benefits of the system to be higher than the costs). If one person chooses to cheat while others conform to the rules, the cheater is usually able to gain substantially to the disadvantage of others. Thus, without monitoring of rule conformance – Design Principle 4 – few systems are able to survive very long at all. The sanctions that are used, however, do not need to be extremely high in the first instance. The important thing about a sanction for an appropriator who has succumbed to temptation is that his or her action is noticed and that a punishment is meted out. This tells all appropriators that cheating on rules is noticed and punished without making all rule infractions into major criminal events. If the sanctions are graduated (Design Principle 5), however, an appropriator who breaks rules repeatedly and who is noticed doing so eventually faces a penalty that makes rule-breaking an unattractive option. While rules are always assumed to be clear and unambiguous in theoretical work, this is rarely the case in field settings. It is easy to have a disagreement about how to interpret a rule that limits appropriation activities or requires input resources. If these disagreements are not resolved in a low-cost and orderly manner, then appropriators may lose their willingness to conform to rules because of the ways that "others" interpret them in their own favor (Design Principle 6).

Design Principles 7 and 8 are related to autonomy. When the rights of a group to devise their own institutions are recognized by national, regional, and local governments, the legitimacy of the rules crafted by appropriators will be less frequently challenged in courts, administrative and legislative settings. Further, in larger resources with many participants, nested enterprises that range in size from small to large enable participants to solve diverse problems involving different scale economies. By utilizing base institutions that are quite small, face-to-face communication can be utilized for solving many of the day-to-day problems in smaller groups. By nesting each level of organization in a larger level, externalities from one group to others can be addressed in larger organizational settings that have a legitimate role to play in relationship to the smaller entities.

7. Theoretical puzzles

In addition to the consensus concerning the variables most likely to enhance self-organization and the design principles characterizing successful, long-term governance arrangements, many unresolved theoretical issues still exist about the self-governance of common-pool resources. Two major theoretical questions relate to the effect of the size and heterogeneity of groups using a resource on their capability to organize effectively.

7.1. Size of group

The effect of the number of participants facing problems of creating and sustaining a self-governing enterprise is unclear. Drawing on the early work of Olson (1965), many theorists argue that size of group is negatively related to solving collective-action problems in general [see also Buchanan and Tullock (1962)]. Many results from game theoretical analysis of repeated games conclude that cooperative strategies are more likely to emerge and be sustained in smaller rather than larger groups [see synthesis of this literature in Baland and Platteau (1996)]. Scholars who have studied many user-governed irrigation and forestry institutions in the field have concluded that success will more likely happen in smaller groups [see, for example, Barker et al. (1984), Cernea (1989)].

On the other hand, several studies of multiple sites have not found that size was positively related to success in organizing. While most of the 37 farmer-governed irrigation systems studied by Tang (1992) were relatively small, ranging in size from 7 to 300 appropriators, he did not find any statistical relationship within that size range between the number of appropriators or the amount of land being irrigated and performance variables (1992, p. 68). In Lam's multiple regression analysis of the performance of a much larger set of irrigation systems in Nepal ranging in size up to 475 irrigators, he also did not find any significant relationship between either the number of appropriators or the amount of land included in the service area with any of the three performance variables he studied (1998, pp. 114–115). Further, in a systematic study of forest institutions, Agrawal (2000) did not find smaller forest user groups as able to undertake the level of monitoring needed to protect forest resources as moderately sized groups.

One of the problems with a focus on size of group as a key determining factor is that many other variables change as group size increases [Chamberlin (1974), R. Hardin (1982)]. If the costs of providing a public good related to the use of a common-pool resource, say a sanctioning system, remain relatively constant as group size increases, then increasing the number of participants brings additional resources that could be drawn upon to provide the benefit enjoyed by all [see Isaac, Walker and Williams (1993)]. Marwell and Oliver (1993, p. 45) conclude that when a "good has pure jointness of supply, group size has a *positive* effect on the probability that it will be provided". On the other hand, if one is analyzing the conflict levels over a subtractable good and the transaction costs of arriving at acceptable allocation formulas, group size may well exacerbate the problems of self-governing systems. Since there are tradeoffs among various impacts of size on other variables, a better working hypothesis is that group size has a curvilinear relationship to performance.

7.2. Heterogeneity

Many scholars conclude that only very small groups can organize themselves effectively because they presume that size is related to the homogeneity of a group and that homogeneity is needed to initiate and sustain self-governance. Heterogeneity is also a highly contested variable. For one thing, groups can differ along a diversity of dimensions including their cultural backgrounds, interests, and endowments [see Baland and Platteau (1996)]. Each may operate differently.

If groups coming from diverse cultural backgrounds share access to a common resource, the key question affecting the likelihood of self-organized solutions is whether the views of the multiple groups concerning the structure of the resource, authority, interpretation of rules, trust, and reciprocity differ or are similar. In other words, do they share a common understanding (A2) of their situation? New settlers to a region may simply learn and accept the rules of the established group, and their cultural differences on other fronts do not affect their participation in governing a resource. On the other hand, new settlers are frequently highly disruptive to the sustenance of a self-governing enterprise when they generate higher levels of conflict over the interpretation and application of rules and increase enforcement costs substantially.

When the interests of appropriators differ, achieving a self-governing solution to common-pool resource problems may be challenging, but not insurmountable [see Baland and Platteau (1999)]. This problem characterizes some fisheries where local subsistence fishermen have strong interests in the sustenance of an inshore fishery, while industrial fishing firms have many other options and may be more interested in the profitability of fishing in a particular location than its sustained yield. The conflict between absentee livestock owners versus local pastoralists has also proved difficult to solve in many parts of the world.

Differential endowments of appropriators can be associated with both extreme levels of conflict as well as very smooth and low-cost transitions into a sustainable, self-governed system. Johnson and Libecap (1982) reason that the difference in the skills and knowledge of different kinds of fishers frequently prevents them from arriving at agreements about how to allocate quantitative harvesting quotas [see also Scott (1993)]. In this case, heterogeneity of endowments and of interests coincide. Heterogeneity of wealth or power may or may not be associated with a difference in interests. As discussed above, when those who have more assets share similar interests with those who have fewer assets (A4), groups may be privileged by having the more powerful take on the higher initial costs of organizing while crafting rules that benefit a large proportion of the appropriators.

Appropriators do, however, design institutions in some settings that cope effectively with heterogeneities. In a series of laboratory experiments very similar to those discussed above, Hackett, Schlager and Walker (1994) divided appropriators into two groups. One group was endowed with three times the tokens of the other group. Despite this substantial heterogeneity in assets, subjects devised rules for investing in the common-pool resource at near-optimal levels when allowed to communicate. Lam (1998) did not find that differences in income among irrigators significantly affected the performance of their irrigation systems. Varughese and Ostrom (2001) examined the effects of locational differences, wealth disparities, and cultural differences on collective action among 18 different forest user groups in Nepal. They found no relationship between these sources of heterogeneity and the likelihood of successful collective action.

Even in a group that differs on many variables, if at least a minimally winning subset of K appropriators from an endangered but valuable resource are dependent on it (A1), share a common understanding of the situation (A2), have a low discount rate (A3), include some with more assets among their members (A4), trust one another (A5), and have autonomy to make rules (A6), it is more likely that expected benefits of governing this resource are greater than expected costs. Whether the rules agreed upon distribute benefits and costs fairly depends both on the collective-choice rule used and the type of heterogeneity existing in the community. Successful groups that have overcome the challenge of heterogeneity appear to have adopted rules that allocate benefits using the same formulae used to allocate duties and responsibilities (Design Principle 2A); appropriators who differ significantly in terms of assets will tend to agree to and follow such rules.

Neither size nor heterogeneity is a variable with a uniform effect on the likelihood of organizing and sustaining self-governing enterprises. The debate about their effect is focusing on the wrong variables. Instead of focusing on size or the various kinds of heterogeneity by themselves, it is important to ask how these variables affect other variables as they impact on the benefit-cost calculus of those involved in negotiating and sustaining agreements. Their impact on costs of producing and distributing information [Scott (1993)] is particularly important.

8. Conclusion

The conventional theory of common-pool resources, which presumed that external authorities were needed to impose rules on those appropriators trapped into producing excessive externalities on themselves and others, has now been shown to be a special theory of the conventional theory of common-pool resources. For appropriators to contemplate changing the institutions they face, a minimal winning coalition of them has to conclude that the expected benefits from an institutional change will exceed the immediate and long-term expected costs. When appropriators cannot communicate and have no way of gaining trust through their own efforts or with the help of the larger political system within which they are embedded, the prediction of the earlier theory is likely to be empirically supported. Ocean fisheries, the atmosphere, and other global commons come closest to the appropriate empirical referents. If appropriators can engage in face-to-face bargaining and have autonomy to change their rules, they may well attempt to organize themselves. Whether they organize depends on attributes of the resource system and the appropriators themselves that affect the benefits to be achieved and the costs of achieving them. Whether their self-governed enterprise succeeds over the long term depends on whether the institutions they design are consistent with design principles underlying robust, long-living, self-governed systems. The theory of common-pool resources has progressed substantially during the past half century. There are, however, many challenging puzzles to be solved.

References

Agrawal, A. (2000), "Small is beautiful, but is larger better? Forest-management institutions in the Kumaon Himalaya, India", in: C. Gibson, M. McKean and E. Ostrom, eds., People and Forests: Communities, Institutions, and Governance (MIT Press, Cambridge, MA) 57–86.

Alexander, P. (1982), Sri Lankan Fishermen: Rural Capitalism and Peasant Society (Australian National University, Canberra).

Baland, J.-M., and J.-P. Platteau (1996), Halting Degradation of Natural Resources. Is There a Role for Rural Communities? (Clarendon Press, Oxford).

Baland, J.-M., and J.-P. Platteau (1999), "The ambiguous impact of inequality on local resource management", World Development 27(5):773–788.

Barker, R., E.W. Coward Jr, G. Levine and L.E. Small (1984), Irrigation Development in Asia: Past Trends and Future Directions (Cornell University Press, Ithaca, NY).

Berkes, F. (1986), "Local-level management and the commons problem: A comparative study of Turkish coastal fisheries", Marine Policy 10:215–229.

Berkes, F. (ed.) (1989), Common Property Resources: Ecology and Community-Based Sustainable Development (Belhaven Press, London).

Berkes, F., D. Feeny, B.J. McCay and J.M. Acheson (1989), "The benefits of the commons", Nature 340:91–93.

Blomquist, W.A. (1992), Dividing the Waters: Governing Groundwater in Southern California (Institute for Contemporary Studies Press, San Francisco, CA).

Blomqvist, A. (1996), Food and Fashion. Water Management and Collective Action among Irrigation Farmers and Textile Industrialists in South India (The Institute of Tema Research, Department of Water and Environmental Studies, Linköping, Sweden).

Bromley, D.W., D. Feeny, M. McKean, P. Peters, J. Gilles, R. Oakerson, C.F. Runge and J. Thomson (eds.) (1992), Making the Commons Work: Theory, Practice, and Policy (Institute for Contemporary Studies Press, San Francisco, CA).

Buchanan, J.M., and G. Tullock (1962), The Calculus of Consent (University of Michigan Press, Ann Arbor).

Cernea, M. (1989), "User groups as producers in participatory afforestation strategies", World Bank Discussion Papers No. 70 (World Bank, Washington, DC).

Chamberlin, J. (1974), "Provision of collective goods as a function of group size", American Political Science Review 68(2):707–716.

Coleman, J. (1988), "Social capital in the creation of human capital", American Journal of Sociology 91(1):309–335.

Cordell, J. (ed.) (1989), A Sea of Small Boats (Cultural Survival, Inc., Cambridge, MA).

Dasgupta, P.S., and G.M. Heal (1979), Economic Theory and Exhaustible Resources (Cambridge University Press, Cambridge).

Dawes, R.M. (1973), "The commons dilemma game: An N-person mixed-motive game with a dominating strategy for defection", Oregon Research Institute Research Bulletin 13:1–12.

de los Reyes, R.P. (1980), 47 Communal Gravity Systems: Organization Profiles (Ateneo de Manila University, Institute of Philippine Culture, Quezon City, Philippines).

Feeny, D., S. Hanna and A.F. McEvoy (1996), "Questioning the assumptions of the 'tragedy of the commons' model of fisheries", Land Economics 72(2):187–205.

Gibson, C., M. McKean and E. Ostrom (2000), People and Forests: Communities, Institutions, and Governance (MIT Press, Cambridge, MA).

Gilles, J.L., and K. Jamtgaard (1981), "Overgrazing in pastoral areas: The commons reconsidered", Sociologia Ruralis 21:129–141.

Gordon, H.S. (1954), "The economic theory of a common property resource: The fishery", Journal of Political Economy 62:124–142.

Hackett, S., E. Schlager and J. Walker (1994), "The role of communication in resolving commons dilemmas: Experimental evidence with heterogeneous appropriators", Journal of Environmental Economics and Management 27:99–126.

Hardin, G. (1968), "The tragedy of the commons", Science 162:1243–1248.

Hardin, R. (1982), Collective Action (Johns Hopkins University Press, Baltimore, MD).

Isaac, R.M., K. McCue and C.R. Plott (1985), "Public goods provision in an experimental environment", Journal of Public Economics 26:51–74.

Isaac, R.M., J. Walker and A. Williams (1993), "Group size and the voluntary provision of public goods: Experimental evidence utilizing large groups", Journal of Public Economics 54(1):1–36.

Johnson, R.N., and G.D. Libecap (1982), "Contracting problems and regulation: The case of the fishery", American Economic Review 72(5):1005–1023.

Lam, W.F. (1998), Governing Irrigation Systems in Nepal: Institutions, Infrastructure, and Collective Action (Institute for Contemporary Studies Press, Oakland, CA).

Lam, W.F., M. Lee and E. Ostrom (1997), "The institutional analysis and development framework: Application to irrigation policy in Nepal", in: D.W. Brinkerhoff, ed., Policy Analysis Concepts and Methods: An Institutional and Implementation Focus (JAI Press, Greenwich, CT) 53–85.

Ledyard, J.O. (1995), "Is there a problem with public goods provision?", in: J. Kagel and A. Roth, eds., The Handbook of Experimental Economics (Princeton University Press, Princeton, NJ) 111–194.

Libecap, G.D. (1995), "The conditions for successful collective action", in: R. Keohane and E. Ostrom, eds., Local Commons and Global Interdependence: Heterogeneity and Cooperation in Two Domains (Sage, London) 161–190.

Libecap, G.D., and S.N. Wiggins (1985), "The influence of private contractual failure on regulation: The case of oil field unitization", Journal of Political Economy 93:690–714.

Marwell, G., and P. Oliver (1993), The Critical Mass in Collective Action: A Micro-Social Theory (Cambridge University Press, New York).

McCay, B.J., and J.M. Acheson (1987), The Question of the Commons: The Culture and Ecology of Communal Resources (University of Arizona Press, Tucson).

McKean, M.A. (1992), "Management of traditional common lands (Iriaichi) in Japan", in: D.W. Bromley et al., eds., Making the Commons Work: Theory, Practice, and Policy (Institute for Contemporary Studies Press, San Francisco, CA) 63–98.

McKean, M.A. (2000), "Common property: What is it, what is it good for, and what makes it work?", in: C. Gibson, M. McKean and E. Ostrom, eds., People and Forests: Communities, Institutions, and Governance (MIT Press, Cambridge, MA) 27–56.

Messick, D.M., S.T. Allison and C.D. Samuelson (1988), "Framing and communication effects on group members' responses to environmental and social uncertainty", in: S. Maital, ed., Applied Behavioral Economics, Vol. II (Wheatsheaf, Brighton).

Moir, R. (1995), "The effects of costly monitoring and sanctioning upon common property resource appropriation", Working Paper (University of New Brunswick, Department of Economics, Saint John, New Brunswick).

Morrow, C.E., and R.W. Hull (1996), "Donor-initiated common pool resource institutions: The case of the Yanesha forestry cooperative", World Development 24(10):1641–1657.

Moxnes, E. (1996), "Not only the tragedy of the commons: Misperceptions of bioeconomics", Working Paper (Foundation for Research in Economics and Business Administration, SNF, Bergen, Norway).

National Research Council (1986), Proceedings of the Conference on Common Property Resource Management (National Academy Press, Washington, DC).

Netting, R.McC. (1972), "Of men and meadows: Strategies of Alpine land use", Anthropological Quarterly 45:132–144.

Olson, M., Jr. (1965), The Logic of Collective Action: Public Goods and the Theory of Groups (Harvard University Press, Cambridge, MA).

Orbell, J.M., A. van de Kragt and R.M. Dawes (1988), "Explaining discussion-induced cooperation", Journal of Personality and Social Psychology 54(5):811–819.

Ostrom, E. (1990), Governing the Commons: The Evolution of Institutions for Collective Action (Cambridge University Press, New York).

Ostrom, E. (1992a), Crafting Institutions for Self-Governing Irrigation Systems (Institute for Contemporary Studies Press, San Francisco, CA).

Ostrom, E. (1992b), "The rudiments of a theory of the origins, survival, and performance of common-property institutions", in: D.W. Bromley et al., eds., Making the Commons Work: Theory, Practice, and Policy (Institute for Contemporary Studies Press, San Francisco, CA) 293–318.

Ostrom, E., R. Gardner and J.M. Walker (1994), Rules, Games, and Common-Pool Resources (University of Michigan Press, Ann Arbor).

Ostrom, E., and J.M. Walker (1997), "Neither markets nor states: Linking transformation processes in collective action arenas", in: D.C. Mueller, ed., Perspectives on Public Choice: A Handbook (Cambridge University Press, Cambridge) 35–72.

Ostrom, V. (1991), The Meaning of American Federalism: Constituting a Self-Governing Society (Institute for Contemporary Studies Press, San Francisco, CA).

Ostrom, V. (1997), The Meaning of Democracy and the Vulnerability of Democracies: A Response to Tocqueville's Challenge (University of Michigan Press, Ann Arbor).

Ruddle, K., and R.E. Johannes (eds.) (1985), The Traditional Knowledge and Management of Coastal Systems in Asia and the Pacific (UNESCO, Jakarta).

Schlager, E. (1990), "Model specification and policy analysis: The governance of coastal fisheries", Ph.D. Thesis (Indiana University, Bloomington, IN).

Schlager, E., and E. Ostrom (1992), "Property-rights regimes and natural resources: A conceptual analysis", Land Economics 68(3):249–262.

Schweik, C.M., K. Adhikari and K.N. Pandit (1997), "Land-cover change and forest institutions: A comparison of two sub-basins in the southern Siwalik hills of Nepal", Mountain Research and Development 17(2):99–116.

Scott, A.D. (1955), "The fishery: The objectives of sole ownership", Journal of Political Economy 63:116–124.

Scott, A.D. (1993), "Obstacles to fishery self-government", Marine Resource Economics 8:187–199.

Sengupta, N. (1991), Managing Common Property: Irrigation in India and the Philippines (Sage, New Delhi).

Shepsle, K.A. (1989), "Studying institutions: Some lessons from the rational choice approach", Journal of Theoretical Politics 1:131–149.

Shivakoti, G., and E. Ostrom (eds.) (2002), Improving Irrigation Governance and Management in Nepal (Institute for Contemporary Studies Press, Oakland, CA).

Singleton, S. (1998), Constructing Cooperation: The Evolution of Institutions of Comanagement (University of Michigan Press, Ann Arbor).

Tang, S.Y. (1992), Institutions and Collective Action: Self-Governance in Irrigation (Institute for Contemporary Studies Press, San Francisco, CA).

Thompson, L.L., E.A. Mannix and M.H. Bazerman (1988), "Negotiation in small groups: Effects of decision rule, agendas and aspirations", Journal of Personality and Social Psychology 54:86–95.

Varughese, G., and E. Ostrom (2001), "The contested role of heterogeneity in collective action: Some evidence from community forestry in Nepal", World Development 29(5):747–765.

Wade, R. (1994), Village Republics: Economic Conditions for Collective Action in South India (Institute for Contemporary Studies Press, San Francisco, CA).

Walker, J.M., R. Gardner and E. Ostrom (1990), "Rent dissipation in a limited-access common-pool resource: Experimental evidence", Journal of Environmental Economics and Management 19:203–211.

Walker, J.M., R. Gardner, A. Herr and E. Ostrom (2000), "Collective choice in the commons: Experimental results on proposed allocation rules and votes", The Economic Journal 110(460):212–234.

Weissing, F.J., and E. Ostrom (1991), "Irrigation institutions and the games irrigators play: Rule enforcement without guards", in: R. Selten, ed., Game Equilibrium Models II: Methods, Morals, and Markets (Springer-Verlag, Berlin) 188–262.

Weissing, F.J., and E. Ostrom (1993), "Irrigation institutions and the games irrigators play: Rule enforcement on government- and farmer-managed systems", in: F.W. Scharpf, ed., Games in Hierarchies and Networks: Analytical and Empirical Approaches to the Study of Governance Institutions (Campus Verlag, Frankfurt am Main; Westview Press, Boulder, CO) 387–428.

Wilson, P.N., and G.D. Thompson (1993), "Common property and uncertainty: Compensating coalitions by Mexico's pastoral Ejidatarios", Economic Development and Cultural Change 41(2):299–318.

Chapter 25

AGRICULTURE AND ECOSYSTEM SERVICES

GEOFFREY M. HEAL

Graduate School of Business, Columbia University, New York, NY

ARTHUR A. SMALL

School of International and Public Affairs and Columbia Earth Institute, Columbia University, New York, NY

Contents

Handbook of Agricultural Economics, Volume 2, Edited by B. Gardner and G. Rausser
© *2002 Elsevier Science B.V. All rights reserved*

Abstract

A broad range of agriculture–environment interactions can be organized around the concept of agriculture as a producer and consumer of *ecosystem services*. Viewed as capital assets, ecosystems embody production technologies that are valuable, complex, and often poorly understood. The quantity and quality of services they deliver depend almost always on the joint actions of many dispersed resource users. Furthermore, ecosystems deliver multiple types of services, across widely varying spatial scales. Efficient delivery of alternative environmental "crops" such as carbon sequestration, water quality, and wildlife habitat requires distinctive institutional forms, and an intellectual integration of ecology into agricultural economics.

Keywords

ecosystem services, natural capital, land, conservation, ecology

JEL classification: Q12

1. Agriculture and global environmental change

Over much of the world's surface, agriculture shapes the environment. Agriculture is by far the most important of the activities through which humanity interacts with the natural world; farming's impact on the global environment is greatly disproportionate to its share in total economic activity. In this story two processes are central: agriculture as a driver of land use changes and agriculture as a source of environmental externalities.

Agriculture is one of the main drivers, if not the main driver, of land use changes leading to habitat loss and environmental destruction [Myers (1995), Tilman et al. (2001)]. Adaptation of land to production has led to widespread deforestation, loss of habitat for many species and consequent loss of biodiversity, and profound changes in significant parts of the Earth's surface [Smith, Daily and Ehrlich (1995)]. Not only has habitat been lost but agricultural use has led to land degradation and soil erosion, a particularly acute problem in many developing countries. Daily, Matson and Vitousek (1997) cite evidence that since 1945 seventeen percent of the Earth's vegetated land surface has undergone soil degradation. López provides a compelling analysis of how poverty, population pressures, unstable institutions, and fragile soils together lead to land degradation throughout the developing world.[1] Lichtenberg cites a substantial body of research that soil erosion is far less of a problem in the U.S. However, the problems also arise in the developed world. In New South Wales, Australia, 30–40 percent of arable land has been lost to selenium and salt drawn up from subsoils by irrigation and land clearing. Similar damage has occurred, on a lesser scale, in the Central Valley of California. Some of these lands whose productivity is being compromised are among the richest in the world.

As detailed by Lichtenberg, agriculture is also a major source of environmental pollution, in the form of pesticides, fertilizers, animal wastes, and soil siltation. These pollutants cause contamination of ground and surface waters [United States Geological Survey (1999)], and create potentially harmful changes in the complex ecological systems supporting agriculture and other activities. They affect the systems that regulate agricultural pests, leading to the decline in populations of pest predators and the buildup of populations resistant to artificial pesticides. Another side effect of agriculture is the eutrophication of water bodies. Runoff of agricultural fertilizers from the American Midwest is implicated in a mammoth eutrophic "dead zone" in the Gulf of Mexico [Doering et al. (1999)].[2] Irrigation demands are also causing the diversion of many streams and rivers, leading to reduced flow to non-agricultural ecosystems, the classic examples being the reductions of stream flow on the West Coast of the U.S. and their impacts on salmon runs. Agriculture can also lead to changes in microclimates, and ultimately to changes in the global climate.

---

[1] Except where noted otherwise, citations to Lichtenberg, López, or Ostrom reference their respective chapters in this volume.
[2] Nitrogen and phosphorus nourish algae that can grow rapidly into large blooms. These can consume all of a water body's available dissolved oxygen, causing other aquatic life to suffocate.

At the same time as it affects the environment, agriculture depends on the environment. Agricultural productivity can be greatly enhanced by services provided by the natural environment – services that range from pollination to irrigation to pest control. Farming can be irreparably damaged by the loss of these services. On occasion, agriculture may reciprocate by contributing to the stability or productivity of the natural environment, as when agricultural crops provide foods for bird or insect populations.

The previous chapters [Lichtenberg (2002), López (2002), and Ostrom (2002)] illuminate the connections between agriculture and its natural environmental base, and develop a range of tools and concepts for analyzing these connections. Their contributions effectively trace out the implications of these interactions for economic modeling and analysis, the design of policies and institutions, and the outcomes for farming and for environmental quality. Yet the linkages they draw between agriculture and the environment are so many and various that they tax our ability to apprehend them as an entirety. Often our mental picture fragments into a disconnected scatter of problems. A piecemeal approach to thinking about the agriculture–environment relationship risks fostering a piecemeal approach to economic analysis and policy design; the history of agricultural policy includes many stories of policies that undercut each other. As language structures our thoughts, it is useful to develop a conceptual framework that organizes the diversity of agriculture–environment interactions into a coherent whole. Such a framework helps us see large-scale patterns, reveals gaps in our knowledge, suggests new connections and new approaches to investigation, and offers insights into the delicate but vital tasks of policy design. Our goal for this chapter is to create such a framework, and to use it as a loom on which to weave together the strands spun out by the authors of the preceding three chapters.

We claim that the connections between agriculture and environment can usefully be organized around the concept that natural environments provide a diverse flow of economically valuable inputs to agriculture – *ecosystem services* that are critical to the agricultural economy. A wide range of agriculture–environment interactions can be seen in terms of their effects on these service flows. Bees provide pollination services to many crops. Systems of roots and soils hold water following a downpour, slowly releasing it during drier weather, thus moderating the extremes of weather. Birds and other predators feast on the insects that would feast on crops. Nature continues its work as wastes leave the farm, as microbes break down orange peels, corn cobs, and other non-edible plant and animal wastes. Lichtenberg's description of agriculture as an activity involving the management of a biological resource base is apt. The farmer is more than anything a supervisor over a legion of other organisms, the manager of a human-dominated ecosystem.

Ecosystem services are appropriate topics for agricultural economics. The services these assets deliver are identifiable, valuable, and in some degree measurable. Indeed, ecosystems constitute a significant part of the economy's capital stock, acting as a form of infrastructure-supporting private enterprise. These stocks of *natural capital* can be increased or diminished through deliberate and accidental human interventions. Human actions – including those by agriculturalists themselves – affect populations of pollinators, populations of insects and their predators, the chemical and microbial "health" of soils, and the maintenance of biodiversity. These and other natural systems each in turn affect farm productivity.

The theme of ecosystems providing services to agriculture provides a natural structure around which to organize many of the insights developed by Lichtenberg, López, and Ostrom. Many of the externality and resource management issues these authors raise can be recast as statements about ecosystems' ability to deliver services. However, as these topics have already attracted abundant scholarship within agricultural and natural resource economics, it is legitimate to question what the concepts *ecosystem services* and *natural capital* actually add to our thinking. Are these merely fashionable ways of restating well-known ideas, or is there really something new here?

These terms do add value, we argue, but not by bringing to light entirely new phenomena. The value accrues, rather, in how they help to organize our thinking. They provide a synthesis, a coherence, to a disparate range of factors that can otherwise appear as a disjointed panoply of special cases and extensions. In acknowledging ecosystems explicitly as a class of capital assets, we bring the conceptual frameworks of economics and finance to bear on ecosystem management. This move has implications for the kinds of questions we ask, and the kinds of tools we use to try to answer them. What, we are tempted to ask, is the financial value of the flows of benefits an ecosystem generates? What options are available for additional investment, and at what rates of return? Most important from a policy perspective, how do alternative institutions affect private incentives to accumulate or liquidate natural capital? As an aerial photograph gives a surprising image of even a well-known landscape, so does the concept of ecosystem services bring a new viewpoint from which to develop a new perspective on agriculture–environment interactions.

These questions are particularly salient because the capacity of healthy, functioning environmental systems to deliver ecosystem services is, in many parts of the world, under considerable stress [Arrow et al. (1995), Vitousek et al. (1997)].[3] Historically, the ecosystem services used and provided by agriculture could often be treated as free and their availability as non-binding when carrying out economic analysis. However, as agriculture and other human activities erode the integrity of many ecosystems, the ability of nature to provide critical services becomes compromised. Shifts in the planet's geophysical, chemical, and biological cycles are already affecting agriculture's productive capacity. Climates already show signs of increasing temperatures, both globally and on a regional basis. These changes are causing shifts in agro-climatic growing regions of a pace and scope unprecedented in the 10,000-year history of agriculture. Some predictions suggest that the southern UK will within the next century be a viable growing region for maize, for example. Changes in the rates, timing,

---

[3] In recognition of the ubiquitous human influence on ecosystems, ecologists increasingly eschew the label "natural" as applied to ecosystems, and refer instead to ecosystems as being, or not being, "functional". A typical quip runs, "If you ever find a 'natural' ecosystem, please call me; I'd love to see it".

and variation of precipitation may affect prospects for both rain-fed and irrigated crop production [National Assessment Synthesis Team (2000)]. Rising temperatures in mountain regions are clearly showing shrinkage of glaciers and snowpack on mountains around the world, so that the role of mountains in making water available throughout the year may be compromised. Rising sea levels may lead to inundation or salination of low-lying coastal regions, or salt-water intrusion of some sources of groundwater serving irrigated agriculture. We have at present only a very incomplete understanding of how agriculture will be affected by these changes in ecosystems and the services that they can provide.[4]

This discussion naturally gives rise to several concerns. One is to manage agriculture to minimize its negative environmental impacts, for example, to minimize the loss of biodiversity and the pollution resulting from agricultural activity. The second is to ensure that in damaging the environment, agriculture does not in the long run damage itself, purchasing short-run productivity gains at the expense of long-run performance. This is the immiserizing cycle noted by López. It underpins the concerns underlying current discussions of "sustainable" agriculture. While it would be inappropriate to view the problems of environmental degradation as strictly modern phenomena, the apparent worldwide decline in production of ecosystem services is unprecedented, and indicates an increasing need for conscious management. As an analogy, the onset of global climate change has made us recognize the atmosphere's carbon absorptive capacity as a scarce resource, and the global carbon cycle as a managed process. Ecosystems' ability to deliver services have likewise become scarce, rendering them legitimate, indeed urgent subjects for economics.

1.1. Organization of the chapter

Our goals in this chapter are to use the concept of ecosystem services to organize an investigation of the links between agriculture and the services provided by natural environmental systems, and to examine what the emerging stresses on these systems imply for economic analysis and institutional design. Section 2 surveys the intricate relationship between agriculture and natural ecosystems, and how their interactions affect the flows of ecosystem services to the economy. Building on this background,

---

[4] Mendelsohn, Nordhaus and Shaw (1994) have argued that agriculture can adapt to climate change reasonably smoothly, without suffering first-order losses in profits. Their studies estimate the economic impacts of climate change by comparing land values under historic agro-climatic conditions to those forecast under a credible simulated climate of the future. These calculations depend on two implicit premises. First, it is assumed that climatic changes proceed slowly, relative to the depreciation rates of the relevant forms of specific physical and human capital. The economic impacts of climate change can then be derived by comparing steady states before and after, without accounting explicitly for transition costs. Second, it is assumed that changes in temperature and precipitation do not induce ecological feedbacks (e.g., in insect or fungal populations) leading to first-order effects on the productivity of agricultural enterprises. In this case, a land parcel in the new steady-state can be compared reliably to one in the old steady-state with similar agro-climatic characteristics. Both premises appear as tenable but unverified hypotheses.

Section 3 extracts a set of common features that characterize ecosystems and ecosystem services as economic objects.

The notion of ecosystems as a distinctive class of production technologies provides the framework for Section 4, a discussion of what is known, and not known, about the features of production functions for ecosystem services. Effective analysis of agro-ecosystems, it is argued, requires new tools and a degree of integration between economics and ecology that is still unusual.

This technical analysis sets the stage for Section 5, an examination of the distinctive challenges that arise in designing institutions for managing agro-ecosystems. The discussion is organized around examples of environmental services, such as carbon sequestration, water quality enhancement, and wildlife habitat, that farms can provide as environmental "crops". The examples provide the setting for a discussion of the menu of institutional types that could be used to organize the production of ecosystem services, and the appropriate role of government as an enabler of these institutions. Section 6 concludes with a discussion of emerging issues at the interface of agricultural economics and ecology.

2. Agriculture and ecosystem services: a brief overview

The term "ecosystem services" denotes the economically valuable services generated by natural ecosystems as byproducts of their normal functioning. The notion centers on natural ecosystems' capacity to process matter – their ability to alter the physical, chemical, or biological characteristics of the materials that pass through them. In an influential recent book, *Nature's Services: Societal Dependence on Natural Ecosystems* [Daily (1997)], Gretchen Daily organizes these services into fourteen categories:

- purification of air and water
- mitigation of droughts and floods
- generation and preservation of soils and renewal of their fertility
- detoxification and decomposition of wastes
- pollination of crops and natural vegetation
- dispersal of seeds
- cycling and movement of nutrients
- control of the vast majority of potential agricultural pests
- maintenance of biodiversity
- protection of coastal shores from erosion by waves
- protection from the sun's harmful ultraviolet rays
- stabilization of the climate
- moderation of weather extremes and their impacts
- provision of aesthetic beauty and intellectual stimulation that lift the human spirit.

In economic terms, natural ecosystems can be viewed as a form of *infrastructure* underpinning human society. Indeed, their services resemble in many ways those provided by conventional utilities [Heal (2000)].[5] A challenge for economic studies and government policy toward agriculture is the need to recognize the importance and increasing scarcity value of ecosystem services.

Scanning down Gretchen Daily's list, one sees immediately that agriculture is a user of many types of ecosystem services. The natural environment provides essential inputs to agriculture, many of which are uncounted and unrecorded. Indeed, the essence of plant agriculture is the capture of public environmental goods – sunlight, wind, and rain – and their conversion into appropriable private goods such as crops. Amongst the ecosystem services used by agriculture are the following:

Pollination of crops and natural vegetation. About one-third by value of the crops, fruits, and vegetables produced in the U.S. require pollination. Historically, "wild" populations of pollinators (bees, other insects, bats or birds) have carried out this function. Recently populations of many of these pollinators have declined sharply, to the point that replacements have been needed. Extensive use of pesticides, usually insecticides, is a significant cause of this decline [Nabhan and Buchmann (1997, 1998)]. There is now an active market in the rental of bees, the most widely used insect pollinator. Beekeepers can increase their income by renting hives of bees to farmers at pollination periods – apple growers and alfalfa growers make extensive use of these services.

Nutrient cycling. Natural ecosystems break down crop and animal wastes and release the nutrients in these to restore the fertility of farmlands. In so doing they maintain soil fertility and also avoid the runoff of wastes into water bodies, preserving their purity and value for humans and other animals.

Pest control. Control of pests is one of the main problems facing farmers. A significant fraction of crops, of the order of one-quarter to one-half, may be lost to pests without extensive intervention by the farmer. Pests are just insects or animals that eat a crop designated for human consumption, and are naturally attracted to huge concentrations of their foodstuffs. Most pests have natural enemies that control their populations in natural ecosystems. In agricultural systems, however, these predators may have been eliminated. For example, the predators of many insect pests may be insects that are eliminated by the very insecticides aimed to kill the pests. Or they may be birds, which have been driven away by the destruction of nesting sites or other cover.

Agriculture is a producer of ecosystem services, as well as a consumer. Indeed, agricultural systems are themselves ecosystems, a form of human-dominated ecosystem. The distinction between cultivated lands and undisturbed areas is always a matter of degree, rather than of kind: farms lie on a spectrum between lands completely free of

---

[5] Lest the term collapse from the strain of overuse, it is important also to clarify what the phrase ecosystem services does not convey. The term does not cover all agriculture–environment interactions. Many environmental problems connected to agriculture, such as workers' exposure to toxic pesticides, are not mediated through their effects on ecosystem function. Likewise, although no sharp distinction can be drawn, we do not intend here to emphasize "ecosystem goods" – renewable natural resources such as wood, and fresh water.

human impact (an essentially hypothetical state, on today's Earth) and completely built environments. The services that agriculture could in principle produce include the following:

Carbon sequestration and stabilization of the climate. Trees and other growing vegetation sequester carbon, as does soil. Decay of vegetable matter releases carbon, as does tilling soil. So farming practices can affect the carbon cycle both positively and negatively. This is now the focus of much political negotiation concerning the future of the Kyoto Protocol and the various flexibility mechanisms that have been proposed to lessen the costs of implementation to industrial countries. Agricultural management is central to this debate.

Beauty and tourism. Tourism is the world's largest industry in terms of employment, and also rapidly growing. Management of the landscape affects its attractions to tourists, and farmers are the principal landscape managers in the U.S. Many farm landscapes are unattractive, but some can retain their natural beauty, as have those in Tuscany and the Swiss Alps.

Habitat for endangered species and other wildlife, especially in wetlands. Farms that retain or restore some measure of the original vegetation provide habitats for indigenous species that are otherwise likely to become endangered. These farms may also help themselves because original vegetation may provide habitat for predators of pests and for pollinators.

Purification of air and water; detoxification and decomposition of wastes. It is now increasingly recognized that wetlands can play a major role in removing a range of pollutants from stream water and so in preventing eutrophication by nitrates and phosphates. Retention or restoration of wetlands is therefore a mechanism through which farms may contribute to the resolution of some of the environmental problems they create.

Mitigation of droughts and floods. We are increasingly recognizing that many floods are caused by human alterations to the landscape that have reduced the ability of natural ecosystems to buffer irregular rainfalls. Forests, wetlands, and floodplains have traditionally preformed this function, and the destruction of the former two and the canalization of rivers have destroyed natural flood control systems. Land management practices by farmers can to some degree restore these functions.

3. A conceptual framework for the economics of agriculture and ecosystem services

In economic terms, ecosystem services and the natural capital assets that provide them have become scarce resources. This observation argues for incorporating their role into economic theory. However, this step must be taken cautiously, as ecosystems are unlike other forms of economic capital in important ways. In spite of our ability to catalog the interactions between agricultural systems and ecosystems at the broadest level, we do not have a good, operational understanding of even the qualitative properties of ecosystem service production at any fine-grain level, such as productivity by type of ecosystem. Because of the vast heterogeneity of ecosystems, and of their connections to agriculture, it is challenging to make general statements about their economic function or value. To ensure sound analysis, we are well advised to return to first principles, and to identify the technical and economic features of ecosystems that characterize them as economic assets. These characteristics have first-order implications for economic analysis and policy design.

The contributions of ecosystem services to agriculture are pervasive. They are, like the air we breathe and the water we drink, so ubiquitous that we tend not to notice them, to take them for granted. As Lichtenberg correctly notes, agriculture is in its essence an activity involving the extraction of renewable resources from a biological base.

In many parts of the world, the ability of ecosystems to deliver services to agriculture is under threat. This characteristic is in some ways the most important of all, the one that motivates our study in the first place. What response to this threat, if any, is called for? What options does the menu of policy responses offer, and what are the implications of choosing each?

Ecosystems are complex and unpredictable. This observation is made so often as to risk becoming a bromide. Nonetheless, the point is critical. Ecosystems can often exhibit non-linear behavior – small changes in one variable can result in large changes in others. They can exhibit threshold effects. Furthermore, there are large numbers of variables at play. Univariate analysis is not appropriate, since there may be interaction effects between variables that unitary analysis does not capture well.

Ecosystems are incompletely understood, especially as concerns the determinants of their ability to deliver economically valuable services. We are powerfully ignorant about the technology that produces ecosystem services. We have in general only a poor idea of how marginal changes in land cover, pollution, or other key factors affect ecosystem function, for example. We can expect that the partial equilibrium calculus used to identify optimal conditions one externality at a time will need substantial improvement. The problems extend to understanding the economic functions of ecosystems, to mapping the locations of ecosystems.

Ecosystems typically deliver multiple services jointly, in non-separable bundles. This "jointness" of the production outputs is a particularly salient feature of ecosystems. A healthy watershed ecosystem that delivers abundant flood control and water filtration services is likely also to provide viable habitat for wildlife. Whatever services an ecosystem delivers, their outputs are likely to exhibit high positive correlation. As a consequence, policies designed to preserve or increase one type of service will often serve to enhance the general state of the ecosystem, increasing the flow of other services as a consequence. Ecologists refer to this phenomenon as the "conservation umbrella" [Heal et al. (2001)]. When a market, government, or other agent pays a farmer to sequester carbon, to what extent will the provision of this service automatically create habitat for wildlife? To what extent will the "production" of sequestration services automatically yield improvements in water quality for downstream consumers? To answer such questions, we must investigate the degree to which processes for producing the several types of ecosystem service exhibit economies of scope. To the extent that they do, policy-making becomes easier. An agent need not ponder carefully which measure of environmental quality to use; the generation of any one service will automatically lead to production of the others. To the extent that they do not, or even interfere with one another, policymakers may need to confront tough choices between several desired environmental outcomes.

The spatial structure of habitats has important effects on ecosystem composition and function. These spatial issues can operate at a much more fine-grain scale than those on which economics usually operates. The provision of ecosystem services to and from agriculture can depend on intricate details of the spatial layout of farms and other land uses. The provision of ecosystem services can be affected by intricate technical complementarities between different types of land use. The spatial "tiling" matters.

Ecosystems commonly span large numbers of property claims. In many cases, the producers of ecosystem services to agriculture are other farms. This dispersed pattern of ownership and control leads to all the issues of common property management described by Ostrom and López.

The consumption, or "demand", side of the ecosystem service market likewise follows certain broad regularities.

Different types of ecosystem services are consumed at many different spatial scales. Many have the character of public goods. Some ecosystem services, such as management of insect pests, mainly benefit agriculturalists in a very local area. Others, such as sequestration of carbon in soils, deliver benefits that accrue to the global commonweal. Wildlife habitat delivers use value to local residents and tourists, while rendering additional non-use value to environmentalists elsewhere. Because "ownership" of natural ecological capital is widely distributed, ecosystem services fall into the category of privately produced public goods.

Finally, there are important general features that characterize current policies and institutions for influencing the ecosystem–agriculture relationship.

Public institutions for managing natural capital are generally inadequate to promote economic efficiency. As noted by Heal et al. (2001), "Societies invest a great deal of effort in monitoring and cultivating their physical, financial and human capital. By comparison, they typically pay scant attention to their natural capital, especially that embodied in ecosystems".

To summarize, the view of ecosystems we take from the vantage of economics and finance suggests certain general salient characteristics. As producers of economically valued services, these assets are technically complex and poorly understood. Control of these assets is often distributed over large numbers of agents, whose actions are not necessarily coordinated through any explicit system of governance. Finally, each ecosystem typically delivers a bundle of multiple services to consumers across many different spatial and temporal scales. A comprehensive view of how to manage ecosystems needs to be informed by an appreciation of these distinctive characteristics.

4. Integrating ecosystem services into production economics

Ecosystem services are scarce, make material contributions to economic welfare, cannot be taken for granted, and can be affected by conscious choices. These features place them within the purview of economic analysis. We need to understand how human actions affect the production of ecosystem services, and how these services combine with other factors of production to create economic value. To that end, the next task is to translate a scientific understanding of ecosystem service production into forms that are useful for economic analysis, and to identify important gaps in our knowledge. Lichtenberg's chapter in this volume delivers a summary of the current mainstream view of how economists see the relationship between agriculture and natural resources. We wish to understand how this view might need to shift if analysis of ecosystem services is to become routine in the profession. The focus here is on methodology – on how we study these systems, and on the formal properties of the models we use to represent them. Two themes structure this discussion: the need for new tools with which to study systems in which standard economic assumptions often fail; and the need for close cooperation with ecologists and other area specialists to provide information that economists cannot get for themselves.

4.1. Ecological production theory

Peering through an economic lens, ecosystems can be viewed as capital assets that embody certain production technologies. To understand how these assets fit into economic production, the first step is to develop an understanding of these technologies – to extend our qualitative itemization of Nature's Services into a formal, potentially quantifiable explication of Nature's Production Functions. Ecological technologies, like other technologies, can be viewed as mechanisms by which to transform a specified vector of inputs into another vectors of outputs. At the broadest level, we have already identified the outputs: these are exactly the ecosystem services described in Section 2. What are the corresponding inputs? Since ecosystems are not designed and constructed to satisfy human needs, answering this question requires unusual care.

Identifying the inputs in ecological production functions. A production function is a mathematical representation of a process by which a human agent can transform scarce economic resources in one form into scarce economic resources in some other form. In its essence, the concept of a production function involves *human choices.* The formalism should evoke a picture of a human agent making decisions about how to allocate scarce resources between alternative competing uses.

Not all of the physical inputs to a production process count as economic inputs. To describe an input as an economic factor of production, it must satisfy at least three conditions. First, the input must be a *limiting factor* in the production process, over at least some part of the relevant domain. (It takes oxygen to bake a cake, but more oxygen will not make it taste better.) Second, the input must be *discretionary*: its availability must be at least to a degree under the control of some human agency. (The baking process also relies on gravity, but the oven has no corresponding dial.) Third, the input must be *scarce*: its use must involve an opportunity cost.

By remembering that the arguments to ecological production functions must represent scarce resources, we can avoid two conceptual mistakes that sometimes arise in this work. Ecosystems are sometimes described as consuming *no* economic inputs, under the logic that they lie outside the economy and provide their services freely, without human agency or effort. It is true that most ecosystems do not require managerial skill or any manufactured feedstocks. Yet all ecosystems require physical space, and the maintenance of suitable environmental conditions. Terrestrial ecosystems take up land (by definition), and often require fresh, clean water. In many instances these resources could profitably be reallocated to other uses. (Where this is not true, there are generally no real economic or policy controversies to be addressed.) Even if the consumption of scarce resources by ecosystems involves no explicit accounting cost, it implies an economic opportunity cost. This principle is particularly salient for agro-ecosystems, where the choice may involve taking land out of crop production to enroll in a conservation program, or diverting water from irrigation to wetlands. In economic terms, ecosystem services are typically not "free".

Another conceptual error lies at the opposite extreme. This is to enumerate *all* the physical inputs that an ecosystem uses, including those that are not scarce, discretionary, or limiting. Sunlight, for example, is an essential input to almost all ecosystems – indeed, their ultimate motive force. Many branches of ecology pay acute attention to the role of sunlight in ecosystem structure and function. Mathematically oriented ecologists often include solar radiation as an input in whole-ecosystem computer simulation models. Some forest ecologists examine sunlight as the scarce resource driving the spatial configuration of plants in a canopy. When analyzing an ecosystem for its own sake, close attention to the role of sunlight is natural, and appropriate. However, when describing an ecosystem's capacity to produce economically valuable services, sunlight is usually not an important limiting factor. Even when it is, its rate of delivery is rarely a choice variable for any human agent. Furthermore, the consumption of sunlight by an ecosystem typically carries no opportunity cost, no potentially valuable alternative usage that must be forgone. In most cases, sunlight is simply part of the *donnée*, an element of the world that matters for ecosystem function, but is no more a factor under human control than the length of the seasons or the strength of the gravitational force.[6] In typical cases, the physical environmental conditions that support an ecosystem should properly be treated as *features of* an economic production process, rather than as inputs to it.

In most applications, these environmental conditions will be bundled and rented together with the land on which production takes place. If one cannot buy a sunny

---

[6] It should be conceded, though, that environmental history includes many examples of factors once thought fixed that are later regrettably discovered to be very much subject to human influence – the global climate, the ozone layer, and the planet's stock of biodiversity being only the most recent and prominent examples.

day, one instead rents the land on which the sunlight falls. Land – differentiated by location, quality, and other characteristics – is by far the most important economic factor in the production of ecosystem services. The second most important factor is probably water, which can often be purchased and deployed separately from land. Other inputs might be treated explicitly in particular applications. For example, the conservation of agricultural genetic resources *in situ* may depend on the maintenance of traditional farming practices. Likewise, installation of wetlands, hedgerows, buffer strips, and other forms of natural capital may require machinery, skill, and other expensive inputs. Many important issues in our analysis can be cast as questions about how the prices of these factors affect the supply of different types of ecosystem services.

The formal properties of ecological production functions. Having identified the economic inputs and outputs to an ecological production process, the next task is to represent the production relationship formally – to the extent possible, in mathematical notation. Describing ecological relationships in formal language is a crucial step in bringing ecosystem services into economics. A move toward formalization clarifies some of the key questions the theory should address. How does the output of various types of services depend on the type of ecosystem, its size, its spatial configuration, and its other characteristics? How do changes in these characteristics affect the mix of outputs? In particular, how do marginal changes in ecosystem properties yield *marginal* changes in service outputs? Understanding at this level is indispensable if ecosystem services are to be brought fully into economic analysis. It is apparent that economists are not able to provide such answers themselves. Expertise from ecology and other relevant natural sciences is essential.

Unfortunately, ecological science is rarely ready to provide answers at this level of precision. Marginal analysis has only a tenuous tradition in ecology, even among theorists who are often highly sophisticated in applied mathematics. This situation does not necessarily represent a failure on the part of ecologists; many of the questions that interest ecologists do not draw on these methods. A more fundamental problem is that ecological processes are often poorly understood. We do know from our ecologist friends that they are frequently characterized by profound complementarities, non-linearities, irreversibilities, and threshold effects [Carpenter, Ludwig and Brock (1999)]. We also know that time matters: the effects of perturbations may exhibit lags, sometimes very long lags.

The complexity of ecosystems can lead to highly unpredictable behavior. An illustration is provided by an account of a possible link between the extinction of the passenger pigeon and the emergence of Lyme disease as a threat to humans [Blockstein (1998)]. Passenger pigeons once flourished in North America, sustained on a diet that included acorns and beechnuts, both of which were abundant in the forests of the northeastern United States. A combination of massive hunting and equally massive destruction of the bird's habitat brought about its extinction. The demise of the pigeons led to an increase in the food available for other animals that ate these, including mice. Mice are the main breeding ground and hosts of the parasites that cause Lyme disease. It is more than plausible that the explosion of food for mice led to a jump in their population and thus in the population of Lyme disease vectors. (Abundant acorn crops always lead to increases in the population of mice.) The disease vectors transfer from mice to deer, which browse in the same forests and on the same foods, and then move across territory likely to be used by humans, grazing on grass on lawns and fields. So the extinction of passenger pigeons could have been instrumental in causing the spread of Lyme disease to humans. This example illustrates well the extraordinary complexity of the web of life, of the connections between different species, and between species and human welfare. No one could reasonably have anticipated this connection between passenger pigeons and Lyme disease. No ex ante analysis of the consequences of the loss of this bird could have anticipated such an outcome. Indeed, the bird was so abundant that it must have been difficult to anticipate that human activity could ever drive it extinct.

In the face of such complexity, economists approaching a discussion of ecological production processes need to be cautious about casually imposing modeling assumptions that are standard in other applications. Researchers should be particularly wary about assuming convexity and smoothness properties. Many economic production processes are routinely represented by smooth production functions. A farm or factory can add a little more capital, a little less labor, and still be a functional economic entity, operating reliably for an indefinite period. In more abstract terms, the production possibilities set offers a continuous range of options for generating a positive level of outputs. An ecosystem however is a dynamical system, not a set of static relationships, and may in consequence have only a few stable equilibria.

Closely related to the smoothness assumption is the ubiquitous assumption of convexity – of production functions, utility functions, and anything else where wrinkled features would cause tedious mathematical trouble. The assumption is undeniably convenient. It makes the math go through, and underpins an almost fetishistic enthusiasm for dual approaches. When the production process being modeled is an ecosystem, the realism of this assumption is suspect, however. Indeed, the assumptions of standard production theory are that technology sets are convex *on the economically relevant range*. A system that is carefully managed by an optimizing agent who understands how it works – a factory, say – is not likely to also be near a potentially devastating break point. The very fact that an economic production process is observed suggests its stability, its "smoothness". An ecosystem that is not managed (at least, not deliberately, by a single optimizing intelligence) is far less likely to be at or near equilibrium. In addition, there is a fundamental connection between external effects and non-convexities, to the point that under certain conditions external effects in production imply non-convexities in the underlying production processes.

The standard approach to analyzing an externality problem calls for an intervention to move a system from one equilibrium to another. This notion of equilibrium, and the constantly repeated assumption that we are dealing with systems near equilibrium, runs throughout our analysis. The assumption is, in fact, intimately related to the assumption of convex production functions. It underpins all of duality theory. When we think of an ecosystem as a productive technology, however, we need to take another look at this assumption. In the ecological literature, the notion that ecosystems ever settle to stable, fixed equilibria is controversial. They may exhibit cyclic dynamics, or even chaotic dynamics. Furthermore, many of the ecosystems that interact with agriculture are already heavily perturbed by various human actions. The assumption of equilibrium is often very poor, given the profound changes that human interventions have caused.

Ecosystem services as factors of agricultural production. The outputs of ecological production processes have, in many cases, direct consumption benefits. In other cases, they serve in turn as inputs to other production processes, to be used in the creation of marketable outputs. To integrate ecosystem services into agricultural economics, the next step is a discussion of economic production processes in which ecosystem services play an important role as inputs. What is particularly salient is the potential to manipulate the characteristics of landscapes in ways that affect the productivity of manufactured inputs, and of labor.

Many important questions for management and policy pivot on the technical properties of these production relationships. A key issue concerns the degree to which labor, manufactured capital, and other inputs can substitute for lost ecosystem services. To the extent that they can, the economic imperative to conserve these resources for direct production purposes is apparently lessened. As the populations of pollinators decline in the Northeast United States, we see New York farmers make do by renting the services of bees from Texas. Advocates for "strong sustainability" and the application of the Precautionary Principle in environmental decision making are implicitly arguing that such specific examples of substitutability do not underpin a general rule. The degree of substitutability between natural capital and manufactured inputs is in principle a researchable topic. More exactly, it forms a class of researchable topics, as the answers are likely to depend very much on the particular context. The growing literature on asset complementarities may find profitable application in this domain.

4.2. Methods for studying agro-ecosystems

Lichtenberg and López review just some of the many important issues concerning agriculture–environment interactions that have been addressed in agricultural and natural resource economics. However, as López notes, the treatments in this literature have mostly been in a partial-equilibrium framework. Attention is usually focused on the effects of marginal perturbations to systems that are assumed implicitly to be at or near equilibrium, and to be sufficiently robust so that small changes in parameter values yield small changes in outcomes. These assumptions are embedded in the very structure of the tools we generally use. In particular, when we use calculus to derive statements that express the state of the system, we assume implicitly that the system responds smoothly to perturbations.

The standard mathematical tools of economic analysis – multivariate calculus, Lagrangian methods of constrained optimization, partial equilibrium analysis – are inadequate to study formal models with the non-standard features that apply to ecological production functions. An almost definitional characteristic of complex systems is that partial equilibrium tools are inadequate for their full analysis. In such systems, small changes in single variables can induce large and unpredictable changes in other variables throughout the system. To address economically productive systems that exhibit pervasive non-convexities, non-linearities, threshold effects, and out-of-equilibrium behavior, new tools and approaches are needed. New techniques will expand the utility of formal analytic modeling, econometric studies, controlled experiments, and computer simulation modeling.

Formal analysis of systems that never settle down to single-point equilibria requires mathematical tools beyond those normally conveyed in graduate training in agricultural economics. Differential geometry and differential topology can be very useful in studying systems for which equilibria lie on manifolds of one or more dimensions. Dynamical systems provide methods for studying transitional behavior, movements toward equilibria. Entry-level dynamical systems theory is now used routinely in resource economics and macroeconomics, but more advanced versions are needed to study transition dynamics in such systems. The utility of chaos theory has probably been oversold, yet it may have value in some applications to linked ecological-economic systems. Advanced mathematics is probably not for everybody, however, and its use carries a risk of sparking fetishistic fads that are long on technique and short on insight. Using more to say less does not constitute progress.

Another promising scholarly technique is enhanced cross-disciplinary cooperation with ecologists. In such partnerships, however, each side needs to show patience with the other's intellectual style. Ecologists can sometimes offer detailed mechanistic accounts of ecosystem structure and function, but such information is not precisely what is needed to conduct economic analysis. What we need for economic analysis is to understand in reduced form the quantitative relationships between ecosystem characteristics and service outputs – what might fairly be termed a "statistical" understanding. Ecology does have summary or reduced-form models, such as the species-area curve relating the number of species an island supports to the area of the island. (An empirical regularity holds that this relationship is log-linear.) These kinds of models have been adapted to address management questions concerning biodiversity conservation. There is an opportunity to develop analogs of the species-area functions for human-dominated ecosystems, and to determine more broadly how the relationship shifts in response to various human impacts and stresses. Jointly designed empirical studies of these relationships could make fruitful use of both fields' relative sophistication in statistics.

Controlled experiments on complex systems are always difficult to design, execute, and interpret. Yet these hold perhaps the most promise as a means to understand how ecosystems function, how they deliver services, and how these systems are affected by shocks. In the early days of agricultural economics, we did not as a profession have a good understanding of the production functions governing agricultural production. Controlled experiments on agricultural experiment stations gave us the data we needed. Controlled experiments seem entirely feasible for at least significant parts of the analysis of ecosystem services.

For some systems, we may have little choice but to accept computer simulation modeling as a valid mode of inquiry, alongside formal analytic theorizing, econometric estimation, and controlled experimentation. Most studies modeling linked ecological and economic systems are based on computer simulations in which sub-systems (geophysical, biological, human) are modeled and simulated separately, with the output of one sub-model serving as (exogenous) parameters for other sub-models. Truly coupled models are not unknown; Aillery, Shoemaker and Caswell (2001), Tschirhart (2000), and Antle et al. (2000) provide recent exceptions. However, fully coupled models remain relatively uncommon.

4.3. Interactions between agricultural economics and ecology

Ecology and economics share a number of commonalities that serve to increase the ease of cooperation.[7] Many questions in ecology have clear analogs in economics. For example, one perennial question in conservation biology concerns the optimal design of conservation reserves subject to a budget constraint: Is it better to have one large reserve, or several smaller ones? The question is clearly recognizable as reflecting a trade-off between increasing returns to scale and diversification in response to risk. Another considers whether diverse ecosystems are unusually productive and resilient to shocks [Wardle, Bonner and Barker (2000)]. Here again we see a parable with finance concerning the benefits of portfolio diversification.

The correspondence between the fields continues in the area of methodology. Some theoretically minded ecologists employ methods of constrained optimization to represent the survival strategies of organisms or functional groups. Indeed, some ecological models represent equilibria as arising from the interactions of maximizing individual agents, thereby taking the parallel with economics down to the foundation.

Differences between the fields cannot be brushed aside, however. Ecology's essence is the understanding of complex systems with high degrees of interdependence and a lot of important detail. Ecologists are usually concerned with how natural systems behave when left to their own devices. Ecology is less concerned with how ecosystems respond to intentional stimuli. The science of *human-dominated ecosystems* is in its infancy. Historically the field has not been concerned with questions of deliberate management of ecosystems, in the sense of intervening in their operation with an eye on some pre-defined objective. When the study comes from a perspective of management rather than understanding for its own sake, the field has shifted from ecology to agronomy, silviculture, or one of the other applied arts and sciences. (An exception is conservation biology, the science of biodiversity preservation.) This suggests that a new discipline yet developing – that of ecosystem management – will be central to the agriculture and agricultural economics of the future.

---

[7] One commonality is etymological: both fields take their name from the Greek word *oikos* ("house").

5. Institutions and ecosystem services

As we have seen, ecosystem services play an incompletely understood but enormously important role in economic activity, particularly in connection with agriculture. There is substantial reason to believe that this role is not given appropriate weight by our economic and political institutions, a failure that might call for policy correctives. The cause seems largely to be the "invisibility" of the services that are provided by ecosystems, which in general do not pass through the marketplace and are rarely explicitly itemized.

In this section, we examine how alternative institutional forms influence the delivery of ecosystem services. Following López, we look at situations in which ecosystem management decisions are under the control of private households, and then at communal or collective agencies. We also investigate corporate ownership as a distinctive form of private control, and direct government management. We then examine the intentions and outcomes associated with various governmental interventions. A brief comparative institutional analysis follows, in which we highlight general principles about how institutions for ecosystem management perform under various conditions.

5.1. The policy problem posed by ecosystem services

Ecosystem services *are* recognized in the market to a large degree, but not separately: They are treated as if bundled with more conventional private goods and assets. In many cases, these values are capitalized into the prices of fixed factors, most especially of land. Insofar as the value of ecosystem services are capitalized into land prices, they show up in national accounts as land rents. Some have argued that to the contrary the value that ecosystems deliver to agriculture, and to the rest of the economy, are not represented in, for example, national income accounts. This erroneous view is at the base of the exercise by Costanza et al. (1997) to estimate the value of the world's ecosystem services, for example. They may not be represented fully but they are represented to some degree.

When a farmer rents a plot of agricultural land for a term, what does he get in return? What make arable land valuable? A substantial part of the value is derived from prior investments in clearing, drainage, leveling and complementary infrastructure. Yet all these investments are aimed precisely at accessing the land's biological capacity, its suitability as an environment for growing crops. An owner or renter of agricultural land gains a complex bundle of nature's services: sunshine and rain; the action of microbial communities that fix nitrogen in forms plants can use as nutrients; pollination of crops by bees; predation of crop pests by insectivores. Insofar as these services make crop production possible, their value is reflected in the rental price of land, and their contribution will be capitalized into land values. For this reason, the value of ecosystem services cannot easily be identified separately from land values. If the local ecosystems were to change in ways that required compensating increases in application of manufactured inputs or labor – if, say, the insect populations required more frequent applications of pesticide – then the returns to farming would decline. Land rents would, necessarily, decline accordingly.

This identification issue applies even if the services are provided by ecosystems concentrated off-site. Part of what a landowner buys is the location of the parcel near public infrastructure assets that generate value for the owner. These assets include roads that reduce the costs of marketing, networks carrying electricity and other utility services, schools and other nearby amenities. Ecosystem services that enhance farm productivity may likewise depend on ecological dynamics playing out on spatial scales far larger than that of a single farm. Insofar as ecosystem services are genuine economic factors of agricultural production, then, they are embedded in land, purchased with land, provided as a function of patterns of land use.

In other words, at least part of the value of the ecosystem services used by agriculture are capitalized into the prices for land and for other fixed productive factors. This is a fundamental principle. The claim that ecosystem services enter the economy without leaving any traces in the national income accounts is false.[8]

The policy problem posed by ecosystem services is therefore not one of incorrect valuation or national income accounting. The problem is, rather, the canonical issue in environmental and natural resource economics – that misaligned incentives for private agents can lead to inefficiencies in situations involving externalities and public goods. Accurate valuation is, however, neither a necessary nor sufficient condition for redressing these incentive problems.

Externalities and public goods are pervasive in the interactions between agriculture and natural ecosystems. In practice, almost all economically significant interactions between agriculture and natural ecosystems are not mediated through market transactions. Consequently agents' economic incentives do not reflect the full social costs and benefits of their actions. Alternative institutional arrangements involving collective or government action can also suffer from a variety of difficulties involving incentives, coordination, and commitment. A key task of economic policy is to design institutions that close these loops, to give the agents who control the fate of ecosystems the incentives to assure that these ecosystems maintain their integrity. This task may require a review of a host of agricultural and environmental policy designs. Policy must be based on a view that agricultural production and environmental management are inseparable. Institutional analysis and design requires a keen understanding of agents' *incentives for modifying ecosystems*. These are shaped by the institutional environment, as well as by the technology of ecosystems. We need to design institutions for ecosystem management with explicit attention to ecosystem service production.

---

[8] Small, strictly local changes in the quantity and quality of ecosystem services will be fully reflected in changes in land values. Changes that alter productivity on a large scale may lead to movement in commodity prices and, therefore, in consumer surplus. In the latter case, the distribution of rents between consumers, land, and other fixed factors will depend, as usual, on the relative price elasticities of demand and supply, and on the elasticities of substitution between fixed factors. These numbers are in principle measurable.

A natural step in getting incentives correct is to connect agents who control ecosystems with the beneficiaries of ecosystem services. This can happen in several ways: through simple (or complicated) contracts; through common-property management regimes; through governmental agro-environmental payment schemes; or through changes in the market itself, extending it to cover services that were previously free. What types of problems can we expect might be solved through voluntary cooperation between farmers (or landowners), perhaps through established or new associations?

We consider several examples, organized according to the spatial scale of the producer and consumer groups. In some cases, farmers will deliver environmental quality privately, as a by-product of profit-maximizing individual actions. Other cases may require coordination with neighbors within small local areas. These can naturally be viewed as common-property management problems. Still other cases involve "fee-for-service" payments from downstream consumers of environmental quality. Finally, there are environmental quality issues that cover such large spatial scales that it is difficult to imagine solutions that do not involve a direct role for government. This role might involve the establishment of a market in carbon offsets. It might involve direct payments from the government treasury in exchange for environmental services.

5.2. Correcting externalities and supporting public goods – incentives for the provision of ecosystem services

The problems facing us in providing a framework that supports the provision of ecosystem services are classical public policy problems in a rather novel setting. The usual policy measures in response to externalities are the use of Pigouvian taxes to correct externalities, or the introduction of property rights à la Coase and the use of a cap and trade system buttressed by a total maximum daily loading of a pollutant. Alternatively we can think of setting up markets in goods or services that are not currently traded – water, for example – and in the case of public goods we can make the public sector the buyer and have them purchase on behalf of the community. Several of these methods have already been introduced on small scales for the management of ecosystem services provided or compromised by agriculture.

5.2.1. Cap and trade mechanisms

The Kyoto Protocol proposed a cap and trade mechanism to control the emissions of greenhouse gases. There has been extensive discussion of how this might apply to agriculture. While the most important sources of greenhouse gases are industrial, agriculture plays a significant role in the carbon cycle, as noted in López (2002). Agriculture contributes to carbon emissions as forested lands are cleared for cultivation. In addition, methane from livestock is a significant contributor to atmospheric greenhouse gases. These contributions are particularly important: methane is twenty-one times more effective than carbon dioxide as a greenhouse gas. These contributions are partly offset by the value of agro-forestry (trees on farms) as carbon sinks. A farm's net emissions depend substantially on farming practices. Recently, agriculture has received attention as a vehicle for carbon sequestration.

Several large transactions based on this capacity to sequester carbon have already taken place. In one prominent case, a consortium of ten Canadian electric utilities purchased 2.8 million tons of carbon credits from IGF, the fourth-largest crop insurer in the U.S. [Cooper (1999)]. IGF will in turn acquire "certified emissions reduction credits" (CERCs) from landowners in Iowa and elsewhere. The reductions are achieved by reducing the frequency of tillage, planting trees, and converting animal wastes and other biomass into methane and power. There is apparently broad excitement among growers at the prospect for selling carbon credits as a new crop, an enthusiasm spurred in part by wildly unrealistic predictions that these will fetch up to $100 per ton per year. With political support from farming interests, the prospects for agricultural carbon credits seem at least reasonably promising.

If agriculture is to play a significant role as part of national and global strategies for reducing net emissions of greenhouse gases, a number of issues will require careful economic analysis. One set of issues concerns the measurement and verification of reductions in net emissions. Actuarial techniques can partly resolve these problems. Farmers could be credited with reductions according to the adoption of techniques that are easily verifiable. The development of standardized measurement and verification protocols is essential to underpin such a system. If farmers are to have adequate incentives to make costly investments to improve the productivity of their natural capital as a provider of carbon sequestration services, they must be able to rely on accepted techniques that allow them to estimate returns with a reasonable degree of confidence. To the extent that farmers are required to absorb the risk that actual reductions are less than those estimated, they will be reluctant to undertake those investments. More generally, we see that in addition to controls on initial emissions there are various potential controls on exposure. Some of these involve the deliberate management of ecosystems for their ability to deliver purification services. (Indeed, phytoremediation refers exactly to the creation of an ecosystem specifically for the purpose of capturing these services.)

Carbon sequestration is not the only agro-ecosystem service that might be supported by a cap and trade system. The use of nitrogen-based fertilizers could be similarly controlled, and one by-product of such a control system would be the provision of incentives to remove nitrates from stream waters. This in turn would support the restoration of wetlands, which have proven efficacy in removing nitrates and other fertilizer residues from river waters. Such policies would illustrate well the jointness of ecosystem service production, for wetlands would not only restore water quality but would also provide habitat for birds and in some cases act as fish nurseries.

5.2.2. Introducing markets in ecosystem services

Organic farming provides an example of a "market-based" mechanism for delivering ecosystem services. The business model behind organic agriculture is to rely more heavily on ecosystem services, and less on purchased chemical inputs, than is typical in agriculture generally. The grower typically suffers some yield loss, but produces a product that commands a price premium as some fraction of the market derives utility from the characteristics of the crop and of the production process. In this case, the value of ecosystem services is reflected in lower production costs and a higher unit price. Buyers are paying for ecosystem services as well as for the physical product.

The quality of nearby stream water is greatly affected by farming practices, and this provides another mechanism through which we may make payments for ecosystem services. The classic case here is that of the New York City watershed. In this case, the Catskills watershed acts as a large filter and pre-processor for New York's drinking water supply. Beginning in 1997, the City has made substantial payments to upstate farmers in its watershed to recompense them for using farming methods that lead to lower pollution levels in the water flowing into the watershed area. They are paid to use riparian buffer strips on cropland, and to keep animals away from stream boundaries. In effect they are being paid not to compromise the provision of ecosystem services, that is, being paid to allow ecosystem services to reach others. Similar systems are in operation elsewhere – in Germany, water utilities make payments to farmers to limit their use of fertilizers and thus maintain water quality, and in the catchment district for Perrier bottled water in France a similar regime has been introduced by the Perrier company, eager to maintain its brand quality.

5.2.3. Government purchase of ecosystem services

A number of countries have experimented with systems of agro-environmental payments. Under these systems, a governmental authority pays farmers to adopt practices that bring environmental benefits but would otherwise reduce profits. Agro-environmental programs are growing in importance as vehicles by which governments enhance environmental quality while supporting farm incomes [Claassen et al. (2001), Wu, Zilberman and Babcock (2001)]. Several factors are moving the governments of developed countries in this direction.[9] National agricultural support policy formulation is increasingly constrained by international trade agreements that limit distortionary interventions in markets for farm products, and in addition, there remains in all these jurisdictions a political imperative to transfer wealth to the farming sector. As incomes in developed countries grow, demand for environmental services and amenities has grown, so the ability to combine agricultural support with environmental support is politically attractive [Becker (2001)]. At the same time research is revealing the intimate connections between farm production, ecosystem services, and environmental health.

Specific illustrations of such policies are the Conservation Reserve Program (CRP) in the U.S., under which the USDA invites farmers to offer land to be held in the Conservation Reserve. In effect the selection of land from that offered is run

---

[9] Also commonly termed "agri-environmental" policies.

like an auction, with the USDA ranking offers according to the rent requested by the farmer and the environmental significance of the land. Currently this program holds about 10 percent of all U.S. cropland, making a significant contribution to environmental conservation, the provision of ecosystem services, and the support of the farm community. In effect the USDA is paying farmers for the provision of ecosystem services under the CRP. Similar systems are in operation in Europe – for example, in the UK farmers may be paid for maintaining or establishing wetlands, hedgerows, and native tree cover. In all of these cases the motivation is that these are integral parts of the native ecosystems and are important to the services that these can provide. A similar but more comprehensive system has been introduced in parts of Costa Rica, involving attempts to quantify ecosystem services and to pay for the provision of specific services as a function of the scale of provision [Castro and Tattenbach (1997), Moura Costa (1998)]. In other countries the policy has been to pay for the maintenance of habitat conducive to the provision of a bundle of services without going to the next step of itemizing specific services for which payment will be made and measuring these.

5.3. Additional issues of institutional design

A major area of research considers how these institutions depend on the technical characteristics of the resource under management, and of the services it provides [Hanna (1998)]. Another closely related (meta-) question concerns the conditions under which institutional forms are likely to change. Ostrom extends and expands on López's insightful discussion in endogenous formation of institutions for environmental management. A major theme is that common property systems arise to manage externalities. As in the "static" case, however, the discussion has far to go.

Financing investments in ecosystem capital raises interesting policy issues of a rather different type from those discussed so far. For example, tree plantings take land out of production immediately, yet only yield their full complement of environmental benefits over many years. If a farmer receives payment for environmental services only "upon delivery", then capital will need to be raised to finance investments in natural capital. In view of this, one of the most high-value roles a government can play is to finance and facilitate the creation of measurement and verification protocols that allow the estimation of investment returns for ecosystem upgrade projects. Rather than absorbing the risk directly, government can play a very constructive role by providing private market actors – farmers and banks – with tools to evaluate and manage risks. An analog is provided by the International Measurement and Verification Protocol for energy efficiency investments.

If environmental assets are to be treated as genuine assets, they must be "bankable". In principle, a promised stream of Pigouvian payments should be usable as collateral for a loan. Several pre-conditions are necessary. First, the loan applicant must hold a clear and enforceable claim to the stream of payments. Usually, this claim will take the form of a clear title to some land to which the payment stream is attached. Second, the payments must be committed credibly for some time in the future. For the purpose of securing financing for other projects, a program subject to annual re-authorization and re-budgeting is not much better than no program at all.

6. Reprise, and directions forward

Our project for this chapter has been to examine critically the concept of ecosystem services in the context of agriculture, drawing on the contributions of Lichtenberg, López, and Ostrom. The term "ecosystem services" does not comprehend some entirely new category of economically important natural phenomena that had previously escaped all notice. Rather, the concept provides a way of viewing and organizing a range of agriculture–environment interactions so numerous and diverse that they are difficult to manage conceptually. By directing our attention to agriculture's ecological setting, it delivers value not so much in the new phenomena it identifies, but in the new questions it inspires us to pose.

There are several potential research programs that would enhance the understanding of the economics of ecosystem services, its connections to agricultural economics, and to policy analysis. If our goal is to construct institutions that recognize and respond to the value of ecosystem services for agriculture, what do we need to know that we do not know now?

One obvious requirement is information about the types and levels of economically valuable services produced by ecosystems, as functions of ecosystem type, size, and other characteristics. These need to be specified at a level of detail fine enough to allow marginal analysis. They should make specific notice of non-convexities, non-linearities, and threshold effects. There needs to be an analysis of the complementarities and substitutabilities between different characteristics in the ecological production process.

The effect of seasonal variation in precipitation and temperature on the flows of various services apparently represents a class of very "accessible" projects. As global climate change creates shifts in regional patterns of temperature and precipitation, these studies become particularly timely. To a limited extent, these projects admit the possibilities of controlled experiments. Getting this information, though, will require working with ecologists. Economists can pose the questions, but must rely on area specialists to give the answers.

For the context of agricultural production, we would like also to know more about how ecosystem services interact with labor, capital, and manufactured inputs of various kinds. To what extent, in what ways, and under what conditions do chemical pesticides substitute for the action of insectivores, for example? These production processes can be studied with a diversity of methods, including controlled experiments, natural experiments, standard regression analysis, analytic modeling, and computer simulation modeling. Here again, there appears to be a large potential for mutually beneficial cross-pollination between agricultural economics, agronomy, and ecology. Especially promising is the emerging area of ecological research on human-dominated ecosystems.

A related issue is: What determines the rate of return (both public and private) to investments in natural capital? Answers to questions of this form require input from both ecologists and economists. Ecologists can identify the technical relationships between actions taken (or refrained from), and resulting outcomes. Economists need to identify how these relationships translate into financial terms of risk and reward, and how the various institutional regimes affect the distribution of risk and reward among agents.

From a policy implementation perspective, it is essential to have summary metrics of ecosystem services. In designing a Pigouvian payment scheme, some choices must be made about the variables that will be used to calculate the payment formula. Ideally, the variables must be directly and verifiably measurable, and transparent to both the government and the payee. They should also be correlated to the land manager's actions, even if these are not directly observable. And, of course, they should be correlated with some notion of ecosystem service benefits. One of the research tasks is to develop such measurable, verifiable indices of success.

Another is to develop measurement techniques and equipment that permits the variables to be measured at low cost, and without undue risk of tampering or fraud.[10] As pointed out by Lichtenberg in this volume, agriculture is characterized by significant heterogeneity in producer scale, crop type, farming system, and ecological footprint. One-size-fits-all policies are generally not efficient. Tools of mechanism design are especially applicable in the design and analysis of effective agro-environmental policy.

Valuation studies do have their uses. They can be used, for example, as part of the background discussion about whether the benefits of creating a new institution justify the costs. (The exchange between Simpson, Sedjo and Reid (1996), and Rausser and Small (2000) about the viability of bioprospecting as a source of financing for biodiversity conservation provides an example.) It merits repeating, however, that "correct" non-market valuation of ecosystem services is neither a necessary nor sufficient condition for creating systems in which economic agents appropriately recognize the contributions of ecosystems to production. The challenge, rather, is to create institutional arrangements that deliver appropriate incentives to foster and maintain ecosystem integrity.

At the highest level, we need principles that guide us in designing institutions for managing agro-ecosystems. To that end, we need a richer framework for examining the economics of various types of ecosystems under alternative institutional arrangements. It may be useful to begin from the premise that institutions arise to solve certain coordination problems. The challenge, then, is to discover which coordination problems are characteristic of various types of ecosystems and their services, and to then

---

[10] Cautionary tales on this score come from the realm of weather derivative contracts. These call for payments between parties based on measurements taken at designated weather stations, usually located at airports. In one alleged case, a contract was annulled after it was revealed that the roof above a temperature gauge had been repainted in a new and different color. The paint job, it was argued, altered the albedo of the structure, thereby changing daytime temperature readings systematically from the historic baselines used to derive the actuarial tables underpinning the contract. Litigation, it is said, ensued.

examine the efficacy of different institutions for redressing the potential coordination failures. Lichtenberg's discussion of stewardship provides a baseline, an examination of conservation incentives under private property, with little or no coordination between agents. López makes further contributions to our understanding of these questions, by comparing environmental outcomes under private, communal, and open-access regimes. Ostrom's work provides a set of guiding principles about the construction of common-property systems. We need much more detail, though. For example, there are many different types of "private" management – owner-operated family farms, share-cropping, corporate management. There is a great diversity of agro-climatic settings that may be more or less suited to common-property management. We do not yet have a clear idea about how institutions can best be contoured to specific environmental settings.

In particular, we do not have a theory that tells us when intervention by a central government is called for, or when local or private initiatives can adequately minimize economic inefficiencies and environmental degradation [Gjertsen and Barrett (2001)]. In this connection the concept of *scale matching* – that the scale of management institutions should conform to the scale of the environmental system being managed [Levin (1999)] – has an obvious intuitive appeal: use a global regime to treat global warming, but a local district to manage a wetland. The task remains to give the concept formal expression, and to identify what value it adds to practical economic analysis. Since ecosystems provide benefits across many different spatial and temporal scales, the simplest version of the scale matching concept is clearly problematic. Perhaps what is called for is a hierarchy of institutions, nested like Matryoshka dolls, with successive layers responsible for larger and larger scales. Yet then we would need an additional, constitutional theory concerning the optimal relationship between the layers. We expect that the notion of scale matching will eventually take hold as a useful principle for designing environmental institutions, but only after further elaboration.

Central to this discussion is the question of whether current agricultural practices give sufficient consideration to the sustainability of agricultural productivity in the long run. We care about how agriculture interacts with ecosystems because we care about the potential costs of lost ecological services to agriculture, about the potential costs of lost ecological services to the rest of society, and because as humans we care about the state of the ecological world. What is at stake, in a growing number of places, is the long-run viability of agriculture itself.

Acknowledgements

We are especially grateful to our editors, Bruce Gardner and Gordon Rausser, for their extraordinary patience and support, and for their many insightful comments. We also thank Joshua Graff Zivin, Eric Lichtenberg and Glenn Sheriff for detailed and thoughtful comments and assistance. Given the range of topics we address, some lying outside our professional expertise, the usual disclaimer applies with unusual force.

References

Aillery, M., R. Shoemaker and M. Caswell (2001), "Agriculture and ecosystem restoration in South Florida: assessing trade-offs from water retention development in the Everglades agricultural area", American Journal of Agricultural Economics 83(1):183–195.

Antle, J., S. Capalbo, E. Elliott, W. Hunt, S. Mooney and K. Paustian (2000), "Understanding and predicting the behavior of managed ecosystems: lessons from agroecosystem research", Prepared for the Workshop on Developing a Research Agenda for Linking Ecological and Socioeconomic Systems, Tempe, AZ, June 5–8, 2000, Mimeo (Department of Agricultural Economics, Montana State University).

Arrow, K.J., B. Bolin, T. Constanza, P. Dasgupta, C. Folke, C.S. Holling, B.-O. Jansson, S. Levin, K.-G. Maler, C. Perrings and D. Pimental (1995), "Economic growth, carrying capacity and the environment", Science 268:520–521.

Becker, E. (2001), "Unlikely allies press to add conservation to farm bill", New York Times, June 18.

Blockstein, D. (1998), "Lyme disease and the passenger pigeon", Science 279:1831.

Carpenter, S.R., D. Ludwig and W.A. Brock (1999), "Management of eutrophication for lakes subject to potentially irreversible change", Ecological Applications 9(3):751–771.

Castro, R., and F. Tattenbach (1997), "The Costa Rican experience with market instruments to mitigate climate change and conserve biodiversity", Paper presented at Workshop on Global Climate Change and Biodiversity, Toronto, Canada, June 24, 1997, Mimeo (Ministry of the Environment and Energy, San Jose, Costa Rica).

Claassen, R., L. Hansen, M. Peters, V. Breneman, M. Weinberg, A. Cattaneo, P. Feather, D. Gadsby, D. Hellerstein, J. Hopkins, P. Johnston, M. Morehart and M. Smith (2001), "Agri-environmental policy at the crossroads: guideposts on a changing landscape", Agricultural Economic Report No. 794 (Economic Research Service, U.S. Department of Agriculture, Washington, DC).

Cooper, G. (1999), "Canada gets appetite for U.S. carbon credits", Environmental Finance 1(2):6–7.

Costanza, R., R. d'Arge, R. de Groot, S. Farber, M. Grasso, B. Hannon, K. Limburg, S. Naeem, R.V. O'Neill, J. Paruelo, G.G. Rakin, P. Sutton and M. van den Belt (1997), "The value of the world's ecosystem services and natural capital", Nature 387(15):253–260.

Daily, G.C. (ed.) (1997), Nature's Services: Societal Dependence on Natural Ecosystems (Island Press, Washington, DC).

Daily, G.C., P. Matson and P. Vitousek (1997), "Ecosystem services supplied by the soil", in: G.C. Daily, ed., Nature's Services (Island Press, Washington, DC) Chapter 7.

Doering, O.C., F. Diaz-Hermelo, C. Howard, R. Heimlich, F. Hitzhusen, R. Kazmierczak, J. Lee, L. Libby, W. Milon, T. Prato and M. Ribaudo (1999), "Evaluation of the economic costs and benefits of methods for reducing nutrient loads to the Gulf of Mexico", Topic 6 Report for the Integrated Assessment on Hypoxia in the Gulf of Mexico, NOAA Coastal Ocean Program Decision Analysis Series No. 20 (U.S. Department of Commerce, National Oceanic and Atmospheric Administration, Washington, DC).

Gjertsen, H., and C. Barrett (2001), "Context-dependent biodiversity conservation management regimes", Mimeo (Department of Applied Economics and Management, Cornell University).

Hanna, S. (1998), "Institutions for marine ecosystems: economic incentives and fishery management", Ecological Applications 8(1):170–174.

Heal, G.M. (2000), Nature and the Marketplace: Capturing the Value of Ecosystem Services (Island Press, Washington, DC).

Heal, G.M., G.C. Daily, P.R. Ehrlich, J. Salzman, C. Boggs, J. Hellmanmn, J. Hughes, C. Kremen and T. Ricketts (2001), "Protecting natural capital through ecosystem service districts", Stanford Environmental Law Journal 20(2):333–364.

Levin, S. (1999), Fragile Dominion: Complexity and the Commons (Perseus Books, Reading, MA).

Lichtenberg, E. (2002), "Agriculture and the environment", in: B.L. Gardner and G.C. Rausser, eds., Handbook of Agricultural Economics, Vol. 2 (North-Holland, Amsterdam) 1249–1313.

López, R. (2002), "The economics of agriculture in developing countries: the role of the environment", in: B.L. Gardner and G.C. Rausser, eds., Handbook of Agricultural Economics, Vol. 2 (North-Holland, Amsterdam) 1213–1247.

Mendelsohn, R., W.D. Nordhaus and D. Shaw (1994), "The impact of global warming on agriculture: a Ricardian analysis", American Economic Review 84(4):753–771.

Moura Costa, P. (1998), The Costa Rican System of Direct Payment for Environmental Services (EcoSecurities, Oxford, UK).

Myers, N. (1995), "Tropical deforestation: population, poverty and biodiversity", in: T. Swanson, ed., The Economics and Ecology of Biodiversity Decline: The Forces Driving Global Change (Cambridge University Press, Cambridge).

Nabhan, G.P. and S.L. Buchmann (1997), "Services provided by pollinators", in: G.C. Daily, ed., Nature's Services (Island Press, Washington, DC) 133–150 (Chapter 8).

Nabhan, G.P. and S.L. Buchmann (1998), Forgotten Pollinators (Island Press, Washington, DC).

National Assessment Synthesis Team (2000), Climate Change Impacts on the United States: The Potential Consequences of Climate Variability and Change (U.S. Global Change Research Program, Washington, DC).

Ostrom, E. (2002), "Common-pool resources and institutions: toward a revised theory", in: B.L. Gardner and G.C. Rausser, eds., Handbook of Agricultural Economics, Vol. 2 (North-Holland, Amsterdam) 1315–1339.

Rausser, G.C., and A.A. Small (2000), "Valuing research leads: bioprospecting and the conservation of genetic resources", Journal of Political Economy 108(1):173–206.

Simpson, R.D., R. Sedjo and J. Reid (1996), "Valuing biodiversity for use in pharmaceutical research", Journal of Political Economy 104:163–185.

Serageldin, I. (1994), Water Supply, Sanitation, and Environmental Sustainability: The Financing Challenge (The World Bank, Washington, DC).

Smith, F.D.M., G.C. Daily and P.R. Ehrlich (1995), "Human population dynamics and biodiversity loss", in: T.M. Swanson, ed., The Economics and Ecology of Biodiversity Decline: The Forces Driving Global Change (Cambridge University Press, Cambridge).

Tilman, D., J. Fargione, B. Wolff, C. D'Antonio, A. Dobson, R. Howarth, D. Schindler, W.H. Schlesinger, D. Simberloff and D. Swackhamer (2001), "Forecasting agriculturally driven global environmental change", Science 292(13):281–284.

Tschirhart, J. (2000), "General equilibrium of an ecosystem", Journal of Theoretical Biology, February.

United States Geological Survey (1999), The quality of our nation's waters – nutrients and pesticides (USGS Circular 1225, Reston, VA).

Vitousek, P.M., H.A. Mooney, J. Lubchenco and J.M. Melillo (1997), "Human domination of the Earth's ecosystems", Science 277(5325):494–499.

Wardle, D.A., K.I. Bonner and G.M. Barker (2000), "Stability of ecosystem properties in response to above-ground functional group richness and composition", Oikos 89(1):11–23.

Wu, J.-J., D. Zilberman and B. Babcock (2001), "Environmental and distributional impacts of conservation targeting strategies", Journal of Environmental Economics and Management 41(3):333–350.

PART 4

AGRICULTURE IN THE MACROECONOMY

Chapter 26

APPLIED GENERAL EQUILIBRIUM ANALYSIS
OF AGRICULTURAL AND RESOURCE POLICIES

THOMAS W. HERTEL

Center for Global Trade Analysis, Department of Agricultural Economics, Purdue University, W. Lafayette, IN

Contents

Handbook of Agricultural Economics, Volume 2, Edited by B. Gardner and G. Rausser
© *2002 Elsevier Science B.V. All rights reserved*

Abstract

This chapter reviews the literature on applied general equilibrium analysis of agricultural and resource policies. It begins with a historical overview, followed by an assessment of the benefits of this methodology for examining sectoral policies. The chapter then turns to questions of disaggregation of commodities, households, regions and factors of production. Parameter specification and model closure are discussed, as well as problems of modeling policies which affect agriculture. There are also special sections on agriculture and the environment, product differentiation and imperfect competition, and model validation. The chapter closes with a discussion of future challenges to the field.

Keywords

general equilibrium, agricultural policy, international trade modeling

JEL classification: Q11

1. Introduction

Applied general equilibrium analysis as we know it today has intellectual origins in the debate over the feasibility of the centralized computation of a Pareto optimal allocation of resources within an economy [Whalley (1986)]. During the first half of this century, quantitative economists were preoccupied with the question of whether or not it was computationally feasible to solve the associated system of behavioral equations. Since that time, rapid developments in operations research have proven the optimists correct. It became possible to solve very large models representing national economies and indeed, the global economy. Initially these were solved as centralized planning problems, intended to deduce the optimal allocation of resources in the economy. With the demise of central planning, decentralized "computable" general equilibrium models have become dominant. While this has not brought an end to the debate over the operational relevance of general equilibrium theory, the increasing use of such models in policy analysis has served to sharpen the debate. It now focuses heavily on questions of model specification, parameter choice, and the appropriate representation of policies [Whalley (1986)]. In this sense, many of the issues raised in this survey are no different from those which arise in other areas of applied economics. This is why I prefer to use the term "applied" general equilibrium (AGE), in place of the popular "computable" general equilibrium (CGE) label.

Leif Johansen (1960) developed the first operational AGE model in the late 1950s. Variants of this model are still used in Norway [Schreiner and Larsen (1985)]. Since Johansen's path-breaking contribution, AGE models have been applied to a very wide range of topics. John Shoven and John Whalley and their students spearheaded work in the analysis of tax issues [Shoven and Whalley (1992)] and Whalley (1985) led the way with multiregion AGE modeling of trade policy questions. The Australian school of AGE modeling, led by Peter Dixon, has been analyzing issues of protection in the Australian economy for more than twenty years [e.g., Dixon et al. (1982)]. Applied general equilibrium models have also been popular in the development economics literature [Dervis et al. (1982), Robinson (1988)].

This survey focuses on AGE modeling issues and applications related to agricultural policy analysis. In order to keep this task manageable, I have elected to limit the bulk of the discussion to issues arising in comparative static, AGE analysis of agricultural policies in national market economies, as well as globally. As noted above, there are a number of surveys of AGE analysis focusing specifically on developing economies. To this might be added the work of Sadoulet and de Janvry (1995), which has a strong developing economy orientation. While many of the issues are common, regardless of the level of economic development, there are some salient differences having to do with underdeveloped markets and other rigidities. I will not have much to say about these "structural" issues here, as they tend to be locationally and institutionally specific.

Additionally, I will not attempt to cover the specialized topics relating to AGE analysis under uncertainty or dynamics.[1]

Another area of modeling omitted in this survey has to do with the incorporation of financial variables in the model. This work, aimed at a synthesis of micro- and macro-economics, is quite challenging. In his 1991 review, Sherman Robinson highlights the theoretical tension between the neoclassical paradigm and AGE models with financial behavior. "We are still far from a theoretical reconciliation between Walras and Keynes and empirical models cannot help but reflect the theoretical gap" (p. 1522). Nevertheless, the need for this type of synthesis remains. In their recent survey of issues arising in this area, Bevan and Adam (1997) point out that many of the structural adjustment packages presented to developing countries and economies in transition ignore the real sector consequences of their macroeconomic prescriptions. Analysis of monetary variables in an AGE model could help to fill this gap, and this clearly represents an important topic for research [see, for example, McKibbin and Sachs (1991)]. However, as the Bevan and Adam survey indicates, no clear consensus exists and many difficult issues remain to be resolved. Consequently, all of the work reviewed below will relate only to *real* models, in which monetary variables, such as the money supply, price levels, and nominal exchange rates, have no role to play.

2. Why applied general equilibrium analysis of agriculture?

2.1. Benefits of AGE analysis

An important question to be raised at the outset of this survey bears on the relevance of AGE analysis for agriculture. With food and agriculture representing an ever-shrinking share of GDP and consumer expenditure, why should we go to the trouble of constructing an economy-wide model to analyze policies in these sectors? There are several important advantages offered by this approach to policy analysis.

Household focus: Traditional agricultural economic analysis has tended to focus on commodities, and associated factor returns. In contrast, AGE models begin with households as the primitive concept. Households supply factors of production and consume goods and services. Welfare in the model is computed directly in terms of household utility and not some abstract summation of producer, consumer, and taxpayer surplus. After all, most households embody a combination of all three of these attributes, namely, income generation, consumer expenditure, and the payment of taxes or the

---

[1] For a recent AGE application with uncertainty, which focuses on agriculture, see Boussard and Christensen (1997). Readers interested in intertemporal models are referred to Keuschnigg and Kohler (1997), McKibbin and Wang (1998), Wilcoxen (1989). Recursive-dynamic applications are quite common in agriculture [Fischer et al. (1988), Burniaux and van der Mensbrugghe (1991), Wang (1997), and Diao et al. (1998)] have an application drawing on endogenous growth theory.

receipt of subsidies. The focus also on people, services, resources, and the environment, instead of just commodities, is increasingly important, as the share of farm household income generated outside of agriculture increases.[2]

Finite resources and accounting consistency: AGE models rely on social accounting matrices (SAMs) for their empirical structure [Pyatt and Round (1979), Hanson and Robinson (1988)]. These SAMs detail all the basic accounting identities which must hold for the economy to be in equilibrium. Those who work with AGE models quickly recognize that these identities are as important as the behavioral assumptions. The fact that households cannot spend more than they earn, or that the same unit of labor, land or capital cannot be simultaneously employed in two different places, serves to tightly circumscribe the range of possible GE outcomes.

A related issue has to do with the fiscal integrity of the analysis. Historically, agricultural economists have rarely posed the question, Who pays for farm subsidies? [Alston and Hurd (1990)]. Yet it has been shown, using AGE methods, that the marginal excess burden of raising revenue in the United States is often very high [e.g., Ballard et al. (1985b)]. By incorporating an explicit budget constraint for the government, AGE models can capture the cost of higher levels of agricultural subsidies – or alternatively, the fiscal benefits of reducing expenditures on farm programs. Chambers (1995) takes the distortionary effect of taxation into account in his general equilibrium analysis of alternative forms of agricultural subsidies. He shows that traditional, partial equilibrium calculations of farm subsidy incidence misrepresent social losses and systematically overestimate the benefits agricultural producers derive from farm programs by ignoring the impact on government revenue requirements.

A final benefit resulting from the exhaustive accounting in AGE analysis derives from the applicability of Walras' Law. This "law" states that if (a) all households are on their budget constraint (subject to explicitly defined inter-household transfers or borrowing), (b) all firms exhaust their revenues on factor payments, taxes, and transfers of excess profits to households, and (c) all markets are in equilibrium (i.e., supply = demand), then one of the equilibrium relationships in the model will be redundant and may be dropped. This provides an extremely powerful check on the consistency of the AGE model, since the redundant equilibrium condition may be checked – after the fact – to verify that there were no errors in data base management, model coding, or possibly in the theoretical structure. Indeed, most AGE modelers will admit to having discovered many errors via the use of this check.[3] Given the complexity of implementing a large-scale empirical model, this can be a very powerful tool indeed.

---

[2] The latest information from the U.S. indicates that 88 percent of farm household income is derived from nonfarm sources [United States Department of Agriculture (USDA) (1995)].

[3] For example, if one decided to introduce imperfect competition in an existing AGE model, but forgot to distribute the excess profits to owners of the enterprise, Walras' Law would reveal this in the form of insufficient demand in the omitted market.

Second-best analysis: One of the distinguishing features of agricultural policy analysis is the high degree of public intervention in the farm and food sector. This includes programs which (a) subsidize inputs such as credit, water, and fertilizer, (b) restrict acreage planted to certain crops, (c) intervene in output markets with subsidies or production quotas, (d) subsidize (or tax less) the consumption of food relative to other goods and services, and (e) intervene at the border with export subsidies, import tariffs and quotas, etc. This complex web of policy interventions makes it very difficult to anticipate the efficiency consequences of a marginal perturbation in, or reform of, farm and food policies [Clarete and Roumasset (1990)]. Chambers (1995) derives conditions under which, *at the margin*, land retirement may dominate decoupled transfers to producers due to their impact on the government budget and hence existing levels of distortionary taxation.

In an AGE application focusing on U.S. agriculture in the mid-1980s, Hertel and Tsigas (1991) show that, *at the margin*, tradable output quotas could have been welfare-enhancing. This stemmed from the fact that existing agricultural, food, and tax policies had retained excessive resources in agriculture and the quotas would provide a mechanism for moving some of these inputs out of the farm sector. However, those authors also show that the supply control approach which was preferred at the time, namely acreage restrictions, would have reduced efficiency in the economy. Finally, they demonstrate that the first-best alternative of removing all of the distortions would generate welfare gains an order of magnitude larger than the tradable quotas. In summary, AGE models provide an excellent vehicle for conducting welfare analysis in a second-best setting, and this makes them particularly well-suited for use in agricultural policy analysis.

Inter-industry linkages: Often when one is conducting policy analysis in the farm sector, it is difficult to know where to draw the line between the commodities and sectors affected by a given policy and the rest of the economy. More generally, distinguishing agriculture from non-agriculture in the modern, industrialized economies has become quite difficult. Increasingly, large, commercial farms contract out some of their operations. The firms providing these services – ranging from pesticide applications to financial services – may not be exclusively tied to agriculture. Sayan and Demir (1988) assess the degree of interdependence between agriculture and non-agriculture industries in Turkey using techniques from input–output analysis. They find that when backward linkages from agriculture to non-agriculture are ignored, the agricultural multipliers are understated by about 20 percent. Linkages from the agriculture to non-farm sectors producing energy, fiber, and other nonfood items are also important. When backward linkages from non-agriculture to agriculture are omitted from Sayan and Demir's analysis, the non-farm multipliers for Turkey are about 8 percent too low. A final, important reason for capturing the non-farm linkages has to do with the diversification of farm households' earnings. They often have significant financial or wage earning interests in other sectors, so that their welfare depends on much more than the changes in agricultural activity.

Economy-wide perspective: AGE analysis also provides a valuable tool for putting things in an economy-wide perspective. Microeconomic theory emphasizes the importance of relative, as opposed to absolute, levels of economic variables. For example, in the case of technological progress, it is not the absolute rate of total factor productivity (TFP) growth that matters for agricultural production and prices, but rather the rate of TFP growth *relative to* the non-farm sector [Simon (1947), Gruen (1961)]. Similarly, a tax reform which raises tax rates for agriculture may not discourage farming activity if the non-agricultural tax rates rise by more. In an AGE analysis of the U.S. tax system, Hertel and Tsigas (1988a) find that relatively low tax rates on capital, labor, and output in agriculture, as well as relatively lower consumption taxes on food, have all conferred an implicit subsidy on the farm and food sector. Nowhere is the importance of relative vs. absolute comparisons more evident than in international trade. It is very common for agricultural economists to compare production costs in different regions, and, when they are lower in one country than another, to conclude that country is more competitive. However, this ignores the most fundamental proposition of international trade, namely, that countries will export the product in which they have a *comparative advantage*. Where do they go wrong? Any partial equilibrium comparison of costs invariably must make an assumption about the terms of trade. Yet the terms of trade are fundamentally endogenous. They adjust to ensure external balance. In equilibrium, a given economy may be the most efficient producer of both agriculture and manufactures. But if its comparative advantage is in manufactures, it will import agricultural products.

In order to better understand where partial equilibrium analysis of competitiveness can lead one astray, it is useful to think about a specific example. Consider the case whereby the U.S. embarks on an effort to become more competitive by investing in the skill-base of its workforce. *A priori* we might think that this should result in an increase in agricultural output, since a more highly skilled workforce will result in more productive farmers. However, once we take into account general equilibrium constraints, we will find that the opposite conclusion is more likely correct. The reasoning is as follows. First of all, more productive labor will tend to boost output across the board. Consequently, at constant prices, exports will increase and imports will be displaced by domestic production in all sectors. Furthermore, foreign investment is also likely to increase in response to the higher level of labor productivity. This leads to a violation of the general equilibrium condition for external balance:

$$S - I = X + R - M, \tag{1}$$

where S = national savings, I = investment, X = exports, R = international transfers, and M = imports.

Without any general equilibrium adjustment, the left-hand side of (1) becomes more negative (I) and the right-hand side becomes more positive (X, M). Something clearly must adjust to ensure that (1) will hold. In general equilibrium, this is the real exchange rate. Goods produced in the U.S. must become more expensive abroad, and imports must become relatively cheaper. As the system re-equilibrates, what will happen to farm output? Since agriculture is relatively more intensive in land, the availability of which is unchanged, and relatively less intensive in skilled labor, the supply of which has increased, we expect agricultural outputs (and exports) to *fall* in this instance. (This is the well-known Rybczynski theorem.) In summary, here we have a case where the economy-wide constraints are strong enough to actually reverse partial equilibrium intuition.

2.2. Hidden challenges to AGE analysis

Having made the argument that general equilibrium analysis is called for in some circumstances, the next question is, What type of AGE model is appropriate? In a paper titled "Hidden challenges in recent applied general equilibrium exercises", Whalley (1986) emphasizes the need to move from general to special-purpose models if AGE analysis is to become more policy relevant. He notes that the AGE models of the 1960s, 1970s, and early 1980s were developed partially in order to "demonstrate the feasibility of constructing applied general equilibrium models... showing they could handle much larger dimensions than theoretical models" (p. 37). Application of such models to particular policy issues often involved redesigning the basic model, while carrying along considerable excess baggage. With model construction and computational cost now less burdensome, Whalley suggests that future efforts be directed at developing special purpose models, tailored to address specific issues. He notes that particular attention should be paid to parameter specification and the manner in which policies are modeled. The remainder of this survey may be viewed as an overview of recent attempts to meet some of these "hidden challenges", which have often limited the impact which general purpose AGE models have had on agricultural policy issues.

Most of the early AGE models of developed market economics (DMEs) treated agriculture (possibly along with forestry and fisheries) as a single, aggregate sector, producing one homogeneous product [e.g., Ballard et al. (1985a)]. This type of aggregation was essential in order to permit complete commodity coverage at a relatively uniform level of aggregation. Also, this is often the level of aggregation provided in published input–output tables. However, when it comes to analyzing farm policies, more detail is required. This is because intervention varies widely across farm commodities, with some receiving a great deal of support (1985 U.S. sugar prices were 500 percent of the world price), while others (such as the U.S. poultry industry) are virtually free of intervention. By lumping all of these products into one single aggregate, little can be said that would carry any weight with agricultural policymakers. The question of appropriate disaggregation of AGE models for agricultural policy analysis will be addressed in Section 3 of the chapter.

A second important feature of general purpose models which has limited their applicability to agricultural issues is their failure to distinguish land from other capital inputs. Yet the presence of farmland in the agricultural production function is critical. It is perhaps the most distinguishing feature of this sector of the economy. Furthermore, land can also be an important instrument of public policy. Historically, a significant aspect of intervention in U.S. agriculture involves the idling of productive acreage in order to raise commodity prices. The European Union and Japan have recently also directed more of their policies towards limiting land use. In addition, farmland prices are themselves often a policy target. With relatively limited alternative uses (outside of agriculture), the price of farmland not adjacent to cities tends to be determined predominantly by expected farm product prices. Therefore land prices are potentially quite volatile. Since land usually represents the major form of wealth-holding for the farm population, the impact of public policy on farm prices and hence returns to landowners is of paramount importance to farmers and agricultural policymakers. There is simply no way around dealing with land markets if one wishes to appropriately model the agricultural sector, and so disaggregation of factors of production, including land, is also dealt with in Section 3.

A third critical limitation of the most common, general purpose AGE models of the last two decades is their tendency to devote too little attention to the specification of key behavioral parameters in the farm and food system. As a consequence, there is a wide gulf between the partial equilibrium models currently used in agricultural policy analysis, and the partial equilibrium behavior of their AGE counterparts. In some cases these discrepancies may be justified. However, in most instances the AGE models' parameters simply lack sufficient empirical justification. As a consequence, they often generate implausible results.

Generous federal and state funding, and close working relationships with other scientists and with industry, have combined to result in an agricultural economic data base which is the envy of many applied economists. There is also more than half a century of applied econometric analysis of supply and demand behavior in agricultural markets upon which to draw. To be effective, any AGE modeler who wishes to seriously tackle farm and food policy issues must be willing and able to capitalize on this wealth of data and behavioral information. In some cases this will require use of more general functional forms for representing preferences and technology in the AGE model. Section 4 of this chapter addresses the issue of parameter specification as well as the related questions of length-of-run and model closure.

Section 5 of this chapter focuses on one of the specific hidden challenges identified by John Whalley – namely the need for explicit modeling of public policies. There are many cases in which simple *ad valorem* equivalent representations, common among general purpose models, give rise to inaccurate, or even misleading, conclusions. Of course, time spent on detailed modeling of individual policies must be balanced against the need to provide a comprehensive picture of distortions in the economy. For some purposes this extends to analyses of agriculture and the environment, which is the topic of Section 6.

Section 7 addresses a few of the issues which arise in the context of product differentiation and imperfect competition. This can be very important when it comes to validation of AGE models, which is the subject of Section 8. The chapter closes with some thoughts about future directions for AGE analysis of agricultural and resource policies.

3. Data and aggregation issues: How detailed should the model be?

3.1. Sectoral and commodity disaggregation

Obviously there are limits to the amount of detail which can be provided by an economy-wide model. The general purpose models have logically opted for a relatively balanced treatment of the entire economy, given the constraints imposed by national accounting conventions. For example, the U.S. tax model outlined in Ballard et al. (1985a, Table 4.13), has nineteen sectors. Sectoral gross output, as a percentage of the U.S. total, ranges from slightly less than one percent (mining) to a little more than 10 percent (services). But most sectors fall in the 2–8 percent range.

A special purpose model focused on agricultural policy will necessarily be more lopsided in order to focus attention on particular issues. Perhaps the most extreme example of this is the world wheat model of Trela et al. (1987). In their framework, each country consumes two goods: wheat, and everything else. This permits them to focus on the global effects of wheat policies within a consistent AGE model. It also makes data and calibration particularly straightforward. Benchmark equilibrium wheat production and consumption data are readily obtained from, for example, the Food and Agriculture Organization (FAO), and they may then obtain data on the other sector as a residual. Constant elasticity of substitution (CES) or transformation (CET) preferences and technology are calibrated to reproduce published supply and demand elasticities for wheat, and they are "off and running" with a model. The IIASA model was based on the same idea, only its authors disaggregated agricultural production into ten commodities, with one residual, "nonagriculture" commodity [Fischer et al. (1988)]. The multiple commodity work of Horridge and Pearce (1988) – based on the Tyers and Anderson (1992) partial equilibrium (PE) trade model – as well as that of Peterson et al. (1994) and McDonald (1990) – both based on USDA's SWOPSIM model [Roningen et al. (1991)] – are similar in spirit.

Given the difficulty of constructing a benchmark equilibrium data base for an AGE-trade model, there are obvious advantages in a model specification which has a large "residual" sector. However, there are important drawbacks associated with this backdoor approach to arriving at a complete AGE model. The first of these is due to aggregation bias. Gehlhar and Frandsen (1998) illustrate how aggregation of agricultural sectors changes key qualitative findings with respect to Asia-Pacific Economic Cooperation (APEC) trade liberalization. This is due to the tendency to create false competition between countries producing fundamentally different products (e.g., rice and wheat). Excessive aggregation also can alter the welfare effects by smoothing out tariff peaks which may exist at a disaggregate level. Bach and Martin (1997) show how this problem can be overcome via the use of a Trade Restrictiveness Index (TRI) in concert with an AGE model. They find that the welfare gains from tariff reform in China double when their analysis begins at the level of individual tariff lines, as opposed to simple aggregation to 10 sectors.

Another problem with excessive sectoral and commodity aggregation stems from the fact that the dividing line between the agricultural and nonagricultural economy is not at all clear. Furthermore, in the case of some agricultural policies, the "gray" area between these two groups of sectors is where the most interesting "action" is. Consider, for example, the U.S. sugar program. Support for U.S. sugar producers is achieved indirectly by administering an import quota on partially refined sugar, which is adjusted until the domestic price of sugar reaches a pre-specified target. The greatest source of pressure on the U.S. sugar quota has come not from the farm sector's supply response, but rather from the manufacturers of substitute sweeteners – in particular, high fructose corn sweeteners (HFCS). The HFCS industry is dominated by a handful of firms that have become a very effective lobby for the sugar program. They have also made a concerted attempt to mobilize corn producers in support of this import quota on sugar, arguing that the derived demand for corn generated by production of this sweetener substitute lends considerable support to the market price of corn. While it has already been partially processed, traded sugar must be further refined for use in the domestic market. As a consequence, successive tightening of the quota has seriously hurt domestic sugar refiners.

Rendleman and Hertel (1993) show how the sugar quota can be analyzed using a special purpose AGE model. They conclude that short-run losses to sugar producers and the manufacturers of substitute sweeteners are, to a great extent, offset by gains to the ailing sugar refiners when the quota is eliminated. They also conclude that corn producer support for the U.S. sugar program is likely misplaced, since the HFCS industry produces by-products, corn oils and glutenous feed, which compete with corn grain. Consequently analysis of the sugar program which ignored the livestock sector seriously overstated the impact on corn prices. The message here is that analysis of particular commodity programs often requires disaggregation of nonfarm, food manufacturing activity as well.

Applied GE models attempting to address the overall impact of farm and food programs need to disaggregate sufficiently to isolate distinct types of commodity market intervention. Hertel, Thompson and Tsigas (1989) distinguish nine different farm products and about a dozen agri-processing sectors in their attempt to assess the impact of unilateral agricultural policy liberalization in the United States. In their work on U.S. agricultural policies, Robinson et al. (1989) began with a model in which three farm sectors were broken out. They subsequently found it desirable to disaggregate to eight agricultural and eight food processing sectors [e.g., Hanson et al. (1989), Kilkenny and Robinson (1990)] in order to capture the major differences among various farm and food policies.

The question of disaggregation becomes more difficult in those cases where the general equilibrium modeler wishes to deal explicitly with agricultural trade and related domestic policies, among a variety of countries. This is because multiple data sources must be used, making disaggregation more difficult. The OECD "Rural-Urban, North–South" (RUNS) model [Burniaux and van der Mensbrugghe (1991)] had 15 commodities, of which 8 pertain to farm and food products. More recently, the Australian Industry Commission developed a 16-region, 37-commodity model with 11 farm and food sectors, nicknamed SALTER [Dee et al. (1992)]. Much of the data base underpinning SALTER was adopted by the Global Trade Analysis Project and built into the GTAP model [Hertel (1997)]. The most recent version of the GTAP database disaggregates 20 farm and food products and 30 non-food products. However, obtaining this degree of sectoral detail for many different countries necessarily involves some compromises. Also, even with that degree of sectoral detail, the breakdown may not be sufficient for a particular policy issue in a specific country.

3.2. Household disaggregation

From the point of view of welfare analysis, disaggregation of *households* in the economy is probably even more important than sectoral disaggregation. Unfortunately, data on factor payments to households is difficult to obtain. For this reason many researchers choose to aggregate all private consumption into a single household. Some notable exceptions in the case of research on U.S. agriculture include Boyd (1988), who distinguishes households by income class, and Kilkenny (1993), who distinguishes rural and urban households. Of course income distribution is often much more skewed in the case of developing countries, and consequently there has been more of this sort of work done in that context [e.g., Brandao et al. (1994), de Janvry and Sadoulet (1987), Robinson et al. (1993), Warr and Coxhead (1993)]. If AGE analysis is to address the important *distributional* implications of farm and food policies, this type of household disaggregation must become standard practice. This will require additional data work on the part of the researcher.

Given the strong interest in income distributional consequences of public policies, some researchers have adopted a second-best approach to the problem. In particular, they first solve a household-aggregated model for a set of relative price changes for commodities and factors of production. They then engage in *ex post* calculations of the implied welfare changes for different household groups. This can make it feasible to examine the welfare implications for thousands of different household types. A recent example of this approach in the analysis of Vietnamese rice policies is provided by Minot and Goletti (1997). Provided the implied changes in income distribution have minimal implications for aggregate commodity demand, this is a very attractive approach to the problem of household disaggregation, since it permits the researcher to report results at a very high level of detail.

3.3. Regional disaggregation

Just as it is often necessary to disaggregate sectors and households, so too is regional disaggregation frequently required to adequately capture the impact of agricultural and resource policies. Such disaggregation can take place at the sub-national level. For example, Kraybill et al. (1992) disaggregate the U.S. into the State of Virginia and the rest of the U.S. in order to analyze the regional incidence of national macroeconomic policy. A major challenge in such efforts at sub-national disaggregation arises from the scarcity of state-level social accounting matrices or input–output tables. Typically these must be "estimated" based on national accounts and selected state level information (e.g., employment by sector and final demand). Another problem arises from the absence of observations on intra-national (inter-state) trade flows. As a consequence, multi-region AGE models are more common at the international level, where researchers can build on national accounts and international data sources on trade-flows.

International AGE models may be broken into two groups: those with a regional focus, and those with global coverage. In some cases, the issue being considered has a clear regional dimension which suggests analysis in the context of a two- or three-country model. The U.S.–Mexico component of the North American Free Trade Agreement (NAFTA) was successfully analyzed by Robinson et al. (1993) in a two-region (U.S.–Mexico) model wherein the rest of the world responses were simply captured with excess supply and demand equations. Harrison et al. (1989, 1991) develop a disaggregated data base for the European Union in order to analyze the welfare and distributional consequences of policies associated with the European Community.

Increasingly, however, many policymakers are seeking answers to global economic policy questions. In this case, global applied general equilibrium analysis is often the most appropriate tool. The drawn-out negotiations under the Uruguay Round of the GATT/WTO provided ample opportunity for quantitative analysis. The volume edited by Martin and Winters (1996) offers the most comprehensive analysis of the Uruguay Round Agreement. All five of the quantitative assessments contained therein are based on global AGE models. While these global models generally share the same basic structure as the national and regional models, there are some specific issues which arise in making the transition from one to the other. Hertel, Ianchovichina and McDonald (1997) provide an extensive discussion of these differences.

In some cases, global modeling is desired, not because the policy scenario under consideration is global in nature, but rather because the consequences of a regional shock are expected to be widespread. Thus Arndt et al. (1997) use a global AGE model to analyze which countries gain, and which lose, from rapid economic growth in China. Coyle, McKibbin and Wang (1998) use a global AGE model to analyze the impact of the Asian financial crisis on U.S. agriculture. One reason why the list of global AGE analyses has been growing so rapidly in recent years is the public availability of a global economic database to support such studies. Nicknamed GTAP (Global Trade Analysis Project), this database is now in its fourth release [Hertel (1997)].[4]

---

[4] For a comprehensive listing of references to global AGE studies based on the GTAP data set (450 at the time of this writing), the reader may visit the following web site: *www.gtap.agecon.purdue.edu*

3.4. Agriculture as a multiproduct industry

The generic, general purpose AGE model is typically characterized by single-commodity, constant returns to scale industries. However, agriculture departs significantly from this mold. Econometric tests for nonjointness in aggregate agricultural production are consistently rejected [e.g., Ball (1988)]. There are numerous explanations for this apparent jointness in production, including technological interdependence, the presence of lumpy/shared inputs, and the presence of an allocatable fixed input, namely land [Shumway et al. (1984)].

The problem posed by the presence of multi-product sectors in an AGE model is that the addition of potential output–output and input–output interactions vastly increases the number of parameters to be specified. One common solution is to impose input–output separability [e.g., Dixon et al. (1982)]. The implication of this particular restriction is that the optimal output mix is invariant to changes in relative input prices. This is a strong assumption which violates one's intuition (e.g., the optimal mix of corn and soybeans is sensitive to the price of fertilizer). It also is persistently rejected by the data [e.g., Ball (1988)].

Another problem confronting the modeler seeking to treat agriculture as a multiple product sector is the presence of commodity-specific factor market interventions. For example, in order to qualify for corn output subsidies in the U.S., it was previously necessary to idle a certain percentage of one's established corn acreage. This in turn had a differential effect on the shadow price of land in corn versus, for example, soybean production. Lee and Helmberger (1985) demonstrate how this can result in own-price effects which are "too small" relative to cross-price effects. As a result, nonconvexities can arise in a multi-product profit function representation of the farm sector.

If one is willing to argue that jointness in agricultural production is due solely to the presence of an allocatable fixed input, then it is possible to revert to modeling commodity production as a set of single product activities – bound together by the presence of a fixed amount of land. Indeed, attempts have been made to estimate agricultural technology under these assumptions [Just et al. (1983)]. It is also a common specification in agriculturally focused AGE models, and has the advantage of facilitating commodity-specific interventions in the land market [Hertel and Tsigas (1991), Kilkenny (1991)].

3.5. Producer heterogeneity

Another type of heterogeneity in the farm sector is that which arises due to differences in producers. This could arise due to differences in entrepreneurial capacity, as hypothesized by Friedman (1976), or due to differences in risk preferences, or for other reasons. In any case, we observe a great deal of variation in farm size as well as production technology in the farm sector. One reason such differences can persist in the face of market forces is the tendency for farmland to absorb any differences in profitability. As long as the farmer owns his or her own land, and as long as he or she is willing to take a sub-market return on this asset, then they can remain in farming in spite of lower levels of efficiency. This is particularly likely in the case of smaller, part-time operations in which farming is part of the household's lifestyle.

In the U.S., a relatively small group of commercial farms produces the majority of agricultural output. There are a great number of small farms, many of which are part-time operations. For example, in 1987, 52 percent of the farms had sales of less than $10,000 and consequently accounted for only 6 percent of gross farm income [Sumner (1990)]. The inexorable downward slide of average costs leaves small producers with below average, sometimes negative, returns to their equity and own-labor. This process is driven by persistent technological change, and at any particular moment, the agriculture sector is in a state of disequilibrium with regard to the composition and size of farms. For example, in their econometric analysis of the period from 1947–74, Brown and Christensen (1981) show that, while family labor in agriculture dropped by two-thirds over this period, the estimated optimal level of this input also dropped dramatically. As a result, the ratio of observed to optimal family labor hardly changed.

While the issue of farm size is an important one, it is essential that AGE modelers with an interest in agriculture focus on aspects of the farm sector (a) which are central to the questions they seek to answer, and (b) to which they can contribute some added insight. I would argue that neither of these applies (in most instances) to the farm size issue in developed market economies. Most production comes from a relatively small group of commercial farms. These operations dominate the data used to estimate price elasticities, and their behavior is more nearly consistent with the neoclassical paradigm prevalent in AGE analysis. Thus, in most cases, we should focus on modeling representative commercial farm operations. Modeling the evolution of the distribution of farms by size is an important policy issue, but not one in which AGE models have any comparative advantage.

Of course there are exceptional cases in which farm size becomes relevant for AGE analysis of agricultural policies. A good example is provided by the Canadian dairy program, whereby individual farms are assigned a production quota. Econometric evidence indicates that this has contributed to the presence of unexploited scale economies [Moschini (1988)]. Thus it is important to build this inefficiency into the initial equilibrium. Robidoux et al. (1989) have done this (both for dairy and poultry) in their analysis of Canadian farm policies. They find that agricultural policy liberalization generates considerable "rationalization" in the dairy industry as some farms exit and the remaining operations move down their long-run average cost curve.[5]

---

[5] In addition to the differences in farm size, there are other observed types of heterogeneity which can have important policy implications. Using USDA survey data, Hertel et al. (1996) show that Indiana corn producers exhibit strikingly different propensities to apply nitrogen fertilizer to their crops. Even after controlling for terrain, soil type, manure applications, and crop rotation, those authors observe application rates ranging from 30 to more than 200 lb./acre in 1989. In the face of a proposed tax on nitrogen fertilizer, the authors argue that this producer heterogeneity can give rise to an additional source of nitrogen-land substitution –

3.6. *Establishing an appropriate benchmark*

The vagaries of weather, long gestation periods, price-inelastic demands, and heavy (but unpredictable) intervention by governments all contribute to greater volatility of agricultural assets, relative to their nonfarm counterparts [Irwin et al. (1988)]. It is not uncommon to find enormous swings in the components of agricultural value-added reported in the national accounts. This volatility in observed "cost shares" can translate directly into volatile model results, as has been demonstrated for Australia by Adams and Higgs (1990), using the ORANI model. Since the share of fixed capital and land in the primary factor aggregate is a key parameter in the calibration of ORANI's agricultural supply response (see also Section 4 below), variation in this share translates directly into variation in the supply elasticity. The authors show that such variation can even alter the predicted macroeconomic consequences of farm sector shocks. This led Adams and Higgs to the development of a "representative year" database for Australian agriculture.

In a somewhat more ambitious undertaking, Harrison et al. (1989) construct a sequence of SAMs for the European Community with which they proceed to analyze the same experiment (removal of the Common Agricultural Policy) over a period of 12 years. A logical extension of this effort would be to use this time series data to estimate a representative benchmark equilibrium for the entire economy. A more modest undertaking might involve the econometric estimation of cost shares for the agricultural sector alone.

Finally, there is a question of what benchmark should be used to assess the impact of policies which are due to be implemented over a relatively long period of time. A good example is provided by the Uruguay Round Agreement (URA), concluded in 1995 but due to be phased in over ten years. Furthermore, in the most contentious areas – agriculture and apparel – many of the reforms are "back-loaded", with the deepest cuts in protection scheduled for the later years. Yet most of the studies of this agreement employed data bases which described the global economy in the early 1990s. Bach et al. (1999) evaluate the difference between the welfare effects of the URA in 1992 vs. 2005, where the latter benchmark is constructed by projecting the global economy forward using World Bank estimates of endowment and productivity growth. Since the deepest URA cuts are in Asia, and since this region was projected to grow rather rapidly as well, the authors found that the global gains from the URA were larger in 2005. In addition, they projected that without the URA, the textile and apparel quotas would have become significantly more binding. This, too, serves to make the URA more valuable in 2005 than would have been foreseen in the context of the 1992 global economy.

---

namely a composition effect. As the price of fertilizer rises, it has a strong negative impact on profitability for the most profligate users of this input. This induces a shift of corn land from the high-intensity users to the low-intensity farm managers.

3.7. Treatment of land in AGE models

The role of land in agricultural production is arguably one of its most distinguishing features in terms of AGE analysis. This section focuses on the treatment of farmland in these markets. Here there are two key issues which I will address. The first pertains to the sector-specificity of land. That is, are there significant alternative nonfarm uses for this input which might contribute to determining its price in the long run? The second issue has to do with the heterogeneity of farmland and subsequent limitations on its mobility among uses within the agricultural sector.

Sector-specificity of farmland: Unlike labor and capital, land is geographically immobile. As a result, it is common to assume that it is a sector-specific asset which ultimately bears all of the producer burden of a reduction in farm support. For example, Hertel, Thompson and Tsigas (1989) estimate an 18 percent reduction in land rents following unilateral elimination of U.S. farm programs. Vincent (1989) estimates that Japanese farmland rents would fall by 68 percent following unilateral liberalization in that country's agricultural sector. Is there a chance that such price reductions might stimulate nonagricultural uses of farmland? If so, this type of quantity adjustment would serve to dampen the landowner losses [e.g., McDonald (1990)]. The answer to this question will clearly vary by region and by country. In the U.S., nonagricultural uses have been shown to play a role in determining the value of farmland in selected metropolitan areas [López et al. (1988)], but this has not proven to be an important determinant of aggregate agricultural land values. Furthermore, most of the commodities grown near urban areas are not the traditional program commodities which are most dramatically affected by U.S. farm policy. Thus the potential for nonfarm uses of agricultural land dampening the downward adjustment of rental rates following unilateral agricultural liberalization would seem to be limited.

The case of Japan is quite different. There, the capitalized value of farm program benefits represents a larger share of land's claim on agricultural output. Furthermore, the proximity of farmland to major population centers is much greater. Thus the demand for residential, recreational, and commercial land may be expected to place a significant floor under farmland values. Of course, the degree to which such adjustment can occur depends on accommodating changes in land use legislation. In Japan, "landowners must obtain the permission of the prefecture or of the Ministry of Agriculture, Forestry, and Fisheries in order to transfer farmland into other uses" [ABARE (1988, p. 75)]. Extremely favorable property and inheritance taxation of farmland, coupled with high rates of capital gains taxation, serves to further discourage movement of land into nonfarm uses. As a result, the percentage of land devoted to agricultural uses in the three major metropolitan areas in Japan (16 percent) exceeds the share of this land devoted to residential, commercial, and industrial plant uses (11.5 percent). It also exceeds the share of farmland in Japan's total land area (15 percent) [ABARE (1988, p. 316)]. Despite these distortions in the land market, there is evidence that nonfarm demands support agricultural land values. For example, between 1979 and 1985 the relative price of rice to rice paddy land fell by about 20 percent [ABARE (1988, p. 321)].

Heterogeneity of land: Abstracting from the question of how much land might move between farm and nonfarm uses, there are important modeling issues deriving from the heterogeneity of such land in agricultural production. The capacity of a given acre of land to produce a particular farm product varies with soil type, location in the watershed, and climatic conditions. These characteristics all combine to determine the yield, given a certain level of nonland inputs. To treat all farmland as homogeneous is to assert that one can grow oranges in Minnesota at the same cost as in Florida (i.e., without greenhouses)! Models based on this structure will overstate supply response, since they do not take into account the agronomic and climatic constraints placed on the production of specific farm commodities. The trick for an AGE model is to capture the essence of such constraints without being forced to develop a full-blown model of agricultural production by locality and land type.

Perhaps the simplest method of constraining acreage response in an AGE model is that employed by Hertel and Tsigas (1988a). They specify a transformation function which takes aggregate farmland as an input and distributes it among various uses in response to relative rental rates. Given a finite elasticity of transformation, rental rates will differ across uses, and acreage response may be calibrated to econometrically estimated values.

The next level of complexity in modeling the heterogeneous nature of agricultural land involves drawing a distinction between land types and land uses. In this framework, equilibrium in the land market involves the equalization of after-tax rates of return on any given type of land. However, provided these land types substitute imperfectly in the production of a given crop, there may exist differential rental rates across land types. Robidoux et al. (1989) adopt this type of specification in their AGE model of Canada. They specify CES aggregator functions that combine three land types, each of which is used – to some degree – in the production of six different farm products. An interesting wrinkle in their approach is the way in which they estimate benchmark equilibrium rental rates, by land type. These are obtained by regressing total land rents in each sector on the observed quantity of each land type used in that sector. In equilibrium, the land-specific rental rate (i.e., the coefficient on acreage) must be equal across uses.

The Robidoux et al. approach deals with differences in land type, but not regional or climatic differences. Models designed to assess the effects of climate change, or the regional implications of policy shocks, must disaggregate land endowments still further. Darwin et al. (1995) have taken a similar approach to their analysis of the economic impacts of climate change in a global AGE model focused on agriculture. They disaggregate land classes into six types, each of which is characterized by its length of growing season. These land classes are employed differentially across farming and forestry sectors, according to current patterns of production. In addition, the authors explicitly identify water as an input into the production function of each crop. The authors then turn to the results of the global climate simulation models in order to assess, by region, the impact of alternative climate change scenarios on temperature and precipitation. This causes a shift in each region's land endowment across land classes and therefore causes patterns of agricultural production to change. Darwin et al. are then able to assess the consequences of climate change for patterns of trade, consumption, and welfare.

3.8. The role of water

As can be seen from the previous example, it is often important to distinguish farmland by its access to water. Berck et al. (1991) provide an overview of the use of AGE models to assess water policies. A key question is how to model water supply. Decaluwe et al. (1997) have wrestled with this issue in the context of an AGE model of the Moroccan economy. In particular, they distinguish between groundwater and surface water collected by dams. Supply response is modeled via a Weibull distribution, and their analysis focuses on the economy-wide implication of water pricing policy in Morocco. In contrast, Robinson and Gehlhar (1995) develop an AGE model of Egypt in which land and water are combined in a linear fashion in the sectoral production function. As water scarcity becomes an increasingly important issue in the drier areas of the world, appropriate modeling of the water supply and demand in AGE models will become a pressing area for research.

4. Parameter specification and model closure

4.1. Specification of preferences and technology

Consumer demand: The long history of applied econometric work in agricultural economics represents an asset which AGE modelers must capitalize on if their work is to have an impact on farm and food policy analysis. In the area of consumer demand, for example, there is a considerable body of work available which reports the results of disaggregated, complete demand systems for food and nonfood commodities [e.g., George and King (1971), Huang and Haidacher (1983)]. While there is a strong tendency for food products to be price- and income-inelastic, individual elasticity values vary widely among food groups, with consumer demands for grains being quite unresponsive to price and income, while livestock products are more responsive. It is impossible to capture this diversity of price responses with simple, explicitly additive demand systems such as the Constant Elasticity of Substitution (CES) or the Linear Expenditure System (LES). Some studies simplify even further, by assuming Cobb–Douglas preferences [e.g., Robidoux et al. (1989), Robinson et al. (1989)]. In so doing, the authors risk overstating some uncompensated price elasticities by a full order of magnitude. This is particularly problematic when agricultural price policies are being examined, since consumer demand elasticities are critical in determining the incidence of changes in these policies. By overstating consumers' ability to respond to a price increase, such models will overstate the backward shifting of the effects of such a shock.

This naturally takes us to the problem of functional form, which lurks beneath the surface in any discussion of parameter specification for AGE models. Since the demand (and supply) relations in these models are the outcome of well-defined optimization problems, it is not possible to arbitrarily specify some elasticities and then plug them into the model equations. Any elasticities must be compatible with the parameters of the underlying utility function. This part of the "calibration problem" can be quite challenging. Most of the work on functional forms has focused on "fully flexible" forms, i.e., those which do not arbitrarily restrict the matrix of $N \times (N - 1)/2$ partial substitution elasticities, where N is the number of commodities. Here the work of Diewert and Wales (1987) and Perroni and Rutherford (1995, 1997) on global well-behaved flexible forms is particularly important. However, for significant disaggregations of commodities and sectors, obtaining this much information is simply not possible. Therefore some intermediate ground is often needed.

In a somewhat overlooked 1975 article, Hanoch proposed a class of implicitly additive functional forms which are associated with N independent substitution parameters. He made precisely the argument alluded to above – namely that there may be cases where a generalization of the CES which falls short of being "fully flexible" might be useful. Furthermore, under implicit additivity, N is precisely the number of free parameters required to match up with a vector of N own-price elasticities of supply (demand). In addition, unlike explicitly additive functions, implicit additivity does not rule out complementary relations. The implicit additivity restriction was first employed empirically in order to represent production possibilities in Australian agriculture, within the context of the ORANI model [Vincent et al. (1977)]. These authors used the CRETH (Constant Ratio Elasticity of Transformation Homothetic) system, which is a primal specification. The Constant Difference Elasticity (CDE) functional form is a dual (potentially non-homothetic) specification. It has been employed to estimate demand relationships in agriculture [Hjort (1988), Surry (1989), Herrard et al. (1997)]. Recently, it has been used in AGE analysis to calibrate consumer demand to a vector of own-price and income elasticities of demand [Hertel et al. (1991)].

Most of the literature on functional forms has focused on flexibility in price space. This is generally the most relevant dimension for comparative static analysis of agricultural policies with highly aggregated households, since the impact of these policies on aggregate income is generally quite small, compared to the impact on relative prices. However, when the AGE analysis involves accumulation of factors of production, as in a dynamic AGE model, or exogenous shocks to endowments in a comparative static AGE model [e.g., Anderson et al. (1997)], then the income elasticities of demand can play a very important role in the results. In such cases it will be important to not only capture variation in income elasticities of demand across commodities, but also the tendency for the income elasticity of demand for food products to fall over time. The need for this type of "Engel-flexibility" has been emphasized by Rimmer and Powell (1994), based on non-parametric analysis. This precipitated development of a new functional form, nicknamed AIDADS, which restricts the price space via implicit additivity, but which provides third-order Engel flexibility [Rimmer and Powell (1996)]. AIDADS can capture the change in the income elasticities of demand for food over time, as per capita incomes rise [Cranfield et al. (1998)].

Producer technology: The predominance in AGE models of Leontief (fixed coefficient) technology with CES substitution in value-added has its origins in the computational advantages which once flowed from this specification. By assuming fixed intermediate input coefficients, the entire equilibrium problem can be reduced to one of finding a fixed point in factor price space [Ballard et al. (1985a)]. This vastly reduces the computational cost of AGE analysis, which was an important consideration prior to the development of more efficient algorithms and more powerful computers. However, intermediate input substitution plays an important role in the farm and food system.

Wohlgenant (1987) shows that substitution of agricultural products for marketing-inputs plays a key role in determining farm-level demand elasticities. The potential incidence of farm programs is also closely circumscribed by the ability of livestock producers and food processors to substitute among raw agricultural products. As noted above, high fructose corn syrup has been widely substituted for sugar in the U.S. food and beverage sectors, as a consequence of the sugar import quota. In the EU, the gains from price support programs for grains have been shared with non-grains producers in the EU and overseas. Peeters and Surry (1997) review the literature on price-responsiveness of feed demand in the EU, where this issue has received a great deal of attention due to the constraints it has placed on the Common Agricultural Policy. They distinguish between three approaches: linear programming, the synthetic modeling approach, and econometric approaches. One of the more innovative is offered by Folmer et al. (1990) who incorporate a detailed treatment of feed demand into the European Community Agricultural Model (ECAM) using the Linear Expenditure System.

Substitution among intermediate inputs and between intermediate and primary inputs also plays an important role at the farm level. Empirical evidence from U.S. agriculture [e.g., Hertel et al. (1989)] indicates greater potential for such substitution, than for substitution within the primary factor aggregate (land, labor, and capital). Warr (1995) also finds significant substitution possibilities between fertilizer and some primary factors. Because many important farm policies represent interventions in the primary factor markets (e.g., acreage reduction programs and subsidized investment), proper assessment of their impact on target variables such as employment and land rents hinges crucially on the specification of farm technology.

Trade elasticities: Since cross-price effects play an important role in the domestic farm and food economy, it is no surprise that they also show up in the rest of the world's response to domestic price movements, and hence in the trade elasticities facing food exporters [Carter and Gardiner (1988)]. Unfortunately such cross-price export demand elasticities are notably difficult to estimate [Gardiner and Dixit (1986)]. Thus, single region models are forced to rely on simulation results from global trade models to measure them. Based on Seeley's (1985) work with the IIASA model, these cross-price effects are empirically quite important. For example, while he estimates a four-year own-price elasticity of export demand for U.S. wheat of -2.15, he finds that the *total elasticity* (when all grain and oilseed prices move together) is only -0.54. Since most farm sector interventions affect these commodities simultaneously, cross-price elasticities of export demand can be expected to play an important role in any policy simulation. Yet most one-country, general purpose AGE models abstract from cross-price effects in export demand.

One of the special features about agricultural trade – particularly in grains – is that it is controlled by state marketing agencies in many regions. This has led Abbott et al. (1997) to conclude that the appropriate model for analysis of grains trade does not treat the individual agents in the economy as the decision makers for imports, but rather focuses on the problem faced by the individuals managing the state trading agencies. The resulting "plans and adjustment" model, which these authors propose, appears to fit the data quite well. Given the emerging importance of state-trading as a topic in multilateral trade negotiations, it may be worthwhile for AGE modelers to work on ways of incorporating this type of behavior as an explicit policy regime into their analysis of grains trade.

Implications for policy analysis: There will always be limitations in the way one is able to represent the basic structure of an economy in an AGE model, and so the critical question becomes: Are these limitations sufficient to warrant the extra effort involved in remedying them? In order to investigate this issue, consider the policy of idling productive acreage in order to boost farm prices. Results are based on a special purpose AGE model outlined in Hertel et al. (1989), which utilizes a flexible representation of consumer preferences and producer technology. I then ask the question, What is the cost of successively restricting preferences and technology along the lines suggested by some of the general purpose models?

The results from the unrestricted experiment are summarized in Hertel and Tsigas (1991). Results for the simplified cases are reported in an appendix which is available on request from the author.[6] They indicate that a generic, general purpose AGE model which oversimplifies consumer preferences (Cobb–Douglas case) and producer technology (no intermediate input substitution), and which omits cross-price effects in export demand, will overstate the welfare costs of acreage controls. In particular, the welfare cost of incremental acreage controls designed to raise program crop prices by 10 percent is overstated by 60 percent ($4.2 billion vs. $2.6 billion in the unrestricted model). This follows from two basic flaws in the general purpose models. First of all, they tend to overstate the farm-level demand elasticity for these crops. Second, they tend to overstate the ability of farmers to substitute away from the land input. It should be

---

[6]   Readers can access this appendix on the worldwide web at *www.agecon.purdue.edu/gtap/wkpapr.*

noted, however, that the direction of bias is ambiguous. For example, when taken alone, the assumption of no substitutability in intermediate uses leads to an understatement of these welfare costs. Of course none of these parameters can be specified without some reference to the time frame for the simulation, and this is the subject to which we now turn.

4.2. Short, medium, or long run?

Commodity stocks: The time frame chosen for an AGE simulation has important implications for a variety of features which are critical to the outcome of the experiment. In the very short run, crop production has little scope for adjustment and, in the absence of stocks, supply shocks cause wide swings in commodity prices. As a result, there are substantial incentives for stockholding – either private or public – in the case of nonperishable crop commodities. In the longer run, the importance of stocks is diminished, since continued stock accumulation or decumulation quickly becomes infeasible in the context of a global agricultural economy.

Since the majority of AGE analyses focus on deterministic, comparative static analysis with respect to the medium run (which I take to be 3–4 years), it is common to abstract from commodity stockpiling – assuming that the associated price effects will be only transitory. However, any annual agricultural data set will include this type of "inventory demand" (or supply). One solution is to purge such demands from the benchmark equilibrium data set, in the process of constructing a representative year data set [Adams and Higgs (1990), James and McDougall (1993)].

An alternative approach is to explicitly incorporate the stockpiling of commodities into the AGE analysis. Harrison et al. (1989) develop a model of the European Community's Common Agricultural Policy in which excess market supplies are purchased, and either stored or unloaded onto world markets (with the help of an export subsidy). Stored commodities "are 'eaten' by EC government agents" (presumably they are stored until they spoil). Thus, they do not return to the marketplace, and hence do not generate future utility for private agents in this model.

Factor mobility: As the time horizon for an AGE model lengthens, there is increased potential for production to adjust in response to a policy shock. In the limit, if all factors were perfectly mobile and the farm sector were relatively small, supply response would be perfectly elastic. However, some farm factors of production are probably never perfectly mobile. As noted above, farmland in particular often has few alternative uses and thus experiences more of a price adjustment than other factors in the long run. Also, family labor, farm structures, and some types of capital are relatively immobile in the short to medium run [Vasavada and Chambers (1986)].

To highlight the importance of factor mobility assumptions in determining the incidence of farm programs, consider the following evidence taken from Hertel, Thompson and Tsigas (1989). [See also Kilkenny and Robinson (1990), for further analysis of factor mobility.] They analyze the impact of unilateral elimination of U.S.

agricultural support policies in both the short run and the long run. The short run is characterized as the period over which both U.S. and foreign farm labor and capital are unable to adjust to this major shock. Thus short-run export demand elasticities are used, and U.S. farm labor, crop, and livestock capital are all assumed immobile out of agriculture. The estimated short-run loss to these factors (in 1987 dollars) is $12.8 billion. The distribution of these losses is determined by the estimated elasticities of substitution in the farm sector. In this case the losses are distributed as follows: labor, 37.3 percent; land, 36.5 percent; livestock capital, 18.2 percent; and crop capital, 8.0 percent. In the medium run, the effect of mobile labor and capital on the elasticity of farm supply dominates the impact on farm-level demand of larger export demand elasticities. As a result, the total producer burden falls to $5.7 billion. However, now all of this is borne by the sector-specific factor – land. Thus the pattern of factor incidence can vary considerably, depending on assumptions about factor mobility.

Exactly how "long" is the medium run in models which assume perfect mobility of labor and capital? This depends in part on the size of the shock. In the above experiments, the adjustments to attain a new equilibrium include a 5.5 percent reduction in the agricultural labor force, and a 14 percent decline in the stock of farm capital. Are these adjustments large? Not when compared to other forces at work in the farm sector. For example, Hertel and Tsigas (1988b) estimate that the average *annual* decline in the derived demand for farm labor as a consequence of technological change during the post World War II period was 4.3 percent. The needed capital stock adjustment is also not too large when compared to average annual rates of economic depreciation for farm machinery, which range from about 10 percent to 25 percent depending on the equipment in question. Of course, these relatively modest adjustments likely mask more dramatic regional and farm-specific effects. Also, if yours is the farm that goes under as a result of the new policies, the adjustment is hardly marginal! Nevertheless, in view of the fact that (a) rigidity is greatest for downward price movements, and (b) this policy experiment is the most dramatic one that could be inflicted on U.S. agriculture (policies are *completely and unilaterally* eliminated), it seems reasonable to expect that the period of adjustment required to obtain a new equilibrium is not more than the 3–4 year time horizon usually assumed.

It would be inappropriate to conclude this section without mentioning the increasing importance of *international* factor mobility. Given the relatively small share of the total national capital stock employed in agriculture, international capital mobility is probably not an area of central concern. However, concerns about international migration of labor have placed that issue at the center of the debate over possible effects of the North American Free Trade Agreement (NAFTA). Advocates of NAFTA cited the need to stem the tide of migration from Mexico into the United States. In their AGE analysis of this issue, Burfisher et al. (1992, 1994) conclude that such an agreement would likely *increase* migration from Mexico to the U.S., largely due to its negative impact on the demand for agricultural labor in Mexico. This reversal of conventional wisdom is an important reminder of the need for careful empirical analysis of agricultural and trade policy questions.

4.3. Supply response

Assumptions about factor mobility and technology combine to determine the supply elasticities for agricultural commodities in an AGE model. In order to highlight this interaction, it is useful to consider a simple CES production function which combines two groups of inputs with a constant elasticity of substitution (σ). The first group of (variable) inputs is assumed to be in perfectly elastic supply and comprises a share of costs equal to C_v. The second group is in fixed supply with cost share C_F. In this case, the sectoral supply elasticity may be computed as $\eta_s = \sigma(C_v/C_F)$. Calibration of this model may proceed by one of two routes. The first is to take some estimate, $\hat{\eta}_s$, such as that from the cross-section study of Peterson (1988), and combine this with the benchmark equilibrium values for C_v and C_F to obtain $\hat{\sigma}$. The problem with this approach is that η_s varies as a function of relative prices (provided $\sigma \neq 1$). In the developed market economies in Peterson's sample, where purchased inputs are cheap relative to the opportunity cost of family labor, we observe a large value of C_v relative to C_F. In this case, Peterson's cross-section estimation of η_s will understate supply response. In the poorer economies the opposite will be true.

The second approach to calibration of supply response in an AGE model involves estimating σ directly and inferring something about η_s based on alternative factor mobility assumptions. Problems with conventional estimates of supply response led Griliches (1960) to this type of indirect approach. Using factor demand relationships, he estimated a long-run supply elasticity for U.S. agriculture to be between 1.2 and 1.3. [This is quite close to the cross-section estimate by Peterson (1988) of 1.19.]

Hertel (1989) generalized the indirect approach to estimation of supply response to the case of multiple, quasi-fixed factors, and a fully flexible production technology. He combines an estimated matrix of Allen partial elasticities of substitution with two alternative factor mobility assumptions. In the first case, land and capital are assumed fixed, and aggregate farm labor is partially mobile with a factor supply elasticity of 0.5. This generates a commodity supply elasticity of 0.84. In the second case, with labor and capital perfectly mobile, the aggregate supply elasticity is simply equal to the absolute value of the own-Allen partial elasticity of substitution for land, which is estimated to be 3.2.

These indirect estimates of supply response are all considerably larger than those obtained using single equation models fitted to time series data. Such studies have generally yielded aggregate agricultural supply elasticities in the range of 0.1 to 0.4 [Peterson (1988)]. In such an environment output subsidies look a lot like lump sum transfers! One problem with such studies is that multicollinearity often precludes inclusion of a complete set of disaggregate prices (or quantities). Consequently, it is unclear what is being assumed about particular decision variables facing the farm firm. Are they fixed or variable? To overcome such problems a preferred approach to the direct estimation of supply response from time series data involves specification of a restricted profit function, which, in turn, gives rise to a complete system of supply and demand equations in which the treatment of decision variables is explicit. Use of symmetry, homogeneity, and curvature restrictions helps to overcome the problem of collinearity in such a system.

One example of the profit function approach is provided by Ball (1988), who estimates a 5-output, 6-input system for U.S. agriculture. It is restricted on an exogenously determined quantity of own-labor (i.e., self-employed farmers). He obtains individual commodity supply elasticities ranging from 0.43 to 1.11. Furthermore, his outputs all exhibit gross complementarity [the so-called "normal case" in Sakai (1974)]. Thus aggregate supply response is larger than individual commodity response. Indeed, revenue share-weighted row sums of the output price submatrix sum to an aggregate supply elasticity of 3.6, which is again much larger than traditional estimates. If this is correct, then agricultural price support policies are much more distorting than is indicated by the agricultural sector models based on conventional time series estimates of supply response.

4.4. Model closure

Economists using the comparative static, AGE framework face a fundamental problem in closing their models. This is because any SAM will have an activity related to investment, yet there is no intertemporal mechanism for determining the level of this activity in a static model. Sen (1963) defined this as a problem of *macroeconomic closure*. Following Dewatripont and Michel (1987), four popular solutions to this problem may be identified. The first three are non-neoclassical closures in which investment is simply fixed and another source of adjustment is permitted. In the fourth closure, investment adjusts endogenously to accommodate any change in savings. This neoclassical closure is the most common one in comparative static AGE models.

In addition to adopting a closure rule with respect to investment, it is necessary to come to grips with potential changes in the current account. (Recall from Equation (1) from Section 2 above that the difference between national savings and investment must equal exports plus international transfers less imports.) How much of the investment will be financed by domestic savings and how much by foreign savings? This question is difficult to address in the context of a single-region, comparative static model. Therefore, it is common to fix the trade balance exogenously, in which case any change in investment must be financed out of national savings. In opting to exogenize this balance, the modeler is acknowledging that it is largely a macroeconomic phenomenon. To a great extent, the causality in Equation (1) runs from left to right. That is, changes in global capital markets dictate what will happen on the current account. This approach also facilitates analysis by forcing all adjustment onto the current account. In addition, if savings do not enter households' utility function, then fixing the trade balance is the right approach for welfare analysis, since it prevents an arbitrary shift away from savings towards current consumption from being confused with a welfare improvement.

Finally, there is the question of labor market closure. The most common alternatives involve either assuming flexible wages and full employment on the one hand, or fixed real wages and unemployment on the other. In their review of alternative modeling approaches and the implications for the incidence of agricultural policy in India, de Janvry and Sadoulet (1987) explore the implications of these two extreme specifications, as well as an intermediate case in which wages are partially indexed to the cost of living. They find that the labor market closure plays a significant role in determining the incidence of technological change in agriculture on the rural population – particularly the landless poor.

4.5. *Equilibrium demand elasticities*

One very useful way of summarizing the combined effect of all of the assumptions about preferences, technology, factor mobility, and model closure is via a matrix of equilibrium demand elasticities. Each column in this matrix captures the change in demand for all products in the model, when the market price of one particular product, say corn, is raised by one percent and all other markets in the model are permitted to clear. Brandow (1961) was the first to use this technique for summarizing his multi-market, farm-to-retail model of U.S. agriculture. Hertel et al. (1989) updated Brandow's work in a general equilibrium setting. They find, for example, that feed grains and food grains are general equilibrium, farm-level substitutes, while feed grains and livestock products are complements.

4.6. *Systematic sensitivity analysis*

We cannot conclude this section on parameters in AGE models without a discussion of systematic sensitivity analysis. Anyone who has been involved in quantitative economic analysis is familiar with the concept of sensitivity analysis. It is also common in AGE modeling to vary key assumptions and parameters. However, given the large number of parameters involved in any economy-wide model, some sort of *systematic* sensitivity analysis (SSA) is advisable [Harrison et al. (1993)]. Unfortunately, since most realistic AGE models require more than a few seconds to solve, standard Monte Carlo analysis (typically involving thousands of solutions) is generally infeasible. Pagan and Shannon (1987) proposed an approach based on a local, Taylor series approximation of the model results, expressed as a function of the model parameters. Harrison and Vinod (1992) have proposed an approach based on a numerical integration procedure, whereby they sample from a discrete approximation to the true distribution of parameters.

Recently a new approach to SSA has been proposed by DeVuyst and Preckel (1997). Like Harrison and Vinod, their approach is based on numerical integration techniques. They use multi-variate Gaussian Quadrature, which draws a sample and associated weights in order to satisfy a set of conditions equating the moments of the approximating distribution to the moments of the true parameter distribution up to some finite order of moments (usually 3 to 5). This has proven to be a very powerful tool. For example, in their SSA of the Whalley–Wigle carbon tax model, DeVuyst and Preckel find that a Gaussian Quadrature requiring only 12 model evaluations dominates both the

Pagan and Shannon approach using 25 evaluations and the Harrison and Vinod approach using 64 model evaluations. Indeed, the *error* from the true mean of the carbon tax required (to obtain a prespecified reduction in omissions) is only one-tenth of that with Pagan and Shannon's method and one-hundredth of that with Harrison and Vinod's method. The good news for AGE modelers is that the Gaussian Quadrature approach to SSA has now been automated for the case of symmetric, independent distributions [Arndt (1996), Arndt and Pearson (1996)].

5. Modeling policies that affect agriculture

As noted in the introduction, one of the important areas for future work identified in Whalley's (1986) "Hidden Challenges" paper involves improved modeling of public policies. This is nowhere more important than in agriculture, where, for some commodities in certain countries, the value of policy transfers exceeds the gross domestic value of production [United States Department of Agriculture, Economic Research Service (ERS) (1988)]. Such interventions are not only large, they are also diverse. For example, it is not uncommon for agricultural policies to send conflicting signals regarding resource allocation. Input subsidies frequently coexist with supply control measures. Furthermore, many agricultural policies are not easily amenable to "ad valorem equivalent" modeling [Gohin et al. (1998), Kilkenny (1991), Kilkenny and Robinson (1988), McDonald (1990), Veenendaal (1998), Whalley and Wigle (1990)].

5.1. Modeling voluntary participation

One of the more vexing problems in agricultural policy modeling has involved the search for an appropriate framework with which to model voluntary farm programs. Voluntary participation has been a hallmark of the U.S. grains programs. Until recently, they required farmers to idle a certain proportion of their base acreage in order to qualify for a variety of program benefits including payments on output. The fact that participation rates varied from year to year indicated that producers are an economically heterogeneous group (see discussion of this topic above). The most common approach to modeling these programs was to derive an average "incentive price" which, when combined with the supply shift due to idled acreage, would have induced the observed market supply of the crop in question [Gardner (1989)]. However, such efforts ignored the impact that changing program parameters have on important components of the problem such as variable costs per acre, optimal yields, and the nature of the supply shift. In reality, this is a complex, highly nonlinear problem.

Whalley and Wigle (1990) propose an alternate approach to modeling participation in the U.S. grains programs. They specify an explicit distribution of farms that reflects differences in their underlying cost structure such that the incentive to participate varies across five broad classes of farms. As program parameters or market conditions change, the participation rate varies endogenously. Hertel et al. (1990) extended this framework to incorporate a continuous distribution of land capacities, which in turn provides the motivation for differential participation. Shoemaker (1992) incorporates the voluntary participation decision in a dynamic model and examines steady-state effects of the farm programs. All of this work highlights the differential incidence of farm programs on participants, nonparticipants, and those who are roughly indifferent to participation.

5.2. Interventions in the processed product markets

A large void in many AGE models with an agricultural policy focus rests in their treatment of the food manufacturing and marketing sectors. In the U.S., only about one-third of every dollar spent on food goes to the farmer. Value-added in food manufacturing, and in wholesale/retail activities, are each roughly equal to that of agriculture. Furthermore, in many cases, support for farm commodities is provided indirectly, by purchase of (or protection for) processed products. For example, the primary mechanism for supporting U.S. fluid milk prices involves purchases of cheese, butter, and skim milk powder by the Commodity Credit Corporation (CCC). This type of indirect approach to supporting the farm sector can have important implications for policy analysis, and hence for the appropriate structure of AGE models. For example, CCC purchases of dairy products have generated considerably more processing capacity in the industry than would otherwise be required. Any lowering of support prices translates into redundant capacity. As a consequence, dairy processors have moved into the forefront of the dairy lobby. Similarly, as noted above, the U.S. sugar quota generated a new set of advocates in the corn milling industry. These processing sector impacts, in addition to the change in returns to dairy and sugar farms, must be captured by any model choosing to focus on such policies.

5.3. Agricultural policies in a changing world economy

In many cases agricultural policies are tied to particular targets. For example, the policymakers may be required to defend a given level of domestic price, to maintain farm incomes, or to ensure a given level of self-sufficiency. Also, it is not uncommon for those seeking reform to legislate constraints on budgetary outlays. In the case of the Uruguay Round Agreement on Agriculture, export subsidies were constrained both in terms of volume (21 percent reduction in the volume of subsidized exports) and value (36 percent reduction). Such policy targets introduce the potential for endogenous changes in policy regimes once the constraint becomes binding. Of course whether, for example, the EU export subsidy commitments become binding will depend on conditions in the EU, as well as those in the world markets. Frandsen et al. (1998) have explored this issue in the context of a global AGE model. Their analysis focuses on the eastward enlargement of the European Union to include a number of Central and Eastern European countries (CEECs). They consider projections from 1992 to 2005 with the Uruguay Round commitments, as well as the explicit specification of compensatory payments, set-aside requirements, base area restrictions, and milk quotas. The authors conclude that the current specification of policies is likely to render EU enlargement infeasible. Some sort of reform of the Common Agricultural Policy will be necessary.

5.4. Political economy of policies: General equilibrium dimensions

The AGE framework can also provide valuable insights into the political economy of agricultural policies.[7] For example, there is a strong tendency for relative rates of protection to shift as countries grow wealthier. Poor countries tend to tax agriculture and subsidize industry, while wealthier countries tend to subsidize agriculture, relative to industry [Anderson and Hayami (1986)]. Anderson (1995) has used a small AGE model to illustrate why this particular pattern of intervention is so compelling.[8] The model that he employs has three sectors: agriculture, industry, and non-tradables (services). Capital is sector-specific, and the welfare of farmers and industrialists is closely tied to the return to their respective capital stocks. Anderson then proceeds to analyze the relative impact of trade policies on farmer and industrialist returns in each of these two archetype economies. He concludes that farmers who successfully seek agricultural price supports in poor countries reap only one-sixth to one-ninth the percentage improvement in returns, as compared with their counterparts in the rich economy. This has to do with a variety of features of lower income economies, including (a) the relatively large share of agriculture in GDP, (b) the large share of food in household consumption, and (c) the relatively lower dependence of farming on industrial inputs. By contrast, industrial protection in the lower income country yields ten times the benefits for manufacturing lobbyists, as compared to their counterparts in the industrialized economy. These findings lead Anderson to conclude that these *general equilibrium,* structural differences in rich and poor countries are a key force between observed differences in protection patterns.

AGE analysis also has an important role to play in the political economy of reforming agricultural and trade policies. The IMPACT project in Australia turned to AGE analysis in the early 1970s in an attempt to stem the tide of special interests in tariff deliberations [Powell and Snape (1993)]. The goal of the AGE modeling work developed under this project was to explicitly identify the opportunity cost of pursuing protectionist policies. While any individual tariff hike might not cost the average consumer very much, when taken together the costs of protection were quite substantial. It is interesting to note that, in the wake of these studies, the position of Australian agriculture with respect to policy reform was eventually reversed. AGE analysis showed that the effects of trade liberalization in Australia were to leave agriculture *better off* after removal of support

---

[7] Some authors have used AGE models in conjunction with game theory to examine the endogenous formation of agricultural and trade policy [Rutstrom (1995), Rutstrom and Redmond (1997)].

[8] De Janvry et al. (1992) also seek to explain the differences in observed policies affecting agriculture and the rural sector in India and Ecuador using an applied general equilibrium framework which captures linkages between rural and urban activity. They develop an index of political feasibility which permits them to take six different determinants of political power into account.

– provided similar measures are taken in the industrial sectors [Higgs (1989)]. The insight that relatively higher support for the Australian manufacturing sector amounted to an implicit tax on agriculture was an important revelation which could not have been communicated without AGE analysis. Similarly, in those economies where agriculture is relatively heavily protected, one of the best hopes for reform involves enlistment of export-oriented manufacturers who stand to benefit from a more competitive economy.

In sum, appropriate modeling of agricultural policies is an important, but difficult task. There is much to be gained by focusing on a particular policy and doing a good job of modeling it. However, in some circumstances it will be essential to incorporate a relatively complete set of economy-wide distortions in order to capture the consequences of potentially second-best interventions. This tradeoff between breadth of coverage and depth of analysis is evident in most areas of AGE analysis. There is no simple answer as to which approach is correct. Indeed, in many cases, both will be needed.

6. Agriculture and the environment

Increasingly agricultural policy is being driven by environmental considerations. Therefore, demand for analyses of the impact of agricultural and trade policies on the environment has been rapidly increasing [Gardner (1993), Bredahl et al. (1996)]. Many environmental issues are very location-specific. This might lead one to conclude that there is little role for AGE analysis. However, Shively (1997) shows that general equilibrium interactions can also be important at the level of an individual watershed. He examines the case where deforestation and erosion from an upland region lowers productivity in lowland agriculture. In addition to being linked through erosion, the two regions are also linked through the labor market, and diminished productivity in lowland agriculture puts downward pressure on wages, thereby reducing off-farm income opportunities for upland farmers. This leads to more deforestation and a downward spiral. Technological change aimed at increasing employment opportunities for upland farmers in the lowland region can have the opposite effect, by relieving pressure on the upland forest, thereby improving downstream productivity and wages.

In the context of national-level, environmental applications, it is most common for AGE modelers to focus on the economy-wide costs of restricting pollution. Rendleman (1993) analyzed the impact of chemical restrictions on U.S. agriculture. Komen and Peerlings (1995) used an AGE model to calculate the costs of manure restrictions in the Netherlands as well as to assess the impact of environmentally motivated energy taxation on agriculture [Komen and Peerlings (1998)]. However, ultimately the policy problem is one of weighing the costs of abatement against the benefits of a cleaner environment. Perroni and Wigle (1994) argue that, despite the conceptual and empirical pitfalls, it is essential to build the benefits of environmental clean-up into AGE models. They do so by specifying an initial endowment of environmental quality, some of which gets consumed by pollution activities. Firms can abate pollution by substituting commercial inputs (e.g., new machinery) for emissions. Households value the environment as a consumption good, and the marginal valuation rises with per capita income. They use this model to explore the interactions between trade policy and environmental policy.

Tsigas et al. (1997) have built upon the approach proposed by Perroni and Wigle with an application which focuses on agriculture in the Western Hemisphere. In particular, they incorporate estimates of soil erosion, pesticide toxic releases, and nitrogen releases from agriculture, in addition to industrial pollution. Like Perroni and Wigle, they are forced to extrapolate from the U.S., where relatively good emissions data are available, to other regions in their analysis (Canada, Mexico, Brazil, and Argentina). The authors use this AGE model to analyze the impact of Western Hemisphere free trade on environmental quality in the region. They find that environmental damages in Mexico, Brazil, and Argentina are likely to increase under free trade, unless trade liberalization is combined with more stringent environmental policies. When the two are undertaken in concert, the welfare gain to these three countries is considerably enhanced.

However, agriculture not only generates pollution, it also provides environmental amenities [Legg and Portugal (1997)]. There is increasing interest in linking farm payments to the level of such amenities provided. The Organization for Economic Cooperation and Development's Joint Working Party between the Committee for Agriculture and the Environment Policy Committee is currently developing a set of agri-environmental indicators to support policy analysis in this area [OECD (1998)]. The initial set of indicators will cover the areas of farm management and financial resources, agricultural land conservation, soil and water quality, nutrient balance, pesticide use, greenhouse gases, biodiversity and wildlife habitat, landscape, and the agricultural use of water resources.

7. Product differentiation and imperfect competition

The theme of product differentiation has come to play an increasingly important role in analysis of agricultural trade policies [Carter et al. (1990)]. A computational motivation for product differentiation is the specialization problem in small open economies facing exogenous world prices [de Melo and Robinson (1989)]. By differentiating home and foreign goods, the elasticity of world price transmission into the domestic economy is dampened and drastic swings in the sectoral composition of output are avoided. This also opens the possibility of intra-industry trade, which is a commonly observed phenomenon. The oldest tradition in this area is the so-called Armington approach in which products are *exogenously* differentiated by origin. This seems most appropriate in the case of those agricultural products for which agronomic and climatic considerations limit the scope for production of particular types of commodities [e.g., wheat (by class) or fruits and vegetables (by season)]. The market share rigidity provided by the Armington specification also serves as a proxy for non-price considerations which often play an important role in agricultural trade [Hjort (1988)]. This specification may also be modified so that the law of one price applies in the long run [Gielen and van Leeuwen (1998)]. However, in light of the increased importance of trade in processed food products, and the globalization of the food manufacturing industry, the Armington approach seems increasingly irrelevant for many sectors. Consumers pay less and less attention to the origin of the products which they consume.[9]

While consumers are growing less concerned with the country of origin, they appear to be growing more aware of brand names. The fact that firms have become important actors in the field of product differentiation fundamentally changes the appropriate modeling approach, since this differentiation is now *endogenous*. That is, firms invest fixed costs in research and development and marketing activities in order to establish a market niche, which then permits them to mark up price over marginal cost. This type of formulation was originally introduced by Dixit and Stiglitz (1979) in order to investigate the trade-off between fixed costs and the benefits which accrue to consumers as additional varieties are provided. It has since provided a foundation for much of the work on international trade under imperfect competition. This approach seems highly relevant for large parts of the farm and food complex. Food manufacturers are among the most important sources of advertising expenditures, accounting for 32 percent of all manufacturer outlays but only 12 percent of total sales [Connor et al. (1985)].[10] In these circumstances, product differentiation is quite clearly endogenous, and supported by firms pricing above marginal cost. Lanclos and Hertel (1995) demonstrate that this alternative approach to product differentiation tends to magnify the impact of trade liberalization on the U.S. food manufacturing industries. Philippidis and Hubbard (1998) find similar magnification effects in their analysis of the European Union's Common Agricultural Policy.

The number of AGE analyses of trade policy incorporating imperfect competition has mushroomed since the path-breaking work of Harris (1984). Many alternative approaches have been identified and the key constraint seems to be availability of high quality data to support the calibration of markups, excess profits, and scale economies. Francois and Roland-Holst (1997) offer a comprehensive survey of this topic. They distinguish between the cases in which products are homogeneous and the market power is derived from barriers to entry, and those in which products are differentiated in the manner discussed above. They also distinguish between the so-called "small group"

---

[9] Another criticism of the Armington approach has to do with functional form. Winters (1984) and Alston et al. (1990) argue that the CES representation is too restrictive and that the non-homothetic, AIDS specification is preferable. Robinson et al. (1993) have used this functional form in their AGE analysis of the North American Free Trade Agreement (NAFTA). As with the specification of consumer and producer behavior, more flexibility is better than less, provided sound estimates and calibration procedures can be provided. The main problem with a non-homothetic specification for import aggregation is the absence of a well-defined price index for the resulting composite commodity, since unit expenditure now depends on the level of utility. This eliminates the viability of the multi-stage budgeting assumption which is the foundation of most disaggregated AGE models of consumer and producer behavior.

[10] Peterson (1989) provides some of the first attempts to incorporate imperfect competition in food manufacturing into an AGE model.

and "large group" cases. In the former instance, markups are endogenous and vary with the nature of inter-firm rivalry, relative prices, and the number of firms in the industry. This is often difficult to implement in AGE models, since industries tend to be highly aggregated. In the small group case, firms ignore potential interactions with other firms and markups are dictated by the degree of product differentiation.[11]

8. Model validation

One question which consumers of AGE model results often ask is, "Has the model been validated?" This is a reasonable question to expect from an analyst seeking advice on a policy reform which may end up shifting hundreds of millions of dollars around the economy. How can we be assured that the model bears any relationship to reality? The typical answer is that the AGE model, like any simulation model, has not been econometrically estimated and therefore cannot be subjected to the usual forecasting tests. To the extent that (a) the individual components of the system are based on plausible, perhaps even econometrically estimated, relationships, (b) the underlying social accounting matrix is accurate and reflects the best economy-wide data available, and (c) the equilibrium assumptions and macro-closure are plausible, then the assertion is that the results will indeed shed relevant light on what might actually happen if the proposed reforms were implemented.

However, if AGE modelers are successful in obtaining a higher policy profile for their results, more will be demanded in the way of model validation. Several relatively ambitious validation efforts have been undertaken in recent years. Kehoe et al. (1991) conducted an *ex post* analysis of the impact of tax reform on the Spanish economy. They conclude that, with some adjustments, their AGE model is able to predict the broad pattern of resource reallocations precipitated by the change in tax policy. Fox (1998) has conducted a similar, *ex post* analysis of the predictions made by Brown and Stern (1989), using the Michigan model to evaluate the U.S.–Canada Free Trade Agreement. He finds that the model performs better for Canada than for the U.S. This is likely due to the fact that this agreement was of much greater significance to the Canadian economy. In contrast, its role in redirecting the sectoral allocation of resources in the U.S. was much more modest, and therefore difficult to detect.

Gehlhar (1997) attempted a somewhat different validation exercise, whereby endowments and productivity are shocked instead of policies. In this "backcasting" exercise he attempts to predict 1982 East Asian export shares based on the multi-region GTAP

---

[11] One important feature of Francois and Roland-Holst (1997) is their approach to handling endogenous product differentiation [see also, Francois (1998)]. By cleverly re-scaling output to obtain "variety-scaled output" they are able to introduce this additional complexity into a standard AGE model at relatively low cost. Anyone thinking about introducing imperfect competition into an existing AGE model should definitely take a look at this before proceeding.

model calibrated to 1992 data. Unlike the usual econometric models, which have hundreds of exogenous variables, he uses only exogenous shocks to primary factor endowments and technology. Once he incorporates a proxy for human capital, he finds that the model performs reasonably well as regards prediction of changes in export shares. Coyle et al. (1998) attempt something similar, but they are more narrowly focused than Gehlhar. They seek to explain the dramatic change in composition of world food trade which occurred between 1980 and 1995. Coyle et al. (1998) employ a modified version of the GTAP model incorporating an econometrically estimated demand system. Their model is able to explain about half of the observed shift from bulk to non-bulk food trade over this period.

Realistically, any such "validation" effort will inevitably involve a certain amount of tinkering with the model in order to improve its performance. In this sense, such exercises are really a more elaborate method of calibration (but something short of formal econometrics) in which the model is fitted to multiple data points.[12] In this sense they do not constitute proof that the model will perform well in future simulations. However, such efforts to compare model performance to economic history will go a long way in addressing the criticism that AGE models bear little or no relationship to reality. As such, this type of work should be a high priority for future research.

9. Conclusions

As noted in Section 2, this chapter may be viewed as a survey of agriculturally related attempts to meet some of the "hidden challenges" outlined by John Whalley in the mid-1980s. I am happy to report that considerable progress has been made. Many of the AGE-based studies reported in this survey represent excellent applied economic research with important policy insights and implications. In fact, there is a clear parallel with developments in other areas of applied economic research. Most of the hidden challenges that Whalley identifies – appropriate disaggregation, parameter specification, modeling of strategic behavior, and treatment of policies – are universal challenges facing applied economists. Of course, general equilibrium modelers face some special challenges. In particular, the constraints imposed by the requirement for an economy-wide, micro-consistent data set have precluded system-wide econometric estimation. Nor do AGE modelers have the luxury of specifying reduced-form elasticities. Agricultural supply response must be the outcome of producers' constrained optimization decisions subject to an explicitly specified technology, and conditioned by clear assumptions about factor mobility. Nevertheless, there are fewer differences between AGE analysis and other areas of applied economics than many would suggest.

Indeed, I believe that one of the main avenues for improvement in AGE analyses of agricultural policies over the coming decade will be through increased collaboration

---

[12] Arndt and Robinson (1998) have recently used a 5-year time series of data on the Mozambique economy to formally adjust their AGE model parameters based on the maximum entropy approach.

with economists working on partial equilibrium studies. As highlighted in Section 2 of this chapter, the AGE approach has many important benefits in the context of policy analysis. However, in order to be fully effective, those working in this field must learn from economists with detailed knowledge of the sector, industry, households, or policies being analyzed. In order for this collaboration to blossom, AGE modelers will have to extend themselves in a number of ways.

The first area in which improvements need to be made involves the communication of key assumptions and parameters in a form which others can interpret and evaluate. Very few AGE analyses of agricultural policy report their assumed supply and demand elasticities for key products. Yet we all know that these are key parameters in determining the economic incidence of any price intervention. Why this paucity of information? The main problem is that AGE models are not typically specified in terms of supply and demand elasticities. Rather they involve the specification of explicit production and utility functions. Deriving the supply and demand elasticities involves some further computations. In addition, there is no longer one simple "supply elasticity". What is to be assumed about factor market adjustment? Are non-agricultural prices and incomes assumed constant? Similar problems exist with the specification of demand elasticities. However, this multiplicity of options is also a strength. The researcher can report elasticities under a range of assumptions, showing how they are altered as one moves from partial to general equilibrium.[13] In so doing, they will assist the partial equilibrium analyst who is trying to grasp the differences between the two approaches.

A second step which will help to facilitate communication between AGE modelers and other economists involves a more widespread use of systematic sensitivity analysis (SSA). Economists accustomed to dealing with models with only a few behavioral parameters are often quite skeptical of models in which there are dozens of elasticities of substitution. Given the difficulty we have of obtaining robust estimates of such parameters, how can we have any confidence whatsoever in the results from such a model? This is a legitimate question, and it can only be addressed by the use of parametric SSA. In the past, authors of prospective journal articles could plead that their model was so big that it would take several months of computing to implement a complete Monte Carlo analysis. However, as pointed out in Section 4 above, recent developments in this field have rendered SSA eminently practicable. In some cases, researchers have been pleasantly surprised with the robustness of AGE results to parametric uncertainty. This is because the data base and equilibrium assumptions also play key roles in determining the range of possible outcomes. Furthermore, as more of the AGE-based work draws on high quality, published databases, the data dependence of these studies will be viewed as a strength of the approach.

Once non-AGE economists have been convinced that the findings are based on reasonable assumptions and that they are robust, they will want to know more about

---

[13] For a discussion of partial and general equilibrium elasticities of demand in a multiregion AGE model, see Hertel et al. (1997).

what is driving the results. This is where experienced AGE modelers and novices have parted company in the past. While some results are easy to explain (e.g., why output falls in a sector when a subsidy is removed), the welfare impact of a marginal change in policies in the context of a heavily distorted economy can be very difficult to interpret. AGE modelers interested in policy analysis need to invest much more time and energy in techniques of analysis which permit them to understand, and explain to others, the basic mechanisms driving their results. One illustration of this is the welfare decomposition technique derived by Keller (1980).[14] He fully decomposes the change in economy-wide welfare into the efficiency consequences for each market captured by the model. Thus one can make statements such as, "Twenty-five percent of the welfare gain was due to improved allocation of labor in the economy". Or, "The welfare loss came about because the partial tax reform lured resources into the relatively protected agricultural sector". Without recourse to such explanations, backed up by detailed tables of data and results, the consumer of AGE model results is left with a black-box which they must either accept or reject as a matter of faith.

In my experience, once an AGE modeler has convinced the audience that the analysis is not only robust, but also sheds light on an important issue, he or she will very likely face requests by others to replicate the study. Replication is standard practice in other sciences, but it has been slow to penetrate the economics profession [Dewald et al. (1986)]. However, given the availability of a number of relatively easy-to-use software packages for AGE modeling [Harrison and Pearson (1996), Rutherford (1999)], it is now within reach for most studies. In fact, I would like to see journal editors require that all AGE-based articles be submitted along with those files needed for replication. Ideally, reviewers would also have the opportunity to vary key assumptions such as model closure and parameter settings. This would greatly enhance the credibility of work in the area. It would also aid those seeking to build on previously published work, thereby facilitating more rapid scientific progress.

One reason why AGE modelers have been reluctant to make their models easier to use is the fear that they will be misused. This fear is well founded. There is no doubt that as construction and implementation of an AGE model becomes routine and accessible to those outside the close-knit fraternity of modelers, foolish applications will abound. However, this is no different from any other branch of quantitative economics. The only distinguishing feature of AGE analysis is that, due to the size of many of these models, one can generate foolish numbers at an extremely rapid rate! Ultimately it will be up to the process of professional peer review to sort the wheat from the chaff. It will no longer be the case that when one gets an AGE application to review, he or she can assume that the individual writing the paper has assembled the data and built the model themselves. This is a drawback. They may be ill-informed, simply offering a

---

[14] Keller's (1980) technique provides a local approximation to this decomposition for a small, open economy. Huff and Hertel (1996) have adapted Keller's approach to the case of large changes, and apply this in the context of the multi-region GTAP model.

mechanistic set of model runs. However, an experienced reviewer can quickly identify
such papers. Furthermore, since model construction is no longer such an onerous task,
one can now reasonably expect much more from the author in the way of analysis and
exposition of results.

Indeed, I believe that successful AGE applications related to agricultural and resource
policies in the future will increasingly exhibit six key features:

(1) Relevant institutional and behavioral aspects of the sector in question are taken
    into account.
(2) Key policies are modeled explicitly. Voluntary program participation, quantita-
    tive restrictions, price ceilings and floors, as well as state trading, are all common
    types of farm-sector interventions which lend themselves to explicit treatment in
    an AGE framework.
(3) Key behavioral parameters are reported and related to econometric work in the
    literature.
(4) Results are reported in terms of means and standard deviations generated by SSA
    procedures which take parametric uncertainty into account.
(5) Central findings are exhaustively decomposed and explained.
(6) Results can be easily replicated, and key assumptions altered, by the reviewer.

Regardless of how forthcoming partial and general equilibrium analysts are in their
dialogue, one cannot avoid the fact that there is an inevitable tension between the mandate for AGE studies to be comprehensive and the contrasting need to delve into the
specifics of the industries/households directly affected by specific policies. By definition, compromises are required, and the most distinguishing feature of high quality
AGE policy applications is that they make the *right* compromises. In particular, they
must preserve key features of the sector in question. For this, a dialogue with industry
experts is essential. Such dialogue is often cumbersome, and at times tedious. However, it is the only way applied general equilibrium studies can avoid falling prey to
Solow's (1973) criticism of Jay Forrester's early work on global modeling. In that debate, Forrester asserted that rather than "go to the bottom of a particular problem ...
what we want to look at are the problems caused by the interactions". To this, Solow
responded:

> I don't know what you call people who believe they can be wrong about everything
> in particular, but expect to be lucky enough to get it right on the interactions. They
> may be descendants of the famous merchant Lapidus who said that he lost money
> on every item sold, but made it up on the volume. (p. 157)

In summary, after several decades of rapid development and application to many
different areas of economic analysis, AGE models are maturing. They must be subjected
to the same scrutiny and skepticism and validation efforts as other models. Ultimately
their usefulness in delivering policy insights and guidance will determine whether or not
this field of endeavor has been a success. Some striking examples of AGE-based impact

in the policy sphere exist.[15] However, the ratio of policy-oriented, AGE applications to effective policy input is still quite low. If this situation is to be rectified, it is essential that the use of AGE analysis extend beyond the narrow modeling community to a broader group of policy economists. It is my hope that this survey will encourage such cross-fertilization.

Acknowledgements

The author thanks Philip Abbott, Kym Anderson, Glenn Harrison, Garth Holloway, Brad McDonald, Everett Peterson, Matt Rendleman, Sherman Robinson, Gerald Schluter, Serdar Sayan, Yves Surry, Marinos Tsigas, and Randy Wigle for their comments on earlier drafts of this chapter.

References

ABARE (Australian Bureau of Agricultural and Resource Economics) (1988), Japanese Agricultural Policies: A Time of Change (Australian Government Publishing Service, Canberra).

Abbott, P.C., P.M. Patterson and L. Young (1997), "Plans and adjustment: A structuralist approach to modeling grain importer behavior", Unpublished manuscript (Department of Agricultural Economics, Purdue University).

Adams, P.D., and P.J. Higgs (1990), "Calibration of computable general equilibrium models from synthetic benchmark equilibrium data sets", Economic Record 66:110–126.

Alston, J.M., C.A. Carter, R. Green and D. Pick (1990), "Whither Armington trade models?", American Journal of Agricultural Economics 72(2):455–467.

Alston, J.M., and B.H. Hurd (1990), "Some neglected social costs of government spending in farm programs", American Journal of Agricultural Economics 72(1):149–156.

Anderson, K. (1995), "Lobbying incentives and the pattern of protection in rich and poor countries", Economic Development and Cultural Change 43(2):401–423.

Anderson, K., B. Dimaranan, T. Hertel and W. Martin (1997), "Asia-pacific food markets in 2005: A global, economywide perspective", Australian Journal of Agricultural and Resource Economics 41(1):19–44.

Anderson, K., and Y. Hayami (1986), The Political Economy of Agricultural Protection (Allen and Unwin, Sydney).

Arndt, C. (1996), "An introduction to systematic sensitivity analysis via Gaussian quadrature", GTAP Technical Paper No. 2 (Center for Global Trade Analysis, Purdue University), http://www.agecon.purdue.edu/gtap.

Arndt, C., T. Hertel, B. Dimaranan, K. Huff and R. McDougall (1997), "China in 2005: Implications for the rest of the World", Journal of Economic Integration 12:505–547.

Arndt, C., and K.R. Pearson (1996), "How to carry out systematic sensitivity analysis via Gaussian quadrature and GEMPACK", GTAP Technical Paper No. 3 (Center for Global Trade Analysis, Purdue University), http://www.agecon.purdue.edu/gtap.

Arndt, C., and S. Robinson (1998), "Estimating computable general equilibrium model parameters: A maximum entropy approach", Paper presented at the First Annual Conference on Global Economic Analysis, June 8–10 (Purdue University).

---

[15] See Powell and Snape (1993) on the Australian experience. Francois and Shields (1994) describe the importance of AGE analysis in the NAFTA debate.

Bach, C.F., B. Dimaranan, T.W. Hertel and W. Martin (1999), "Market growth, structural change and the gains from the Uruguay round", Review of International Economics (forthcoming).

Bach, C., and W. Martin (1997), "Would the right tariff aggregator please stand up?", Mimeo (The World Bank).

Ball, V.E. (1988), "Modeling supply response in a multiproduct framework", American Journal of Agricultural Economics 70(4):813–825.

Ballard, C.L., D. Fullerton, J.B. Shoven and J. Whalley (1985a), A General Equilibrium Model for The Policy Evaluation (University of Chicago Press, Chicago).

Ballard, C.L., D. Fullerton, J.B. Shoven and J. Whalley (1985b), "General equilibrium computations of the marginal welfare costs of taxes in the United States", American Economic Review 75(1):128–138.

Berck, P., S. Robinson and G. Goldman (1991), "The use of CGE models to assess water policies", in: A. Dinar and D. Zilberman, eds., The Economics and Management of Water and Drainage in Agriculture (XXX Press, Boston).

Bevan, D.L., and C.S. Adam (1997), "Modelling asset markets in developing country CGEs: Some design issues", Paper presented at the DIAL/PARADI Conference on CGE Modeling in Developing Economies, Paris, September 4–5.

Boussard, J., and A.K. Christensen (1997), "Risk and development in Poland and Hungary: An application of CGE models under different agricultural market systems", Paper presented at the DIAL/PARADI Conference on CGE Modeling in Developing Economies, Paris, September 4–5.

Boyd, R. (1988), "An economic model of direct and indirect effects of tax reform on agriculture", ERS/USDA Technical Bulletin 1743.

Boyd, R., and D. Newman (1989), "Tax reform and land using factors in the U.S. economy: A general equilibrium analysis", American Journal of Agricultural Economics 73:398–409.

Brandao, A.S., T.W. Hertel and A. Campos (1994), "The implications of international agricultural trade liberalization for Brazilian agriculture", in: I. Goldin, O. Knudsen and A.S. Brandao, eds., Modeling Economy-Wide Reforms Development Centre of the Organization for Economic Co-Operation and Development (Paris), Chapter 4, pp. 193–222.

Brandow, G.E. (1961), "Interrelationships among demands for farm products and implications for control of market supply", Technical Bulletin 680 (Pennsylvania Agricultural Experiment Station, Pennsylvania State University, University Park).

Bredahl, M.E., N. Ballenger, J.C. Dunmore and T. Roe (eds.) (1996), Agricultural Trade and the Environment: Discovering and Measuring Critical Linkages (Westview Press, Boulder, CO).

Brown, R.S., and L.R. Christensen (1981), "Estimating elasticities of substitution in a model of partial static equilibrium: An application to U.S. agriculture", in: E.R. Berndt and B.C. Field, eds., Modeling and Measuring Natural Resource Substitution (MIT Press, Cambridge).

Brown, D.K., and R.M. Stern (1989), "U.S.–Canada bilateral tariff elimination: The role of produce differentiation and market structure", in: R.C. Feenstra, ed., Trade Policies for International Competitiveness.

Burfisher, M., S. Robinson and K. Thierfelder (1992), "Agricultural policy in a U.S.–Mexico free trade agreement", North American Journal of Economics and Finance 3(2):117–140.

Burfisher, M., S. Robinson and K. Thierfelder (1994), "Wage changes in a U.S.–Mexico free trade area: Migration versus Stolper–Samuelson effects", in: C. Shiells and J. Francois, eds., Modeling Trade Policy: Applied General Equilibrium Assessments of North American Free Trade (Cambridge University Press, Cambridge).

Burniaux, J.-M., F. Delorme, I. Lienert, J.P. Martin and P. Hoelief (1988), "Quantifying the economywide effects of agricultural policies: A general equilibrium approach", Working Paper No. SS (OECD Department of Economics and Statistics, Paris).

Burniaux, J.-M., and D. van der Mensbrugghe (1991), "Trade policies in a global context: Technical specification of the RUNS model", Technical Paper No. 48 (OECD Development Centre, Paris).

Carter, C.A., and W.H. Gardiner (eds.) (1988), Elasticities in International Agricultural Trade (Westview Press, Boulder, CO).

Carter, C.A., A.F. McCalla and J.A. Sharples (1990), Imperfect Competition and Political Economy: The New Trade Theory (Westview Press, Boulder).

Chambers, R.G. (1995), "The incidence of agricultural policies", Journal of Public Economics 57:317–335.

Clarete, R.L., and J.A. Roumasset (1990), "The relative welfare cost of industrial and agricultural policy distortions: A Philippine illustration", Oxford Economic Papers 42:462–472.

Clarete, R.L., and J. Whalley (1988), "Interactions between trade policies and domestic distortions in a small open developing country", Journal of International Economics 24:345–358.

Connor, J., R. Rogers, B. Marion and W. Mueller (1985), The Food Manufacturing Industries: Structure, Strategy, Performance, and Policies (Lexington Book, Lexington, MA).

Coyle, W., M. Gehlhar, T.W. Hertel, Z. Wang and W. Yu (1998), "Understanding the determinants of structural change in world food markets", American Journal of Agricultural Economics 80(5):1051–1061.

Coyle, W.T., W. McKibbin and Z. Wang (1998), "The Asian financial crisis: Impact on the US economy and agriculture", Unpublished paper (ERS/USDA, Washington, DC).

Cranfield, J.A.L., T.W. Hertel, J.S. Eales and P.V. Preckel (1998), "Changes in the structure of global food demand", American Journal of Agricultural Economics 80(5):1042–1050.

Darwin, R., M.E. Tsigas, J. Lewandrowski and A. Raneses (1995), "World agriculture and climate change: Economic adaptations", USDA Agricultural Economic Report No. 703.

Decaluwe, B., A. Patry and L. Savard (1997), "When water is no longer a gift from heaven: A CGE model of the Moroccan economy", Paper presented at the DIAL/PARADI Conference on CGE Modeling in Developing Economies, Paris, September 4–5.

Dee, P., P. Jomini and R. McDougall (1992), "Alternatives to regionalism – Uruguay and APEC", Paper presented at conference on Regionalism in the World Economy: The Case of the North American Free Trade Agreement and the Australian Response, Adelaide, July.

de Janvry, A., and E. Sadoulet (1987), "Agricultural price policy in general equilibrium models: Results and comparisons", 69:230–246.

de Janvry, A., A. Fargeix and E. Sadoulet (1992), "The political feasibility of rural poverty", Journal of Development Economics 37:351–367.

de Melo, J., and S. Robinson (1989), "Product differentiation and the treatment of foreign trade in computable general equilibrium models of small open economies", Journal of International Economics 27(1–2):47–67.

Dervis, K., J. de Melo and S. Robinson (1982), General Equilibrium Models for Development Policy (Cambridge University Press, Cambridge).

Devarajan, S., and D. Go (1995), "The simplest dynamic general equilibrium model of an open economy", Working paper (Public Economics Division, The World Bank).

DeVuyst, E.A., and P.V. Preckel (1997), "Sensitivity analysis revisited: A quadrature-based approach", Journal of Policy Modeling 19(2):175–185.

Dewald, W.G., J.G. Thursby and R.G. Anderson (1986), "Replication in empirical economics", American Economic Review 76:587–603.

Dewatripont, M., and G. Michel (1987), "On closure rules, homogeneity and dynamics in applied general equilibrium models", Journal of Development Economics 26:65–76.

Diao, X., T.L. Roe and E. Yeldan (1998), "A dynamic open economy model of R&D-driven endogenous growth: The case of Japan", Paper presented at the First Annual Conference on Global Economic Analysis, June 8–10 (Purdue University).

Diewert, W.E., and T.J. Wales (1987), "Flexible functional forms and global curvative conditions", Econometrica 55:43–68.

Dixit, A.K., and J.E. Stiglitz (1979), "Monopolistic competition and optimum product diversity", American Economic Review 67:297–308.

Dixon, P.B., B.R. Parmenter, J. Sutton and D.P. Vincent (1982), ORANI: A Multisectoral Model of the Australian Economy (North-Holland, Amsterdam).

Fischer, G., K. Frohberg, M.A. Kegzer and K.S. Parikh (1988), Linked National Models: A Tool for International Policy Analysis (Kluwer Academic Publishers, Dordrecht).

Folmer, C., M.D. Merbis, H.J.J. Stolwijk and P.J.J. Veenendaal (1990), "Modeling EC feed demand", ECAM Report No. 17 (CPB, The Netherlands).

Fox, A.K. (1998), "Evaluating the success of a CGE model of the U.S.–Canada free trade agreement", Paper presented at the First Annual Conference on Global Economic Analysis, June 8–10 (Purdue University).

Francois, J.F. (1998), "Scale economies and imperfect competition in the GTAP model", GTAP Technical Paper no. 14, http://www.agecon.purdue.edu/gtap/techpaper.

Francois, J.F., and D. Roland-Holst (1997), "Scale economies and imperfect competition", in: J. Francois and K. Reinert, eds., Applied Methods for Trade Policy Analysis: A Handbook (Cambridge University Press, New York) Chapter 11.

Francois, J.F., and C.R. Shields (1994), Modeling Trade Policy: Applied General Equilibrium Assessments of North American Free Trade (Cambridge University Press, New York).

Frandsen, E.F., C.F. Bach and P. Stephensen (1998), "European integration and the common agricultural policy: A CGE multiregional analysis", in: M. Brockmeier, J.F. Francois, T.W. Hertel and P.M. Schmitz, eds., Economic Transition and the Greening of Policies: Modeling New Challenges for Agriculture and Agribusiness in Europe (Vauk, Kiel).

Friedman, M. (1976), Price Theory (Aldine, Chicago).

Gardiner, W.H., and P.M. Dixit (1986), "The price elasticity of export demand: Concepts and estimates", USDA/ERS Staff Report No. AGES860408 (Washington, DC).

Gardner, B.L. (1989), "Gains and losses from the U.S. wheat program", Unpublished paper (Department of Agricultural Economics and Resource, University of Maryland).

Gardner, B.L. (1993), "The impacts of environmental protection and food safety regulation on U.S. agriculture" (Agricultural Policy Working Group, Washington, DC).

Gehlhar, M. (1997), "Historical analysis of growth and trade patterns in the pacific rim: An evaluation of the GTAP framework", in: T.W. Hertel, ed., Global Trade Analysis: Modeling and Applications (Cambridge Univ. Press, New York) Chapter 14.

Gehlhar, M., and S. Frandsen (1998), "Trade elasticities, aggregation bias and welfare effects in the GTAP model", Paper presented at the First Annual Conference on Global Economic Analysis, June 8–10 (Purdue University).

George, P.S., and G.A. King (1971), "Consumer demand for food commodities in the U.S. with projections for 1980", Giannini Foundation Monograph, No. 26.

Gielen, A., and N. van Leeuwen (1998), "A note on Armington and the law of one price", in: M. Brockmeier, J. Francois, T. Hertel and M. Schmitz, eds., Economic Transition and the Greening of Policies: Modeling New Challenges for Agriculture and Agribusiness in Europe (Vauk, Kiel).

Gohin, A.H., H. Guyomard, N. Herrard, Y. Le Roux and T. Trochet (1998), "Modelling agricultural policy instruments in a single country, multi-sector general equilibrium framework: Application to France", in: M. Brockmeier, J.F. Francois, T.W. Hertel and P.M. Schmitz, eds., Economic Transition and the Greening of Policies: Modeling New Challenges for Agriculture and Agribusiness in Europe (Vauk, Kiel).

Griliches, Z. (1960), "Estimates of the aggregate U.S. farm supply function", Journal of Farm Economics 42:282–293.

Gruen, F.H. (1961), "Agriculture and technical change", Journal of Farm Economics 43:838–858.

Hanoch, G. (1975), "Production and demand models with direct or indirect implicit additivity", Econometrica 43:395–419.

Hanson, K.A., and S. Robinson (1988), "Data, linkages and models: U.S. national income and product accounts", in: The Framework of the Social Accounting Matrix, Unpublished paper (USDA Economic Research Service).

Hanson, K., S. Robinson and S. Tokarick (1989), "United states adjustment in the 1990's: A AGE analysis of alternative trade strategies", Paper presented at the Fourth IIASA Task Force Meeting on Applied General Equilibrium Modeling, Laxenburg, Austria, August 23–25.

Harris, R.G. (1984), "Applied general equilibrium analysis of small open economies with scale economies and imperfect competition", American Economic Review 74:1016–1032.

Harrison, G.W., R. Jones, L.J. Kimbell and R. Wigle (1993), "How robust is applied general equilibrium analysis?", Journal of Policy Modeling 15(1):99–115.

Harrison, W.J., and K.R. Pearson (1996), "Computing solutions for large general equilibrium models using GEMPACK", Computational Economics 9:82–127.

Harrison, G.W., T.F. Rutherford and I. Wooten (1989), "The economic impact of the European community", American Economic Review 79:288–294.

Harrison, G.W., T.F. Rutherford and I. Wooten (1991), "An empirical database for a general equilibrium model of the European communities", Empirical Economics 16:95–120.

Harrison, G.W., and H.D. Vinod (1992), "The sensitivity analysis of general equilibrium models: Completely randomized factorial sampling designs", Review of Economics and Statistics 74:357–362.

Herrard, N., Y. Le Roux and Y. Surry (1997), "A Bayesian analysis of trade in processed food products: An application to France", Paper presented at the IAAE meetings, Sacramento, August 10–16.

Hertel, T.W. (1989), "Negotiating reductions in agricultural support: Implications of technology and factor mobility", American Journal of Agricultural Economics 71(3).

Hertel, T.W. (1990), "General equilibrium analysis of U.S. agriculture: What does it contribute?", Journal of Agricultural Economic Research 42(3):3–9.

Hertel, T.W. (1997), Global Trade Analysis: Modeling and Applications (Cambridge University Press, New York).

Hertel, T.W., V.E. Ball, K.S. Huang and M.E. Tsigas (1989), "Computing general equilibrium farm level demand elasticities for agricultural commodities", AES Research Bulletin No. 988 (Purdue University).

Hertel, T.W., E. Ianchovichina and B. McDonald (1997), "Multi-region general equilibrium modeling", in: J. Francois and K. Reinert, eds., Applied Methods for Trade Policy Analysis: A Handbook (Cambridge University Press, New York) Chapter 9.

Hertel, T.W., D.K. Lanclos, K.R. Pearson and P.V. Swaminathan (1997), "Aggregation and computation of equilibrium elasticities", in: T.W. Hertel, ed., Global Trade Analysis: Modeling and Applications (Cambridge University Press, New York) Chapter 5.

Hertel, T.W., E.B. Peterson, Y. Surry, P.V. Preckel and M.E. Tsigas (1991), "Implicit additivity as a strategy for restricting the parameter space in computable general equilibrium models", Economic and Financial Computing 1:265–289.

Hertel, T.W., K. Stiegert and H. Vroomen (1996), "Nitrogen-land substitution in corn production: A reconciliation of aggregate and farm-level evidence", American Journal of Agricultural Economics 78(1):30–40.

Hertel, T.W., R.L. Thompson and M.E. Tsigas (1989), "Economywide effects of unilateral trade and policy liberalization in U.S. agriculture", in: A.B. Stoeckel, D. Vincent and S. Cuthbertson, eds., Macroeconomic Consequences of Farm Support Policies (Duke University Press, Durham, NC).

Hertel, T.W., and M.E. Tsigas (1988a), "Tax policy and U.S. agriculture: A general equilibrium approach", American Journal of Agricultural Economics 70(2):289–302.

Hertel, T.W., and M.E. Tsigas (1988b), "Factor market implications of trade and policy liberalization in U.S. agriculture", Paper prepared for the IATRC Symposium on Bringing Agriculture Into the GATT, Annapolis, MD, August 19–20.

Hertel, T.W., and M.E. Tsigas (1991), "General equilibrium analysis of supply control in U.S. agriculture", European Review of Agricultural Economics 18:167–191.

Hertel, T.W., M.E. Tsigas and P.V. Preckel (1990), "An economic analysis of the freeze on program payment yields", ERS/USDA Staff Report No. 9066.

Higgs, P.J. (1989), "The taxation of Australian agriculture through assistance to Australian manufacturing", in: A.B. Stoeckel, D. Vincent and S. Cuthbertson, eds., Macroeconomic Consequences of Farm Support Policies (Duke University Press, Durham, NC).

Hjort, K.C. (1988), "Class and source substitutability in the demand for imported wheat", Unpublished Ph.D. dissertation (Purdue University).

Horridge, M., and D. Pearce (1988), "Modeling the effects on Australia of interventions in world agricultural trade", IMPACT Preliminary Working Paper No. OP-65 (University of Melbourne).

Huang, K.S., and R.C. Haidacher (1983), "Estimation of a composite food demand system for the United States", Journal of Business and Economic Statistics 1:285–291.

Huff, K.M., and T.W. Hertel (1996), "Decomposition of welfare effects in the GTAP model", GTAP Technical Paper No. 5 (Center for Global Trade Analysis, Purdue University), http://www.agecon.purdue.edu/gtap.

Irwin, W.H., D.L. Forster and B.J. Herrick (1988), "Returns to farm real estate revisited", American Journal of Agricultural Economics 70(3):580–587.

James, M., and R.A. McDougall (1993), "FIT: An input–output data update facility for SALTER", SALTER Working Paper No. 17 (Australian Industry Commission, Canberra).

Johansen, L. (1960), A Multisectoral Model of Economic Growth, 2nd edn. (North-Holland, Amsterdam, 1974).

Just, R.E., D. Zilberman and E. Hochman (1983) "Estimation of multicrop production functions", American Journal of Agricultural Economics 65:770–780.

Kehoe, T.J., C. Polo and F. Sancho (1991), "An evaluation of the performance of an applied general equilibrium model of the Spanish economy", Working Paper No. 480 (Federal Reserve Bank of Minneapolis).

Keller, W.J. (1980), Tax Incidence: A General Equilibrium Approach (North-Holland, Amsterdam).

Keuschnigg, C., and W. Kohler (1997), "Dynamics of trade liberalization", in: J. Francois and K. Reinert, eds., Applied Methods for Trade Policy Analysis: A Handbook (Cambridge University Press, New York) Chapter 13.

Kilkenny, M. (1991), "Computable general equilibrium modeling of agricultural policies: Documentation of the 30 Sector FPGG GAMS model of the United States", ERS/USDA Staff Report No. AGES9125 (USDA, Washington, DC).

Kilkenny, M. (1993), "Rural-urban effects of terminating farm subsidies", American Journal of Agricultural Economics 75(4):968–980.

Kilkenny, M., and S. Robinson (1988), "Modeling the removal of production incentive distortions in the U.S. agricultural sector", Invited paper, XX International Conference of Agricultural Economists, Buenos Aires, Argentina, August 24–31.

Kilkenny, M., and S. Robinson (1990), "AGE analysis of agricultural liberalization: Factor mobility and macro closure", Journal of Policy Modeling 12(3):527–556.

Komen, M.H.C., and J.H.M. Peerlings (1995), "Effects of manure policies in the Netherlands", Paper presented at the 6th CGE Modeling Conference, Waterloo, Oct. 26–28.

Komen, M.H.C., and J.H.M. Peerlings (1998), "Environmental indicators in an AGE framework – effects of the Dutch 1996 energy tax on agriculture", in: M. Brockmeier, J.F. Francois, T.W. Hertel and P.M. Schmitz, eds., Economic Transition and the Greening of Policies: Modeling New Challenges for Agriculture and Agribusiness in Europe (Vauk, Kiel).

Kraybill, D.S., T.G. Johnson and D. Orden (1992), "Macroeconomic imbalances: A multiregional general equilibrium analysis", American Journal of Agricultural Economics 74:726–736.

Lanclos, D.K., and T.W. Hertel (1995), "Endogenous product differentiation and trade policy", American Journal of Agricultural Economics 77(3):591–601.

Lee, D.R., and P.G. Helmberger (1985), "Estimating supply response in the presence of farm programs", American Journal of Agricultural Economics 67(2):193–203.

Legg, W., and L. Portugall (1997), "How agriculture benefits the environment", The OECD Observer, No. 205.

López, R.A., A.O. Adelajo and M.S. Andrews (1988), "The effects of suburbanization on agriculture", American Journal of Agricultural Economics 70(2):346–358.

Martin, W., and L.A. Winters (1996), The Uruguay Round and the Developing Countries (Cambridge University Press).

McDonald, B.J. (1990), "Agricultural negotiations and the Uruguay round", World Economy 13(3):299–327.

McKibbin, W.J., and J. Sachs (1991), Global Linkages: Macroeconomic Interdependence and Cooperation in the World Economy (The Brookings Institution, Washington, DC).

McKibbin, W.J., and Z. Wang (1998), "G-Cubed (agriculture) model: A tool for analyzing U.S. agriculture in a globalizing world", Unpublished manuscript (ERS/USDA, Washington, DC).

Minot, N., and F. Goletti (1997), "Rice policy in Vietnam: Analyzing the regional implications with a multimarket spatial equilibrium model", Paper presented at the 1997 AAEA meetings, Toronto, July 28–31.

Moschini, G. (1988), "The cost structure of Ontario dairy farms: A microeconometric analysis", Canadian Journal of Agricultural Economics 36:187–206.

OECD (Organization for Economic Co-operation and Development) (1998), "Work on agriculture and the environment", http://www.oecd.org/agr/publications/AGE_PUEB.HTM.

Pagan, A.R., and J. Shannon (1987), How reliable are ORANI Conclusions?", Economic Record 1:33–45.

Peeters, L., and Y. Surry (1997), "A preview of the arts of estimating price responsiveness of feed demand in the European Union", Journal of Agricultural Economics 48:379–392.

Perroni, C., and T.F. Rutherford (1995), "Regular flexibility of nested CES functions", European Economic Review 39(2):335–343.

Perroni, C., and T.F. Rutherford (1997), "A comparison of the performance of flexible functional forms for use in applied general equilibrium analysis", Computational Economics 11:245–263.

Perroni, C., and R. Wigle (1994), "International trade and environmental quality: How important are the linkages?", Canadian Journal of Economics 27(3):551–567.

Peterson, E.B. (1989), "The farm-retail price spread revisited: A general equilibrium perspective", Unpublished Ph.D. dissertation (Purdue University).

Peterson, E.B., T.W. Hertel and J. Stout (1994), "A critical assessment of supply-demand models international agricultural trade", American Journal of Agricultural Economics 76(4):709–721.

Peterson, W. (1988), "International supply response", Agricultural Economics 2:365–374.

Philippidis, G., and L.J. Hubbard (1998), "Characterizing imperfectly competitive markets using the GTAP model", Paper presented at the First Annual Conference on Global Economic Analysis, June 8–10 (Purdue University).

Powell, A.A., and R.H. Snape (1993), "The contribution of applied general equilibrium analysis to policy reform in Australia", Journal of Policy Modeling 15(4):393–414.

Pyatt, G., and J.I. Round (1979), "Accounting and fixed-price multipliers in a social accounting matrix framework", Economic Journal 89:850–873.

Rendleman, C.M. (1993), "Agrichemical reduction policy", Journal of Agricultural Economics Research 43(3):7–12.

Rendleman, C.M., and T.W. Hertel (1993), "Do corn farmers have too much faith in the sugar program?", Journal of Agricultural and Resource Economics 18:86–95.

Rimmer, M.T., and A.A. Powell (1994), "Engel flexibility in household budget studies: Non-parametric evidence vs. standard functional form", COPS/IMPACT Working Paper No. OP-79 (Monash University, Clayton, Vic.).

Rimmer, M.T., and A.A. Powell (1996), "An implicitly additive demand system", Applied Economics 28:1613–1622.

Robidoux, B., M. Smart, J. Lester and L. Beausejour (1989), "The agriculture expanded GET model: Overview of model structure", Unpublished manuscript (Department of Finance, Ottawa, Canada).

Robinson, S. (1988), "Multisectoral. Models of developing countries: A survey", in: Chenery and Srinivasan, eds., Handbook of Development Economics (North-Holland, Amsterdam).

Robinson, S. (1991), "Macroeconomics, financial variables, and computable general equilibrium models", World Development 19(11):1509–1525.

Robinson, S., M.E. Burfisher, R. Hinojosa-Ojeda and K.E. Thierfelder (1993), "Agriculture in a U.S.–Mexico free trade agreement: A computable general equilibrium model with migration and farm programs", Journal of Policy Modeling (February).

Robinson, S., and C. Gehlhar (1995), "Land, water and agriculture in Egypt: The economywide impact of policy reform", IFPRI TMD Discussion Paper No. 1 (Washington, DC).

Robinson, S., M. Kilkenny and I. Adelman (1989), "The effect of trade liberalization in agriculture on the U.S. economy: Projections to 1991", in: A.B. Stoeckel, D. Vincent and S. Cuthbertson, eds., Macroeconomic Consequences of Farm Support Policies (Duke University Press, Durham, NC).

Roningen, V.O., J. Sullivan and P.M. Dixit (1991), "Documentation of the Static World Policy Simulation (SWOPSIM) modeling framework", Staff Report AGES 9151 (U.S. Department of Agricultural, Economic Research Service).

Rutherford, T.F. (1999), "Applied general equilibrium modeling with MPSGE as a GAMS subsystem: An overview of the modeling framework and syntax", Computational Economics.

Rutstrom, E.E.H. (1995), "Political preference functions, trade wars and trade negotiations in agriculture", Empirical Economics 20:49–73.

Rutstrom, E.E.H., and W.J. Redmond (1997), "A quantification of lobbying benefits with an application to the common agricultural policy", Journal of Policy Modeling.

Sadoulet, E., and A. de Janvry (1995), Quantitative Development Policy Analysis (Johns Hopkins University Press, Baltimore).

Sakai, Y. (1974), "Substitution and expansion effects in production theory: The case of joint production", Journal of Economic Theory 9:255–274.

Sayan, S., and N. Demir (1998), "Measuring the degree of block interdependence between agricultural and non-agricultural sectors in Turkey", Applied Economics Letters 5:329–332.

Schreiner, P., and K.A. Larsen (1985), "On the introduction and application of the MSG-model in the Norwegian planning system", in: Forsund, Hoel and Longva, eds., Production, Multisectoral Growth and Planning (North-Holland, Amsterdam).

Schuh, G.E. (1976), "The new macroeconomics of agriculture", American Journal of Agricultural Economics 58:802–811.

Seeley, R. (1985), "Price elasticities from the IIASA world agriculture model", ERS Staff Report No. AGES850418 (USDA, Washington, DC).

Sen, A.K. (1963), "Neo-classical and Neo-Keynesian theories of distribution", Economic Record 39:54–64.

Shively, G.E. (1997), "Erosion and income dynamics in a watershed-based model of tropical agriculture", Paper presented at the meetings of the Soil and Water Conservation Society, Toronto, July 23.

Shoemaker, R.A. (1992), "The incentive effects of agricultural support programs: A dynamic analysis of U.S. agricultural policy", Unpublished Ph.D. dissertation (George Washington University).

Shoven, J., and J. Whalley (1992), Applying General Equilibrium (Cambridge University Press, Cambridge).

Shumway, C.R., R.D. Pope and E.K. Nash (1984), "Allocatable fixed inputs and jointness in agricultural production: Implications for economic modeling", American Journal of Agricultural Economics 66:72–78.

Simon, H.A. (1947), "Effects of increased productivity upon the ratio of urban to rural population", Econometrica 15:31–42.

Solow, R.M. (1973), "Is the end of the world at hand?", Challenge (March–April issue).

Stoeckel, A.B. (1985), Intersectoral Effects of the CAP: Growth, Trade and Unemployment (Australian Government Publishing Service, Canberra).

Sumner, D.A. (1990), "Targeting and distribution of farm program benefits", in: K. Allen, ed., Agricultural Policies in a New Decade (Resources for the Future, Washington, DC).

Surry, Y. (1989), "The 'Constant difference of elasticities' (CDE) functional farm: A neglected alternative?", Contributed paper (AAEA annual meetings, Baton Rouge, LA).

Trela, I., J. Whalley and R. Wigle (1987), "International trade in grain: Domestic policies and trade conflicts", Scandinavian Journal of Economics 89(3):271–283.

Tsigas, M.E., D. Gray and B. Krissoff (1997), "Harmonization of environmental standards in the western hemisphere", Unpublished paper (ERS/USDA, Washington, DC).

Tyers, R., and K. Anderson (1992), Disarray in World Food Markets (Cambridge University Press).

United States Department of Agriculture, Economic Research Service (ERS) (1988), "Estimates of producer and consumer subsidy equivalents: Government intervention in agriculture, 1982–86", Staff Report No. AGES880127 (Washington, DC).

United States Department of Agriculture (USDA) (1995), "Farm operation household income compares favorably with all household income", Rural Conditions and Trends, Spring, pp. 34–35.

Vasavada, U., and R.G. Chambers (1986), "Investment in U.S. agriculture", American Journal of Agricultural Economics 68(4):950–960.

Veenendaal, P.J.J. (1998), "EU agricultural policy implementation using complementarity conditions", Paper presented at the First Annual Conference on Global Economic Analysis, June 8–10 (Purdue University).

Vincent, D.P. (1989), "Effects of agricultural protection in Japan: An economywide analysis", in: A.B. Stoeckel, D. Vincent and S. Cuthbertson, eds., Macroeconomic Consequences of Farm Support Policies (Duke University Press, Durham, NC).

Vincent, D.P., P.B. Dixon and A.A. Powell (1977), "Estimates of the CRETH supply system for Australian agriculture", IMPACT Working Paper No. OP-17 (University of Melbourne).

Wang, Z. (1997), "Impact of China's WTO accession on labor intensive exports and implications for U.S. agricultural trade: A recursive dynamic analysis", Paper presented at the 1997 AAEA meetings, Toronto, July 28–31.

Warr, P.G. (1995), "Factor demand and technical change in Philippine agriculture", Asia-Pacific Economic Review 1(3):23–36.

Warr, P.G., and I.A. Coxhead (1993), "The distributional impact of technical change in Philippine agriculture: A general equilibrium analysis", Food Research Institute Studies 22:253–274.

Whalley, J. (1985), Trade Liberalization Among Major World Trading Areas (MIT Press, Cambridge).

Whalley, J. (1986), "Hidden challenges in recent applied general equilibrium exercises", in: Piggott and Whalley, eds., New Developments in Applied General Equilibrium Analysis (Cambridge University Press, New York).

Whalley, J., and R. Wigle (1990), "Terms of trade effects, agricultural liberalization, and developing countries", in: O. Knudsen and I. Golden, eds., Agricultural Trade Liberalization: Implications for Developing Countries (The World Bank, Washington, DC).

Wilcoxen, P. (1989), "Intertemporal optimization in general equilibrium: A practical introduction", Impact Project Preliminary Working Paper No. IP-45 (Melbourne).

Winters, L.A. (1984), "Separability and the specification of foreign trade functions", Journal of International Economics 1:239–263.

Wohlgenant, M.K. (1987), "Demand for farm output in a complete system of demand functions", American Journal of Agricultural Economics 71(2):241–252.

Chapter 27

AGRICULTURE AND THE MACROECONOMY, WITH EMPHASIS ON DEVELOPING COUNTRIES

MAURICE SCHIFF and ALBERTO VALDÉS

The World Bank, Washington, DC

Contents

Handbook of Agricultural Economics, Volume 2, Edited by B. Gardner and G. Rausser
© 2002 Elsevier Science B.V. All rights reserved

Abstract

Based on an economy-wide perspective, this paper begins with a discussion of the bias against exports and agriculture that characterized the economic literature and the development strategies in many developing countries after World War II. This is followed by an analysis of how the macroeconomic environment affects agricultural price incentives. Specifically, the paper discusses how policies concerning industrial protection, exchange rates, and interest rates and other fiscal policies can strongly influence the economic incentives for agriculture compared with other sectors, identifying the most relevant literature and alternative approaches used on this issue. It then proceeds to examine how the real exchange rate can be affected by exogenous shocks, such as the foreign terms of trade, with emphases on the Dutch disease phenomenon and agriculture. The paper next examines the influence of interest rates on incentives in agriculture, arguing that, surprisingly, this has been a neglected area in the literature.

The paper explores the effects on agriculture of structural adjustment programs implemented since the early 1980s in developing countries. The final section surveys the literature on agriculture and the macroeconomy in industrial countries, focusing on the impact of the exchange rate on export competitiveness in the United States, the cost of agricultural protection for the overall economy in Europe and Japan, and the increased importance of fluctuations in money markets for the farm sector and the additional instability they generate.

Keywords

macro, trade, exchange rate, interest rate policy

JEL classification: Q10

1. Introduction

Until the mid-1980s, most analysts of agricultural policies were preoccupied with the direct effects of sectoral pricing and trade policies on output, resource use, and income distribution. Since that time, however, a number of analyses have suggested that the indirect effects of economy-wide policies on agricultural incentives have been greater than the impact of policies directed specifically toward agriculture. Conversely, in some cases, agricultural policies have had significant effects on macroeconomic variables.

This chapter assesses the state of our knowledge about the relationship and interaction between agriculture and the macroeconomy, with emphasis on less developed countries. It identifies what the authors believe to represent the most significant contributions and shortcomings of the existing scholarship on the subject. We begin with a discussion of the bias against exports and agriculture that characterized development economics following the Second World War and the decolonization of many developing countries. During this time, export pessimism drove the shift from agriculture toward industry, and the substitution of imported industrial products with domestically produced goods. This substitution occurred irrespective of comparative advantage or disadvantage. The effects of import-substituting policies on agricultural incentives and economic growth were profound. A reorientation towards more open economies followed, beginning in South America in the mid-1970s, and becoming more profound in the mid-1980s. The changes were influenced by trade and development economists who began to investigate the potential contribution that opening the trade regime could make to overall economic growth.

In an analysis of agricultural incentives from an economy-wide perspective, it was found that the "indirect" effects of macroeconomic and industrial policies were no less important to agriculture than the "direct" sector-specific agricultural policies. Two key relationships were central in this analysis: the relative price of agricultural to non-agricultural products, and the price of tradable to non-tradable (or "home") goods, i.e., the real exchange rate. We examined the factors that determine the equilibrium real rate of exchange, and that shift actual exchange rates toward equilibrium. These factors include both policy-induced domestic forces (such as changes in technology and productivity), and exogenous international forces (like changes in a country's foreign terms of trade).

Exogenous factors include the relative prices of a country's imports and exports (its terms of trade) and the variables that go into determining them. One of the determinants is an export commodity boom (in some cases resulting in "Dutch disease" phenomenon), whose effect on other tradables has proven to be profound. Foreign capital flows are also significant in determining exchange rates, the price of inputs, and the cost of borrowing money. We discuss below the importance of interest rates to these capital flows, as well as their effects on agricultural investment itself.

We then explore the effects of structural adjustment programs. These began during the 1970s, and gained currency throughout the developing world during the 1980s, as countries sought to correct their macroeconomic imbalances, especially overvalued exchange rates, that resulted from years of industrial protection and budget deficits.

In the final section, we compare and contrast the experience of the industrialized "North", where agriculture accounts for a far lower proportion of national incomes and economic growth, to that of the developing "South", where substantially greater levels of exchange rate misalignment and industrial protection have imposed severe indirect taxation on agriculture. In stark contrast to the Southern experience, Northern agriculture enjoyed substantial protection even while industrial protection declined over time. We explore the macroeconomic implications of agricultural protection in the North for international prices and agricultural competitiveness, giving special attention to U.S. agricultural tradables and the European Community's experience under the Common Agricultural Policy.

2. Development strategies in the South after World War II: A historical perspective

The historical setting in which countries conceived and implemented development strategies in the decades following World War II is an appropriate place to start. The central issue of the time was finding and then cultivating a developing economy's "lead" sector, the sector capable of serving as its "engine of growth". This "engine" would presumably provide the income necessary to nourish and sustain economic development, while fostering a self-reliance that would prevent a society from depending upon international market forces that were outside a small country's capacity to affect. Economists recalled the collapse of primary commodity markets during the Depression, and of the disruptions in these markets during the Second World War. Their fear of such dependency led many development economists to ally themselves with what became known in economics as the "structuralist school" and "dependency theory".

The sector which seemed capable of providing the "engine", particularly in the aftermath of the colonial experience, was industry. Agriculture was viewed, by many, as the station of the colony, the provider of primary products demanded by industrial countries. Persisting in this peripheral role would be tantamount to a *de facto* perpetuation of colonialism, hence the term neo-colonialism. But the nationalistic impulse among developing countries, many of which were newly independent, was not alone in leading many in the developing world to spurn agriculture and to discount its potential contribution to economic growth. Agrarian society by its very nature was regarded as socially and economically backward, governed by tradition, impervious to market signals, and devoid of links to other sectors that could bring the benefits of progress in agricultural production to the economy as a whole.[1]

---

[1] Another concern was the perceived secular decline in real agricultural prices which was blamed on an inelastic demand for agricultural products. The assumption was that the shift in the supply of agricultural

The academic acceptance of these presumptions without proper empirical evidence, and the overwhelming pre-eminence that scholars afforded industrial policy as a result, represented a monumental failure on the part of development economists. The illogic of this course was characterized succinctly by Theodore W. Schultz at the beginning of *Transforming Traditional Agriculture* (1964), when he wrote that "economists who have been studying growth have, with few exceptions, put agriculture aside in order to concentrate on industry, despite the fact that every country has an agriculture sector and in low-income countries it is generally the largest sector". Schultz's work set into motion an academic reexamination of the anti-export, anti-agricultural prejudice of dependency doctrine that would ultimately provide many of the theoretical underpinnings of the policy realignments of the 1980s.

The preoccupation with the limits of traditional and subsistence agriculture that was so characteristic of structuralists and dependency literature led to a neglect of agriculture in general. The fear of depending on agricultural exports led to a neglect of the potential contributions export revenues might deliver to growing, capital-starved economies. And yet, one of the outstanding attributes shared by nearly all developing countries was that their exports were overwhelmingly agricultural.

Another attribute shared by most developing countries was that their imports were, in large measure, industrial products. The unfortunate alternative to pursuing productivity gains in exportables was to replace imports with products made domestically. The prescription of import-substituting industrialization followed from the structural and dependency doctrines' assumptions about agriculture. The reasoning was that if industry lacked competitive advantage, it must be shielded from powerful foreign competitors by import barriers until it became capable of competing, regardless of whether or not this was a realistic expectation. Whatever costs had to be incurred by other sectors, including agriculture, to pay for this protection were justified on these grounds. The costs of this protection were felt widely across entire economies, with disastrous effects on growth.

One theory that had a significant impact on economic policy was that of "balanced growth", articulated by Rosenstein-Rodan (1943) and Nurkse (1952). They predicted that rapid growth in developing economies would not be achieved through increased exports of primary commodities, and argued that development strategies should place greater emphasis on industrialization. Recognizing the limits imposed by the small size of domestic markets, balanced growth theory prescribed the simultaneous promotion of a variety of different industries in a way that would foster complementary demand among those industries for one another's products. A central premise in Rosenstein-Rodan and Nurkse's work (as well as that of Ranis and Fei, Lewis, and others) was the assumption that a large surplus of labor was employed at zero marginal product in rural

---

products over time associated with technical progress was larger than the shift in demand. On the other hand, Martin and Warr (1993), and Gehlhar, Hertel and Martin (1994) have argued that Rybczynski effects associated with the accumulation of capital in the process of growth result in a shift of resources away from the labor-intensive sector (agriculture) to the capital-intensive one (industry), which should dampen the negative effects on relative agricultural prices.

areas. This surplus would prevent labor bottlenecks from occurring that might otherwise constrain balanced growth. Underlying the concept of a balanced growth path was the perception that resources for investment were severely limited. This, coupled with the belief that a certain minimum level of investment was required to capture the external economies of sectoral growth and move a country to a higher growth path, was the "big push" advocated by Rosenstein-Rodan (1943, 1957). And it was here that the debate over where resources should be concentrated came to a choice between agriculture and industry.

The "structuralist school", embodied in the works of Prebisch (1950), Singer (1950), and Myrdal (1957), drew similar conclusions, strongly emphasizing the forces which limited demand for primary products. The structuralist view, prevalent at the time, was that agriculture in general, and the traditional agriculture that was characteristic of developing economies in particular, was slow and weak in its response to market signals, owing to such constraints as imperfect factor mobility.[2]

Pessimism about the potential of agricultural exports to "lead" economic development was based on a number of factors [Valdés (1991)]. Agricultural exports tended to consist of a small number of commodities, more reliant on natural resources as inputs than other commodities. For this reason, the agricultural sector was perceived as having few or weak linkages with the rest of the economy, and thus unable to serve as an "engine of growth". Demand for many of these primary commodities was presumed to be inelastic, both with respect to their prices and to income. It was argued that dependence on a few export commodities implied that import capacity would be determined by the prices of these commodities on the international market, making income subject to boom-bust cycles which governments could do little or nothing about. There were those who felt that the lack of control over foreign exchange earnings made outward-oriented development strategies seem irresponsible.

Given that many countries were indeed experiencing declining demand for their primary agricultural products [Meier (1989)], it is perhaps not surprising that these ideas came to profoundly influence the formulation of development strategies in many developing countries. In the 1950s, these countries began pursuing higher economic growth through policies of import-substituting industrialization. High import tariffs and concessional credit lines favored industry, while low import tariffs and relatively high export taxes on agricultural products revealed the extent to which the prevailing export pessimism was embraced by Third World policy-makers. Resources had to be purposefully channeled to the non-farm sectors which were thought capable of contributing to and sustaining faster growth within the overall economy. Agriculture in this view was there to serve simply as a resource base.

---

[2] The belief that agricultural output was not responsive to changes in price was also propounded in industrialized countries. This arose from the experiences of the U.S. during the Depression (1919–22 and 1929–33), as articulated by Galbraith (1938). However, Johnson (1950) disputed the validity of this hypothesis as applied to the Depression, and also disputed its applicability during times of full employment.

As understandable as the popularity of the structuralist school was, their emphasis on factors that would limit the demand for primary products led them to discount the possible benefits that opening new markets for new primary products might have. Moreover, the assumption that agriculture had few and weak linkages to the rest of the economy caused structuralists to disregard these linkages in their strategy. In fact, little empirical evidence was produced regarding the strength or extent of the interrelationship between agriculture and the larger economy [Valdés (1991)].

Beginning in the early 1960s, the structuralist and dependency-theory schools faced increasing criticism. Schultz's *Transforming Traditional Agriculture*, and pioneering cross-country studies on trade policy and development by Little, Scitovsky and Scott (1970), Krueger (1978), Bhagwati (1978), and Balassa (1982), argued that in terms of both growth performance and employment generation, export-oriented development strategies had performed better than import-substituting ones during the post-World War II period.

By the mid-1980s, developing countries had grown increasingly disillusioned with import-substituting strategies, and a major reorientation has been taking place ever since. The new approach involves a more open economy, and recognizes the active role that agriculture can play as a major tradable sector in most developing countries.

3. The macroeconomic environment and agricultural price incentives

Governments affect agriculture directly through sector-specific measures including tariffs, input and credit subsidies, price controls, quantitative restrictions (QRs), and government expenditures and taxes. Indirectly, government policies often have unintended effects on agriculture. Policies concerning industrial protection, exchange rates and interest rates, and other fiscal and monetary policies can strongly influence the incentives for agriculture vis-à-vis other sectors. For example, border protection has often been used to protect domestic manufacturing, and restrictive trade policies, accompanied by fiscal deficits, often result in exchange rate misalignment. Agriculture is also affected indirectly by exogenous changes in the world prices of non-agricultural commodities, such as oil and minerals, and by foreign capital flows. Because sectoral growth is affected by resource flows between sectors, and because these flows adjust to the relative opportunities offered by different sectors over time, an economy-wide view of returns is necessary for understanding the dynamics of agricultural growth and employment.

Traditionally, agricultural economics has defined the effect of economic policies on incentives in terms of the nominal tariff, or sometimes the tariff equivalent (including QRs), faced by agriculture, or what we referred to above as "direct" price interventions. Alternatively, in a general equilibrium framework, agricultural incentives could be defined in terms of the relative price of agricultural to non-agricultural products. The difference between the two concepts lies in the definition and the measurement of price interventions. Most studies have taken the price of the non-agricultural sector as given, and have restricted their analysis to the effects of sectoral or direct policies on agricultural prices. Some studies did adjust for exchange rate misalignment, generally employing nominal exchange rates (we will argue below that the real exchange rate is more appropriate). For examples of the nominal exchange rate adjustment approach, see Valdés (1973), Taylor and Phillips (1991), Byerlee and Sain (1986), and Lattimore and Schuh (1979).

Agriculture's ability to compete for resources domestically and globally is directly affected by economy-wide policies. These policies have important effects on relative agricultural prices through the real exchange rate and the price of non-agricultural tradable activities. We proceed below with a discussion of nominal and real exchange rates, followed by a description of the evolution of our understanding of how macro-economic policies affect agricultural incentives. The remainder of the section discusses, in turn, exogenous effects (in particular export-commodity booms), interest rates, and structural adjustment programs.

3.1. The real exchange rate

There are two major concepts of the exchange rate, namely the nominal and the real rates. The nominal rate is an undeflated conversion factor between one currency and another. It corresponds to the exchange rate a government can announce or fix. The nominal equilibrium rate is the rate at which the demand and supply of foreign exchange (to finance both current account and autonomous capital account transactions) are equal for a given set of trade taxes. The purchasing power parity (PPP) relates the purchasing power of one currency to that of another, by adjusting the nominal rate for relative inflation. Neither the PPP nor the nominal equilibrium rate necessarily implies an optimum exchange rate, nor does either correspond to the shadow price of foreign exchange used in social project evaluation. The PPP is considered to be misaligned when its value differs from the base period value. The concept of effective exchange rate, a commodity-specific rate that expresses the price of foreign exchange including all import or export taxes, is useful in analyzing individual activities.

In contrast, the real exchange rate (RER) is a relative price that reflects the competitiveness of the tradable sector (import substitutes and exportables). The RER varies according to the definition used (e.g., with respect to the deflator). Following Salter (1959), Swan (1960), Dornbusch (1974), and others, the RER introduces the concept of a home goods (or non-tradable) sector. A key factor on which the distinction between tradables and non-tradables is based is their price-formation mechanism. Both prices and quantities of home goods are determined by domestic supply and demand. In contrast, for small open economies, the domestic prices of tradables are determined by world markets together with the nominal exchange rate, trade taxes, and subsidies.

The various definitions of the RER that are used in agricultural economics literature have resulted in some confusion.[3] One version is the purchasing power parity index

---

[3] See Hinkle and Nsengumiva (forthcoming) for a detailed discussion on the various definitions of the real exchange rate.

mentioned above. Most early studies that attempted to measure the impact of the RER on agricultural incentives used the PPP approach [for example, Valdés (1973), Binswanger and Scandizzo (1983), and more recently Byerlee and Sain (1986)]. There are at least three problems with the PPP concept of the RER. The first is the possibility that the base period RER may be misaligned as a result of macroeconomic disequilibrium. Second, even if the RER is in equilibrium in the base period, there is no reason to assume that this equilibrium will remain unchanged over time, owing to such factors as changes in the terms of trade and international interest rates. Third, the base period PPP is obtained under given trade policy distortions, while we are interested in the equilibrium RER that would prevail in the absence of trade policy distortions. This requires a model of RER determination not found in the PPP adjustment.

A now widely accepted definition of the real exchange rate is the ratio of the price of tradables to non-tradables,

$$\text{RER} = \frac{P_T}{P_{NT}}, \tag{1}$$

in which P_T is the price of tradables and P_{NT} is the price of non-tradables. The RER can serve as a proxy for a country's international competitiveness [Edwards (1988)]. An increase in the RER (a depreciation) represents an improvement in the country's international competitiveness given relative prices in the rest of the world. Conversely, a decrease in the RER (an appreciation) indicates a decline in the country's international competitiveness. Changes in the RER can occur as a result of policy-induced effects that reflect a misalignment in the RER, and as a result of exogenous factors that reflect a change in the equilibrium value of the RER.

In empirical estimation, the RER is often proxied as

$$\text{RER} = \frac{E_0 P^*}{P}, \tag{2}$$

where E_0 is the nominal exchange rate, expressed as local currency per unit of foreign currency, P^* is the foreign price index for tradables (often approximated by the wholesale price index), and P is the domestic price index, presumably heavily weighted by the home goods sector (as with the consumer price index).

It is important to clarify the concept of equilibrium RER (ERER). Several conceptual and empirical definitions of the ERER are used in the literature, including the PPP. Edwards (1988) defined the ERER as that level of RER at which the economy is accumulating or decumulating foreign assets at the "desired rate", and at which the demand for domestic goods equals supply. This definition can be refined to consider an ERER for a given trade policy regime, such as the ERER that would prevail under free trade. An important feature of this definition is its treatment of the ERER as a general equilibrium concept.

Edwards' calculation was based on the idea of "macroeconomic fundamentals", and provides a useful framework for the discussion at hand. The "macroeconomic fundamentals" that determine the RER can be divided into external and internal factors. The internal factors can be divided into those influenced by policy decisions, and those that are exogenous to policy. Domestic policy variables include import tariffs and export taxes, quantitative restrictions on imports and exports, exchange and capital controls, other taxes and subsidies, and the level and composition of government expenditure.[4] Domestic effects that are exogenous to domestic policies include productivity changes and technological progress, among others. External factors include international prices, international transfers (such as private capital flows and foreign aid), and world real interest rates.

Changes in any of the variables will have an impact on the level of the RER, and most will affect the level of the ERER. For example, an increase in the world price of importables relative to exportables (i.e., a deterioration of the terms of trade) reduces the quantity of importables demanded, and induces a change in the level of the ERER (the direction of the change is ambiguous due to the negative income effect). An increase in import tariffs will have a similar effect on the domestic relative price of importables, reducing the quantity of importables demanded, and resulting in demand switching to non-tradables and exportables. This in turn exerts upward pressure on the price of non-tradables, causing the ERER to shift downwards (i.e., to appreciate), given the existing trade policy regime and other determinants. Sustainable, or permanent, increases in government expenditure can also cause the ERER to decrease, owing to the increase in aggregate demand. Even if increases in government spending are financed through taxes, the ERER may appreciate due to the public sector's higher propensity to spend on non-tradables (such as labor).

The ERER is, therefore, not a constant, but follows a discernible trend, a fact of critical importance when considering the effects of policy decisions. Elbadawi (1994), for instance, found India's ERER from 1967 to 1981 not only close to the actual RER, but that the ERER depreciated along with the actual RER. This does not imply that the rupee was not overvalued, but simply that the actual depreciation was just sufficient to offset the reduction in protection, leaving the margin of overvaluation almost unaffected.

Conversely, changes in the RER do not necessarily reflect disequilibrium. For example, technological progress in the production of importables (which will result in an improvement in the foreign terms of trade), or increased capital inflows, will both result in an appreciation of the RER. Insofar as the changes in these factors are permanent, the ERER will also appreciate.

While the ERER is determined by real variables, the actual RER responds to both real and monetary variables. Typically, the RER is misaligned when the monetary and fiscal policies in place are inconsistent with the chosen nominal exchange rate regime. When the nominal exchange rate is fixed, any increase in domestic credit that exceeds

---

[4] Williamson (1994) pointed out that the evidence for the relevance of the composition of government expenditure was weak. Both Edwards (1994) and Elbadawi (1994) included it as a variable in estimating ERERs. In Williamson's view, the size of government expenditure, not its composition, was the important factor.

growth in the domestic demand for money (i.e., expansive monetary policy) will result in excess demand for both tradables and non-tradables. Excess demand for tradables translates into higher trade deficits, loss of international reserves, and/or higher net foreign borrowing, none of which affects domestic prices. Excess demand for non-tradables results in higher prices, and thus appreciation of the RER. If this appreciation is not the result of equilibrium changes in the macroeconomic variables, it implies a deviation of the actual RER from its equilibrium value.

It is also possible to construct another estimate of misalignment by comparing the ERER under the conditions of free trade to the actual RER. This construction was used by Schiff and Valdés (1992a) in computing the indirect effect of trade and macro-economic policies on agricultural incentives.

3.2. Policy-induced effects

In order to examine the impact of policy on agricultural incentives, we examine the impact on the value added among agricultural goods relative to that among non-agricultural goods. Both types of goods can be divided into tradables and home goods, i.e.,

$$\frac{\mathrm{VA}_A}{\mathrm{VA}_{NA}} = \frac{\beta \mathrm{VA}_{A_T} + (1-\beta)\mathrm{VA}_{A_H}}{\alpha \mathrm{VA}_{I_T} + (1-\alpha)\mathrm{VA}_{I_H}}, \quad \alpha, \beta < 1, \tag{3}$$

where VA_A is value added in the agricultural sector, VA_{NA} is value added in the non-agricultural sector, and VA_I is value added in the non-agricultural tradable (or industrial) sector. The subscripts T and H refer to tradable and home (non-tradable) goods, respectively. Since most agricultural goods are tradable, the value of β is usually taken to be very close to 1. The expression simplifies to the following form:

$$\frac{\mathrm{VA}_A}{\mathrm{VA}_{NA}} = \frac{\mathrm{VA}_A}{\alpha \mathrm{VA}_I + (1-\alpha)\mathrm{VA}_H}, \quad \alpha < 1. \tag{4}$$

This can be rewritten as

$$\frac{\mathrm{VA}_A}{\mathrm{VA}_{NA}} = \frac{\mathrm{VA}_A / \mathrm{VA}_H}{\alpha \mathrm{VA}_I / \mathrm{VA}_H + (1-\alpha)}, \quad \alpha < 1. \tag{5}$$

Many studies use relative prices instead of value added, in which case the expression becomes

$$\frac{P_A}{P_{NA}} \equiv \frac{P_A / P_H}{\alpha P_I / P_H + (1-\alpha)}, \quad \alpha < 1. \tag{6}$$

The relative price (or value added) of agricultural goods to non-agricultural goods can change as a result of changes in the price (or value added) of agricultural, industrial, or home goods. Protection of industry will affect agricultural relative prices in three ways. The first is through the real exchange rate, i.e., the price of tradables relative to non-tradables. Appreciation of the RER lowers both P_A/P_H and P_I/P_H, thus lowering P_A/P_{NA}. Second, industrial protection raises the domestic prices of industrial goods (P_I), therefore lowering the relative price of agricultural goods. Third, it lowers agriculture's value added by raising the cost of agricultural inputs.

Protectionist policies could theoretically result in higher P_H, higher P_I, lower VA_A, or any permutation of the three, depending on what macroeconomic policies are followed. An increase in the price of non-agricultural goods, resulting from industrial protection using tariffs or other restrictions, will lower the relative price of agricultural products. Industrial protection may also result in higher prices of agricultural inputs such as fertilizer, which will reduce the value added of agriculture [Schiff and Valdés (1992a)]. Finally, an increase in the relative price of home goods (i.e., an appreciation of the real exchange rate) will adversely affect the relative price of agriculture to non-agriculture (since the value of α is usually significantly less than 1), thus reducing the value of the numerator more than the value of the denominator in Equations (5) and (6).

Early discussions of the bias against agriculture as a result of industrialization policies pursued by developing countries is found in Diaz-Alejandro's (1970) study of Argentina, and Little, Scitovsky and Scott's (1970) study of seven developing economies in the 1950s and 1960s. Diaz-Alejandro used relative prices to examine the impact of protectionist policies on agriculture, while Little, Scitovsky and Scott examined effective protection through an analysis of value added. In the early 1980s, influenced by the work of Sjaastad (1980), the Trade Policy Program at the International Food Policy Research Institute (IFPRI) adapted and extended the "true protection" approach to analyze the issue of how industrial policies affected the price of agricultural tradables relative to non-tradable goods [for a synthesis of this research, see Valdés (1986a)]. Later, Krueger, Schiff and Valdés (1988), and Schiff and Valdés (1992a) adapted the "elasticities" approach to exchange rate determination in conjunction with an explicit treatment of non-agricultural prices (P_{NA}). These works explored the combined effect of direct (sector-specific) and indirect (economy-wide) policies on agriculture in a sample of eighteen developing countries. A sketch of these various approaches is presented below.

3.2.1. The Diaz-Alejandro approach

Diaz-Alejandro (1970) examined the case of Argentina from 1930 to 1964, studying the impact of policy on the relative prices of final goods. He focused exclusively on one ratio, P_A/P_I, finding that exports (virtually all of which were agricultural commodities) and the rural sector in general were effectively discriminated against by Argentine macroeconomic policies. Diaz-Alejandro's hypothesized bias against exports and agriculture was supported empirically by both data on the evolution of the external and internal terms of trade, and crop-specific data.

Diaz-Alejandro focused on the relative prices between agricultural and industrial commodities. He used a proxy that he called the "external terms of trade", or the ratio

Table 1
Argentina: agricultural domestic and external terms of trade (1935–39 $=$ 100)

Years	Internal TOT	External TOT	Ratio Int/Ext
1925–29	132	111	119
1930–34	87	79	110
1935–39	100	100	100
1940–44	62	89	70
1945–46	74	120	62
1947–49	80	169	47
1950–52	68	124	55
1953–55	68	114	60
1956–58	78	93	84
1959–61	85	91	93
1962–64	93	89	104

Source: Diaz-Alejandro (1970).

of export prices to import prices. The second proxy he used was the "internal terms of trade", or the ratio of wholesale prices of rural products to those of non-rural goods. He then calculated an index of the ratio of internal to external terms of trade as a summary measure of the net effect of government policies on relative prices.

Between 1925 and 1949, when the overwhelming majority of Argentina's exports were agricultural products, the internal terms of trade of agricultural goods deteriorated relative to Argentina's external terms of trade as a result of domestic policies. In the period from 1930 to 1939, Diaz-Alejandro calculated the average index value as 105.[5] The second period, from 1945 to 1955, covered the Peron years, during which policies were severely biased against agriculture. This period was characterized by extensive import-substituting industrialization, and the index average dropped to 55. During the final period, from 1955 to 1964, the index averaged 94, as the bias against rural goods diminished.

3.2.2. The effective protection approach

The concept of effective protection, developed by Corden (1966) and Balassa (1965), was used in cross-country studies of the manufacturing sector by Balassa (1965), and by Little, Scitovsky and Scott (1970). In their analysis of seven developing countries in the 1950s and 1960s, Little, Scitovsky and Scott (1970) compared domestic value added to value added at world prices. They found extremely high levels of protection for manufacturing in several of the countries, as high as 313 percent in India in 1961 (the lowest being 27 percent in Mexico in 1960). In four of the seven cases, nominal protection exceeded 100 percent, far higher than could be justified by those who argued in favor of protection of infant industries.

---

[5] Diaz-Alejandro excluded the World War II period, 1940–44.

The protection of manufacturing worked against agriculture by reducing both the relative incentive (or demand) to invest in the production of agricultural goods, and the resources available (supply) for this investment. This was especially true of agricultural tradables, since protection (through quotas, tariffs, and other controls) enabled overvalued currencies to persist. Little et al. found nominal protection for agricultural exports ranging from -10 percent to zero in their sample. Considering that the domestic prices of manufactured agricultural inputs exceeded world prices in general, effective protection of agriculture was even lower, and lower still when compared with the high levels of protection afforded manufacturing.

3.2.3. The "true protection" approach

On the premise that an import tariff is an implicit tax on exports (the Lerner Symmetry Theorem), Sjaastad (1980) derived an incidence parameter, ω, using a three-sector model of a small open economy. The incidence parameter, ω, measures the effect of an increase in import prices (such as would result from an increase in tariffs) on the domestic price of non-tradables. The term $(1 - \omega)$ measures the change in the price of importables to non-tradables, something Sjaastad referred to as the "true tariff". The application of this approach to agriculture by IFPRI's Trade Program during the 1980s focused on the impact of changes in P_I / P_H (true industrial protection) on agricultural prices relative to the prices of non-tradables (P_A / P_H). When a policy of industrial protection such as an import tariff is put into place, the domestic price of imports rises, attracting resources to protected sectors, and shifts consumer demand away from them, resulting in excess demand in the other sectors. This in turn leads to a rise in the price of non-tradables, and a reduction in the relative price of unprotected tradables (including agricultural exportables), in effect acting as a tax on them. This effect is reinforced by wage pressures generated by the higher cost of living due to the rise in the price of imports.

The incidence parameter, ω, reveals the extent to which the burden of the change in relative prices is divided among different sectors. If importables and home goods are close substitutes, either in consumption or production, the most notable effect of higher tariffs is to reduce the price of exportables relative to the price of home goods. The equation that Sjaastad used in his empirical estimation was

$$\ln(P_h / P_x) = a + \omega \ln(P_m / P_x), \tag{7}$$

where ω, the incidence parameter, reflects proportional changes in the price of home goods relative to exportables as a function of proportional changes in the price of importables relative to exportables, P_h is the price of home goods, P_x the price of exportables, P_m the price of importables, and a is a constant.

Table 2 presents the estimated incidence parameters of seven country studies, five of which focused specifically on the agriculture sector. These studies found a fairly high level of substitution between home goods and importables, implying a strong negative

Table 2
Estimates of the incidence parameter (ω) as it affects agriculture

Country	Author	Value of ω
Argentina	Sjaastad*	0.4 to 0.5
Chile	Sjaastad*	0.5 to 0.6
Colombia	Garcia	about 0.9
Nigeria	Oyejide	0.6 to 0.9
Peru	Valdés	about 0.7
Philippines	Bautista	about 0.8
Zaire	Tshibaka	about 0.8

*Sjaastad's studies of Argentina and Chile analyzed the entire tradable sector, while the others analyzed agriculture only.
Source: Valdés (1986a).

impact on the relative price of exportables to home goods. For example, Bautista and Valdés (1993) found a persistent and significant bias in relative price incentives against agricultural exports in the Philippines during the period from 1950 to 1980. The bias was not surprising considering the Philippines' strategy of import-substituting industrialization through the 1950s and 1960s. The surprise was that this bias persisted through the 1970s, when the government was supposedly committed to export promotion. Bautista's study also found that a 10 percent increase in the domestic price of importables was associated with an 8 percent decline in the domestic price of agricultural exports relative to home goods. This was essentially a significant tax on agricultural exportables. In Peru, Valdés (1986a) found that raising the uniform tariff of manufactured goods by 10 percent imposed an implicit 5.6 percent tax (with respect to home goods) on the production of importables (e.g., rice), and an implicit 6.7 percent tax on the production of exportables (e.g., cotton and sugar).

3.2.4. The Mundlak general equilibrium econometric approach

The previous studies examined the impact of policy on incentives, but did not examine the impact of policy on supply response. Most studies of agriculture's aggregate supply response have used a partial equilibrium approach, and thus have failed to take into account the effects of relative price changes on intersectoral resource flows over time. More specifically, they have failed to take into account relative price changes associated with economy-wide macroeconomic policies. An important contribution to correcting this inadequacy was pioneered by Mundlak and his colleagues. Employing a general equilibrium approach, Mundlak, Cavallo and Domenech (1989) analyzed the experience of Argentina from 1913 to 1984. Argentina grew faster than many countries (including Brazil, Canada, and the U.S.) until 1930, at which point it began to lag behind. Mundlak et al. found that Argentine agriculture was heavily taxed post-World War II, directly through export taxes, and indirectly through trade restrictions and protection of non-agricultural goods (note that these findings are consistent with those of Diaz-Alejandro's study of Argentina). Simulations in a general equilibrium framework suggested that Argentina would have achieved a much higher rate of economic growth if it had crafted policies that permitted it to benefit from its comparative advantage in agricultural exports. Such policies would have ensured that incentives reflected true terms of trade, without distortions.

In their study on Chile, Coeymans and Mundlak (1993) applied a five-sector econometric model to the period 1962–82, and found that economy-wide policies were far more important than sector-specific policies in influencing the sectoral allocation of labor, capital, and overall growth. Changes in the RER affected sectoral prices according to the sector's tradability. In the case of Chile, mining and agriculture had the largest tradable components, suggesting that their product prices would be the most responsive to changes in the RER. In their simulations, Coeymans and Mundlak found that mining and agriculture did indeed respond strongly to changes in the RER. Chile's long-run aggregate supply elasticity for agriculture was estimated to be 1.4, while Argentina's was estimated at 1.8.

3.2.5. The Krueger, Schiff, and Valdés approach

The taxation of agriculture through sector-specific price interventions, and through trade, exchange rate, and other macroeconomic policies, was examined for a wider sample of developing countries in Krueger, Schiff and Valdés (1988) and in Schiff and Valdés (1992a, 1992b). They examined direct protection as the difference between relative producer prices and border prices (P_A / P_{NA}) at the official exchange rate. They also measured both the effect of exchange rate overvaluation, using the elasticities approach, and the effect of industrial protection on agriculture's relative price.

As derived in Schiff and Valdés (1992a, Chapter 2) the measures of intervention were calculated as follows. The direct nominal protection rate was estimated as

$$\mathrm{NPR}_D = \frac{P_i / P_{NA} - P_i' / P_{NA}}{P_i' / P_{NA}} = \frac{P_i}{P_i'} - 1, \tag{8}$$

where NPR_D measures the effect of price controls, export taxes or quotas, and other sectoral policies on the domestic producer price, P, of tradable agricultural product i (P_i); P_i' is the border price (P_{iB}) converted into local currency at the official nominal exchange rate E_0 and adjusted for transport, storage and other costs, and quality differences, so that $P_i' = P_{iB} E_0$; P_i^* is the border price of product i at the equilibrium nominal exchange rate E^* and adjusted as before so that $P_i^* = P_{iB} E^* = P_i' E^* / E_0$; P_{NA} is the nonagricultural sector price index, which consists of a tradable share α with a price P_{NAT} and of a nontradable share $1 - \alpha$ with a price P_{NAH}, so that $P_{NA} = \alpha P_{NAT} + (1 - \alpha) P_{NAH}$; and P_{NA}^* is the nonagricultural sector price index, where the price index of the tradable part is evaluated at E^* and in the absence of trade interventions (t_{NA}) affecting nonagricultural tradables, so that $P_{NA}^* = \alpha P_{NAT}[E^* / (1 + t_{NA}) E_0] + (1 - \alpha) P_{NAH}$.

The indirect nominal protection rate would be

$$\mathrm{NPR}_I = \frac{P_i'/P_{NA} - P_i^*/P_{NA}^*}{P_i^*/P_{NA}^*} = \frac{P_i'/P_{NA}}{P_i^*/P_{NA}^*} - 1$$

$$= \frac{P_i'/P_{NA}}{(E^*/E_0)(P_i'/P_{NA}^*)} - 1 = \frac{P_{NA}^* E_0}{P_{NA} E^*} - 1. \tag{9}$$

It measures the effect of the difference between the nominal exchange rate, E_0, and the equilibrium exchange rate, E^*, and of the effect of trade policy on P_{NAT}. NPR_I is the same for all tradable products since P_i does not appear in Equation (9).

The total nominal protection rate is

$$\mathrm{NPR}_T = \frac{P_i/P_{NA} - P_i^*/P_{NA}^*}{P_i^*/P_{NA}^*} = \frac{P_i/P_{NA}}{P_i^*/P_{NA}^*} - 1. \tag{10}$$

Because the denominator of Equation (8) differs from that of Equations (9) and (10), $\mathrm{NPR}_D + \mathrm{NPR}_I \neq \mathrm{NPR}_T$. To make the three measures comparable, we define another direct protection rate,

$$\mathrm{npr}_D = \frac{P_i/P_{NA} - P_i'/P_{NA}}{P_i^*/P_{NA}^*}, \tag{11}$$

which measures the impact of direct policies ($P_i/P_{NA} - P_i'/P_{NA}$) as a percentage of the relative price that would prevail in the absence of all interventions (P_i^*/P_{NA}^*), the same denominator used in Equations (9) and (10). Then, $\mathrm{npr}_D + \mathrm{NPR}_I = \mathrm{NPR}_T$.

Schiff and Valdés (1992a) found that indirect taxation, NP_{RI}, generally exceeded direct taxation, npr_D (see Table 3). Taxation of agriculture as a result of direct price intervention averaged 8 percent, while indirect taxation (the product of macroeconomic policies and industrial protection) taxed agriculture in excess of 22 percent, for a total taxation of 30 percent. Industrial protection policies in most of the countries examined had a more adverse impact on agriculture than did exchange rate overvaluation.

As shown in Table 3, sub-Saharan African countries had both the highest direct and highest indirect taxation of agriculture, with a total tax on agriculture higher than 50 percent. The group of ten representative taxers had an average total rate of taxation of 36 percent. Of the 18 developing countries in the sample, only Korea and Portugal appeared to be net protectors of agriculture.

The most striking findings of Schiff and Valdés were:
- The indirect tax on agriculture from industrial protection and macroeconomic policies was about 22 percent on average for the eighteen countries during 1960–85, nearly three times the direct tax from agricultural pricing policies (which was about 8 percent). The total (direct plus indirect) was thus 30 percent.
- Industrial protection policies taxed agriculture more than did real overvaluation of the exchange rate.

Table 3
Direct and indirect rates of nominal protection, 1960–84 (period averages in percentages)

Country	Period	Indirect protection	Tax due to industrial protection	Direct protection	Total protection
Extreme taxers					−51.6
Côte d'Ivoire	1960–82	−23.3	−23.2	−25.7	−49.0
Ghana	1958–76	−32.6	−32.4	−26.6	−59.5
Zambia	1966–84	−29.9	−21.4	−16.4	−46.3
Representative taxers					−36.4
Argentina	1960–84	−21.3	−39.5	−17.8	−39.1
Colombia	1960–83	−25.2	−37.8	−4.8	−30.0
Dominican Republic	1966–85	−21.3	−20.8	−18.6	−39.9
Egypt	1964–84	−19.6	−27.5	−24.8	−44.4
Morocco	1963–84	−17.4	−13.4	−15.0	−32.4
Pakistan	1960–86	−33.1	−44.9	−6.4	−39.5
Philippines	1960–86	−23.3	−33.0	−4.1	−27.4
Sri Lanka	1960–85	−31.1	−40.1	−9.0	−40.1
Thailand	1962–84	−15.0	−13.9	−25.1	−40.1
Turkey	1961–83	−37.1	−57.4	5.3	−31.8
Mild taxers					−15.8
Brazil	1969–83	−18.4	−21.4	10.1	−8.3
Chile	1960–83	−20.4	−37.4	−1.2	−21.6
Malaysia	1960–83	−8.2	−9.9	−9.4	−17.6
Protectors					10.4
Korea, Republic of	1960–83	−25.8	−26.7	39.0	13.2
Portugal	1960–84	−1.3	−1.0	9.0	7.7
Sample average	1960–84	−22.5	−27.9	−7.9	−30.3

Notes: The tax on agriculture resulting from industrial protection, t_{na}, is given by $[1/(1 + t_{na})] - 1$. Direct protection is measured as the difference between relative producer and border prices at the official exchange rate, after adjusting for transportation, storage, and other relevant margins, and divided by the relative price in the absence of all interventions. Sample average is a simple unweighted cross-country average.
Source: Schiff and Valdés (1992a).

- High taxation of agriculture was associated with low growth in agriculture, and low growth in the economy.
- Surprisingly, most countries protected importables. On average, the direct protection of importables was about 18 percent, and the direct taxation of exportables about 16 percent, for an average impact (on the relative price of importables to exportables) of about 40 percent. These distortions within agriculture increased between the early 1960s and the mid-1980s.
- Direct price policies stabilized domestic agricultural prices relative to world prices, with an average reduction in variability of 25 percent, and even more when world

prices were highly volatile. Indirect policies contributed little, if anything, to price stability.

- Public investment in agriculture did not compensate for adverse price policies.
- The effect of removing agricultural price interventions was not regressive. In most countries, removing direct (or total) interventions changed the real incomes of the poorer urban and rural groups by less than 5 percent (up or down). More often than not, the rural poor gained from removing the interventions.
- The contribution of agriculture to fiscal revenues has fallen over time, and is, on average, small.

Using a similar approach, Dorosh and Valdés (1990) found a strong import-substituting, anti-export bias in Pakistan during the period 1960 to 1987. Import quotas, rather than tariffs, were used as the primary instrument of protection. However, implicit import tariffs on principal importables ranged between 130 and 220 percent in the 1960s, declining to still-high levels of between 40 and 55 percent from the mid-1970s onward. Direct taxation of agricultural exportables averaged 15 percent from 1972 to 1987. The cost of this taxation was compounded by indirect taxation of 38 percent through a combination of trade and exchange rate policies. Transfers out of agriculture, resulting from both direct and indirect policies, averaged about 36 percent of agricultural value added. Simulations revealed that in the absence of all interventions, farm income from Pakistan's five leading crops would have been 40 percent higher between 1983 and 1987.

Using measures of direct and indirect taxation similar to those applied by Schiff and Valdés (1992a), Amin (1996) considered the case of Cameroon. As a member of the *Communaute Financiere Africaine* (CFA), Cameroon has fixed its currency, in nominal terms, to the French franc. During the period 1963 to 1992, the CFA franc became increasingly overvalued, owing to both the mounting strength of the French franc, and to a number of adverse shocks to the country's terms of trade, the most important of which related directly to Cameroon's two major agricultural exports, coffee and cocoa. The study ended before the devaluation of the CFA franc that took place in January 1994. Amin estimated that the level of over-valuation peaked at 77 percent in 1993. The agricultural sector was taxed directly, with coffee and cocoa producers typically receiving less than one-half of the f.o.b. price. The results Amin obtained for Cameroon are in line with those obtained by Schiff and Valdés in their sample, although it should be qualified that under the nominal exchange rate arrangements of the CFA, Cameroon's policy flexibility to accommodate adverse exogenous shocks was severely limited.

Agriculture was similarly taxed elsewhere in sub-Saharan Africa, owing to the widespread perception among developing countries that industrialization was the key to economic growth. Import substitution and tight trade controls conspired to transfer resources out of agriculture and into industry. In his study on Nigeria, Oyejide (1993) found that all crops suffered negative nominal (direct) protection from 1969 to 1983. This taxation declined from −0.27 in 1969–71 to −0.01 by 1981–83, mainly as a result of increased protection of cereals, but export crops remained heavily taxed. Indirect taxation increased throughout the entire period, compounding the effect of direct taxation on exportables, and more than offsetting any direct protection to agricultural importables.

Macroeconomic and industrial policy have come under increasing scrutiny by economists seeking to explain the poor economic performance of agriculture in many sub-Saharan African countries during the past two decades. Ghura and Grennes (1993) confirmed a negative relationship between RER misalignment and economic performance, using pooled data, for the years 1972 to 1987, for 33 sub-Saharan African countries. They tested this relationship with three different measurements of RER misalignment. These included one measure based on purchasing power parity, one derived from an Edwards-type model in which the ERER was estimated as a function of macroeconomic variables, and one that used the black-market premium of the exchange rate.

Ghura and Grennes found that the RER had been substantially overvalued in most of the countries in their sample, regardless of which measure of RER misalignment was used. Botswana, the country with the least misalignment, had experienced the highest rate of growth. The poorest economic performers, such as Ghana and Uganda, also had the most misaligned real exchange rates. Estimates of the RER, irrespective of which measure was used, revealed an unambiguously negative relationship between misalignment of the RER and export growth. Their results also suggest that export growth was adversely affected by macroeconomic instability.

3.3. Exogenous effects including Dutch disease

Having examined the impact of industrial and macroeconomic policies on the real exchange rate, we can proceed to understanding how the RER can be affected by exogenous factors such as changes to an economy's terms of trade. Such changes may result from the boom or bust of an important commodity, from technological change, from changes in productivity, or from medium- or long-term changes in foreign capital flows. The effects these have on the equilibrium RER will, in the absence of intervention, affect the RER. A change in the RER will, in turn, have an impact on all tradables, not confining itself to the sector experiencing the boom, bust, technological change, or change in productivity.

Such phenomena have been popularly referred to as the Dutch disease. Dutch disease has been associated with significant temporary (medium-term) increases in export revenues from oil, gas, coffee, or more recently from the increased foreign capital inflows that tend to follow structural adjustment and trade liberalization. It is characterized by the simultaneous co-existence of advancing and declining subsectors within the traded-goods sector, during which time declining RERs profoundly inhibit the ability of non-booming subsectors to export or compete with imports. In developing countries, the agricultural sector has usually been the traded goods subsector that suffers most from this decline. Examples of Dutch disease associated with commodity booms include the natural gas boom in the Netherlands, oil export booms in the U.K., Nigeria, Mexico, and Venezuela, and coffee booms in Colombia and other countries.

A widely accepted theoretical model of the Dutch disease phenomenon was developed by Corden and Neary (1982), and is summarized here. We then examine several country-specific applications of this model. Corden and Neary developed a variant of the Salter "dependent economy" model to analyze the impact of a booming export subsector on the RER and on the economy as a whole. They were interested in both the short- and long-term impacts of the boom on production, employment, wages, and profitability. They distinguished between two effects, the resource movement effect, and the spending effect.

The spending effect occurs through the higher real income resulting from the commodity boom. As long as neither traded goods nor non-traded goods are inferior, the increase in income will raise demand for both types of goods. The short-term effects of this increased demand will include higher prices for non-traded goods, and an increase in imports. The higher price of non-traded goods relative to traded goods implies an appreciation of the RER, and a loss of competitiveness among non-booming exports.

The higher price of home goods and boom-sector activity attracts factors of production, at the expense of traditional exports, which are usually agricultural in developing countries. This is part of the resource movement effect. Simple models of Dutch disease assume that labor is the only mobile factor, though Corden and Neary also examined cases in which capital is mobile across sectors. For purposes of illustration, we restrict our discussion to cases in which labor is assumed to be the only factor that is mobile across sectors, keeping in mind that some of these outcomes may be reversed when capital is also mobile across sectors [as demonstrated by Corden and Neary (1982)].

With labor the only factor that is mobile across sectors, the impact will remain confined to the wage rate. A commodity boom causes wages to increase in the booming subsector, thereby inducing labor to move out of both the home-goods sector and the non-booming traded-goods sector. The spending effect will tend to raise the price of non-traded goods, placing upward pressure on wages in these sectors as well, also inducing labor to move out of the non-booming traded goods sector. This last sector is squeezed the most, and employment and production in the sector will fall further than in the others.

To the extent that it is the equilibrium RER that changes, policy prescriptions are neither obvious nor unambiguous. One issue is whether it is advisable to pursue a policy that prevents the RER from appreciating fully, by depreciating the nominal exchange rate. In addition, the model assumes that the increase in income is spent by factors, when in reality a significant share of this increase is likely to be collected by the government as taxes. The level and composition of government spending of this revenue increase will therefore influence the subsequent magnitude and direction of the spending effect.

In his analysis of the coffee boom in Colombia, Edwards (1985) found that higher coffee prices resulted in an accumulation of international reserves, and a higher rate of growth of the money supply. The resultant higher rate of inflation, for a given rate of change of the nominal exchange rate, results in an appreciation of the RER, which leads to a loss of competitiveness in the non-coffee tradable goods sectors. The RER will appreciate even more if the fiscal deficit increases, and is financed, even if only partially, by money creation. If, as was the case in Colombia, the rate of devaluation of the nominal exchange rate is decreased, the RER appreciation will be correspondingly greater, as will be the squeeze on the non-coffee tradable goods sector.

Oyejide (1993) found that the structural changes that occurred in Nigeria between 1960 and 1984, particularly during the oil boom of the 1970s, reflected a similar story. Agriculture accounted for almost 60 percent of Nigeria's export revenue prior to the oil boom, when it then dropped to 25 percent. During the same period, agriculture's share of non-oil GDP fell from an average of 60 percent during 1960–65, to about 30 percent between 1978 and 1981. Agriculture's share in employment likewise fell, from 75 percent in 1970 to 59 percent in 1982. The fact that agriculture's share of non-oil GDP fell by 50 percent but agricultural employment fell by only about 20 percent, reflected the low degree of labor mobility in this sector. The two non-oil tradable sectors, agriculture and manufacturing, were both losers relative to oil in the structural changes that occurred in the wake of the oil boom. Oil revenues accrued mainly to the government, and public spending rose rapidly between 1970 and 1980. In spite of increased revenues, fiscal deficits grew between 1975 and 1983, and the current account remained in deficit, as Nigeria accumulated both internal and external debt.

The oil boom did yield one favorable effect on agriculture, as increased revenues from oil reduced the government's reliance on taxation of agricultural exports. Poor agricultural performance during the 1970s led the government to focus more attention on the sector, as evidenced by reforms of Nigeria's agricultural marketing boards, the institution of generous input subsidies, increased direct protection to importables, and lower taxation of exportables. None of these policy changes were sufficient, however, to compensate the agricultural sector for the effects of inflation and appreciation of the RER, as real producer crop prices fell, or, at best, remained constant.

The oil boom of the 1970s led to a similar situation in Venezuela. But the case of Indonesia, another oil-exporting developing country, provides a marked contrast to the experiences of Nigeria and Venezuela, and an instructive counterexample to the Dutch disease phenomenon. Following a more prudent macroeconomic management of their oil-boom windfall, Indonesia's RER did not appreciate to any significant degree, and exports remained diversified. Clearly, how a government manages a commodity boom is important in determining its ultimate effect on the economy and on economic growth.

For Chile and New Zealand, structural reform triggered changes in the equilibrium RER [Valdés (1994)]. Prior to these reforms, both countries were inward-looking and highly regulated. Each had high rates of protection, extensive government intervention in both product and factor markets, and low rates of agricultural and economic growth.

Chile undertook reform in two stages. In the first stage, from 1973 to 1983, the government focused on general economic reforms, in response to an urgent need to correct fundamental macroeconomic imbalances. Sweeping trade liberalization took place, as tariffs were cut drastically, quantitative restrictions were removed, and most price controls and all multiple exchange rates were eliminated. Interest rate ceilings were also gradually withdrawn, and input subsidies eliminated.

Although trade liberalization initially resulted in depreciation of the RER, a turnaround occurred, and the RER began appreciating between 1979 and 1982 as a result of capital inflows and wage indexation. Following a deep recession in 1983 that led to a devaluation and a real depreciation, agriculture began to recover. Around 1990, following capital inflows, the RER began to appreciate, leading once more to a slowdown in agricultural growth.

The stabilization program initiated by New Zealand in 1984 led to high interest rates, an inflow of foreign capital, and the appreciation of its RER. On the trade front, the government liberalized agriculture and removed farm subsidies, even though industrial protection remained high. Sandrey and Scobie (1994) estimated that by 1992, agriculture in New Zealand faced an 11 percent implicit tax as a result of industrial protection. Argentina and a number of other countries in Latin America have recently experienced circumstances similar to those of New Zealand, as capital inflows increased in the wake of structural reforms. Similar evidence is emerging in Russia, Estonia, and Poland.

So far we have stressed the importance of the relationship of capital inflows to competitiveness of agriculture. Long-term capital inflows are essential for development, even though the comparative advantage of some sectors may be affected. Capital inflows do, however, entail some risk, by generating inflationary pressures and appreciation of the RER. These risks are higher with short-term inflows, particularly if international interest rates are expected to rise, and when investors sense financial fragility, as we have seen in relation to the 1994 "Tequila" crisis in Mexico, and the 1997 "Asian flu" crisis in East and Southeast Asia. The result can be abrupt capital outflows which, although less likely to occur in foreign direct investment, remain difficult to anticipate. The recent experience of middle-income countries has demonstrated the difficulty of judging *ex ante* whether a particular inflow is likely to be permanent or transitory. Countries like Chile, Colombia, and India have attempted to restrict short-term capital inflows by imposing high taxes on them, a temporary solution at best. The issue will become increasingly important as a growing number of countries choose to liberalize their economies. It is far from obvious what, if any, policy action is optimal. An obvious one is to first reform the domestic financial sector.

3.4. Interest rates

In spite of the substantial body of literature on rural financial markets in less-developed countries, there is very little applied research on the interface between domestic capital markets and agriculture. This omission is the more surprising in light of economic reforms in Latin America and eastern and central Europe, where dramatic increases in real interest rates have occurred. By raising the cost of capital, higher domestic interest rates have the largest adverse effect on capital-intensive industries. Research presented by Mundlak (1997) on a large sample of developing countries shows that because agriculture is capital intensive, it is more sensitive than non-agriculture to changes in interest rates and less sensitive to changes in the cost of labor. The capital/labor ratio in agriculture increases over time and, Mundlak concluded, "...policies that cause a rise in interest rates are more damaging to agriculture and to agricultural investment in particular".

Changes in the interest rates have macroeconomic consequences well beyond their direct effect on investment and production decisions. An important article by Snape (1989) elucidated the interactions between real exchange rates, interest rates and agriculture, using Salter's "dependent economy" model. Snape considered four scenarios of the interaction between real exchange rates and real interest rates. Two were policy-induced (fiscal and monetary expansion), and two were induced by exogenous changes (in the savings rate and in world interest rates).

In considering the case of fiscal expansion, in which the government would finance its increased budget deficit by borrowing from the private sector, Snape made two assumptions. He assumed that the economy was at full employment, and that an increase in public expenditure would not be offset by an increase in private savings. This meant that no private savings were put aside to pay future taxes that would be necessary to meet payments on interest and principal on the new public borrowing. In the absence of international capital flows, increased public borrowing would result in higher real interest rates, and private investment would be crowded out. Foreign capital inflows would finance increased public borrowing, and real interest rates would remain constant (unless the country risk premium rises with the level of external borrowing). The additional foreign exchange would result in an appreciation of the real exchange rate.

In a floating exchange rate regime, this would occur through an appreciation of the nominal exchange rate. If the nominal exchange rate was fixed, the capital inflow would result in a balance of payments surplus, and an accumulation of foreign exchange reserves. If this increase in international reserves was not sterilized, the rate of inflation would increase, and the real exchange rate would appreciate. Sterilization of foreign exchange reserves (by selling Treasury bills in the open market) could delay appreciation of the RER, but fiscal expansion would result in a higher interest rate, which in turn would continue to attract capital inflows, resulting in further appreciation of the RER. A once-and-for-all fiscal expansion would result in higher interest rates in the absence of capital flows or in an appreciation of the RER in the presence of capital flows, regardless of the nominal exchange rate regime in place. Thus, under both scenarios, agriculture would be harmed by fiscal expansion.

We have already seen that an increase in world real interest rates would raise the cost of borrowing and servicing public debt, resulting in a reduction in real absorption and a depreciation of RER. Thus, while the production of tradables would be positively affected by the depreciation of the RER, it would be negatively affected by an increase in world interest rates.

Prior to economic reforms in the mid-1980s, much of global agriculture benefited from subsidized credit lines. When these subsidies were removed, the farm and agro-processing sectors faced high market interest rates. The experience of early reformers such as Chile and New Zealand, and later Argentina and Mexico, along with others, showed that in spite of the opening of the capital account, domestic real interest rates remained much higher than international interest rates for a period of several years. Interest rates were higher primarily because the cost of intermediation in the domestic capital market remained high. Costs were high due to a relatively uncompetitive capital market in an obsolete regulatory framework. Rodriguez (1994) calculated the spread between local currency lending rates and the U.S. Treasury bill rate, adjusted for exchange rate depreciation, at 23 percentage points in Argentina in 1993, and 59 points in Uruguay in 1992. There is ample evidence, therefore, of the critical importance of including the financial sector early on in the process of overall economic reform.

3.5. Structural adjustment

A growing number of developing countries have implemented structural adjustment programs, with the support of the World Bank, aimed at reducing fiscal imbalances, redefining the role of the public sector, and accelerating growth [Goldin and Winters (1992)]. Structural adjustment programs affect agriculture in a number of ways. Redressing fiscal imbalances typically involves reductions in both agricultural and non-agricultural subsidies. The impact of these reductions on agriculture's relative value added is ambiguous *a priori*, and depends on the initial distribution of subsidies across sectors. We see in Equation (5) that a reduction in subsidies to intermediate inputs would cause value added in all affected sectors to fall, with an ambiguous relative impact on agriculture.

As seen in Equations (5) and (6), a reduction in government expenditures results in a depreciation of the RER, which in turn increases agriculture's relative prices and value added. The relative price changes affect relative factor rewards, the distribution of income, and ultimately rural–urban migration patterns over time.

Trade liberalization, another major component of structural adjustment programs, improves agricultural incentives in two ways, through lower industrial prices, and through the depreciation in the RER.

In view of the potential benefits of structural adjustment, how can it best be carried out? Three issues emerge in response to this question. The first is the sequence of reforms [Edwards (1988)], which reduces to the question of whether trade liberalization should precede capital account liberalization or vice versa. The second issue centers on the "small-country assumption". In the countries that influence world prices, increased exports can theoretically result in lower revenues, but this is, generally, not supported by evidence, with the exception of a few cases such as coffee in Brazil and cocoa in Côte d'Ivoire [Panagariya and Schiff (1991)].

Third, we should be interested in the effects of structural adjustment on public spending. Public expenditure cuts are an inescapable component of structural adjustment, and will undoubtedly include cuts in spending on agriculture. Van Blarcom, Knudsen and Nash (1993) analyzed a sample of 32 countries in which public spending on agriculture had been cut some time after 1970. They concluded that much of the public spending on agriculture in these countries had been directed toward relatively unproductive purposes. In Mexico, for instance, 85 percent of public spending on agriculture in 1989 went to untargeted food and input subsidies administered primarily through state agencies. As a result, public investment in agriculture declined, as fiscal pressures created by funding these subsidies escalated. According to the authors' calculations, if spending on untargeted subsidies was cut in half, spending on irrigation, research, and extension could be doubled at the same time as overall sectoral spending was reduced by 28 percent. The point is, that a reduction in public spending on agriculture need not have a negative impact on agricultural output as long as the allocation of public spending is targeted to public goods.

Van Blarcom, Knudsen and Nash (1993) developed a set of guidelines for structural adjustment in agriculture. These included the following: (i) reduce industrial protection and remove the misalignment of the RER; (ii) reduce subsidies and effectively target the remaining subsidies to services that foster growth; (iii) increase the public goods component of public spending on agriculture (such as research and extension); (iv) privatize state-owned enterprises in conjunction with price liberalization in order to end the drain on fiscal resources; and (v) build greater transparency into the public sector's budget process so that public funds are allocated in a context of clearly defined sector strategies and explicitly stated goals.

Support services that can be transferred to the private sector should be transferred. Recurrent costs should be adequately funded, particularly operations and maintenance costs of public infrastructure. Indeed, the *World Development Report 1994* [World Bank (1994)] identified these recurrent costs as generating some of the highest social returns of any type of public spending. One way of ensuring adequate funding for recurrent costs is through cost recovery measures. The user charges for water, power, and fertilizer often account for a small fraction of their actual cost in many countries, and should be increased to reflect the cost of providing them.

4. The North

Agricultural policies in industrialized countries (the North) have taken fundamentally different forms than those in developing countries (the South), and the contrasts are instructive. Agricultural sectors in the North generally comprise a small proportion of the economy relative to the urban–industrial sectors. Northern agriculture has remained highly protected, while Northern industry is afforded generally low rates of protection. Furthermore, low industrial protection, coupled with lower levels of exchange rate misalignment, has resulted in a substantially lower level of indirect taxation of agriculture than in developing countries.

4.1. The United States

The nature of the relationship between the macroeconomy and relative prices in agriculture for the U.S. was detailed in several pioneering studies by Schuh (1974, 1989). Schuh's (1974) analysis for the U.S. began with the 1950s. The U.S. dollar was considered overvalued, but under the Bretton Woods agreement, the U.S. agreed to a fixed nominal exchange rate relative to gold. The exchange rate overvaluation adversely affected the competitiveness of U.S. agriculture, particularly for exportables, at a time of burgeoning levels of grain stocks. The U.S. resorted to providing massive food aid, in essence as an implicit export subsidy, and by the end of the 1960s had added explicit export subsidies as well. But these efforts did not succeed in sufficiently lowering the level of stocks, given the level of exports at the prevailing exchange rate. By 1970/71, as real price supports were reduced or eliminated, about 60 million acres of land were taken out of production.

In his 1989 article, Schuh argued that the combined effect of an overvalued dollar and the commodity programs in place induced an income transfer to consumers, while the land set-aside program made land more scarce, and induced the adoption of land-substituting inputs. The Bretton Woods system was abandoned when the U.S. devalued its currency in 1972, and the dollar depreciated roughly 25 percent. The depreciation, combined with an unstable monetary policy that resulted in negative real interest rates and varying inflation rates, contributed to an agricultural boom that was sustained through the 1970s. The boom came to an end with the OPEC oil price increase of 1979. In the 1980s, taxes were cut, but public expenditures were not. The result was a growing fiscal deficit at a time when the Federal Reserve chose to maintain tight monetary policies. Real interest rates climbed, and capital inflows increased, leading to an appreciation of the real exchange rate.

The increase in interest rates ended the land market boom, at the same time that the U.S. imposed a grain embargo on the Soviet Union. U.S. agriculture faced three simultaneous shocks: declining domestic prices due to the appreciation in the RER, the collapse of the land market, and the loss of the Soviet grain market. Asset values and farm income also collapsed. U.S. agriculture began to recover only after significant agricultural acreage was retired, and the government has only partially scaled back from the relatively high implicit and explicit subsidies it continues to provide for key commodities.

A number of lessons can be learned from the U.S. experience. First, as with the developing countries, changes in the real exchange rate are important to agriculture. Second, changes in macroeconomic conditions are likely to inspire changes in direct interventions, such as agricultural commodity-support programs. Through their effects on the structure of incentives and on commodity programs, macroeconomic events indirectly influence productivity change as well as the distribution of benefits between producers and consumers.

Another lesson relates to short-term price instability. Traditionally, prior to the early 1970s price instability in agricultural markets was explained largely by the inelastic nature of food demand, and on the supply side, by weather patterns, rapid technological change, and asset fixity. In an important contribution on the U.S. experience, Rausser, Chalfant and Stamoulis (1985) examine the increased importance of money markets on the farm sector and the additional source of instability that it generates. Because agricultural markets behave as "flex price" while other markets behave as "fixed price" (e.g., stickiness of non-food prices) in the short run, overshooting in agricultural commodity markets will occur, even if expectations are formed rationally. This amounts to either a tax (in the case of deflation) or a subsidy (in the case of inflation) to agriculture through relative price changes. For example, anticipated money growth, according to their econometric estimates, causes a much greater response in food prices (the flex-prices) than for non-agricultural goods. Under negative shocks, the implicit taxes resulting from overshooting imposed on U.S. agriculture were limited by the price support policy, which introduced a downward price inflexibility for the supported commodities, but which in turn caused the incidence of the macroeconomic policy tax on agriculture to shift towards the cost of maintaining stocks.

The implications of these findings for other economies need to be examined. One would expect that, unlike the U.S., most LDCs are price takers in grain markets and so (at a given nominal exchange rate) domestic farm prices would change relatively less than those of home goods after a monetary shock, which would not induce overshooting. This is likely to apply to most Latin American countries but not necessarily to other ones. For instance, state trading in agricultural commodities is still pervasive in India. In that case or in the case of non-tariff barriers, the domestic price may be unrelated to the world price and overshooting may occur as well.

4.2. The European Union and its common agricultural policy

The fiscal burden of the Common Agricultural Program (CAP) has inspired substantial analyses of the impact of agricultural protection on macroeconomic variables in studies such as Gylfason (1995) and the volume edited by Stoeckel, Breckling and Cuthbertson (1989). Gylfason argued that although partial equilibrium analysis found that deadweight losses resulting from farm policies represented about 1 percent of GDP, long-term general equilibrium considerations were shown to raise the loss estimates to about 3 percent of GDP. The CAP has been responsible for higher consumer food prices and an increased tax burden. Total per capita agricultural transfers per full-time farmer equivalent[6] averaged $17,700 in the European Union (EU), compared with a median labor income of $12,000 in 1992.

Based on general equilibrium models described in the volume edited by Stoeckel, Breckling and Cuthbertson (1989), various authors quantified the impact of agricultural protection on relative prices to manufacturing, manufacturing output, and employment. The studies found that industrial countries would benefit from removing agricultural protection because manufacturing output and exports would increase, as would employment.

Stoeckel and Breckling (1989) examined the effects of removing both the CAP and national agricultural protection in the four largest EU countries, namely Germany, France, Italy, and the United Kingdom. They found that the elimination of both

---

[6] Full-time farmer equivalent is defined as 2200 hours of work in agriculture annually.

measures of protection could generate an increase in aggregate output of over 1 percent, create 3 million new jobs, and lead to a 5 percent increase in manufacturing exports to the rest of the world.

Dicke et al. (1989) focused on the case of West Germany, the largest economy in the EU and the largest contributor to the CAP. They also found that Germany would experience gains from liberalization similar to those estimated by Stoeckel and Breckling. Total public subsidies to German agriculture are, at present, equal to about 70 percent of the sector's gross value added at domestic prices. Assuming an increase of 10 percent in world agricultural prices and constant wages, agricultural liberalization would result in a reduction in the rate of unemployment from 9 to 5 percent, along with a 3 percent gain in real GDP, and a 5 percent increase in foreign trade. Their results on employment support Stoeckel, Breckling and Cuthbertson's (1989) estimate that continued support of agriculture could result in an increase in unemployment of up to 3 million workers in the EU. Given the small share of agriculture in the economy of the EU and Germany, the effects found in the above studies seem rather large.

4.3. Japan and New Zealand

A similar study by Vincent (1989) on Japan's agricultural economy also appears in the Stoeckel, Breckling and Cuthbertson (1989) volume. Japan, which has the highest agricultural protection levels in the Organization for Economic Cooperation and Development (OECD), would enjoy benefits from liberalization similar to those of the EU. Vincent found that agricultural liberalization in Japan could result in a 3 percent increase in revenues from manufactured exports in the short run, and an increase in average real wages of about 2.5 percent.

In New Zealand, extensive reforms have resulted in the virtual elimination of agricultural protection.[7] The reform program began in earnest in 1984, and during its initial phases had severe adverse effects on agriculture [Sandrey and Scobie (1994)]. Subsidies were removed early in the reforms, at the same time as the real exchange rate experienced a substantial appreciation, aggravating the problems faced by the agriculture sector. Since that time, however, public sector deficits have been eliminated, and compensatory microeconomic reforms have been implemented. As a result, New Zealand's agriculture sector has become increasingly competitive in international markets.

5. Concluding comments

In this chapter, we assessed the state of our knowledge about the links between agri-culture and the macroeconomy, with emphasis on countries. We provided a historical

---

[7] Australia and New Zealand were the only two industrial countries that taxed agriculture by providing relatively higher protection to manufacturing.

perspective of the role of agriculture in development strategies, and an analysis of the various approaches to the concept and measurement of the impact of the real exchange rate and of industrial policy on agriculture. We also examined the role of the Dutch disease, interest rates, and structural adjustment policies. Finally, some of the issues were examined for developed countries.

A basic concept underlying the analysis presented in this paper is that of 'neutrality'. By that, we mean 'intersectoral neutrality' or the equal treatment of all sectors. In other words, we considered the case of intersectorally neutral policies as the counterfactual or 'anti-monde' to which the actual policies were compared. Neutrality was selected as the 'anti-monde' based on efficiency considerations. In the absence of power on the world market and externalities, the Pareto efficient solution is to treat all sectors equally.[8]

We submit this as a paradigm, i.e., from the viewpoint of efficiency, agriculture should not be taxed relative to other sectors and neither should it be favored. Nevertheless, developing countries have traditionally taxed the agricultural sector while developed countries have protected it, and both have incurred efficiency losses.

Based on Schiff and Valdés (1992a), it was shown that the taxation of agriculture in developing countries resulted in a slowdown in agricultural growth and in overall economic growth, and that the slowdown was caused essentially by indirect taxation policies rather than by the direct ones. A number of less developed countries (LDCs) have undertaken structural adjustment reforms in the last fifteen years, including trade policy reform and stabilization efforts, and this has reduced the level of indirect taxation. One reason often given for direct taxation of agriculture is to keep food prices low for urban consumers and to obtain export tax revenue. The benefits from food subsidies were captured mainly by urban households. However, the majority of the poor are often located in the rural areas rather than in the cities, and it is the rural poor who gain most from the removal of price interventions. As for export tax revenues, their contribution to fiscal revenues has fallen over time, and is, on average, small. LDCs that depend heavily on them will have to look for alternative sources of revenue by implementing a tax reform and/or will have to raise the efficiency of the public sector and/or reduce its size.

In the developed countries, protection of agriculture has had adverse general equilibrium effects by raising costs and reducing production and employment in the manufacturing sector. A number of studies have found the cost in terms of higher unemployment to be significant. Moreover, a GATT study found that the policy had a negative impact on poor consumers.

---

[8] This assumes that there are no "non-economic" objectives (such as sectoral production targets or balance-of-payments targets) or other constraints. In the case of a fiscal constraint, Ramsey's rule indicates that the tariff on any given sector is inversely related to the elasticity of import demand. In the real world, however, administering such a complex system of tariffs is costly because of the administrative requirements, lack of transparency, discretionality, and the fact that a tariff structure which is differentiated by sector generates more lobbying pressure and higher tariffs than a uniform tariff structure. The optimal solution may entail a uniform tariff or a few tariff levels.

Since the Uruguay Round, agriculture has been integrated into the trade rules of the World Trade Organization (WTO), and most LDCs have joined the WTO. This gives us hope that future multilateral negotiations will continue to lower the bias against agriculture in LDCs, and in favor of agriculture in developed countries.

Acknowledgements

The authors gratefully acknowledge the helpful comments from William Martin and the anonymous reviewers.

References

Amin, A.A. (1996), "The effects of exchange rate policy on Cameroon's agricultural competitiveness", Research Paper #42 (African Economic Research Consortium, Nairobi).

Balassa, B. (1965), "Tariff protection in industrial countries: an evaluation", Journal of Political Economy 73:573–594.

Balassa, B. (1970), "Growth strategies in semi industrial countries", Quarterly Journal of Political Economics 84:24–47.

Balassa, B. (1982), "Adjustment to external shocks in developing countries", World Bank Staff Working Paper 472 (World Bank, Washington, DC).

Bautista, R.M., and A. Valdés (1993), "The relevance of trade and macroeconomic policies for agriculture", in: R.M. Bautista and A. Valdés, eds., The Bias Against Agriculture: Trade and Macroeconomic Policies in Developing Countries (International Center for Economic Growth and International Food Policy Research Institute, Washington, DC).

Bhagwati, J. (1978), Anatomy and Consequences of Exchange Control Regimes (Ballinger, Cambridge).

Binswanger, H., and P.L. Scandizzo (1983), "Patterns of agricultural protection", Agricultural Research Unit Report 48 (World Bank, Washington, DC).

Byerlee, D., and G. Sain (1986), "Food pricing policy in developing countries: bias against agriculture or for urban consumers?", American Journal of Agricultural Economics 68:961–969.

Coeymans, J.E., and Y. Mundlak (1993), "Sectorial growth in Chile: 1962–82", Research Report 95 (International Food Policy Research Institute, Washington, DC).

Corden, W.M. (1966), "The structure of a tariff system and the effective protection rate", Journal of Political Economy 74:221–237.

Corden, W.M., and J.P. Neary (1982), "Booming sector and deindustrialization in a small open economy", Economic Journal 92:835–848.

Diaz-Alejandro, C.F. (1970), "Essays on the Economic History of the Argentine Republic" (Yale University Press, New Haven, CT).

Dicke, H., J.B. Donges, E. Gerken and G. Kirkpatrick (1989), "Effects of agricultural trade liberalization on West Germany's economy", in: A.B. Stoeckel, D. Vincent and S. Cuthbertson, eds., Macroeconomic Consequences of Farm Support Policies (Duke University Press, Durham, NC).

Dornbusch, R. (1974), "Tariffs and non-traded goods", Journal of International Economics, May:177–185.

Dorosh, P.A., and A. Valdés (1990), "Effects of exchange rate and trade policies on agriculture in Pakistan", Research Report 84 (International Food Policy Research Institute, Washington, DC).

Edwards, S. (1985), "Coffee, money and inflation in Colombia", in: V. Thomas, ed., Linking Macroeconomic and Agricultural Policies for Adjustment with Growth: the Colombian Experience (Johns Hopkins University Press, Baltimore, MD).

Edwards, S. (1988), Exchange Rate Misalignment in Developing Countries (World Bank, Washington, DC).

Edwards, S. (1994), "Real exchange rate determination of real exchange rate behavior: theory and evidence of developing countries", in: J. Williamson, ed., Estimating Equilibrium Exchange Rates (Institute for International Economics, Washington, DC).

Elbadawi, I.A. (1994), "Estimating equilibrium long run real exchange rates", in: J. Williamson, ed., Estimating Equilibrium Real Exchange Rates (Institute for International Economics, Washington, DC).

Galbraith, J.K. (1938), "The maintenance of agricultural production during the depression: the explanation reviewed", Journal of Political Economy XLVI:305–323.

Garcia Garcia, J. (1993), "Effects of the coffee boom and government expenditures on agricultural prices in Colombia", in: R.M. Bautista and A. Valdés, eds., The Bias Against Agriculture: Trade and Macro-economic Policies in Developing Countries (International Center for Economic Growth and International Food Policy Research Institute, Washington, DC).

Gardner, B.L. (1997), "Policy reform in agriculture: an assessment of the results in eight countries", Mimeo (University of Maryland).

Gehlhar, M.J., T.W. Hertel and W. Martin (1994), "Economic growth and the changing structure of trade and production in the Pacific Rim", American Journal of Agricultural Economics 76:1101–1110.

Ghura, D., and T. Grennes (1993), "The real exchange rate and macroeconomic performance in sub-Saharan Africa", Journal of Development Economics 42:155–174.

Goldin, I., and L.A. Winters (eds.) (1992), Open Economies: Structural Adjustment and Agriculture (Cambridge University Press, Cambridge).

Gylfason, T. (1995), "The macroeconomics of European agriculture", Princeton Studies in International Finance #78 (Princeton University, Princeton, NJ).

Hinkle, L.E., and Nsengumiva (forthcoming), "External real exchange rates: purchasing power parity, the Mundell–Fleming model, and competitiveness in traded goods", in: L.E. Hinkle and P.J. Montiel, eds., Estimating Equilibrium Exchange Rates in Developing Countries (World Bank, Washington, DC).

Johnson, D.G. (1950), "The nature of the supply function for agricultural products", American Economic Review 40:539–564.

Krueger, A.O. (1978), "Liberalization attempts and consequences", in: Foreign Trade Regime and Economic Development, Vol. 10 (Ballinger, Cambridge).

Krueger, A.O., M. Schiff and A. Valdés (1988), "Agricultural incentives in developing countries: measuring the effects of sectorial and economy wide policies", World Bank Economic Review 2(3):255–271.

Kyle, S. (1992), "Pitfalls in the measurement of the real exchange rate effects on agriculture", World Development 20(7):1009–1019.

Lattimore, R.G., and G.E. Schuh (1979), "Endogenous policy determination: the case of the Brazilian beef sector", Canadian Journal of Agricultural Economics 27(2):1–16.

Lewis, W.A. (1954), "Economic development with unlimited supplies of labor", Manchester School of Economic and Social Studies 22:139–191.

Little, I., T. Scitovsky and M. Scott (1970), Industry and Trade in Some Developing Countries (Oxford University Press and OECD, Oxford).

Loo, T., and E. Tower (1989), "Agricultural protectionism and less developed countries: the relationship between agricultural prices, debt servicing capacities and the need for development aid", in: A.B. Stoeckel, D. Vincent and S. Cuthbertson, eds., Macroeconomic Consequences of Farm Support Policies (Duke University Press, Durham, NC).

Martin, W., and P.G. Warr (1993), "Explaining the relative decline of agriculture: a supply-side analysis for Indonesia", World Bank Economic Review, September.

Meier, G.M. (1989), Leading Issues in Economic Development (Oxford University Press, New York).

Meier, G.M. (1995), Leading Issues in Economic Development (Oxford University Press, New York).

Mundlak, Y. (1997), "The dynamics of agriculture", in: Proceedings of the XIII International Conference of Agricultural Economics, Sacramento, California, August 10–16, 1997.

Mundlak, Y., D. Cavallo and R. Domenech (1989), "Agriculture and economic growth in Argentina, 1913–84", Research Report 76 (International Food Policy Research Institute, Washington, DC).

Myrdal, G. (1957), Economic Nationalism and Internationalism (Australian Institute of International Affairs, Melbourne).

Nurkse, R. (1952), "Some international aspects of the problem of economic development", American Economic Review 42(Suppl.):571–583.

Nurkse, R. (1961), "Trade theory and development economics", in: H.S. Ellis, ed., Economic Development for Latin America (St. Martin's Press, New York).

Oyejide, T.A. (1993), "The oil boom, macroeconomic policies and Nigerian agriculture: analysis of a 'Dutch disease' phenomenon", in: R.M. Bautista and A. Valdés, eds., The Bias against Agriculture: Trade and Macroeconomic Policies in Developing Countries (International Center for Economic Growth and International Food Policy Research Institute, Washington, DC).

Panagariya, A., and M. Schiff (1991), "Taxes versus quotas: the case of cocoa exports", in: I. Goldin and L.A. Winters, eds., Open Economies: Structural Adjustment and Agriculture (Cambridge University Press, Cambridge).

Prebisch, R. (1950), El Desarrollo de America Latina y sus Problemas Principales (United Nations, New York).

Prebisch, R. (1959), "Commercial policy in the underdeveloped countries", American Economic Review 49(Suppl.):251–273.

Ranis, G., and J.C.H. Fei (1961), "A theory of economic development", American Economic Review 51:533–565.

Rausser, G.C., J.A. Chalfant and K.G. Stamoulis (1985), Instability in Agricultural Markets: The U.S. Experience (International Association of Agricultural Economics).

Rodriguez, C. (1994), "Interest rates in Latin America", World Bank Internal Discussion Paper No. IDP-140 (April), quoted in Brock, P.L. (1996), "High real interest rates, guarantor risks and bank recapitalizations", Mimeo (World Bank).

Rosenstein-Rodan, P.N. (1943), "Problems of industrialization of Eastern and South-Eastern Europe", Economic Journal 53:202–211.

Rosenstein-Rodan, P.N. (1957), Notes on the Theory of the "Big Push" (MIT, Cambridge, MA).

Sadoulet, E., and A. De Janvry (1995), Quantitative Development Policy Analysis (Johns Hopkins University Press, Baltimore, MD).

Salter, W.E.G. (1959), "Internal and external balance: the role of price and expenditure effects", The Economic Record 35:226–238.

Sandrey, R.A., and G.M. Scobie (1994), "Changing international competitiveness and trade: recent experience in New Zealand agriculture", American Journal of Agricultural Economics 78(5):1140–1146.

Schiff, M., and A. Valdés (1992a), The Political Economy of Agricultural Pricing Policy, Vol. 4. A Synthesis of the Economics in Developing Countries (Johns Hopkins University Press, Baltimore, MD).

Schiff, M., and A. Valdés (1992b), The Plundering of Agriculture in Developing Countries (World Bank, Washington, DC).

Schuh, G.E. (1974), "The exchange rate and U.S. agriculture", American Journal of Agricultural Economics 56(1):1–13.

Schuh, G.E. (1989), "Macro linkages and agriculture: the United States experience", in: A. Maunder and A. Valdés, eds., Agriculture and Governments in an Interdependent World, Proceedings of the Twentieth International Conference of Agricultural Economists, Dartmouth.

Schultz, T.W. (1964), Transforming Traditional Agriculture (Yale University Press, New Haven, CT).

Singer, H.W. (1950), "The distribution of gains between investing and borrowing countries", American Economic Review 40:473–485.

Sjaastad, L.A. (1980), "Commercial policy, 'true tariffs', and relative prices", in: J. Black and B. Hindley, eds., Current Issues in Commercial Policy and Diplomacy (St. Martin's Press, New York).

Snape, R.H. (1989), "Real exchange rates, real interest rates and agriculture", in: A. Maunder and A. Valdés, eds., Agriculture and Governments in an Interdependent World, Proceedings of the Twentieth International Conference of Agricultural Economists, Dartmouth.

Stoeckel, A.B., and J. Breckling (1989), "Some economywide effects of agricultural policies in the European Community: a general equilibrium study", in: A.B. Stoeckel, D. Vincent and S. Cuthbertson, eds., Macroeconomic Consequences of Farm Support Policies (Duke University Press, Durham, NC).

Stoeckel, A.B., J. Breckling and S. Cuthbertson (1989), "Overview", in: A.B. Stoeckel, D. Vincent and S. Cuthbertson, eds., Macroeconomic Consequences of Farm Support Policies (Duke University Press, Durham, NC).

Swan, T.W. (1960), "Economic control in a dependent economy", Economic Record 36:51–60.

Taylor, D., and T.P. Phillips (1991), "Food pricing policy in developing countries: further evidence on cereal producer prices", American Journal of Agricultural Economics 73(4):1036–1046.

Valdés, A. (1973), "Trade policy and its effect on the external agricultural trade of Chile 1945–1965", American Journal of Agricultural Economics 55(2):1973.

Valdés, A. (1986a), "Exchange rates and trade policy: help or hindrance to agricultural growth?", in: Agriculture in a Turbulent World Economy, Proceedings of the Nineteenth International Conference of Agricultural Economists, Gower.

Valdés, A. (1986b), "Impact of trade and macroeconomic policies on agricultural growth: the South American experience", in: Economic and Social Progress in Latin America 1986 Report (Inter-American Development Bank).

Valdés, A. (1991), "The role of agricultural exports in development", in: C.P. Timmer, ed., Agriculture and the State (Cornell University Press, Ithaca, NY).

Valdés, A. (1994), "Agricultural reforms in Chile and New Zealand: a review", British Journal of Agricultural Economics 45:189–201.

Valdés, A. (1996), "Surveillance of agricultural price and trade policy in Latin America during major policy reforms", Discussion Paper #349 (World Bank, Washington, DC).

Valdés, A., and A. Siamwalla (1988), "Foreign trade regime, exchange rate policy and the structure of incentives", in: J.W. Mellor and R. Ahmed, eds., Agriculture Price Policy for Developing Countries (Johns Hopkins University Press, Baltimore, MD).

Van Blarcom, B., O. Knudsen and J. Nash (1993), "The role of public expenditures for agriculture", World Bank Discussion Paper #216 (World Bank, Washington, DC).

Vincent, D. (1989), "Effects of agricultural protection in Japan: an economywide analysis", in: A.B. Stoeckel, D. Vincent and S. Cuthbertson, eds., Macroeconomic Consequences of Farm Support Policies (Duke University Press, Durham, NC).

Williamson, J. (ed.) (1994), Estimating Equilibrium Exchange Rates (Institute for International Economics, Washington, DC).

World Bank (1994), World Development Report 1994 (The World Bank, Washington, DC).

Chapter 28

THE MACROECONOMICS OF AGRICULTURE

PIER GIORGIO ARDENI

Department of Economics, University of Bologna, Italy

JOHN FREEBAIRN

Department of Economics, University of Melbourne, Australia

Contents

Handbook of Agricultural Economics, Volume 2, Edited by B. Gardner and G. Rausser
© *2002 Elsevier Science B.V. All rights reserved*

Abstract

The existence of linkages between the agricultural sector and the rest of the economy points to the specificity of that sector and justifies why we can conceive of a *macro-economics of agriculture*. The primary sector is characterized by product homogeneity, a pre-condition for the absence of imperfect competition. Also, agricultural prices are subject to seasonal variations. Moreover, farming activities are often carried on by large fractions of the population and are very dispersed on the territory. Finally, production of commodities relies on an irreproducible factor of production – land – whose availability is finite and whose productivity cannot be individually infinitely increased. Given these features, we expect macroeconomic policy to affect the agricultural sector, and agricultural prices and markets to affect other sectors and the macroeconomy in a specific way (as opposed to the other sectors). In this essay, the transmission mechanisms and linkages – by which changes in one sector alter economic performance in other sectors – are described under the sub-headings of *backward linkages* – from agriculture to the rest of the economy – *forward linkages* – from the macroeconomy and the international economy to agriculture – and second-round feed-back interdependent linkages. Models and studies attempting to quantify the linkages are then discussed in terms of theoretical constructs, structural econometric models, computable general-equilibrium models, and time-series models.

Keywords

macroeconomic backward and forward linkages, monetary policy effect on agriculture, vector autoregression and error-correction, models, structural macromodels, interactions between money and prices

JEL classification: Q10

1. Introduction

The importance of agriculture in the economy and its structure varies across countries and over time. In low-income countries agriculture is usually the largest sector in terms of employment and contribution to national product, much of it is self-sufficient rather than part of a commercial chain, and the linkages are stronger from agriculture to the macroeconomy than vice-versa. By contrast, in high-income countries, agriculture broadly interpreted to include supply of farm inputs, farming, and off-farm marketing accounts for less than 20 percent of employment and national product, with farming itself just a small percent, and there are strong commercial links and intersectoral transfers and competition for inputs and consumers' expenditures. In most high-income countries international trade, either via export markets for large shares of production or via competing imports, is an important part of the agricultural sector environment. Trade and agricultural policies vary in the extent to which agriculture in general, and farming in particular, are insulated from international trade and macroeconomic fluctuations. Relative to lower-income countries, in high-income countries it seems likely that the links between agriculture and the general economy will be less important, and that developments in the macroeconomy and the international markets will be more important determinants of the economic outcomes in agriculture.

Several sources or points of changes in the international economy, the macroeconomy, and the agricultural sector can drive behavioral responses and performance in the other sectors as well as the sector initially affected. Longer-term trends, cyclical fluctuations, and random variations in technology, consumer tastes, real incomes, and relative factor prices generate on-going structural changes. Of particular interest to this paper are government policy changes. These include exchange rate policy, fiscal policy, monetary policy, and trade and industry policies, as well as commodity policies and other policies explicitly directed to the agricultural sector. Of course, policies themselves often are partly endogenous reactions to the state of the general economy and of the well-being of the agricultural sector [Anderson and Hayami (1986)]. Seasonal fluctuations and conditions in international commodity markets directly influence agriculture and potentially flow on to affect the economic performance of the general economy. There is a rich set of *feed-forward, feed-back*, and *interdependent linkages* between policy and other disturbances in the agricultural sector, the rest of the economy, and the international economy.

The existence of linkages between the agricultural sector and the rest of the economy, albeit obvious, points to the specificity of the *primary sector* as opposed to the other sectors of the economy. Such a specificity, in turn, justifies why we can speak of a *macroeconomics of agriculture* as a way to describe the special characteristics of the agricultural sector from the macroeconomic point of view. The *primary* sector, as opposed to the *secondary* (broadly industrial) sector and the *tertiary* (services) sector, comprises the agricultural sector (farming, forestry, and hunting) as well as the fishing sector. If we include the mining and the energy sectors, all these sectors comprise activities relying on the exploitation of natural resources and the transformation of the products thereof. Broadly speaking, in fact, the primary sector plus the mining and energy industries entail the production of raw materials (commodities) and goods from the exploitation of land and natural resources, while the industrial sector comprises all the activities devoted to the transformation of such commodities and goods into *consumer* products.[1]

There are certain features that characterize the primary sector and define its particular role within the economy as well as its relationships with the macroeconomy. These features justify the need for the study of the macroeconomics of agriculture. In the first place, the primary sector is characterized by product homogeneity, broadly speaking, which is a pre-condition for the absence of imperfect competition. As we will see below, one of the reasons why it is expected that agricultural prices are more flexible than industrial prices is that agricultural prices are usually freer to adjust due to (almost) perfect competition. While it is true that in commodity markets cartels, trading bourses, storage policies, government intervention, and other factors alike influence price determination, it can be assumed to a large extent that primary product markets are characterized by product homogeneity and are less prone than industrial markets to imperfect competition. Yet, as it turns out, this is also true of other non-food and non-agricultural markets (other commodities) and many intermediate unfinished industrial products. Hence, the first noticeable feature of primary product markets is a great deal of (almost perfect) competition.

A second distinguishing feature of primary markets is that most agricultural products are subject to seasonal variations and climatic influences (on a broad scale), originating seasonal fluctuations in prices against which sometimes hedging and insurance policies or storage and unstocking cannot do much. Primary product prices are subject to some unpredictable and unpreventable degree of variability.

A third characteristic of most agricultural (and fishing) activities in most countries is that they are carried on by a large fraction of the population (particularly in low-income countries) and they happen to be very dispersed on the territory. This, historically, has been very important in affecting government policies towards the agricultural sector. In Europe, the Common Agricultural Policy (CAP) of the European Union has always held as a benchmark the preservation of the "rural communities" in the countryside, not only for a mere social purpose but also as a way to guard the environment and preserve land deterioration. The backbone of rural America has also always relied on the wealthy development of agricultural activities.

A fourth preeminent feature of primary markets is that the production of commodities heavily relies on an irreproducible factor of production – land – whose availability is finite and whose productivity cannot be individually infinitely increased. Technology and innovation in seeding, cultivating techniques, and capital utilization obviously have limited to a great extent the influence of limited land, but land availability still remains a problem in many circumstances, and greatly affects agricultural prices and markets.

---

[1] In a stylized representation of the economy we can say that all products and goods, as such, come from the primary and secondary sectors, while the tertiary sector only produces services.

All of these features make it clear why the primary sector (and the agricultural one in particular) is "different" from the other sectors in the economy and therefore why we can conceive of a *macroeconomics of the agricultural sector*, by which to analyze the effects of macroeconomic phenomena (monetary and exchange rate policy) on the sector as well as how the developments in the agricultural sector affect the overall economy and interact with the macroeconomy as a whole. Given the features described above, we expect macroeconomic policy to affect the agricultural sector in a specific way (as opposed to the other sectors), and agricultural prices and markets affect other sectors and the overall economy in a way that is not the same as the other sectors.

This essay is structured as follows. The transmission mechanisms and linkages – by which trend and short-term changes in one sector alter economic performance in other sectors – are described initially. This is done under the subheadings of backward linkages from agriculture to the rest of the economy, forward linkages from the macroeconomy and the international economy to agriculture, and second-round feed-back interdependent linkages. Models and studies attempting to quantify the linkages are then discussed in terms of theoretical constructs, structural econometric models, computable general-equilibrium models, and time-series or atheoretic models. A final section draws some key results and areas for further evaluation.

2. Inter-sector linkages

2.1. Agriculture to the general economy (backward linkages)

There are a number of real and monetary links originating from the agricultural sector affecting the economic performance of the general economy. These relationships often are referred to as *backward linkages*.

Agriculture, as one sector of the economy, competes for scarce labor and capital inputs from other sectors, provides raw materials for other sectors, directly provides consumer needs for food and fiber, and generates a component of national income. Trend improvements in technology, much of which have built on extensive public investment in research and development (R&D), have tended to be labor-saving and larger-scale biased, and they have contributed to declining terms of trade between agricultural product prices and overall (economy-wide) prices. Over the longer term, in most cases growth in agricultural productivity has been a significant contributor to rising national income levels, at least in the initial stages of economic take-offs. The structural changes have thus released labor resources for use in the rest of the economy. In many cases the adjustment has been slow, with workers equating their marginal utilities and gradually leaving agriculture due to higher relative industrial wage rates. Sometimes, the abandonment of agriculture has been revealed in disequilibrium outcomes of relatively low farm incomes.[2] Technological change, rising incomes, and changed relative factor

---

[2] The general historic trends of the development of industrial economies and the diminishing importance of agriculture have been analyzed by, for instance, Schultz (1945) and Cochrane (1993).

prices have combined to bring about a more commercial agriculture in which the relative importance of the farm sector has declined. At the same time, the farm purchase of inputs from the rest of the economy and off-farm marketing has expanded. Self-consumption at the farm level has decreased, while marketed agricultural products have become more common. These developments have strengthened linkages between the farm sector and other parts of the economy.

Variability of farm sector activity associated with climatic fluctuations and with volatile international commodity markets has flow-on effects on the rest of the economy. Many agricultural product markets are characterized as flex-price or auction markets in which prices adjust to equilibrate fairly inelastic supply and demand. However, the increasing relative importance of off-farm activities in the food and fiber sector, together with the more fix-price and customer market characteristics of these sectors – sometimes captured under activities of price leveling and averaging – cushion the volatility of farm commodity prices at the retail price level. Agricultural price variability contributes to various extents to price inflation and deflation. In the more advanced economies, food still contributes up to 20 percent of the weight of consumer price indices. Then, poor seasonal conditions shifting agricultural supply and buoyant international demand generate inflationary pressures on the rest of the economy, and of course vice-versa. That is, agriculture can be an important source of cost-push inflationary pressures.

Seasonal changes in farm income directly feed into GDP, often with multiplicative effects, and into expenditures by the agricultural sector on intermediate inputs, investment, and consumption. These effects are larger the greater the volatility, the less the sector indulges in intertemporal smoothing, and the larger is the sector as a share of the economy (both in terms of national product and employment). Agricultural policies also often modify the flow-on effects of agricultural sector disturbances on the rest of the economy, for example, through drought and flood damage assistance, deficiency payments, and price stabilization schemes.

In some countries agriculture is a dominant contributor to the trade balance, in terms of share of total exports and of import substitutes. Seasonal conditions and world price movements can combine to cause significant fluctuations in the current account which, in turn, flow on to offsetting adjustments of the foreign exchange rate.[3] In some conditions, it might be useful to insulate exchange rate movements generated by and affecting the agricultural trade balance only to avoid excessive revaluations (devaluations) that would penalize other more "exposed" sectors.

Agricultural policies and other policies generating budget outlays for the agricultural sector imply that changes in these policies, and in the performance of the sector, will affect government outlays, receipts, and deficits, and, in turn, the stance of fiscal policy. On the other hand, tax expenditures as well as direct budget outlays become relevant for

---

[3] In some countries, such as Australia, the term *commodity exchange rate* has been devised to indicate how the exchange rate varies in a coincident way with world commodity prices, appreciating with booms and depreciating with slumps. The European Union has also adopted for several years the so-called *green exchange rates* to be applied specifically to foreign transactions of agricultural goods.

the performance of the sector whenever fiscal policy is significantly oriented to shielding the sector from the rest of the economy.

Finally, it must be mentioned that agriculture has a major influence on wider environmental outcomes affecting the general economy and the welfare of its inhabitants. It is a major user of land and water resources, its use of fertilizers, pesticides, and herbicides often has externality effects, and rural land often provides direct amenity benefits. Different decision choices in agriculture can thus significantly alter the environmental goods available to the wider population.

2.2. *General economy to agriculture (forward linkages)*

There are a number of long-term and short-term links and real and monetary effects of changes in the general structure of the economy and of macroeconomic policies influencing quantity, price, and income outcomes in the agricultural sector. A growing body of literature in recent years has been devoted to the study of the effects of macroeconomic aggregates on the agricultural sector. In the 1970s and 1980s, for instance, the substantial variation in exchange rates, inflation rates, relative farm prices, and agricultural income induced a new stream of research on the relationships between macroeconomic policy and the agricultural sector [e.g., Schuh (1974, 1976), Tweeten (1980), Gardner (1981), Chambers (1981, 1984), Chambers and Just (1982), Barnett, Bessler and Thompson (1983), Bessler (1984), Rausser (1985a, 1985b), Rausser et al. (1986), Ardeni and Rausser (1995)].

General economic growth brings important structural changes affecting the agricultural sector. Real income growth increases demand for food and fiber, but the income elasticity is low, perhaps as high as 0.7 to 0.9 for developing countries, but down to 0.4 or lower for developed countries. For particular agricultural products the income elasticity is negative, while for others it may be positive. At the same time, economic growth means higher real wages. Thus, while the agricultural sector expands in absolute output, its share in the economy falls and it becomes less labor-intensive in terms of production methods used and the mix of products produced. Also, cyclical fluctuations in real national income generally have relatively small effects on the agricultural sector because of the low income elasticity of demand.

In some countries, large and often unforeseen developments in other sectors of the economy have had significant real implications for the agricultural sector. Particular examples are mineral, gas, and oil discoveries and large changes in prices of these products. Large expansions of these (and other) sectors have significantly boosted export income and have led to higher exchange rates than otherwise. The adjustment process has restored the balance-of-payments equilibrium by reducing agricultural exports [as discussed by, for example, Gregory (1976) and Snape (1977)]. The extra draw on limited national resources and the income boost or booms in other sectors of the economy also have effects on the agricultural sector, but often of a lower order of magnitude than the exchange rate effect.

The effects of general inflation on the agricultural sector involve different casual effects on the sector depending on the source of the inflation. Cost-push inflation, for example, associated with wage agreements ahead of (or greater than) productivity growth and with oil price shocks, often squeezes agriculture returns. As a competitive sector and a sector dependent on export sales, agriculture finds it hard to pass on cost increases, with residual rents on fixed factors (like land) taking the adjustment. By contrast, demand-pull inflation may have a relatively favorable effect on agriculture. Here it is argued that agricultural commodity prices have more of a flex-price or *auction* market characteristic than manufactured and services prices, which are usually a more fixed-price or *customer* market. Then, aggregate demand stimuli flow into larger price increases in the short run for agriculture commodity prices than for manufactured goods prices (a sort of over-shooting behavior). Both the demand-pull and demand-push inflationary effects on real agricultural sector returns would tend to be washed out in the longer run as relative prices readjust, thanks to the higher degree of competitiveness and price flexibility of the sector.

Inflation may also affect land asset values. In the longer run, and in the shorter run for expected inflation, land prices will tend to move with inflation. However, some authors, such as Feldstein (1980), argue that the interaction of different tax treatments of agricultural land, stocks, and other assets, together with inflation, can alter relative prices of agricultural land and alternative assets. Felstein uses a portfolio model to show that inflation increases the relative value of land and reduces the real value of corporate equities.

Since Schuh's paper (1974) the exchange rate has been recognized as an important determinant of real farm prices, through its effects on the trade balance. Several theoretical and empirical studies on the effects of agricultural commodity trade have shown, for instance, the importance of an overvalued currency on U.S. agricultural production and exports [Vellianitis-Fidal (1976), Chambers and Just (1979, 1982), Devadoss, Meyers and Johnson (1986), Orden (1986)].

Exchange rate policies, trade policies, and international commodity markets generally have a large influence on agriculture in most countries. World trade markets, either as export markets or as import substitutes, often set domestic agricultural commodity price levels. As Carter, Gray and Furtan (1990) note, some sectors of agriculture import inputs as well as export output so that the exchange rate effects on output prices can be partly muted by adjustments to costs.[4] Typically the "law of one price" (LOP) holds with fairly homogeneous bulk agricultural commodities [Richardson (1978), Roll (1979)].[5] However, many countries impose a range of quantitative restrictions on trade and partly insulate domestic prices from world price fluctuations. But such policies at

---

[4] As Jabara and Schwartz (1987) have pointed out, little work has been done to estimate exchange rate pass-through in the case of commodity prices. As a matter of fact, "certain commodity prices may not be as flexible as commonly perceived" (p. 581).

[5] Following the usual definition, commodity price arbitrage ensures that each good has a single price (defined in terms of a common currency unit) throughout the world [Isard (1977)].

the same time cause exaggerated volatility of world market prices, as argued by Johnson (1973), Tyers and Anderson (1992), and others. Also, empirical studies on international commodity prices frequently find significant and persistent deviations from the long-run equilibrium values [Isard (1977), Ardeni (1989)].

Government policy on exchange rates often influences agricultural terms of trade and incomes. Many countries, particularly up to the 1970s, adopted fixed exchange rate regimes. For instance, even in recent years, low-income countries have often set artificially high exchange rates which adversely affected agricultural exports and the sector generally [World Bank (1994)].

Freely floating exchange rates have a number of potential implications for the fortunes of the agricultural sector. For countries in which agricultural exports are a major share of total exports, agricultural sector declines (or booms) due to seasonal and price fluctuations will be partly cushioned by offsetting currency depreciations (appreciations). Similarly, relatively high (low) domestic inflation rates – when compared with those of other countries – are often largely offset by currency depreciations (appreciations), although the underlying purchasing-parity exchange-rate model often has poor explanatory power, especially in the short run. As Ardeni (1989) has summarized it, "in the simplest version of monetary models of exchange rate determination, deviations from the LOP are not expected for any commodity and, thus, purchasing-power parity holds strictly. In other models ... deviations from the LOP are expected for non-traded goods only. Empirical studies at the level of general price indices generally treat purchasing-power parity (PPP) as a long-run proposition but frequently find significant and even persistent deviations" (p. 662).[6] The short-term effects of monetary policy on interest rates, international capital flows, and exchange rates are sometimes considered important. For the U.S., many have argued that low interest rates and a low exchange rate in the 1970s were important to good agricultural outcomes compared to the tight monetary policy, high interest rates, and high exchange rate of the 1980s [Chambers and Just (1982)].

The stance of fiscal policy, both in terms of the aggregates and in terms of specific provisions for agriculture, may directly and indirectly enhance or detract from agricultural sector returns. Expansionary fiscal policy usually aims to stimulate real output, which will have limited implications for agriculture because of the low income elasticity mentioned above. In general it will also bring in some demand-pull inflationary pressure, which may lead to short-term gains for agriculture via the "overshooting" model recognizing the flex-price characteristic of agricultural commodity markets. Tighter aggregate fiscal policy would have the reverse effects.

A more disaggregated view of government taxing and spending policies indicates more specific direct links between fiscal policy and performance of the agricultural sector. Tax mix switches increasing the tax burden on labor incomes and on expenditure

---

[6] An example of these significant and persistent deviations of actual exchange rates from long-run purchasing-power parity values is given by Ardeni and Lubian (1991).

and away from saving and investment would favor the relatively capital-intensive agricultural sector (making capital cheaper via interest rate effects). Many concessions and deductions, including accelerated depreciation allowances, exemptions from capital gains tax, and investment allowances, often are particularly favorable to investment in agriculture. On the expenditure side, agricultural policies find expression in deficiency payments, export grants, reduced loan rates, storage support, and so forth, which effectively redistribute or transfer wealth from taxpayers generally to the agricultural sector. Most of the concessions and expenditures become capitalized into higher land values than otherwise.[7]

Monetary policy has real as well as nominal effects on the general economy and the agricultural sector in the short and medium run, but generally no real effects in the long run.[8] In a general macroeconomic sense, looser monetary policy involving expanded growth of the money supply and lower interest rates than otherwise induces a short-run combination of faster real output growth and higher inflation; tighter monetary policy has the opposite effects.

There are a number of more direct linkages between monetary policy, and especially its effect on interest rates, and the agricultural sector. Interest rates have a direct effect on costs of agricultural production with agriculture being a relatively capital-intensive sector and one dependent on debt finance. Higher (lower) interest rates reduce (increase) land asset values by raising (lowering) the discount rate on future income flows.[9] Higher (lower) interest rates also reduce (increase) the rewards from holding stocks of grain crops and inventories of breeding animals. The stock and inventory responses alter intertemporal market supplies and the time pattern of prices. To the extent higher nominal interest rates signal higher inflation expectations, the higher interest rates induce a flow out of money assets to other assets, including commodities. With freely floating exchange rates and increased international capital mobility, interest rate changes affect the capital component of the balance of payments and in turn the exchange rate. Lower (higher) domestic interest rates than otherwise discourage (encourage) net international capital flows, both by foreign and domestic players. In turn, the lower (higher) net capital inflow via the balance of payments identity induces a currency depreciation (appreciation) in order to increase (decrease) net exports, and a boost (contraction) to returns in the export-intensive agricultural sector and relief (more pressure) for import competitors. These types of monetary linkages have been argued as important in the U.S. to high agricultural returns and land prices in the 1970s period of loose monetary policy, and poor returns and falling land prices in the 1980s period of tight monetary policy.

---

[7] Another specific link is between fiscal policy and land prices. In general, fiscal policy amounts to a wealth transfer (through time) from taxpayers to landowners at the start of the policy and until land is sold, when some portion of the future expected benefits will get collected by the buyers in increased land prices.

[8] See the literature reviewed in Ardeni and Rausser (1995).

[9] And also by reducing (raising) income flows due to higher (lower) production costs for all farmers who borrow operating capital.

An important building block for understanding the short-term nominal and real effects of monetary policy on the agricultural sector is differences in the "stickiness" of different prices in the economy. A somewhat extreme view to illustrate the price-stickiness story is to consider financial asset and primary commodity markets as flex-price markets, and the rest of the economy as much closer to fix-price markets [e.g., Frankel (1986)]. Then, a change in monetary policy affecting nominal demand leads to much greater price responses, in fact *overshooting*, in the flex-price markets relative to the fix-price markets. That is, relative prices change and there are short-run real effects. The agricultural sector gains during periods of loose monetary policy and loses during periods of tight monetary policy. Ultimately, however, the reality and importance of the flex-price/fix-price dichotomy appears to be an empirical issue.

Studies on relative prices and aggregate inflation have supported the hypothesis that instability in aggregate demand causes instability in relative farm prices, and that variability in real farm income and prices increases with the general price level variability [Vining and Elwertowski (1976), Parks (1978), Cukierman (1979), Cukierman and Wachtel (1979, 1982), Hercowitz (1981), Fisher (1982), Rotemberg (1982), Stockton (1988), Lapp and Smith (1992)]. This area of research has stemmed from the idea that if an unanticipated exogenous shock (like a monetary expansion) occurs, all the subsequent price and interest-rate adjustments will happen in some sectors earlier than in others. Assuming that prices adjust more quickly in competitive markets than in imperfectly competitive ones, farm prices will rise faster than non-farm prices, provided that agricultural markets are indeed more competitive.

Explanations for these relative price movements include differences in the supply and demand elasticities of specific goods [which go back to Cairnes (1873)], and the effects of contract length (timewise) and hence of price-setting on the speed of adjustment [Bordo (1980)]. According to Bordo, a change in money supply causes a faster response for crude (raw materials and unfinished) product prices than manufactured (finished) product prices, a faster response for farm prices than industrial prices, and a faster response for non-durable than durable good prices.

The existence of nominal influences on real variables in a market in which long-term contracting was held as not important – the agricultural market – has been tested in a number of studies. Tweeten (1980), for instance, analyzing the period 1963–1977, concluded that prices *received* by farmers increased at the same rate as the general price level, while prices *paid* by farmers increased at a slower rate. Gardner (1981) concluded that although overall macroeconomic stability had real sectoral effects on agriculture, there is no predictable direction in which real farm prices are affected by general inflation.

In a more general context, Fisher (1982) has studied three sets of hypotheses linking aggregate price changes to relative-price variability: the *adjustment cost* hypothesis; the *rational-expectations–unanticipated-disturbances* hypothesis; the *asymmetric price response* hypothesis. The first two hypotheses imply that relative-price variability is affected by macroeconomic disturbances, whereas the third hypothesis implies that autonomous relative (i.e., sectoral) disturbances have macroeconomic effects. Under the first two hypotheses, both changes in price levels and relative-price variability are caused by the same aggregate supply and demand interactions (like changes in real aggregate output, interest rates or money supply).

The asymmetric price response hypothesis is based on the assumption that prices respond asymmetrically to disturbances, and are downward-rigid. Under this hypothesis, "if the disturbances that induced relative prices to change were primarily supply-side, resources should be moving out of the industries where prices have risen towards the industries where prices have yet to fall. If the disturbances were demand-side, resources should be moving towards the higher-prices sectors" [Fisher (1982, p. 180)]. Hence, differential responses in prices are in this case due to asymmetry more than to price-stickiness alone. The empirical results presented by Fisher were not totally supportive of the first two hypotheses, whereas the third one could not be rejected.

Most of the studies mentioned above have focused on one single aspect (like exchange rate and price interactions or relative-price movements), rather than analyzed specific questions within a broader macroeconomic framework. Frankel (1986), among others, has pointed out the importance of monetary policy for agricultural commodity prices, besides the exchange rate alone. Also, as Rausser (1985a) has noted, "since the 1970's the emergence of a well integrated international financial market has meant that agriculture, through domestic and foreign money exchange-rate markets, has become increasingly more dependent on capital flow among countries". From this perspective, the literature on the *macroeconomics of agriculture* has focused on a wider set of issues, relating in a more integrated way macroeconomic aggregates with agricultural-sector variables.

Stemming from Dornbusch's (1976) "overshooting" model of exchange-rate determination, Frankel (1986) proposed a model in which exchange rates, money supply, interest rates, and aggregate demand determine commodity prices. He emphasized the distinction between commodity prices, which are free to adjust instantly in response to changes in supply or demand, and the prices of most goods and services, which are not. In Frankel's model, a decline in nominal money supply is a decline in real money supply in the short run. This raises the real interest rate, which in turn depresses real commodity prices. The latter then "overshoot" (downward) their new (long-run) equilibrium value in order to generate expectations of a future appreciation sufficient to offset the higher interest rate. In the long run, however, all real effects vanish.

Within a framework similar to Frankel's, Rausser and other researchers later studied, in a more extensive fashion, the macroeconomic *linkages* between the agricultural sector and the aggregate economy [Rausser (1985a, 1985b), Rausser et al. (1986), Andrews and Rausser (1986), Stamoulis and Rausser (1987), Ardeni and Rausser (1995)]. As Rausser (1985a) noted, the heightened importance of macroeconomic factors on U.S. agriculture *does not* represent a structural change in long-run patterns. The linkages with the macroeconomic and international sectors did not emerge in the early 1970s and were in fact previously witnessed, according to Rausser. As a matter of fact, macroeconomic disturbances and their links to the agricultural sector should be central to any historical account of policy developments in the agricultural sector.

Rausser and associates have analyzed the macroeconomic linkages between the agricultural sector and the aggregate economy using a fix-price/flex-price type of model [à la Hicks (1974) and Okun (1975)]. The farm sector was modeled as a set of auction markets (flex-price markets) while the non-farm sectors are characterized by price inertia and gradual price adjustment (fix-price markets). In their model, the dynamics of agricultural markets was studied by explicitly taking into account not only the real demand and supply forces directly related to the farm sector, but also the effects of monetary and fiscal policies. As a result, monetary and fiscal policies can have substantial effects on prices and income in the agricultural sector in the short run, whereas sector-specific policies appear to have a more significant influence in the long run.

The definition of the *macroeconomic linkages* between the agricultural sector and the rest of the economy appears to be, to date, one of the most thorough attempts to identify the channels through which the farm sector interrelates with the aggregate economy. This notwithstanding, the "state of the art" in this area of research, with regards to the theoretical developments, is still not quite satisfactory. In the first place, not all the linkages have been fully investigated. The "macroeconomic linkages" model itself is based on some crucial assumptions that limit the full potential impact of further research hypotheses (such as, for instance, the perfect flexibility of farm prices). In the second place, the major emphasis has been put on what have been named the *forward linkages*, that is, those effects that go *from* the aggregate economy *to* the agricultural sector. The *backward linkages* have been, on the other hand, quite neglected. And yet the latter linkages appear to be of some importance, particularly those from the agricultural sector to the money and foreign exchange markets.

Although Gardner (1981) has pointed out that a thoroughly specified model is not necessary to identify *macroeconomic effects* upon agriculture (since agriculture is a small part of the overall economy), there are reasons to assume, at least as a research hypothesis, that agriculture can have a feedback effect on the monetary side of the economy. A policy of strong sectoral support, for instance, can have effects either on the government budget or on prices (besides distribution effects). *A priori*, we could expect both of these *sectoral effects* to have an influence on monetary policy (e.g., money supply), if the monetary authority's "reaction function" is not fully exogenous. While some facts, put forth by the literature mentioned above, have already been acknowledged, some others that are more neglected need further investigation.

In light of the previous considerations, in order to analyze in detail the macroeconomic interactions between the agricultural sector and the aggregate economy a more thorough model must be developed. The need for a fully specified model is not difficult to justify. As we have seen above, a large part of the literature focuses just on single aspects, ignoring the potentiality for interactions among neglected variables. As Chambers (1981, p. 934) stated, "as far as the agricultural sector is concerned, these variables [money supply, interest rates, and exchange rates] are, by and large, predetermined". Yet, to neglect their interactions with agricultural-sector variables (prices, as well as demand and supply) can lead to misleading results.[10] In the "macroeconomic linkages" model developed by Rausser et al. (1986) and Ardeni and Rausser (1995), a full-equilibrium dynamic monetary model in the Keynesian Mundell–Fleming tradition, several forward and backward linkages from agriculture to the rest of the economy are specified.

In the model, an economy with two sectors (farm and non-farm) is defined, in which output is demand-determined and prices are sticky in the short run (although they can adjust at different speeds). A balance-of-payments equation determines the rate of accumulation of reserves as a fraction of the total money stock: thus, either the capital-account or the current-account balances can be non-zero in the short run (imperfect capital mobility). The monetary authority intervenes on the foreign exchange market in order to keep the rate of depreciation of the exchange rate in line with the domestic trend of monetary growth (the target rate of credit creation). Total money-supply growth is given by the rate of credit creation (controlled by the monetary authority) and the rate of accumulation of reserves (controlled through the foreign exchange intervention rule).

Price inflation in the farm and non-farm sectors depends on excess demand pressures and on the money growth rate. In the long run, price inflation and output growth are the same in the two sectors and are equal to the money growth rate. This is equal to the target rate of credit creation as well as to the rate of currency depreciation. Real income is given in the long run. Price inflation in the two sectors, money growth, and the exchange-depreciation rate are the endogenous variables. The money stock, the price level in the two sectors, and the exchange-rate level are exogenously given, as well as output, interest rates, and all the foreign variables (assuming the home country is small).

Changes in exchange rates have a direct effect on prices, since they imply changes in relative prices, especially of tradables relative to non-tradables. They also have indirect effects, through the foreign-exchange intervention rule, since the latter implies a change in domestic supply, a consequent change in income, and thus a pressure on prices. All of these are *forward linkages* from exchange rates to prices. Changes in money have also an effect on prices (although not a direct one, since prices are sticky in the short run) via changes in domestic demand. They have an indirect effect also through the induced change in interest rates, the change in the capital-account balance, and the consequent pressures on the exchange rate. Changes in money have also depreciating effects on the exchange rate through the non-sterilized foreign-exchange intervention (another feedback channel on prices). All of these are *forward linkages* from money to prices.

Autonomous changes in prices have an effect both on money and on the exchange rate. An exogenous supply shock to the whole economy (like an "oil shock") with stag-flationary effects induces changes in the terms of trade (the real exchange rate and sectoral relative prices), and hence in the trade balance, in domestic output, and therefore in domestic money demand. An accommodating monetary policy and a

---

[10] Several studies on money causality and price-stickiness are subject to the same kind of criticism.

cautious "leaning-against-the-wind" foreign-exchange policy will let the autonomous changes in prices be fully reflected in changes in money and the exchange rate. Sectoral changes in prices, due to autonomous supply shifts, also have an effect on money and the exchange rate through the trade balance and domestic demand. All of these effects from prices to money and the exchange rate are *backward linkages*.

The transmission channels depicted above extend rather naturally to the possibility that exogenous shocks to demand and supply in the goods markets be not related to macroeconomic policy or to government policy measures directed to the farm sector. While several stylized facts establish a relationship between money and the exchange rate and farm prices which is easy to acknowledge, there is no validated framework wherein to assess the influence of government policy in agriculture at the macroeconomic level. As pointed out by Stamoulis and Rausser (1987, p. 3), in stressing the importance of focusing on relative prices, "(1) a policy that leaves relative prices of agricultural products unchanged is of no interest from a policy perspective. (2) Admitting monetary policy effects on *relative* prices requires identification of the special characteristics that separate or distinguish the farm sector from other sectors of the economy. Therefore, a model is needed that distinguishes agriculture from other sectors so that effects of monetary policies on the farm sector can be isolated".

Within the "macroeconomic linkages" model outlined above, Ardeni and Rausser (1995)[11] have analyzed the effects of government policy (specific to the farm sector, such as farm-support programs) on the dynamics of agricultural prices, in response to changes in monetary and exchange rate policy. Two typical farm-policy measures are *target prices* and *supply reduction* measures. The first puts a "lower bound" on prices received by domestic farmers, while the second is a compensation measure aimed at reducing excess agricultural supply.

The effect of a target price is such that, if the government wanted to fully "protect" the farm sector, then all downward changes in relative prices are paid back to domestic producers. Thus, changes in market prices will not be "natural" anymore, and the higher the government protection, the smoother they will be. Supply reduction measures help producers to face exogenous falls in demand and to alleviate excessive stock accumulation. Reducing excess supply has therefore dampening effects on price variability. If agricultural output is kept at the market-clearing level, price inflation in the farm sector will be the same as price inflation for the overall economy. These measures entail an expenditure by government, which obviously faces a budget constraint. Thus, either government revenues balance out expenditures, or the budget deficit must be financed out of some money-market operations. If one assumes this is the case, since the cumulative budget deficit must be zero in the long run, then it will be either monetized or debt-financed. Either choice will have obvious effects on the money market, the capital account, and the trade balance. This way, if some of the effects of monetary policy on agricultural prices are smoothed by government support, some others will

---

[11] Based on Ardeni's 1989 unpublished Ph.D. thesis.

be exacerbated (excessive money creation, trade balance overburden, etc.). This shows, once more, the strict linkages between the agricultural sector and the overall economy.

From the empirical point of view, the forward linkages hypothesis basically reduces to a one-way effect from money to exchange rates and prices. Under this hypothesis, the effect of prices on money is null. Likewise, the backward linkages hypothesis allows one-way effects from prices to money and exchange rates. Under this hypothesis, in its strict form, the effect from money or exchange rates to prices is zero. Obviously, a nested backward/forward linkages hypothesis will admit two-way effects.

2.3. Feedback effects

In many cases the feed-forward and feed-back linkages between the agricultural sector and the macroeconomy described above represent just the first-round effect. Often there will be second-round repercussions which bring an element of simultaneity to interactions between sectors of the economy as it adjusts to exogenous shocks. Second-round adjustments also highlight the likelihood of complex dynamic response patterns.

Consider, for example, inflation. A cost-push inflation coming from the agriculture sector, for example, as a result of unfavorable seasonal conditions, would likely induce a tightening of monetary and fiscal policies [e.g., Phelps (1978)]. Those policy reactions would work to offset at least some of the overall inflation outcome. Again, the initial adverse effects of general inflation on the agricultural sector may be partly, fully, or even more than fully offset by a depreciation of the currency.

Biological production lags and the importance of inventories lead to complex dynamic response patterns of agricultural production, especially in the case of livestock, to changes in macroeconomic circumstances. Initial improvements in profitability due to price increases or interest rate falls may reduce quantity supplied as animals are diverted from slaughter to breeding. In time the extra production enters the market and starts to exert downward pressure on prices.

In many senses macroeconomic and agricultural policies are not exogenous but really endogenous reaction functions [Anderson and Hayami (1986)]. Given the importance of the U.S. economy in the world economy, it is often the case also that changes in U.S. macroeconomic policies will influence macroeconomic policies in other countries. In turn, overseas policy reactions affect international markets and world prices for agricultural exports and imports.

3. Quantitative studies and the empirical evidence

3.1. Structural models

A vast array of econometric studies from single equations to macro-econometric models have been estimated to test hypotheses and quantify interactions between the agricultural sector and the rest of the economy.

Many structural equations for demand, supply, and inventory decisions, and for price, quantity, and income outcomes in the agricultural sector include general macro-economic variables as explanatory variables, and in most cases as exogenous explanatory variables. Income and general price indices typically are found to be significant explanatory demand variables. Indices of prices of non-farm input costs, including interest rates, are significant explanatory variables in production and investment equations. Inventory decisions often are found to respond significantly to interest rate changes. Where international trade is important, overseas prices, exchange rates, trade, and agricultural policies are found to be significant determinants of domestic commodity prices [see, e.g., Gemmill (1977), Johnson, Grennes and Thursby (1977), Bale and Lutz (1979)].

In some macroeconomic econometric studies of wage and price equations, agricultural product prices entered either in their own right or as an important component of a general price index [see, e.g., Hathaway (1974), Cooper and Lawrence (1975), Phelps (1978), Eckstein and Heien (1978), Lamm (1980)]. Studies for the 1970s sometimes found different and more important effects for agricultural product prices than for other product prices [e.g., Hathaway (1974), Lamm (1980)]. These and other estimated structural equations explaining decisions and behavior in the agricultural sector and in the general economy provide useful evidence that outcomes in one sector are affected by other sectors.

Most macro-econometric models, including those first built in the 1960s up to the present, seldom include explicit endogenous variables for the agricultural sector. Sometimes agricultural prices and exports enter as exogenous variables, and even more rarely is the performance of the model to shocks to these variables studied. The exception is a short period in the early 1970s when volatile energy and food prices were of interest.

Early econometric models of the agricultural sector included a number of macroeconomic variables as exogenous variables [see, e.g., Cromarty (1959), Fox (1965), Egbert (1969), Arzac and Wilkinson (1979)]. These variables included GDP, aggregate price indices, and interest rates, and after the floating of exchange rates, the exchange rate. Agricultural policy variables also were used as important components of supply and price equations, but typically only as exogenous variables. Generally, the macro variables were important in terms of contribution to explaining variations in performance of the agricultural sector.

In an effort to better capture interdependencies between the agricultural sector and the rest of the economy, a second generation of econometric studies initially sought to iteratively solve a general macro-econometric model and a more detailed separate model for the agricultural sector [for example, Fox (1965)]. Soon efforts were made to build and use more detailed econometric models of the agricultural sector with a sound macroeconomic component, detailed equations for supply, demand, and inventories for crop and livestock products, and to capture many of the linkages between the sectors described previously.

One of the more ambitious examples is the suite of models reported by Rausser (1985a, 1985b) and Rausser et al. (1986).[12] They find support for the earlier more conceptually based claim of Schuh (1976) that in the short run macroeconomic policies may be more important to agriculture than are specific commodity policies. In particular, their policy simulations found monetary policy to have major effects via its influence on the exchange rate and via overshooting effects associated with their characterization of agriculture as a flex-price sector versus a fix-price rest-of-the-economy. Also of interest were the findings that agricultural policies helped to cushion the effects, especially the downward commodity price effects, of monetary and fiscal policy disturbances, and that the dynamic responses of the crop and livestock sectors were different.

At a more disaggregated agricultural product level, Lapp and Smith (1992) have found that general inflation, and especially uncertain inflation, at the macroeconomic level causes the variability of relative agricultural product prices to increase by 20 to 40 percent. That is, macroeconomic policy can alter relative prices within agriculture, as well as between the sector and the rest of the economy. The study by Krueger, Schiff and Valdés (1988) illustrates the extent to which policies directed to facilitate development of the general economy – including overvalued exchange rates, ceiling prices on food, export taxes, and so forth – in many low-income countries effectively tax the agricultural sector and retard its income and development.

Structural econometric models seem to be powerful analytical tools. They allow for inclusion of considerable complexity and detail, they allow the various interactions to be included, and for them to be resolved in dynamic adjustment solution paths. Yet structural models have had to face considerable criticism and questioning. Much *a priori* specification is imposed on the model. This can involve the choice of macro-economic paradigm – for example, classical, Keynesian, new-Keynesian; the choice of fix-price versus flex-price adjustment mechanisms; the form of competition – i.e., perfect competition, oligopoly or monopoly; the expectations mechanism – for example, backward-looking adaptive expectations to various forms of forward-looking rational expectations; and the choice of variable exogeneity/endogeneity, including of policy variables. These and other choices give rise to misspecification errors and in many respects they can predetermine the general character of the model results. Further, the estimation phase inevitably involves long processes of specification searching, even data mining. Many estimated models have poor explanatory powers, and even less success at forecasting, and the latter raises doubts about using historical results for policy assessments with perhaps quite different future circumstances. Good modeling practices, and extensive sensitivity studies, can help to minimize the impact of the criticisms.

Clearly, however, criticisms of the use of econometric models based on structural equations to study interactions between the agricultural sector and the rest of the economy cannot be dismissed. But the studies give empirical support to the theoretically

---

[12] See also O'Mara, Wallace and Meshios (1987).

derived hypothesis of significant and important inter-sector linkages. More sensitivity analyses using competing specifications is desirable to evaluate the robustness of the available conclusions.

3.2. Computable general equilibrium models

Computable general equilibrium (CGE) models are suitable for and have been used for assessing the effects of supply and demand shocks to the agricultural sector on other sectors and on the overall economy, and they have been used for assessing the effects of changes in other sectors of the economy on the agricultural sector [see, e.g., Dervis, de Melo and Robinson (1982), Higgs (1986), Greenaway and Milner (1993)]. Agriculture is one of many sectors, sometimes with disaggregations of more than 100 industries, interlinked by input–output tables. National-account, balance-of-payment, and product and factor market-clearing identities ensure that general equilibrium effects across industries and sectors of the economy are captured. In most cases CGE models are expressed in real terms and are not well suited to analyzing monetary phenomena. Earlier models were restricted to comparative static assessments, but more recent developments trace out dynamic adjustment paths as well. Generally they are used to assess policy effects and other "what if" questions.

Disturbances to the agricultural sector analyzed include production shocks, such as drought and flood and technological change, international commodity price changes, and policy changes affecting quantities and wedges between buyer and seller prices. Initial effects on the agricultural sector, sometimes referred to as the direct effects in input–output terminology, are magnified by indirect effects on the input-supplying industries and the output-using industries. The total effects on the economy can be large in low-income countries and some regions of higher-income countries [Kilkenny and Otto (1994)]. However, in the high-income countries where farming makes up only a small percentage of the economy, it takes a shock of 50 percent or more in the agricultural sector to affect GDP or general price indices by more than a half percentage point [e.g., Greenaway and Milner (1993)].

Real changes in the rest of the economy such as changes in the real exchange rate, a wage increase as a form of cost-push inflation, a boom or slump in a significant export competition sector, and changes in other industry policies, such as tariffs, often are shown to have significant effects on quantities, prices, and returns in the agricultural sector [see, e.g., Higgs (1986)]. Total effects are found to be sensitive to the model closure assumptions imposed on the particular CGE model simulations, or by implication on the allowable second-round adjustments. For example, the adverse effects of a wage push on the agricultural sector, and on other tradable sectors, are more benign if a constant current account and endogenous exchange rate is imposed, relative to the contrary. Currency changes have larger effects if nominal or real wages are rigid and employment adjusts as opposed to a constant aggregate employment and endogenous wages. In many cases the appropriate model closure is ambiguous and worthy of sensitivity assessments.

In summary, computable general-equilibrium models explicitly impose considerable theoretical structure and *a priori* constraints on analysts. They effectively capture second-round general equilibrium effects. Often key elasticities and parameters have not been formally estimated, and very few attempts to evaluate the explanatory and forecasting properties of the models have been undertaken and reported.

3.3. Time-series studies

Criticisms of econometric model and computable general-equilibrium model proce-
dures, particularly concerned with the dominant role of imposed constraints and the influence of specification errors, have encouraged the use of time-series techniques to quantify economic linkages between agriculture and the rest of the economy. Observed data is used to tell most of the story with very little weight given to *a priori* reasoning. Several procedures are used to test for *directions of causality* between variables (in the sense of Granger),[13] and *impulse response functions* as well as *variance decomposi-
tions* are used to trace out the time pattern and magnitudes of response of endogenous performance variables to a shock or perturbation to different variables.

Consider, for example, the simple bivariate relationship between the two variables "money" and "agricultural prices" (a price index). A time series of data – often for quarterly intervals but maybe monthly, annual or something else – on both variables is available. Then, money is said to *cause* agricultural prices if variations in prices are significantly better explained with the addition of the money variable; and vice-
versa; and causality may be in both directions [e.g., Bessler (1984)]. *Impulse response functions* are used to simulate the time path response of the money and price variables to a shock in either the money or the price variable. Using vectors, these procedures can be generalized to handle many variables, although proceeding beyond four endogenous variables obviously becomes increasingly cumbersome.

Behind the simple time-series model idea, there are a number of important details and options to consider which often have a large impact on the results. The choice of variables to include in the analysis is partly arbitrary, its guidelines coming from theory, the issues of interest, data availability, and parsimony. Statistical results largely guide variable classifications as *endogenous* and *exogenous* [Engle, Hendry and Richard (1983)]. Often there is discretion on the choice of the actual variable, for example, the various measures of money from base money, M1, M3, and so on, and measures of agricultural prices at the farm, wholesale, or retail levels. Results and implications of time-series studies of links between the agricultural sector and the rest of the economy have often been found to be sensitive to variable choices [e.g., Barnett, Bessler and Thompson (1983), Robertson and Orden (1990)].

---

[13] See Sims (1972) and Granger (1988). See also Stock and Watson (1989).

Time-series models generate robust and reliable results when applied to data with stationary or I(0) properties.[14] Most economic data on the levels of prices, money, and quantities used to study intersectoral linkages appear to be non-stationary.[15] They require transformations, sometimes but not always as easy as taking first differences, to achieve stationarity and to avoid the problems of spurious regressions [Granger and Newbold (1974), Plosser and Schwert (1978)]. Failure to test for stationarity and to make appropriate transformations in most early *vector auto-regression* (VAR) studies of intersectoral linkages requires extreme caution in interpreting their results.[16]

Where the time-series variables being studied also are found to be *cointegrated*,[17] a *vector error correcting model* (VEC)[18] rather than a VAR model should be used. In some studies of linkages between the rest of the economy and the agricultural sector, an *unconditional* VEC model, which has endogenous variables only, has been extended to a *conditional* VEC model by adding exogenous policy variables [e.g., Robertson and Orden (1990), Ardeni and Rausser (1995)]. Provided the policy variables are exogenous or not caused by the included endogenous variables, the conditional VEC model makes use of more information and can provide stronger and more robust results.

VAR and VEC studies passing appropriate tests provide useful insights on backward and forward linkages between agriculture and the rest of the economy. All studies find significant effects of changes in macroeconomic variables for monetary policy and exchange rates on agricultural prices in the short run [Orden (1986), Orden and Fackler (1989), Robertson and Orden (1990)]. These results are associated with greater flexibility of farm commodity prices. By contrast the studies provide mixed results on the longer-run neutrality effects of monetary policy and exchange rate shocks [Choe and Koo (1993)]. However, there is growing consensus in more recent studies in favor of the long-run money neutrality hypothesis [Boschen and Otrok (1994), Haug and Lucas (1997)]. Non-agricultural price changes frequently are found to have both short- and long-term effects on the agricultural sector. That is, events in the rest of the economy, and especially monetary and exchange rate policies in the short run, have significant effects on prices, incomes, and asset values in the agricultural sector.

Dorfman and Lastrapes (1996) use Bayesian methods to investigate the effects of monetary policy on crop prices and on livestock prices. They are unable to reject a long-run neutrality constraint and in fact find it holds after about four years. But easier

---

[14] A time series is said to be *non-stationary*, or *integrated of order* 1, i.e., I(1), if its associated polynomial has one unit root, or if its first differences are *stationary*, or *integrated of order* 0, i.e., I(0) [see Fuller (1976)]. Unit-root tests have been proposed by, for example, Dickey and Fuller (1979, 1981).

[15] Since Nelson and Plosser's (1982) findings of non-stationarity on U.S. macroeconomic time series, unit-root tests have become standard practice.

[16] VAR models were popularized by, for instance, Sims (1980). See also Litterman and Weiss (1985).

[17] In the sense of Engle and Granger (1987). Cointegration refers to the stochastic properties of linear combinations of time series. Two or more non-stationary time series are said to be cointegrated if there exists a linear combination which is stationary.

[18] "Error correcting" models were discussed at length in the famous paper by Davidson et al. (1978). See also Granger and Weiss (1983).

monetary policy favors agricultural prices in the short run, initially more so livestock relative to crops. While monetary policy significantly affects agricultural prices, they find that monetary shocks explain less than 10 percent of the short-term variation of relative agricultural prices.

Many time-series studies find significant influences of agricultural sector fortunes, especially prices, on the general economy. In part, monetary policy, fiscal policy, and exchange rate policy are themselves policy reaction functions responding to shocks in the agricultural sector. Such second-round effects indicate the desirability of analyzing total effects of disturbances to the agricultural sector using a general equilibrium framework rather than an isolated agricultural sector model.

The conditional VEC model proposed by Ardeni and Rausser (1995) provides intuitively attractive results on the role of agricultural commodity policies on the intersectoral linkages. Using public expenditures on farm programs and government inventory holding of agricultural products as indicators of policy intervention, they find that sector policies, in addition to the longer-term direct assistance to the sector, partly insulate and cushion the magnitude of short-run effects of monetary policy, exchange rates, and non-farm price shocks on the agricultural sector. That is, commodity policies have a general stabilizing effect on shocks from the general economy on the agricultural sector.[19]

The use of time-series methods to study linkages between the agricultural sector and the rest of the economy has some pros and cons. The willingness to let the data speak avoids the problem of *a priori* predetermining much of the results and of incurring spec-ification errors. While the important process of computing impulse functions requires prior assumptions about the recursive structure of variable causation and orthogonality of error disturbances and their assignment, the lag structures are freely determined by the data. As argued by Orden and Fackler (1989), results are sensitive to the imposed assumptions. Further, these requirements in using impulse response functions make it increasingly difficult to study more than a few variables. Time-series models are data-demanding, particularly for more than a few variables. The parsimony of variables and associated high levels of aggregation required to simplify and restrict the assessment to a few variables can disguise interesting dynamics. For example, agricultural prices seem to have different dynamics as between crops and livestock and between different levels of the marketing chain. Diagnostic tests to assess lag lengths, statistical tests, and the results all are subject to sampling errors. This means that selected models and results of-ten require judgment and are sensitive to selections of variables, of their measurement, and of time periods of the data. Thus, time-series models, like econometric models, are not free of art and judgment, even though the data carries more weight with time-series studies.

The empirical time-series studies on monetary effects on agriculture have produced controversial results. As it turns out, different theoretical hypotheses have often yielded

---

[19] Phillips and Bewley (1991) likewise find that Australian buffer stock schemes for wool partly insulate agriculture from exchange rate volatility.

opposite outcomes, whereas the empirical research has revealed a great deal of method-ological and statistical problems. The effects of money-supply changes on agricultural prices have been shown to be significant under the hypothesis that agricultural prices are perfectly flexible. However, rather than "perfect" flexibility, one could just assume different degrees of "rigidity" among prices. And yet different speeds of adjustment to changes in money supply and, hence, in money demand,[20] will naturally make money *effective* in the short run [Fisher (1982)]. Yet, the *neutrality* of money (vis-à-vis sec-toral prices) and the timing of adjustment of agricultural prices are still unsettled issues. As shown by Gordon (1982), an interesting research hypothesis can successfully incor-porate Lucas' (1973) model as a special case, as well as adjustment-costs or contract-length models.

On the basis of some results it is difficult to find a justification for the apparently existent feedbacks from prices to money demand (and supply). For this, in fact, we must go back either to the idea of *accommodating money* or to the *differentials-in-demand-elasticities* explanation. But feedbacks can rise through the balance of payments and non-sterilization policies also. Money supply will adjust according to changes in the monetary base (capital movements induced by trade via the exchange rate).

The theoretical effects of exchange-rate changes on the (aggregate) price level are clearly defined in Dornbusch's (1976) model, as well as in Frankel's (1979, 1986) mod-ifications of it.[21] If we have more than *one* price (i.e., two sectors), the overall result will be the same, although it will differ in the two sectors due to their different prices' speeds of adjustments. The thrust is that, unless the degree of rigidity is the same for both prices, the short-run disequilibrium can last longer [due to relative-price effects as in Fisher (1982)]. Besides, in a Dornbusch-type model, such as Frankel's, there is a feedback from prices to real exchange rates.

A related issue is the extent of exchange-rate *pass-through* to prices. In a way, this corresponds to a long-run neutrality concept in the foreign-exchange market. How much of the changes in exchange rates are "passed through" to prices and how long does that "pass-through" take? Some theoretical developments have provided promising insights [Dornbusch (1988), Krugman (1989)], and the empirical evidence has suggested some answers [Jabara and Schwartz (1987)]: domestic farm prices appear to be downward-rigid to changes in exchange rates, but upward-flexible.

Overall, the time-series empirical literature on the relationships between the macro-economy and agriculture can hardly be judged as satisfactory. On the issue of farm-price flexibility versus manufacturing-price rigidity, the evidence basically confirms Bordo's findings (1980). One problem is the robustness of these results: in principle, there is a simultaneity bias and a mis-specification problem. Moreover, as Bordo himself ac-knowledged (in footnotes 37 and 38), income effects are ignored and the feedbacks are not explicitly modeled.

---

[20] The underlying hypothesis of these models is the monetary assumption that the money market is in equilibrium.

[21] See, also, Dornbusch (1980).

On money *neutrality* there is a great deal of conflicting evidence. Causality and exogeneity tests have not always been correctly performed, particularly in the early 1980s. In this respect, there is still the need for an appropriate reassessment of the major results. Some of the studies were conducted using univariate models. Yet the problem with univariate (auto)regressions is that of inconsistency and misspecification. Vector autoregressions (i.e., multivariate) models, on the other hand, suffer from "omitted variable" problems, as well as from dubious orthogonalizations. One example is given by the following "money neutrality" test, sometimes carried out. By regressing

$$p_t = a + \sum_j b_j m_{t-j} + u_t,$$

where p is price and m is money, in order for the estimated b_j coefficients to be consistent, the residuals u_t and m_{t-j} must be independent for all t. If they are independent, and the b_j are significantly different from zero, then we say that *money causes prices* (in Granger's sense). If they are not, the estimated b_j are inconsistent and, more important, there is a feedback from prices to money. Similar tests for independence are seldom carried out in the literature.

One of the most striking observations about the time-series literature is that, in any case, little exploratory data analysis is usually done. Filtering (or seasonal filtering) is sometimes applied, but somewhat blindly [even by Sims (1980)]. Non-stationarity has by now been acknowledged as a major problem in time-series data analysis [after Granger and Newbold (1974) and the subsequent literature]. If a time-series variable is non-stationary *within the sample*, then standard asymptotic theory cannot be applied in judging the estimates. Although time-differencing (or filtering, for that matter) can solve the problem, in a multivariate context one has to make sure that the variables have a *common root*. The common-root problem [Davidson et al. (1978)] leads to two different sets of problems: overdifferencing [Plosser and Schwert (1978)] or moving-average residuals with one unit root (i.e., non-invertible polynomials). Moreover, time-series variables can be individually non-stationary, i.e., they can be *integrated*, but there can exist linear combinations of them that are stationary. In that case, they are said to be *co-integrated*. If two variables, x_t and y_t, are both integrated of order one (they are I(1)), i.e., their first time-differences are stationary, and they are also co-integrated and one estimates a VAR in the first difference such as

$$\Delta x_t = a_1 + \sum_j^k b_j \Delta x_{t-j} + \sum_j^h c_j \Delta y_{t-j} + u_{1t},$$

$$\Delta y_t = a_2 + \sum_j^g d_j \Delta x_{t-j} + \sum_j^l e_j \Delta y_{t-j} + u_{2t},$$

then the system is *misspecified* since a term $z_t = x_t - Ay_t$ (the so-called *co-integrating term*) is missing in one or both equations.[22] This also makes all the results on causality and exogeneity (and hence money neutrality) flawed whenever the time-series variables under investigation were I(1) and co-integrated. Conversely, non-stationary time-series variables in econometric models (even after the inclusion of a time-trend variable) cause *spurious* correlations [Granger and Newbold (1974)].

The evidence presented by Ardeni and Rausser (1995) using U.S. data shows that farm prices increase more than non-farm prices in the short run as money supply or the exchange rate increase, even though the long-run responses are qualitatively similar. Yet these results appear to be dependent on the *orthogonalization* of the moving-average representations of the cointegrated vector autoregressions used for estimation. Different orthogonalizations imply different *orderings* among the time-series variables. Under a money-to-prices causation ordering the result is in line with Robertson and Orden (1990), who concluded that "positive monetary shocks induce a shift in relative prices in favor of agriculture in the short run". Conversely, under a prices-to-money causation ordering, short-run price responses are the same while agriculture is pushed in a "cost–price squeeze" in the long run. Under a non-orthogonalized representation, both monetary and manufacturing-price shocks imply just the same cost–price squeeze effect on agriculture, thus confirming Tweeten's (1980) findings.

Several time-series studies on the relationship between money and prices have found evidence that is consistent with the hypothesis that relative prices change as money supply changes, because price levels in the different sectors change differently. Also, these studies point out that even though the short-run effects of money-supply changes may be different, the long-run effects are equal, and in particular money will have no real effects in the long run. Several authors have shown that farm prices respond faster than non-farm prices to money-supply changes [e.g., Bordo (1980), Devadoss and Meyers (1987), Orden and Fackler (1989), Robertson and Orden (1990)]. Others have found evidence of Granger causality from money supply to agricultural prices with no reverse feedback [e.g., Barnett, Bessler and Thompson (1983), Bessler (1984)]. Most of those studies, however, lack an appropriate treatment of the time-series properties of the data, which makes the results questionable.

The assumption of money exogeneity with respect to farm prices justifies the causality from money to prices and the absence of causality from prices to money. However, as Bessler (1984, p. 29) has also acknowledged, this assumption is not neutral with respect to the effect of money-supply changes on prices. Under this assumption, i.e., under the assumption of a structural recursive money-to-prices ordering, Ardeni and Rausser (1995) find that farm prices respond faster than non-farm prices to money innovations in the short run, while in the long run both prices revert to their initial equilibrium level. That is, money is not neutral in the short run, both prices overshoot their long-run value, agricultural prices are more flexible than manufacturing prices, and money has no real effects in the long run.

---

[22] This result was first proven by Engle and Granger (1987).

4. Assessment

There is an impressive set of conceptual arguments and supporting empirical assessments indicating significant real and monetary linkages and short-term and long-term effects of the general economy on the agricultural sector. In developed economies the short-run monetary and exchange rate policies often have a larger effect on the agricultural sector than do sector policies and other shocks. Agricultural policies often modify the effects of macroeconomic disturbances on the sector and may themselves be partly endogenous. Backward linkages from the agricultural sector to the rest of the economy are very important for developing countries, but, according to most studies, they are not important in developed countries, except for infrequent very large rural sector disturbances.

The variety of policy issues and economy contexts means it is difficult to provide meaningful summaries of the pattern and magnitude of effects of the different linkages between the macroeconomy and the agricultural sector. Policies may be largely anticipated or a surprise, and other policies react to circumstances rather than being even quasi-exogenous. Clearly the structure and behavior of economies vary from country to country, and within a country over time. The empirical evidence indicates complicated leads and lags and feedback reactions driving dynamic responses and the observed data. And price, quantity, income, and asset path responses vary across agricultural products, and in particular between crops and livestock, and across different levels of the marketing chain.

The comparative strengths and weaknesses of structural models and of time-series models recommend their applications as complementary tools to further understand and quantify linkages between agriculture and the macroeconomy – a point made much earlier in the debate by Sims (1989). In particular, all modeling efforts could usefully focus on evaluating the robustness of results to alternative specifications, variable measures, and time periods.

Acknowledgements

We gratefully acknowledge the comments of two anonymous referees and the Editors for helpful comments and additional references.

References

Anderson, K., and Y. Hayami (1986), The Political Economy of Agricultural Protection (Allen and Unwin, Sydney).

Andrews, M.S., and G.C. Rausser (1986), "Some political economy aspects of macroeconomic linkages with agriculture", American Journal of Agriculture Economics 68:413–417.

Ardeni, P.G. (1989), "Does the law of one price really hold for commodity prices?", American Journal of Agricultural Economics 71:661–669.

Ardeni, P.G., and D. Lubian (1991), "Is there trend reversion in purchasing-power parity?", European Economic Review 35:1035–1055.

Ardeni, P.G., and G.C. Rausser (1995), "Alternative subsidy reduction paths: the role of fiscal and monetary policy linkages", in: G.C. Rausser, ed., GATT Negotiations and the Political Economy of Policy Reform (Springer-Verlag, Berlin) Chapter 11, 315–345.

Arzac, E., and M. Wilkinson (1979), "A quarterly econometric model of the US livestock and feed grain markets and some of its policy implications", American Journal of Agricultural Economics 61:297–308.

Bale, M.D., and E. Lutz (1979), "The effects of trade intervention on international price instability", American Journal of Agricultural Economics 61:512–516.

Barnett, R.C., D.A. Bessler and R.L. Thompson (1983), "The money supply and nominal agricultural prices", American Journal of Agricultural Economics 65:303–307.

Bernanke, B.S. (1986), "Alternative explanations of the money–income correlation", Carnegie–Rochester Series on Public Policy 25:49–100.

Bessler, D.A. (1984), "Relative prices and money: a vector autoregression on Brazilian data", American Journal of Agricultural Economics 66:25–30.

Bordo, M.D. (1980), "The effects of a monetary change on relative commodity prices and the role of long-term contracts", Journal of Political Economy 88:1088–1109.

Boschen, J., and C. Otrok (1994), "Long-run neutrality and superneutrality in an AR/MA framework: comment", American Economic Review 84:1470–1473.

Box, G.E.P., and G.M. Jenkins (1976), Time Series Analysis, Forecasting, and Control (Holden Day, San Francisco).

Burt, O. (1986), "Econometric modeling of the capitalization formulae for land prices", American Journal of Agricultural Economics 68(1):10–26.

Cairnes, J.E. (1873), Essays on Political Economy: Theoretical and Applied (Reprint 1965) (Kelley, New York).

Carter, C., R. Gray and W. Furtan (1990), "Exchange rate effects on inputs and outputs in Canadian agriculture", American Journal of Agricultural Economics 72:738–743.

Chambers, R.G. (1981), "Interrelationships between monetary instruments and agricultural commodity trade", American Journal of Agricultural Economics 63:934–941.

Chambers, R.G. (1984), "Agricultural and financial market interdependence in the short run", American Journal of Agricultural Economics 66:12–24.

Chambers, R.G., and R.E. Just (1979), "A critique of exchange rate treatment in agricultural trade models", American Journal of Agricultural Economics 61:249–257.

Chambers, R.G., and R.E. Just (1981), "Effects of exchange rate changes on U.S. agriculture: a dynamic analysis", American Journal of Agricultural Economics 63:32–46.

Chambers, R.G., and R.E. Just (1982), "An investigation of the effect of monetary factors on agriculture", Journal of Monetary Economics 9:235–247.

Choe, Y.C., and W. Koo (1993), "Monetary impacts on prices in the short and long run: further results for the United States", Journal of Agricultural Economics Research 18:211–224.

Cochrane, W. (1993), The Development of American Agriculture: An Historical Analysis (University of Minnesota Press, Minneapolis).

Cooper, R., and R. Lawrence (1975), "The 1972–75 commodity boom", Brookings Papers on Economic Activity 3:671–715.

Cromarty, W. (1959), "An econometric model for United States agriculture", Journal of American Statistical Association 5:556–574.

Crouhy-Veyrac, L., M. Crouhy and J. Melitz (1982), "More about the law of one price", European Economic Review 18:325–344.

Cukierman, A. (1979), "The relationship between relative prices and the general price level: a suggested interpretation", American Economic Review 69:444–447.

Cukierman, A., and P. Wachtel (1979), "Differential inflationary expectations and the variability of the rate of inflation: theory and evidence", American Economic Review 69:595–609.

Cukierman, A., and P. Wachtel (1982), "Relative price variability and non-uniform inflationary expectations", Journal of Political Economy 90:146–157.

Davidson, J.E.H., D.F. Hendry, F. Srba and S. Yeo (1978), "Econometric modeling of the aggregate time-series relationship between consumers' expenditure and income in the United Kingdom", The Economic Journal 88:661–692.

Dervis, K., J. de Melo and S. Robinson (1982), General Equilibrium Models for Development Policy (Cambridge University Press, Cambridge).

Devadoss, S., and W.H. Meyers (1987), "Relative prices and money: further results for the United States", American Journal of Agricultural Economics 69:838–842.

Devadoss, S., W.H. Meyers and S.R. Johnson (1986), "Exchange rates, trade deficits, and U.S. prices", Working Paper 86-WP 10 (Center for Agricultural and Rural Development, Iowa State University).

Dickey, D.A., and W.A. Fuller (1979), "Distribution of estimates for autoregressive time series with unit root", Journal of the American Statistical Association 74:427–431.

Dickey, D.A., and W.A. Fuller (1981), "The likelihood ratio statistics for autoregressive time series with a unit root", Econometrica 49:1042–1057.

Dorfman, J., and W. Lastrapes (1996), "The dynamic responses of crop and livestock prices to money-supply shocks. A Bayesian analysis using long-run identifying restrictions", American Journal of Agricultural Economics 78:530–541.

Dornbusch, R. (1976), "Expectations and exchange rate dynamics", Journal of Political Economy 84:1161–1176.

Dornbusch, R. (1980), Open Economy Macroeconomics (Basic Books, New York).

Dornbusch, R. (1988), Exchange Rates and Inflation (MIT Press, Cambridge).

Driskill, R. (1981), "Exchange rate overshooting, the trade balance, and rational expectations", Journal of International Economics 11:361–377.

Duloy, J., and J. Nevile (1965), "The effects of a reserve price scheme for wool on the balance of payments and gross national product", Economic Record 41:254–261.

Duloy, J., and A. Woodland (1967), "Drought and the multiplier", Australian Journal of Agricultural Economics 11:82–86.

Eckstein, A., and D. Heien (1978), "The 1973 food price inflation", American Journal of Agricultural Economics 60:186–196.

Egbert, A. (1969), "An aggregate model of agriculture: empirical estimates and some policy implications", American Journal of Agricultural Economics 51:71–86.

Engle, R., and C.W.J. Granger (1987), "Co-integration and error correction: representation, estimation, and testing", Econometrica 55:251–276.

Engle, R.F., D.F. Hendry and J.F. Richard (1983), "Exogeneity", Econometrica 51:277–304.

Feldstein, M. (1980), "Inflation, portfolio choice, and the prices of land and corporate stock", American Journal of Agricultural Economics 62:910–916.

Fisher, S. (1982), "Relative price variability and inflation in the United States and Germany", European Economic Review 18:171–196.

Fox, K.A. (1965), "A submodel of the agricultural sector", in: J.S. Dusenberry et al., eds., The Brookings Quarterly Econometric Model of the United States (North-Holland, Amsterdam).

Frankel, J. (1979), "On the mark: a theory of floating exchange rates based on real interest differentials", American Economic Review 69:610–622.

Frankel, J. (1986), "Expectations and commodity price dynamics: the overshooting model", American Journal of Agricultural Economics 68:344–348.

Fuller, W.A. (1976), Introduction to Statistical Time Series (John Wiley & Sons, New York).

Gardner, B. (1981), "On the power of macroeconomic linkages to explain events in U.S. agriculture", American Journal of Agricultural Economics 63:871–878.

Gardner, B. (1987), The Economics of Agricultural Policies (Macmillan, New York).

Gemmill, G. (1977), "An equilibrium analysis of US sugar policy", American Journal of Agricultural Economics 59:609–618.

Girton, L., and D. Roper (1977), "A monetary model of exchange market pressures applied to the postwar Canadian experience", American Economic Review 67:537–548.

Godden, D. (1997), Agricultural and Resource Policy (Oxford University Press, Melbourne).

Gordon, R.J. (1975), "The impact of aggregate demand on prices", Brookings Papers on Economic Activity 6:183–204.

Gordon, R.J. (1982), "Price inertia and policy ineffectiveness in the United States, 1890–1980", Journal of Political Economy 90:1087–1117.

Granger, C.W.J. (1988), "Some recent developments in a concept of causality", Journal of Econometrics 39:199–211.

Granger, C.W.J., and P. Newbold (1974), "Spurious regressions in econometrics", Journal of Econometrics 26:1045–1066.

Granger, C.W.J., and A.A. Weiss (1983), "Time-series analysis of error correction models", in: Studies in Econometrics, Time Series, and Multivariate Statistics (Academic Press, New York) 255–278.

Greenaway, D., and C. Milner (1993), Trade and Industrial Policy in Developing Countries (University of Michigan Press, Ann Arbor).

Gregory, R. (1976), "Some implications of the growth of the mining sector", Australian Journal of Agricultural Economics 20(1):71–91.

Hathaway, D.E. (1974), "Food prices and inflation", Brookings Papers on Economic Activity 5:63–116.

Haug, A., and R. Lucas (1997), "Long-run neutrality and superneutrality in an AR/MA framework: comment", American Economic Review 87:756–759.

Hercowitz, Z. (1981), "Money and the dispersion of relative prices", Journal of Political Economy 89:328–356.

Hicks, J.R. (1974), The Crisis in Keynesian Economics (Basil Blackwell, Oxford).

Higgs, P. (1986), Adoption and Survival in Australian Agriculture (Oxford University Press, Melbourne).

Isard, P. (1977), "How far can we push the law of one price?", American Economic Review 67:942–948.

Jabara, C.L., and N.E. Schwartz (1987), "Flexible exchange rates and commodity price changes: the case of Japan", American Journal of Agricultural Economics 69:580–590.

Johnson, D.G. (1973), World Agriculture in Disarray (Fontana, London).

Johnson, P.R., T. Grennes and M. Thursby (1977), "Devaluation, foreign trade controls and domestic wheat prices", American Journal of Agricultural Economics 59:619–627.

Kilkenny, M., and D. Otto (1994), "A general equilibrium perspective on structural change in the rural economy", American Journal of Agricultural Economics 76:1130–1137.

Kravis, I.B., and R.E. Lipsey (1977), "Export prices and the transmission of inflation", American Economic Review 67:155–163.

Krueger, A., M. Schiff and A. Valdés (1988), "Agricultural incentives in developing countries: measuring the effect of sectoral and economy wide policies", World Bank Economic Review 2:255–271.

Krugman, P.R. (1989), Exchange-Rate Instability (MIT Press, Cambridge).

Lamm, R.M. (1980), "The role of agriculture in the macroeconomy: a sectoral analysis", Applied Economics 12:19–35.

Lapp, J., and V. Smith (1992), "Aggregate sources of relative price variability among agricultural commodities", American Journal of Agricultural Economics 74:1–9.

Litterman, R.B., and L. Weiss (1985), "Money, real interest rates, and output: a reinterpretation of postwar U.S. data", Econometrica 53:129–156.

Lucas, R.E. (1973), "Some international evidence on output-inflation tradeoffs", American Economic Review 63:326–334.

Myers, R., R. Piggott and W. Tomek (1990), "Estimating sources of fluctuations in the Australian wool market: an application of VAR methods", Australian Journal of Agricultural Economics 34:242–262.

Nelson, C.R., and C.I. Plosser (1982), "Trend and random walks in economic time series", Journal of Monetary Economics 10:139–162.

Officer, L.H. (1976), "The purchasing-power theory of exchange rates: a review article", IMF Staff Papers 23:1–60.

Okun, A.M. (1975), "Inflation: its mechanics and welfare costs", Brookings Paper on Economic Activity 2:351–401.

O'Mara, P., N. Wallace and H. Meshios (1987), "The current account, monetary policy, market sentiment and the real exchange rate: some implications for the farm sector", Australian Journal of Agricultural Economics 31:219–241.

Orden, D. (1986), "Money and agriculture: the dynamics of money–financial market–agricultural trade linkages", Agricultural Economics Research 38:14–28.

Orden, D., and P. Fackler (1989), "Identifying monetary impacts on agricultural prices in VAR models", American Journal of Agricultural Economics 71:495–502.

Orden, D., and L. Fisher (1991), "Macroeconomic policy and agricultural economics research", American Journal of Agricultural Economics 73:1348–1354.

Parks, R.W. (1978), "Inflation and price variability", Journal of Political Economy 86:79–95.

Phelps, E.S. (1978), "Commodity-supply shocks and full-employment monetary policy", Journal of Money, Credit and Banking 10:206–221.

Phillips, S., and R. Bewley (1991), "The effects of flexible exchange rates in Australian wool prices", Australian Journal of Agricultural Economics 35:49–90.

Plosser, C.I., and G.W. Schwert (1978), "Money, income, and sunspots: measuring economic relationships and the effect of differencing", Journal of Monetary Economics 4:637–660.

Protopapadakis, A., and H.R. Stoll (1983), "Spot and futures prices and the law of one price", Journal of Finance 38:1431–1455.

Rausser, G.C. (1985a), "Macroeconomics and US agricultural policy", in: B. Gardner, ed., US Agricultural Policy: The 1985 Farm Legislation (American Enterprise Institute, Washington, DC).

Rausser, G.C. (1985b), "Agriculture, trade, and macroeconomics", Giannini Foundation Working Paper 407 (University of California, Berkeley).

Rausser, G., J. Chalfant, H.A. Love and K. Stamoulis (1986), "Macroeconomic linkages, taxes and subsidies in US agricultural sector", American Journal of Agricultural Economics 68:399–413.

Richardson, J.D. (1978), "Some empirical evidence on commodity arbitrage and the law of one price", Journal of International Economics 8:341–351.

Robertson, J., and D. Orden (1990), "Monetary impacts on prices in the short and long run: some evidence from New Zealand", American Journal of Agricultural Economics 72:160–171.

Roll, R. (1979), "Violations of the 'law of one price' and their implications for efficient international commodity markets", in: M. Sarnat and G. Szego, eds., International Finance and Trade, Vol. I (Ballinger, Cambridge) 133–176.

Roop, J., and R. Zeitner (1977), "Agricultural activity and the general economy: some macroeconomic experiments", American Journal of Agricultural Economics 59:117–125.

Rotemberg, J.J. (1982), "Sticky prices in the United States", Journal of Political Economy 90:1187–1211.

Runkle, D.E. (1987), "Vector autoregression and reality", Journal of Business and Economic Statistics 5:437–442.

Saunders, P.J. (1988), "Causality of U.S. agricultural prices and the money supply: further empirical evidence", American Journal of Agricultural Economics 70:588–596.

Schuh, G.E. (1974), "The exchange rate and U.S. agriculture", American Journal of Agricultural Economics 56:1–13.

Schuh, G.E. (1976), "The new macroeconomics of agriculture", American Journal of Agricultural Economics 58:802–811.

Schultz, T.W. (1945), Agriculture in an Unstable Economy (McGraw-Hill, New York).

Sims, C.A. (1972), "Money, income, and causality", American Economic Review 62:540–552.

Sims, C.A. (1980), "Macroeconomics and reality", Econometrica 48:1–48.

Sims, C. (1989), "Models and their uses", American Journal of Agricultural Economics 71:489–494.

Snape, R. (1977), "Effects of mineral development on the economy", Australian Journal of Agricultural Economics 21:147–156.

Stamoulis, K.G., J. Chalfant and G. Rausser (1986), "Monetary policy and relative farm prices", Mimeo (University of California, Berkeley).

Stamoulis, K.G., and G. Rausser (1987), "Overshooting of agricultural prices", Mimeo (University of California, Berkeley).

Starleaf, D., W. Myers and A. Womack (1985), "The impact of inflation on the real income of US farmers", American Journal of Agricultural Economics 67:384–389.

Stock, J.H., and M.W. Watson (1989), "Interpreting the evidence on money-income causality", Journal of Econometrics 40:161–181.

Stockton, D.J. (1988), "Relative price dispersion, aggregate price movement, and the natural rate of unemployment", Economic Inquiry 26:1–22.

Thorton, D., and D. Batten (1985), "Lag length selection and tests of Granger causality between money and income", Journal of Money, Credit and Banking 17:164–178.

Tweeten, L. (1980), "An economic investigation of inflation pass-through to the farm sector", Western Journal of Agricultural Economics 5:89–106.

Tyers R., and K. Anderson (1992), Disarray in World Food Markets (Cambridge University Press, Cambridge).

Vellianitis-Fidal, A. (1976), "The impact of devaluation on U.S. agricultural exports", Agricultural Economics Research 28:107–116.

Vining, D.R., and T.C. Elwertowski (1976), "The relationship between relative prices and the general price level", American Economic Review 66:699–708.

World Bank (1994), Adjustment in Africa (Washington, DC).

Chapter 29

AGRICULTURE AND ECONOMIC DEVELOPMENT

C. PETER TIMMER

Graduate School of International Relations and Pacific Studies, University of California, San Diego, La Jolla, CA

Contents

Handbook of Agricultural Economics, Volume 2, Edited by B. Gardner and G. Rausser
© *2002 Elsevier Science B.V. All rights reserved*

Abstract

This chapter takes an analytical look at the potential role of agriculture in contributing to economic growth, and develops a framework for understanding and quantifying this contribution. The framework points to the key areas where positive linkages, not necessarily well-mediated by markets, might exist, and it highlights the empirical difficulties in establishing their quantitative magnitude and direction of impact. Evidence on the impact of investments in rural education and of nutrition on economic growth is reviewed. The policy discussion focuses especially on the role of agricultural growth in poverty alleviation and the nature of the market environment that will stimulate that growth.

Keywords

poverty alleviation, economic growth, structural transformation

JEL classification: O13

1. Introduction

How does agriculture contribute to economic development? This is an old and honorable question, tracing back at least to the Physiocrats in the mid-eighteenth century, and one that was central to the early development of analytical economics by Adam Smith, David Ricardo, and Thomas Malthus.[1] Even the first modern, comprehensive effort to address the question, the seminal article, "The role of agriculture in economic development", by Johnston and Mellor, appeared as long ago as 1961. And yet the question continues to be debated, as D. Gale Johnson's Ely lecture to the American Economic Association on "Agriculture and the wealth of nations" indicates [Johnson (1997)].

The present chapter addresses the issue from two perspectives. The first is analytical, where the potential role of agriculture in contributing to the growth of the rest of the economy is examined within the context of the new growth economics [Barro and Sala-i-Martin (1995)]. The second is policy oriented, where the question is how to stimulate the positive linkages between agriculture and the growth process while minimizing the structural lag in labor productivity between the two sectors that seems to be an inevitable result of rapid economic growth [Schultz (1953), Anderson and Hayami (1986), Timmer (1992)].

These two perspectives are integrated by recognizing two important intellectual developments that have occurred since World War II. The first is the scientific revolution in agriculture, which has transformed the potential productivity of land and rural people from subsistence levels using traditional techniques to levels producing substantial commercial surpluses that are available to feed rapidly increasing non-farm populations [Johnson (1997)]. The second is the growing understanding of the role of markets in the process of economic development and what governments must (and must not) do to foster that role. At the start of the 21st century there is now general agreement that agricultural development is best served by a market-oriented strategy capable of stimulating rapid technological change in the agricultural sector.

But this agreement in principle masks considerable controversy over policy design and implementation, for three reasons. First, agriculture is a declining industry during the process of economic growth. The smaller share for agriculture of economic output and workers as incomes increase over time is the most robust "stylized fact" describing the structural transformation [Chenery and Syrquin (1975), Syrquin (1988)]. Does a (relatively) smaller agricultural sector in the future mean that investments should be diverted to the industrial sector, where long-run payoffs might be higher? In other words, does a development strategy of "rapid industrialization", apparently the surest path to higher incomes, mean that agriculture should be squeezed for resources [Timmer (1988)]?

---

[1] The reverse question, how economic development affects agriculture, should be treated simultaneously, and is the main focus of "The agricultural transformation" in *The Handbook of Development Economics* [Timmer (1988)].

Second, in a market-oriented development strategy, how will appropriate technology for raising the productivity of each country's agriculture be developed? Historically, a very substantial share of agricultural research and extension activities has been in the public sector. Even private sector research usually builds on basic agricultural science produced in public universities and research centers. Beyond research, how will the basic infrastructure that supports private sector investment, especially in agricultural marketing, be funded and managed? "Privatization" as a development strategy runs a risk of eliminating the public investments and institutions that are needed to make a private market economy profitable [Rausser (1990)].

Third, the agricultural sector in the poorest countries seems to be crucial to the economic growth process in ways that are often not well reflected in markets and market prices. If so, "getting prices right" as a development strategy is vastly more complicated than using free trade to transmit world commodity prices to domestic producers and consumers. The failure of markets, on their own, to provide price stability and food security, to alleviate poverty and stimulate rapid economic growth, and to protect the environment, gives rise to a search for appropriate government interventions to overcome these broad failures.

A road map is useful as a guide to the ground to be covered. The next section provides the analytical framework for understanding and quantifying agriculture's contribution to the process of economic growth. This framework points to the key areas where positive linkages might exist, and it highlights the empirical difficulties in establishing their quantitative magnitude and direction of impact. The few empirical studies that have tried to cope with these difficulties are reviewed.

Another approach to overcoming these difficulties is through a historical perspective, so the next step is to review the intellectual environment in the early days of development economics, when squeezing agriculture for industrial growth seemed so logical. This stage in thinking about the role of agriculture in economic development is capped by the Johnston–Mellor article, which provides the first systematic integration of agriculture as a sector, requiring its own development strategy, into the overall growth process.

The final section of the analytical half of the chapter then traces the growing emphasis in the 1970s and 1980s on the role of markets, price incentives, and new technology as the foundation of agricultural development. The emphasis on markets and prices began to alleviate the bias against agriculture in development plans but it also required a more careful integration of agricultural strategies with macroeconomic policies. The analytical complexities of this policy integration forced the development of new general equilibrium models capable of reflecting not just macroeconomic relationships but also the capacity of agricultural decision makers to choose new crops, techniques of production, and intensity of cultivation as economic and technological conditions changed. These models have turned out to be extraordinarily complex to build as tools for policy analysis [de Janvry and Sadoulet (1987)].

Attention then turns to policy issues. If agriculture is so important to economic development, priority must be given to "getting agriculture moving", to use Arthur

Mosher's title of a famous book [Mosher (1966)]. How to do that involves a facilitating macroeconomic environment, investments in rural infrastructure, new technology and productive inputs, and financial incentives. Next, the special role of agriculture in poverty alleviation is quantified through new statistical analysis of the Deininger–Squire data set [Deininger and Squire (1996)] on changes in income distribution over time. The results raise crucial questions about the political economy of sustaining rapid growth. Some speculative answers conclude the chapter.

2. Modeling the role of agriculture in economic development

Consider a standard neoclassical production function that incorporates human capital and a vector of variables that determine whether the economy functions at its technological potential:

$$y^* = T^* Z_j^* f(k^*, h^*) = \text{"frontier" per capita income,}$$

where

$T^* = $ technological frontier,

$Z_j^* = $ vector of conditioning variables that determine whether the frontier is reached, e.g., "property rights", "stability", "distortions", and so on, $0 < Z_j^* < 1$,

$k^* = $ "optimal" physical capital per worker,

$h^* = $ "optimal" human capital per worker.

Assume that population growth $=$ labor force growth $= 0$. Then $dy^*/dt = dT^*/dt$, if all $Z_j^* = 1$ (or $dZ_j^* = 0$). For any country i at time t,

$$y_{it} = T_{it} Z_{jit} f(k_{it}, h_{it}).$$

In principle,

$$dy_{it}/dt = g\big[A_i(T^* - T_{it}), B_{ij}(Z_j^* - Z_{jit}), C_i(k^* - k_{it}), D_i(h^* - h_{it}),$$
$$E_i(k^* h^* - k_{it} h_{it})\big],$$

where A_i, B_{ij}, C_i, D_i, and $E_i > 0$ measure convergence rates.
Empirically,

$$y_{it_1} - y_{it_0} = g[y_{it_0}, Z_{jit_0}, Z_{jit_1} - Z_{jit_0}, k_{it_0}, k_{it_1} - k_{it_0}, h_{it_0}, h_{it_1} - h_{it_0}, k_{it_0} h_{it_0},$$
$$k_{it_1} h_{it_1} - k_{it_0} h_{it_0}].$$

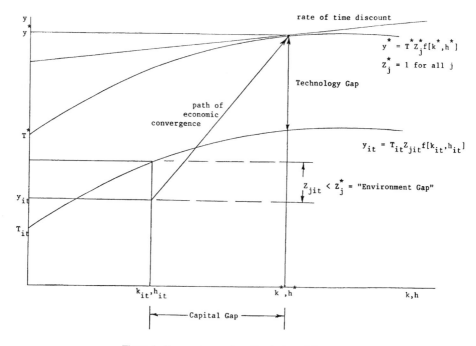

Figure 1. Economic growth as the closing of three gaps.

With panel data, all variables should have estimable coefficients, if suitable instruments are available to correct for endogeneity. With fixed effects models, only coefficients for the "difference" variables are estimable. The approach here can also be shown schematically (see Figure 1).

It is apparent from the figure that economic growth in the non-frontier countries (i.e., "latecomers") is decomposable into the closing of three gaps – a technology gap, a capital gap (both physical and human), and an "environment" gap. Thus if $dT^* = 0$, $dZ^* = 0$ for all j, and $dk^* = dh^* = 0$, then $dy_i = y_{it_1} - y_{it_0} > 0$ requires one or more of the following to hold:

Technology gap	$d(T^* - T_i) < 0$,
Physical capital gap	$d(k^* - k_i) < 0$,
Human capital gap	$d(h^* - h_i) < 0$,
"Environment" gap	$d(Z_j^* - Z_{ji}) < 0$ for at least some Z_{ji}.

This is an alternative representation of neoclassical growth, similar empirically to the model developed by Barro (1997) for estimation with time-series, cross-country data.

The question is, how does agriculture affect economic growth? Formally, if dA_i is growth in the agricultural sector, in what way is dy_i a function of dA_i? First, there is the obvious national income accounting identity:

$$dy_i = S_{A_i} \, dA_i + (1 - S_{A_i}) \, dNA_i,$$

where

S_{A_i} = share of agriculture in GDP, and

dNA_i = growth in the non-agricultural economy.

It is worth noting that where S_{A_i} is large, the direct contribution of agriculture to total economic growth can also be substantial. This obvious but often forgotten fact is also an ingredient in the fast growth of city-states such as Singapore and Hong Kong, which never faced the drag of a large, slow-growing agricultural sector or the need to make large infrastructure investments to modernize that sector.

Assume that any indirect effects of dA_i on dy_i will be exerted through an impact on T, Z, k, or h. For simplicity, assume that $dT^*/dA = dZ_j^*/dA$ (for all j) $= dk^*/dA = dh^*/dA = 0$. That is, agriculture is such a small component of the frontier economy that it has no indirect impact on the rate of technological change, changes in "environmental" variables, or the rate of accumulation in physical or human capital.

For latecomers, however, and especially for countries where S_{A_i} is not trivial, changes in agricultural productivity might plausibly influence the growth process through a set of indirect and roundabout linkages. They can be categorized by each of the variables in the neoclassical production function:

A. Impact on $d(T^* - T_i)$, the rate of shift in the local technological frontier T_i:

dA earns foreign exchange that permits imports of foreign T, where new technology is embodied in physical capital. It should be noted that agricultural exports have a very high ratio of value added, unlike many manufactured exports that rely heavily on imported materials and components. On the other hand, there may be few knowledge spillover effects from exporting traditional agricultural products, thus forgoing one of the main growth stimulants from foreign trade specified in the endogenous growth literature. Earning foreign exchange is one of the Johnston–Mellor linkages.

B. Impact on $d(k^* - k_i)$, the rate of physical capital deepening:

1. Savings from the agricultural sector are a function of dA, and in a semi-closed economy, or one with imperfect capital markets, higher savings translate into faster physical capital deepening [Feldstein and Horioka (1980)]. The sector in which the investment takes place will depend on financial intermediaries (for private savings), or mechanisms of savings extraction (for example, taxation or pricing policy). This is a standard Lewis linkage [Lewis (1954)].

2. Savings may be less productive for growth if in government hands rather than private hands, after minimum government revenues are available to fund affairs

of state. It should be recognized, however, that these public revenues can have very high productivity when invested in public goods and infrastructure that raise the profitability of private sector investment in agriculture [Teranishi (1997)]. If agriculture is more easily taxed than nonagriculture in the early stages of development, perhaps by border taxes on exports, the agricultural sector may well provide revenue for this important, initial stage of public sector investment.

C. Impact on $d(h^* - h_i)$, the rate of human capital deepening:

1. Rural education levels can be influenced by growth in agricultural productivity and rural incomes [Chai (1995), Birdsall, Ross and Sabot (1995)]. Such education can raise farm productivity directly [Jamison and Lau (1982)]. It can also make the migration process much less painful and more economically rewarding for children who leave the farm [Johnson (1997), Larson and Mundlak (1997)].

2. Improved nutritional intake can raise labor productivity through the processes examined in historical England and France by Fogel (1991, 1994). Although in principle staple foods are tradable, in fact there is a very high correlation between increases in food production and increases in food consumption within regions and countries. The "Fogel linkages" can thus be stimulated by growth in agricultural output, especially food output.

D. Impact on $d(Z_j^* - Z_{ji})$, the rate of change in "environmental" variables:

A wide range of variables might cause economies to produce at less than their technically efficient level. Lack of economic freedom, poor institutions, ineffective economic policies, and political instability all have been shown to slow down economic growth, when controls are included for initial conditions and factor accumulation [Barro (1997)]. How changes in agricultural productivity might affect these "efficiency shifters" is a matter of considerable speculation and relatively little empirical evidence. Two mechanisms for which evidence is accumulating involve price stability, because investments are more efficient when signal extraction problems are reduced [Lucas (1973)], and political economy considerations, because restive rural populations can challenge political leaders if they are left behind during the process of rapid economic growth [Anderson and Hayami (1986)].

Other linkages that Johnston and Mellor identified might also work through these Z variables. For example, producing raw materials for industrial processing suggests that capacity utilization in the industrial sector might depend on agricultural productivity. Earning foreign exchange might have the same impact on imported intermediate goods, which are often crucial for producing manufactured exports.

None of these effects is easy to measure empirically because dy_i and dA_i are simultaneously determined by Z_{ji} and by each other. The trick is to find an empirical specification, and the data, that solve this simultaneity problem. There are three promising results so far: Chai's work disaggregating human capital stocks into rural and urban components; Fogel's historical analysis of the impact of gains in nutritional intake on labor productivity and the modern test of the impact by Nadav (1996); and

Dawe's analysis of the impact of commodity price instability on economic growth [Dawe (1996)].

It is, of course, important not to forget the critical direct contribution that agricultural development has made historically to economic growth. As stressed by Lewis (1954) analytically and by Johnson (1997) empirically, lower food prices stimulated by rapid technological change in agriculture have contributed substantially to higher living standards directly, especially for the poor who spend a large share of their budget on basic foodstuffs, and indirectly by keeping real wage costs low in the industrial sector, thus fostering investment and the structural transformation. It is argued, however, that these benefits of low food prices are as easily accessed by trade as by investing in the domestic agricultural sector [Sachs (1997)]. What is the significance of other contributions from agricultural modernization that would be missed with a pure trade strategy?

Surprisingly, in view of the length of time the debate has been going on, there are still no satisfactory tests of the impact of changes in agricultural productivity on the four mechanisms of catch-up growth outlined above. There is evidence generated from a large data-gathering project at the World Bank led by Don Larsen, Will Martin, and Yair Mundlak, that total factor productivity in agriculture tends to grow faster than in manufacturing [Martin and Mitra (1996)]. This result alone argues that past investments in agriculture have had large economic returns [Mundlak (2000)].

3. The rural economy and growth in the macro economy: Specifying the mechanisms

The most satisfactory approach to measuring the nonmarket impact of agriculture on economic growth is to begin by augmenting recently developed theories of economic growth, which are summarized in Barro and Sala-i-Martin (1995). Typical empirical specifications of modern growth models control for initial conditions, factor accumulation, and quality improvements in labor and capital and then proceed to search for control variables that affect the overall efficiency of resource allocation. Openness of the economy, size of government, price distortions, and instability in the macro economy all influence this efficiency, but the potential contribution of agricultural growth to economic efficiency has not been directly tested in the new models.

At the most basic level, a positive relationship between the rate of economic growth and growth in rural economies shows clearly in the historical record. In a sample of 65 developing countries, a highly significant positive relationship existed, from 1960 to 1985, between growth in the agricultural sector and growth in the nonagricultural sector; about 20 percent of the growth rate in agriculture was added to the exogenous growth rate in nonagriculture (see Table 1). This direct and positive association between growth in the two sectors does not, of course, show causation. Sound macroeconomic policy, for example, could have caused both sectors to grow independently, or each sector could have simultaneously caused the other to grow [Timmer (1996a)]. However, rates of

Table 1
Impact of agricultural growth on non-agricultural growth, 1960–1985

Independent variable*	Regression coefficients		
Constant	0.046	0.044	0.038
	(16.1)	(12.3)	(9.8)
Growth in agricultural GDP	0.197	–	0.199
	(3.8)		(3.3)
Growth in agricultural GDP, lagged one five-year period	–	0.136	0.162
		(2.1)	(2.6)
Number of observations	307	244	244
Adjusted R^2	0.041	0.014	0.053

*The dependent variable is the rate of growth in GDP in the nonagricultural sector.
Note: t-statistics are shown in parentheses. When separate intercept terms are included for each five-year time period and for regional dummy variables for Latin America, Africa, and East Asia, the coefficient for *current* growth in agricultural GDP remains significant, whereas the coefficient for *lagged* growth in agricultural GDP remains positive but becomes insignificant.
Source: Calculated from data for seventy countries and five 5-year time periods from 1960 to 1985, in Chai (1995).

agricultural growth in the previous five years were a separate, significant additional factor influencing the dependent variable, growth in the nonagricultural economy, and such a lag suggests a more causal relationship because of the predetermined nature of the lagged variable.

The linkages that help produce this causal relationship are indirect and hard to measure because the direct market-mediated linkages through Lewis and Johnston–Mellor mechanisms are automatically included at their market values in traditional growth accounting. However, at least three of these nonmarket linkages have been identified with enough analytical clarity that empirical tests can be specified and estimated. These are an "urban bias" linkage with an impact that depends on political undervaluation of, and hence underinvestment in, the economic contribution of the rural economy; a "nutritional" linkage that depends on a poverty trap caused by low labor productivity due to inadequate nutrient intake; and a "stability" linkage that connects unstable food prices and food insecurity with a consequent reduction in the quality and quantity of investment. Each of these mechanisms links performance in the agricultural sector to overall economic growth, after accounting for the market contributions of the higher agricultural output through the Lewis and Johnston–Mellor linkages.

Again, it should be emphasized that these are "second-order" effects on the growth process, as lower food prices, labor migration, and capital flows from agriculture account for the main contributions. However, with an economy truly open to goods and capital, there is no theoretical reason why these "first-order" contributions cannot be obtained from world markets. Hence the desire to test empirically the contribution of agriculture to economic growth within the context of an open-economy, general equilibrium model.

3.1. Urban bias and economic growth

Only in East and Southeast Asia did agriculture have a high priority in national plans because of its importance in feeding people and providing a spur to industrialization. In much of Africa and Latin America, a historically prolonged and deep urban bias almost certainly led to a distorted pattern of investment [Lipton (1977, 1993)]. Too much public and private capital has been invested in urban areas and too little in rural areas. Too much capital has been held as liquid and nonproductive investments that rural households use to manage risk. Too little capital has been invested in raising rural productivity.

This historical record suggests that such distortions have resulted in strikingly different marginal productivities of capital in urban and rural areas. A new growth strategy, such as those pursued in Indonesia after 1966, China after 1978, and Vietnam after 1989, which alters investment priorities in favor of rural growth, should be able to benefit from this disequilibrium in rates of return, at least initially. Such a switch in investment strategy and improved rates of return on capital would increase factor productivity because of improved efficiency in resource allocation [Schultz (1978)]. The mechanisms involved include the relatively greater efficiency with which rural households allocate the resources at their disposal and the low opportunity cost of much household labor.

The basic approach to measuring the contribution to growth of a strategy that balances marginal productivity in urban and rural areas is to create a variable that captures the important dimensions of urban bias and then to use regression analysis to measure the impact of this variable in a standard Barro-style growth model. The variable chosen here, the per capita stock of education in rural and urban areas separately, is relevant for two reasons. First, education levels are a common proxy for human capital in modern growth empirics (enrollment rates are even more common), and separating urban stocks from rural stocks should be revealing about the mechanisms by which education influences the growth process.

Second, the ratio of the two stocks, that is, average education levels in rural areas compared with urban areas, is arguably a proxy for the broader influence of urban bias. Rural education levels will depend on both supply and demand factors and urban bias will affect each in reinforcing ways. Thus restricting rural investments means building fewer schools, reducing the supply of educational facilities in rural areas. Biasing the terms of trade against agriculture through a variety of direct and indirect policies reduces rural incomes, thus reducing the demand for rural education, which further reduces rural incomes relative to urban incomes, starting a vicious circle that runs in the opposite direction from the "virtuous circle" identified by Birdsall, Ross and Sabot (1995). The net outcome, the average rural stock of education as measured by years of schooling per capita, reflects the joint impact of both sources of urban bias, especially when the comparison is in relation to urban education levels. The ratio of rural education levels to urban education levels should be a very revealing measure of urban bias. If urban bias is an important drag on economic growth, the impact should show up when this variable is entered into a standard growth model.

The difficulty, of course, is disaggregating the level of educational stocks into their rural and urban components. The starting point is the data set developed by Barro and Lee (1994) to measure the impact of educational stocks instead of enrollment ratios, the readily available but badly flawed proxy for human capital that had been used in growth empirics until that time. Through a combination of country statistical records, UNICEF surveys, and creative analytics that enforced consistency across sectors with the Barro–Lee aggregates, Chai (1995) was able to disaggregate educational stocks into their rural and urban components for a sample of 65 developing countries, including 19 from sub-Saharan Africa. The time period is from 1960 to 1985, with each five-year subperiod used as an individual observation. With five subperiods and 65 countries, there are 325 possible observations. Appendices A–D list definitions of variables used, the means and standard deviations of these variables, the countries in the sample, and the value of the rural and urban educational stock for each observation.

The results of testing a number of specifications of the urban bias hypothesis are highly satisfactory. When the dependent variable is the growth rate in real per capita GDP for the total economy, rural human capital is a significant and positive contributor to growth, while the urban human capital variable has a negative and significant coefficient (see Equation (1) in Table 2).[2] All other variables are significant with expected signs, including the level of initial income. The significantly negative coefficient on this variable indicates that per capita incomes of poorer countries grow faster than richer ones, thus leading to convergence of incomes.

Significant convergence is found for all equations reported here, which is slightly surprising because the sample is restricted to developing countries and convergence has sometimes been difficult to confirm for such samples. Investment share has a very significant positive coefficient, whereas both government expenditures as a share of GDP and the black market premium on foreign currency have a significantly negative impact on economic growth. Interestingly, when a dummy variable for regions is included in the regressions, the coefficient on the variable for sub-Saharan Africa is always negative, is the largest in absolute terms, and is the most significant of the regional variables. Economic growth in sub-Saharan Africa is retarded even after controlling for the high degree of urban bias found in the region.

---

[2] The negative coefficient on urban human capital occurs whenever rural human capital is in the regression. Dropping rural human capital allows the coefficient on urban human capital to become positive, but it is never as significant as when rural human capital is included alone. The likely cause of this strange result is the importance of urban bias in reducing the rate of economic growth. When rural human capital is in the regression, thus controlling for the most important form of human capital to growth of poor countries, *additional* urban capital reflects additional urban bias, which has a negative effect on growth. Specifying the regression with the ratio of these two variables confirms this result.

Table 2
Determinants of the growth rate of real per capita GDP, 1960–1985

Independent variable*	Regression coefficients			
	Eq. (1)	Eq. (2)	Eq. (3)	Eq. (4)
Constant	0.17338 (0.02413)	0.14396 (0.02066)	0.15119 (0.03121)	0.13930 (0.02777)
LNGDPSH5	−0.02093 (0.00325)	−0.02025 (0.00316)	−0.01727 (0.00403)	−0.01741 (0.00396)
RHUM	0.01071 (0.00316)		0.00508 (0.00325)	
UHUM	−0.00773 (0.00277)		−0.00187 (0.00286)	
RUHUMRAT		0.03520 (0.01241)		0.02861 (0.01186)
INVSH5	0.15017 (0.02452)	0.14469 (0.02464)	0.11185 (0.02415)	0.11128 (0.02385)
GOVSH5	−0.10872 (0.02589)	−0.09640 (0.02582)	−0.06344 (0.02496)	−0.05589 (0.02480)
BMPL	−0.02359 (0.00478)	−0.02413 (0.00480)	−0.02087 (0.00443)	−0.02131 (0.00443)
DUMMIES?	no	no	yes	yes
Number of observations	294	294	294	294
Adjusted R^2	0.298	0.292	0.426	0.427

*The dependent variable is the rate of growth in real GDP per capita (GRSH5). See Appendix A for variable definitions.
Note: Standard errors are shown in parentheses. When DUMMIES? is "yes", separate intercept terms are included for each five-year time period and for regional dummy variables for Latin America (19 countries), sub-Saharan Africa (19 countries), and Asia (12 countries). The dummy variables are jointly significant, but individual dummy variables often are not.
Source: Chai (1995).

When dummy variables for each time period and three regions are added, the separate significance of the two human capital variables is lost. The rural human capital variable remains positive and marginally significant; urban human capital remains negative but becomes completely insignificant (see Equation (3) in Table 2). Multicollinearity between these two variables produces these results. One obvious approach to overcoming this problem is to use the ratio of the two stocks of human capital as a single variable. The results of doing so are shown in Equations (2) and (4) in Table 2.

In both specifications, the ratio of rural to urban human capital, as proxied by the per capita stock of education, performs extremely well. Even with the full set of dummies included, this ratio has a highly significant and positive coefficient. Countries grow faster when the per capita stock of human capital in rural areas does not lag too far behind the per capita stock in urban areas (although the urban stock per capita is always higher than the rural stock per capita – see Appendix D).[3]

Many of the mechanisms suggested by the urban bias literature for its impact on economic growth operate primarily in the rural economy itself. Thus reducing the degree of urban bias should speed up growth in the rural economy, at some cost to growth in the urban economy. Factor productivity should rise for the economy overall as the efficiency of resource allocation is enhanced, but with more resources used in the rural areas and fewer resources in the urban areas, the non-rural economy might be expected to show slower growth for a number of years as urban bias is redressed.

This expectation turns out to be wrong. Including the rural and urban human capital variables in growth equations where the dependent variable is growth in the non-rural economy produces results similar to those when the dependent variable is the growth rate in GDP per capita for the entire economy (see Table 3). The standard errors on all variables are somewhat larger, so statistical significance is often reduced, but the pattern of results is remarkably similar. Macroeconomic distortions caused by a large share of government in the economy and black market premia on foreign currency extract a higher cost on the non-rural economy alone than on the overall economy, and the payoff to investment seems to be smaller. All of these variables remain highly significant.[4]

The pattern of impact of the human capital variables is also the same. Rural human capital is a significant contributor to growth in the non-rural economy; urban human capital is not, or has a slightly negative impact (see Table 3, Equation (5)). When the full set of dummy variables is added, the multicollinearity between the two variables becomes severe enough that neither is significant (see Equation (6)). But dropping urban human capital, as in Equation (7), or using the ratio specification, as in Equation (8), fully restores the positive significance of rural human capital. Again, the ratio speci-

---

[3] The ratio variable has quite different statistical characteristics from the rural and urban human capital variables individually. It increases much more slowly over time and has much smaller variance, compared with the mean, than the variables that measure stocks of human capital in each sector. Accordingly, the ratio variable is likely to proxy for general urban bias rather than the contribution of human capital to the growth process.

[4] The relatively larger impact of distortions on the non-rural economy alone than on the overall economy, which includes agriculture, is somewhat puzzling. In most circumstances, the rural economy produces a higher share of tradable goods than does the non-rural economy, and thus exchange rate distortions would be expected to have a larger impact there than on the more protected non-rural economy. One possible explanation is that the rural economy may be somewhat less vulnerable to the direct effects of rent seeking on economic growth that are discussed below. These effects seem to be very large, as the collapse of economies under the weight of "crony capitalism" in the late 1990s would suggest.

Table 3
Determinants of the growth rate of real per capita GDP in the non-rural sector, 1960–1985

Independent variable*	Regression coefficients			
	Eq. (5)	Eq. (6)	Eq. (7)	Eq. (8)
Constant	0.23849	0.22749	0.23024	0.21410
	(0.03171)	(0.04215)	(0.03861)	(0.03788)
LNGDPSH5	−0.02827	−0.02556	−0.02588	−0.02547
	(−0.00430)	(0.00543)	(0.00507)	(0.00532)
RHUM	0.01064	0.00421	0.00486	
	(0.00422)	(0.00429)	(0.00171)	
UHUM	−0.00606	0.00062		
	(0.00367)	(0.00376)		
RUHUMRAT				0.03432
				(0.01616)
INVSH5	0.13360	0.08700	0.08766	0.09600
	(0.03256)	(0.03229)	(0.03198)	(0.03188)
GOVSH5	−0.13584	−0.08890	−0.08941	−0.08095
	(0.03390)	(0.03291)	(0.03271)	(0.03299)
BMPL	−0.03504	−0.03078	−0.03075	−0.03112
	(0.00666)	(0.00620)	(0.00619)	(0.00623)
DUMMIES?	no	yes	yes	yes
Number of observations	280	280	280	280
Adjusted R^2	0.273	0.393	0.395	0.387

*The dependent variable is the rate of growth in real GDP per capita in the non-rural sector (GRNAGSH5). See Appendix A for variable definitions.
Note: Standard errors are shown in parentheses. When DUMMIES? is "yes", separate intercept terms are included for each five-year time period and for regional dummy variables for Latin America (19 countries), sub-Saharan Africa (19 countries), and Asia (12 countries). The dummy variables are jointly significant, but individual dummy variables often are not.
Source: Chai (1995).

fication is likely to be capturing rather different forces in the growth process than the human capital stock variables.

The significance of the rural human capital variable is puzzling in view of the potential mechanisms already identified by which urban bias might affect the rate of economic growth. These mechanisms worked almost entirely through the rural economy itself, with little impact expected outside of agriculture. Some other mechanisms must be at work for such a strong link to exist between the level of rural human capital, or the ratio of rural to urban human capital, and the rate of growth of non-rural GDP per capita.

One plausible link is identified in the political economy literature, where urban bias is caused by extensive rent seeking on the part of powerful urban-based coalitions, such as government workers, students, industrialists, or the military [Bates (1981)]. Such rent seeking not only distorts the relative balance between urban and rural areas, it also has the potential to distort investments in the urban economy itself, thus lowering the rate of growth there as well as in the rural economy.

These potential distortions from urban-based rent seeking are in addition to the losses caused by large government spending and macroeconomic policies that create sizable black market premia for foreign currency (because these factors are also included in the regressions in Tables 2 and 3). Thus, urban bias seems to be a separate factor distorting the allocation of resources, reducing their efficiency in both the rural and urban sectors. By reducing the degree of urban bias, a government may well be able to increase the rate of growth in both sectors. That, at least, is what the empirical record from 1960 to 1985 suggests.[5]

3.2. *Agricultural productivity and nutritional status of workers*

In a long-run, dynamic context, rapid economic growth that differentially benefits the poor is the key to sustainable poverty alleviation. One reason is the important link between agricultural productivity and the nutritional status of workers. Fogel (1991), in his work on the factors causing the end of hunger and reductions in mortality in Western Europe, provides strong evidence for the importance of increasing caloric intake in reducing mortality and increasing productivity of the working poor. Using a robust biomedical relationship that links height, body mass, and mortality rates, Fogel calculates that increases in food intake among the British population since the late eighteenth century contributed substantially to increased productivity and income per capita. "Thus, in combination, bringing the ultrapoor into the labor force and raising the energy available for work by those in the labor force explains about 30 percent of the British growth in per capita incomes over the past two centuries" (p. 63).

Fogel's analyses are not concerned about the sources of food that supplied the increased caloric intake needed to raise labor productivity. But for both economic historians and development economists seeking to explain differential growth experiences in terms of potentially exogenous policy choices, where the food came from is crucial. Indeed, the debate over the impact of the Corn Laws focused on precisely this issue. Empirically, the answer is clear for Britain.

In Britain, during the early stages of the process analyzed by Fogel, until the end of the third quarter of the nineteenth century, nearly all of the food that permitted

---

[5] These results are highly complementary to those reported by Schiff and Valdés (1992) from their extensive analysis of 18 case studies that investigated the impact of macroeconomic policy and commodity pricing distortions on the agricultural sector. The results presented here, however, are stronger in the sense that they draw on a much larger sample of countries and they use a broader measure of urban bias to capture its impact on both the rural and non-rural economies.

the increases in nutrient intake was produced domestically, a result of the agricultural revolution in the late eighteenth and early nineteenth centuries [Chambers and Mingay (1966), Timmer (1969)]. This agricultural revolution was not a simple response of private farmers to market signals. It was heavily stimulated by the protection offered by the Corn Laws, which both raised average prices for cereals and stabilized them with respect to prices in world markets. Much investment in rural infrastructure and technology was also stimulated by these incentives. Grain production, the source of most of the calories of the poor, was significantly enhanced by the Corn Laws, but at the same time bread prices were kept high, contributing to a skewed distribution of income [Williamson (1985, 1990)]. In Fogel's judgment, only the Poor Laws, funded to a large extent from taxes on land rents that were enlarged by the Corn Laws themselves, prevented a French-style revolution [Fogel (1991, p. 47)]. By extension, the argument is that the Corn Laws caused the agricultural revolution instead, and they contributed in important ways to the Industrial Revolution.

3.2.1. The impact of the Corn Laws on the Industrial Revolution

Ricardo was wrong about the Corn Laws, at least when he entered the debate with Malthus in 1815. By the time the Corn Laws were repealed in 1846, however, they had probably outlived their paradoxical (and unplanned) role as an optimal tariff that raised profits of manufacturers by turning the terms of trade against cotton exporters and importers of British manufactured goods [McCloskey (1980), Irwin (1988), Williamson (1990)]. Although startling and still somewhat controversial, this revisionist interpretation of the Corn Laws has its foundation firmly in neoclassical trade theory.

A second role of the Corn Laws, however, is less well appreciated. The much-praised English agricultural revolution had nearly all of its roots enriched by significant price protection for cereals and stabilized by the Duke of Wellington's "sliding scale". With higher and more stable prices than those faced by farmers in France, Holland, or Germany, grain producers in England (and their local governments) invested heavily in new agricultural technology and rural infrastructure [Chambers and Mingay (1966), Timmer (1969)].

Nearly all of the increases in average caloric intake per capita that Fogel sees driving up workers' heights and weights, and hence their potential for productive work, stemmed from food grown on English farms. France, with a "provisioning" policy designed to keep food prices low, was unable to increase agricultural productivity [Bates (1988)]. Imports were not sufficient to provide increases in caloric intake per capita, especially in rural areas where three-quarters of the labor force lived and worked; hence, labor productivity in France lagged behind England by several decades [Fogel (1991), O'Brien and Keyder (1978)].

The Corn Laws were linked to the Industrial Revolution and history's first sustained process of intensive economic growth by several mechanisms (see Figure 2). The Fogel linkages that connect increased caloric intake, made possible by greater food availability, to higher labor productivity and faster economic growth are only one of several

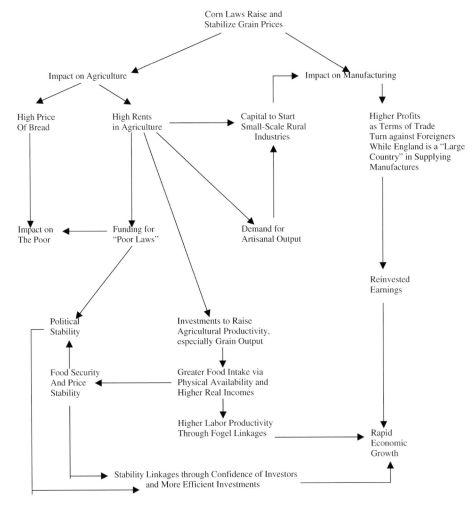

Figure 2. The Corn Laws and the Industrial Revolution.

routes by which greater incentives for agricultural production might be translated into faster economic growth. For developing countries, one other mechanism seems important: the confidence of investors and the improved efficiency of their investments as signal extraction problems are reduced. This might be called the "stability linkage". In the food-oriented context discussed here, investor confidence and efficiency will be a function of political stability and food security (see Figure 2). These linkages help explain the surprisingly important role that agricultural productivity played historically in the economic development of the countries that make up the "East Asian economic miracle" [World Bank (1993)], even accounting for the nutritional effect of greater food supplies.

Table 4
Determinants of the growth rate of real GDP per worker between 1960 and 1985

Independent variable*	Regression coefficients			
	Eq. (9)	Eq. (10)	Eq. (11)	Eq. (12)
Constant	1.674 (0.768)	2.766 (0.697)	−2.453 (1.708)	−1.545 (1.623)
ln(Rgdp 1960)	−0.137 (0.048)	−0.282 (0.048)	−0.448 (0.065)	−0.447 (0.059)
ln(I/Y)	0.615 (0.094)	0.496 (0.099)	0.387 (0.103)	0.413 (0.093)
ln($n + d + g$)	−0.360 (0.235)	−0.5S6 (0.210)	−0.077 (0.276)	0.290 (0.266)
ln(school)		0.227 (0.059)	0.205 (0.061)	0.037 (0.072)
ln(nutrition)			0.960 (0.303)	0.933 (0.270)
LATAM				−0.237 (0.074)
SAFRIC				−0.501 (0.100)
N obs	97	97	97	97
Adjusted R^2	0.371	0.455	0.507	0.628

*The dependent variable is the log difference in real GDP per worker between 1960 and 1985.
Note: Heteroscedasticity consistent standard errors in parentheses. Population growth rates and investment are averages for the period 1960–85. School is the average percentage of the working-age population in secondary school for the same period. Nutrition is the average of calories adjusted for quality for the period 1961–81. Source: Nadav (1996).

Efforts to quantify the impact of nutritional intake on labor productivity within the framework of modern theories of economic growth have just begun. Using the extended Solow model developed by Mankiw, Romer and Weil (1992) to test the importance of human capital in a neoclassical framework, Nadav (1996) included "nutritional" capital as well as more traditional human capital (as proxied by school enrollment rates). With a sample of 97 countries, including 34 "poor" countries and 34 "intermediate" countries, Nadav found that nutrition *levels* had a large and highly significant impact on economic *growth*, even when dummy variables for Latin America and sub-Saharan Africa were included (see Table 4). Indeed, nutrition remained significant in explaining economic growth at the same time that variables measuring schooling rates and growth in the labor force became insignificant. Nadav interpreted this evidence, and the results from splitting the sample into three nutrition "clubs", as evidence that a low productivity trap exists that is at least partially caused by inadequate nutritional intake.[6]

Much more research needs to be carried out to identify the mechanisms that cause these low productivity traps and to determine how efforts to raise agricultural productivity might help poor countries to break out of such traps [Dasgupta (1993)]. In particular, understanding why a strong connection exists between domestic food production and domestic food consumption, especially by the poor, would help policy-makers design appropriate investments and price interventions to stimulate this linkage [Timmer (1996c)]. Much of the answer probably lies in the difficulty and expense of marketing staple food *imports* in rural areas, far from ports and efficient transportation links. With most poverty in poor countries located in these rural areas, a strategy of economic growth built on manufactured exports, with foreign exchange earnings used to pay for food imports, will have little impact on this poverty trap.

4. Food security, food price stability, and economic growth

An important reason for investing in a country's agricultural sector is the potential to stabilize the domestic food economy and thus enhance food security. This potential is greater in large countries that affect world prices when they import, in rice-based economies because the world rice market is very thin and unstable, and for cropping systems in which reliance on irrigation makes domestic production less variable than prices in the world market. Food imports may well provide a more reliable base for food security than domestic food production in small countries, in wheat- and corn-based food systems, and in rain-fed agriculture. There are many circumstances, however, in which imports of food may not offer greater stability.

For both microeconomic and macroeconomic reasons, no country has ever sustained the process of rapid economic growth without first solving the problem of food security. At the microeconomic level, inadequate and irregular access to food limits labor productivity and reduces investment in human capital [Bliss and Stern (1978), Strauss (1986), Fogel (1994), Williamson (1993)]. At the macroeconomic level, periodic food crises undermine political and economic stability, reducing both the level and efficiency of investment [Alesina and Perotti (1993), Barro and Sala-i-Martin (1995), Dawe (1996), Timmer (1989, 1996b)]. The political importance of food security has not been entirely lost on government leaders [Kaplan (1984), Timmer (1993), Islam and Thomas (1996)]. But its connection to economic growth raises the potential of linking the political economy of food security to macroeconomic efficiency.

---

[6] As with the results produced by Chai on the impact of urban bias, Nadav's regressions show a significantly retarded rate of economic growth for sub-Saharan African countries, in relation to other regions, when a dummy variable is included for this effect. Concerns that the positive coefficients for nutrition are the result of reverse causation should be alleviated by the fact that the nutrition variable is specified as a level whereas the dependent variable is the rate of growth in per worker GDP.

4.1. The macroeconomic impact of stabilizing food prices

An important class of benefits from stabilizing food prices is macroeconomic in nature. Price stabilization affects investment and growth throughout the entire economy, not just in the food sector. These effects can be large when food is a large share of the economy and when world grain markets are unstable.

Unstable food prices can increase or decrease the level of savings and investment in an economy. The rationale for a decrease is intuitively clear – greater uncertainty drives investors to brighter horizons. The rationale for an increase in the rate of savings and investment draws on the need for precautionary savings in an economy with imperfect capital markets [Deaton (1992)]. Consumers need to save to protect themselves against the effects of a possible increase in food prices, whereas farmers save to insure themselves against a sudden drop in the crop price. These precautionary savings will be kept in liquid form to be called upon in the event of a sudden change in food prices, and might not contribute much to economic growth in the absence of efficient financial intermediation.

Also, the quantity of investment is not the only determinant of growth. The efficiency, or quality, of that investment is equally important. Food price instability can affect the quality of investment in at least two distinct ways. When food prices increase (because of a poor harvest or an increase in world prices), consumer expenditures on food also increase, because demand is price inelastic – that is, the percentage increase in price is greater than the percentage decline in the quantity consumed. The increase in expenditures on food causes expenditures for other commodities to fall, which lowers demand for all other commodities in the economy. The opposite situation occurs in the event of a good harvest, when consumer expenditures on food decrease. This reduction causes demand for other commodities to increase temporarily, putting upward pressure on prices in other sectors. Over time, if food is important in macroeconomic terms, instability in food prices causes instability in all other prices in the economy.

These "spillover" effects from the food economy into other sectors have two separate consequences. First, risk is increased in all sectors, because non-food prices fluctuate more than if food prices were stable. Second, the price changes that occur throughout the economy contain relatively little information about long-run investment opportunities – a classic example of a "signal extraction" problem [Lucas (1973)].

The fundamental role of prices in a market economy is to serve as signals for allocating both consumption and investment resources. If demand curves shift because of sustained growth in incomes or a change in consumer preferences, or supply curves shift because of changes in technology used in the production process, then relative prices should change accordingly. These price changes convey information to investors about fundamental shifts in expected returns on investment opportunities, shifts that should lead to a reallocation of investment. If prices are changing frequently in various sectors throughout the economy because of temporary and unexpected fluctuations in the domestic grain harvest or in the world price of food, however, prices convey less information about attractive opportunities for long-run investment than if food prices were stable. Rapid and variable rates of inflation cause serious signal extraction problems and hence slow down the rate of economic growth. When food is a significant share of the economy, highly variable food prices can cause similar problems.

The quality of investment might decline for another reason. If spillovers from the food and agricultural sector increase risk throughout the economy, investment is biased toward more speculative activities and away from fundamentally productive activities, such as investment in machinery and equipment, or away from investments in the long-term development of human capital. Both types of investment are closely associated with higher rates of economic growth [DeLong and Summers (1991)].

Consequently, instability in the food sector can have three important macro-level effects. It can affect the quantity of investment through an increase in precautionary savings or a decrease caused by greater uncertainty. It can *decrease* the quality of investment (rate of return) because prices contain less information that is relevant for long-run investment. Finally, because of spillovers creating additional risk throughout the economy, instability can induce a *bias* toward speculative rather than productive investment activities and thereby slow down economic growth.

4.2. Empirical evidence relating price instability and economic growth

Historical data offer empirical evidence about these effects. Dawe (1993, 1996) analyzes these data with respect to instability of export earnings as a share of GDP from 1970–1985 for a cross-section of eighty-five countries. The results support the theoretical arguments presented above. Higher export instability (mostly caused by variations in export prices) is associated with *increased* investment, presumably driven by precautionary savings. After controlling for the *quantity* of investment, export instability *decreases* the efficiency of investment. Both effects are statistically significant and robust to changes in the specification of the regressions [in the Levine and Renelt (1992) sense of robustness in growth equations]. The net sum of these two effects is *negative* – that is, on balance, instability in export prices, when exports are measured as a share of the total economy, leads to a *slower* rate of growth.

It is interesting, if somewhat controversial, to apply the parameters estimated in these regressions to rice in Indonesia, a country that had – until 1997 – an excellent record of stabilizing rice prices through the interventions of its national food logistics agency (BULOG). The logic for such an application is as follows: when the rice economy as a share of GDP is unstable because of unstable prices, the relative impact on the macro economy will be similar to the shocks to the economy from unstable export prices, for the same share of exports in GDP. In fact, the impact of unstable rice prices should be greater than a similar instability in export prices because rice prices also have a large weight in the consumer price index. Instability in inflation has an independent and negative impact on the rate of economic growth. Thus using only the net coefficient (after allowing for the larger investment induced by price instability) for impact of export price instability on growth should yield a lower bound on the impact of unstable rice prices on growth.

Using this net coefficient, one can generate rough measures of the quantitative impact of BULOG's rice price stabilization activities on the historical rate of economic growth in Indonesia. The results reveal two important facts: BULOG made large contributions to the growth process from 1969 to 1995 by stabilizing rice prices; and BULOG's role in the growth process declined in importance over time.

The contribution of BULOG's rice price stabilization activities in the early years of President Suharto's New Order regime was very large. During the first Five-Year Plan (Repelita I), from 1969 to 1974, the rice price stabilization program alone generated nearly one percentage point of economic growth each year, which was more than one-sixth of the total increase in output during that period. In the second Five-Year Plan, from 1974 to 1979, the contribution was 0.61 percent per year, or 13.5 percent of the total growth in per capita income. In absolute terms, rice price stabilization contributed more than $300 million (in 1991 U.S. dollars) per year to increased output in the first Five-Year Plan and more than $270 million in the second [Timmer (1996b)]. As noted above, these estimates are lower bounds because they do not include the direct contribution of rice price stabilization to reduced variance in the rate of inflation. Perhaps of equal importance, they also do not credit the rice price stabilization program with any benefits from enhanced political stability and the greater confidence felt by investors because of such stability.

The second important fact, however, is that the benefits from stabilizing rice prices fell markedly over time. By the middle of the fifth Five-Year Plan, in 1991, stabilization activities contributed only 0.19 percentage points a year to economic growth, just 3.8 percent of the total increase in per capita income during that period. Because the Indonesian economy was much larger, the absolute contribution to increased output did not fall nearly so fast, and this contribution still averaged more than $180 million per year between 1989 and 1991.

The decline in benefits from stabilizing rice prices occurred mostly because the share of rice in the economy fell sharply over time, and this decline reduced the importance of spillovers from rice into other sectors of the economy. In other words, the impact of rice price stabilization on investment and economic growth declines as per capita income increases. Still, when instability in both the domestic and world rice economies is as great as in the mid-1990s, unstable rice prices are capable of slowing the rate of economic growth significantly.

Between 1969 and 1995, BULOG's stabilization of rice prices contributed on average approximately 0.5 percent per year to Indonesia's economic growth, leaving total GDP more than 11 percent higher at the end of the period than it would have been without the stabilization program. Of course, this contribution is now built into the Indonesian economy, and those historic benefits continue to be reaped by the current population. But the contribution each year is clearly on a declining trend.

In summary, this section has tried to address empirically the impact of greater food supplies on economic growth. Three roles were considered. First, if the additional food production is stimulated by policies that redress urban bias, the greater efficiency of resource allocation stimulates economic growth. Second, additional food supplies can have a direct effect on nutrient intake and thus impact labor productivity through the "nutritional" linkages. Third, if additional domestic food production helps stabilize food prices and leads to greater food security, it will have an impact through the quantity and efficiency of investment because of the "stability" linkages.

Each of these contributions is discussed somewhere in the early literature on the role of agriculture in economic development. But no systematic model was ever developed of the mechanisms by which growth in agricultural productivity could speed up this process, apart from its direct contributions that might equally be gained from an open economy and trade. A review of this literature indicates why such a model has been difficult to develop and verify.

5. The early debate on the role of agriculture – origins of discrimination

The debate over the role of agriculture in the process of economic development has both economic and political roots of considerable depth.[7] As the Physiocrats in eighteenth century France were arguing that agriculture was the sole productive activity in a society, Jefferson was arguing that the yeoman farmer was the sole foundation for an American democracy. The development of analytical economics through the nineteenth century eroded this place of honor in economic accounting just as industrialization and urbanization shifted the center of gravity of politics (although not nearly as rapidly as people themselves shifted).

By the middle of the twentieth century, the analysis of agriculture's role was largely in the hands of institutionalists and historians. It was these analysts, especially Clark (1940) and Kuznets (1966), who provided the general facts about the role of agriculture during the growth process that were available to economists and planners at the beginning of the drive for economic growth in the less-developed countries. These facts formed the basis for the prevailing neoclassical view that agriculture was a declining sector, a "black box" in Little's phrase (1982), which contributed labor, food, and perhaps capital to the essential modernization efforts in industry. No policy efforts on behalf of agriculture's own modernization were needed because the sector declined naturally.

Most interpretations of Lewis' (1954) model of "Economic development with unlimited supplies of labor", especially the Fei and Ranis versions (1964), which became the main teaching paradigms, ignored the factors needed to modernize traditional agricultural sectors so that they could play positive contributory roles in the development of the rest of the economy. The structuralist views of Prebisch (1950) about declining terms of trade for traditional products and the importance Hirschman (1958) attached to linkages to "modern" economic activities further diminished any apparent rationale for actively investing in the modernization of agriculture itself. As Hirschman wrote in 1958, "agriculture certainly stands convicted on the count of its lack of direct stimulus to the setting

---

[7] The summary of this debate presented here builds on an earlier version in Timmer (1988).

up of new activities through linkage effects – the superiority of manufacturing in this respect is crushing" [Hirschman (1958, pp. 109–110)].

It is easy to see why the agricultural sector itself was neglected as a source of growth in early strategies of economic development. The historical record shows that it always declines in relative importance in growing economies. It is the home of traditional people, ways, and living standards – the antithesis of what nation builders in developing countries in the 1950s and 1960s envisioned for their societies. Moreover, agriculture was thought to provide the only source of productivity that could be tapped quickly to fuel the drive for modernization, implicitly a drive that took place in cities and factories. Surplus labor, surplus savings, and surplus expenditures to buy the products of urban industry, and even surplus foreign exchange to buy the machines to make them, could be had from an uncomplaining agricultural sector. Nothing more was needed to generate these resources than the promise of jobs in the cities and a shared nationalistic pride in the growing power of the state.

Despite how simplistic these promises sound after the collapse of centrally planned economies in Eastern Europe and the Soviet Union, the success of the Soviet approach from the 1930s to the 1950s caused the rhetoric to be very appealing when first uttered by such charismatic leaders of the developing world as Sukarno, Nkrumah, Nasser, and Nehru. The unique features of agriculture as a sector were simply not widely understood in the 1950s, and continued investment in the sector would seem to endorse the policies of colonial exploitation, which usually focused on the agricultural sector.

The mindset of national leaders, especially those newly in power at the head of revolutionary movements against colonial occupation, clearly reflected this bias against agriculture. Moreover, this mindset was reinforced by the basic model of economic development taught in the 1950s and 1960s by academics and used by policymakers. This model can be shown in a simple schematic diagram (see Figure 3). The driving force of development is the flow of savings, allocated to their "best" uses by a national plan, into the modern factories built to produce the higher physical output that counted as "development". High profits from these factories were one important source of increased savings, and it was easier to redirect these savings directly into industrial investments if the factories were owned by the state.

The other important source of savings in the hands of the state (the only savings that were "productive") was the agricultural sector. Agricultural savings arose from direct taxes on exports, low agricultural prices, high prices for manufactured goods sold in the rural areas, and an overvalued domestic currency. In combination, these policies toward the agricultural sector kept wages low and imported inputs cheap for manufacturers, thus guaranteeing high profits from the industrial sector. The structural transformation meant that increased profits from a rising share for industrial output would replace the important role of agricultural savings in the early stage of industrialization. Reducing the extraction of resources from agriculture was not desirable at this early stage because it would slow the expansion of industry. Later, agriculture was no longer important, and there was no point in developing it. In this simple but influential model, the discrimination against the agricultural sector is revealed not as an urban bias but as

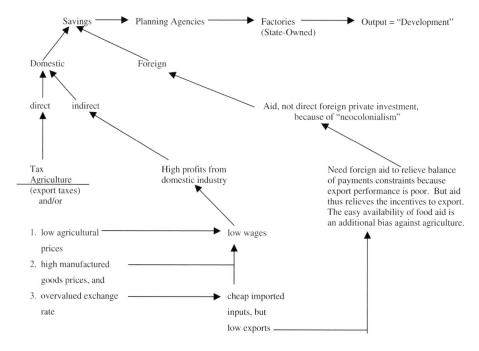

Figure 3. The "traditional" development paradigm. Note that there are direct trade-offs between agriculture and industry throughout the model. This is the source of the deep-seated bias that helping agriculture will slow down the pace of industrialization, equated with development.

the core of the development process itself. Any efforts to help the agricultural sector would inevitably slow down the rate of economic growth, a point that was reinforced by the empirical observations of Hirschman and Prebisch.

This mindset was widespread among national leaders in developing countries. Historical studies of England and Japan that showed the importance of an agricultural revolution to their modern economic growth were deemed irrelevant to countries in a hurry to industrialize. Better to follow the Soviet model that explicitly followed the path of extracting resources from agriculture. The rise of Soviet industrial and military power to challenge the West – the "first" world – had a powerful validating influence on national leaders and their economic policymakers in the Third World. Unfortunately, the strategy of central planning and discrimination against agriculture ruined the economies of the poorest developing countries a decade or more before its ultimate unsustainability was demonstrated in the Soviet Union itself.

As early as the 1960s a more positive attitude about the agricultural sector was beginning to emerge. First, emphasis was placed on "role" rather than the more forced concept of "contribution" of agriculture. The classic article by Johnston and Mellor (1961) listed five roles for agriculture in economic development:

- increase the supply of food for domestic consumption;
- release labor for industrial employment;
- enlarge the size of the market for industrial output;
- increase the supply of domestic savings; and
- earn foreign exchange.

Although the second, fourth, and fifth roles are certainly consistent with the earlier "extractive" views of agriculture, Johnston and Mellor insisted that all five roles are equally important. Agriculture in the process of development is to provide increased food supplies and higher rural incomes to enlarge markets for urban output, as well as to provide resources to expand that urban output:

> It is our contention that "balanced growth" is needed in the sense of simultaneous efforts to promote agricultural and industrial development. We recognize that there are severe limitations on the capacity of an underdeveloped country to do everything at once. But it is precisely this consideration which underscores the importance of developing agriculture in such a way as to both minimize its demand on resources most needed for industrial development and maximize its net contribution required for general growth. [Johnston and Mellor (1961, pp. 590–591)]

Second, Nichols (1963), Schultz (1953), and Jorgenson (1961) emphasized the interdependence between a country's agriculture and its industry. Myint (1975) stressed a curious inconsistency between the "closed economy" model implicit in this domestic interdependence and the fifth role, earning foreign exchange, which obviously implies the country is open to international trade. This trade perspective returns in the 1970s and 1980s to dominate thinking about appropriate development strategies, but it was largely ignored in the 1960s, perhaps because of the dominance of the "Indian model" in development thinking, in which sheer size keeps the importance of foreign trade quite small, even apart from the "inward looking" strategy being pursued.

Despite the early insistence by agricultural economists that the agricultural sector must be viewed as part of the overall economy and that the emphasis be placed on the sector's interdependence with the industrial and service sectors rather than on its forced contributions to them, the notion of agriculture as a resource reservoir, available to be tapped by economic planners and refilled by natural forces, has persisted in general development models. Reynolds (1975) emphasized an important but usually overlooked distinction between static and dynamic views of the resource transfers:

> In most development models, modern industry is the cutting edge of economic growth, while agriculture plays the role of a resource reservoir which can be drawn on for supplies of food, labor, and finance to fuel the growth of urban activities. It is argued that this is both a logical necessity and a matter of historical experience, illustrated by the case of Japan.
>
> In commenting on this view, I must emphasize a distinction that is often not clearly drawn: (1) It is one thing to assert that, in an economy where agricultural output is not rising, the agricultural sector contains potential surpluses of labor time, food output, and saving capacity requiring only appropriate public policies for their

release. This we may term the static view of resource transfer. (2) It is quite a different thing to assert that, in an economy where agricultural output is being raised by a combination of investment and technical progress, part of the increment in farm output and income is available for transfer to non-agriculture. This we may term the dynamic view of resource transfer. The model-building implications of this approach are different, and its policy implications are decidedly different. (pp. 14–15)

The welfare consequences of the two views are also sharply different. Forced extraction of resources from a stagnant agricultural sector almost always creates widespread rural poverty, sometimes famine. Market linkages that connect a dynamic agricultural sector to rapidly growing industrial and service sectors offer an opportunity for rural inhabitants to choose in which sector they wish to participate. There are certainly losers in this process: high-cost producers in unfavorable ecological settings who cannot compete with low-cost producers in favored locales who have access to new technology; or newly landless laborers who have lost their tenancy access to land when commercial relationships replace patron–client relationships.

But new technology and market linkages have shown the potential to create more opportunities than they destroy if both the agricultural and nonagricultural sectors are growing together. An emphasis on finding the policy environment that creates such mutual growth is needed. For agriculture, that environment must call forth rapid technical change, a point repeatedly stressed by Schultz (1964). Experience since the mid-1960s has demonstrated how to do that, but the key has been to understand why the agricultural sector is different from the industrial and service sectors [Hayami and Ruttan (1985), Timmer, Falcon and Pearson (1983)].

6. Agricultural decision making and the role of market signals

Research in the 1970s into the links between technical change and the decision-making environment at the farm level led to at least two significant changes in thinking about agriculture and development. First, and no doubt the most important for the long run, agricultural decision makers – farmers and traders – began to be thought of as an integral part of the rest of the economy, connected to it by rational decision making in the face of new technologies or income and price changes. Acceptance of this principle by economic modelers and policymakers led to a fundamental shift in attitudes about how agriculture should be treated in the development process – not as an isolated appendage but as a key component essential to the health of the overall organism.

Second, new importance was given to developing and choosing appropriate technologies, whether in agriculture directly, in processing, or in the industrial sector. If millions of farmers, or thousands of traders and small industrialists, were making rational decisions about investment, the nature of the technology set facing them would be at least as critical as the set of prices in determining the consequences of economic growth for employment and income distribution. In addition, farm-level decision making was obviously conditioned by farm-level constraints and opportunity costs for household resources, especially unskilled labor. Technical packages that were inappropriate in the face of those constraints – especially packages imported largely intact from Western agricultural systems – were not adopted, and agricultural development failed to take place.

Sparked by the world food crisis in 1973–74, but guided by this earlier understanding of the importance of fitting technology to field-level conditions, nearly all the international centers for agricultural research devoted a significant share of their budgets to discovering the nature of farm-level constraints on the adoption of new technology and to developing specific crops as well as entire farming systems that dealt more effectively with these constraints [see International Rice Research Institute (IRRI) (1978), CIMMYT (1984)]. The analysis of farming systems is the microeconomic equivalent of general equilibrium analysis, where agriculture is one of several interacting sectors. Just as commodities and household activities are connected at the farm level by complex biological and economic relationships, so is agriculture heavily influenced by the rest of the economy. In poor countries, the reverse causality is often equally important.

In their summary of research in the 1970s, Eicher and Staatz (1990) make the following observations:

> The results of microeconomic research during the 1970s contributed to an accumulation of knowledge about the behavior of farmers; constraints on the expansion of farm and nonfarm production, income and employment; the linkages between agricultural research and extension institutions; and the complexity and location-specific nature of the agricultural development process. ... But the increased orientation to micro-level research resulted in relatively less attention being paid to macroeconomic research on food policy and the role that agriculture can play in the structural transformation of Third World economies. (p. 20)

These latter themes dominated the research agenda of the 1980s, as growing debt burdens, a slowdown in the world economy, and a collapse of commodity prices at mid-decade forced developing countries to undergo wrenching structural adjustment policies that often directly contradicted the state-controlled development strategies that had been followed for decades. The role of the state in the agricultural sector became the critical question for research during the decade, and the answer turns out to depend on two factors: whether the private sector and free markets can provide adequate growth in the agricultural sector without government intervention; and whether a market-determined agricultural output provides optimal stimulus to the overall process of economic growth.

7. The role of the state – evolution of the debate

In some important sense, modern economic policy analysis was developed to address the issue of state intervention in agriculture. The debate over the Corn Laws in early nineteenth century Britain pitted Ricardo's increasingly sharp and focused micro-economic models against Malthus' vague but realistic concerns for dynamic macro-economic and general-equilibrium effects. A general equilibrium model of the Corn Laws shows that Malthus was probably right, at least for an England in the early stages of the Industrial Revolution [Williamson (1990)].

The foundation of the neoclassical approach to this question is Schultz' volume *The Economic Organization of Agriculture* [Schultz (1953)]. Scholars who are familiar only with Schultz' later writings on rational farmers and the importance of price incentives will be surprised to find a careful analysis of imperfections in factor markets in United States agriculture coupled with a pervasive concern for the powerful negative welfare effects generated by the instability seen in commodity prices and incomes of American farm families. Only the government is capable of dealing with the macroeconomic forces that were the basic cause of this instability, and Schultz provides a carefully analyzed set of interventions that would lessen the social impact of commodity price instability, including income transfers during periods of depressed economic activity. But no satisfactory approach to dealing with instability within agriculture is found:

> The instability of farm prices is an important economic problem. It is, however, exceedingly difficult to organize the economy so that farm prices will be on the one hand both flexible and free and on the other relatively stable. Farm price supports and efforts to control agricultural production by acreage allotments, marketing quotas, and related public measures are not satisfactory. Diversion operations, subsidized exports, and efforts to shelter the domestic market from foreign competition are also unsatisfactory. [Schultz (1953, p. 365)]

Schultz does quote approvingly the work of Johnson on forward pricing for agriculture as an approach to improving the efficiency of resource allocation in the agricultural sector (although Johnson himself later became skeptical of the approach).

Schultz' preference for dealing with fundamental causes rather than symptoms shows up in 1964 in his most influential work, *Transforming Traditional Agriculture*. The low level of farm incomes in developing countries is not because peasants are irrational or lack knowledge of how to farm efficiently with the resources at their disposal, but because of the lack of technology that would generate higher streams of income. The demise in the late 1960s of community-action programs and the emphasis of donors and policymakers on research and development of new agricultural technology can be traced fairly directly to Schultz' influence. The subsequent failure of the Green Revolution to transform the agricultural sectors of poor countries at anything like its advertised potential is explained by Schultz in 1978, in *Distortions of Agricultural Incentives*, as the consequence of government policies that prevent prices in world markets from reaching farmers in developing countries. Pressures from urban consumers, the need for tax revenues, and instability in world markets served to reinforce policymakers' biases against a positive role for agriculture in the development process. In this view of the world, government intervention into agricultural markets is almost always wrongheaded and harmful. Left alone, markets, with all their failures, work better to serve the interests of agriculture and the rest of the economy.

The debate over the role of government in agricultural development has, then, become increasingly focused on the tensions between market failures and government failures. A series of contributions starting in the 1980s clarified the issues analytically. Binswanger and Rosenzweig (1986) attempted to draw on fundamental characteristics of agricultural production processes and household behavior to explain patterns of organization for different crops and the potential for government interventions to improve the efficiency of resource allocations. Several of these characteristics, especially the importance of imperfect and asymmetric information, led Stiglitz to examine the prevalence and efficiency of linked markets in agriculture. In many cases, the underlying market failures that prevented unconstrained Pareto optimal outcomes were not susceptible to improvements by cost-effective government intervention, especially land tenure arrangements and rural credit markets [Stiglitz (1987, 1989)]. On the other hand, the failure of risk markets may offer important opportunities for governments to stimulate rural investments and "learning by doing" by appropriate pricing policies for inputs and outputs. Most important, Stiglitz (1987) emphasizes the empirical nature of the debate:

> Simple prescriptions have one obvious advantage: they enable economists to make policy judgments with virtually no knowledge of the country in question. But the flaws in the simplistic approach make it all the more important to accumulate detailed information on most of the developing world. The first step in any systematic analysis of agriculture policies is therefore to describe as accurately as possible the consequences of each policy. This requires a model of the economy concerned – and a model appropriate for one country may not be for another. Recent work has clarified some of the essential ingredients of these models: wage-setting policies in the urban sector, the nature of rural–urban migration, and the organization of the rural sector – labor, land, and credit markets. ...
> In any analysis of agricultural policies, the hardest part is to incorporate political economy considerations – to decide what are to be taken as political constraints. (p. 54)

Precisely because it is the core of the problem, the political economy of agricultural policy has also attracted the attention of economists and political scientists. Anderson and Hayami (1986), Bates (1981), Binswanger and Deininger (1997), Rausser (1990), Srinivasan (1985), and Varshney (1993) have used political economy models of rent seeking, rational choice, and organizational costs to explain pervasive patterns of government intervention into the agricultural sectors at different levels of development. Two of these patterns, the "development paradox", whereby rich countries protect their relatively few farmers while poor countries discriminate against their many farmers, and the "anti-trade bias", where both imports and exports of agricultural commodities are taxed in rich and poor countries alike, are analyzed in considerable historical detail by Lindert (1991). What is still missing in the literature, however, is much consideration of how actual policy settings shift and evolve and how policy analysts can use sudden shifts in economic or political environments as "windows of opportunity" to pursue more effective policies for the economy, including the agricultural sector.

8. The policy issues

In view of the evidence that agricultural productivity must increase if increases in industrial productivity are to be sustainable, the issue becomes how to do it. The next section argues that "getting agriculture moving" involves coordinated policy initiatives in four areas: the macroeconomic environment, rural infrastructure, new technology, and the level of incentives facing farmers. The final section asks whether the unique role played by the agricultural sector in developing countries includes a differential contribution to poverty alleviation.

8.1. The macroeconomic environment and agriculture

The nature of the macroeconomic environment that will support vigorous agricultural development is a major topic covered by others in this volume. The key elements are well known: a balanced internal and external account, macro-price stability, a competitive exchange rate that favors exports, and a trade regime that is transparent and unbiased. The agriculture minister seldom has much say in these policies, and if history is any guide, is often on the wrong side of the debate. But one of the costs of integrating the agricultural sector into the rest of the economy is its dependence on the macroeconomic environment. It is virtually impossible to "get agriculture moving" unless this environment is highly supportive [Schuh (1976), Timmer, Falcon and Pearson (1983)].

Beyond a supportive macroeconomic environment, it is widely agreed that governments should provide public goods and correct important market failures. The debate is over levels of funding, appropriate institutional organization, and relative roles for public agencies and private firms and households. Since Pigou, this debate has formed an integral core of analytical economics, and the modern field of public economics has evolved to deal directly with these issues. The major topics in agricultural development are government support and organization for research, extension, irrigation, and the rural marketing infrastructure.

8.2. Agricultural technology

8.2.1. Research

The public good aspects of agricultural research have been recognized by governments for centuries, well before economists provided a formal analytical rationale for the widespread public support for improving agricultural technology. Optimal incentives to private firms to invest in the discovery of new technology require that the new income streams generated be appropriable to a significant degree by the firm incurring the costs of research. Although hybrid seeds with secret inbred lines, patented chemical formulae, or specific brand-name farm implements meet this criterion and are consequently activities of the private sector in developed countries, most technology for food grains, livestock, and inputs falls outside this category. The inability of private firms to capture more than a tiny fraction of the increased financial flows made possible by innovations in these commodities means that research activity by them will be quite small unless directly funded (and probably carried out) by the public sector. Biotechnology using patentable genetic manipulations offers far greater opportunities for private sector investment. Little of this investment seems destined to take place in developing countries until well into the twenty-first century.

Scale economies in modern research also militate against optimal levels of research being carried out by the private sector in developing countries. Indeed, agricultural *producers* now conduct only a trivial amount of research on new seeds and techniques in all countries, in contrast to earlier in the century when most productivity-enhancing innovations arose on the farm and were spread by word of mouth. Modern science and technology have nearly eliminated the role of the "farmer improver" championed in the eighteenth century by Arthur Young in Great Britain and in the nineteenth century by Charles Warren in the United States.

Partly because modern science has stimulated a technological revolution in the way agricultural research is done (and the subsequent productivity of the innovations) and partly because public goods often receive inadequate budgetary support, the returns to public-sector investment in agricultural research are typically very high. Research by Griliches (1958), Evenson and Kislev (1975), and others document internal rates of return on such investments at double and more the social opportunity cost of capital. As already noted, the absolute necessity for new technologies to generate higher income streams for traditional farmers was stressed by Schultz (1964) in the volume that provided the analytical foundations for an entirely new approach to agricultural development. Clearly, only in those countries with the capacity to fund and conduct the agricultural research that yields these new technologies can agricultural development take place at a rapid enough pace for the sector to play its broader role in stimulating the entire development process. Building this capacity in both financial and scientific terms deserves very high priority.

8.2.2. Extension

Although "research and extension" are often said in the same breath as though they were one concept, in fact the "extension" part of the story is much more controversial than the research part. To be sure, there are empirical counterparts to the high economic returns from agricultural research (although sometimes the high payoff to extension is a result of lumping research and extension costs together in the analysis), but there are also many documented failures and doubts about the capacity of public sector extension services to deliver anything of value to farmers. Because research results are virtually without value unless adopted by farmers, nearly all public research programs are designed to have outreach components to extend their results to the farm level. The controversy over extension programs arises not because of the need for such components as a public-sector activity – the public good aspect is clear enough – but over program design itself. An intense intellectual discussion is taking place in this field that is impossible to capture in this chapter. See Evenson (2001), this Handbook, for a review of the issues.

8.3. Rural infrastructure

8.3.1. Irrigation investments

The appropriate mix between public and private investments becomes a lively issue in irrigation. Although there is no intrinsic reason why large-scale dams and delivery canals cannot be a private-sector activity, it seems to be beyond the capacity of private firms in developing countries to manage the substantial problems in coordination, design, finance, and execution. Only tube-well irrigation and low-lift pumps from rivers and canals are primarily a private activity in developing countries (and the developed world, for that matter).

With large-scale irrigation schemes almost always a public-sector activity, a number of policy issues arise. At one level, concerns exist over the public health and environmental impact of many irrigation facilities.[8] Diversion of water from natural flows inevitably has some consequences for the environment, including the potential for downstream salinity problems, the creation of breeding grounds for such public-health hazards as schistosomes and malarial mosquitoes, and depletion of underground aquifers that may be important water sources some distance away. These externalities should in principle be included in the evaluation of costs and benefits to the public-sector irrigation project. Indeed, the presence of such important externalities is a major reason why large-scale irrigation projects "should" be a public-sector activity. But the actual track record of incorporating environmental and public health costs into the design and evaluation of irrigation projects is dismal indeed, whether the projects were funded by external donors such as the World Bank or came directly from the country's own budget.

At a similar level of concern, Hayami and Kikuchi (1978) have demonstrated the existence of a powerful "irrigation cycle" of public sector investments. When grain prices are high in world markets, signaling scarcity to both private and governmental buyers, countries increase their budgetary commitments to expanding agricultural output, especially through investments in irrigation facilities to grow rice and wheat. Multilateral and bilateral donors follow the same short-run economic logic in evaluating their investments. The result is a surge in irrigation investments shortly after world markets signal a grain shortage. Of course, grain production from these investments does not

---

[8] For a useful overview of the public health dimensions of agricultural development in Africa, see Ohse (1988).

appear on domestic and international markets for nearly a decade, because of the long lags between identification of a need for an irrigation investment and its construction and operation. As these supplies flow to markets more or less in synchronous fashion, world prices are depressed. The low prices then cause governments and donors to reject further investments in irrigation, thus setting the stage for the next iteration of the cycle. The failure, of course, is the short time horizon for price expectations on the part of governments and donors. Although this behavior is partially understandable on the part of governments that must pay the current market price for imports, the failure of donors to take a longer-term perspective on the impact of commodity prices on their investment decisions is distressing and perplexing.

At a more grass-roots level, several issues exist with respect to water pricing. Simple concerns for allocative efficiency suggest that farmers should pay some type of fee related to the volume of water they use and the economic cost of delivering or replacing it. Bureaucratic efficiency in operation and maintenance of irrigation facilities by public-sector employees suggests that the fees paid by farmers should also be connected to the timeliness of water deliveries and the quality of water services. And a broader concern for the integrity of public-sector budgets suggests that full cost recovery from beneficiaries of public-sector irrigation projects is needed to provide the resources for continued investments.

Virtually none of these private charges is actually paid. Most countries have provided irrigation water free (or at modest fixed charges) to farmers, with both investment costs and operations and maintenance charges paid out of the budget of the central government (or sometimes by state or regional authorities). As a consequence, actual budgets for operations and maintenance are usually seriously inadequate even for an efficient bureaucracy. More important, there are no incentives to perform the operations and maintenance activities in a timely and effective manner, and most irrigation systems need complete rehabilitation well before their economic and technical designs would indicate. Investment costs are then spread much more thinly than is necessary, thus slowing the expansion of agricultural output.

These are precisely the sorts of government failures that have led to calls to privatize a greater proportion of development-related investments, including in the irrigation sector. But it is not easy to see how the private sector can overcome the barriers to its effective involvement either. Two kinds of compromise are possible. One draws on the best features of the two sectors to produce the right volume of irrigation projects, in the right places, and with appropriate concern for externalities, while design, construction, and operation are efficiently managed by the private sector. The other compromise, of course, combines the worst of the two sectors. Then public-sector funding subsidizes private investors to ignore cost-recovery issues, to scrimp on operations and maintenance programs, and to evade any responsibilities for negative externalities. The risk of the second approach is sufficiently large in most countries that efforts to improve public-sector capacity to design, finance, and manage their irrigation programs are probably better investments than trying to find new institutional arrangements that privatize most of these decisions.

8.3.2. Marketing infrastructure

After two decades of declining support for public investment in the rural infrastructure that supports efficient marketing of agricultural commodities, the direct and indirect contributions of this infrastructure to rural growth and reductions in poverty are again being recognized.[9] The decline had been caused to some extent by tighter budgets in most developing countries, but sharp criticisms in the 1970s of the supposed failure of investments in rural infrastructure to reach the "poorest of the poor" also reoriented donor priorities toward meeting basic needs through rural development programs.

The importance of an efficient marketing system in raising the productivity of an impoverished rural population is now recognized, but public-sector investments to provide the physical infrastructure for such a system were badly neglected in the 1970s and early 1980s. The impact of this neglect shows clearly in the empirical record of agricultural exports reported by Valdés (1991), and on changes in labor productivity in the agricultural sector in Asia [Timmer (1991)]. And yet substantial controversy remains over how many public resources should be devoted to rural infrastructure and what share of the needed investments should come from the private sector.

An examination of the key areas of concern reveals the reasons for the controversy. For a rural marketing system to work efficiently, an entire set of interlinked components must be in place and mesh relatively smoothly. These components include farm to market roads, regional highways, railways, trucks, and rolling stock; communications networks involving telephones, radios, and information-gathering capacity; reliable supplies of electricity for lighting, to operate office equipment, and to power rural industries; market centers and wholesale terminals with convenient access to both transport facilities and financial intermediaries; and a set of accepted grades and standards for traded commodities that permit reliable "arms-length" contracts to be written and enforced at low cost.[10]

Each individual component of a well-functioning marketing system has a major role for private-sector involvement, perhaps even to the exclusion of any necessary public role. Certainly trucking companies, warehouse operators, and rural and regional banks can be entirely in the private sector, and, indeed, the empirical record suggests that they should be if reasonable efficiency standards are to be maintained. But a marketing system is more than the sum of these private firms, partly because the *links* that connect these firms – the roads, railways, telephone networks, and so on – have important public good dimensions or problems of coordination that markets alone have a difficult time

---

[9] See research on Bangladesh carried out by the International Food Policy Research Institute (IFPRI) and the Bangladesh Institute of Development Studies reported in Ahmed and Hossain (1990) and Kumar (1988). Results from India are in Binswanger, Khandker and Rosenzweig (1993). The role of marketing infrastructure in agricultural commercialization and diversification is discussed in C.P. Timmer (1997).

[10] Chapter 4 of Timmer, Falcon and Pearson (1983) discusses at greater length these components of an efficient marketing system and analyzes the types of government policies that stimulate its development. Abbott (1993) also provides a broad review of the topic.

solving. A further part of the story, however, involves substantial economies of scale and externalities in the construction and operation of the marketing system itself. No private firm can hope to capture the full economic benefits accruing to an efficient marketing system, even when the firm's own investment is a crucial component needed to make the system work at all.

The existence of these externalities and system-wide scale economies that are not appropriable by individual private firms creates an important role for the public sector in guaranteeing that the basic rural infrastructure is in place and operates efficiently. Clearly, direct public investment, ownership, and operation is neither necessary or even desirable in many contexts, and regulation, indicative plans, and appropriate investment incentives may well be sufficient. But equally clearly, a direct public role may also be needed in many circumstances, especially in the building of roads, railroads, and communications networks. It is precisely these types of capital-intensive investments, however, that came under fire in the 1970s as failing to help the poor. Expanded funding for them, especially in the context of universally tighter public budgets, requires a clear rationale.

Investment in infrastructure has two important economic payoffs. Rural infrastructure, in the form of irrigation and drainage works, roads, ports and waterways, communications, electricity, and market facilities, provides the base on which an efficient rural economy is built. Much of the investment needed to provide this base comes from the public sector, even when the private sector is playing the predominant role in agricultural production and marketing. Without this public investment, rural infrastructure is seriously deficient in stimulating greater production of crops and livestock. Investment by the private sector is also less profitable in the absence of adequate rural infrastructure, thus further reducing rural dynamism. Public-sector investment in rural areas has a "crowding in" effect rather than a "crowding out" effect on private investment, and for this reason the main role of investments in infrastructure is this longer-run stimulation of agricultural production, which has important positive effects on rural employment and income distribution.

A second role needs to be stressed as well. The investments in infrastructure themselves can generate substantial rural employment directly, and this potential has not been lost on planners seeking both long-run employment creation and short-run work programs to alleviate rural poverty or even famine conditions. "Food for Work" and "Employment Guarantee" schemes almost always are designed to build rural infrastructure using low-cost or unemployed workers. Large-scale irrigation and road construction projects offer the potential to employ vast numbers of unskilled rural laborers if project designers are sensitive to employment issues in the choice of technique and are willing to address the managerial problems that arise from labor-intensive techniques in construction.

The progressive commercialization of agriculture – as more productive inputs are purchased and a greater share of output is marketed, made possible by the development of an efficient marketing system – is a major stimulus to agricultural productivity and creates substantial employment in the agriculturally related industries. In modern economies far more workers are engaged in agribusiness than in farming itself. In the less-developed agricultural economies, such nonfarm but agriculturally linked employment is not quite so important. Even so, the single most important sector of the industrial labor force is usually in agricultural processing. Employment in rice or wheat milling, jute mills, cotton spinning and weaving, and cigarette manufacture is often the main source of organized factory jobs. When small-scale traders, food wholesalers, retailers, and peddlers are also included, the volume of indirect employment begins to rival direct employment on farms. Many of the workers are the same, or at least live in the same household. Half of the income for farm households on Java now comes from off-farm labor. Not all of the jobs are in large- or small-scale agribusiness, of course, but most are linked via well-functioning commodity and factor markets to the health of the rural economy (and the strength of the urban construction industry). Such jobs are usually a critical step on the path out of poverty for many rural inhabitants [Mellor (1976, 2000)].

9. Agriculture and poverty alleviation

There is little doubt that rapid economic growth reduces poverty. Even cursory analysis of the Deininger–Squire data set on changes in income distribution over time reveals only a small handful of examples where economic growth on average failed to increase per capita incomes in the bottom twenty or forty percent of the income distribution [Deininger and Squire (1996), Fields (1997), Gallup, Radelet and Warner (1997), Ravallion and Chen (1997), Roemer and Gugerty (1997)]. However, a statistical result that reports a strong linkage between economic growth and poverty alleviation under nearly all circumstances seems somehow to miss the growing numbers of poor, as well as the anecdotal stories about widening income gaps and the poor being left behind, stories with powerful political resonance. It would be useful to know if it is possible to improve the connection between growth and poverty alleviation, especially through the sectoral composition of growth.

Sectoral growth rates clearly have a differential impact on the poor. Ravallion and Datt (1996) can find no impact on the poor from growth in the Indian manufacturing sector, even in urban areas, whereas rural growth reduces poverty in both rural and urban areas. Analysis of the expanded Deininger–Squire data set by Gallup, Radelet and Warner (1997) also hints at the potential for strengthening the linkage from economic growth to poverty alleviation through sectoral priorities. They find that a one percent growth in agricultural GDP per capita leads to a 1.61 percent increase in per capita incomes of the bottom quintile of the population in 35 developing countries. A similar one percent increase in industrial GDP increases the incomes of the poor by 1.16 percent. And the incomes of the bottom quintile increase by only 0.79 percent with a one percent increase in service sector GDP [Gallup, Radelet and Warner (1997)]. Although these differences are not statistically significant because of noise in the data, they do suggest that, on average, the sectoral composition of growth affects the strength of the linkage between economic growth and poverty.

Further, historical experience argues that development strategies and economic policies can significantly strengthen the contribution of the overall growth process to poverty alleviation [Dasgupta (1993), Fogel (1994)]. In some countries, growth strategies permitted an improvement in the distribution of income at the same time that rapid growth was sustained [World Bank (1993)]. In these countries, declines in the levels of absolute poverty were the fastest in history [Timmer (1996d)], although the financial crisis that started in Thailand in 1997 has threatened some of these gains, especially in Indonesia.

The approach to understanding the role of the agricultural sector in poverty alleviation taken here is straightforward. A carefully chosen sub-set of the Deininger–Squire data [Deininger and Squire (1996)] is subjected to an econometric procedure that utilizes the availability of five separate (but linked) observations – the per capita income of each quintile in the income distribution – for each year in which Deininger and Squire judge the distributional data to be of good quality. Data for 27 developing countries, with a total of 181 observations, pass the Deininger–Squire quality test as well as the "relevance" test for the approach taken here. Relevance required reasonable size – only Jamaica (2.5 million) and Costa Rica (3.4 million), each included for geographical representation, have populations smaller than the 5.9 million in Honduras, the next smallest country in terms of population. The population represented in the sample totaled more than 3.3 billion in 1995, or two-thirds of the total population of the low and middle income countries, as classified by the World Bank (1997).

In view of the motivating hypothesis that the rural economy is likely to have especially important linkages to incomes of the poor, all countries included in the sample have significant agricultural sectors. The least important is the 5 percent of GDP contributed by the agricultural sector of Venezuela in 1990, but the average for the countries is 25 percent. Perhaps more telling, the average share of agricultural workers in the overall labor force is 51 percent in this sample, reflecting the importance of the sector in employment and income generation for the poor.

The sample is also reasonably representative of the developing world. If population share is the criterion, the 10 countries from Latin America with 57 observations over-represent that region, and Africa, East Asia, and South Asia are somewhat under-represented. If regional GDP is the criterion, South Asia is over-represented and Latin America is under-represented. Only Africa is significantly under-represented in the sample if a simple average of these two criteria is used (see Table 5).

Thus the data set consists of 181 observations from 27 countries over a time period that extends from 1960 to 1992. The most observations for individual countries are for India, Brazil, China, Taiwan, and Korea, with 22, 15, 12, 12, and 11 observations, respectively. For Chile, Dominican Republic, Guatemala, Honduras, Morocco, Tunisia, and Uganda, just two observations each are available, the minimum needed for the statistical procedure used here.

Table 5
Basic data

Country and regional group	# of obs	1995 pop (millions)	1995 GDP per capita USD	1995 GDP per capita $PPP	1995 GDP (billion $PPP)	Average relative income gap[*]	Avg. GNP growth p.c. 1965–1985	Avg. GNP growth p.c. 1985–1995
Latin America								
Brazil	15	159.2	3,640	5,400	860	2.99	4.3	−0.8
Chile	2	14.2	4,160	9,520	135	2.57	−0.2	6.1
Colombia	7	36.8	1,910	6,130	226	2.63	2.9	2.6
Costa Rica	7	3.4	2,610	5,850	20	2.52	1.4	2.8
Dom. Republic	2	7.8	1,460	3,870	30	2.35	2.9	2.1
Guatemala	2	10.6	1,340	3,340	35	2.81	1.7	0.3
Honduras	2	5.9	600	1,900	11	2.90	0.4	0.1
Jamaica	5	2.5	1,510	3,540	9	2.14	−0.7	3.6
Mexico	6	91.8	3,320	6,400	588	2.81	2.7	0.1
Venezuela	9	21.7	3,020	7,900	171	2.22	0.5	0.5
East & SE Asia								
China	12	1,200.2	620	2,920	3,505	1.53	4.8	8.3
Indonesia	7	193.3	680	3,800	735	1.72	4.8	6.0
S. Korea	11	44.9	9,700	11,450	514	1.76	6.6	7.7
Malaysia	5	20.1	3,890	9,020	181	2.56	4.4	5.7
Philippines	5	68.6	1,050	2,260	155	2.49	2.3	1.5
Taiwan	12	21.0	11,236	13,240	291	1.49	–	–
Thailand	8	58.2	2,740	7,540	439	2.39	4.0	8.4
South Asia								
Bangladesh	9	119.8	240	1,380	165	1.75	0.4	2.1
India	22	929.4	340	1,400	1,301	1.64	1.7	3.2
Sri Lanka	8	18.1	700	3,250	59	2.04	2.9	2.6
Pakistan	9	129.9	460	2,230	290	1.59	2.6	1.2
South Asia								
Ivory Coast	4	14.0	660	1,580	22	1.98	0.9	4.6[†]
Ghana	3	17.1	390	1,990	34	1.80	−2.2	1.4
Morocco	2	26.6	1,110	3,340	89	1.98	2.2	0.9
Tunisia	2	9.0	1,820	5,000	45	2.09	4.0	1.9
Uganda	2	19.2	240	1,470	28	1.87	−2.6	2.7
Other								
Turkey	3	61.1	2,780	5,580	341	2.58	2.6	2.2

[*](Per capita income in quintile V minus per capita income in quintile I) divided by average per capita income, all in $PPP.
[†] 1985–1994.

9.1. The statistical approach

By merging data on shares of income (or, more commonly, expenditures) by quintile from the Deininger–Squire data base with time series data on real per capita incomes in purchasing power parity equivalents from the Penn World Tables [Summers and Heston (1991), with 1996 update], it is possible to generate for each observation in the sample the per capita income in each quintile. Most researchers have used such data to calculate growth rates for the incomes of the bottom twenty or forty percent of the income distribution, with the time period of the calculation determined by data availability for each country in the sample [Deininger and Squire (1996), Ravallion and Chen (1997), Roemer and Gugerty (1997), Gallup, Radelet and Warner (1997)]. In what is now the standard approach to explaining the factors that cause economic growth, these growth rates are regressed on a variety of factors – structural, institutional, political, and economic – that help to explain their variation [Barro and Sala-i-Martin (1995)].

The approach here is different. Advantage is taken of the panel nature of the data to estimate a fixed-effects model of per capita income in each country for each year data on income distribution are available. The income data are meant to be comparable because they are in purchasing-power-parity dollars, so merging the data in this form is a promising avenue. With five observations for each country for each year of data on income distribution, multiple degrees of freedom are available to track the impact of variables on the functioning of each economy, including the impact of economic growth on income distribution itself, and vice versa.

The simplest approach replicates the spirit of the analysis conducted by Roemer and Gugerty (1997), which determined the "elasticity of connection" between growth in the overall economy and growth in per capita incomes of the poor, specified as either the bottom twenty or forty percent of the income distribution. Table 6 presents the results of estimating this elasticity for the present data set, where the dependent variable is specified as the logarithm of the per capita income of each quintile and the independent variable is the logarithm of average per capita income for the entire economy (Log Avg Y). The estimating equation also includes "fixed effects", separate dummy variables for each country in the sample (excluding Ghana, whose impact is included in the intercept term), as well as separate dummy variables for data from the 1960s, the 1970s, and the 1980s (thus accounting for high R^2 for each quintile regression). The impact of data from the 1990s is also included in the intercept term. Table 6 reports how many of these fixed effects coefficients are significant in each regression.

It is obvious from basic national income accounting identities that the sum of the elasticities for the five quintiles should equal one when each elasticity is weighted by the share in national income of the respective quintile. Table 6 also presents in Panel B the results of estimating a complete system of all five equations that imposes this "adding up" constraint. It is a reassuring test of the quality of the data that the weighted sum of the unconstrained elasticities reported in Table 6 totals 0.989, not significantly different from 1.0. Imposing the adding-up constraint changes the individual elasticities

Table 6
Estimates of the "elasticity of connection" between average per capita income (in $PPP) and per capita income by quintile

	Quintile I (poorest)	Quintile II	Quintile III	Quintile IV	Quintile V (richest)
Panel A: Sum of weighted elasticities not constrained to equal one					
Constant	0.408	−0.206	−0.080	0.097	0.622
(*t*)	(0.8)	(0.3)	(0.3)	(0.2)	(3.2)
Log Avg *Y*	0.790	0.948	0.975	0.992	1.022
(*t*)	(11.4)	(21.2)	(27.4)	(11.5)	(36.6)
Countries*	12	14	12	1	15
Decades*	2	0	0	0	0
$\hat{R}^2$	0.909	0.966	0.981	0.907	0.993
Panel B: Sum of weighted elasticities constrained to equal one					
Constant	0.343	−0.292	−0.179	−0.011	0.588
(*t*)	(0.973)	(0.8)	(0.5)	(0.0)	(3.0)
Log Avg *Y*	0.800	0.961	0.990	1.012	1.029
(*t*)	(15.8)	(19.3)	(20.3)	(21.8)	(38.5)
Countries*	16	12	9	4	12
Decades*	2	0	0	0	0
$\hat{R}^2$	0.908	0.966	0.981	0.907	0.993
Panel C: Percent change in "elasticity of connection" due to constraining the weighted sum of the elasticities to equal one					
Percent change	1.27%	1.37%	1.54%	2.02%	0.68%

*Numbers for "countries" and "decades" indicate the number of variables in each category significant at 10 percent or higher.
Source: Author's estimates from data in Deininger and Squire (1996).

very little. Panel C reports that only in quintile IV does the coefficient change by as much as two percent.

Interestingly, not all five elasticities are equal to one. As Figure 4 shows, the elasticity for the poorest quintile is only 0.8 (and is significantly less than one), with the value rising steadily to slightly greater than one for the richest quintile. Despite its unfamiliar shape, Figure 4 can be interpreted as part of a Kuznets curve, the "early" part when income distribution deteriorates with rising incomes [Kuznets (1955)]. The curve in

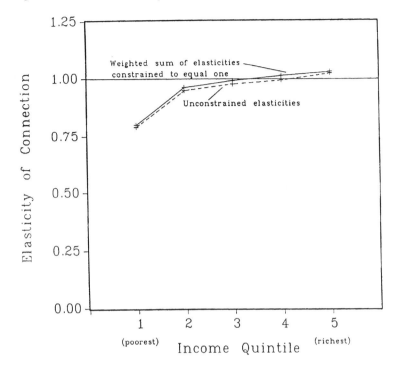

Figure 4. "Elasticity of connection" between average per capita income (in $PPP) and per capita income by quintile. Source: Data in Table 2.

Figure 4 was generated by the structure of economic growth in a representative sample of developing countries, and shows clearly that the distribution of income worsened as a result of this growth process.

9.2. The impact of income distribution on the distribution of growth

At one level, it would seem to be a tautology that the distribution of income will affect the distribution of growth in incomes. Upon reflection, of course, the connection is not so obvious. For example, Gallup, Radelet and Warner (1997) find that the initial level of per capita income in the lowest quintile is negatively associated with growth in income for that quintile. Although some of this effect may be simple regression to the mean caused by measurement error in the quintile shares, part of it may be due to a genuine convergence effect that tends to reduce skewing in the distribution of income, both within and across countries. The convergence effect – based on the logic of the neoclassical Solow growth model – provides an alternative, and contradictory, mechanism to the more popular view that "it takes money to make money". In this view, traceable to the Bible and Adam Smith, a skewed income distribution is likely to be self-reinforcing over time, as only the rich can accumulate assets that provide faster income growth than comes from wage labor.

Which mechanism is dominant is an empirical issue. The test here relies on the "self-reinforcing" logic of the asset distribution mechanism sketched above. A variable is constructed that measures the relative income gap between the rich and the poor, and this variable is then used to define a dummy variable that is equal to one when the observation reflects a highly unequal distribution of income. Specifically, the per capita income of the bottom quintile is subtracted from that of the top quintile, and this "income gap" is then compared with average per capita income for that particular observation. When the resulting value exceeds two – the gap is twice as large as average income – the dummy variable (W2) is equal to one; it is zero otherwise.

Simply adding this dummy variable to the regressions that produced Figure 4 produces few surprises. The "elasticities of connection" are little changed, but in general are estimated more precisely. When W2 is equal to one – the income gap is relatively large – incomes of the poor are shifted downward significantly. In the bottom quintile the shift is 27 percent; it is 21 percent and 10 percent, respectively, in the next two quintiles. The shift in the fourth quintile is not significant, whereas the highest quintile experiences a 15 percent increase in its per capita income. There is not much more than accounting to these results, although it is interesting to see the magnitudes of the changes by quintile.

A more revealing exercise is to permit the elasticities to shift as well as the intercept term in those economies with relatively large income gaps. By and large, the results are not significant in statistical terms, although the coefficient of most interest, the shift in the bottom quintile, is significant at the ten percent level. The negative direction of the shift suggests that the poor in "unequal" economies are not just poor, they are not nearly as well connected to the growth process in the rest of the economy as their poor cousins in economies with smaller relative income gaps, a result consistent with those reported by Birdsall, Ross and Sabot (1995) and Ravallion (1996).

These results are suggestive, but they merely hint at the underlying structure that might actually cause economies with different relative income gaps to generate systematically different connections to each income quintile. The obvious starting point in a search for this structure is to divide the economy into its agricultural and non-agricultural components to see if these systematic differences can be traced to basic sectoral patterns of income growth [Anand and Kanbur (1993), Timmer (1995)].

9.3. The "elasticity of connection" from agriculture and non-agriculture

National income data are generally reported by sectoral origin of gross domestic product (GDP). These data can be used to calculate the share of GDP originating each year in agriculture and non-agriculture. For the countries and years in the data set used here, 25 percent of GDP originated from the agricultural sector on average, with 75 percent from non-agriculture.

From the data set on agricultural labor force constructed by Larson and Mundlak (1997), it is also possible to estimate the share of the total labor force working in agriculture for each country and year. Again, for this sample, the average was 51 percent. These data, when combined with data on share of GDP from agriculture and the PPP estimates of average real per capita income used earlier, can be used to construct estimates of agricultural GDP per agricultural worker, which serve as a proxy for per capita productivity of workers in this sector. Simple accounting identities permit construction of a similar series for non-agricultural workers. On average, agricultural GDP per capita is PPP$1,021 per year compared with average GDP per capita of PPP$2,393. Since 51 percent of the labor force is in agriculture on average, non-agricultural GDP per capita works out to PPP$3,636. On average, agricultural workers produce less than a third of what workers outside of agriculture produce. This relatively low productivity is a structural characteristic of nearly all poor countries, and raising it is a key source of growth during the structural transformation [Kuznets (1966), Timmer (1988)].

The question to be examined is whether the sectoral composition of labor productivity matters in a significant way to incomes earned by each quintile. When weighted by their share in the labor force, do the per capita labor productivities of workers in agriculture and non-agriculture have differential effects on the average earnings in each income quintile?

Figure 5 shows the rather startling answer. The disaggregation into "good" and "bad" levels of the relative income gap is maintained in the regressions that provide these results. That is, elasticity "shifters" are included for both the agricultural and non-agricultural coefficients, and they are highly important for understanding the underlying structure and dynamics of the countries in this sample (see Table 7). Two fundamentally different growth processes seem to be at work with respect to the roles of labor productivity in agriculture and non-agriculture, and how these affect incomes in each of the five quintiles of the income distribution.

In countries where the income gap is relatively small, labor productivity in agriculture is slightly but consistently more important in generating incomes in each of the five quintiles. Furthermore, agricultural productivity has a noticeable "anti-Kuznets" effect in these countries. Using the results in Panel B of Table 7, where weighted elasticities are constrained to add up to one for each of the sub-samples, the elasticities of connection for the bottom two quintiles average 1.087, about 8 percent greater than the average for the top three quintiles of 1.005. A similar "anti-Kuznets" effect is seen from the non-agricultural sector, and this impact is even more important to the poor because the non-agricultural sector makes up, on average, 75 percent of the overall economy. It also has the capacity to grow significantly faster than the agricultural economy over sustained periods of time.

The contrast with countries where the relative income gap is large – more than twice the average per capita income – is striking. In the poorest quintile, workers are virtually disconnected from the national economy. A 95 percent confidence interval includes zero for both sectors! The elasticity of connection rises sharply by income class and exceeds one for the top quintile. For countries with large income gaps, the "early" (and

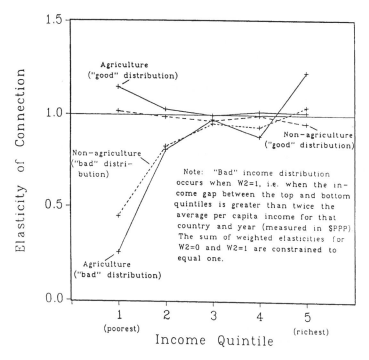

Figure 5. "Elasticity of connection" between labor productivity in agriculture and non-agriculture and income per capita by quintile, for "good" and "bad" income distributions. Source: Data in Table 7.

Table 7

Estimates of the "elasticity of connection" between per capita income by quintile and average per capita income (in $PPP) for agriculture and non-agriculture separately, for countries with "good" and "bad" distribution of income*

	Quintile I (poorest)	Quintile II	Quintile III	Quintile IV	Quintile V (richest)
	Panel A: Sum of weighted elasticities not constrained to equal one				
Constant	−1.695	−0.712	−0.235	−0.120	0.578
(t)	(1.6)	(1.0)	(0.4)	(0.1)	(1.0)
Log Ag Y	1.160	1.049	1.021	1.050	1.073
(t)	(6.2)	(8.0)	(9.2)	(4.1)	(10.6)
Log Non-Ag Y	1.026	0.999	0.981	1.012	0.988
(t)	(9.2)	(12.9)	(14.9)	(6.6)	(16.5)
W2	5.096	1.306	0.169	0.801	−0.724
(t)	(3.5)	(1.3)	(0.2)	(0.4)	(0.9)
W2* Log Ag Y	−0.900	−0.238	−0.043	−0.161	0.181
(t)	(3.6)	(1.3)	(0.3)	(0.5)	(1.3)

Table 7
Continued

	Quintile I (poorest)	Quintile II	Quintile III	Quintile IV	Quintile V (richest)
W2* Log Non-Ag Y	−0.576	−0.172	−0.027	−0.074	0.071
(t)	(3.8)	(1.6)	(0.3)	(0.4)	(0.9)
Net when W2 = 1					
[Ag]	[0.260]	[0.811]	[0.978]	[0.889]	[1.254]
[Non-Ag]	[0.450]	[0.827]	[0.954]	[0.938]	[1.059]
Countries[†]	12	18	16	3	24
Decades[†]	1	1	1	0	3
$\hat{R}^2$	0.922	0.966	0.978	0.904	0.989

Panel B: Sum of weighted elasticities constrained to equal one

	Quintile I (poorest)	Quintile II	Quintile III	Quintile IV	Quintile V (richest)
Constant	−1.622	−0.598	−0.085	0.084	0.944
(t)	(2.1)	(0.8)	(0.1)	(0.1)	(2.0)
Log Ag Y	1.146	1.028	0.994	1.013	1.008
(t)	(8.4)	(7.7)	(7.9)	(8.1)	(11.7)
Log Non-Ag Y	1.018	0.987	0.965	0.991	0.949
(t)	(12.6)	(12.5)	(12.5)	(13.4)	(18.1)
W2	5.032	1.213	0.054	0.653	−0.920
(t)	(4.8)	(1.2)	(0.1)	(0.7)	(1.6)
W2* Log Ag Y	−0.889	−0.221	−0.022	−0.135	0.216
(t)	(4.8)	(1.2)	(0.1)	(0.8)	(2.1)
W2* Log Non-Ag Y	−0.569	−0.163	−0.015	−0.059	0.090
(t)	(5.2)	(1.5)	(0.1)	(0.6)	(1.5)
Net when W2 = 1					
[Ag]	[0.257]	[0.807]	[0.972]	[0.878]	[1.224]
[Non-Ag]	[0.449]	[0.824]	[0.9S0]	[0.932]	[1.039]
Countries[†]	15	16	13	15	22
Decades[†]	1	1	1	1	3
$\hat{R}^2$	0.922	0.966	0.978	0.904	0.989

*Agricultural value added per agricultural worker, in $PPP, is used as a proxy for agricultural income and similarly for non-agriculture. The dummy variable W2 is set equal to one when the gap between per capita income of the top quintile and the bottom quintile exceeds twice the average per capita income, for that particular country and time period.

[†]Numbers for "countries" and "decades" indicate the number of variables in each category that are significant at 10 percent or higher.

Source: Author's estimates from data in Deininger and Squire (1996).

discouraging) part of the Kuznets curve is a dramatic reality of their economies. And growth in agricultural productivity is no more successful in alleviating poverty than growth in the non-agricultural economy. Indeed, the rich benefit considerably from agricultural growth in countries with large income gaps, no doubt because of highly skewed distributions of land. But neither sector reaches the poor very effectively.

10. Insights on the political economy of growth

These results raise intriguing possibilities about the political sustainability of rapid economic growth. When the relative income gap is less than twice the level of average per capita incomes, economic growth is roughly equal in all income quintiles and is especially stimulated by growth in agricultural productivity (see Figure 5). Alternatively, when the relative income gap exceeds twice the average per capita income, the poor are nearly left out of the growth process altogether, and agriculture is no more effective in reaching them than non-agriculture.

These results raise the possibility that the relatively good income distributions in some countries of East, Southeast, and South Asia produce a growth process that is more sustainable than in countries with highly skewed income distributions, and this effect could be magnified by emphasizing growth in the agricultural sector. The reasons are almost certainly political and may hinge importantly on the extent of political liberties and flexibility in the labor market. Economies with few political choices, low and stagnant labor productivity in agriculture, and structural rigidities in moving that labor to more productive sectors are likely to find a visibly growing income gap between the rich and the poor to be more destabilizing than in economies that are open and flexible [A.S. Timmer (1997)].

Evidence from the record of economic growth from 1965 to 1985 and from 1985 to 1995 provides a rough confirmation of this line of speculation (see Table 8). When the difference in the rate of growth of per capita incomes between these two periods (GRDIFF) is regressed on the average relative size of the income gap for each country (RELGAP, data from Table 5), the result is a large, negative coefficient that is significant at the one percent level. Controlling for the (logarithm of the) level of per capita income at the end of the period (LPCYPPP) and the growth rate in the first period (GR6585), a larger income gap is significantly associated with a sharp slowdown in the rate of economic growth from the first to the second period. Richer countries experience a smaller slowdown than poorer countries, suggesting that it is possible to "buy" political stability [A.S. Timmer (1997)]. And controlling for the other two factors, a faster rate of economic growth in the first period is also associated with a slower rate in the second, suggesting that there is considerable "luck of the draw" in individual growth rates.

These political economy insights suggest that changes in relative incomes are more likely to influence political stability than changes in the degree of absolute poverty. Because Gini coefficients and "top quintile/bottom quintile" ratios rarely blend easily into populist speeches, the more visible measure of inequality is the gap between the

Table 8

Impact of relative income gap on sustainability of economic growth for 26 countries between 1965 and 1995

Independent variable	Dependent variable	
	GRDIFF	RELGAP
Constant	−12.68	−1.34
	(1.83)	(1.34)
RELGAP	−3.57	
	(2.90)	
LPCYPPP	2.78	0.46
	(2.82)	(3.82)
GR6585	−0.85	
	(3.27)	
GR8595		−0.08
		(3.20)
Adjusted R^2	0.33	0.38

Note: *t*-statistics are shown in parentheses.
GRDIFF = difference in rate of economic growth per capita between 1965–85 and 1985–95, RELGAP = per capita income in quintile V minus per capita income in quintile I, divided by average per capita income, all in $PPP, LPCYPPP = logarithm of per capita income in 1995, in $PPP, GR6585 = rate of growth of per capita incomes from 1965 to 1985, and GR8595 = rate of growth of per capita incomes from 1985 to 1995.
Source: Data from Table 5.

rich and the poor. For the empirical analysis conducted here, this gap is measured by the difference between the incomes of the top and bottom quintiles and, because the data actually report on expenditure patterns rather than income patterns, this gap is likely to be quite visible to most citizens, at least in urban areas.

This measure of the relative gap is positively associated with the level of per capita incomes, confirming the "early" stage of the Kuznets curve for the countries in this sample (see Table 8). For the countries and time period examined here, there is a very clear and significant tendency for the gap to widen with higher incomes per capita. Interestingly, countries able to grow fastest from 1985 to 1995 were associated with a narrowing of the income gap. This result again suggests the role of the income gap in sustaining the growth process.

The evidence presented here argues that an income gap that is twice as large as the average per capita income is an effective dividing line between societies with "good" and "bad" income distributions, with sharply different growth processes in the two types of economies. The dividing line is not particularly sensitive to a gap that is exactly 2.0 times the average income per capita. When all the results were re-estimated with values of 1.9 and 2.1, there was little change in the basic patterns. Large changes, to 1.5 or 2.5

for example, produce more significant changes in the results, partly because the sample size for the smaller sub-sample becomes too small for us to have much confidence in the coefficients. It is reasonable to conclude that when the income gap between the top and bottom quintiles exceeds twice the average per capita income, it is large enough for citizens to notice and to affect the political economy of the growth process.

The apparent failure of economic growth to reach the poor in precisely those environments where the connection would seem to be most crucial is clearly disappointing, but should not be taken as a council of despair or a general indictment of economic growth itself. Even in societies that start with a wide income gap, growth has a positive, although small, impact on the poor, and failure to grow will certainly hurt the poor. More positively, visible and pro-active measures to reach the poor as a concomitant part of trade opening, structural adjustment, and privatization programs designed to speed economic growth will help to sustain the growth-friendly initiatives. Clearly, the role for agriculture in these measures will depend on land distribution and the structure of the sector. But the failure to sustain rapid economic growth in countries with wide (and widening) income gaps is no mystery when viewed in the context of these results.

Appendix A. Definitions of variables used in regressions

ASIA: Dummy variable for countries in Asia

BMPLx: Log(1 + black market premium exchange rate)

DTIMEx: Time dummy variable

GOVSH5x: Ratio of real government "consumption" expenditure to real GDP

GRNAGSH5x: Growth rate per year of real per capita GDP in the nonagricultural sector

GRSH5x: Growth rate per year of real per capita GDP

HUMxx: Sum of rural human capital and non-rural human capital

INVSH5x: Ratio of real domestic investment (public plus private) to real GDP

LATAMERI: Dummy variable for countries in Latin America

LNFERTx: Log of total fertility rate (measured in children per woman)

LNGDPSH5xx: Log of real per capita GDP

LNGSH5SQxx: Square of the log of real per capita GDP

POPGROWx: Rate of population growth per year

RHUMSHFTx: Product of the starting level of rural human capital and the current rate of sectoral migration from rural to non-rural areas

RHUMxx: Level of rural human capital

RUHUMRATxx: Ratio of rural human capital to non-rural human capital

SUBAFRIC: Dummy variable for countries in sub-Saharan Africa

UHUMxx: Level of non-rural human capital

Note: The term "x" behind a variable denotes the average of a sub-period among five-year sub-periods (1960–64, 1965–69, 1970–74, 1975–79, 1980–84), while the term "xx" denotes a starting-value year (1960, 1965, 1970, 1975, 1980).

Appendix B

B.1. Means and standard deviations of variables when GRSH5 is the dependent variable

Variable	Mean	St. dev.	Variable	Mean	St. dev.
BMP1L	0.201	0.263	RHUMSHFT1	0.042	0.066
BMP2L	0.207	0.268	RHUMSHFT2	0.084	0.114
BMP3L	0.253	0.316	RHUMSHFT3	0.067	0.075
BMP4L	0.304	0.457	RHUMSHFT4	0.074	0.086
BMP5L	0.383	0.497	RHUM60	1.85	1.297
GOVSH1	0.15	0.055	RHUM65	2.063	1.428
GOVSH2	0.152	0.061	RHUM70	2.281	1.577
GOVSH3	0.157	0.067	RHUM75	2.65	1.781
GOVSH4	0.179	0.082	RHUM80	3.014	1.855
GOVSH5	0.188	0.079	RUHUMRAT60	0.572	0.18
GRSH51	0.028	0.025	RUHUMRAT65	0.592	0.184
GRSH52	0.031	0.024	RUHUMRAT70	0.609	0.188
GRSH53	0.026	0.037	RUHUMRAT75	0.635	0.187
GRSH54	0.023	0.036	RUHUMRAT80	0.658	0.197
GRSH55	−0.01	0.029	UHUM60	2.956	1.489
INVSH51	0.155	0.085	UHUM65	3.188	1.539
INVSH52	0.163	0.082	UHUM70	3.424	1.648
INVSH53	0.185	0.093	UHUM75	3.828	1.779
INVSH54	0.18	0.081	UHUM80	4.245	1.682
INVSH55	0.168	0.079			
LNGDPSH560	7.035	0.679			
LNGDPSH565	7.17	0.7			
LNGDPSH570	7.332	0.729			
LNGDPSH575	7.503	0.757			
LNGDPSH580	7.613	0.81			

B.2. Means and standard deviations of variables when GRNAGSH5 is the dependent variable

Variable	Mean	St. dev.	Variable	Mean	St. dev.
BMP1L	0.208	0.265	LNGDPSH560	7.033	0.69
BMP2L	0.191	0.211	LNGDPSH565	7.196	0.696
BMP3L	0.244	0.292	LNGDPSH570	7.365	0.718
BMP4L	0.296	0.441	LNGDPSH575	7.539	0.741
BMP5L	0.373	0.482	LNGDPSH580	7.645	0.802
GOVSH1	0.151	0.055	RHUM60	1.897	1.297
GOVSH2	0.152	0.061	RHUM65	2.14	1.43
GOVSH3	0.157	0.068	RHUM70	2.363	1.581
GOVSH4	0.181	0.083	RHUM75	2.738	1.778
GOVSH5	0.19	0.079	RHUM80	3.106	1.85
GRNAGSH51	0.038	0.032	RUHUMRAT60	0.582	0.174
GRNAGSH52	0.044	0.033	RUHUMRAT65	0.606	0.178
GRNAGSH53	0.029	0.045	RUHUMRAT70	0.624	0.182
GRNAGSH54	0.032	0.046	RUHUMRAT75	0.649	0.179
GRNAGSH55	−0.009	0.037	RUHUMRAT80	0.673	0.189
INVSH51	0.159	0.085	UHUM60	2.993	1.504
INVSH52	0.168	0.081	UHUM65	3.248	1.56
INVSH53	0.19	0.092	UHUM70	3.481	1.675
INVSH54	0.184	0.081	UHUM75	3.892	1.795
INVSH55	0.171	0.079	UHUM80	4.298	1.703

Appendix C. List of countries in samples

	Country	Regional dummy		Country	Regional dummy
(1)	Algeria		(36)	Chile	LATAMERI
(2)	Botswana	SUBAFRIC	(37)	Colombia	LATAMERI
(3)	Ghana	SUBAFRIC	(38)	Ecuador	LATAMERI
(4)	Kenya	SUBAFRIC	(39)	Guyana	LATAMERI
(5)	Lesotho	SUBAFRIC	(40)	Paraguay	LATAMERI
(6)	Liberia	SUBAFRIC	(41)	Peru	LATAMERI
(7)	Malawi	SUBAFRIC	(42)	Uruguay	LATAMERI
(8)	Mauritius	SUBAFRIC	(43)	Venezuela	LATAMERI
(9)	Mozambique	SUBAFRIC	(44)	Bangladesh	ASIA
(10)	Niger	SUBAFRIC	(45)	Myanmar (Burma)	ASIA
(11)	Senegal	SUBAFRIC	(46)	India	ASIA
(12)	Sierra Leone	SUBAFRIC	(47)	Indonesia	ASIA
(13)	Sudan	SUBAFRIC	(48)	Israel	
(14)	Swaziland	SUBAFRIC	(49)	Korea	ASIA
(15)	Tanzania	SUBAFRIC	(50)	Malaysia	ASIA
(16)	Togo	SUBAFRIC	(51)	Nepal	ASIA
(17)	Tunisia		(52)	Pakistan	ASIA
(18)	Uganda	SUBAFRIC	(53)	Philippines	ASIA
(19)	Zaire	SUBAFRIC	(54)	Sri Lanka	ASIA
(20)	Zambia	SUBAFRIC	(55)	Syria	ASIA
(21)	Zimbabwe	SUBAFRIC	(56)	Thailand	ASIA
(22)	Barbados		(57)	Cyprus	
(23)	Dominican Republic	LATAMERI	(58)	Greece	
(24)	El Salvador	LATAMERI	(59)	Malta	
(25)	Guatemala	LATAMERI	(60)	Portugal	
(26)	Haiti	LATAMERI	(61)	Spain	
(27)	Honduras	LATAMERI	(62)	Turkey	
(28)	Jamaica		(63)	Yugoslavia	
(29)	Mexico	LATAMERI	(64)	Fiji	
(30)	Nicaragua	LATAMERI	(65)	Papua New Guinea	
(31)	Panama	LATAMERI			
(32)	Trinidad and Tobago				
(33)	Argentina	LATAMERI			
(34)	Bolivia	LATAMERI			
(35)	Brazil	LATAMERI			

Appendix D

D.1. Panel data set of rural human capital (average years of education per person over the age of 25)

Country	RHUM60	RHUM65	RHUM70	RHUM75	RHUM80	RHUM85
Algeria	0.6	0.44	0.54	0.76	1.27	1.63
Ghana	0.55	0.93	1.62	1.61	1.82	2.46
Kenya	1.07	1.03	1.16	1.25	2.09	2.6
Lesotho	2.42	2.63	2.48	2.64	2.88	3.07
Liberia	0.32	0.39	0.35	0.62	0.68	0.95
Malawi	1.53	1.55	1.8	1.97	1.99	2.22
Mauritius	2.08	2.52	2.73	3.16	3.73	4.15
Mozambique	0.39	0.43	0.69	0.73	0.76	0.9
Niger	0.79	0.64	0.52	0.44	0.43	0.45
Senegal	1.29	1.1	1.29	1.47	1.5	1.87
Sierra Leone	NA	0.63	0.8	1.27	1.3	1.41
Sudan	0.23	0.24	0.27	0.35	0.47	0.67
Tanzania	1.16	1.8	1.93	1.75	2.14	1.98
Togo	0.17	0.28	0.39	0.72	1.21	1.58
Tunisia	0.29	0.46	0.58	0.8	1.35	1.8
Uganda	1.09	1.06	0.97	1.17	1.52	1.79
Zaire	0.48	0.69	0.81	0.98	1.11	1.45
Zambia	1.34	1.7	1.7	2.03	2.71	3.44
Zimbabwe	1.48	1.58	0.73	1.86	2.01	2.23
Dominican Republic	1.92	2.1	2.39	2.72	2.98	3.4
El Salvador	1.12	1.32	1.57	2.06	2.69	3.02
Guatemala	0.76	0.94	1.13	1.25	1.63	1.84
Haiti	0.43	0.5	0.57	0.68	0.81	0.9
Honduras	1.33	1.43	1.53	1.67	2.13	2.83
Mexico	1.91	2.21	2.63	2.78	2.84	3.71
Nicaragua	1.28	1.31	1.47	1.41	1.62	2.28
Panama	3.4	3.38	3.55	4.14	4.97	5.36
Argentina	4.5	4.91	5.24	5.32	5.84	6.17
Bolivia	2.41	2.93	2.59	2.68	2.83	3.11
Brazil	1.86	1.82	2.03	2.05	2.05	2.48
Colombia	2.12	2.39	2.48	3.17	3.6	4
Ecuador	2.4	2.58	2.52	3.25	4.52	4.64
Guyana	3.79	3.59	3.33	3.73	3.89	4.17
Paraguay	3.02	3.22	3.42	3.92	4.32	4.48
Peru	2.05	2.2	2.47	2.87	3.59	3.94
Uruguay	3.72	4.05	4.32	5.19	5.21	5.86
Bangladesh	0.73	0.86	0.76	0.9	1.5	1.76
Myanmar (Burma)	0.76	0.76	0.82	0.7	1.01	NA
India	1.12	1.29	1.5	1.91	2.13	2.4
Indonesia	1.02	1.47	2.1	2.42	2.85	3.49
Korea	2.96	4.06	5.08	5.42	6.33	7.44
Malaysia	2.1	2.57	3.13	3.73	4.17	5.08

Country	RHUM60	RHUM65	RHUM70	RHUM75	RHUM80	RHUM85
Nepal	0.06	0.09	0.03	0.33	0.46	0.74
Pakistan	0.42	0.72	1.04	1.04	1.1	1.24
Philippines	3.3	3.7	4.24	4.68	5.1	5.61
Sri Lanka	3.29	3.89	4.76	4.9	5.04	5.3
Syria	0.79	1.1	1.33	1.88	2.61	3.39
Thailand	3.34	3.14	3.43	3.64	3.62	4.88
Cyprus	4.03	4.55	5.2	6.73	6.76	6.92
Greece	3.91	4.46	4.62	5.23	5.88	6.25
Portugal	1.69	1.56	1.07	1.85	2.93	3.53
Spain	3.18	3.59	4.5	4.15	4.85	5.37
Turkey	1.68	1.84	1.66	1.81	2.22	2.9
Yugoslavia	3.91	4.98	4.82	5.4	5.96	6.69
Papua New Guinea	1.33	1.12	0.68	0.82	0.89	1.51
Botswana	1.24	1.28	1.26	1.71	2.12	3.43
Swaziland	1.6	1.52	1.71	2.82	2.78	3.36
Barbados	4.72	5.6	8.12	7.52	6.23	7
Jamaica	2.04	2.22	2.66	2.83	2.88	3.38
Trinidad and Tobago	4.32	4.35	4.17	4.86	6.35	6.36
Chile	4.04	4.08	4.41	4.57	4.94	5.61
Venezuela	1.29	1.33	1.5	1.91	2.5	2.88
Israel	5.64	5.93	6.44	7.06	8.09	8.7
Malta	3.35	3.39	3.92	4.34	5.1	6.06
Fiji	4.06	5.31	4.27	4.37	5.24	5.92

D.2. Panel data set of non-rural human capital (average years of education per person over the age of 25)

Country	UHUM60	UHUM65	UHUM70	UHUM75	UHUM80	UHUM85
Algeria	1.39	0.98	1.17	1.58	2.63	3.24
Ghana	1.04	1.76	2.98	3.13	3.57	4.77
Kenya	2.19	2.16	2.52	2.5	4.16	5
Lesotho	6.42	6.34	6.24	5.53	5.67	5.58
Liberia	1.32	1.55	1.35	2.28	2.42	3.12
Malawi	3.73	3.68	4.34	4.67	4.8	5.07
Mauritius	3.01	3.57	4.1	4.29	4.84	4.98
Mozambique	0.69	0.74	1.15	1.31	1.51	1.8
Niger	1.73	1.33	1.06	0.98	0.94	0.99
Senegal	2.34	1.95	2.33	2.69	2.79	3.18
Sierra Leone	NA	1.17	1.46	2.34	2.49	2.62
Sudan	0.69	0.7	0.78	0.96	1.23	1.66
Tanzania	2.21	3.34	3.48	3.03	3.56	3.06
Togo	0.51	0.82	1.1	1.97	3.17	3.85
Tunisia	0.65	1.01	1.24	1.65	2.31	2.88
Uganda	2.29	2.17	1.91	2.22	2.78	3.04
Zaire	1.09	1.5	1.71	2.17	2.91	3.56

Country	UHUM60	UHUM65	UHUM70	UHUM75	UHUM80	UHUM85
Zambia	2.52	3.09	3.01	3.44	4.43	5.23
Zimbabwe	2.7	2.92	1.33	3.23	3.63	3.72
Dominican Republic	3.34	3.3	3.42	3.83	4.14	4.4
El Salvador	2.59	2.76	2.99	3.6	3.93	4.11
Guatemala	1.91	2.3	2.68	2.86	3.58	3.77
Haiti	2.02	2.28	2.5	2.87	3.32	3.44
Honduras	2.8	2.91	2.88	2.88	3.53	4.39
Mexico	2.81	3.15	3.64	3.7	3.62	4.41
Nicaragua	3.16	3.15	3.43	3.16	3.49	4.57
Panama	5.32	5.2	5.37	5.78	6.41	6.44
Argentina	5.03	5.31	5.91	5.99	6.56	6.46
Bolivia	4.83	5.7	4.88	4.85	4.93	5.04
Brazil	3.41	3.24	3.5	2.96	3.17	3.57
Colombia	3.2	3.49	3.5	4.31	4.36	4.51
Ecuador	3.87	4.04	3.83	4.74	5.84	5.57
Guyana	6.24	5.92	5.39	5.69	6.03	6.88
Paraguay	3.84	3.97	4.08	4.51	4.77	4.61
Peru	3.91	4.07	4.43	4.94	5.94	6.08
Uruguay	4.39	4.63	4.79	5.53	5.61	6.2
Bangladesh	1.64	1.9	1.61	1.85	2.83	3.1
Myanmar (Burma)	2	1.82	2.05	1.82	2.58	NA
India	2.82	3.05	3.34	4.01	4.25	4.45
Indonesia	1.59	2.23	3.09	3.39	3.81	4.35
Korea	3.61	4.8	5.83	5.98	6.7	7.44
Malaysia	2.82	3.34	3.95	4.57	4.96	5.63
Nepal	0.24	0.34	0.12	1	1.16	1.75
Pakistan	1.32	2.21	3.09	3.06	3.11	3.26
Philippines	4.2	4.55	5.07	5.63	6.17	6.33
Sri Lanka	3.98	4.59	5.45	5.51	5.55	5.44
Syria	1.3	1.71	2.02	2.56	3.32	4.08
Thailand	4.05	3.68	3.91	3.98	3.8	4.88
Cyprus	4.63	5.07	5.77	7.36	7.11	6.92
Greece	4.87	5.39	5.41	5.97	6.54	6.48
Portugal	2.66	2.33	1.49	2.41	3.59	4.06
Spain	3.58	3.92	4.75	4.32	4.96	5.37
Turkey	2.5	2.66	2.32	2.43	2.87	3.48
Yugoslavia	4.94	6.11	5.73	6.24	6.7	7.01
Papua New Guinea	2.37	1.84	1.09	1.33	1.44	2.33
Botswana	2.12	2.11	2.01	2.62	3.13	4.72
Swaziland	2.79	2.45	2.56	4.17	3.85	4.72
Barbados	6.88	7.82	10.53	9.39	7.23	7.69
Jamaica	3.24	3.4	3.88	4.03	4.28	4.77
Trinidad and Tobago	5.49	5.4	5.07	5.64	6.62	6.41
Chile	5.35	5.26	5.54	5.6	5.93	6.28
Venezuela	3.05	3.05	3.35	4.1	5.14	5.51
Israel	6.82	6.96	7.33	7.72	8.5	8.7
Malta	5.68	5.64	5.87	6.11	6.45	6.91
Fiji	6.28	8.14	6.32	6.1	6.95	7.58

Acknowledgements

I would like to thank the editors and an anonymous reviewer for helpful comments. Both my daughter Ashley and my wife Carol have contributed more to this effort than I really care to acknowledge, and I thank them both profusely for their continued willingness to struggle with my ideas and manuscripts.

References

Abbott, J.C. (ed.) (1993), Agricultural and Food Marketing in Developing Countries: Selected Readings (CAB International).

Ahmed, R., and M. Hossain (1990), "Developmental impact of rural infrastructure in Bangladesh", IFPRI Research Report No. 83 (International Food Policy Research Institute, Washington, DC).

Alesina, A., and R. Perotti (1993), "Income distribution, political instability, and investment", Working Paper No. 4486 (National Bureau of Economic Research (NBER), Cambridge, MA).

Anand, S., and S.M.R. Kanbur (1993), "The Kuznets process and the inequality-development relationship", Journal of Development Economics 40(1):25–52.

Anderson, K., and Y. Hayami (with associates) (1986), The Political Economy of Agricultural Protection: East Asia in International Perspective (Allen and Unwin, London).

Barro, R.J. (1997), "Determinants of economic growth: a cross-country empirical study", Development Discussion Paper No. 579 (Harvard Institute for International Development).

Barro, R.J., and J.-W. Lee (1994), Sources of Economic Growth, Carnegie–Rochester Conference Series on Public Policy (North-Holland, Amsterdam) 1–46.

Barro, R.J., and X. Sala-i-Martin (1995), Economic Growth (McGraw-Hill, New York).

Bates, R.H. (1981), Markets and States in Tropical Africa: The Political Basis of Agricultural Policies (University of California Press, Berkeley, CA).

Bates, R.H. (1988), "Lessons from history, or the perfidy of English exceptionalism and the significance of historical France", World Politics 40(4):499–516.

Birdsall, N., D. Ross and R. Sabot (1995), "Inequality and growth reconsidered: Lessons from East Asia", World Bank Economic Review 9(3):477–508.

Binswanger, H.P., and M.R. Rosenzweig (1986), "Behavioral and material determinants of production relations in agriculture", Journal of Development Studies 22:503–539.

Binswanger, H.P., S.R. Khandker and M. Rosenzweig (1993), "How infrastructure and financial institutions affect agricultural output and investment in India", Journal of Development Economics 41.

Binswanger, H.P., and K. Deininger (1997), "Explaining agricultural and agrarian policies in developing countries", Journal of Economic Literature 35.

Bliss, C., and N. Stern (1978), "Productivity, wages and nutrition: Parts I and II", Journal of Development Economics 5(4):331–398.

Chai, C.P. (1995), "Rural human capital and economic growth in developing countries", Senior Honors Thesis (Department of Economics, Harvard University, Cambridge, MA).

Chambers, J.D., and G.E. Mingay (1966), The Agricultural Revolution, 1750–1880 (Schocken, New York).

Chenery, H.B., and M. Syrquin (1975), Patterns of Development, 1950–1970 (Oxford University Press, London).

CIMMYT Economic Staff (International Maize and Wheat Improvement Center) (1984), "The farming systems perspective and farmers participation in the development of appropriate technology", in: C.K. Eicher and J.M. Staatz, eds., Agricultural Development in the Third World (Johns Hopkins University Press, Baltimore, MD).

Clark, C. (1940), The Conditions of Economic Progress (Macmillan, London) (3rd edn. 1957).

Dasgupta, P. (1993), An Inquiry into Well-Being and Destitution (Clarendon Press, Oxford).

Dawe, D. (1993), "The effects of export instability on investment: The information content of prices and growth", Ph.D. Dissertation (Economics Department, Harvard University, Cambridge, MA).

Dawe, D. (1996), "A new look at the effects of export instability on investment and growth", World Development, December.

Deaton, A.S. (1992), Understanding Consumption (Clarendon Press for Oxford University Press, Oxford).

Deininger, K., and L. Squire (1996), "A new data set measuring income inequality", The World Bank Economic Review 10(3):565–591. Data available at http://www.worldbank.org/html/prdmg/grwthweb/growth_t.htm.

de Janvry, A., and E. Sadoulet (1987), "Agricultural price policy in general equilibrium models: results and comparisons", American Journal of Agricultural Economics, May:230–246.

DeLong, J.B., and L.H. Summers (1991), "Equipment investment and economic growth", Quarterly Journal of Economics 106(2):445–502.

Eicher, C.K., and J.M. Staatz (eds.) (1990), Agricultural Development in the Third World, 2nd edn. (Johns Hopkins University Press, Baltimore, MD).

Evenson, R.E. (2001), "Economic impact of agricultural research and extension", in: B.L. Gardner and G. Rausser, eds., Handbook of Agricultural Economics, Vol. 1 (Elsevier, Amsterdam) 573–628.

Evenson, R.E., and Y. Kislev (1975), "Investment in agricultural research and extension: an international survey", Economic Development and Cultural Change 23:507–521.

Fei, J.C.H., and G. Ranis (1964), Development of the Labor Surplus Economy: Theory and Policy (Irwin, Homewood, IL).

Feldstein, M., and C. Horioka (1980), "Domestic saving and international capital flows", Economic Journal 90:314–329.

Fields, G.S. (1997), "Poverty, inequality, and economic well-being: African economic growth in comparative perspective", Paper prepared for presentation to the African Economic Research Consortium, Nairobi, Kenya, mimeo.

Fogel, R.W. (1991), "The conquest of high mortality and hunger in Europe and America: Timing and mechanisms", in: P. Higonnet, D.S. Landes and H. Rosovsky, eds., Favorites of Fortune: Technology, Growth, and Economic Development since the Industrial Revolution (Harvard University Press, Cambridge, MA) 35–71.

Fogel, R.W. (1994), "Economic growth, population theory, and physiology: The bearing of long-term processes on the making of economic policy" (Nobel prize lecture), American Economic Review 84(3):369–395.

Gallup, J., S. Radelet and A. Warner (1997), "Economic growth and the income of the poor", Prepared for the CAER II Project, mimeo (Harvard Institute for International Development).

Griliches, Z. (1958), "Research costs and social returns: hybrid corn and related innovations", Journal of Political Economy 66:419–431.

Hayami, Y., and M. Kikuchi (1978), "Investment inducement to public infrastructure: irrigation in the Philippines", Review of Economics and Statistics 60:70–77.

Hayami, Y., and V. Ruttan (1985), Agricultural Development: An International Perspective, revised and expanded edition (Johns Hopkins University Press, Baltimore, MD).

Hill, H. (1995), The Indonesian Economy Since 1966: Southeast Asia's Emerging Giant (Cambridge University Press, Cambridge).

Hirschman, A.O. (1958), The Strategy of Economic Development (Yale University Press, New Haven).

International Rice Research Institute (IRRI) (1978), Economic Consequences of the New Rice Technology (International Rice Research Institute, Los Banos, Philippines).

Irwin, D.A. (1988), "Welfare effects of British free trade: debate and evidence from the 1840s", Journal of Political Economy 96(6):1142–1164.

Islam, N., and S. Thomas (1996), "Foodgrain price stabilization in developing countries: issues and experiences in Asia", Food Policy Review No. 3 (International Food Policy Research Institute (IFPRI), Washington, DC).

Jamison, D., and L. Lau (1982), Farmer Education and Agricultural Productivity (Johns Hopkins University Press, Baltimore, MD).

Johnson, D.G. (1997), "Agriculture and the wealth of nations" (Ely lecture), American Economic Review 87(2):1–12.

Johnston, B.F., and J.W. Mellor (1961), "The role of agriculture in economic development", American Economic Review 51(4):566–593.

Jorgenson, D.W. (1961), "The development of a dual economy", Economic Journal 71:309–334.

Kaplan, S.L. (1984), Provisioning Paris: Merchants and Millers in the Grain and Flour Trade during the Eighteenth Century (Cornell University Press, Ithaca, NY).

Kumar, S.K. (1988), Rural Infrastructure in Bangladesh: Effects on Food Consumption and Nutrition of the Population (International Food Policy Research Institute, Washington, DC).

Kuznets, S. (1955), "Economic growth and income inequality", American Economic Review 49(1):1–28.

Kuznets, S. (1966), Modern Economic Growth (Yale University Press, New Haven, CT).

Larson, D., and Y. Mundlak (1997), "On the intersectoral migration of agricultural labor", Economic Development and Cultural Change, 295–319.

Levine, R., and D. Renelt (1992), "A sensitivity analysis of cross-country growth regressions", American Economic Review 82(4):942–963.

Lewis, W.A. (1954), "Economic development with unlimited supplies of labor", The Manchester School 22:3–42.

Lindert, P.H. (1991), "Historical patterns of agricultural policy", in: C.P. Timmer, ed., Agriculture and the State: Growth, Employment, and Poverty in Developing Countries (Cornell University Press, Ithaca, NY) 29–83.

Lipton, M. (1977), Why Poor People Stay Poor: Urban Bias in World Development (Harvard University Press, Cambridge, MA).

Lipton, M. (1993), "Urban bias: of consequences, classes and causality", in: A. Varshney, ed., Beyond Urban Bias (Frank Cass, London) 229–258.

Little, I.M.D. (1982), Economic Development: Theory, Policy, and International Relations (Basic Books, New York).

Lucas, R.E. (1973), "Some international evidence on output-inflation tradeoffs", American Economic Review 63:326–334.

Mankiw, N.G., D. Romer and D.N. Weil (1992), "A contribution to the empirics of economic growth", Quarterly Journal of Economics 107(2):407–437.

Martin, W., and D. Mitra (1996), "Productivity growth in agriculture and manufacturing", Preliminary draft (International Trade Division, The World Bank, Washington, DC).

McCloskey, D.N. (1980), "Magnanimous Albion: free trade and British national income, 1841–1881", Explorations in Economic History 17(3):303–320.

Mellor, J.W. (1976), The New Economic of Growth: A Strategy for India and the Developing World (Cornell University Press, Ithaca, NY).

Mellor, J.W. (2000), "Agricultural growth, rural employment, and poverty reduction: Non-tradables, public expenditure, and balanced growth", prepared for the World Bank Rural Week 2000, March.

Mosher, A.T. (1966), Getting Agriculture Moving: Essentials for Development and Modernization (Praeger, New York).

Mundlak, Y. (2000), Agriculture and Economic Growth: Theory and Measurement (Harvard University Press, Cambridge, MA).

Myint, H. (1975), "Agriculture and economic development in the open economy", in: L.G. Reynolds, ed., Agriculture in Development Theory (Yale University Press, New Haven, CT).

Nadav, C. (1996), "Nutritional thresholds and growth", processed (Department of Economics, Ben-Gurion University, Israel).

Nichols, W.H. (1963), "An 'agricultural surplus' as a factor in economic development", Journal of Political Economy 71:1–29.

O'Brien, P., and C. Keyder (1978), Economic Growth in Britain and France, 1780–1914: Two Paths to the Twentieth Century (Allen and Unwin, London).

Ohse, T. (1988), "Epidemiology of hunger in Africa", in: D.E. Bell and M.R. Reich, eds., Health, Nutrition, and Economic Crises (Auburn House Publishing, Dover, MA) 223–240.

Prebisch, R. (1950), The Economic Development of Latin America and Its Principal Problems (U.N. Department of Economic Affairs, Lake Success, NY).

Rausser, G. (1990), "A new paradigm for policy reform and economic development", American Journal of Agricultural Economics 72(3):821–826.

Ravallion, M. (1996), "Can high-inequality developing countries escape absolute poverty?", mimeo (Policy Research Department, The World Bank, Washington, DC).

Ravallion, M., and S. Chen (1997), "What can new survey data tell us about recent changes in distribution and poverty?", The World Bank Economic Review 11(2):357–382.

Ravallion, M., and G. Datt (1996), "How important to India's poor is the sectoral composition of economic growth?", The World Bank Economic Review 10(1):1–25.

Reynolds, L.G. (ed.) (1975), Agriculture in Development Theory (Yale University Press, New Haven, CT).

Roemer, M., and M.K. Gugerty (1997), "Does economic growth reduce poverty?", CAER II Discussion Paper No. 4 (Harvard Institute for International Development, Cambridge, MA).

Sachs, J. (1997), "Nature, nurture, and growth", Economist, June 14:19–27.

Schiff, M., and A. Valdés (1992), The Political Economy of Agricultural Price Policy, Vol. 4 (Johns Hopkins University Press, Baltimore, MD).

Schuh, G.E. (1976), "The new macroeconomics of agriculture", American Journal of Agricultural Economics 58:802–811.

Schultz, T.W. (1953), The Economic Organization of Agriculture (McGraw-Hill, New York).

Schultz, T.W. (1964), Transforming Traditional Agriculture (Yale University Press, New Haven, CT).

Schultz, T.W. (ed.) (1978), Distortions of Agricultural Incentives (Indiana University Press, Bloomington, IN).

Srinivasan, T.N. (1985), "Neoclassical political economy, the state, and economic development", Asian Development Review 1(1):38–58.

Stiglitz, J.E. (1987), "Some theoretical aspects of agricultural policies", The World Bank Research Observer 2(1):43–60.

Stiglitz, J.E. (1989), "Market failures and development", American Economic Review 79(2):197–203.

Strauss, J. (1986), "Does better nutrition raise farm productivity?", Journal of Political Economy 94(2):297–320.

Strauss, J., and D. Thomas (1998), "Health, nutrition, and economic development", Journal of Economic Literature XXXVI(2):766–816.

Summers, R., and A. Heston (1991) (updated 1996), "The Penn world table (mark 5): An expanded set of international comparisons, 1950–1988", Quarterly Journal of Economics 106(2):327–368.

Syrquin, M. (1988), "Patterns of structural change", in: H. Chenery and T.N. Srinivasan, eds., Handbook of Development Economics, Vol. 1 (North-Holland, Amsterdam) 203–273.

Teranishi, J. (1997), Presentation at World Bank seminar on research project documenting importance of investment in agricultural infrastructure.

Timmer, A.S. (1997), "Exit options and political stability", Paper presented to the Harvard/MIT Research and Training Group (RTG) Seminar in Positive Political Economy, mimeo.

Timmer, C.P. (1969), "The turnip, the new husbandry, and the English agricultural revolution", Quarterly Journal of Economics 83(3):375–395.

Timmer, C.P. (1988), "The agricultural transformation", in: H. Chenery and T.N. Srinivasan, eds., Handbook of Development Economics, Vol. 1 (North-Holland, Amsterdam) 275–331.

Timmer, C.P. (1989), "Food price policy: the rationale for government intervention", Food Policy 14(1):17–42.

Timmer, C.P. (1991), "Agricultural employment and poverty alleviation in Asia", in: C.P. Timmer, ed., Agriculture and the State: Growth, Employment, and Poverty in Developing Countries (Cornell University Press, Ithaca, NY) 123–155.

Timmer, C.P. (1992), "Agriculture and economic development revisited", in: P.S. Teng and F.W.T. Penning de Vries, special editors, Agricultural Systems 38(5):1–35.

Timmer, C.P. (1993), "Rural bias in the East and Southeast Asian rice economy: Indonesia in comparative perspective", in: A. Varshney, ed., Beyond Urban Bias (Frank Cass, London) 149–176.

Timmer, C.P. (1995), "Getting agriculture moving: do markets provide the right signals?", Food Policy 20(5):455–472.

Timmer, C.P. (1996a), "Food supplies and economic growth in Great Britain, Japan and Indonesia", typescript (Harvard Institute for International Development, Harvard University, Cambridge, MA).

Timmer, C.P. (1996b), "Does BULOG stabilize rice prices in Indonesia? Should it try?", Bulletin of Indonesian Economic Studies 32(2):45–74.

Timmer, C.P. (1996c), "Agriculture and poverty alleviation in Indonesia", in: R.A. Goldberg, ed., Research in Domestic and International Agribusiness Management, Vol. 12 (JAI Press, Greenwich, CT).

Timmer, C.P. (1996d), "Food security strategies: The Asian experience", Prepared for a conference on food security in Central America sponsored by the Food and Agriculture Organization of the United Nations.

Timmer, C.P. (1997), "Farmers and markets: the political economy of new paradigms", American Journal of Agricultural Economics 79(2):621–627.

Timmer, C.P., W.P. Falcon and S.R. Pearson (1983), Food Policy Analysis (Johns Hopkins University Press for the World Bank, Baltimore, MD).

Valdés, A. (1991), "The role of agricultural exports in development", in: C.P. Timmer, ed., Agriculture and the State: Growth, Employment, and Poverty in Developing Countries (Cornell University Press, Ithaca, NY) 84–115.

Varshney, A. (ed.) (1993), Beyond Urban Bias (Frank Cass, London) 149–176.

Williamson, J.G. (1985), Did British Capitalism Breed Inequality? (Allen and Unwin, London).

Williamson, J.G. (1990), "The impact of the Corn Laws just prior to repeal", Explorations in Economic History 27:123–156.

Williamson, J.G. (1993), "Human capital deepening, inequality, and demographic events along the Asia–Pacific rim", in: N. Ogawa, G.W. Jones and J.G. Williamson, eds., Human Resources in Development along the Asia–Pacific Rim (Oxford University Press, Singapore).

World Bank (1993), The East Asian Miracle: Economic Growth and Public Policy (Oxford University Press for the World Bank, Oxford).

World Bank (1997), World Development Report: The State in a Changing World (Oxford University Press for the World Bank, New York).

Chapter 30

THE RURAL SECTOR IN TRANSITION ECONOMIES

KAREN BROOKS and JOHN NASH

The World Bank, Washington, DC

Contents

Handbook of Agricultural Economics, Volume 2, Edited by B. Gardner and G. Rausser
© *2002 Elsevier Science B.V. All rights reserved*

Abstract

Inefficiencies in agriculture in Eastern and Central Europe and the Soviet Union contributed to the financial collapse of the socialist system. Yet during the transition, agricultural production has declined. Low profits, high real interest rates, slow progress in reforms in some countries, and uncertainty have restricted producers' ability to respond to reforms. When China's collectivized agriculture was dismantled after 1978, producers' incentives improved and the economy remained stable, fueling a large supply response. In several Central European countries where reforms are well advanced, agricultural growth has resumed. The difficulties of ten years of rural transition offer lessons about the high costs of embedded distortions and inflexibility in institutional evolution.

Keywords

central planning, collective agriculture, transition, state-owned enterprises, privatization, EU accession, land reform

JEL classification: O13

1. Introduction: From isolation to integration in Eastern and Central Europe and Central Asia

Among the paradoxes of the socialist experience in Europe and Central Asia is the poor showing of agriculture. The agricultural institutions of central planning – e.g., large unwieldy farms, distorted incentives, and inefficient investment policies – were poorly suited to modern agriculture [Pryor (1992), Johnson and Brooks (1983)]. Agriculture is widely perceived to have been a major failing of the communist model of economic organization. Yet the fall of communism in Eastern and Central Europe and the Soviet Union has not yet brought growth and recovery in agriculture. On the contrary, agriculture has been in steep decline throughout the region during the transition. Declines in aggregate production of from one-quarter to one-third over a seven-year period, as shown in Table 1, have been commonplace in this region. That the rest of the economy has contracted in many cases more than agriculture does not lessen the impact on rural people.

Table 1

Agricultural production, selected countries of Eastern and Central Europe and Central Asia (1989–1991 = 100)

	1989	1990	1991	1992	1993	1994	1995	1996	1997
Bulgaria	110.2	101.7	88.1	87.4	69.9	68.6	78.1	63.8	59.6
Czech Republic					98.7	81.4	85.8	84.7	79.9
Hungary	103.0	96.6	100.4	75.6	70.9	71.7	70.9	80.1	80.8
Poland	101.7	102.4	95.8	85.2	90.5	78.5	83.3	87.3	77.5
Romania	108.1	105.7	86.3	88.4	96.8	93.8	100.8	94.0	103.4
Slovakia					81.7	77.2	73.8	76.7	75.9
Armenia				85.6	76.2	75.6	77.4	81.3	77.9
Azerbaijan				72.2	61.2	55.5	52.0	54.7	49.2
Belarus				77.0	78.1	59.8	58.9	59.2	59.2
Estonia				74.1	66.7	55.2	51.5	49.0	47.5
Georgia				62.1	59.0	57.5	63.2	64.9	66.8
Kazakhstan				81.8	98.1	82.9	66.5	64.4	66.9
Kyrgyzstan				86.8	80.2	76.6	80.0	72.2	n.a.
Latvia				97.3	84.1	59.4	56.3	47.7	47.2
Lithuania				82.9	85.8	69.9	66.0	69.3	73.4
Moldova				73.2	74.6	58.4	61.5	55.0	55.5
Russia				82.0	78.1	67.2	60.9	63.2	64.0*
Tajikistan				69.1	74.9	72.9	66.6	60.5	63.0
Turkmenistan				92.5	92.0	97.8	100.0	63.8	73.7
Ukraine				87.6	82.5	68.0	71.1	62.9	70.6
Uzbekistan				92.1	94.7	94.1	96.8	88.5	85.1

n.a. = Not available; * = provisional.
Sources: 1989–96, FAO (1989–98); 1997, FAO (1989–98); Yearbook of Labor Statistics, 1997.

Agriculture's poor showing to date derives from several factors. The rural institutions and behaviors inherited from decades of central planning are in many respects opposites of those needed for successful integration into a dynamic global agricultural economy. Fundamental rural reforms are proceeding in an environment of national macroeconomic crisis that dampens domestic demand for food, limits resources for adjustment, and impedes establishment of needed stability. Agricultural producers have absorbed a shock to profitability as relative prices for inputs and output adjust to international trading prices without the traditional cushion of credit subsidies and debt write-off.

In addition, the understanding of those who must guide the process of reform and those who participate in it is incomplete. Important changes in the global arena, including agricultural technology, financial flows, and trading opportunities, bound the range of appropriate policies. Many policymakers in formerly planned economies are only partially informed about recent changes in the global environment of agriculture. In some cases they seek to use as a reference point the interventionist paradigms of the early post-war decades in the United States and Western Europe. These paradigms are now recognized to be costly for closed economies and unworkable in open economies, but policymakers even in developed market economies have had difficulty shifting from the interventionist paradigms to approaches more consistent with a globally integrated agricultural economy. Where the ideological constraints of the prior era weakened intellectual as well as economic integration, the knowledge base for designing appropriate policies is still weak.

Despite these current difficulties, agriculture throughout Eastern and Central Europe and the former Soviet Union shows significant potential for recovery. In some countries the recovery has already begun, as seen in Table 1. The European and Central Asian countries in transition hold approximately 15 percent of global agricultural land, and productive use of this resource has global as well as regional significance. Transfer of known and proven technology of temperate agroclimatic zones can bring increases in productivity once institutions, incentives, and resources for adoption are in place. The East Asian countries in transition, with their very different demographics and agricultural technology, face different issues from different starting positions. Here, too, the Chinese experience since 1978 has shown that substantial productivity gains are achievable when the institutional constraints of central planning are relaxed.

The transition has been underway for almost a decade, if the start is dated from the initial political events of 1989 in Central Europe. A number of preliminary observations about agriculture's role can be made at this point. In virtually all countries of the region, agricultural production has declined, reflecting over-expansion under the high levels of support and low productivity of the old regime. The two exceptions, Romania and Albania, were among the few countries in which agriculture was not highly supported, and may have been net taxed in the late socialist period.

The fall in output is a natural response to deteriorating incentives exacerbated by the rupture of traditional institutional arrangements and, in some cases, by civil unrest. Underneath the aggregate figures of decline lie three quite separate experiences. In one set of countries, civil peace either was not threatened or has been restored.

Macroeconomic stabilization has succeeded enough that inflation is moderate and real interest rates have been around 10 percent or less annually for at least three years. Sector specific reforms have proceeded far enough that investors are confident of their property rights and willing to invest. At prevailing interest rates commercial financial institutions are willing to work with promising rural clients, and recapitalization of the agricultural sector, albeit on a small scale, is beginning. In these countries growth on some farms and in some sub-sectors counterbalances continued decline in more traditional activities, and rural life has a dynamism not yet fully evident in the aggregate statistics. Macroeconomic policy, sectoral reforms, and civil peace complement and reinforce each other to promote rural regeneration. Hungary, the Czech Republic, and Poland are among these countries, and Latvia, Slovenia, Slovakia, and Croatia show similar positive trends.

Where real interest rates are consistently higher than 10 percent, agriculture remains largely cut off from commercial finance even if sectoral reforms are well underway. Inability to finance new rural ventures, in turn, constrains the response of producers to opportunities available, and dampens political support needed to push the reforms ahead. Under these circumstances reforms already implemented yield little apparent benefit, and momentum is lost. Russia in 1998 fell into this category. Although reforms in trade liberalization, privatization, and farm restructuring in Russia were significant, rural areas showed little dynamism because governmental fiscal policy pushed real interest rates out of a range accessible to rural clients, particularly since land rights – a traditional celluteral for rural credit – remained in limbo.

Much of the remainder of the former Soviet Union lags behind Russia on sectoral reforms and lacks key elements of macroeconomic stability. In some regions civil unrest has flared up sporadically, with terrible consequences for affected rural areas. Countries of the southern tier of Central Europe, notably Romania and Bulgaria, like much of the former Soviet Union, have shown uneven progress with sectoral reforms and macroeconomic stability, and are missing one or all of the triad associated with renewed rural growth although Bulgaria has recently (since 1998) stabilized its macroeconomic policy, implemented extensive sectoral reforms, and begun to show rural dynamism. Although in most of the lagging countries the imperative for reform is generally accepted, political opponents have succeeded in delaying implementation or deleting key measures. In three countries – Belarus, Uzbekistan, and Turkmenistan – the highest political leadership explicitly rejects reforms oriented toward global integration at present, and opts instead for programs of import substitution, paid for in the latter two cases largely through high implicit taxation of agriculture. In these countries the macroeconomy remains largely closed and sectoral reforms have barely started.

Agriculture's vulnerability to macroeconomic policy is consistent with the experience of more mature market economies, and is perhaps a clear indication that the economic mechanism is functioning. The difficult situation of agriculture at present reflects in large part the sector's role in destabilizing the macroeconomic and political order of the late communist era. Collectivist agriculture was economically unsustainable ultimately because the rest of the economy was unable to generate the increasingly large transfers needed to operate it at acceptable levels of output. The enormous windfall gains from the rise in energy prices after 1973, if invested wisely, could have put the Soviet Union and all of Eastern Europe in the forefront of global technological innovation for the next century. Instead they were squandered, in part on military adventurism and the arms race, but in significant part on production of ever greater quantities of subsidized sausage from unproductive herds tended by poorly motivated workers. The thoroughness with which agricultural policy and other ill-advised measures of the old order bankrupted the economy becomes clear as successive financial crises unfold, and makes the task of rebuilding even more difficult.

2. The legacy of the plan

The legacy of central planning consists of the institutions, policies, and behaviors left over from the past, and the intellectual understanding of what went wrong and why. Size is a salient feature of the legacy. Agricultural sectors in Eastern and Central Europe and the former Soviet Union are relatively large, contributing at the outset of the transition from 10 percent to as much as one-third of GDP. With a few exceptions, these countries were largely rural at the time of the adoption or imposition of central planning, and the policies of socialist agriculture slowed the exit of resources from the sector. Most countries entered the transition with more labor, capital, and land in agriculture than could be sustained as central planning was dismantled.

Socialist agriculture displayed a range of institutional variation around a core of defining characteristics, of which collective forms of organization and ownership, primacy of physical rather than financial indicators of performance, and authority of political and administrative officials in decisions on production and marketing are central. These defining characteristics derive from the political struggles, ideological debates, and economic dogmas of Soviet communism in 1928, when the first five-year plan was adopted. Once implanted forcibly into the structure created at that time, they proved only modestly amenable to subsequent reform. Many of the well-known features of socialist agriculture – e.g., the huge farms, soft budget constraints, low quality of production, merging of social and economic functions within farm enterprises, and environmental damage – derive from these defining characteristics. The features were replicated to varying degrees wherever socialist agriculture was adopted or imposed.

Despite administrative and institutional features in common, Eastern and Central Europe and the Baltics, the former Soviet Union minus the Baltics, and East Asia displayed distinct differences in their conditions at the outset of the transition, and in the course of reforms in the rural sector. In most countries of Eastern and Central Europe, communism was imposed or adopted after World War II. Input, product, and financial markets remained active even under central planning, more so than was the case in the Soviet Union. Commercial agricultural production in the private sector continued, and economic agents in the private and collective sectors had experience with market transactions. Although land was collectivized except in Poland and parts of Yugoslavia, much of the collective land in Eastern and Central Europe remained formally privately owned. Landowners could not make meaningful decisions regarding use and disposition of their property, but many nonetheless retained deeds and a knowledge of the physical boundaries of their holdings. Formal property rights in land in this part of the region were thus more mixed than in the Soviet Union, where land ownership was nationalized and management collectivized.

The decision to collectivize agriculture in the USSR was taken at the time of the adoption of the first five-year plan (1928–33). Actual planning was largely wishful thinking on the part of the political leadership until advances in linear programming techniques and computational capacity, which came much later, but the ideology accompanying the plan left no useful economic role for markets. Arguing that the market-based policies of the New Economic Policy (1921–28) had failed to deliver sufficient quantities of grain into central stocks, Stalin proclaimed that henceforth administrative orders would move resources according to politically determined objectives of production, consumption, and investment. No economic or political mechanism served as an equilibrating force, but Stalin implicitly recognized the limits of planning by allowing rural households in collectives to retain small plots of land for personal consumption and local sales. The private sector, relegated to the tiny household plots of farm members and employees, became an enduring and very important feature of Soviet agriculture [Wadekin (1973)]. The Soviet private sector, in contrast to its Eastern and Central European counterpart, was confined exclusively to the household plots. Legal and quasi-legal contractual relations between individual households and the collective sector that became common in, for example, Hungary after 1968 [Braverman, Brooks and Csaki (1993)], were never as fully developed in the USSR.

The traditional Soviet farm structure consisted of collective and state farms supplemented by the household plots of farm members and employees. On state farms workers were employees and received wages and job security determined by the economy-wide wage scale and general labor regulations. On collectives (and cooperatives in Eastern Europe), employees were members and in theory owned the non-land assets of the farm jointly. Ownership was not meaningful, and members had little voice in the operation of the farm. Until the 1960s collective farm members in the USSR could not even freely abandon their property, since they did not have guaranteed rights to the internal passports needed to move away from their villages of origin. As farm members, rather than employees of the state, they were not entitled to pay scales and benefits of the state sector.

Until reforms of 1965 in the USSR, earnings in the collective sector were lower than in the rest of the economy. Rural people carried the burden of inefficiencies in agricultural organization, as well as that of the government's policy to redistribute earnings from rural areas for investment in industry. This policy was softened after Stalin's death, and reversed under Brezhnev. Under the Brezhnev reforms after 1965, farm earnings were manipulated through price policy and cheap credit to deliver agricultural wages approximately equal to earnings in other sectors on average, as shown in Table 2.

Table 2
Average monthly wages in agricultural sector (% of the average wages in the national economy)

Country	1960	1965	1970	1975	1980	1985	1990	1995
USSR								
State sector	68.5	77.3	82.7	87.0	88.3	95.8		
Collective sector	35.0	53.2	61.4	63.1	70.2	80.5		
Czechoslovakia*	81.5	87.6	93.2	97.1	97.3	101.8	103.2	
Hungary*	91.2	91.2	98.6	96.3	95.9	95.4	85.6	75.4
Bulgaria*	95.0	89.1	86.3	94.5	86.5	85.5	113.8	69.4
Poland*	81.2	80.2	83.5	88.7	100.2	100.5	91.0	100.1
Romania*	85.6	90.5	92.5	95.8	96.5	97.3	106.1	83.2

* = Average monthly wages of employees in the state and cooperative agricultural sectors.
Source: Narodnoe khozyaistvo of the USSR in 1985 (Statistical Yearbook) Moscow, 1985, pp. 277, 397.
Statistical Yearbook; Member Countries of the Council for Mutual Economic Assistance, 1976, pp. 422–424.
Statisticheskii ezhegodnik stran-chlenov Soveta ekonomicheskoi vzaimopomoshi, 1989, pp. 417–420.
Rossijski Statisticheski Ezhegodnik, 1997, pp. 115, 122.

Collective farm members in the USSR after 1965 came under many of the same labor regulations as did employees of state farms, and many collective farms were converted into state farms. As shown in Table 2, farm earnings in Eastern and Central Europe were close to those of the non-farm sector throughout the period after 1960. By the final decades of central planning, the differences between state, collective, and (in Eastern and Central Europe) cooperative farms had diminished. Agricultural employees throughout the region worked for wages in a highly regulated environment with job security and very little linkage between productivity and earnings. The economic position of farm laborers in Eastern and Central Europe and the Soviet Union immediately prior to reforms differed markedly from that of Chinese farm laborers before the introduction of the household responsibility system after 1978. At the outset of the Chinese reforms, earnings of farm workers lagged far behind those of employees in the urban state sector, and agriculture was still taxed to provide subsidized food for urban populations [Pryor (1992)].

With the reforms in agricultural wage policy of the 1960s throughout the European and Central Asian socialist region, governments began to shift the high costs of collectivized agriculture onto their own budgets. This was a major step toward reduction of rural poverty, but it was ultimately unsustainable since it was not accompanied by reforms to increase productivity. As a consequence, agricultural subsidies contributed to cumulative macroeconomic imbalance that eventually, together with distortions in other sectors, toppled the system. Although quantification of the level of support under communism raises severe measurement issues, recent efforts by the Organization for Economic and Cooperative Development (OECD) to estimate producer subsidy equivalents in the final years of the communist period yield figures in the range of 30 to 50 percent for Hungary, the Czech Republic, and Poland, and approximately 80 percent for Russia and the Baltic Republics [OECD (1998)]. The highest levels of support in the

Table 3
Average size of farm enterprises (hectares of agricultural land)

Country	Year	State sector*	Cooperative or collective sector
USSR	1960	26104	6463
	1970	20529	6094
	1978	17548	6599
Romania	1960	3071	1495
	1970	2881	1728
	1978	5149	1660
Bulgaria	1960	5627	4865
	1970	6000	5496
Poland	1960	398	117
	1970	509	214
	1978	1894	258
Hungary	1960	2598	734
	1970	4906	1658
	1978	6394	3097
Czechoslovakia	1960	3104	421
	1970	4265	631
	1978	7663	2426
East Germany	1960	592	238
	1970	867	490
	1978	760	781

Source: For USSR: Narodnoe khozyaistvo SSSR za 60 let (Moscow, 1997), pp. 355–356, 371; for all other countries: CMEA statistical annual, 1979, pp. 224–225, 229–230, 278. Wadekin (1982).

OECD at the time were in the Scandinavian countries, Switzerland, and Japan (in the range of 70 to 80 percent), and the average producer subsidy equivalent for the OECD at the time was approximately 45 percent. Since agriculture was a larger part of the aggregate economy in socialist countries than in OECD countries, the macroeconomic burden of sectoral support was correspondingly higher.

The high costs and low efficiency of socialist agriculture derive in part from excessively large farm size, and related difficulties in management and monitoring of resource use. Farm size reflected the ideological conviction that economies of scale in agricultural production are substantial. As shown in Table 3, farms in much of Eastern and Central Europe were smaller than in the Soviet Union. The very large farms of the USSR were created through amalgamations and mergers in the period following World War II. The initial collectives of the 1930s had encompassed the land and labor force of a single village. When the village level collectives experienced financial difficulties or consistently failed to meet production plans, administrators made them larger in the belief that they would become more efficient.

Despite the assumed superiority of large farms, land, capital, and labor remained in agriculture under the planned system in quantities that were subsequently shown to be unsustainable when market pressures for efficiency emerged. The apparent resource intensity of socialist agriculture and its relatively low indicators of partial productivity (yields and labor productivity) led a number of economists outside the socialist bloc to argue that socialist agriculture is inherently inefficient compared to agriculture in developed market economies [Stuart (1983), Johnson and Brooks (1983)]. This view was not universally shared, however, either before or after the fall of communism. Even after seven years of sharp contraction during the transition, many observers within the region remain convinced that large-scale collectivist agriculture is well suited to compete with the types of farms prevalent in market economies, and that the innate advantages of the system would be apparent if producers received levels of support commensurate with those of the United States or the European Union. Lack of intellectual consensus on the inherent efficiency and competitiveness of socialist agriculture impeded efforts at reform within the socialist framework, and contributes now to difficulty in reaching political consensus on needed changes.

The theoretical basis for assessment of the relative efficiency of socialist agriculture depends critically on assumptions about the presence or absence of economies of scale, the economics of labor incentives within groups, transactions costs of monitoring hired labor in agriculture, and incentives for innovation and dynamic efficiency. Taken together, the weight of theoretical argument when wielded by an economist trained in the neoclassical tradition, including the recent innovations in institutional economics, leads to the conclusion that socialist agriculture is likely to be inefficient [Lin (1987, 1988)]. There is, however, no comprehensive or unified theory of comparative efficiency. Instead there are separate pieces of theoretical reasoning, some of which can be accepted or rejected only through empirical tests. Rigorous empirical measurement with data generated and disclosed under the strictures of central planning was difficult to undertake and not fully reliable. Measurement of total factor productivity in the USSR and climatically comparable areas of North America during the 1970s and 1980s suggested that Soviet agriculture was substantially less productive than that in the Canadian and American versions of developed market economies [Johnson and Brooks (1983)]. Empirical comparisons of productivity were imprecise and ambiguous, however, and even the practitioners were cautious about interpreting their findings, and did not always publish the results [Wyzan (1985), Koopman (1989), Brada and King (1989)]. Measurement problems abounded and many standard econometric tools were of dubious applicability to data generated under disequilibrium conditions and nonoptimizing behavior of centrally planned economies.

With neither an accepted general theory of comparison of socialist and market agriculture nor a solid body of empirical evidence, economists and observers raised in the separate Western and socialist traditions have made differing assumptions and applied differing weights to the pieces of evidence that are relevant to the whole picture. For example, a belief in economies of scale in agricultural production remains very widespread throughout Eastern Europe, Russia, and Central Asia, and in many parts of the West, as well, even though the empirical record does not support this belief. Researchers who have tested for economies of scale in market economies have in general not found them. Available evidence suggests that for farms above the very smallest range of the size distribution, major inputs are in reality quite divisible when rental possibilities exist. Johnson and Ruttan (1994), Binswanger, Deininger and Feder (1995), and Kislev and Peterson (1982) do not find evidence of economies of scale in farming. Van Zyl, Miller and Parker (1996) argue that in the case of Poland apparent economies of scale are created by policy-induced distortions in factor markets, and that the apparent advantages of larger size disappear when the distortions are removed.

Empirical tests of economies of scale are only of moderate interest where farm size is an endogenous variable of choice, and where farms of a wide range of sizes are observed to be economically viable. A finding against economies of scale is not particularly controversial because neither policy decisions nor managerial choices are based on the finding. Researchers remain interested in the topic in an effort to understand factors that affect endogenous changes in enterprise size and industry structure, but the findings are ambiguous and not high on the policy agenda.

In contrast to the relatively agnostic approach to economies of scale in the Western tradition of economic thought, under the socialist tradition the concept is sacrosanct. Where farm size is not an endogenous decision of the farm operator, and where rural people were forced onto enormous farms with a capital stock redesigned to serve large-scale production, the finding that economies of scale are either nonexistent or insignificant was in the past heretical, and is even now controversial. Many people raised in the socialist tradition require incontrovertible empirical evidence against economies of scale before they will abandon the belief that big is better. Moreover, the observed increase in average farm size in North America and Western Europe serves to confirm the belief in economies of scale among those who do not understand how changing costs of labor, information, management, and land affect farm size. Many policymakers and trained agriculturalists in Eastern and Central Europe and Central Asia fear that the reduction in farm size associated with land reform will lead inexorably to a reversion to pre-modern agricultural practices.

The organization of socialist agriculture was based on the beliefs, in addition to that of economies of scale, that collective production provided insurance against risk, encouraged adoption of advanced technology, and allowed efficient provision of public goods. Deininger (1995) examines each of these in turn. Following Binswanger and Rosenzweig (1986) he notes that the combination of moral hazard and spatial covariance of production makes agriculture an arena in which collective production is particularly unlikely to be an efficient way of insuring against risk. Moreover, price policy under central planning increased income risk, since bonuses for plan fulfillment created a positive correlation between price and quantity of production. Cooperative production could in principle speed up the adoption of technology, but collective practices discouraged individual experimentation and adaptation to varying circumstances of farmers. Uniform decisions that apply to all farms increase the risks of new technology, and Deininger (1995) cites examples from China and Cuba of clear and very costly mistakes in adoption of technology. Nikita Khrushchev's corn campaign and Trofim Lysenko's successful war against modern genetics provide a few of many examples of the high cost of politically motivated choice of agricultural technology in the Soviet experience [Joravsky (1970), Nikonov (1995)]. Deininger also examines the rationale for provision of public goods through cooperatives, and finds that in virtually all cases, more efficient vehicles are available.

Collective production suffered from serious managerial shortcomings. One problem is the difficulty of effectively monitoring effort, emphasized by Lin in the Chinese context [Lin (1996)]. This is a case study of the more general principal-agent "control problem" [Jensen and Meckling (1979)]. While monitoring is easier for processing and provision of services than for farming per se (because of the spatial dispersion of farmers), even these other activities of the collectives could not be effectively monitored. Furthermore, some disciplinary mechanisms, such as firing, were not available under this mode of production. The integrated nature of collectives encouraged cross-subsidization among different lines of business, blurring distinctions between profitable activities and loss-makers. These factors in combination led to weakening of the incentive mechanisms that promote efficiency in a market economy.

Western economists are trained to accord high importance to incentives. Most will accept the behavioral implications of theoretically demonstrated incentive failures even without extensive empirical testing. People educated under economic theories of central planning, however, do not naturally accord the same importance to incentives. Adverse economic behavior implicit in collectivist land tenure and farm organization, such as shirking or pilfering, is more likely to be identified as a moral failure of individuals, amenable to remedy by exhortation or punishment, than as a systemic failure of incentives. The importance of incentives is superficially recognized in post-communist intellectual and cultural life, but a deeper understanding of the implications of incentives for design of institutions is not yet fully in place. For example, people can simultaneously hold the views that mortgage of land should be allowed, but purchase and sale of land forbidden.

The empirical case that socialist agriculture was a failure has been clouded by the apparent high growth in output and reported gains in partial factor productivity shown during periods of growth. For example, gross agricultural output in constant prices in the USSR was reported to grow by 50 percent in the two decades following 1960. Growth was shown, however, to be due to increases in input use, not to technical change [Johnson and Brooks (1983)]. Wong and Ruttan (1990) found that the highest growth rates of land productivity were in the most industrialized socialist economies, since they could provide inputs, especially fertilizer, cheapest (that is, with the highest subsidy). Land productivity grew more slowly in the 1970s than in the 1960s [Carter and Zhang (1994)], as diminishing marginal productivity set in. Hatziprokopiou, Karagannis and Velentzas (1996) found that 90 percent of Albania's output growth was accounted for by increased input use.

The intellectual judgment on the legacy of central planning is thus read somewhat differently by those who still accept the basic premises of the collectivist tradition and those who reject them. The former believe that large farms are inherently more pro-ductive than small, and that adverse behavior can be curbed by firing managers and by public exhortation. These people are not convinced by the empirical evidence regarding economies of scale, and do not fully understand the implications of the economics of incentives. People who hold these beliefs are likely to argue in favor of minimal institutional reforms, stronger labor discipline, and massive public investment in agriculture to provide the modern technology that captures economies of scale. This is the intellectual agenda of the conservative agrarian lobbies of the region. The agrarian lobbies are often assumed to be motivated solely by rent-seeking behavior and a desire to maintain political power. In addition to other motives they may have, these people subscribe to an intellectual framework that leads naturally to rejection of institutional reforms.

Even within the Western economic tradition, the consensus that socialist agriculture is inefficient is relatively recent, and derives largely from the developments in institutional economics. The earlier economic literature on growth and development of the 1960s and 1970s focused on mechanisms for mobilization of savings and intersectoral transfer of resources in poor economies. Collectivist forms of organization of production and mandatory marketing through public sector entities such as marketing boards appeared to offer effective instruments for transfer of capital from agriculture to industry. The literature on growth and development of the 1960s and 1970s looked favorably on the apparent high growth rates achieved earlier under central planning, and did not accord much importance to the comparative statics of institutional performance; that is, to the longer-term costs or sustainability of growth. Moreover, the work on the institutions of collectivist production, such as that of Sen (1967), Oi and Clayton (1969), Israelsen (1980), and Putterman (1981), did not directly address the issue of comparative efficiency, and suggested that labor incentives would be superior in production teams than for individual laborers. Models constructed under the assumption that collective farms were genuine producer cooperatives misspecified conditions under which real socialist institutions functioned. They led to conclusions that were not relevant in practice, such as the prediction that collective farms would voluntarily understaff themselves in order to increase average returns to labor. The early analyses underemphasized the implications of soft budget constraints, the exclusion of the farm labor force from decision making, and high costs of monitoring performance of poorly motivated and spatially dispersed hired workers.

Subsequent developments in institutional economics – in particular, in the economics of contracts, moral hazard, and principal-agent theory – and Janos Kornai's (1982) seminal work on the implications of soft budget constraints provided a theoretical foundation for the argument that collective forms of organization entail high costs of monitoring and result in inefficient use of labor and purchased inputs. Justin Yi-fu Lin (1987, 1988) used this theoretical framework in an imaginative decomposition of the gains from Chinese decollectivization after 1978, and concluded that a substantial portion derived from the superior contractual incentives inherent in the household responsibility system. Lin's work offers important insight into the differing experiences of agricultural sectors in China and Eastern and Central Europe and Central Asia during the transition. A number of observers initially expected that the reforms in the former Soviet bloc would bring an early recovery in agriculture such as that experienced in

China after 1978. Lin's work confirmed that a significant portion of China's remarkable agricultural growth derived from the incentives to reduce shirking and waste, increase hours worked, and improve the quality of labor when households were assigned their own plots of land. Under the previous collective farm system, an individual worker was in principle rewarded in such a way that his private incentives at the margin exceeded the value of his production; however, because of the difficulty of monitoring, in reality his marginal incentive was much lower. For this reason, when households became the primary unit of production, and monitoring was no longer an issue, production grew rapidly for 15 years, in spite of some other underlying problems. Lin (1989b) estimates that total factor productivity increased at a rate of about 15 percent per year due to this change. Kalirajan, Obwona and Zhao (1996), using a different methodology, estimate that growth of total factor productivity increased from -5.6 percent per year during 1970–78 to 7.7 percent during 1978–84, then fell to 2.7 percent in 1984–87.

Another significant portion of the improvement in Chinese productivity was correlated with the partial market liberalization, i.e., increase in state procurement prices and reduction in procurement quantities, introduced at the same time. The price changes reduced implicit taxation of the sector, and offered rural households the opportunity to assume tenure of their land at a time when agricultural profitability was increasing. The synergy between higher output prices and decollectivization explains the residual increment in productivity. These effects, however, eventually played out, largely because of the failure to adopt a broader package of reforms. While several other factors contributed to the stagnation of grain output around 1984, each of which is emphasized by different investigators, there is a broad consensus that the continuation of the administrative pricing and large-scale consumer subsidies for grain was the major cause [on this, see Johnson (1994), Lin (1990), Sicular (1993), Putterman (1993)].

In contrast to China, where reforms were accompanied by lower net sectoral taxation, liberalization in Eastern and Central Europe and Central Asia brought reduced net subsidies and consequent decline in profitability. Agricultural producers in most of the region had received net subsidies throughout the last two decades of central planning, as expressed in the high measured producer subsidy equivalents of the OECD's analysis, and in additional subsidies delivered through soft budget constraints and not necessarily captured by conventional estimates of distortions. When prices of inputs rose relative to the price of outputs (when the energy-exporters of the region began increasing prices), the profitability of state enterprises – farms, in particular – eroded more than that of smaller, more labor-intensive private firms and farms [Van Zyl, Miller and Parker (1996), discuss this in the context of Poland].

In addition to producer subsidies, communist budgets had carried large consumer subsidies, bridging the gap between rising producer prices and controlled consumer prices. Citizens of the Council for Mutual Economic Assistance (CMEA) countries were regularly informed that increased consumption of meat at stable nominal prices was one of the benefits that a socialist economy conferred. Meat consumption increased; for example, in the USSR it increased from a reported 41 kilos per capita in 1965 to 67 kilos per capita in 1990. The inefficiencies of socialist agriculture were greatest in the livestock sector, and growth in production was achieved at increasing unit costs. With rising incomes and constant nominal prices for meat, disequilibrium grew along with per capita consumption, and perceived shortages worsened even as people consumed more. The meat subsidies were regressive, since wealthier urban consumers benefited more than poor people and rural residents. The subsidies and growing disequilibrium on food markets contributed substantially to the erosion of the ruble as a meaningful unit of exchange and store of value, and had similar, but lesser effects on currencies of other countries in the region.

Liberalization after 1990 under these circumstances brought a shock to producer incomes and declining demand for many basic food items, particularly for those with high income elasticities. The agricultural reforms of the transition were introduced when the generalized macroeconomic crisis required reduction of producer and consumer subsidies. Governments responded with often inconsistent measures. In an effort to continue support to producers, they retained some subsidies, often those targeted to the least productive activities. At the same time, to reduce the impact on consumers, price controls and export restrictions were imposed on key commodities, especially grains. As a consequence of macroeconomic crisis and discriminatory sectoral policy, the reforms in land tenure and farm structure associated with decollectivization were introduced along with changes in price and credit policy that depressed, rather than enhanced, farm profitability. Producers prior to the reforms used more inputs per unit of output than in competitive market-based agricultural economies. They thus experienced a substantial shock to earnings when exposed to relative prices prevailing outside the region without the cushioning effect of the subsidies. The array of inputs used in socialist agriculture generated sizable losses at post-socialist relative prices, even when the cost of land was excluded.

The experience of Eastern Germany (former GDR) illustrates the magnitude of the fall in profitability resulting from rapid change in relative prices imposed on existing technology of production. As shown in Table 4, East German technology in both the crop and livestock sectors was unprofitable at West German prices, and the difference was most pronounced in the livestock sector. East Germany was atypical of the region because prices of purchased inputs adjusted immediately to West German levels, and so the shock to profitability was sharper and more sudden than in other countries. East German productivity prior to unification was considered to be higher than in other countries of the region, and less efficient sectors in other countries experienced a shock even when price change was more gradual.

The shock to earnings at the farm level and to budgets at the national level resulted in a scarcity of resources available from domestic public and private sources to ease the costs of adjustment in the rural sector. In this situation, the financial contributions of the multilateral institutions and bilateral programs are crucial to easing costs of adjustment and facilitating reinvestment. Even here, however, the legacy of old institutions and lack of consensus on how to build new ones has limited the capacity of transition economies to absorb assistance from outside. Under the best of circumstances, the resources of the multilateral community would be modest compared to the magnitude of the sectoral contraction and the resources required for reinvestment. The only part of the region to

Table 4
Financial indicators of East German agriculture at West German prices (values in million DM)

Financial indicators	Crop production	Livestock production	Total agricultural production
Value of production	13,237.7	18,921.7	32,159.4
Purchased input	10,061.1	19,102.7	29,163.8
Gross value added at market prices	3,176.6	−181.0	2,995.6
Subsidies[a]	515.9	208.1	7,24.0
Taxes[a]	933.9		9,33.9
Gross value added at factor costs[a]	2,758.6	27.1	2,785.7
Depreciation[a]	1,817.4	1,305.8	3,123.2
Net value added at market prices	1,359.2	−1,486.8	−127.6
Net value added at factor costs	941.2	−1,278.7	−337.5
Wages[b]	3,875.0	4,741.7	8,616.7
Interest payments	773.2	583.2	1,356.4
Net income	−3,707.0	−6,603.6	−10,310.6

[a]Quantities are an average of 1986–1989 and prices of 1990.
[b]Inclusive wages for members of collective farms.
Monetary values directly translated into DM at the official exchange rate of 1:1.
Source: Boese et al. (1991).

experience the transition without a contraction in agricultural production is the former GDR, and the total budgetary allocation for agricultural and rural adjustment between 1990 and 1995 was DM 17.4 billion for a land area covering just over 6 million hectares, or about US$1600 per hectare [Koester and Brooks (1997)]. A program offering comparable assistance, for example, for Russia's 170 million hectares would cost approximately US$270 billion. The resources needed to manage rural adjustment according to the German approach are clearly of a magnitude exceeding the delivery capacity of the external community and the capacity of the institutions in the transition countries to absorb assistance effectively.

Strategies to finance the transition must therefore rely on three potential sources of money. Remaining budgetary resources for the rural sector must be carefully targeted to complement adjustment, rather than to prolong the life of the old order. Judicious supplemental borrowing from the multilateral organizations and bilateral donors can finance needed public goods and services, and supply additional capital for the private financial system as it begins to seek rural clients. Private capital, both domestic and foreign, will be the dominant source of finance for reinvestment.

The reform agenda should be designed with the overarching objective to attract private capital into the sector. As the rural sector is able to attract and retain capital, rural growth can recommence and new opportunities can link rural people with the rest of the domestic and global economy. A strategy to attract capital for reinvestment in the rural sectors includes land reform, restructuring of farms, reforms in the financial sector, creation of markets, improved linkage between and among markets, and more efficient public investment and expenditure. These issues form the core agenda of reform in the rural sectors of transition economies.

The reforms can thus be seen as a strategy to achieve competitiveness through reintegration in order to overcome the economic legacy of isolation and exceptionalism under the rural institutions of communism. In many respects the problems of the transition economies are not unique; throughout Africa and Latin America the state is reducing its interventionist role and providing greater scope for markets. Important lessons can be derived from the developed market economies and from the developing world. The scope of change needed, however, together with the intellectual heritage and the extremely unfavorable macroeconomic context for the reforms, makes the challenges unique in their difficulty, if not in their character.

3. The agenda of transition

3.1. Land and farms

Changes in land tenure throughout the region have proceeded at varying paces and with different outcomes. Land markets based on transactions between private agents have begun to function, although financial constraints and institutional shortcomings limit the frequency of transactions. Land values tend to be depressed by the persistent low profitability of agriculture in the transitional period. Governments within the region remain sharply divided on the risks and benefits of private ownership, the role of land markets, and how to develop them.

In Eastern and Central Europe and the Baltics, private ownership of land predominates, and land markets are gradually beginning to function. In Poland and much of the former Yugoslavia, most of the land remained privately owned and operated even in the socialist period. Throughout much of the rest of this part of the region, restitution programs returned land to those who had owned it prior to collectivization, either directly in the boundaries previously owned, or, as in Hungary, in parcels of equivalent value and approximate location allocated through an auction process [Swinnen (1997), Swinnen and Mathijs (1995)]. Restitution applied in large part to collective lands, since the collective or cooperative sector was formed through coerced amalgamation of privately owned land.

In many of these countries, state farms were originally created on land from confiscated large holdings of the church or other groups that were not made eligible under the restitution process. Separate procedures had to be designed to privatize the land in state farms. The initial emphasis on restitution of collective lands and the need to agree on procedures for privatization of state-owned land tended to slow down the privatization of the latter. Land reform in the collective sector proceeded first, and the state retained ownership of approximately 15 percent of land until 1996 and 1997, when privatization of state land accelerated in Hungary, Poland, and Romania. In the Czech Republic, state farms were privatized in a process similar to that for other state-owned enterprises. They were transformed into joint stock companies, and citizens could redeem privatization vouchers for shares, with some shares being reserved for workers and managers. This mechanism was designed in response to pressure, especially from workers and managers, not to break the farms into smaller units [Ash (1992)].

With the exception of the Baltics, restitution has not been adopted in the former Soviet Union. Land in Moldova and Western Ukraine was collectivized at the same time and through similar procedures as in Central Europe, and political pressures for restitution could have developed as they did across the borders. Legislatures in countries of the former Soviet Union have been less supportive of privatization of agricultural land than was the case in Central Europe. The constitutions of Belarus, Kazakhstan, Uzbekistan, Tajikistan, and the Kyrgyz Republic do not recognize private ownership of agricultural land. In the Russian Federation, the federal constitution of 1993 recognizes private ownership, and grants broad authority to the regions in jurisdiction over land issues. Drawing on this authority, ten constituent republics of the federation do not recognize private ownership of land. Other regions have drawn on the same constitutional authority to pass their own land laws that create a relatively liberal environment for transactions in land. The constitution specifies that the regulatory framework governing the functioning of land markets will be determined by federal law, i.e., a land code. The land code has become the most politicized of the measures of economic reform in Russia, and struggles between the legislative and executive branches of government, among factions in the Duma, and between levels of government have been protracted. The conservative position, i.e., that land cannot be an object of market transactions, would essentially isolate the agricultural sector from the growth process in the economy in general. This position has not been adopted, but neither has it been definitively put to rest. The legal guarantees for property rights in agricultural land in Russia in 1998 are therefore ambiguous; private ownership is recognized and transactions in principle are legal, but procedural issues remain unclear. Elsewhere, primarily in Central Asia, private ownership is not recognized, but legislatures have in some cases nonetheless been willing to pass land codes sanctioning long-term leaseholds with marketability that create quasi-ownership rights and allow land markets to begin to function. This is the case in the Kyrgyz Republic and in Kazakhstan.

Land markets have been slow to develop even where purchase and sale of land is legal. One survey in Poland and Hungary, two of the "cutting edge" reformers, showed that only 0.2–0.4 percent of the land in the survey area had been or was being bought or sold approximately three years into the reform process [Euroconsult (1995)]. This compares to 0.8 percent in the United Kingdom, which has a 2 to 4 times larger turnover rate. Even this difference is misleading, since the land market in the United Kingdom is presumably more or less in equilibrium, while markets in transitional countries are not, and should be very active. Because land turnover is low, consolidation of fragmented parcels occurs very slowly. This can be a problem in countries where the restitution programs resulted in fragmented small holdings, as in Hungary and Romania, or where small farms dominated the farm structure even prior to the reforms, as in Poland. Polish authorities have pursued an active policy to try to consolidate land holdings, but average farm size increased by only 6 percent between 1990 and 1996 [Christensen and Lacroix (1997)], despite incentives to older farmers to sell their land in return for higher pension benefits and subsidized credit to buy land. In many countries where ownership is widely dispersed, such as in Hungary, leasing results in consolidation of operation [Csaki and Lerman (1998)].

In part the slow pace of activity on land markets reflects the need for complementary legal institutions, such as cadastral services, titling, registration, notary services, and adjudication of conflicting claims. For example, of the five to six million land claims adjudicated in Romania since 1989, about one million were still under dispute in 1996. In addition, the legal framework in many cases constrains transactions through, for example, restrictions on the size of holdings, bans or restrictions on foreign ownership, setting of minimum purchase prices, and provision of pre-emptive purchase rights to renters, neighbors, relatives, and others.

The low volume of transactions on land markets suggests that few new landowners seek to sell their land at present, even if they have little intention to farm. Rental markets are more active than markets for purchase and sale. The restitution programs passed a portion of land in kind, usually in identified small parcels, to urban heirs of original owners, and a portion to rural people still working in agriculture. Many of the urban landowners chose to lease their parcels to cooperatives that had managed them in the past, or to new private operators seeking to enlarge their holdings. Members of cooperatives remained initially within the larger units that employed them and leased the land to the larger farm. According to one estimate, rented rural land in Poland increased from 9 percent of total rural land in 1990 to 12 percent in 1995 [Christensen and Lacroix (1997)]. Other surveys show that 7 percent of respondents in Romania and 14 percent in Armenia rent land from someone else. The proportion of leased land in Eastern Germany (former GDR) is particularly striking; approximately 90 percent of arable land in East Germany is operated under leasehold [Koester and Brooks (1997)]. Active rental markets in Eastern Germany allow enterprising private farmers to establish operations averaging 150 hectares for individual operators and over 400 hectares for partnerships. These are profitable and competitive operations when financed through leasehold, but would have required much higher start-up costs had operators chosen to purchase the land.

Conservative legislatures and rural constituencies opposing fully functioning land markets often argue that unrestricted purchase and sale will lead to rapid consolidation of land ownership in the hands of a few large speculators, with resulting increased landlessness of the rural population. The observed early dominance of leasing over purchase and sale even where the latter is permitted suggests that these fears are not well grounded. Rights of new landowners can be adequately protected by identifying and allocating land parcels, documenting ownership, and educating new owners about the relative merits of leasing compared to sale. Consolidation of holdings is likely to proceed over time, particularly where the initial allocations of parcels are small and where pensioners received a large portion of land. Excessive concentration in the short run has not been a feature of land markets where they have been allowed to function relatively freely and where land has been allocated in kind to households and individuals.

Where land was not returned to former owners through restitution, privatization took place in most cases by distributing shares of collectively owned land and assets to the farm work force, pensioners, and some other rural residents. This approach was developed in Russia in 1991, and most countries of the former Soviet Union adopted similar approaches soon thereafter [Brooks and Lerman (1994), Brooks et al. (1996), Wegren (1998)]. Recipients of shares had the right to withdraw land and assets (or the monetary equivalent of assets) from the collective to start individual private farms. Some did so, with the results that in Russia approximately 9 percent of land is cultivated individually, either in household subsidiary gardens (3 percent) or on individual farms (6 percent) [OECD (1998)]. In Ukraine, the corresponding figure is about 15 percent, including 2 percent in individual farms, and the remainder in the household gardening sector [Csaki and Lerman (1997b), Lerman, Brooks and Csaki (1994)]. Most recipients of land and asset shares, however, have chosen to remain at present with the collective entities, now restructured as various types of shareholding companies.

Where farmland and assets were privatized through share distributions, therefore, reorganizations of farm enterprises started more slowly than where restitution prevailed, as in Eastern and Central Europe. In Russia and Ukraine, much of the reorganization has been pro forma, and the resulting enterprises retain key features of the collective farm, such as employment of all shareholders and continuation of loss-making product lines. Enterprises that have gone through a well-defined process of reorganization, such as that pioneered in Russia in Nizhegorodskaia Province, tend to have better-informed shareholders, and more private farms and service firms are created in the process. The collective and corporate entities resulting even from these well-defined processes tend to be relatively large, and likely to undergo further changes in structure in the future.

Shareholders who have not reassigned land rights to corporate entities retain the right to exit from the collective with a parcel of land and a share of non-land assets. In Moldova, an initial slow exit from collective structures accelerated in 1996 as remaining members sought not to be the last to leave with the least desirable assets [Lerman and Csaki (1998)]. The Moldavian experience indicates that when exits reach a critical point, the process triggers a full-scale reorganization, resulting often in creation of a number of private farms of one or several households with private or cooperative service firms created from the nondivisible assets. Over most of Russia, Ukraine, and Kazakhstan, even after seven years of experience within the moribund old enterprises, few shareholders are yet leaving. The share distribution system has thus not brought the change in structure inherent in its legal potential. Shareholders report that they are reluctant to exit because risks are high and supporting institutions delivering services are poorly developed [Euroconsult (1995), Brooks and Lerman (1994), Brooks et al. (1996), Lerman, Brooks and Csaki (1994)]. In addition, the current structure allows shareholders to channel earnings and assets (and in many cases, subsidized inputs) to their household farming operations that are shielded from taxes, while writing off losses on the enterprise accounts.

The extent of reorganization, including the new expanded role for the household sector, may thus be greater than that indicated in official statistics. In 1998 approximately half of the value of agricultural production in Russia is reported to have originated in the household sector managing 3 percent of land. The shift in volume of production and marketing from the enterprise to the household sector will very likely shift back, at least in part, as the tax treatment of enterprises and households becomes more even, and as financial accountability strengthens.

Many remaining large enterprises report financial losses and are in arrears in payments to the budget, to employees, and to suppliers. They have remained in this status for several years because the legal framework for enforcing bankruptcy in the agricultural sector either did not exist or was not enforced. The large number of agricultural enterprises in quasi-bankrupt status reduces the volume of commercial transactions and impedes efforts to improve tax collection. A second round of reorganization in Russia, Ukraine, and Kazakhstan is likely, therefore, to focus on legal and financial restructuring of insolvent farm enterprises. Russia passed a new bankruptcy law in 1998 that, unlike its predecessor, includes agriculture. The outcome of this round will be an increased number of enterprises of various forms with a clear structure of ownership, including individual family farms, farms consisting of contiguous holdings of several households, and various other business forms. Enforcement of bankruptcy has proceeded normally in Central Europe; liquidation of a number of enterprises in Hungary early in the reform period freed assets for resale through markets and demonstrated commitment to enforce financial discipline.

There is some concern that implementation of bankruptcy procedures, while necessary for the economic health of the rural sector, could nonetheless lead to widespread unemployment and landlessness. In cases in which shareholders have invested both their land rights and their asset shares in the corporate structure of an entity that subsequently goes bankrupt, the original shareholder loses rights to the corporate land. In general, however, shareholders have been advised not to invest the ownership of the land share in the corporate entity, and to invest only the use right if they choose to remain within a larger enterprise. In that case ownership of the land remains with the individual when the corporate entity is liquidated. If additional assistance is available for start-up capital, the landowner has greater opportunity to start a new and potentially viable operation than was the case when the former enterprise dominated production in the locality. Thus even if bankruptcy procedures must be implemented on a large scale, they will not necessarily lead to landlessness and unemployment unless the enterprise sector has been formally corporatized, and ownership of land has passed to the corporations.

The same conservative agrarian lobbies that oppose purchase and sale of land in order to protect individuals against speculators often favor corporatization of the existing large enterprises. Given the precarious financial health of many of the enterprises, shareholders who invest land rights in these entities will face a high risk of losing their land along with the value of the asset share. Thus the greater threat to an egalitarian structure of land ownership comes from corporatization of the large enterprises rather than from normally functioning land markets.

3.2. Rural finance

Rural finance is arguably the most critical bottleneck in the reforms, since implementation of other measures depends on financial flows through channels that function normally in a market economy. Institutions to deliver rural financial services have proven difficult to establish, and macroeconomic conditions have constrained financial flows even when institutions exist. As a consequence, access of rural clients to financial services at competitive and affordable interest rates remains a problem throughout the region.

Prior to achievement of macroeconomic stabilization, government borrowing is high, domestic savings are low, and real interest rates are high. Even a well-developed financial sector under these conditions would reorient away from many rural activities, especially those with high risk and modest returns, such as agriculture. While real interest rates remain high, there are simply no palliative policies able to isolate the rural sector from the general macroeconomic stress. For that reason the key measure needed to initiate solutions to the problems of rural finance is not an agricultural policy instrument at all, but rather adoption and implementation of a credible program of macroeconomic stabilization.

Even under favorable macroeconomic conditions, banks have difficulty working with rural clients for a number of reasons, some unique to the transition economies, and some not. The countries of Central and Eastern Europe have been more successful in rebuilding the financial sector than has the former Soviet Union [Csaki and Nash (1998)], in part because the banks in this part of the region retained more traditional banking functions under socialism than was the case in the Soviet Union. Even in Central and Eastern Europe, however, private financial institutions willing and able to lend to farmers have been slow to emerge. In Poland, a 1993 survey found that only 7 percent of private farmers had received investment loans. In the 1994 agricultural census in Poland, 82 percent of farmers reported using no debt [Pedersen (1996)]. Even in the relatively advanced Slovak Republic, 80 percent of farm investment is from own-resources [Csaki and Nash (1998)]. Small operators seek small loans that entail high transactions costs for the banks. New farmers do not have established credit histories. Nor, in many cases, do they have sufficient collateral to secure a risky loan, since land values are depressed or impossible to know in the absence of a land market. Moveable property is either insecure as collateral or too old to have much market value. The market environment is subject to sudden shifts associated with changes in price and trade policy and currency movements.

Constraints on land markets and incomplete registration limit the value of land as pledge. For example, in Hungary a restriction on corporate land ownership intended to favor individuals and partnerships has had the unforeseen effect of precluding foreclosure by a bank, since the bank would temporarily own the asset. In Poland, in the absence of a central registry of pledged collateral, borrowers have reportedly engaged in widespread fraud by mortgaging the same land at several banks simultaneously. Banks, in turn, require collateral far in excess of the size of the loan. Even where there is no history of fraud on a substantial scale, banks require high collateral because foreclosure is expensive and risky, and the value of collateral uncertain.

Where governments have not been able to achieve stable and modest real interest rates and to strengthen rural financial institutions, they are often nonetheless under political pressure to ease the distress of rural people by providing special programs of subsidized credit. The political strength of rural constituencies and the general scarcity and high cost of commercial credit has made it difficult for the state to withdraw from subsidizing and directing rural credit. Remnants of the old system linger in many countries in the form of directed credits allocated through local governments or state banks and debt rescheduling or cancellation. Large government-owned banks have been forced to use their scarce resources to underwrite the losses of state farms or state-owned enterprises. In Romania, for example, directed loans from the agricultural bank, even at negative real interest rates, had a recovery rate of only 60–70 percent as late as 1996 [Csaki and Nash (1998)]. In other countries, government budgets are used to subsidize interest rates of commercial loans. Their political popularity notwithstanding, there is no evidence that these subsidies have a significant impact on the volume of loans reaching farmers. In Bulgaria, the subsidies have been largely unused because banks are reluctant to lend and farmers to borrow even at subsidized rates. In Poland, data indicate much the same story – the large subsidies, while they were utilized, generated little additional credit for farmers, since most of the recipients were viable farms that could have borrowed at market rates. Little of the subsidized credit went to the other farmers, who were unable to borrow even at the subsidized rates. Consequently, the increment in total credit to agriculture through the subsidy program was very little [Christensen and Lacroix (1997)].

These schemes entail a high fiscal cost in economies that can ill afford them. More important in the long run, they displace commercial lending and impede the emergence of new private financial institutions and corresponding behaviors. Administratively allocated subsidized rural credit increased from 58 percent of all rural lending to 72 percent in Poland from 1993 to 1995 [Christensen and Lacroix (1997)]. Subsidized credit programs also focus attention exclusively on lending, to the detriment of mobilization of rural savings and development of other rural financial services, such as leasing and insurance.

Creating new institutions can be more productive than offering subsidized credit, but this, too, carries risks if the demand for services is not properly understood. It is widely recognized that rural credit cooperatives can play a positive role, and these are well established in Central and Eastern Europe. Many operated even in the socialist era, and governments have assisted them in adapting to market conditions. They have been slow to expand their operations, however, in part because savings of members are low at present, and in part because they face many of the same risks as their commercial competitors. Moreover, where the traditional state banks for agriculture or private commercial banks with access to government subsidies continue to offer subsidized and directed credit to agricultural producers, the cooperative banks cannot compete. In most countries the rural cooperative banks mobilize deposits, but do little lending in rural areas. Hungary's experience with cooperative banking has been somewhat more positive than elsewhere. The government recapitalized the existing network of credit cooperatives in the early 1990s, and integrated them into a network with an apex institution and a fund to give technical assistance, training, and auditing services, with positive results.

Mechanisms for pledging collateral can be improved. In addition to land, a number of other assets commonly serve this function in Western economies, including warehouse receipts (especially in grain markets) and more generally other moveable assets. This will require substantial amendments and additions to the legal framework in most transition countries, but some have already begun using warehouse receipts on a small scale (Poland), and others are moving quickly to put the framework in place. Credit from input suppliers and advance payments from agrobusiness are other potentially important sources of credit for farmers, and these are developing slowly throughout the region.

Government guarantees for commercial bank lending can be used successfully, but, because they echo the role that the government played in the prior financial system, they carry considerable risk. Guarantees can create moral hazard on the part of the lenders, who will have less incentive to exercise due care in evaluations of loan applications. They increase contingent liabilities for the treasury. However, a guarantee does address the problem of missing markets for collateral in a way that can distort markets less than do interest subsidies and administratively allocated credit. Moreover, partial guarantees may increase the experience of commercial banks with rural clients, leading to better knowledge of clients and reduced costs of service in the future. If structured in such a way that banks assume a significant share of the default risk, and borrowers pay commercial rates, this may be a reasonable temporary response while the other mechanisms for collateralization of loans are developing. Experience in Hungary has been relatively positive with a partial guarantee fund. Excessive use of governmental guarantees for commercial lending, however, has clear risks increasingly evident, for example, in Ukraine and in some regions of Russia. Where governments have provided guarantees to finance provision of inputs, they have also sometimes required that producers benefiting from the program deliver output to designated agencies, such as a regional food fund providing products to local consumers at preferential prices. Under these circumstances, unlike those in Hungary, the governmental guarantee serves to perpetuate the administrative relations of central planning, rather than to bridge the changeover to more fully functioning private markets.

Community-based micro-credit programs have been successful in some countries, particularly those in which institutional breakdown has been most severe and income levels are lowest. In these countries large numbers of rural small-holders have little access to subsidized credit, even if it exists. Households want to borrow very small amounts – for example, enough to buy one cow. Although people emerging from enforced cooperative relationships are sometimes reluctant to enter into new ones, community-based micro-credit schemes designed on principles of joint and several liability have been successfully introduced in some countries, e.g., Albania and Georgia. The performance of these credit schemes in the early period has been acceptable. In

Albania repayment rates were 99 percent until the collapse of the financial sector in 1996/97, and have never fallen below 90 percent.

3.3. Reforms of price policy and trade

In periods of radical reform, it is not unusual for governments to revise drastically the roles of various participants in markets, by redistributing property rights, changing the regulatory framework for transactions, and changing the policies that affect incentives. Rarely have governments had to create, in a short period of time, markets *de novo*. In this respect, the transition is unique, and different in kind as well as degree from other episodes of reform. In Eastern and Central Europe, nascent markets existed and could be developed, but in the former Soviet Union, the pre-existing black markets did not provide a foundation for a normal market economy, since they were part of the framework of the administered economy. Market development in the transition has had three critical elements: reforms in pricing and associated trade policy to integrate domestic and global markets; privatization to create new economic agents; and institutional and regulatory reforms to govern transactions.

The trade policy of socialist countries relied more on explicit export restrictions, and less on import controls, than did that of most developing countries. A very large part of the exports of the CMEA countries comprised raw materials. Export controls simultaneously allowed domestic users of raw materials to benefit from lower prices, and prevented exporters from appropriating gains from arbitrage as they moved products onto higher-priced international markets. The pervasive and chronic shortages, particularly of consumer goods, fueled an attitude that local production should be reserved for markets within the socialist bloc. Travelers leaving the Soviet Union as recently as in the late 1980s faced notices informing them that it was illegal to carry out products in domestic short supply, such as toothpaste. This attitude survived the breakup of the bloc and was reflected in a variety of taxes, regulations, and foreign exchange surrender requirements on exports, and in some cases outright bans [Michalopoulos and Tarr (1994a)].

On the import side, state trading organizations and the state monopoly on foreign trade allowed the implicit taxes on exports to subsidize priority imports. Thus, the socialist economies followed the pattern common in developing countries, and documented by Krueger, Schiff and Valdés (1991), of penalizing exportables, and generally subsidizing consumption of staples.

Trade policy early in the transition retained a number of these features, although the explicit role of state trading organizations was reduced, and the state monopoly on trade dismantled. As private traders gained a legal position, tariffs, export taxes, and non-tariff trade barriers replaced the administrative actions of the state trading boards. Retention of trade barriers implicit in the traditional trading patterns exacerbated the reduction in the volume of trade resulting from financial crisis and rupture of traditional institutional arrangements. Even barter trading arrangements began to break down, though some survived well into the mid-1990s. Currency problems added to barriers created or retained by trade policy. Payments were required in hard currency, which was in short supply and rationed in most countries. In particular, as Russia and other energy exporters in the bloc began to charge market prices, their trading partners experienced a large adverse shock in terms of trade, which further shrank the supply of convertible currency available for other imports. The ruble survived in the former Soviet Union as a common currency and medium of exchange until 1993. Central banks of the former republics retained the right to create rubles, however, and their countries ran unchecked trade surpluses with Russia, leading to the dissolution of the ruble zone. By the end of 1993 all of the countries resulting from the breakup had introduced their own currencies. These for the most part, however, were not convertible, and efforts to create a clearing mechanism for inconvertible currencies came to naught [Gros (1994a)]. All these factors led to a virtual collapse in trade between countries of the former Soviet Union and their foreign partners. Central European countries with long-established currencies did not face the same problems, but still had to dismantle state trading companies and the procedures of the state monopoly on foreign trade.

Given this initial situation, the first order of priority in trade policy was to move to convertible currencies and to reduce export controls. Decontrol of exports other than industrial raw materials and food products proceeded fairly quickly. Countries have moved at different speeds toward convertible currencies, but some now have currencies that are fully convertible on current account and trade regimes that resemble those of OECD countries. Removal of direct controls on consumer prices and reduction of subsidies proceeded fairly early in most Central European countries. These were carried out in Poland, Hungary, and Czechoslovakia in 1990–91, and initiated in Russia and a number of neighboring countries in January of 1992. There was virtually no targeted food assistance program, but consumers were given some cash assistance. Food prices increased by about 30–40 percent, and consumers adjusted quickly. Prices later declined as supply responded to the higher prices [Csaki (1993)].

Agricultural products and raw materials have typically been the last products for which export controls were removed. The Slovak Republic, its advanced reform status notwithstanding, still in 1998 had non-automatic export licensing requirements for a number of "sensitive" products. For raw materials, in this region as elsewhere, the motive in retaining export controls is to benefit manufacturers that use these inputs. For food staples, the motivation is somewhat different. Countries fearing domestic shortages, usually because of policy-induced production problems, see the export controls as a tool for food security. Even traditional grain exporters, such as Bulgaria and Romania, have instituted export controls for grains under generalized economic difficulties that have caused production to collapse. Trade restrictions and implicit taxation of the grain sector during the global rise in grain prices in the mid-1990s were particularly costly for agricultural sectors already burdened with high costs of adjustment.

Several Central European countries introduced agricultural trade policies resembling those of the members of the European Union, with no quantitative controls, but relatively high tariff protection afforded to import substitute products (Poland, Hungary,

Lithuania) [on this, see Ash (1992); Safin and Guba (1996) quantify the anti-export bias in Poland's trade regime]. Though tariffs are still moderate by standards of the EU, they are higher than those on most non-agricultural imports and have been rising. Pressure for increased protection has been exacerbated by the real appreciation of the exchange rate in countries that have attracted significant capital inflows and by the example of the EU and its subsidized exports. This has led in some cases to over-reaction, with increased protection more than offsetting the exchange rate effect, as in Poland [Christensen and Lacroix (1997)]. In spite of a significant appreciation of the real exchange rate, producer support prices of most major crops in Poland have risen in real terms since 1991.

Also in common with the Western European countries' past policy, most of these more advanced reformers use export subsidies for selected commodities (sugar in Poland, milk in the Slovak Republic, several crops in Hungary). In addition to their budgetary implications (Hungary's export subsidies in 1998 amounted to around 0.5 percent of GDP), the subsidies in Hungary have breached its World Trade Organization (WTO) commitments and created a major irritant with other WTO members.

Some of the Central European countries are already WTO members (Bulgaria, Czech Republic, Hungary, Poland, Romania, Slovak Republic, Slovenia) and joined before the reforms, though as centrally planned economies they did not formerly enjoy all the privileges of membership. In particular, the rules applied to them made it easier to impose large anti-dumping penalties on their exports [Kaminski (1994)]. With the exception of Bosnia, those that were not members before have applied and are at various stages of accession.

As WTO members, these countries accepted the Uruguay Round obligations to remove quantitative restrictions, to reduce tariffs and export subsidies, and to lower aggregate measures of support in agricultural products. However, WTO membership has not led to much reduction in tariff levels in agriculture. Like developing countries, transition countries were allowed to make offers in the Uruguay Round unrelated to base period conditions [International Policy Council on Agriculture, Food, and Trade (1997)]. As a result, tariffs were generally bound at levels much higher than rates currently applied. Poland's weighted average tariff on agricultural products went from about 20 percent before WTO membership to 24 percent after, and is scheduled to fall to 18.6 percent by 2000. Poland did, however, have to quit using its variable levy scheme and convert its specific tariffs to ad valorem equivalents. Few of these countries have an entitlement to subsidized exports, but of those that do, WTO commitments have not reduced the subsidies significantly. Although the commitments under the Uruguay Round have not had a major impact on levels of protection in Central Europe, countries have nonetheless been drawn into the general framework governing international trade. For example, Hungary was called to account for its performance with regard to commitments to reduce export subsidies and aggregate support. After considerable acrimonious negotiation, and clarification of the original commitment, Hungary was granted an extended time to meet its obligation.

All but four countries of the former Soviet Union have applied for WTO membership. The Kyrgyz Republic has acceded (December 1998), as has Latvia (February 1999), and some others are close as of mid-1999, including Estonia. Others are on a slow track [Michalopoulos and Tarr (1994a)]. Some have followed a strategy of applying for membership as developing countries. This has the disadvantage that because of the great latitude allowed developing countries, membership under this status is a much less convincing signal of a commitment to maintain an open trade regime.

Most OECD countries have granted Most Favored Nation status and eligibility for the Generalized System of Preferences (GSP) to the Central European countries and, starting with the Baltics in 1992, to the countries of the former Soviet Union. Nonetheless, because GSP provisions exclude many of the major exports of the region, and because a number of the countries are still treated as state trading countries in trade disputes, barriers to trade with the West have declined relatively little. In early 1998 Russia shed its designation as a state trader, and achieved the status of a market economy (a development noted with bemused irony by the domestic financial community preoccupied at the time with perilously volatile financial markets).

As the countries of the region seek new trading relationships, some have explored signing and in some cases signed free trade agreements. The Baltic countries have signed free trade agreements with several Scandinavian countries and Switzerland (excluding agriculture, however). The EU has negotiated Partnership and Cooperation Agreements with most of the former Soviet countries, beginning with the Baltics. These provide for mutual Most Favored Nation treatment, removal of quantitative restrictions on trade, and eventually a free trade area. The latter, however, depends on progress in the transition to a market economy [Kaminski (1994)]. Poland, Hungary, and the Czech Republic signed the Central European Free Trade Agreement (CEFTA). In addition to the CEFTA arrangement, countries are actively pursuing bilateral preferential arrangements among themselves.

Although trade under the CEFTA agreement, for example, grew quickly (though from a low base), the economic effects of regional trade agreements are ambiguous. For most products, an agreement to eliminate tariffs among regional partners will not result in any reduction in prices within the regional market, as long as marginal requirements continue to be supplied by imports from outside the region. This implies that no trade will be created in these products; rather, the only effect will be that exporters receive the money formerly collected by importing country governments as tariff revenues on intra-regional trade. Thus, in each product market where this occurs, regional exporters gain and governments in the importing countries lose. The net effect on each country depends on the sum of these product-specific impacts in its own import and export markets, but in general, the biggest losers are treasuries in high-tariff countries that are net importers from within the region [Panagariya (1998)]. In any case, agricultural products are not fully incorporated into the CEFTA agreement, and there are a number of loopholes that are likely to minimize trade in "sensitive" products, that is, the heavily protected food products in which increased trade could be most beneficial.

Creation of a common agricultural market or free trade agreement among Russia, Belarus, Kazakhstan, and the Kyrgyz Republic, with possible expansion to include additional regional members, has been under discussion for several years, and agreements have been signed. Although the volume of trade in agricultural commodities among former trading partners of the socialist bloc increased after the nadir of 1993 and 1994, the improvement is due to better establishment of the currencies and bank clearing arrangements. For political and economic reasons there is little expectation that a common agricultural market with much practical impact can be formed.

All of the Central European countries officially aspire to membership in the European Union, and most (including the Baltics) have signed agreements known as Europe Agreements to join. Albania and the countries of former Yugoslavia (except for Slovenia) have not yet signed agreements. Based on the EU's mid-1998 evaluation, it is generally expected that the first countries to accede (though not necessarily simultaneously) will be Poland, Hungary, the Czech Republic, Slovenia, and Estonia.

Accession poses thorny issues for the EU. Extension of the current version of the Common Agricultural Policy to new Central European members would be expensive for both the old and new members. [Both Buckwell et al. (1994) and Tangermann and Josling (1994), contain surveys of estimates for different countries and for the EU as a whole.] As an example, Orlowski (1996) estimates costs of over $3 billion per year for taxpayers and consumers in Poland, with a reduction in GDP growth of about 0.2 percent per year. Inclusion of even a few Central European countries, with agricultural sectors relatively larger than in current EU members, would almost certainly result in exportable surpluses that would break the EU's commitments under the Uruguay Round agreements [Buckwell et al. (1994)]. Accession-related concerns such as these have added weight to the traditional arguments for reform of the Common Agricultural Policy, including proposals for radical reforms that would completely eliminate support prices. Alternative programs would focus instead on stabilization, payments for environmental and cultural services, rural development incentives, and transitional assistance [Buckwell (1997)].

The Europe Agreements differ in details among countries, but generally grant some immediate preferential access to EU markets for designated products, expand this access over time, and stipulate the process by which accession will occur, without a fixed timetable. Over time since 1990 barriers to importation of non-agricultural products from Central Europe into the European Union have declined or been eliminated, but constraints on agricultural imports remain.

Accession to the European Union will require a major effort to revise legislation, regulatory standards, and testing institutions to ensure their compatibility with those of the EU. For agricultural inputs (seeds, livestock breeding material, chemicals) and unprocessed outputs, phytosanitary and environmental norms will have to be considered as well. Harmonization will require investment in testing equipment, and this is difficult in the current fiscally stringent environment; in some countries, this is an important bottleneck [Network for Agricultural Policy Research and Development (1997)]. Laws affecting investment will also have to be harmonized. In agriculture, one implication of this is that the current restrictions on foreign land ownership (as in Poland) will have to be revised.

The prospect of accession has undoubtedly hastened the reform process in most Central European countries, and the incentive to harmonize legislation, institutions, and standards with those of the EU has had beneficial results. However, in agriculture, one adverse consequence unique to this sector has been a temptation to increase protection in order to harmonize with the mechanisms and rates of support given by the Common Agricultural Policy. Indeed, one of Poland's first steps in 1994 was to introduce some of the CAP measures as they existed before the MacSharry reforms. Thus the incentive structure has come to resemble that of the EU, with the producer subsidy equivalents for agriculture increasing from negative levels immediately at the outset of the transition to 21 percent in 1994, while the consumer subsidy equivalent went from slightly positive to a negative 18 percent [World Bank (1997)].

This tendency has arisen in spite of the ongoing debate on the future of the Common Agricultural Policy within the European Union. With land productivity in Poland about a third of that in the EU, and labor productivity in the sector about a tenth, adoption of high support prices would not contribute to making the sector more competitive. Furthermore, the consequences would be highly negative for Polish consumers, who spend a larger share of their incomes on food than do their counterparts in the EU.

Understanding of the full implications of membership in the European Union has not yet become widespread among the populations. There is, however, a dawning recognition that the impact on agriculture is likely to be greater than in other sectors. Agricultural parties in Hungary, Poland, and Slovenia have expressed some misgivings about the process, but the prevalent political sentiment for the countries as a whole is an overriding desire to grasp an historic opportunity to solidify linkage with the West. The domestic politics of accession within the countries will be complex, and agricultural constituencies are likely to agree to policies that will entail even more adjustment than has taken place so far.

3.4. Privatization

Privatization of assets in marketing and input supply has moved relatively slowly. Only in a few countries (e.g., Hungary, Slovak Republic) has the privatization process been largely completed for the larger industries. The privatization process in agroindustry has paralleled that in other industries, and has shared the same financial constraints and administrative bottlenecks. At the same time, additional concerns particular to food markets have arisen. Governments have been reluctant to allow full privatization of the grain and bread complex, due to concerns about food security. Thus grain storage facilities in Bulgaria and Romania, for example, and bakeries in Georgia remained in state ownership long after most other assets were privatized. State control over the grain sectors in Turkmenistan and Uzbekistan is complete, with retention of mandatory state orders and state-owned processing and marketing monopolies. Concerns about food security and reliability of the private sector have also delayed privatization of key input providers, such as for fertilizer and seed. In addition to concerns about food security, governments (for example, in Moldova, Ukraine, and Russia) have attempted to privatize processing facilities in ways that give local producers of raw materials a dominant share of ownership. This is intended as a measure to reduce the potential monopoly power of privatized processors.

Slowness in developing the legal framework and court system for enforcing bankruptcy also stalled the process. Many of the enterprises were allowed to accrue large losses, without being forced into bankruptcy or liquidation. Management and workers lobbied to ensure that they were given priority in the privatization process. The slow pace of the process had the consequence that in those cases where it was clear that the current management and employees would not become owners, they had no incentive to care for the plant and equipment. Vandalism and theft resulted.

State farms have retained privileged access to subsidized credit, either explicitly or through debt forgiveness, as well as preferential input supply from state-owned suppliers. They have had little need to purchase inputs from private suppliers, and the small family farmers are constrained by their cash flow and their inability to take advantage of scale economies in purchase. Thus private suppliers and marketers have little incentive to enter the market. Nonetheless, where fundamental restructuring of the former large farms was mandated through the land reform and restitution process, as in Hungary, a number of enterprises spun off small companies providing services and inputs. In contrast, in Russia, Ukraine, and other countries where the enterprise sector is still largely intact, there has been little creation of such firms in marketing and input supply. Competition from foreign suppliers of inputs is constrained by trade barriers and by the difficulty of arranging trade finance. Under these circumstances, although domestically produced inputs, such as machinery and fertilizer, are available in more than adequate supply, the level of service provided by the input supply industry has not improved, and may have even deteriorated.

As a result of all these obstacles to private sector development, state agencies or parastatal successors to the state agencies remain active in input supply. In a survey in a group of countries (Albania, Bulgaria, Hungary, Poland, and Romania), Albanian farmers showed the lowest dependence on state sources of input supply [Euroconsult (1995)]. There, the fraction of farmers who bought from state suppliers was between 26 and 58 percent of all farmers who used purchased inputs (depending on type of input), though input use was very low overall. But in the other countries, this figure was much higher, around 80–95 percent in Bulgaria, Romania, and Hungary, and 45–50 percent in Poland. The role of the state in input supply has declined over time but remains higher than in other sectors.

The state also retained an active role in marketing of output in all these countries, though the majority of private farmers responding to farm surveys report that they have a choice of buyers. Primary commodity marketing agencies have been particularly resistant to full privatization, primarily because the state is reluctant to relinquish its ability to use these as channels for direct procurement. In Poland, where 70 percent of agroindustrial firms have been privatized, the major hold-outs are in the cereals and sugar subsectors. Poland's grain agency has even increased its role as measured by intervention purchases, up from 23 percent of marketed surplus in 1993/94 to 52 percent in 1994/95. One effect of this is to destabilize domestic prices, partially because the agency has been a very poor predictor and has bought and stored large quantities of wheat expecting shortages, only to be forced to sell in a declining market (and further depress prices) when it became obvious its forecasts were wrong. Even where parts of these agencies were spun off, the remaining state agency sometimes kept the best storage and handling facilities, as in Romania.

Privatization of non-farm enterprises in rural and urban areas alike has been carried out through two basic types of legal mechanisms: case-by-case and mass privatization. The former has the benefits of generating revenue, establishing clear shareholder control, and providing access to capital and skills, while the major advantages of the latter are that it is (or can be) fast, promotes widespread participation, and generates political support for the process [Goldberg, Jedrzejczak and Fuchs (1997)]. There was, early in the transition process, also another form, euphemistically referred to as "spontaneous privatization", which was largely an appropriation of state assets by enterprise managers, but this was eventually brought under control [Johnson and Kroll (1991)].

Many countries have relied on some variant of vouchers for mass privatization, especially for small businesses of all types. This involves the distribution to the general population of vouchers to be used in bidding on shares in the firms being privatized. In some cases, the state maintains control of some fraction of the vouchers [about 20 percent in the Czech and Slovak Republics, for example, see Network for Agricultural Policy Research and Development (1997)]. Funds have emerged in several countries as vehicles for voucher recipients or shareholders in enterprises being privatized to pool their resources. In the Czech Republic and Russia, these funds were not directly allocated shares, but rather had to form spontaneously and then advertise to attract investment of vouchers from the public, which the funds then used to bid for shares in companies. In Poland and Kazakhstan, however, the national investment funds were given shares in the companies being privatized, and then individual voucher recipients could exchange their vouchers for shares in the funds. Each fund took a lead role in particular firms. The biggest part of the vouchers in the Czech Republic is controlled by investment funds, which in turn are owned by large Czech banks. This arrangement was in some ways fashioned after the German model, in which banks and industry have close ties.

In Hungary or Poland bank-owned funds have been much more reluctant than creditors to force poorly performing firms into liquidation or restructuring. More than 30,000 firms in Hungary have gone through bankruptcy, but not a single important one has in the Czech Republic. Reluctance to pursue bankruptcy may have contributed to the poor competitiveness of Czech firms, resulting in a large trade deficit and in 1997 a currency crisis. In Russia, the voucher privatization scheme was a hybrid. Voucher-holders received 29 percent control of each company, with the rest of the shares allocated in such a way that management and employees usually kept controlling interest. The right to purchase assets being privatized has been restricted in various ways. The government of Romania, for example, restricts the sale of state-owned agricultural machinery companies to workers, farmers, and residents of the surrounding areas.

The system used in Poland took considerably longer to set up than did the schemes in other countries, delaying the mass privatization program there. While awaiting privatization, the state-owned farms and agroindustries were transferred to a large off-budget holding company. The privatization agency has moved relatively slowly, and in the meantime the industries continue to incur losses. Some state farms have largely ceased to function, while the land of others is leased out. The agency has large unserviced debts.

Where foreign firms have been attracted into processing sectors, they have done so largely through the case-by-case process. Hungary and Estonia have been particularly successful in attracting foreign investment, with around 45 percent of the food processing industry in Hungary now foreign-owned. In other countries, civil unrest and perceived high risk limit the interest of foreign partners, and the privatization process itself does not encourage participation of foreigners in the early round.

In general, privatization of the small-scale businesses proceeded much faster than large-scale, partially because privatizing the latter has more significant implications for employment. Retail, trading (except primary commodity market agencies), and small service sectors have been largely privatized by now. Large-scale domestic and international firms have made inroads in the retail food sectors in some countries, with salutary impact on quality control.

Several attempts have been undertaken to evaluate on a theoretical or empirical level the optimality of different schemes for privatization [see, for example, Boycko, Shleifer and Vishny (1994), Katz and Owen (1995)]. Katz and Owen (1997) construct a formal model to evaluate the Czech, Polish, and Russian systems, based on the degree to which vouchers are allocated to individuals or funds best able to govern the companies. Their conclusion is rather agnostic, however, with the outcome depending on whether the general public or government is better able to judge the ability of funds to govern specific companies, and on the ability of insiders to restructure from within. In the end, they conclude that voucher privatization is probably a better tool for mobilizing popular support than for assuring economically optimal outcomes. Glaeser and Scheinkman (1996) focus on the optimal sequencing of privatization. In their model, the major advantage of private over non-private firms is the ability to assimilate and diffuse market information. They therefore argue that privatization should take place first in sectors where information is most critical. They rate the importance of privatizing sectors in ascending order as retail trade, upstream production, and downstream production. Retail trade is lowest priority because no production decisions are made there. The downstream sector dominates the upstream because of its importance in both production and in transmitting information on market demand to the upstream sector. While it is hard to dispute the importance of information, it is also important to note the contribution that upstream sectors can make to technology transfer, particularly in agriculture and agroindustry. Failure to restructure input and capital equipment manufacturers, and to allow farmers and food manufacturers access to imported technology, has impeded their ability to improve efficiency.

Experience suggests that speed is more important than technique in privatization. Quick progress gives opponents less time to organize resistance, generates tangible benefits faster, and allows a new government to take advantage of a honeymoon period to signal its commitment and begin a virtuous cycle of investment [Rodrik (1989)]. While tradeoffs should be taken into account – including the possibility of a backlash from politically powerful losers [Wei (1993)], the danger that a fast-moving privatization process might be overly centralized [Rausser and Simon (1992)], and the disruptions that may be necessary to kick out the old guard [emphasized in the formal model of Lyons, Rausser and Simon (1996)] – experience here as elsewhere has shown that slow or piecemeal reform efforts often get bogged down. Slow privatization, in particular, creates uncertainty, which has been disruptive of production, as collective farms were reluctant to invest resources into sowing when it was unclear who would harvest [Ash (1992)]. Delay also creates opportunities for rent-seeking and corruption, particularly since corporate governance of firms that are in limbo between state and private ownership has proven to be difficult [Lieberman et al. (1995)]. Kaufmann and Siegelbaum (1996) emphasize this and, in evaluating different types of privatization for their potential to breed corruption, give the most positive marks to vouchers for mass privatization, and to liquidation, of which there has probably been too little in most countries (Hungary and Estonia are possible exceptions). Vouchers and liquidation are swift and give less room for bureaucratic meddling. Kaufman and Siegelbaum recognize that the German privatization was based on very different principles (tenders and trade sales) without being marked by corruption, but note that this was due to the institutional framework in which it was carried out, which differs greatly from that in most transition economies.

An important but under-emphasized component of a privatization strategy is the removal of barriers to competition to ensure that public monopoly is not replaced by private monopoly. This may not require an "antitrust policy" as that term is sometimes used, with laws and agencies to evaluate the market power of particular firms, an approach which has had mixed results in the West. An open trade policy and low barriers to entry (for new firms) and exit (for old ones) can effectively limit how much market power can be exercised by both newly privatized enterprises and those awaiting privatization. Governments in the former Soviet Union have in several instances created special procedures for privatization of agroindustry, and passed a dominant share of ownership to primary producers, thereby attempting to delegate market power rather than to disperse it. When the new strategic owners are traditional local agricultural enterprises, the new ownership structure is not likely to bring an infusion of capital or new ideas about management or marketing. The producers themselves are often insolvent, and facing reorganization through bankruptcy.

Privatization of marketing and input supply has received considerable attention and is controversial, but new entry has arguably had a greater impact on competitiveness of the sector. There is relatively little that governments can do to stimulate new entry, although small business incubators offering physical space, communications, and advice to new entrepreneurs have had some success in Poland. The government's greatest contribution is to reduce barriers to entry, such as cumbersome licensing requirements, and to avoid granting privileges to existing enterprises.

3.5. Legal and regulatory reform

Required legal and regulatory reforms span the entire range, from new constitutions to new standards for product quality. Some observers have argued that policy prescriptions for countries in transition are of distinctly secondary importance, since with an appropriate constitutional framework, correct policies will emerge endogenously [Rausser (1990)]. Rausser (1992) surveys some of these issues and lays out a number of principles of constitutional design, arguing that among the most important principles to be embodied in the constitutions are diffusion of political power, ease of representation of alternative views in the political arena, rule of law widely accepted as fair, and clear limitations on governmental authority. The constitutional order needs to be embodied in the legal systems. Posner (1998) surveys some critical issues here, including the questions of to what extent foreign laws can be transplanted (he is optimistic) and what the tradeoffs are between investing in complex legal systems which require a strong judiciary and legal profession, versus simple laws that are not very comprehensive but are relatively cheap to enforce. While these are not very relevant issues for the countries that will accede to the EU and will harmonize legal systems with the EU fairly closely, other countries will need to resolve these issues.

Constitutions and civil codes are in place throughout the region, and yet agricultural activity continues to suffer from gaps in the regulatory and legal framework, suggesting that the large issues and the detailed regulatory reforms are equally important. For example, regulatory lacunae constrain trade finance. This issue is one of a number that must be addressed to facilitate integration of these economies into global markets [Nash (1994), United Nations Economic Commission for Europe (1995)]. Even for transactions that are likely to be profitable, local banks demand full cash collateral to issue letters of credit. Correspondent banking relations are slow to form because of the lack of track record of countries as well as firms, and foreign correspondent banks generally refuse to confirm letters of credit issued by banks of the region without full collateral by those banks in the form of deposits. Export credit insurance markets are very slow to develop, stifled by the shallowness of financial markets, which makes it difficult to pool risks. Insurance is available for some import transactions, provided by export credit insurance agencies in the selling countries, but this is generally restricted to short-term transactions or to firms that are backed, implicitly or explicitly, by government guarantees. Small private firms find themselves at a strong disadvantage.

Regulatory deficiencies constrain the flow of new technology into the region. Lack of legal protection for intellectual property obstructs transfer of technology in agriculture, particularly in seeds. In the absence of appropriate protection, multinationals are reluctant to sell some of their best products. While these kinds of issues are often viewed as secondary to more general trade policy reform, they present barriers to flow of technology needed to increase productivity.

Seed regulations of the transition economies are generally more similar to the developing country pattern than to those of developed economies. The former tends to be more restrictive; it prohibits the import of seed varieties that have not undergone fairly extensive in-country tests to prove their superiority over existing varieties. In part, this reflects the paternalistic attitude common in the developing countries, and in part the perceived threat to the local research establishment represented by improved inputs from abroad. Introduction of new varieties is delayed and farmers are denied access to productivity-enhancing technology until it is virtually obsolete, since the effective commercial life of new varieties is often not much longer than the required testing period. And for small markets, the expense of testing makes it unprofitable for international companies to introduce new varieties. More advanced countries either require no testing or waiting other than what is needed to ensure that seeds are carrying no pests (U.S. model) or pool the lists of allowed varieties, so that varieties approved in one country are automatically allowed into others (EU model). The EU model is more restrictive than the U.S., but dramatically expands the potential market and increases returns to introduction on new varieties. Romania and Bulgaria, for example, have adopted the EU's Common Catalogue of Seeds, and automatically allow import of varieties on this list (upon satisfaction of phytosanitary requirements), with no additional performance testing. This may be a reasonable approach for all the countries in line for accession. For countries not joining the EU in the near future, a better strategy may be to eliminate compulsory varietal registration totally, as in the United States.

Similarly, old-style pesticide regulations impede access to the new generations of environmentally friendly biopesticides. By requiring new chemicals to pass efficacy tests based on the same criteria, regardless of the level of risk, these regulations keep farmers locked into the old broad-spectrum poisons. Among the transition countries, Slovenia has the most advanced regulations. These allow registration of a new low-risk biopesticide without efficacy tests if it is already registered in two EU countries, and allow import of pheromones without registration. Other transition economies would benefit from adoption of similar regulations.

Regulatory reforms are needed to allow markets for risk management to function. Mechanisms and knowledge for managing risk have become increasingly important in the global agricultural economy. Although fluctuation of agricultural commodity prices will be reduced as barriers to trade are lowered, domestic producers will be more exposed to variability than under the socialist regime because of the closer links between domestic and world prices. A wider array of risk management tools exists than ever before, but taking advantage of them demands specialized skills and appropriate institutional and policy frameworks.

While governments in some transition countries have expressed interest in developing commodities futures exchanges to manage risk, little progress has been made. Commodity exchanges exist in several countries, but these are spot markets or at best forward markets that rely on eventual physical delivery. Traders may be better served by improved access to commodity futures markets that already exist, since a number of related problems must be addressed before genuinely functioning futures markets can be established in the region. The most serious among these is the destabilizing role that governmental interventions play in domestic markets and the resulting lack of transparency in price formation, as noted above in the context of Poland. Other problems include the lack of standards and licensed warehouses, which form the foundations of futures market systems in other countries. Jump-starting these markets will require a sustained commitment of governments to not undertake ad hoc interventions, as well as technical assistance from donors to establish the appropriate legal framework.

3.6. Public goods and services

Under severe budget constraints and political pressure from sectoral lobbying groups, many governments of the region have spent more than is warranted on intervention programs, and less than warranted on provision of much needed public goods and services.

Collection and dissemination of statistical data is in large part a public good or service, and governments can play a useful role in this area. Market information is vital for decision-making in both the public and private sectors, and private agents will not in general provide the basic statistics. Lack of information is one reason for the perceived high risk in the region. The Central European countries have made considerable progress in setting up the public framework for data collection, but the responsibility is fragmented among different agencies and dissemination of useable information to market agents is poor. The Russian Ministry of Agriculture and Food has begun design and implementation of a market information system, but access and dissemination over the vast geography of the Russian Federation requires additional work. In much of Central Asia and the Caucasus, basic statistics tracking the performance of the sector and indicators of rural well-being have ceased to be collected or to be reliable.

Governments have historically been active in support for research and extension in developed economies, although this role has changed as more activities are undertaken by private firms and individuals [Umali (1992)]. Research institutes in the Soviet Union and Eastern Europe were traditionally overstaffed and over-centralized, with the ratio of researchers per US$ million of sectoral output 0.46 in Russia and 0.72 in East Germany, compared to about 0.15 in the U.S. and West Germany [Pray and Anderson (1997)]. Institutions maintained relatively few links with researchers outside the region.

During the transition, budgets for agricultural research have declined by 50–80 percent [Csaki (1998)]. The retrenchment has not been implemented in a way that protects the quality of work in activities of high priority. Rather, redundant staff have largely been retained, without resources to pay salaries or buy equipment. Few countries have undergone a systematic assessment to determine which parts of the inherited research establishment to retain in the public sector, which to privatize, which to liquidate, and followed up with an appropriate funding program [Srivastava and Reinhardt (1996)].

Under the old system, trained specialists able to advise on issues of choice and application of technology were on the staff of the large enterprises. Specialists typically had links to the research establishment, but there was no extension service, public or private, of the kind usually functioning in market economies. During the transition, new clients with new needs for advice have appeared, and within the limitations of severely constrained budgets, governments have responded. In Poland and Hungary at the beginning of the transition, extension services focused on technical issues, but they subsequently reoriented to address the needs of farmers to make good business decisions. In Hungary, the system has also been developed as a private-public activity, with an attempt to target government support to low-income producers. A low tier of services is provided free by government agents. Other services are provided on a fee-for-service basis by consulting firms, research institutes, and universities, with the government reimbursing users for a portion of the cost. This de facto privatization of extension has occurred in other countries as well (e.g., Bulgaria, Slovak Republic), though driven less by a fundamental re-thinking of the role of the state than by budgetary stringency.

4. Outcomes and prospects

The collapse of socialist agriculture, along with the other sectors of the economies in Eastern Europe and Central Asia, revealed it to be unsustainable. The arguments about its relative merits diminish when viewed against the fact of collapse. Factors that caused the failure of agriculture are basically the same as those underlying the aggregate collapse. Severely distorted economic incentives and poor institutions combined to create a system that rewarded behaviors that did not produce wealth. In the end, "it did not fail because aggregate growth was too low, but because this growth occurred at a high cost" [Pryor (1992, p. 357)]. Growth was achieved by investing resources rather than by developing or adopting improved technology to improve total factor productivity. The high cost of socialized agriculture contributed to the macroeconomic imbalances and environmental degradation that eventually became so manifestly unsustainable that they led to a political upheaval and the end of the whole system. Throughout the region agriculture was costly, but the relative burden probably varied by country.

Even with full acknowledgment of the costly legacy, the state of the rural sector in much of Eastern and Central Europe and the former Soviet Union in 1998 must be judged as poor, in many cases shockingly so. Output has fallen severely, rural incomes have declined even more, and investment has come to a standstill. That this has happened at a time without major war or natural calamity in a region with a rich agricultural endowment, educated people, roads, and telecommunications, is all the more sobering.

Without understating the severity of the present situation, one can observe that it could have been worse. In fact, worse was feared at the outset of the reforms, particularly in the USSR in the fall of 1991. At that time, a potential massive disruption in the system of food production and distribution was feared to threaten the food security of 290 million people, in an awful echo of the famines of 1921 and 1932. Multilateral and bilateral programs assessed the situation and lined up supplies of food assistance, which would, if needed in the worst event, have been insufficient simply for logistical reasons. The worst did not occur, largely due to the timely and appropriate, if imperfect, responses of governments, producers, and consumers.

Not only could the situation be worse now and could have been worse in the past; in select countries of the region it is not in fact bad at all. Within the overall very difficult experience of the past ten years lies a range of performance from "very bad indeed" to "not so bad, considering the starting point". Where rural growth has started again and sectoral dynamism is evident, as in Hungary, performance can be judged to be poor only relative to an inappropriate reference point – the protected, noncompetitive, and oversized sector of 1990 that was the culmination of socialist agricultural policy.

Hungary and other nascent success stories are, however, exceptions within a region where rural life has deteriorated markedly over the past decade and rural poverty is pervasive. Whether the state of the rural sector in 1998 is an outcome of too much reform or too little is a matter hotly debated in parliaments throughout the region and, to a lesser degree, abroad as well. The fires of this debate are fanned by statistics showing lesser declines in gross production in some of the countries that have undertaken the least significant reforms (Table 1). To those of the old school who measure success by gross production, this is an indication that reform does not pay. What these statistics do not reveal is the high cost of that production, which argues that reform is inevitable if the sector – and these economies as a whole – are ever to become competitive with the rest of the world.

Although data are still preliminary and time series are short, it appears that the countries that started to recover first were those that adopted relatively quick and comprehensive reform programs, not only – arguably not most importantly – in agriculture, but economy-wide. While the issue of sequencing has been extensively discussed, sequencing per se does not appear in practice to have been as important as its prominence in the literature might suggest. Nonetheless, lessons regarding the sequencing of macroeconomic reforms appear to be emerging from the crucible of the Russian crisis of 1998. Early attention to tax collection and administration can lower real interest rates and prevent the crowding of the real sector out of financial markets. Agriculture, with its needs for regular financing of working capital and investment, suffers particularly from high interest rates, and benefits from fiscal measures that reduce rates. Early priority must also be accorded to setting up an appropriate exchange rate regime. Insufficiently flexible exchange rate pegs can lead to overvaluation of the exchange rate and interest rate spikes prior to devaluation, heightening risks to the financial and real sectors. Especially in countries where credibility is at issue, there is a strong argument that exchange rate regimes should be either free-floating or firmly anchored by, for example, a currency board. Intermediate regimes risk pressures producing overvaluation, capital flight, and currency crises. Improved banking regulation and supervision should precede full removal of capital controls to minimize the scorched earth left in the path of fast-flowing hot money. Each of these are sequencing issues predominantly in the macroeconomic realm, but with a significant impact on agriculture.

Within the agricultural sector, sequencing has not been shown to be as important as speed, comprehensiveness, and political will to move ahead despite resistance by sometimes powerful lobbies. Speed is especially important where vested interests are likely to be significant opponents of reform. This is consistent with the political economic theory that new governments, especially those born in dire circumstances, have a honeymoon period in which their mandate for change is broad and deep, and the population is willing to endure sacrifice [see Haggard and Webb (1993)]. In this period, the efficiency gains are large relative to the rents that will be re-distributed [Rodrik (1994)]. Reforms not carried out then may languish indefinitely. In a number of cases, this has been the experience in the transition countries. Poland and others, for example, carried out sweeping reforms early on, but a number of measures not undertaken in that first rush of reform – especially agricultural policy – have still not been taken. If anything, the lesson of experience is to do as much as possible as quickly as possible, and to focus first on whichever measures are likely to encounter the greatest resistance in the country in question, rather than to worry too much about adopting each category of reform in its proper sequence.

In the political economy of reform, the countries of Eastern and Central Europe differ in a fundamental way from other transition economies. One does not need sophisticated theories of political economy to observe that in these countries, the historic chance to join Europe provided a degree of political consensus that overrode countervailing pressures toward rent-seeking or nostalgic reaction. This facilitated the adoption of early reforms across the board [de Melo (1998)], and will ensure that these countries continue to make progress toward completing the agenda of privatization and institutional reform. There will, of course, be some vacillation, and short-term crises and changes of governments will lead to some policy reversals, as they have already, but these are likely to be minor. As electorates become more experienced in democracy and as accession looms nearer, it will be increasingly difficult for populist promises to attract support for policies that are inconsistent with those of the European Union. Agricultural policy debates will revolve – as they do now in some of these countries – around the same issues as in the EU, such as levels of specific support measures and ways to assist backward regions to integrate and catch up with the rest of the country. On balance, for these countries the future looks promising.

For other countries, the future is murkier. Nonetheless, the slow accretion of positive indicators in selected countries over time offers evidence that where progress on civil peace, macroeconomic stability, and sectoral reform can be achieved, rural recovery is likely to follow. This is an encouraging message for rural people living through the transition in these countries, particularly if their political leaders accept the message and translate it into subsequent reforms. The prospects for success are relatively good, since the potential for improvement is so great. The experience of much of Latin America and Africa, however, confirms that potential is not enough. The outcome is not yet clear, and will depend on actions taken by policymakers and by rural people themselves.

For the agricultural economics profession, the drastic decline of agriculture during the transition period offers evidence for the unconvinced that socialist agriculture was unproductive, unsustainable, and, moreover, very costly to dismantle. This lesson is of limited policy relevance, since recollectivization does not currently appear to be on the agenda of any political groups actually or potentially in power, even those most sympathetic to large-scale government intervention. More fundamentally, the transition provides a cautionary lesson in the high costs of cumulative distortions built into institutions lacking an internal mechanism permitting and forcing them to evolve. Although all societies place bounds on the permissible range of institutional innovation, clearly the bounds set by communist societies were too narrow, and the mechanism of innovation – i.e., decrees issued from the administrative center – ineffective. Future understanding of the mechanisms of institutional formation and innovation may be enriched by careful examination of the experience under socialist agriculture. In the meantime, the day-to-day task of recreating viable institutions continues, as rural people reconstruct their livelihoods and communities.

Acknowledgements

The authors would like to thank the editors of this volume, Bruce Gardner and Gordon Rausser, as well as two anonymous reviewers, for comments on earlier drafts of this chapter. Johnson Appavoo's assistance with the text is gratefully acknowledged. The views are those of the authors, and not of the World Bank.

References

Ash, T.N. (1992), "Agricultural reform in Central and Eastern Europe: Marketisation, privatization, developing a new role for the state", Communist Economies and Economic Transformation 4(4):513–536.

Binswanger, H., and K. Deininger (1997), "Explaining agricultural and agrarian policies in developing countries", Journal of Economic Literature 25:1958–2005.

Binswanger, H.P., K. Deininger and G. Feder (1995), "Power, distortions, revolt and reform in agricultural land relations", in: J. Behrman and T.N. Srinivasan, eds., Handbook of Development Economics, Vol. 3 (Elsevier, New York) Chapter 42, 2659–2772.

Binswanger, H., and M.R. Rosenzweig (1986), "Behavioral and material determinants of production relations in agriculture", Journal of Development Studies 22(3):503–539.

Boese, Ch., J. Welschof, H. Neumetzler and G. Schmidt (1991), "Auswirkungen der geanderten Rahmenbedingungen auf die Landwirtschaft der neuen Bundeslander", in: H. Henrichmeyer and K. Schmidt, eds., Die Integration der Landwirtschaft der neuen Bundeslander in den Eurapäischen Agrarmarkt, Agrarwirtschaft, Sonderheft 129 (Buchedition Agrarmedia, Hamburg and Frankfurt). Presented in Koester and Brooks (1997).

Boycko, M., A. Shleifer and R.W. Vishny (1994), "Voucher privatization", Journal of Financial Economics 35:249–266.

Brada, J.C., and A.E. King (1989), "Is private farming more efficient than socialized agriculture?", Unpublished paper.

Braverman, A., K. Brooks and C. Csaki (1993), The Agricultural Transition in Central and Eastern Europe and Former USSR (The World Bank, Washington, DC).

Brooks, K., and Z. Lerman (1994), "Land reform and farm restructuring in Russia", World Bank Discussion Paper 233 (The World Bank, Washington, DC).

Brooks, K., et al. (1996), "Agricultural reform in Russia: A view from the farm level", World Bank Discussion Paper No. 327 (The World Bank, Washington, DC).

Buckwell, A. (1997), "Potential developments in the CAP: EU perspective", in: SAEPR (1997) (reproduce from SAEPR, p. 73).

Buckwell, A., J. Haynes, S. Davidova, V. Couboin and A. Kwiecinski (1994), "Feasibility of an agricultural strategy to prepare the countries of Eastern and Central Europe" (Commission of the European Communities, Brussels).

Carter, C.A., and B. Zhang (1994), "Agricultural efficiency gains in centrally planned economies", Journal of Comparative Economics 18:314–328.

Christensen, G., and R. Lacroix (1997), "Competitiveness and employment: A framework for rural development in Poland", World Bank Discussion Paper No. 383.

Clague, C., and G.C. Rausser (eds.) (1992), The Emergence of Market Economies in Eastern Europe (Blackwell, Cambridge, MA).

Csaki, C. (1993), "Transformation of agriculture in Central–Eastern Europe and the Soviet Union: Major issues and perspectives", in: A.J. Rayner and D. Colman, eds., Current Issues in Agricultural Economics (MacMillan, London).

Csaki, C. (1998), "Agricultural research in Central and Eastern Europe and the former Soviet Union: Issues in transition", World Bank ECSRE Rural Development and Environment Sector Working Paper No. 2 (April).

Csaki, C., and Z. Lerman (1996), "Agricultural transition revisited: Issues of land reform and farm restructuring in East Central Europe and the former USSR", Quarterly Journal of International Agriculture 35(3):211–240.

Csaki, C., and Z. Lerman (1997a), "Land reform and farm restructuring in East Central Europe and the CIS in the 1990s: Expectations and achievements after the first five years", European Review of Agricultural Economics 24(3/4).

Csaki, C., and Z. Lerman (1997b), "Land reform in Ukraine: The first five years", World Bank Discussion Paper No. 371 (World Bank, Washington, DC).

Csaki, C., and Z. Lerman (1998), "Land reform and farm restructuring in Hungary during the 1990's", in: S.K. Wegner, ed., Land Reform in the Former Soviet Union and Eastern Europe (Routledge).

Csaki, C., and J. Nash (1998), "The agrarian economies of Central and Eastern Europe and the Commonwealth of Independent States: Situation and perspectives, 1997", World Bank Discussion Paper No. 387 (World Bank, Washington, DC).

Deininger, K. (1995), "Collective agricultural production: A solution for transition economies?", World Development 23(8):1317–1334.

de Melo, J. (1998), "Macroeconomic management and trade reform: A political economy perspective", reproduce from Nash and Takacs (1998), p. 72.

Euroconsult (1995), "Farm restructuring and land tenure in reforming socialist economies: A comparative analysis of Eastern and Central Europe", World Bank Discussion Paper 268 (The World Bank, Washington, DC).

European Commission (1995), "Agricultural situation and prospects in the Central and Eastern European countries", Summary Report and Country Reports (Directorate-general for Agriculture).

European Commission (1997), "Agenda 2000. Vol. 1: Communication: for a stronger and wider union", Doc/97/6 (European Commission, Strasbourg).

FAO (1989–98), Yearbook of Labor Statistics, 1997.

Fernandez, R., and D. Rodrik (1991), "Resistance to reform: Status quo bias in the presence of individual-specific uncertainty", American Economic Review 81:1146–1155.

Figiel, S., T. Scott and P. Varangis (1997), "The relationships between cash wheat prices in Poland and wheat futures prices", WB Working Paper WPS 1778.

Glaeser, E.L., and J.A. Scheinkman (1996), "The transition to free markets: Where to begin privatization", Journal of Comparative Economics 22(1):23–42.

Goldberg, I., G. Jedrzejczak and M. Fuchs (1997), "A new approach to privatization: The IPO-plus", Transition 8(3):20–22.

Gros, D. (1994a), "Comment on Ch. 11: The genesis and demise of the interstate bank project", in: C. Michalopoulos and D. Tarr, eds., Trade in the New Independent States (Word Bank/UNDP, Washington, DC) 229–236.

Gros, D. (1994b), "Comment on 'Russian trade policy' ", in: C. Michalopoulos and D. Tarr, eds., Trade in the New Independent States (Word Bank/UNDP, Washington, DC) 52–57.

Haggard, S., and S. Webb (1993), "What do we know about the political economy of economic policy reform?", World Bank Research Observer 8(2):143–168.

Haggard, S., and S. Webb (eds.) (1994), Voting for Reform: Democracy, Political Liberalization and Economic Adjustment (Oxford University Press for the World Bank).

Hatziprokopiou, M., G. Karagannis and K. Velentzas (1996), "Production structure, technical change, and productivity growth in Albanian agriculture", Journal of Comparative Economics 22:295–310.

Hoff, K., and A.B. Lyon (1994), "Non-leaky buckets: Optimal redistributive taxation and agency costs", Working Paper 4652 (National Bureau of Economic Research, Cambridge, MA).

International Policy Council on Agriculture, Food, and Trade (1997), "Agriculture and EU enlargement to the east", Position Paper No. 4 (March) (Washington, DC).

Israelsen, L.D. (1980), "Collectives, communes and incentives", Journal of Comparative Economics 4(4):99–124.

Jensen, M.C., and W.H. Meckling (1979), "Rights and production functions: An application to labor managed firms and co-determination", Journal of Business 52(4):469–506.

Johnson, D.G. (1994), "Does China have a grain problem?", China Economic Review 5(1):1–14.

Johnson, D.G., and K. Brooks (1983), Prospects for Soviet Agriculture in the 1980s (Indiana University Press, Bloomington, IN).

Johnson, N.L., and V.W. Ruttan (1994), "Why are farms so small?", World Development 225:691–706.

Johnson, S., and H. Kroll (1991), "Managerial strategies for spontaneous privatization", Soviet Economy 7(4):281–316.

Joravsky, D. (1970), The Lysenko Affair (Harvard University Press, Cambridge, MA).

Kalirajan, K.P., M.B. Obwona and S. Zhao (1996), "A decomposition of total factor productivity growth: The case of Chinese agriculture before and after the reforms", American Journal of Agricultural Economics 78(2):331–338.

Kaminski, B. (1994), "Trade performance and access to OECD markets", in: C. Michalopoulos and D. Tarr, eds., Trade in the New Independent States (Word Bank/UNDP, Washington, DC) Chapter 12, 237–244.

Katz, B.G., and J. Owen (1995), "Designing an optimal privatization plan for restructuring firms and industries in transition", Journal of Comparative Economics 21(1):1–28.

Katz, B.G., and J. Owen (1997), "Optimal voucher privatization fund bids when bidding affects firm performance", Journal of Comparative Economics 24(1):25–43.

Kaufmann, D., and P. Siegelbaum (1996), "Privatization and corruption in transition economies", Journal of International Affairs (Winter).

Kislev, Y., and W. Peterson (1982), "Prices, technology and farm size", Journal of Political Economy 90(3):578–595.

Koester, U., and K. Brooks (1997), "Agriculture and German reunification", World Bank Discussion Paper No. 355 (World Bank, Washington, DC).

Koopman, R.B. (1989), "Efficiency and growth in agriculture: A comparative study of the Soviet Union, United States, Canada, and Finland", Staff Report No. AGES 89–54 (Agriculture and Trade Analysis Division, Economic Research Service, U.S. Department of Agriculture).

Kornai, J. (1982), Growth, Shortage and Efficiency (University of California Press, Berkley and Los Angeles).

Krueger, A. (1992), "Political economy of agricultural pricing policy", in: A Synthesis of the Political Economy in Developing Countries (Johns Hopkins Press, Baltimore).

Krueger, A., M. Schiff and A. Valdés (1991), Political Economy of Agricultural Pricing Policy (Johns Hopkins University Press, Baltimore).

Lerman, Z., K. Brooks and C. Csaki (1994), "Land reform and farm restructuring in Ukraine", World Bank Discussion Paper 270 (The World Bank, Washington, DC).

Lerman, Z., and C. Csaki (1998), "Land reform and farm restructuring in Moldova", World Bank Discussion Paper No. 398 (World Bank, Washington, DC).

Lieberman, I.W., M. Mejstrik, J. Burger, S. Rahuja and J. Mukherjee (1995), "Mass privatization in Central and Eastern Europe and the former Soviet Union: A comparative analysis", Studies of Economies in Transformation No. 16 (World Bank, Washington, DC).

Lin, J.Y. (1987), "The household responsibility system reform in China: A peasant's institutional choice", American Journal of Agricultural Economics 69(2):410–415.

Lin, J.Y. (1988), "The household responsibility system in China's rural reform: A theoretical and empirical study", Economic Development and Cultural Change 36(3):199–225

Lin, J.Y. (1989a), "The household responsibility system in China's rural reform", in: A. Mander and A. Valdes, eds., Agriculture and Governments in an Interdependent World: Proceedings of the XX International Conference of Agricultural Economists (Dartmont, Aldershot, England).

Lin, J.Y. (1989b), "Rural reforms and agricultural productivity growth in China", UCLA Working Paper No. 576 (Los Angeles).

Lin, J.Y. (1990), "Institutional reforms in Chinese agriculture", in: J. Dorn and W. Xi, eds., Economic Reform in China: Problems and Prospects (University of Chicago Press, Chicago).

Lin, J.Y. (1996), "Household farm, cooperative farm, and efficiency: Theory and evidence from the Chinese experience", in: J. Antle, ed., Papers in Honor of D. Gale Johnson (University of Chicago Press, Chicago and London).

Lyons, R., G. Rausser and L. Simon (1996), "Putty-clay politics in transition economies", Mimeo (University of California at Berkeley).

Maticic, B. (1993), "Agricultural research and development in Eastern European countries: Challenges and needs", Technology in Society 15:111–129.

McCloskey, D. (1991), "The prudent peasant: New findings on open fields", Journal of Economic History 51(2):343–355.

Michalopoulos, C., and D. Tarr (1994a), "Summary and overview of development since independence", in: C. Michalopoulos and D. Tarr, eds., Trade in the New Independent States (Word Bank/UNDP, Washington, DC) Chapter 1, 1–20.

Michalopoulos, C., and D. Tarr (eds.) (1994b), Trade in the New Independent States, Studies of Economies in Transition (World Bank/UNDP, Washington, DC).

Nash, J. (1994), "Institutional policies for export development", in: C. Michalopoulos and D. Tarr, eds., Trade in the New Independent States (Word Bank/UNDP, Washington, DC) Chapter 11, 211–228.

Nash, J., and W. Takacs (eds.) (1998), Lessons in Trade Policy Reform, World Bank Regional and Sectoral Series (World Bank, Washington, DC).

Network for Agricultural Policy Research and Development (1997), "Keystones of a strategy for an institutional framework in the Central and Eastern European agrofood sector", Document for the Fourth Meeting of the Ministers of Agriculture from Central and Eastern Europe, Bucharest, 2–4 May.

Nikonov, A. (1995), Spiral Mnogovekovoi Dramy: Agrarnaia Nauka i Politika Rossii (XVIII–XX vv.) (Moscow, Russia).

OECD (1996), Agricultural Trade, Agricultural Incomes and Rural Development in Poland (Paris).

OECD (1998), Review of Agricultural Policies, Russian Federation (Paris).

Oi, W.Y., and E.M. Clayton (1969), "A peasant's view of a soviet collective farm", American Economic Review 59(1):37–59.

Orlowski, W. (1996), "Price support at any price? Costs and benefits of alternative agricultural policies for Poland", Policy Research Working Paper 1584 (World Bank, Washington, DC).

Panagariya, A. (1998), "Rethinking the new regionalism", in: J. Nash and W. Takacs, eds., Lessons in Trade Policy Reform (World Bank, Washington, DC) Chapter 4, 87–146.

Pedersen, G. (1996), "Rural finance policy in Poland", Consultant report for the World Bank, Unpublished manuscript.

Piesse, J., C. Thirtle and J. Turk (1996), "Efficiency and ownership in Slovene dairying: A comparison of econometric and programming techniques", Journal of Comparative Economics 22(1):1–22.

Pomfret, R.W.T. (1996), "Economic reform in China, 1978–94", in: R.W.T. Pomfret, ed., Asian Economies in Transition (Edward Elgar, Cheltenham, UK).

Posner, R.A. (1998), "Creating a legal framework for economic development", World Bank Research Observer 13(1):1–11.

Pray, C.E., and J.R. Anderson (1997), "The agricultural research system of the former Soviet Union: Past and future", Journal of International Development 9(4):517–527.

Pryor, F.L. (1992), The Red and the Green: the Rise and Fall of Collectivized Agriculture in Marxist Regimes (Princeton University Press, Princeton).

Putterman, L. (1981), "On optimality in collective institutional choice", Journal of Comparative Economics 5(4):392–402.

Putterman, L. (1993), Continuity and Change in China's Rural Development (Oxford University Press, New York).

Rausser, G.C. (1990), "Implications of the structural adjustment experience in the developing world for Eastern Europe: Discussion", American Journal of Agricultural Economics 72(5):1252–1256.

Rausser, G.C. (1992), "Lessons for emerging market economies in Eastern Europe", in: C. Clague and G.C. Rausser, eds., The Emergence of Market Economies in Eastern Europe (Blackwell, Cambridge, MA) Chapter 19, 311–333.

Rausser, G.C., and L. Simon (1992), "The political economy of transition in Eastern Europe: Packaging enterprises for privatization", in: C. Clague and G.C. Rausser, eds., The Emergence of Market Economies in Eastern Europe (Blackwell, Cambridge, MA) Chapter 14, 245–270.

Rayner, A.J., and D. Colman (eds.) (1993), Current Issues in Agricultural Economics (MacMillan, London).

Rodrik, D. (1989), "Political economy and development policy", European Economic Journal 36(2–3):326–336.

Rodrik, D. (1994), "The rush to free trade in the developing world: Why so late? Why now? Will it last?", in: S. Haggard and S. Webb, eds., Voting for Reform: Democracy, Political Liberalization and Economic Adjustment (Oxford University Press for the World Bank).

Rodrik, D. (1996), "Understanding economic policy reform", Journal of Economic Literature 34:9–41.

Rosenzweig, M., and K. Wolpin (1993), "Credit market constraints, consumption smoothing, and the accumulation of durable goods: Investment in bullocks in India", Journal of Political Economy 101(2):223–244.

SAEPR (Agricultural Policy Analysis Unit, Ministry of Agriculture) (1997), "Polish agricultural and rural policies pre-EU accession: Conference proceedings from conference in Jablonna, December 6–7, 1996" (Ministry of Agriculture (SAEPR), Warsaw).

Safin, M., and W. Guba (1996), "Agricultural price policy impacts in Poland, regional and income distribution perspective", Report for WB, cited in Christensen.

Sen, A. (1967), "Labor allocation in a cooperative enterprise", Review of Economic Studies 33:361–371.

Sicular, T. (1993), "The quest for sustained growth in Chinese agriculture", in: A.J. Rayner and Colman, eds., Current Issues in Agricultural Economics (MacMillan, London) Chapter 6.

Srivastava, J., and C. Reinhardt (1996), "Agricultural knowledge system in the transitioning economies" (World Bank and CGIAR).

Stuart, R. (1983), "Russian and soviet agriculture: The western perspective", ACES Bulletin 25(3):43–52.

Swinnen, J. (1997), "Agrarian reform policies in Central Europe and the Baltics: A political economy perspective", in: J. Swinnen, ed., Political Economy of Agrarian Reform in Central and Eastern Europe (Ashgate, Aldeshot).

Swinnen, J., and E. Mathijs (eds.) (1995), Agricultural Privatization, Land Reform and Farm Restructuring in Central Europe (K.U. Leuven).

Tangermann, S., and T.E. Josling (with W. Munch) (1994), "Pre-accession agricultural policies for Central and Eastern Europe and the European Union", Final report (European Commission (with PHARE Program), DG I (12 December), Brussels).

Truszczynski, J. (1997), "Prospects for Poland's accession negotiations: the view from Brussels", in: SAEPR (1997).

Umali, D. (1992), "Public and private sector roles in agricultural research", World Bank Discussion Paper No. 176 (World Bank, Washington, DC).

United Nations Economic Commission for Europe (1995), Ways and Means of Promoting the Expansion of Trade in Transition Economies (17 February)

Van Zyl, J., B.R. Miller and A.N. Parker (1996), "Agrarian structure in Poland: The myth of large farm superiority", Policy Research Working Paper 1596.

Wadekin, K. (1973), The Private Sector in Soviet Agriculture (University of California Press, Berkley).

Wadekin, K.E. (1982), "Agrarian policy in communist Europe", in: Studies in East European and Soviet Russian Agrarian Policy, Vol. 1.

Wegren, S. (ed.) (1998), Land Reform in the Former Soviet Union and Eastern Europe (Routledge, London).

Wei, S.-J. (1993), "Gradualism versus the Big Bang: Speed and sustainability of reforms", Working Paper R93-2 (John F. Kennedy School of Government, Harvard University).

Wong, L.-F., and V. Ruttan (1990), "A comparative analysis of agricultural productivity trends in centrally planned economies", in: K. Gray, ed., Soviet Agriculture (Iowa State University Press, Ames) 23–47.

World Bank (1997), Poland Country Economic Memorandum: Reform and Growth on the Road to EU Membership (Central Europe Department, May).

Wyzan, M.L. (1985), "Soviet agricultural procurement pricing: A study in perversity", Journal of Comparative Economics 9:24–45.

Chapter 31

RURAL DEVELOPMENT AND RURAL POLICY

ALAIN DE JANVRY and ELISABETH SADOULET

Department of Agricultural and Resource Economics, University of California, Berkeley, CA

RINKU MURGAI

The World Bank

Contents

Handbook of Agricultural Economics, Volume 2, Edited by B. Gardner and G. Rausser
© *2002 Elsevier Science B.V. All rights reserved*

Abstract

Rural development policy addresses the welfare of rural households and communities. With a majority of the world's poor located in rural areas, the resilience of rural poverty in industrialized countries, and a significant share of environmental degradation the byproduct of rural poverty, the design of effective rural policies remains an important theme. There is a long history of economic thought as to how to address rural development. In the last 15 years, the context for rural development has changed markedly. At the same time, there have been major theoretical and empirical advances in household behavior, institutional economics, community behavior, and endogenous regional growth. They allow us to rethink approaches to rural development and to experiment with novel initiatives.

Keywords

rural development, agrarian institutions, household behavior, community behavior

JEL classification: Q18

1. Agricultural economics and rural economics

Agricultural economics has been principally concerned with the economics of agriculture as a sector. The elementary unit of analysis is the farm. The major fields of analysis are farm production, the marketing of agricultural commodities and the demand for food, the performance of product and factor markets, the linkages between agriculture and other sectors of the economy and the rest of the world, sustainability in resource use, and agricultural and food policy.

Rural economics and the design of rural policies to achieve rural development constitute a broader subject than agricultural economics, with a spatial as opposed to a sectoral definition. The elementary unit of analysis is the household, with the farm as a typical subset of economic activity. The fields of application of rural economics include resource allocation by households and their choices of income strategies, the emergence and performance of agrarian institutions, income levels achieved by specific categories of rural inhabitants, poverty and inequality, income and food security, the satisfaction of basic needs (in particular access to public goods and services such as health and education), intergenerational equity, and the broad characterization of the quality of life for rural households (which includes features such as individual freedoms, the range of available opportunities and "capabilities" [Sen (1985)], community relations and congeniality, the rule of law and respect of human rights, political rights, etc.). Rural economics requires focusing importantly on the heterogeneity of rural populations that inhabit a particular region since the determinants of welfare are highly varied. For rural development, who produces in agriculture matters for efficiency and welfare, for instance smallholders as opposed to large commercial farmers. Where agricultural production takes place also matters, for instance in better-endowed versus marginal areas. What non-farm sources of income exist in particular regions and which particular classes of households are able to participate in those is important for the determination of household incomes. How households aggregate in communities and the level of social capital they contain explains the efficiency of rural institutions and the ability to cooperate in the provision of public goods and the appropriation of common pool resources. And how sizable the local linkages are between farm and non-farm activities, particularly the multiplier effects created by the expenditure of farm incomes, matters for the creation of non-farm incomes that supplement for farm households the incomes derived from agriculture and create employment opportunities for rural non-farm households.

In spite of the importance of the subject, rural economists have been a rare breed in the economic profession compared to agricultural economists. As a result, analyses of rural societies have more frequently been done by sociologists, anthropologists, and geographers than by rural economists, and by extension agents rather than research faculties. In spite of the many insights derived from these studies, the scarcity of rural economists creates two important voids. One is a deficit of rigorous economic theories explaining the determinants of behavior among households and communities and the logic of agrarian institutions. This is detrimental to conducting solid empirical analyses of these subjects. The other is insufficient policy purpose in the research conducted since these other social sciences tend to be more interested in positive than in normative analysis. Systematic primary data have also been scarce, particularly long series panel data that are needed to analyze the successive rounds of response to change while controlling for many non-observables. Interdisciplinary approaches using rapid and participatory rural appraisal techniques [Chambers (1993)] are extremely powerful in revealing the perceptions of actors and in identifying new hypotheses, but are a weak basis for the formulation of economic policy due to lack of representativity and of quantification. As a result, rural policy has all too often been based on highly incomplete understandings of the material and behavioral determinants of household, community, and institutional responses. Heroic controversies about the determinants of household behavior, for instance between formalists and substantivists in peasant anthropology [LeClair and Schneider (1968)], have been based largely on misinterpretation of the structural context within which households exercise their choices [see de Janvry, Fafchamps and Sadoulet (1991)]. The highly complex trade-offs between the multidimensional objectives of rural policy remain poorly measured. And prescriptions for rural development have all too often followed simplistic bandwagon ideas, where the presumed silver bullet for success has failed to recognize the heterogeneity of households and communities and the complexity of determinants of behavior, creating waves of enthusiasm and disillusionment.

Because agriculture remains an important source of dynamism for rural areas, even when the sector directly generates only a small fraction of regional income, agricultural policy that stimulates investment and productivity gains is a necessary, if not a sufficient, condition for rural development. In most LDCs (less developed countries) agricultural policy, either made at the macro level via the exchange rate and the intersectoral terms of trade for agriculture, or at the sectoral level via commodity-specific trade interventions, taxes, and subsidies, has played against rural policy [Lipton (1977), Krueger, Schiff and Valdés (1988)]. By discriminating against agriculture, policy has created disincentives to invest in agriculture and undervalued the conservation of natural resources. Hence, not only has agricultural policy been made ignoring rural policy, but it has often been its worst enemy, creating widespread suspicion among rural development advocates about the ability of economists to contribute useful prescriptions for the improvement of rural welfare [Altieri (1989), Chambers (1993), Norgaard (1994)].

Very important changes have, however, occurred in recent years, with major advances in rural economics and in the design of new approaches to rural development. From the angle of theory, these changes derive from progress in household and community economics, the theory of agrarian institutions, and understanding the endogenous determinants of regional growth. From the angle of empiricism, extensive data bases have allowed uncovering regularities and testing new ideas for rural development as never could have been done before. And from the angle of the practice of rural development, a new economic, institutional, and political context that emerged largely in the 1990s has opened the possibility of experimenting with novel approaches to rural development, some of which show definite promise. It is the objective of this chapter to map out these changes, analyze the nature of their contributions to rural development, and identify important gaps that remain to be filled.

2. Why the need for a rural policy?

2.1. The less developed countries

In the LDCs, rural underdevelopment remains a fundamental determinant of overall underdevelopment. Nearly three-fourths of the 1.3 billion world poor who subsist on less than one dollar a day live in rural areas [World Bank (1997)]. Three-fourths of the world's 800 million underfed also live in rural areas. In spite of rapid urbanization, a majority of the world poor and underfed will remain in rural areas for the next several decades. And levels of poverty are typically much deeper in rural areas. In 19 Latin American countries with data, for instance, the poverty headcount ratio was 55 percent in the rural sector compared to 34 percent in the urban sector in 1994 [ECLAC (1997)]. And the incidence of extreme poverty was 33 percent in the rural sector compared to only 12 percent in the urban sector. With typical public underinvestment in rural areas combined with higher costs of delivery, levels of basic needs for amenities such as health, education, potable water, and sanitation are also lower than in the urban areas. This situation of chronic poverty in rural areas has often led to backlashes against the economic models pursued by governments at the national level. In Peru, Colombia, Guatemala, and Mexico, as well as many African nations, rural violence has, on repeated occasions, been a source of political destabilization, with heavy macroeconomic costs.

Rural poverty can also create serious negative externalities on a country's metropolitan population. Rapid migratory flows crowd out urban residents on non-farm labor markets and displace rural poverty to the urban slums, adding to urban welfare budgets. And environmental abuse associated with the pressures of rural poverty contributes to national and global externalities under the form of siltage, exhaustion of underground water reserves, desertification, deforestation, loss of biodiversity, and climate change.

In many countries, smallholders are a fundamental source of agricultural supply. In this case, the problem of rural development becomes confounded with that of agricultural development. This is particularly true in sub-Saharan Africa, where most of the land is cultivated by smallholders. With population expected to triple by 2025 and low tradability of many staples, food security is at risk. To face up to this challenge, it is thus essential to raise the productivity and efficiency of rural households in using resources and to enhance their ability to protect the environment. In other countries, particularly in Latin America, even though the national food security problem can be addressed through trade or through production in a large sector of commercial farms (making the problem one of agricultural as opposed to rural policy), agriculture remains a major source of income for many rural poor households. In this case, using rural development interventions to boost access to productive assets for these households and to increase their productivity of resource use should be a major objective for rural policy.

2.2. The more developed countries

Poverty is also differentially widespread and more severe in the rural areas of MDCs (more developed countries) than in metropolitan areas, justifying rural development interventions. Per capita rural incomes are well below national averages in most OECD countries and in many cases are falling further behind [OECD (1993)]. In the United States, the gap in earnings per job between non-metropolitan and metropolitan counties was widening until 1980, and has remained about constant since then. In 1994, per capita income in non-metropolitan counties was 26 percent below that in metropolitan counties [United States Department of Agriculture, Economic Research Service (ERS) (1997)]. Rural areas (non-metropolitan counties) have 21 percent of the national population but only 18 percent of the jobs, they generate 14 percent of national income, and they harbor 30 percent of the poor [Duncan and Tickamyer (1988)]. In 1986, the poverty headcount ratio was 18 percent in the non-metropolitan counties compared to 12 percent in the metropolitan. Poverty differentially affects specific social categories: 43 percent of all rural blacks, 59 percent of children in rural female-headed households, and 83 percent of black children in rural female-headed households are in poverty. Rural areas typically lack a middle class as middle income and better-educated adults have left for metropolitan environments with more abundant opportunities. Poverty is highly concentrated by regions, creating conditions of social exclusion and a culture of poverty similar to those that prevail in urban ghettos. Economic disadvantages of many rural areas include (1) low-density settlements and geographical isolation, implying poorly funded public sectors and costly provision of basic needs services, (2) lack of diversification in economic activity, implying high income exposure to sudden displacements of employment, (3) low-skilled labor force employed in low-wage traditional industries that face enhanced foreign competition with progress in globalization, (4) declining employment in resource-based industries (agriculture, mining), and (5) rigid social stratification that limits social mobility for specific groups of citizens [Galston and Baehler (1995)]. Compared to metropolitan areas, these disadvantages have translated into higher rates of unemployment, larger falls in real wages, lower returns to education, and growing differentiation among rural areas to a large extent according to their degree of economic integration with metropolitan areas.

In Europe, agriculture accounted for less than 25 percent of rural employment, even in the most agricultural areas of the European Union. Hence, agricultural policy can only be a minor component of rural policy. In the United States, the percentage of the rural workforce employed in farming declined from 14.4 percent in 1970 to 7.6 percent in 1990, largely as a consequence of successful agricultural development that doubled labor productivity during that period [United States Department of Agriculture, Economic Research Service (ERS) (1995)]. Farm employment dropped from some

8 million in 1948 to 3 million in 1991, while the number of farms fell from 5.8 million to 2.1 million. In 1990, 58 percent of U.S. farm operators received off-farm wages and salaries. As a share of total employment, services accounted in 1992 for 50.6 percent, and this share is rising; government accounts for a stable 17.2 percent; and manufacturing for 16.9 percent, and this share is falling. Among services, activities with expanding employment include recreation, retirement, finance, insurance, real estate, retail stores, restaurants, telemarketing, and data processing. In general, counties dependent on farm and traditional manufacturing activities have lost population, while counties with recreation opportunities, retirement development, and proximity to urban areas have gained population. Persistent poverty is a characteristic of extensive geographical areas that do not have these desirable characteristics, particularly in the Southeast.

The need for a rural policy thus derives from the differential incidence and persistence of poverty between rural and urban areas in both LDCs and MDCs, the pervasiveness of environmental degradation associated in part with the very same determinants of poverty, and negative spillovers on metropolitan areas. Rural poverty is associated with inefficiency in resource use since many of the resources controlled by the poor (including most prominently their labor and entrepreneurship) are locked into low-level equilibrium traps where they are underused. We will show that the determinants of these problems can be traced back to the structural features of rural areas (distance, dispersion, resource-based activities, incomplete property rights, inequality in the distribution of assets, etc.), the pervasiveness of market failures for a significant share of households (particularly for credit, insurance, and information as well as high transactions costs in accessing product and factor markets), serious gaps in agrarian institutions essential for productivity and welfare, lags in the intersectoral reallocation of resources, lack of coordination to escape regional low-level equilibrium traps, pro-urban policy biases, and lack of bargaining power for the rural poor. While economic growth is a precondition for the elimination of poverty, it has not been sufficient for a high share of rural households. What needs to be questioned is the nature of growth and the differential ability of a heterogeneous rural population to participate in and benefit from this process. This is where a rural policy coordinated with the nation's agricultural and macroeconomic policy has an essential role to play.

3. Approaches to rural development in a historical perspective

While the problem of rural underdevelopment has been persistent, the design of rural policies to solve this problem has changed markedly over time as the context for development was transformed, correspondingly modifying the opportunities for and the constraints on success, and as ideas about development in general and rural development in particular evolved. To characterize the evolution of thought on rural development, we can contrast theories according to the relative importance which they attribute to market forces, the role of the state, and the role of civil society. All theories recognize a certain balance between market, state, and civil institutions. In what follows, we classify schools of thought (names italicized) according to the element among those three on which greater normative emphasis is placed. To each school of thought regarding economic development corresponds a position (or at least an implication) regarding rural policy. We discuss here only the most influential bodies of thought that help explain past attempts at rural development and that will help us in the next section to characterize current attempts in contraposition to those.

3.1. From World War II to 1980: Role of the state in rural development

Following the destruction caused by World War II and emergence of the problem of accelerating growth in the occupied Asian countries, two schools of thought immediately confronted each other regarding the roles of the market and the state in catching up. Advocates of *modernization theory* looked at the history of successful industrialization in the West and recommended an evolutionary approach that would emulate these achievements in the context of market economies. Economies were to transit through a set of stages [Rostow (1971)] and follow "normal patterns" of structural transformation [Chenery and Taylor (1968)] that would lead them to the structure of advanced economies. For rural policy, this meant promoting the diffusion of innovations [Rogers (1983)] to emulate the technologies, institutions, and behavioral patterns of Western economies.

Reliance on markets for catching up faced, however, formidable adversaries. The intellectual context was the recent experience of running war economies through strong state interventions, success of the Marshall Plan in reconstructing Europe, the powerful role of the state under Cold War tensions, the early success of the Soviet experience with central planning, emergence of the Third World movement as an alternative to both market capitalism and state ownership of the means of production, and the role of the Bretton Woods institutions in the developing world with their ability to finance large-scale investment projects. The dominant paradigm in development economics focused on the role of market failures in preventing catching up and on the role of the state in compensating for these failures. In *radical dependency theory*, this took the form of advocating collectivization, central planning, and delinking from the international market [Frank (1969)]. Rural policy correspondingly imposed collectivization of the land and the coercive extraction of an agricultural surplus for the financing of heavy industry.

For most countries, the relevant theoretical thinking to engineer a catching up was to be found in an extraordinarily creative body of thought that assumed the name of *"development economics"*. A shared principle was belief in the pervasiveness of market failures for latecomers, and hence the need for an active role of the state in protecting infant industries, mobilizing domestic savings, and coordinating private investment. The *"pioneers" of development* thus focused on the need to promote capital accumulation by raising saving rates [Domar (1947)], implementing import-substitution industrialization (ISI) policies [Prebisch (1962)], accepting increased inequalities as the inevitable social cost of rapid growth [Lewis (1954)], relying on trickle-down effects via labor markets to reduce poverty [Hirschman (1958)], and extracting a surplus from agriculture to finance industrial development. Agricultural policy was subjected to industrial policies clearly unfavorable to agriculture as exchange rates appreciated under industrial protectionism or were fixed at overvalued levels to subsidize capital goods imports for industry, and industrial protectionism turned the domestic terms of trade against agriculture. This urban bias in policy design was in part justified by a presumed lack of supply response in agriculture which could allow surplus extraction via price without adverse effects on agricultural output [see Mellor (1976)]. Agricultural policy was at best seeking compensations for agriculture to remedy the harshness of price distortions, principally via input and interest rate subsidies. In the occupied Asian countries, rural policy successfully focused on land reform and the creation of a large class of smallholders effectively organized in village communities to access the market and the state. Elsewhere, the main initiative in rural policy was the community development movement of the 1950s and early 1960s, which sought to promote the organization of members of rural communities so they could jointly plan the allocation of resources under their control [Holdcroft (1978)]. This movement was the guideline for rural policy interventions by USAID and the United Nations in much of the world, but particularly in India and Africa. This early attempt at decentralized rural development, however, rapidly failed because it was not transferring to communities new resources that could raise incomes and because it reinforced the power of traditional elites by refusing to address issues of land distribution and local power structures. In the United States, rural policy was similarly under the aegis of strong state intervention, with the New Deal policies implementing a variety of federal programs with the intent of mitigating market failures in rural areas.

The *first development decade* (1960–70) saw extraordinary success in promoting economic growth, not only in the newly industrialized countries (NICs) of East and South East Asia, but also in many Latin American and some African countries. For agricultural policy, the main lesson from this period was the key role of technological change in agriculture. This had been advocated by theories belonging to *neo-classical economic development*: Schultz's (1964) "poor but efficient" farmers for whom technological change was the only option for higher incomes, Jorgenson's (1961) dual economy model where full employment implied the need to use technological change in agriculture to keep nominal wages for industry low in spite of labor transfers, and Hayami and Ruttan's (1985) induced technological innovations where changes in relative factor scarcities, translating in changes in relative factor prices, induce corresponding factor-saving biases in technological innovations. The role of technological change in agriculture was also central to theories belonging to *development economics*: this is captured in the dual economy models of Fei and Ranis (1964) and Lele and Mellor (1981), where technological change in agriculture allows lowering nominal wages for industry in spite of surplus labor and constant real wages. While neo-classical economic development reasoned on the basis of perfect markets and development economics of market failures, both looked at technological change in agriculture as the dynamic source of growth for industry. With yield-increasing agricultural technologies largely public goods, the state was to be the main source of these necessary technological changes. Rural policy was largely subjected to the logic of agricultural policy, with the achievements of the Green Revolution and their diffusion among smallholders seen to be the key instruments for rural development. Land reform, more often of the modernizing (i.e., using the threat of expropriation to induce modernization) than of the redistributive type [see de Janvry (1981)], was also used as a policy instrument to promote the diffusion of technological change in agriculture and thus contribute to the success of industrial policies via cheap food and expanding domestic markets.

The *second development decade* (1970–80) was marked by a slowdown in economic growth (oil and food crises, rising inefficiencies of ISI strategies, and accumulation of debt) but also by increasingly evident failure of economic growth to reduce poverty and inequality, with the exception of the East and South East Asian NICs that thus provided a source of inspiration for a set of policies to achieve growth with equity. Thought in development was thus dominated by a set of propositions to reconcile growth and equity [Adelman (1975), Chenery et al. (1974)] and cover the basic needs of populations [Streeten (1979)], with again the state as the key instrument to achieve these goals. In rural policy, this quest took the form of integrated rural development projects. The core instrument was the technology of the Green Revolution, seen as the missing piece in the failed community development movement of the 1950–65 period. Because of pervasive market failures for smallholders, the state was to coordinate and usually subsidize the delivery to smallholders of services complementary to the new technologies, particularly credit, technical assistance, access to markets, and crop insurance. Massive support was provided to these projects by USAID and the World Bank. These attempts were, however, generally not successful beyond the level of pilot projects, and even these limited projects were rarely sustainable without continued inflow of government resources. This failure was due to a combination of (1) generally adverse policy environments, with urban biases undermining the profitability of investment in agriculture, (2) excessive focus on agriculture, even though it generates only a small fraction of household income for a majority of the rural poor, (3) failure to address the problem of access to assets, land most particularly, (4) serious coordination failures among government agencies in the delivery of expected complex packages of "integrated" services, (5) imperfect information in enabling government agencies to deal with heterogeneity in rural areas and define alternative paths out of poverty for different classes of households and communities, (6) failure to decentralize decision-making to the community level and to enlist the participation of beneficiaries into project definition and project implementation, and (7) insufficient attention to building political coalitions in support of a continuing commitment to rural development [Crener et al. (1984)]. By the early 1980s, integrated rural development projects had fallen into disfavor with governments and international development agencies.

3.2. *The 1980s: Restoring the role of the market*

The gradual exhaustion of import-substitution industrialization policies, explosion of the debt crisis in 1982, the need to implement stabilization and adjustment policies under conditionalities from the IMF and the World Bank, ideological shifts against the pervasiveness of government intervention, and critiques of the urban bias in agricultural policy led to a frontal attack on the role of the state in development, a movement that has been called the *neo-liberal response*. The success of open economy industrialization (OEI) was contrasted to the deadlocks of import-substitution industrialization [Chenery, Robinson and Syrquin (1986)], frequently forgetting [Edwards (1993)] that ISI had been an essential step toward OEI in allowing entry into activities characterized by economies of scale and learning-by-doing [Rodrik (1996)]. A new set of theoretical contributions exposed the limits and frequent malfeasance of government intervention in assuming functions that could be fulfilled by the market and in perverting the allocative functions of the market. Incapacity of the state to solve incentive and informational problems [Hayek (1989)], to defeat rational expectation responses of private agents to policy interventions [Lucas (1983)], and to countervail the logic of rent seeking [Krueger (1974)] all provided arguments for those calling for a descaling of the role of the state and a restoration of the role of market forces. In agricultural policy, the calculations of Krueger, Schiff and Valdés (1988) exposed the magnitude of price distortions, and the long-term extrapolations of Cavallo and Mundlak (1982) quantified the devastating costs on aggregate growth of price policies systematically distorted against agriculture. Stabilization and adjustment policies led to a sharp compression of the role of the state, extensive trade and financial liberalization, and implementation of the further recommendations of the *Washington Consensus* [Williamson (1990)].

For rural policy, this set of policies implied the weakening of the urban bias in price formation, but also the removal of a set of explicit or implicit subsidies and public services to agriculture and rural areas. In the U.S., agricultural commodity programs as well as area and rural development programs were widely criticized as inefficient and regressive [Gardner (1987)]. In much of the developing world, parastatals that had serviced agriculture, often at great social costs, were closed or privatized [Bates (1989)]. Subsidies to credit given through development banks were eliminated. From then on, the rules of market competitiveness were to determine success or failure in rural development. Where the state had been stifling on individual initiatives, the new freedoms gained by rural households could lead to important one-time gains in productivity, such as the household responsibility system in China and liberalization of the ejido from state controls in Mexico. In most places, however, market incentives were matched by massive de-institutionalization of agriculture, making it impossible for smallholders to adapt to the new competitive rules. This period was thus one of retrogression in rural development, but at the same time one of setting the context for new approaches to rural development in terms of market incentives and new roles for civil society.

4. The 1990s: New context for rural development

Following the general failures of community development, redistributive land reform, and integrated rural development under state-led initiatives, and the retrogression of rural areas under adjustment policies and descaling of government interventions, the question to be asked for rural policy is whether there are new perspectives for rural development in the context of (1) the recovery of growth following the years of debt crisis and structural adjustment, and (2) the theoretical progress made by rural economists in the understanding of the behavior of households and communities, the logic of agrarian institutions, and the endogenous determinants of regional growth. The answer seems to be a cautious yes. To argue this, we first identify in this section the context for rural development that emerged in the 1990s. We will then proceed to characterize what recent theoretical advances have to offer as instruments for a better understanding of rural households, communities, institutions, and growth. This in turn will allow us to identify rural development initiatives consistent with this new context and the recent theoretical advances, which differ markedly from the past attempts we have surveyed.

We use again the trilogy between market, state, and civil institutions to characterize the new context for rural development.

4.1. Role of the market

4.1.1. Globalization

The most remarkable change in the role of the market for rural development in the 1990s is the rapid progress toward globalization of competition. Following the progress of GATT and numerous regional agreements, as well as implementation of adjustment policies, trade and international capital movements have been extensively liberalized. This implies an homogenization across households and communities of the rules of the game for rural development, with the need to achieve competitiveness for smallholders to survive in markets largely ruled by international competition. This, in turn, implies the need for these smallholders to modernize and diversify their cropping patterns, identify market niches particularly for non-traditional exports (organic foods and coffee, exotic forest products, labeling of the quality and social origin of products), and capitalize on opportunities (for instance through contract farming) to access international markets.

The overarching requirement of achieving competitiveness is visible in the evolution of the design of rural development projects financed by IFAD (the International Fund for Agricultural Development). This United Nations rural development bank was set up 20 years ago in the aftermath of the oil and food crises with the objective of sheltering smallholders from the harshness of the market, largely by helping them achieve food security through greater food self-reliance. Today, this philosophy has been transformed into the quest for market opportunities to sell cash or food crops. Production of non-traditional export crops and contract farming with agroindustry figure prominently in the recommended strategies [Jaffee and Morton (1995)]. The objective is to achieve income security, and through this food security, without necessarily seeking greater food self-sufficiency (at least within the idiosyncratic possibilities offered by food markets and their specific transactions costs) [Jazairy, Alamgir and Panuccio (1992)].

In the United States, deregulation has eliminated a set of implicit subsidies for the rural areas in transportation, telecommunications, and banking. The Federal Agricultural Improvement and Reform Act of 1996 has largely decoupled farm income support from commodity prices, except in a few commodities such as sugar and milk. With the removal of these subsidies, market forces determine the competitiveness of family farms in agricultural production [Tweeten and Zulauf (1997)].

Exposure of smallholders to international markets creates new opportunities but also new challenges for rural development. In countries with weak domestic savings, economic recovery is associated with foreign capital inflows which appreciate the real exchange rate, undermining incentives to invest in agriculture. International commodities markets in which smallholders with low ability to cope with risk are drawn to participate are notably unstable and frequently fraught with new forms of protectionism in the importing countries. Large segments of smallholders are at a clear disadvantage in facing the challenges of modernization and competitiveness relative to commercial farmers due to low quality assets, market failures for credit and insurance, limited access to new technologies and information, and high transactions costs on markets. In the more developed countries, globalization hurts unskilled labor-intensive industries, which typically had moved to rural areas in quest of cheap, unskilled labor before globalization shifted comparative advantage to unskilled labor in the less developed countries. With low diversification of sources of industrial employment in most rural communities, displacement of these firms toward LDCs can have devastating effects on rural residents.

4.2. Role of the state

There are both positive and negative aspects to the changes in the role of the state for rural development in the emerging context.

4.2.1. Policy instruments

In the context of liberalization and adjustment, agricultural policy increasingly has been subservient to macroeconomic policy. Dominance of macro over sectoral policy is not new. Under import-substitution industrialization, Krueger, Schiff and Valdés (1988) have shown that indirect price distortions attributed to real exchange rate appreciation and to industrial protectionism were a more important source of anti-agriculture price biases than direct trade interventions on farm products. In this context, agricultural policy was often a reactive set of interventions to compensate for these anti-agriculture biases through input and interest rate subsidies. These biases have been significantly weakened by floating exchange rates and trade liberalization [Valdés (1996)], but so has also the ability of government to compensate for the remaining price distortions on the product side via costly price distortions on the factor side. In addition, underinvestment in research and development, infrastructure, health, and education for rural populations remains pervasive, and these investments have been systematically biased against smallholders and the rural poor. The new context also implies a loss of instruments for agricultural policy since commodity prices are no longer supposed to be intervened and strict fiscal balances confine the magnitude of farm subsidies. The main instruments for rural policy are instead to be found in direct income transfers, the definition and targeting of public goods, regulation of competition and environmental effects, selected assistance to entrepreneurship, and targeted welfare interventions such as food subsidies and food-for-work programs.

4.2.2. Institutional gaps

Stabilization policies, regional integration agreements, and neo-liberal philosophies in policy-making in general have sharply attacked the practice of running large government deficits that characterized previous periods. This has led to a decline in government budgets for rural development. State contraction has led to the foreclosure, devolution, or privatization of an array of parastatals formerly serving rural development (in research and development, extension services, marketing, development loans, infrastructure, irrigation management, etc.). The expectation was that, wherever the state was involved in the delivery of private or club goods, the private and associative sectors would enter where the state had withdrawn. This has, however, been very partial at best, leaving huge institutional gaps that constrain response to the reforms for large segments of the rural population. In that sense, state contraction has often contradicted the expected positive effects of market liberalization on supply response [Lipton (1990)]. Due to small market size, high risks, and information failures, private services have been slow to replace public services. In addition, when they have emerged, private services have selectively focused on subsets of the rural population with lower transactions costs, lesser risks, and greater ability to respond, excluding most of the traditional clients of rural development programs. And declines in public investment in true public goods such as infrastructure, agricultural research, rural education, primary health care, and marketing facilities have undermined the profitability of private investment in rural areas.

The new context for rural development is thus one that begs a redefinition of the role of the state. This redefinition must accommodate severe budget constraints on and contraction of public agencies, seek cooperation with the private and associative sectors in the co-production of public goods, and maximize coordination between public and private initiatives [Evans (1996)].

4.2.3. Decentralization of governance

Most countries have implemented a process of decentralization of governance toward states (if federal), regions, and municipalities. This has been done under a variety of motives including the quest for greater efficiency in governance, greater accountability of locally elected officials, the unloading of expensive tasks onto lower levels of governance, and the deepening of democracy, but also sometimes substitutes for democratization at the national levels [Manor (1997)]. Decentralization has taken three forms [Parker (1995)]: (1) The deconcentration of administrative tasks to local offices of the central government. This allows governmental organizations to better access local information, but does not imply greater participation by local clients. (2) Delegation of decision-making to local governments or to a parastatal. In this case, local governments or the selected agencies have the responsibility of project organization. (3) Devolution to local governments with political and fiscal control over projects.

Potential benefits of decentralization include: (1) Access to local private information about agents for decision-makers and, reciprocally, to information about policy-making (e.g., budgets) for local populations. (2) Possibility of mobilizing local social capital for the enforcement of rules and contracts, the sustainability of cooperation, and greater accountability of elected officials. (3) Mobilization of local underused assets, most particularly entrepreneurship for the definition and implementation of projects, and labor for the co-production of public goods and services. (4) Participation of beneficiaries in decision-making, allowing the formulation of demand-led projects that account for local heterogeneity and induce commitment derived from project ownership. (5) Improved local coordination in the delivery of public goods and services, and consultative planning for decisions regarding consistency between public and private investment. And (6), shift in the balance of political power toward poor minorities if they have territorial representation [Piriou-Sall (1997)].

Decentralization is, however, also fraught with risks for rural development. Potential liabilities of decentralization include: (1) Increased private cost for the community of activities with economies of scale and increased social cost of activities with negative externalities as the size of local administrative units decreases. (2) Weaker fiscal base, for precisely the communities that need more costly rural development programs. (3) Projects open to capture according to the local power structure, creating in particular: (i) potential discrepancies between central and local objectives, (ii) loss of control over targeting within the community, and (iii) potential exclusion of minorities with no territorial base. (4) Potential cooperation failures due to heterogeneity of local populations, excessive group size, lack of leadership, lack of trust and shared social norms, etc. (5) Coordination problems across units of local governance (for instance, over the positive externalities across localities created by educational expenditures) and between local and central governments [e.g., in Bolivia, see Cossio (1997)]. However, incentives to coordinate in order to decrease the inefficiencies created by externalities also increase with decentralization since the magnitude of the externalities to be internalized (and hence the gains from coordination) increase with decentralization.

Hence, large externalities created by greater decentralization could eventually lead to smaller inefficiencies if they trigger coordination [Klibanoff and Morduch (1995)]. (6) Imperfect local information about global opportunities and constraints.

While a process about which there is considerable controversy (for instance implementation of the concept of subsidiarity in the European Union) and insufficient information is available, the decentralization of governance opens new possibilities to manage rural development in a markedly different manner than the top-down approach followed by integrated rural development in the 1970s.

4.2.4. Participatory democracy

During the last 15 years, significant progress has been made toward democratic forms of governance. This is true in Latin America where backlash effects from the debt crisis have delegitimized the remaining dictatorships [Haggard and Kaufman (1989)]. Today, a large majority of developing countries have democratic governments, at least formally. In South East Asia, many countries that boomed under authoritarian regimes have subsequently transited to democratic regimes, responding to clamors for more accountability in governance to secure the economic gains achieved. Even in Africa, where political liberalization is lagging most, many countries have shifted to democracies and there are strong pressures in this direction in most of the other countries. Democratization, particularly in the context of the decentralization of governance, opens up important roads for alternative approaches to rural development. Yet, while this opens the possibility of greater participation by the rural poor and greater accountability by elected officials, young democracies are often characterized by fragmented and unstable political parties, oscillation between corporatism and populism, and high levels of cronyism and corruption. Importantly for democratic decentralization, local elected officials may represent the old authoritarian political order instead of the new class of politicians who appropriated control over the central government, creating conflicts in policy objectives between central and local governments [Fox (1996)]. This raises complex questions as to whether these local levels of governance should, in the name of expediency, be bypassed by central governments and international agencies in reaching directly the poor, or whether the pursuit of rural development includes the arduous task of transforming local governance to secure the political sustainability of rural development programs.

4.2.5. Property rights and access to land

The issue of access to land is far from resolved, and redefinitions of property rights open new fronts for rural development. Old-style approaches to land reform basically used the coercive powers of the state to expropriate and redistribute [Lipton (1993)]. While there are exceptional historical circumstances where this is still possible, seeking new forms of access to land consistent with the prevailing balance of forces in the political economy is a fundamental premise of rural development. Today, extraordinary opportunities for land reform do exist in the context of decollectivization of land use in transition economies. This includes Central and Eastern Europe, Russia, China, and Vietnam [Mathijs and Swinnen (1997), Rozelle et al. (1997)]. In Africa, there are strong pressures to reform property rights away from the open access regimes that nationalization of land ownership created after decolonization. Where land is most fertile or under irrigation, individual titling of open access land has progressed rapidly, often at the cost of exclusion of the poor and serious inequities in the process of enclosure [Baland and Platteau (1998)]. In other places, collective titling offers the possibility of controlling incentives to overuse via cooperation while preserving the advantages of economies of scale, geographical risk diversification, and solidarity relations among community members [Baland and Platteau (1996), Nugent and Sanchez (1998)]. The end of white rule in Southern Africa and massive titling of community lands in Mexico offer the unique historical possibility of creating a large rural middle class of family farmers [Van Zyl, Kirsten and Binswanger (1996), de Janvry, Gordillo and Sadoulet (1997)]. In all cases, successful land reform hinges on instrumenting complementary rural development programs, particularly in redesigning the institutions assisting the competitiveness of rural households consistently with the new set of property rights.

There are other paths of access to land that can serve as prerequisites for rural development. Where different household members cultivate separate plots, intra-household rules for the allocation of resources across land plots have important efficiency and equity implications [Udry (1996)]. Rural development interventions can then be targeted at women's plots if they display lower productivity. Inheritance rights typically discriminate against women and have implications for incentives to conserve [Otsuka and Quisumbing (1997)]. Land rental markets open very important channels of access to land, but they often (as in Latin America, the Philippines, and many African nations) have been undermined by weak property rights for landlords and unprotected contracts for tenants. In addition, the rising capital intensity of agriculture induces landlords to look for sharecroppers endowed not only in cheap family labor, but also in capital and managerial expertise, limiting entry into the agricultural ladder for the rural poor [Sharma and Drèze (1996)]. Finally, important new experiments are in place to organize efficient land markets [Carter and Salgado (1997)] and assist the landless and smallholders in gaining access to land through these markets [Deininger (1997)]. These "land market-assisted approaches to land reforms" require putting into place complementary institutions to register and title land, facilitate access to long-term credit, broker transactions between sellers and buyers, and reduce transactions costs in dividing large properties among small buyers (land banks) [Dorner (1992)].

4.2.6. Environmental externalities

A large share of the rural poor are located in fragile areas with advanced levels of degradation. They are often trapped in a vicious circle where poverty induces more degradation and degradation worsens poverty [Reardon and Vosti (1997)]. There are, however, increasing domestic and international pressures to reduce the negative externalities associated with rural poverty and to achieve greater sustainability in resource use. Urban society in the MDCs places new demands on rural areas such as the management of rural landscapes to support recreation and tourism. Environmental regulations have entered regional trade agreements and international treaties, giving new incentives to reduce these negative externalities. Examples include regulations to reduce the devastation created by slash-and-burn agriculture in watersheds and to reduce the loss of biodiversity associated with burning tropical forest to create farm lands that, in turn, rapidly degrade into low-productivity pastures [Hecht (1985)]. By reducing low-value slash-and-burn agriculture, watersheds could instead become producers of high-value clean water for irrigation and hydroelectricity for the rest of the nation. Burning tropical forests to create low-productivity pastures produces very little value added compared to the same quota of emissions created by modern industry, opening opportunities for mutually beneficial international agreements on trading emission quotas. The same applies to the depletion of water tables for inefficient irrigation compared to use under precision technologies like drip irrigation [Zilberman, Khanna and Lipper (1997)] or for urban development. In all cases, either internalizing these externalities through taxation or, if property rights are clearly assigned, creating markets to reallocate the sources of these externalities to the most efficient producers opens a vast new space for rural development. Massive resources could thus be transferred in support of conservation-oriented and restoration-oriented rural development. New technological options for peasant farming systems in fragile lands need to be explored by combining the contributions of formal scientific research (e.g., the Consultative Group on International Agricultural Research [CGIAR] and the U.S. Land Grant College system) with the traditional wisdom embodied in heterogeneous peasant farming systems. Even though they offer considerable promise, these institutional and technological options have barely begun to be explored [see, however, Altieri and Hecht (1990) and ICRAF (1997)].

4.3. Role of civil society

4.3.1. Local organizations

The last 15 years have witnessed an explosion in the number, diversity, and complexity of forms of organizations in civil society, a phenomenon that has been referred to as the "thickening of civil society" [Fox (1996)]. Combined with the decentralization of governance and progress in participatory democracy, these organizations offer new opportunities for a radically new approach to rural development. They include both corporatist institutions and non-profit organizations [principally non-governmental organizations (NGOs) and grassroots organizations (GROs)]. While well established in the United States since the mid-nineteenth century [de Tocqueville (1835)], they are a phenomenon of the 1970s in Latin America and of the 1990s in Africa and countries formerly under central planning. Their emergence can be traced back to (1) the failures of the development model based on a strong role of the state in economic and social affairs and the subsequent dismantling of government institutions in support of rural development; (2) the need for rural households to organize on a variety of ad hoc fronts to face a multiplicity of issues in income generation (pluriactivity, microenterprises) and the organization of social life (school, neighborhood, youth activities, etc.) not attended to by the state and that cut across the mandates of traditional class positions [Touraine (1980)], and (3) responses to the lack of democratic rights at the national level and to the frequent dismantling of political parties, labor unions, and producer cooperatives as the traditional forms of organization. Increasingly, however, civil institutions that originated as a response to market failures (e.g., seeking survival in spite of the debt crisis) and government failures (e.g., seeking representation at the local level to compensate for lack of democratic rights at the national level) have become complementary to the market and the state [Nugent (1993)]. For income generation, they are playing the role of assisting members in accessing services or achieving economies of scale that they could not obtain individually. Hence, they can be instrumental in facilitating access for their members to credit, insurance, technical assistance, and markets which could not be reached by the individual. For political representation, they are assuming the role of lobbies to exercise pressure for the definition and targeting of public goods and to influence relevant legislation. For rural development, NGOs and GROs open the possibility of new partnerships with the state, where each institution, public and private, focuses on what it can do best. The comparative advantages of NGOs and GROs are in accessing local private information for monitoring programs and targeting transfers, capturing local social capital for the enforcement of contracts and cooperation, promoting local entrepreneurship, coordinating the emergence of new institutions when there are positive externalities and hence private underinvestment, and mobilizing grassroots pressures for a multiplicity of progressive causes [Besley (1996)]. At the same time, these organizations can be plagued with serious limitations that include weak financial and administrative capacities, dispersion, lack of continuity, territorial conflicts, attachment to ideological doctrines, exclusion of segments of civil society, and lack of social accountability [Carroll (1992)].

4.3.2. Agrarian institutions

In response to the de-institutionalization of rural areas that followed state compression, the construction of new agrarian institutions complementary to the market and the state is thus a fundamental element of rural development [Hoff, Braverman and Stiglitz (1993)]. This has taken the form of either private or cooperative organizations. Private organizations include technical assistance firms (sometimes paid with government vouchers distributed to smallholders, as in Chile), merchants replacing parastatals in supplying inputs and marketing commodities, commercial banks capturing clienteles formerly attended by public development banks, and private insurance companies absorbing clients from failed public insurance schemes. Organizations based on cooperative principles include informal financial institutions that provide access to credit to households without collateral (group lending with joint liability, village banks, rotating savings and credit associations), mutual insurance schemes among self-selected sub-coalitions of villagers, and service organizations to reduce transactions costs in accessing markets. Complementarity between civil organizations and the state often allows for the co-production of public goods and services, for instance through private financial contributions or labor participation to public projects of infrastructure development. The design of these institutions is one of the main challenges of the new context for rural development.

In many parts of the world, rural households have been organized in communities since ancestral times. For rural development, an important issue of debate is whether the traditional rural community can serve as the basis for the emergence of modern organizations in support of rural development. Looking at the experience of Japan and Korea, Hayami (1988) argues that the village-based community is a fundamental organizational unit. Rising resource scarcity has induced these communities to organize to conserve and manage local commons such as irrigation systems. In this context, landlords are under social pressure to participate in provision in the commons, serve as patrons to their tenants, and invest to raise labor productivity. The relations of trust and the norms of reciprocity that prevail among community members have helped sustain efficient contractual relations with local merchants and develop community-based service organizations [Hayami and Kawagoe (1993)]. Hence, local information, social capital, and repeated interactions in the community have been assets for institutional development and growth. By contrast, looking at the tribal community in sub-Saharan Africa, Hayami and Platteau (1997) argue that land abundance and high weather risks have structured community relations around redistributive norms of mutual insurance as opposed to concerns for productivity growth and reciprocity. Pressures to share, even if doing well is not due to random shocks but to entrepreneurship, have as a purpose the prevention of social differentiation and block exit from the community of the most successful entrepreneurs. As a result, redistributive norms tend to act as a retardant to investment and growth. The community is consequently not an effective basis on which growth-promoting rural development initiatives can be organized, unless growth benefits the whole community in a sufficiently egalitarian fashion. Successful entrepreneurs can escape the redistributive constraints imposed by the community only through urban migration, by moving to other communities where as newcomers they are not subjected to redistributive pressures, by converting to other religions and thus adopting outsider norms, or by coordinating with other entrepreneurs to achieve a sufficient critical mass to subvert traditional norms.

4.3.3. Heterogeneity, gender, and ethnicity

Empirical analyses of rural populations reveal a rising degree of heterogeneity in income strategies among households. This is due to the progressively greater integration of rural households into a variety of markets as a consequence of improved infrastructure, more complete markets, better flows of information, and rising land scarcity that pushes household members into agricultural diversification and non-agricultural activities. The result is increasing social differentiation where some households accumulate assets while others decumulate. Better data have allowed more detailed understanding of the complexity of household income strategies, perhaps exposing aspects of heterogeneity that had been overlooked in the past.

To be effective, rural policy has to account for this heterogeneity. The main determinants of heterogeneity that need to be taken into account in distinguishing types of rural households are the following: heterogeneity in asset positions, in technologies available to them, in transactions costs in product and factor markets, in exposure to credit constraints and insurance market failures, in access to public goods and services, and in access to agrarian institutions. Corresponding to household heterogeneity, sources of income for rural households have become more diversified. This pluriactivity characterizes rural households both in the LDCs [Reardon and Taylor (1996)] and in the MDCs [Bryden et al. (1992)]. In addition to traditional farming activities, farm households are increasingly participating in agricultural and non-agricultural labor markets, in microenterprises often linked to agriculture through forward, backward, and final demand linkages, and also in manufacturing, tourism, retirement activities, and a range of services. It is this diversification of income sources for farm households that increasingly distances rural from agricultural economics.

In most countries, the role of women in agriculture has become more important. This is associated with the permanent outmigration of men (Mexico, Russia), pluriactivity that draws male labor off farm seasonally on labor markets, improved (even if still highly deficient) legal rights for women in accessing land through government programs or inheritance [Meinzen-Dick et al. (1997), Deere and León (1997)], and the expansion of labor-intensive activities which are well fit to women's participation (e.g., tobacco, fruits and vegetables, and dairy cattle). In Africa, in part because of the pervasiveness of polygamy, women cultivate separate plots which are less intensively used than household plots or those cultivated by men, suggesting opportunities for efficiency gains through factor reallocation [Udry (1996)]. The new context for rural development thus places explicit emphasis on the role of women in agriculture, not only as an equity issue but as a fundamental efficiency question [Collier (1988)]. In many countries, rural women manage a majority of the rural microenterprises, a sector which has been in rapid expansion.

There is a close correlation between poverty and ethnicity. In Latin America, 80 percent of the region's indigenous population lives in poverty [IADB (1996)]. Indigenous populations have often lost access to land due to poor information about their property rights, abuse, and discrimination. There exists a vast backlog of rural development initiatives to redefine and enforce their legal rights (both property rights and human rights), promote their access to income sources while respecting the choice of attachment to place, and involve ethnic communities in the management of resource conservation programs.

5. Modeling household responses

In recent years, important theoretical advances have been made in applying the new institutional economics (NIE) to issues relevant for the design of rural development. This has opened a fast-growing field of modeling and empirical analysis of household behavior, agrarian institutions, community behavior, and regional determinants of growth. While it is beyond the scope of this chapter to review exhaustively these many advances, we selectively discuss each of these levels of analysis for the sake of illustrating how these efforts open new perspectives for the design of rural development. This link between theoretical advances and rural policy design is, however, not trivial. Indeed, much of the work on households, institutions, communities, and growth has been motivated by positive rather than normative purposes. Using these models for rural policy-making remains seriously underdeveloped.

5.1. Static household behavior under market imperfections

There exists a class of static household models that stresses the role of pervasive risks, limited information, and imperfect markets on household behavior. The predictions derived from these models differ markedly from those of the standard household model where all markets are assumed to work, and hence where there is separability between production and consumption decisions [Singh, Squire and Strauss (1986)]. Under separability, allocation of resources in production can be decided independently of consumption decisions. Once farm profits have been realized, consumption decisions are taken under the budget constraint that includes farm profits, other incomes that can be obtained given the time constraint, and exogenous transfers. Separability breaks down when there are market failures. In this case, production and consumption decisions need to be taken jointly.

Models with market failures stress the following determinants of household behavior:

(a) Asset endowments with multiple dimensions. These include natural capital, man-made capital (fixed capital used in farm and microenterprise production), human capital, institutional capital (access to local organizations, access to public goods and services), and social capital (interlinkages with community members that help reduce transactions costs, local availability of organizations, and migration capital).

(b) Unitary transactions costs in accessing markets. Effective prices received at the farm gate are below market price and effective prices paid at the farm gate are above market price by the corresponding transactions costs.

(c) Credit constraints and/or high transactions costs in accessing financial services.

(d) Risk aversion and limited access to risk-coping instruments (credit, mutual insurance).

A simple example of a model of this class is one where there are transactions costs in the food market. It allows one to classify households endogenously regarding participation in the food market and to derive supply responses to changes in exogenous prices and fixed assets conditional on food market participation.

The household chooses a consumption vector c, a production vector q (with positive values for products and negative values for inputs), a sales vector e, and a purchases vector m. With an initial endowment E_i for good i, the commodity balance is $c_i + e_i = E_i + q_i + m_i$. Let us denote by I the set of all goods, I_c the set of consumption goods (with $c_i > 0$), and I_q the set of production goods (with $q_i \neq 0$).

Assume that food is both consumed and produced and that there are unitary transactions costs in accessing the food market. The effective prices for the sale, p_a^s, and the purchase (p_a^b) of food are $p_a^s = p_a - t^s$ and $p_a^b = p_a + t^b$, where p_a is the market price of food and t^s and t^b are unit transactions costs in sales and purchases, respectively. These transactions costs are household-specific and expressed as functions of household characteristics z_t that include not only factors such as distance to market but also elements of the household's social and institutional capital, $t^s(z_t)$ and $t^b(z_t)$. All other commodities are transacted at a unique price p_i.

The household problem is:

$$\max_{c,q,e,m} u(c; z_u); \tag{1}$$

subject to:

$$g(q, z_q) = 0, \qquad \text{technology;} \tag{2}$$

$$(p_a - t^e)e_a - (p_a + t^m)m_a + \sum_{i \neq a} p_i(e_i - m_i) + T = 0, \quad \text{budget constraint;} \tag{3}$$

$$c_i + e_i = E_i + q_i + m_i, \quad i \in I, \qquad \text{commodity balance;} \tag{4}$$

$$c_i \geqslant 0, \; e_i \geqslant 0, \; m_i \geqslant 0, \quad i \in I, \qquad \text{non-negativity constraints.}$$

In these equations, z_u are exogenous shifters of the utility function such as demographic characteristics, z_q are exogenous shifters of the production function such as the household's endowments in productive assets, and T is exogenous non-farm income.

The solution of this model shows that:

(1) Households sort themselves into three regimes of participation in the food market – buyers, sellers, and self sufficient – according to the relation between what would be the shadow price p_a^* of food under self-sufficiency and the two effective market prices p_a^s and p_a^b.

(2) Households make production and consumption decisions as if they were separately maximizing profit and utility, with a decision price for food $\tilde{p}_a$ equal to the effective market price when they participate in the market and equal to its shadow price when they are self-sufficient.

This is written as follows:

$$q_k = q_k(\tilde{p}_a, p_j, z_q), \qquad k \in I_q, \; j \in I_q - \{a\},$$
$$c_l = c_l(\tilde{p}_a, p_i, \tilde{y}, z_u), \qquad l \in I_c, \; i \in I_c - \{a\}, \tag{5}$$

with income

$$\tilde{y} = \tilde{p}_a(q_a + E_a) + \sum_{j \in I_q - \{a\}} p_j(q_j + E_j) + T.$$

The shadow price under self-sufficiency is the solution to the self-sufficient equilibrium condition:

$$c_a(p_a^*, p_i, y^*, z_u) = q_a(p_a^*, p_j, z_q) + E_a, \tag{6}$$

with income

$$y^* = p_a^*(q_a + E_a) + \sum_{j \in I_q - \{a\}} p_j(q_j + E_j) + T.$$

The three regimes and the corresponding decision prices are:
- (a) If $p_a^* \leqslant p_a^s = p_a - t^s$, the household chooses to be a net seller of food, and its decision price is $\tilde{p}_a = p_a^s$.
- (b) If $p_a^s < p_a^* < p_a^b$, the household chooses food self-sufficiency, and its decision price is $\tilde{p}_a = p_a^*$.
- (c) If $p_a^* \geqslant p_a^b = p_a + t^b$, the household chooses to be a net buyer of food, and its decision price is $\tilde{p}_a = p_a^b$.

For households who are buyers or sellers of food, the price of food is determined by the market price and the transactions costs. There is separability. Hence, production decisions are not a function of the determinants of p_a^*. By contrast, if the model holds true, for households who are self-sufficient in food, the shadow price of food

$$p_a^* = p_a^*(p_i, E_i, E_a, z_q, z_u), \qquad i \in I_c \cup I_q - \{a\},$$

affects production decisions, and food production is a function of the household's demand characteristics, namely of endowments, prices of pure consumption goods, and utility shifters. There is non-separability. The same model applies if there is a price band on the labor market rather than on the food market [Sadoulet, de Janvry and Benjamin (1998)]. Transactions costs in the labor market include supervision costs for hired labor, and search costs and involuntary unemployment on household members' off-farm labor.

What are some of the implications for rural development that derive from this general class of models?

5.1.1. Elasticity of supply response of food crops

Food production of self-sufficient households is perfectly inelastic to the food price, unless the change in price is sufficiently large to induce them to enter in the market either as sellers or as buyers. This implies that the regional price elasticity, equal to the average, over all producers, of individual price elasticities, will depend on the share of production which is produced by market participants, and will be smaller than under complete market participation if a fraction of the households opt for self-sufficiency. Oversight of this heterogeneity in household market participation can explain some of the huge discrepancies in estimated supply elasticities across studies, even for the same commodity and the same country [see, e.g., Askari and Cummings (1976)].

The transactions costs that we have considered so far are proportional to the quantity traded, and hence are modeled as raising or lowering the price for the transaction. Transactions costs also include fixed costs, invariant to the quantity exchanged, such as search costs, costs of seeking information, cost of bargaining, and time involved in accessing the market. As under unit transactions costs, behavior under fixed transactions costs creates a set of autarkic households. However, a price change that induces a household to enter the market is accompanied by a discrete increase in production, while production is incremental when households only face proportional transactions costs. The consequence of this behavior is to further reduce the aggregate price elasticity of the marketed surplus [see Key, Sadoulet and de Janvry (1999)].

For households which are autarkic in food, an increase in productive assets or in technology will not induce as large an increase in food production as for households integrated into the market. This is because, as food production increases, its shadow price declines, making it a less attractive activity. This, however, should not be used as an argument against the need to include these households in efforts of technological diffusion. The benefit of technology to these households is in allowing them to free some of their resources for other activities such as the production of cash crops and labor market participation.

5.1.2. Covariation between production and market prices

If local markets are shallow, there will exist a high negative covariance between output and prices. As a result, price bands widen with output fluctuations, keeping households in self-sufficiency: as prices fall in good years, households are eventually unable to sell even though they have a bumper harvest; as prices rise in bad years, they are eventually unable to buy even though they have little home production to consume [de Janvry and Sadoulet (1994)]. Households in shallow local markets are thus prevented from using market transactions to stabilize welfare when yields fluctuate. Shadow prices fluctuate widely, reflecting the changing scarcity value of the goods they cannot market. Regions with poorly integrated markets expose producers to such fluctuations, stressing the advantages of better infrastructure and of integration into deeper markets, for instance through international trade. Hence, an important dimension of rural development is to deepen the markets to which households have access.

5.1.3. Elasticity of supply response of cash crops

In a model where food and cash crops compete for fixed factors, the elasticity of supply response of cash crops will be low if the household is in the self-sufficiency range for food and/or labor [de Janvry, Fafchamps and Sadoulet (1991)]. This is because, as cash crops prices rise, for instance as a consequence of a real exchange rate depreciation, the household will not reduce food production to plant more cash crops if access to food through the market remains too expensive (i.e., although the household's shadow price of food increases, it remains below the market price plus transactions costs in buying). And it cannot increase labor allocated to cash crops without reducing leisure, precisely at a time when the household is better off due to a higher price of cash crops and hence is more inclined to increase leisure as opposed to working more. Policies for increasing the elasticity of supply response of cash crops include:

(1) Reduce the incidence of market failure for food by reducing transactions costs. This calls on infrastructure investment, improved access to information about markets, and greater competitiveness in marketing.
(2) Promote technological change in the production of food crops to reduce resources locked into food production.
(3) If "food" includes the set of nontradable maintenance activities which the household needs to perform to survive (particularly the collection of firewood and the fetching of water), improving the productivity of labor in these activities will free time to respond to the incentive to produce cash crops.

Hence, improving the elasticity of supply of cash crops requires looking beyond cash crops as such into the set of other constraints that limit household resource reallocation toward these crops.

5.1.4. Change in the price of manufactured consumption goods

If the price of manufactured consumption goods falls, for instance as a consequence of reducing industrial protectionism as a country shifts out of import-substitution industrialization policies, this creates a shift in consumption demand for food. This shift induces a change in the marketed surplus of food and in net labor supply, but does not affect the production decision of separable households. By contrast, for households not participating in the food and/or labor markets, it creates an incentive to produce more cash crops in order to have the liquidity necessary to acquire more of these goods. This is one of the important complementarities between successful industrialization and agricultural growth [Berthélémy and Morrisson (1987)]. The policy implication is thus that access to low-priced industrial consumption goods is a necessary complement to rural development as it offers farm households a reward for the delivery of a marketed surplus. Otherwise, forced savings (as in Cuba and formerly the Soviet Union) or low rewards in the consumption of manufactured goods create disincentives to the production of cash crops.

5.1.5. Infrastructure development

Infrastructure investment serves to narrow the width of price bands. In so doing, more producers are exposed to price incentives. The result is that infrastructure investment helps increase the elasticity of regional supply response by raising market participation, an externality of infrastructure investment usually not accounted for in project appraisal. Hence, infrastructure investments to reduce transactions costs pertain prominently to rural development initiatives.

5.1.6. Risk aversion

To look at the impact of price risk, one can ignore autarkic households and concentrate on market participants. This can be done with a model similar to the one presented above without transactions costs in the food market and an expected utility specification [Finkelshtain and Chalfant (1991), Fafchamps (1992a)]. Home consumption of part of production helps a household reduce exposure of its real income to price fluctuations. Intuitively, this is because both full income y and the aggregate consumer price P move with the price of food:

$$\frac{dy}{y} = s_q \frac{dp_a}{p_a} \quad \text{and} \quad \frac{dP}{P} = s_c \frac{dp_a}{p_a},$$

where s_q and s_c are the shares of food in income and in consumption respectively. Hence, the variance of real income y/P is lower than the variance of nominal income. When facing these risks, net sellers will reduce production, but less so than pure producers. Net buyers may react to price risks by producing more instead of less: they protect their household consumption by securing more of their food supply through higher food self-sufficiency, particularly if yield risks are low compared to price risks. The response to price risk among risk averse producers is thus highly differentiated: pure producers (commercial farms) produce less; net seller households reduce production, but by less than commercial farms; and net buyers may insure themselves by producing more.

Households can reduce exposure to consumption risk through risk management (interventions which are ex-ante relative to income realizations) and through risk coping (ex-post relative to income), and there is hence a tradeoff between the two [Alderman and Paxson (1992)]. Since risk management has an opportunity cost on expected income, improved access to risk-coping instruments may allow households to take higher risks in production and achieve higher expected incomes [Binswanger and Rosenzweig (1993), Morduch (1992)]. Rural policy should thus promote access to risk-coping instruments such as flexible credit, particularly for poor risk-averse households, as a way of raising expected incomes.

5.1.7. Liquidity constraints and suboptimal resource allocation

Because the expenditure and income profiles are markedly seasonal in agricultural production, the problem of liquidity constraints in financing production can be particularly acute. This prompts households to adjust their income-generating strategies and their expenditure patterns to bring the distance between the two profiles within the range of available credit. A simple way to think about a liquidity constraint for a lean season, for example, is to consider commodities consumed and produced in the two seasons as being different commodities. Let us call I_K the subset of commodities consumed or produced in the lean season and I_{nK} the complement set of commodities, and let K be the exogenous amount of liquidity available for the season above the cash generated by the productive activities themselves. Adding the liquidity constraint

$$\sum_{i \in I_K} p_i (e_i - m_i) + K = 0 \tag{7}$$

to the model above introduces a decision price for all commodities subject to the liquidity constraint:

$$\tilde{p}_i = p_i (1 + \lambda_c), \quad i \in I_K,$$

where λ_c is the shadow price of the liquidity constraint. With this modification to the definition of $\tilde{p}_i$, the solution to the model is otherwise similar to the system of equations (5) and (6). With higher decision prices, households will bias their resource allocation toward the activities that generate or save cash in the lean season. This liquidity constraint may considerably reduce their capacity to seize opportunities of increasing production in response to higher prices [de Janvry et al. (1992)]. The ability of farmers to benefit from higher prices, offered for example by a price liberalization policy, depends on relaxation of the liquidity constraint, confirming the fundamental importance of a credit component to accompany these policies if they are to induce supply response.

5.1.8. Poverty traps and heterogeneity of rural populations

Because there are set-up costs in any income-generating activity, minimum asset endowments are required to enter these activities [Eswaran and Kotwal (1986)]. To keep within the same framework of analysis, the set-up costs can be conceptualized as composed of a fixed cost K_0 and a subset I_K of credit-constrained variable inputs. The model is obtained by: (a) subtracting the fixed entry cost K_0 from the budget constraint (3), (b) replacing commodity balance equalities by inequalities, and (c) imposing an additional constraint:

$$K_0 - \sum_{i \in I_K} p_i q_i \leqslant \sum_{i \in I_K} p_i E_i + K,$$

where the right-hand side represents the resources available to the household to finance the set-up costs. Households with resources below the K_0 threshold are caught in poverty traps, with underused resources (shown in this model by unused resources E_i that cannot be consumed or sold). This opens an important area for rural development interventions. Asset thresholds to enter farming can be reached either through transfers or loans. The role of donors in supporting rural development programs (e.g., foundations, international development agencies) can be understood as efforts at capitalizing households to reach the minimum thresholds needed to enter income-earning activities that will bring them above the poverty line. Because these transfers mobilize otherwise idle resources held by the poor, the internal rate of return on these social investments can be extremely high. Targeting transfers to achieve these multipliers should be an important principle in organizing rural development interventions.

5.2. Dynamic household models: Asset accumulation and evolution of agrarian structure

Rural development is a dynamic issue where success or failure for particular households depends on their ability to accumulate productive assets. Accumulation of financial assets, man-made and natural resource assets, as well as human capital assets is potentially important to enhance household production and consumption. We focus on investment behavior in each of these assets, with particular attention on the implications for rural policy. We also derive implications of household asset accumulation for the evolution of agrarian class structure in a context where the determinants of accumulation are highly heterogeneous across classes of households.

Households engage in intertemporal asset accumulation to optimize the trade-off between consumption today and consumption in the future. Motives underlying asset accumulation vary across households as they differ in their objectives and the constraints they face in attaining them. Traditionally, household asset accumulation has been explained by the 'investment' motive: with access to multiple investment opportunities, households adjust the relative amounts of investment in different types of capital to keep the rates of return in step, or to maximize the return to their portfolio. Early models of savings behavior also focused on 'life-cycle and bequest' motives, which stem from the relationship between optimal consumption (which changes with household characteristics such as age and demographic structure) and income. For an exogenous income path and total lifetime resources, the savings profile depends on the desired consumption profile, the rate of return to assets, and life expectancy of the households. Finally, because saving provides resources that are available in the future when uncertainties (e.g., in future income, rate of return on savings, and utility of consumption, say because of health status) are resolved, the decision to save is intimately related to the nature and extent of uncertainty – the 'precautionary' motive [Gersovitz (1988)]. Saving in assets not only allows for growth in income and increases in consumption but also provides a means to 'smooth' consumption over time.

The optimal asset accumulation path is also influenced by the constraints faced by a household. For instance, a household's exposure (and, therefore, its precautionary savings response) to uncertainty depends on the opportunities it has for insurance and on borrowing constraints. In response to future income uncertainty, a borrowing constrained household will increase savings to reduce the probability of having to decrease consumption when faced with a negative income shock [Deaton (1992a)]. Since there is considerable evidence of high degrees of uncertainty and of borrowing constraints in rural economies, the impact of constraints on savings behavior has been the focus of much recent research. Further, since there are arguments to suggest that asset accumulation to mitigate the impact of these constraints can significantly overwhelm life-cycle savings motives and reduce income growth, understanding precautionary savings behavior is naturally very important for rural policy.

Although asset accumulation is an inherently dynamic issue, a large part of the empirical literature on the determinants of investment in different assets has proceeded with cross-sectional data, in part due to the paucity of panel household surveys. Most of these empirical models are static, but yield useful insights into investments that can be treated like a stock and determinants that do not change over time. There are also studies that are explicitly interested in the dynamics of asset accumulation, and that tackle issues such as the impact of unexpected shocks, anticipated constraints, and technological change on asset accumulation behavior. In this section, we focus primarily on these dynamic household models.

5.2.1. Accumulation of financial and production assets

Dynamic household models which analyze the factors that affect investment in financial or production assets usually stress the precautionary savings motive, focusing on the impact of riskiness in agricultural production (both yield and asset price risk) and the lack of contingency markets (credit and insurance). Early models of consumption smoothing and asset accumulation focused on savings in the form of a single interest-earning asset in response to exogenously determined risky incomes. In reality, savings can take a variety of forms such as demand deposits, cash, physical assets, or the storage of consumption goods. Some stores of saving such as physical assets or human capital assets may be used directly as inputs in production. Others may be preferred for their liquidity (e.g., draft animals are easier to sell than tube-wells), their degree of access (access to credit may be limited), or their low-risk returns (e.g., grains). Each of these asset attributes affects the optimal asset portfolio and the incentives for asset accumulation. The ability to smooth consumption depends on initial asset stocks while the evolution of asset stocks depends importantly on the sequence of income shocks and borrowing constraints faced by the household.[1]

---

[1] For reviews of the literature on savings and asset-buffering behavior, see Gersovitz (1988), Deaton (1992b), and Besley (1995).

An example of a model of consumption smoothing and asset accumulation behavior is one where there are constraints on unlimited borrowing and households must rely on other assets they control to shield consumption from shocks to income or consumption.[2] Consider a simple multiperiod model in which the household chooses consumption each period to maximize the present value of lifetime utility over a finite horizon. Household income derives from two sources. First, the household faces an income shock T_t which is exogenous to the household's behavior. Second, the household derives income from production each period. Production combines two types of assets which differ in their degree of liquidity – a composite 'liquid' asset (B, such as livestock and tools) and a 'nonliquid' asset (M, such as tube-wells, threshers, and cane crushers) – with a fixed amount of land according to the following technology:

$$Y_t = f(B_t, M_t), \quad t = 0, \ldots, T.$$

The production function $f(\cdot, \cdot)$ is assumed to be continuously differentiable, concave, and requires both liquid and nonliquid inputs for nonzero production. Both the income shock and farming income are realized at the beginning of each period and are allocated between consumption and savings.[3] Savings can either be in physical production assets (B and M) or in financial instruments such as bank deposits and loans to others, or in both. That is,

$$C_t + p_b(B_{t+1} - B_t) + p_m(M_{t+1} - M_t) + (1+r)L_{t-1} - L_t \leqslant Y_t + T_t,$$
$$t = 0, \ldots, T$$

and

$$B_t \geqslant 0, \quad M_t \geqslant 0, \quad t = 0, \ldots, T.$$

L_t is the amount borrowed for consumption in period t when $L_t > 0$, or financial savings when $L_t < 0$. p_b and p_m are the unit prices of the liquid and nonliquid assets respectively.[4] In summary, the household chooses B_{t+1}, M_{t+1}, and L_t in each period t

---

[2] Indeed, consumption-smoothing needs arise whenever the path of optimal lifetime consumption diverges from the income path. While much of the literature focuses on income uncertainty as the motivating factor, equally valid reasons for consumption smoothing include variable optimal consumption paths with steady income or differentially fluctuating consumption and income streams.

[3] In this simple model, even though both exogenous income shocks and farming income are assumed to be nonstochastic, smoothing needs arise since the desired consumption profile differs from the endogenously determined income path.

[4] We have assumed that prices for the two assets are not stochastic. If prices were stochastic, changes in asset holdings would reflect expectations of changes in asset prices over time and portfolio diversification. In reality, these are important considerations that should be borne in mind when taking the model to data. However, in order to allow a focus on the consumption-smoothing role of assets, we have ignored portfolio diversification motivations in the model.

to maximize the present value of lifetime utility from time t to T subject to the budget constraint. The household is, however, subject to a ceiling on the amount that can be borrowed each period

$$L_t \leqslant \bar{L}_t, \quad t = 0, \ldots, T-1.$$

To analyze asset accumulation when not all assets are equally liquid, we impose an additional constraint which states that asset B is more liquid than asset M. In the extreme case, when investment in M is irreversible, the constraint is

$$M_{t+1} \geqslant M_t, \quad t = 0, \ldots, T-1.$$

The solution to this problem is characterized by the familiar Euler equations which state that the intertemporal marginal rate of substitution is equal to the marginal rate of transformation. In the absence of borrowing constraints, in the first period the household chooses an asset portfolio to equate the rates of return across all assets – physical and financial:

$$\frac{f_B(B_{t+1}, M_{t+1}) + p_b}{p_b} = \frac{f_M(B_{t+1}, M_{t+1}) + p_m}{p_m} = 1 + r.$$

This optimal portfolio condition determines the stocks of B and M (and therefore farming income). It implies that allocation of savings between the two production assets is determined by production or investment considerations alone, without regard to the smoothing role played by the assets. A change in the rate of return in either the physical assets or the financial asset induces the household to readjust its asset portfolio until the returns to all assets are equalized, thereby maximizing investment income. Consumption smoothing is achieved via participation in financial markets: in response to income shocks, the household prevents consumption from falling by borrowing more on the credit market. In *anticipation* of income shocks, the household reduces its debt to reduce its repayment obligations in a future unlucky period. If per-period utility changes from one period to the next, say for life-cycle considerations, the optimal consumption profile changes. Again, consumption is smoothed by saving and dissaving in the financial asset.

However, when the household faces credit constraints, asset accumulation behavior is very different since the household has to rely on production assets to smooth consumption. In response to current or anticipated income shocks, the household adjusts total investment in physical assets accordingly; it increases investment in anticipation of a negative shock and sells these assets to maintain consumption when faced with the income shock.[5] This sort of dissaving in income-generating assets can be a costly

---

[5] For a positive income shock, investment behavior is reversed: the household reduces investment carried over to the next period when it anticipates a positive shock to its exogenous income.

strategy since it reduces farming income in subsequent periods and makes the household more susceptible to future borrowing constraints.

Further, since M is illiquid, in anticipation of income shocks, the asset portfolio is biased towards B, with resulting over-investment in the liquid asset. When faced with negative shocks, consumption is protected from the full impact of the shock by reducing investment in physical assets. Since only asset B can be sold, this results in under-investment in this liquid production asset. Consumption-smoothing needs, therefore, bear upon production decisions in the form of allocative inefficiencies and output losses. A sequence of binding constraints and negative income shocks forces a household to enter a cycle of both allocative inefficiency and input depletion, which further erodes its capacity to cope with credit constraints. The cycle can be broken if there are intermittent periods of relief in which the household can accumulate assets.

The results of this simple model are suggestive of new areas for rural policy focus. For better or for worse, governments and other development agencies have made the development of credit markets a focus for policy interventions [Besley (1995)]. Our focus on savings in production assets illustrates one example of how borrowing constraints combined with the absence of formal deposit institutions (or other remunerative savings opportunities) results in allocative inefficiencies, output losses, and lower incomes. An understanding of which assets people save in and the incentives underlying that choice may elucidate other markets or institutions that warrant attention. To this end, we summarize the results of selected studies that have been engaged in this research agenda.

When access to credit and alternative assets for savings are limited, households engage in costly strategies to both smooth consumption *ex-post* to income realizations and reduce income fluctuations *ex-ante* [Alderman and Paxson (1992)]. If, for instance, a household is liquidity-constrained during the planting season, it will bias its portfolio of activities towards crops and income sources (such as labor market, microenterprise activities, and migration) that generate cash flows during that season and away from input use (purchased factors), type of activities (activities with a higher cash flow and a faster turnover), and expenditures (purchased consumer goods) that absorb liquidity during that season. This burden of liquidity management through the adjustment of resource allocation, income strategies, and consumption patterns can be eased by saving and dissaving. In this case, the quality of savings instruments matters in the cost of managing liquidity. Policies that increase the return on savings can thus have a positive effect on output for credit-constrained households.

Focusing on which assets are used for saving and dissaving, Rosenzweig and Wolpin (1993) provide evidence that south Indian households which are credit constrained resort to the use of relatively liquid production assets such as draft animals to smooth consumption in periods of crisis. Household production and consumption decisions become non-separable: in response to negative shocks, households divest in liquid production assets and invest disproportionately in these in response to positive shocks. With successive shocks, households can be forced into a cycle of under-investment in production assets [Murgai (1997)]. Since reliance on production assets as a buffer is a costly strategy, as long as a household has stocks of an asset which is not used in production, this asset will be used to smooth consumption [Udry (1995)]. If the assets that are used to buffer consumption from income fluctuations are themselves used in the production process, then there can be important effects on future income from temporary shocks to current income. Farmers' aversion to risk combined with borrowing constraints, low income, and the absence of formal deposit institutions thus not only results in output losses and lower incomes but also exacerbates the susceptibility to income shocks.[6]

Under-investment, poverty, and inequity are exacerbated when input investments are non-divisible and irreversible, as in the case of tube-wells [Fafchamps and Pender (1997)]. With low returns to savings, poor households are unable to accumulate enough wealth to make a profitable investment and are in effect forced to accept a lower return on divisible wealth.[7] Focusing on household heterogeneity, Zimmerman and Carter (1996) extend the asset accumulation literature to look at the role of wealth levels in determining portfolio composition of households facing risky yields, risky asset prices, and subsistence constraints. Wealthy households are farther from the subsistence constraint, and therefore are willing to bear more risk than poorer households. Households too poor to support subsistence consumption eventually stock out, driving their asset base to zero. This is in marked contrast to the rich who are endowed with large enough stocks of productive assets to avoid a subsistence crisis even in a bad year. The rich, therefore, continue to accumulate high-return, high-risk assets over their life-cycle. The model thus predicts increasing polarization in asset positions over time, with disappearance of a middle class of farmers.

Results from this class of models provide insights into why there might be a 'poverty trap' for select groups of households. Households that are credit constrained, that have small wealth endowments, and limited access to remunerative savings opportunities have a tendency to pursue safer but lower-return asset portfolios, to refrain from profitable but non-divisible investments, and to rely on costly strategies for smoothing consumption. These are the vulnerable groups that are the natural focus of rural policies

---

[6] These studies are part of a growing literature with empirical evidence both in support and against the use of production assets in consumption smoothing. Using the same data as Rosenzweig and Wolpin (1993), Chaudhuri and Paxson (1993) and Lim and Townsend (1994) show that grain stocks and cash are used for high-frequency smoothing in the Indian ICRISAT villages. Kochar (1995) contends that rather than resort to costly risk-coping strategies, households rely on participation in the labor market to shield consumption from negative income shocks. Fafchamps, Udry and Czukas (1998) use the Burkina Faso ICRISAT data and find that cattle sales offset on average only 15 percent and at most 30 percent of the income losses resulting from aggregate rainfall shocks. Alderman (1996) finds considerable variation across income classes in the ability to cope with risk. Rich households are able to shield consumption most effectively against transitory income changes, and can capitalize increases in permanent income into physical savings.

[7] A similar point is made by Rosenzweig and Binswanger (1993) who find that the composition of asset portfolios is influenced significantly by farmers' aversion to risk and their wealth. The trade-off between profit variability and average profit returns is significant, and the loss in efficiency associated with risk mitigation is considerably higher among the poorer farmers.

for poverty alleviation. Policies and programs to improve access to credit will reduce the need to bias resource allocation towards liquidity saving and create efficiency and welfare gains, stressing the importance of institutional innovations in micro-lending as a key element of rural development.

Equally important, and generally overlooked in rural policy, is the need to focus attention on improving the quality of savings instruments to reduce reliance on production assets for risk coping and to facilitate investment in profitable but non-divisible or irreversible assets. Compared to credit programs, savings programs do not suffer from problems of moral hazard, adverse selection, and enforcement. Increasing the rate of return on saving and making savings secure in the face of regional shocks may thus be a better alternative than subsidizing credit. There is hence a need to develop financial institutions that can mobilize the savings of the poor as a fundamental component of rural development initiatives [Wickrama and Keith (1994)].

5.2.2. Investment in human capital assets

Evidence of knowledge-driven endogenous growth at the macro-level [Romer (1994)] underscores the importance of research on investment in human capital at the micro-level. Human capital can be broadly defined as education and health. Unlike investment in physical or financial assets, analysis of human capital investment is complicated by its role as both a 'consumption good' as well as a 'capital good' that contributes to income via its impact on productivity. It is difficult to allocate human capital expenditures between current and future consumption. Further difficulties in analyzing human capital investment stem from the fact that human capital is multi-dimensional. Different dimensions of human capital (e.g., anthropometrics, schooling, morbidity, nutrient intakes, etc.) can have different effects on productivity and preferences. There is a large empirical literature [reviewed in Strauss and Thomas (1995)] that focuses on the determinants of investment in these multiple facets of human capital and on the impact of human capital investment on asset returns, productivity, and income. Most of these empirical models are static, typically being concerned with outcomes that may be treated as a stock, such as completed schooling or child height. Considerable insights on the determinants of human capital investments (such as the impact of parents' schooling on human capital investments in children, or the impact of permanent income on longer-run measures of human capital) have been gained from this literature. There are relatively few studies that have looked at human capital investment in the context of dynamic household models, with attention to considerations such as the impact of unexpected shocks, future credit constraints, or technological change. We summarize selected studies and insights for rural policy from this relatively young literature.

The effect of technology shocks on schooling investment by households in rural India has been analyzed by Foster and Rosenzweig (1996). They estimate the dynamic schooling decision rule in period t as a function of household assets (including human capital) in that period, variables affecting current income (such as the level of technology, wages, and weather realizations), and variables affecting expectations about the future (parameters of the technology distribution). They find that technological change both increases the returns to as well as results in greater private investment in schooling. Availability of schools in the area complements the effects of technological change: returns to investment in technological change increase when primary schooling is accessible, and returns to investment in schooling increase when technological change is more rapid. From a rural policy point of view, their study has important implications that have often been neglected in interventions aimed at spurring rural investment. Since schooling has an opportunity cost to the household in terms of earnings foregone or education expenditures, households choose to invest in it only if the returns can outweigh these costs. Foster and Rosenzweig's study shows that schooling has a payoff if there exist technologies or other processes that increase the returns to education. That is, simply increasing the availability of schools in an area may not spur investment in human capital if the returns to education are small. In addition to supply-side interventions, it is thus essential to intervene on the demand-side to increase the payoff to schooling.

However, a household that wishes to invest in human capital may be prevented from doing so when it faces credit constraints. For example, Jacoby (1994) asks how borrowing constraints affect the timing of human capital investments by looking at how quickly children with different family backgrounds progress through the primary school system in Peru. For an unconstrained household, the 'timing' of human capital investment should be independent of parental income, and part-time schooling is never optimal. Children in a household that derives income from both parental income and child earnings may, in contrast, attend school part-time if the credit constraint is binding. To test this hypothesis, Jacoby splits the sample into 'constrained' and 'unconstrained' households on the basis of the predicted probability of being constrained. Using a profit regression on the probability of part-time schooling, he finds that higher family income and durable asset stocks do not significantly increase school progress in unconstrained households, but do in constrained households. Similarly focusing on the impact of borrowing constraints, Foster (1995) argues that fluctuations in child weight growth in rural Bangladesh after the flood of 1988 reflect variations in access to credit. He finds that both landless and landed households made substantial use of credit to shore consumption after the flood. However, borrowing was more costly for the landless households, as a result of which their children suffered greater fluctuations in growth. Both studies identify select groups of households that are disadvantaged in their investment decisions and suggest policy-prone instruments that can be targeted appropriately for maximum benefit.

In addition to differences in constraints, heterogeneity in household behavior also arises due to differences in asset positions and production patterns. Foster and Rosenzweig (1996), in the study mentioned above, found that anticipated technological change had a positive effect on investments in schooling by farm households but did not affect decisions made by non-farm households. Based on these results, they suggest that human capital in the context of the Indian Green Revolution technologies affected productivity through its impact on managerial abilities. Thus, rates of return to schooling were affected more strongly for children in farm than non-farm households. For rural policy, this study implies that investment in schooling responds to technical change but, conditional on the nature of the technology, only select groups of households may reap benefits.

Dynamic household models are particularly important for human capital accumulation decisions since there can be significant time-lags between the investment and its productivity or health returns. Moreover, the return to human capital (and hence the relationship between human capital investment and its determinants) can vary across seasons or stages of agricultural production. For instance, Behrman, Foster and Rosenzweig (1997) obtain radically different estimates of the calorie-income elasticity across seasons for rural households. They suggest that there are difficulties in transferring resources across stages of production, which leads to a greater caloric response to income in the lean than in the harvest season. This study points to the importance of being attentive to the timing of income and production activities within the year when designing rural policies, measures directed at certain agricultural stages might be much more effective at influencing human capital investments than those directed at other stages of the production cycle.

5.2.3. Selective investment and dissipation of natural capital

The importance of natural capital – in particular, land – as a central income-generation asset for rural households has long been recognized. However, conceptualizing natural capital (e.g., soil fertility) as a produced rather than primary input analogous to other inputs used in agriculture opens new perspectives [Coxhead (1996)]. This raises the potential of using rural policy to promote the conservation and sustainable use of natural resources. Research on the factors that influence household choices of adoption and maintenance of soil conservation techniques is an important step towards realizing this potential.

The possibility of soil-enhancing investments expands the range of household options with respect to production and resource allocation: in addition to choosing current production and consumption levels, the household optimizes a dynamic trade-off between current consumption and investment in future soil quality. Focusing on this trade-off, Pender and Kerr (1996) provide evidence that investment in soil and water conservation measures is greater among small landowners who have more education, a higher percentage of off-farm income, and more adult males, results which are indicative of significant transactions costs in participating in land, credit, and labor markets.

Similarly, in a study of the Sierra highlands of the Dominican Republic, de la Brière (1997) finds that adoption of soil conservation techniques is highly selective, with many households choosing to not adopt. The main determinants of soil conservation are the perceived security of access to land, idiosyncratic market failures for food, casual labor constraints for the poorest households, remittance and off-farm income, and collaboration with Plan Sierra, a rural development project geared towards poverty alleviation and environmental sustainability. Further, households selectively abandon soil conservation practices over time as efficiency-enhancing effects of learning by doing and efficiency-reducing effects of soil fertility loss create a dynamic trade-off. Analysis of the factors which determine the duration of adoption suggests that households strongly vested in agriculture for their livelihood, with few exit options, and large families to feed (in the context of high transactions costs on food markets) are more likely to adopt. However, since they are likely to be using their land more intensively, they are also more sensitive to the continued, though lower rate of fertility loss.[8]

For rural policy, the study suggests that dynamic aspects of the determinants of both *adoption* and *maintenance* of soil conservation techniques need to be taken into account in the design of soil conservation programs. Otherwise, the promotion of adoption could be misleading as policies may affect the adoption and sustainability of use differently. Adoption under the auspices of rural development programs may end in subsequent abandonment, thus failing to achieve sustainability of conservation in spite of initial success in diffusion.

5.2.4. Evolution of agrarian structure: The role of asset accumulation under imperfect factor markets

The dynamic issues discussed so far have for the most part been restricted to problems of savings and investment decisions at the household level. These models illustrate that asset accumulation behavior varies across households that differ in their asset endowments and face idiosyncratic constraints or transactions costs in their access to credit, labor, food markets, etc. However, household heterogeneity also has ramifications for divergence in household behavior which extends beyond asset accumulation to consumption choices, the organization of production, and eventually the formation of agrarian classes. Eswaran and Kotwal (1986) show that along a continuum of endowments and transactions costs, households optimally choose their labor allocation strategies and can therefore be endogenously classified into agrarian classes. To simplify the analysis, they assume that the initial distribution of asset endowments is static and exogenous. In equilibrium, there is a misallocation of resources: land-to-labor ratios differ across farm sizes and there is scope for welfare- and output-improving transfers of resources across households, justifying the implementation of redistributive land reform.

Therefore, how patterns of production, asset distributions, and agrarian structure evolve over time is a central concern for rural policy from both an efficiency and equity point of view. Recent research has addressed these questions by integrating

---

[8] Other recent studies that explore the effect of imperfect factor market on conservation investments in a dynamic context include Shiferaw (1996) and Wik and Holden (1996). Grepperud (1997) develops a theoretical model to analyze soil conservation adoption decisions by subsistence households in a context of imperfect markets for insurance.

dynamic asset accumulation with endowment continuum models to analyze the extent to which initial asset endowments (and class structure) perpetuate themselves over time. Banerjee and Newman (1993) focus on the evolution of the pattern of occupational choice. They consider an economy in which, because of capital market imperfections, the pattern of occupational choice (wage worker, self-employment, etc.) depends on the initial distribution of wealth. But the occupational choice in turn determines how much households save and how much risk they bear. These factors give rise to a new distribution of wealth. Over time, the economy stabilizes into a pattern of occupational choice and economic growth that depends on the initial distribution of wealth.

Carter and Zimmerman (1993) model intertemporally rational land and wealth accumulation decisions with imperfect labor and credit markets. Labor market imperfections stem from search costs when farmers wish to hire out labor and supervision costs on hired-in labor. In the credit market, there is a fixed transactions cost that is paid by all borrowers, making credit more attractive to large farmers than to small ones. Together, these two market imperfections endogenously generate classes – each with distinct production strategies – that depend on the distribution of land and wealth endowments. Since each of these classes faces different shadow prices for inputs, the economic returns to land and wealth also differ across classes. Over time, it is these differences in asset returns or the 'class competitiveness regime' that determine the ability to accumulate land or wealth and thereby induce structural changes in the distribution of land.[9]

Whether incentives generated by the shifts in competitive regime actually affect structural change depends on how well the land market works [Carter and Zegarra (1995)]. Whether agrarian structure evolves towards increasing polarization or towards a more equitable distribution depends on whether the likely labor advantages of small farms outweigh their disadvantages in the capital market. Ultimately, which rural policies – land, labor, or credit market reforms – can generate a significant shift towards a more equitable agrarian class structure depends on these empirical questions.

6. Modeling agrarian institutions: Informal finance

We have seen that the pervasiveness of institutional gaps, which has worsened in the context of economic transitions and adjustment policies, is one of the important current hurdles for successful rural development. Recent advances in the NIE applied to agrarian institutions provide important guidelines for rural policy directed at this task. Institutional gaps concern a wide array of agrarian institutions including rural finance, marketing arrangements, research and development, technical assistance, and rural insurance. One area in which there has been remarkable progress in both theory and implementation is rural informal finance. In this section, we focus on this subject as an example of successful theoretical advances in support of rural policy.

---

[9] The term 'class competitiveness regime' comes from Carter and Zegarra (1995) who examine agrarian class evolution in Paraguay.

6.1. Formal and community-based finance: Limitations and comparative advantages

To be successfully completed, credit transactions require control of adverse selection (AS) and moral hazard (MH), and provision of some insurance to avoid losing good borrowers who face a bad shock. Insurance itself requires control of AS and MH, and sufficient resources to absorb the negative shock.

Control of AS and MH is demanding in information and punishment instruments. Acquiring adequate information for a bank can be prohibitively expensive. Hence, banks resort to second-best devices such as:

(a) Requirement of collateral that could be seized if repayment does not take place. This mechanism controls for AS and MH, but does not per se offer access to insurance. The main problems are exclusion of those who do not own collateral and absence of insurance, leading to both inefficiency and inequity.

(b) By incorporating limited liability (i.e., insurance, which assumes sufficient control of moral hazard) in a contract, AS can be mitigated by a combination of keeping the interest rate lower than the equilibrium level and credit rationing [Stiglitz and Weiss (1981)]. This mechanism also entails efficiency costs due to the interest rate distortion and the rationing mechanism that cannot identify the best projects under imperfect information.

Members of rural communities have access to local private information and to instruments for enforcement not available to banks. Banks have a comparative advantage in securing resources for lending and diversifying risk over space and activities. This calls for the design of intermediary institutions that provide access to the banking sector's resources while at the same time mobilizing the community's informational, monitoring, and enforcement advantages to improve the delivery of credit [Aryeetey (1996)].

Some informal financial institutions like money lenders and RoSCAs (rotating savings and credit associations) are based on community relationships only. Interlinked credit contracts (for instance with merchants who themselves have access to the formal banking system), village agents working for commercial banks, credit and savings cooperatives, and group lending call upon both formal financial institutions and community relationships.[10] Among such alternative institutions, we develop the theory of group lending which is particularly promising for rural development finance.

6.2. The theory of group lending: Peer selection, peer monitoring, and mutual insurance

Group lending is generally organized by a specific financial institution that serves as an intermediary between a bank, which is the original source of funds, and borrowers.

---

[10] Descriptions of alternative institutions are given in Otero and Rhyne (1994) and Krahnen and Schmidt (1994).

Borrowers form groups to access loans. The financial institution may extend loans to all group members individually or to the group as a whole. Individual loan amounts may be equal or different, although for successful functioning of the group itself, differences cannot be too wide across borrowers. Even though some institutions require initial savings deposits, all members are net borrowers. Interest rates paid by borrowers are usually high, although less than on funds obtained from money-lenders. The fundamental characteristics of a group-lending scheme are (1) groups form voluntarily and members self-select, and (2) group members are jointly liable for the loans. Joint liability implies that members cannot obtain further credit until all outstanding loans in the group have been repaid, or that they may be required to pay a penalty if any member defaults.

Using simple models, we show how the joint liability clause creates incentives for members to use locally public information for the purpose of exercising peer selection and peer monitoring, to apply social pressure to force repayment of loans, and to extend insurance to each other or help with repayment in case of genuine difficulties. In all these models, we assume that there is an infinite supply of capital at a fixed cost ρ. The bank's function is to design a contract that will allow the delivery of this capital to borrowers, and we assume that the bank makes no profit, i.e., all benefits are returned to borrowers.

6.2.1. The benchmark equilibrium of individual credit with adverse selection

Following Morduch (1999), imagine that there are two types of potential borrowers, "safe" S and "risky" R, in given proportions s and $1 - s$. Project i has probability of success π_i, net return R_i per dollar invested, and thus an expected return $\bar{R}_i = \pi_i R_i$. Risky borrowers have a lower probability of success ($\pi_R < \pi_S$) but a higher return if they succeed. Borrowers are assumed to be risk neutral, with m their fall-back option without a loan. To focus on the issue of adverse selection, we assume that there is no moral hazard, i.e., the bank can enforce payment when the project is successful. The bank extends insurance to borrowers through a limited liability clause which pardons dues in case of project failure.

If the bank knows each borrower's type, its first best option is to offer a loan contract with a gross interest rate (including both principal and interest) $r_i = \rho/\pi_i$ to borrowers of type i. Safe borrowers, who repay their loan more often, have a lower interest rate than risky borrowers, but all borrowers on average pay the cost of capital ρ. With this personalized contract, all socially profitable projects, i.e., with expected return $\bar{R} \geqslant \rho + m$, are financed and credit delivery is efficient.

However, when the borrower type is not known, the bank can only offer the same rate r to all borrowers. The rate that ensures zero profit to the bank is $r = \rho/\pi$, where $\pi = (1 - s)\pi_R + s\pi_S$ is the average probability of success in the population. The average cost of capital to safe borrowers is $r\pi_S$ which is higher than ρ. Safe borrowers subsidize risky borrowers, and will only take loans for projects with expected return $\bar{R}_S > \rho\frac{\pi_S}{\pi} + m$. At the same time, risky borrowers pay an average cost that is lower than the opportunity cost of capital, and hence are likely to undertake projects that are not socially profitable. Asymmetric information on borrower types thus penalizes safe borrowers and subsidizes risky borrowers, inducing a misallocation of capital, i.e., inefficiency in credit delivery.

6.2.2. Peer selection improves the pool of borrowers and increases efficiency in credit delivery

Adapting the model of assortative matching developed by Becker (1981), Ghatak (1997) shows that the joint liability clause induces borrowers to sort into homogeneous groups. This process allows for lower interest rates and raises the social efficiency of credit distribution.

In a two-person group contract, a borrower is liable to a fine c if his associate fails to repay his loan (i.e., if his associate's project fails since there is no moral hazard), and he himself has a successful outcome. A borrower of type i, associated with a borrower of type j, will therefore expect to repay $\pi_i(r+(1-\pi_j)c)$. Comparing these expected costs across borrower-types, we can see that any borrower would prefer to associate with a safe rather than a risky borrower. However, the benefit that a risky borrower would gain in teaming up with a safe borrower rather than a risky borrower is lower than the cost that the safe borrower would incur in the mixed group. Hence there is no mutually beneficial way for risky and safe borrowers to form mixed groups. Joint liability thus leads to assortative matching into homogeneous groups.

With assortative matching, safe borrowers when successful pay an interest rate $r+(1-\pi_S)c$ which is lower than $r+(1-\pi_R)c$ paid by risky borrowers when they themselves are successful. Increasing the fine c creates an effective price discrimination between safe and risky borrowers that brings the contract closer to the social optimum. This is shown as follows. The bank's zero profit rule creates a link between r and c, allowing in particular a lower r when higher fines c are imposed. Substituting this relation into the average cost for safe borrowers shows that safe borrowers will find it profitable to borrow whenever the expected return of their project is sufficiently high:

$$\bar{R}_S > \rho\frac{\pi_S}{\pi}+m-c\frac{\pi_S\pi_R}{\pi}(\pi_S-\pi).$$

Can the bank set a sufficiently high level of c to achieve the efficient price discrimination of the first best contract? Not necessarily, because there is an upper limit to the fine c set by the fact that the total liability, interest plus fine, cannot exceed the net return to the project $r+c \leqslant R_S$.

One can show that group credit lowers the limit $\bar{R}_S$ for safe borrowers and raises it for risky borrowers. This simple model thus shows that group liability can attract back into the credit scheme the projects of safe borrowers that are socially profitable but are excluded in an individual loan scheme, and can eliminate some socially inefficient projects by risky borrowers who benefit from the subsidy they receive in the individual scheme.[11] Thanks to peer selection, group lending is thus a more constrained-efficient institution.

In a different set-up where losing access to credit after a default represents a large loss to any borrower, Sadoulet (1997) shows that groups may form heterogeneously provided the safer borrowers receive transfers from the riskier borrowers in compensation for the insurance provided. In essence, this is obtained by adding a term $(1 - \pi_i)(1 - \pi_j)L$ in the expected cost of the loan, where L represents this loss. This is another scheme by which incorporation of the poorer segments of the population, that often face a more precarious and riskier set of options for their activities, is made possible.

6.2.3. Peer monitoring

Group lending can also curb opportunistic behavior that would induce default. The peer monitoring mechanism is illustrated in a simplified version of a model by Stiglitz (1990), similar to the one developed by Besley (1995). Borrowers are assumed to be homogeneous, but can choose between a risky and a safe project. Suppose, for the sake of the argument, that the safe project is socially optimal, i.e., $\pi_S R_S > \pi_R R_R$. Under an individual loan program, there is a critical r above which $\pi_R(R_R - r) > \pi_S(R_S - r)$ and the risky project is always chosen. Thus, if the zero profit rate for safe projects, ρ/π_S, is above this critical limit, the risky project will be chosen in equilibrium, resulting in socially inefficient distribution of credit.

Under a group lending scheme, joint liability will induce both borrowers to choose either the risky or the safe project, for the same reason that makes heterogeneous borrowers exercise peer selection. With interest rate r and fine c, the expected return for an individual of a group having chosen project i is $\pi_i(R_i - r(1 - \pi_i)c)$. This indicates that an increase in the fine raises the relative profit of the safe project if the variance of the risky project is higher than the variance of the safe project, $\pi_R(1 - \pi_R) > \pi_S(1 - \pi_S)$. Under these circumstances, a sufficiently high level of fine induces the choice of safe projects. With peer monitoring, joint liability improves social efficiency in allocating credit to the safer projects.

6.2.4. Insurance

A third dimension of group lending is to provide an environment conducive to mutual insurance among borrowers [Besley and Coate (1995)]. In its simplest form, the idea is that the bank only needs to assess a fine for group default greater than twice the interest rate. This naturally leads borrowers to prefer to pay for their partner whenever they can rather than letting the group default. The equilibrium group solution is that each partner pays for the other when he himself can cover the total dues and his partner does not

---

[11] A rigorous analysis of incorporation of borrowers should go further in allowing for the shares of safe and risky borrowers to be endogenous, and jointly determined with the participation of borrowers.

pay his own share. Assuming further that the group has the ability to control for moral hazard internally, the equilibrium is that each borrower will pay if he can, and pay for both loans if he can and his partner cannot pay his share. The capacity to punish in order to control moral hazards often draws on interlinked transactions among members or on the mobilization of social collateral or pressure from the community which can ostracize a member for his bad behavior. This provision of insurance increases the repayment rate for the bank. The drawback of the scheme is that whenever one of the partners can repay his loan but not both loans, the whole group will default. Overall, joint liability increases the repayment rate if the incidence of mutual insurance overweights the incidence of group default when one of the partners would have been able to pay his share.

In most contexts, the bank has no ability to control moral hazard behavior and hence cannot provide limited liability. If one thinks of the fine as being the denial of future loans, mutual insurance increases the ability for borrowers to remain in the credit scheme when they face adverse shocks. This is clearly welfare-improving compared to no insurance at all, and it explains why some borrowers may choose group credit even when they have access to individual credit [Sadoulet (1997)]. It is noteworthy, however, that this mechanism keeps the burden of insurance within the group, which is second best compared to what could be achieved if the less risk-averse bank could play the role of insurer.

6.3. Evidence on the importance and impact of group-lending programs

The group-lending approach to credit delivery started in the early 1970s in El Salvador, India, and notably in Bangladesh with the Grameen Bank and the Bangladesh Rural Advancement Committee (BRAC). Since the 1970s, group lending programs have expanded in number, size, and geographical coverage.[12] At present, there are 168 Grameen Bank replications in 44 countries. In Latin America, Acción Internacional provides assistance to implement a well-defined lending technique to affiliates in 14 countries. An important characteristic of the program is institution-building and the transformation of NGOs into regulated institutions, a status achieved by BancoSol in Bolivia, for example. In Africa, several initiatives have sought to develop the group-lending methodology, and there also we see the development of second-level organizations such as the Kenya Rural Enterprise Program (KREP), an umbrella organization that provides technical and financial assistance to local NGOs. Group lending has also been introduced in the United States: Acción Internacional has established six programs geared towards the poor in Southern California, New Mexico, Texas, Chicago, and New York. In its Directory of Microenterprise Programs, which covers 195 programs assisting 210,000 low income microentrepreneurs in 44 states, SELP (Self-Employment Learning Project, from the Aspen Institute) notes that 20 percent of the programs operate group-lending schemes.

---

[12] Sources of information on group-lending programs are: Zeller et al. (1997), Otero and Rhyne (1994), and the web pages of Acción Internacional and FINCA.

Most group-lending programs are still relatively young and small, with fewer than 10,000 borrowers. Some of them, however, have reached a sizable scale: the Grameen Bank now lends to two million clients, mostly women, BRAC was serving 700,000 microentrepreneurs in 1992, Acción Internacional and its affiliates reached 176,000 microentrepreneurs in 1996, and BancoSol serves one-third of all the banking sector clientele in Bolivia. The rapid growth of these institutions creates challenges of internal organization and source of funding that we will address in the next section.

While the purpose of these programs is to improve the welfare of their clientele, few impact analyses are available. The main difficulty in addressing this question is proper control for selectivity of clientele and non-random program placement. Econometric correction for these selection bias problems would require identification variables, i.e., variables that affect program participation but do not affect directly the effects of participation. Short of finding such variables, survey design needs to include proper control groups [Coleman (1997)]. Controlling for these effects, Pitt and Khandker (1998) find that each dollar lent by Grameen raises annual household expenditure by 17 cents. If the program has a permanent effect on income generation, then the proper value of the program should be an income stream of 17 cents per year rather than just 17 cents [Morduch (1998)].

While group lending was born and expanded mostly in urban contexts, village banking was developed mainly in rural settings. Village banks are community-managed credit and savings associations of 20 to 50 members. Members of the village bank self-select and offer a collective guarantee. An important difference from group lending is the building of local resources through a compulsory savings program, and an expectation that the village bank will become self-sufficient. FINCA, a pioneer of this lending technology, was working in 14 countries, serving approximately 70,000 borrowers in more than 2,600 village banks in 1997. Recently introduced FINCA programs in the United States, in the Washington–Baltimore metropolitan area and in rural Minnesota, differ in many ways from their counterparts overseas: borrower groups in the U.S. are comparatively small, averaging six members, with members mostly in the service sector, and loans are much larger. However, group solidarity remains an essential characteristic. The village banking method has been replicated in more than 80 other programs in 32 countries, notably by CARE, Catholic Relief Services, Freedom from Hunger, and Save the Children.

A critical issue when judging the effectiveness of these institutions for rural development is to assess their capacity to include the poor. Targeting the poor is embedded in the rules of eligibility, with for example upper limits on land holdings (Grameen Bank and BRAC) and targeting of women (Grameen Bank and FINCA). While there is evidence of substantial mis-targeting [Morduch (1998)] and loss of control by women over the loans [Goetz and Sen Gupta (1996)], statistics on clientele from the institutions' records and from surveys show that group lending reaches a clientele that would not be served by the formal banking system. Borrowers do not have collateral acceptable to banks and loans are substantially smaller than what banks deal with. In that sense, these institutions allow inclusion of poorer borrowers more than allowed by the previously existing financial system. What is not clear, however, is who the excluded are. Due to lack of information on the excluded, one can only infer exclusion by any institution from the rules and criteria for eligibility or from descriptive statistics on the clientele population. Genesis, for example – an affiliate of Acción Internacional in Guatemala – requires that merchants had a fixed location and stall on the local market for at least one year in order to qualify. The reason for this is easy to understand. In a market environment where merchants are fluid and residence unknown, the only element that constitutes some sort of membership to a community is permanence in the workplace. On the other hand, this very condition excludes all potential new entrepreneurs who need start-up capital.

There is an unsettled debate about whether it is appropriate for a financial institution to try to reach the "poorest of the poor", rather than concentrating only on the segment of "bankable poor" and, if the latter, how far it can go in successfully transforming poorer households into bankable poor. This debate relates to another issue on whether these lending institutions should strictly follow the rules of good business and at a minimum financial self-sufficiency, or also be seen as welfare agencies efficiently channeling transfers and subsidies.

6.4. Lessons for institutional building for rural development

The financial institutions described above illustrate some basic principles of a new approach to institution-building for rural development. These institutions are designed to harness the comparative advantages of communities in information and enforcement and to link them to the larger market. Their success relies on the conditions that ensure that (1) community information and enforcement capacity are sufficient, and (2) members become full partners in the market place.

6.4.1. Building on communities

A community's advantage in accessing information on its members' actions comes from geographical and sociological factors. Proximity of living quarters or businesses, frequent encounters and interactions, stability of the community and long-term relationships – all contribute to reduction in information costs. Homogeneity in ethnicity, religious affiliation, caste membership, or wealth is also found to be conducive to tighter links among members. While these conditions are typically satisfied in rural areas, credit institutions have also managed to build on whatever embryonic community exists in urban market settings. Training in "community" behavior is an important element of group-lending programs that are located in urban environments.

Contract enforcement depends on the incentives that members have to stay in the program and on the community's capacity to exclude or punish for opportunistic behavior. A major difference in types of community endeavors is whether the group of beneficiaries is predetermined, or whether there is selective inclusion/exclusion. In group-lending programs, exclusion from access to credit is in itself an important deterrent to opportunistic behavior, and this all the more if the institution has built in dynamic incentives by increasing loan size in reward for good repayment performance. Exclusion is not, however, possible when programs dispense public goods for the community, or when members have inalienable rights (right to grazing on common property, right to access water, etc.). The expected benefit of remaining in the program depends on the long-term prospects of the program. Many failures in microlending were precipitated when clients, perceiving some weakness in the program, assumed that it would be short-lived, and then defaulted on their loans. The unfortunate historical experiences with short-lived development programs have in certain areas generated a culture of opportunistic appropriation of loans. A third determinant of the relative benefit of a program is the value of the exit option. Microcredit financial institutions prefer to operate in a context of monopoly, where clients' exit option is the moneylender with a much higher interest rate. If financial institutions were competing, borrowers could always default and join another program. This situation has drawbacks, as monopolies always have, with limited product differentiation and non-competitive prices. This is partially avoided when informal financial institutions are non-profit, but it recreates another set of incentive problems typical of NGOs [Bebbington and Farrington (1993)]. The threat of exclusion can be an effective punishment if institutions that compete share their blacklists of defaulters, like credit bureaus in the MDCs. When potential exclusion is not a sufficient threat, communities can resort to other means of pressure to curb opportunistic behavior. Means of enforcement range from the interruption of other interpersonal linkages, to the mobilization of social norms of behavior to have the community denounce, shame, and eventually ostracize the offender.

The mesh of interpersonal and community relations which facilitate communication, information, and control is part of what has been coined "social capital" [Coleman (1990)]. There is the interesting issue here of how much social capital can be "created" by development agencies, as opposed to being taken as an exogenous attribute of history. Can new communities be formed around common interests or needs (such as professional associations and interest groups), build linkages, and learn to cooperate? How much is cooperation "habit-forming" [Seabright (1997)], and can cooperation be sustained beyond the initial phase of intensive training programs?

The issue of exclusion relates to a larger concern for social differentiation. In the context of microenterprise finance, social differentiation will obviously increase between those who have the minimum start-up "capital" or meet the minimal conditions to qualify for the program and those who do not. Furthermore, in group-lending, groups tend to form homogeneously, as theory predicts, with wealthier and better entrepreneurs joining together and less skilled or endowed borrowers joining in other groups. This is bound to increase differentiation among groups and individuals. Incorporation and support of the weaker by the stronger requires another type of social network, based on patronage relationships [Fafchamps (1992b)] or transfers for insurance services rendered [Sadoulet (1997)]. In general it takes very peculiar circumstances for better-endowed individuals to actually need the less well endowed and hence pull them into participation and support them on some unequal exchange basis [Ostrom and Gardner

(1993)]. Identifying best practices to extend as much as possible inclusion of the poorer rural households into solid credit groups is thus an important, pending issue in the use of microfinance for rural development.

6.4.2. Institutional requirements

At the level of the institutions themselves, two issues are of importance: (1) the process of their emergence, and (2) their sustainability.

Comparing village banks and rotating savings and credit associations (RoSCAs) illustrates the role of external agents for the emergence of new institutions. A RoSCA is a group whose members meet at regular intervals to contribute a predetermined amount of money, with members taking turns collecting the total amount contributed. The RoSCAs offer to their members the possibility of accumulating savings for a lumpy purchase, and serve as intermediaries between depositors and creditors [Besley, Coate and Loury (1993)]. RoSCAs are for the most part indigenous institutions that have emerged throughout the world and particularly in Africa. While the range of services they offer is quite limited, they are simple to operate, with minimum administration, no start-up costs, and simple rules to design and enforce. For this reason, they spontaneously emerged and spread without external intervention. In contrast, the emergence of group-lending or village banks almost always required the involvement of an external leader or agency.

Initialization of a financial service in a new area entails higher costs than the subsequent operation of the service due to start-up costs (equipment, recruitment, and training of local agents) and provision of a range of services, without having yet a sufficient scale to spread the costs. One can argue that innovative institutions have costs of diffusion of techniques and training that are higher than standard commercial banking services but entail positive externalities beyond the community that is served. This justifies the allocation of subsidies at the onset of new programs. Acción Internacional, for example, supports its new affiliates with subsidies and training for three years, after which the operation is expected to be self-sufficient. Another important role of external agents is the transmission of expertise. Management techniques to lend to the microenterprise sector are being tried, tested, and improved in experiences that take place all over the world, and considerable benefits and lower risks of failure can be achieved by allying with a larger organization, such as Acción Internacional, FINCA, and other similar large NGOs which have the benefit of cumulative experiences. Most of these institutions depend on strong leaders, especially at the onset of the program when he or she may be under strong pressure to accommodate individual needs. External promoters may sometimes find it easier to pressure community members to comply with regulations. As time passes, rules become institutionalized, patterns are established, and local institutions may be able to function on their own [Holt (1994)].

Beyond the start-up years, financial self-sufficiency is almost a prerequisite for sustainability of the services offered. Programs that perform poorly with revenues falling short of costs and that require a continuing flow of grants are vulnerable to the willingness of donors to continue providing them with funds. The very vulnerability of a program weakens its credibility and may induce rational borrowers to default on loans. Even when they cover their operating costs and loan losses, programs that depend on soft sources of funds at below market rates receive an important implicit subsidy. Dependence on soft sources of funds represents a constraint for expansion of the programs as these funds are limited. This restriction prevents institutions from reaching economies of scale to spread their fixed management costs, which further hampers financial self-sufficiency. Hence, programs that want to develop need to reach a level of efficiency and cost reduction that allows them to borrow from the commercial sector. Only when this level of self-sufficiency has been attained can we consider that the institution has fulfilled the goal of linking the local community to the larger market, and in doing so has both helped the poor gain access to market opportunities and provided the capital market opportunities for profitable operations. Many of the well-known programs have reached this level where most subsidies are eliminated, with only a small share of their funds acquired at subsidized rates. A few programs now aspire to transform to take on financial intermediation, i.e., to expand their services to the full array of credit and savings services offered by banks [Otero and Rhyne (1994)].

The participation of NGOs in financial intermediation poses challenges to them in terms of sophistication and technicality of management which they did not need to have in their previous activities. It also highlights an important dilemma between the social development objective of the original NGO and the donors, and the profit objective of a banking institution [Otero (1994)]. The social agenda of these organizations is to incorporate a certain number of poor into the capital market. While this has proved to be feasible and financially viable, the more the institution goes in the direction of financial intermediation, relying on banking procedures to remain viable and cover its costs, the more difficult it may be to incorporate the more risky clientele with costly lending techniques, and the more the wealthier clientele may seem attractive. The institution thus risks being caught between two worlds, with criticisms from the NGO community for having lost its commitment to the poor, and from the banking community for not being credibly viable.

The debate about self-sufficiency of the Grameen Bank illustrates another important dilemma, even in the realm of an NGO organization [Morduch (1998)]. Although the Grameen Bank has been reporting profits every year since 1986, a detailed accounting of implicit subsidies in the form of concessional interest rates for the capital obtained from foreign donors and the Bangladesh Central Bank shows that beneficiaries received an overall subsidy of about 25 cents per dollar borrowed. This is in contrast with some of the more advanced group-lending programs initiated by Acción Internacional and Indonesia's BRI, which are free of any subsidy. However, Grameen has focused its attention on a substantially poorer segment of the population than these other institutions. This population would probably be excluded from the lending operation if Grameen were to charge full costs. Yet, impact studies show that households clearly benefit from the loans, not only in terms of higher income, but in many other aspects of welfare including empowering women, encouraging better health practices, promoting education, and encouraging social cohesion [Morduch (1998)]. For these functions, the proper counterfactual to which Grameen should be compared is the cost of alternative welfare programs, implying the need to clarify objectives when designing new financial institutions for rural development.

Financially sustainable programs are less limited in their scope and, while reaching a population which is less poor, can have a strong impact on poverty by their scale. The issue is not so much to argue for one or the other of these programs, but to accept that each serves different population groups.

7. Community relations and behavior[13]

The community is an important unit of intervention for rural development. It serves functions that support individual decentralized actions and contracts. These functions include the circulation of information among members (e.g., on market opportunities, new technologies, and strategies to migrate) and the mobilization of social capital (through permanence of the community, interlinkages, and social norms) for the enforcement of contracts. In particular, the strength of local social norms can be a powerful substitute to costly enforcement mechanisms, thus helping community members manage informal financial institutions and mutual insurance schemes. The community can also organize to undertake centralized functions such as governance for the provision of local public goods, the management of common property resources, the creation of incentives for local investment, and the organization of local safety nets.

Community failures in collective action arise when prisoner's dilemma behavior prevails, leading to the breakdown of cooperation. This incentive structure has been used to explain a range of community outcomes including the under-provision of public goods and the over-appropriation of rival resources extracted from common access resources [Hardin (1968)]. This is, however, not an inevitable outcome – far from it [Ostrom (1990), Baland and Platteau (1996)]. There are two types of situations that lead to this virtuous community outcome. One is when the payoff from community-level non-cooperative games is identical to cooperative outcomes. This is the case for instance with the Chicken Game where some community member will perform a provision task irrespective of the behavior of others, simply because it is so important that the task be done [Bardhan (1993)]. The other is based on the ability of the group to genuinely cooperate, although this ability is conceptualized in two quite different ways. One type of model is based on social stability in the community, limited availability of exit options, and the observability of individual actions. Dynamic repeated games lead to applicability of the Folk Theorem. Credible threats of punishment are necessary to trigger cooperation, such as exclusion of community benefits. Social norms of trust in reciprocity are important in helping start an intertemporal cooperative process, such as tit-for-tat arrangements. An alternative framework assumes that the community has

---

[13] See Ostrom (2002) in this Handbook.

instruments of observability and enforcement, although these are costly. If the costs of enforcement are fixed, cooperative behavior will be triggered by benefits that exceed fixed costs. If, in addition, the costs that the community has to incur to observe and enforce cooperative behavior depend on the incentives that members have to cheat, then the quality of cooperation will depend on the community's efficiency in countervailing these incentives [McCarthy, Sadoulet and de Janvry (1998)].

The literature is replete with identification of conditions that promote community cooperation. They include factors that (1) Increase the benefits from cooperation (a truly closed-access resource with well-defined boundaries and a well-defined set of members [Ostrom (1992), Wade (1987)]; involve a smaller number of members over which to distribute the gains from cooperation [Olson (1965), Bendor and Mookherjee (1987)]; have a resource abundance that is neither too high nor too low [Bardhan (1993)]). (2) Lower monitoring costs (smaller groups, greater proximity and homogeneity [Wade (1987)], longer-term relationships [Hirschman (1970)]). And (3) increase the ability to enforce rules (leadership, high cost of exit option [Hirschman (1970)], homogeneity and perception of fairness in the distribution of gains from cooperation [Johnson and Libecap (1982)], interlinkages among community members [Besley and Coate (1995)], credibility of threats and commitment of sanctions, availability of conflict resolution mechanisms [Ostrom (1992)], shared social norms [Sethi and Somanathan (1996)], and trust capital [Seabright (1993)]).

While the village-based community is a natural organizational unit, many cooperative institutional functions are not fulfilled at the community level but within specialized sub-coalitions. In many situations, the community is too large, too heterogeneous, and too ridden with conflicts to prevent free riding. Sub-coalitions allow better monitoring and enforcement, both by reducing the number of participants and by allowing screening (which cannot be done at the community level). Mutual insurance thus rarely occurs at the community level. For instance, mutual insurance along irrigation canals (water smoothing) occurs among self-selected subgroups, usually on a kinship basis [Murgai et al. (1998)]. This is the reason why tests of mutual insurance that looked for consumption smoothing at the community level may have been misspecified and found evidence of imperfect smoothing [see, e.g., Deaton (1992b), Townsend (1994), Ligon, Thomas and Worrall (1997), and Gertler and Gruber (1997)]. Among ejidatarios, regulation of grazing on common property pastures frequently occurs within sub-coalitions [Wilson and Thompson (1993)]. Sharecropping contracts among close kin allow mitigation of Marshallian disincentives through interlinked transactions and are thus preferred to contracts with non-kin [Sadoulet, de Janvry and Fukui (1997)]. Hence, the community is frequently not the social unit in which cooperation occurs and from which new institutions emerge. And, reciprocally, these arrangements could emerge and be efficient for rural development without functional rural communities if making private information locally public, building social capital, and repeated interactions can be engineered over alternative social units. Assisting rural communities in achieving higher levels of cooperative behavior in the provisioning of local public goods and the extraction of common property resources is thus an important and much neglected dimension of rural policy, particularly in the context of extensive devolution of resource control to local communities [Arnold (1999)]. Improved cooperation can lead to efficiency, welfare, and environmental gains.

8. Regional linkages and endogenous growth

Rural policy has a regional dimension that creates opportunities to induce income effects via complementarities among economic activities. A number of analytical tools that apply at the national level to study multiplier effects, market effects, and external economies effects thus also have validity for rural development. There has been extensive use of multiplier analysis to quantify the regional income effect of an increase in autonomous income (e.g., migrant remittances) or the effect of a technological change in an export sector on the regional production of nontradables [Haggblade, Hazell and Brown (1989)]. Multiplier effects have been generalized in the Social Accounting Matrix Framework to account for backward linkage and final demand effects [Subramanian and Sadoulet (1990), Taylor and Adelman (1996)]. For rural areas, final demand effects are typically larger than intersectoral linkage effects due to the low intermediate demand content of agriculture and microenterprise activities. Since there are markets that close at the regional level, multimarket [Quizon and Binswanger (1986), Braverman and Hammer (1986)] and computable general equilibrium (CGE) models with regional disaggregation have also been used. In some instances, these models have been applied at the village level [Taylor and Adelman (1996)]. Such models are effective in tracing the short-run effects of exogenous shocks, changes in price and tax policies, technological change, and different income redistribution schemes. Social disaggregation allows an analysis of the income distribution effects of these shocks and reforms across land or income classes. These models are, however, weak in allowing for market and institutional failures and for non-linear effects associated with externalities and economies of scale.

The endogenous growth literature has much to offer to the understanding of regional development and the design of rural development interventions. Positive externalities in specific firms and activities create complementarities whereby one action reinforces other actions. This is the case for the adoption of new technologies by one firm or the decision to invest by one firm in a particular location. Adoption and investment by one firm will reduce costs for other firms and induce them to do the same. This behavior, conceptualized for instance in the assurance game, typically creates multiple growth equilibria based on different expectations about the behavior of others. Hence, a region or a community may find itself locked in a low-level equilibrium trap because agents have mutually low expectations about the behavior of others. Coordination among actors is thus necessary to escape the low-level equilibrium and switch to a higher income equilibrium. This may apply to market expansion effects for regional nontradables produced with economies of scale, or to the use of intermediate inputs produced with economies of scale [Ciccone and Matsuyama (1996)]. Coordination in investment (Rosenstein–Rodan's "big push") will create these market expansion effects.

Coordination may thus help a region switch from an equilibrium based on activities with decreasing returns to scale to an equilibrium based on activities with increasing returns to scale, escaping a low-level equilibrium trap and entering into self-sustaining growth. When there are time lags in achieving scale and capital markets fail, activities with increasing returns to scale, when more efficient industries are already in place in other regions or countries, will typically require a phase of protection or subsidies. This is the infant-industry approach that has justified implementation of import-substitution industrialization policies. In rural development, economies of scale are typically due to high fixed costs in setting up new institutions and reaching critical levels of learning-by-doing and learning-from-others. Subsidies to cover these costs or long-term loans to future beneficiaries are needed for these institutions to be introduced in the region.

There are many reasons why coordination may fail, maintaining regions in poverty traps. Gains and losses from a rural policy reform may be hard to value, particularly if there are many market failures. The interpersonal distribution of gains and losses may be uncertain, leading agents to prefer the status quo over the risks of change [Fernandez and Rodrik (1991)]. Financing may not be available, for instance for a land reform that redistributes land from inefficient large farms to efficient small farms. And, when there is a lag between future benefits for gainers and present losses for losers, commitment devices may be lacking to guarantee that compensation will indeed be paid, creating a time consistency problem. Useful commitment devices for this purpose may include reputation based on exposure to democratic elections, delegation to specialized agencies with legal and administrative rules removed from political pressures, guarantees of future transfers by reputable foreign institutions, and sunk costs that create irreversibilities. Social norms may also block the emergence of new patterns of behavior until a critical mass of individuals abiding to these new patterns has emerged, a process of change analyzed in evolutionary economics [Basu (1995)]. Unless coordination allows this critical mass to emerge, the status quo will prevail, even if highly inefficient [Akerlof (1976)]. Triggers to the emergence of this critical mass, as we have seen for financial institutions, include charismatic leadership, better information on the expected gains from cooperation [Hirschman (1984)], and external catalytic agents such as NGOs. Identifying best practices to activate these triggers is a key dimension of rural policy.

9. Conclusions: Toward a new approach to rural development [14]

Combining the new context for rural development with the theoretical advances in household behavior, institutional economics, community behavior, and endogenous

---

[14] There are three additional areas of theoretical advances that would need to be covered to give a complete background for the design of rural policy: (1) the decentralization of governance, (2) the political economy of pro-rural development coalitions, and (3) the definition and targeting of welfare programs for the poor who cannot benefit from income generation oriented programs. We refer the reader to other chapters of the Handbook for these subjects.

local growth has allowed a rethinking of approaches to rural development and to experiment with novel initiatives. We only briefly mention here some of the key features of this new approach. It remains in general only weakly conceptualized and experiments are dispersed and poorly informed, suggesting a rich research agenda for rural economists.

The general principles on which a new approach to rural development are based are: (1) a macroeconomic and sectoral policy context that does not discriminate against rural development, (2) decentralization of governance and improved capacity of local governments, (3) coordination between local agencies and between local and national agencies, (4) organization of households in grassroots organizations and mediation by non-governmental organizations for relations to the state and the market, (5) empowerment through the participation of organized local agents in the definition of priorities for public investment and the allocation of subsidies, (6) mobilization of resources both locally through taxation and user fees, and for transfer to the region, (7) devolution of management of common property resources and local public services to user groups, (8) institutional reconstruction to mitigate market and government failures and complement opportunities offered by the market and the state, (9) greater access to assets for households to help them escape poverty traps and initiate a process of accumulation, (10) improved performance of markets and reduction of anti-poor biases in the performance of markets [Carter and Barham (1996)], and (11) political pressures to deal with environmental issues which offer opportunities for significant resource transfers in support of rural development initiatives that promise conservation and sustainability.

Progress in the theory of rural economics allows a better understanding of the following elements of rural development interventions:

(1) *Household behavior.* Accounting for the role of private information, transactions costs, limited commitment, costly enforcement, market constraints, and exposure to risk helps provide interpretations of the static and dynamic behavior of households. We have seen that this second-best context explains why there are important spillovers across activities in resource allocation (e.g., between food and cash crops), biases in investment portfolios (e.g., toward liquid productive assets), and rigidities in supply response as many households opt for self-sufficiency or are constrained on other markets. These behavioral patterns all have efficiency costs that can be reduced by perfecting markets and promoting mitigating institutions. In particular, seeking to reduce transactions costs opens a whole array of rural development interventions beyond the farm.

Ex-ante adjustments to price risk differ considerably across households according to market integration, with net sellers reducing production, although less than pure farmers, while net sellers may increase it. Anticipated constraints and shocks induce households to smooth their long-term consumption paths, for which they need access to remunerative and secure savings opportunities and to financial institutions for borrowing. Unanticipated constraints and shocks have large negative impacts on welfare as households need to cope with them as they come. Reducing the welfare costs of these risks requires access to flexible lines of credit less costly than money lenders and to safety nets such as guaranteed employment programs [Subbarao et al. (1997)].

Many households are susceptible to poverty traps. In static analysis, these traps are due to under-endowments in assets when there exist minimum threshold requirements for their productive use. This calls upon making socially profitable transfers and long-term loans to help households escape these traps and initiate sustainable income growth. In dynamic analysis, use of liquid income-generating assets for consumption smoothing creates persistence in income shocks and potential collapse into poverty traps. This also can be prevented by emergency assistance programs to avoid decapitalization of productive assets and help stabilize assets prices. Duration analysis of household behavior stresses the volatility of participation in new activities. Hence, not only must adoption be induced but abandonment prevented. This suggests paying attention to investment in maintenance and conservation activities if booms are not to be followed by busts, as has been the sad story of too many rural development programs.

Household asset endowments and circumstances are highly heterogeneous, inducing households to pursue a broad range of investment and income strategies. This includes not only on-farm activities but, importantly for the rural poor, off-farm activities and especially rural non-agricultural employment. The implication is that there are many roads out of poverty and that rural development initiatives must capitalize on this diversity. Rural development must consequently be organized on a territorial basis, as opposed to following a sectoral approach as was traditionally done in integrated rural development projects where agriculture was seen as the main activity to be promoted. Hence, there is no silver bullet for successful rural development. Heterogeneity calls upon rural development interventions that differ across classes of households according to their potential and go beyond agriculture. For instance, program interventions must differentiate between households with agricultural potential, with no agricultural potential, and with potential to pursue multiple sources of income (pluriactivity), calling in each case on a sharply different set of instruments for rural development [see de Janvry et al. (1995), Echeverría (1997)]. Interventions must also differ across time periods, for instance to relax specific seasonal credit constraints or target nutrition interventions during the lean season. It is precisely because of this heterogeneity in a context of asymmetric information between households and development agencies that the fundamental task of rural development is to help households reveal their demands for intervention, stressing the importance of decentralization and participation.

(2) *Institutions and contracts.*   Institutional failures need to be addressed not at the level of their symptoms (e.g., by providing subsidized loans to credit-constrained households), but of their structural determinants. This requires identifying the sources of market failures (the causes of adverse selection and moral hazard) and the role of institutional innovations in making markets work for rural households or in mitigating market failures. Markets for credit, insurance, technical assistance, staple foods, labor, and modern inputs are typically ridden with incompleteness and distortions. The development of new institutions must capitalize on the advantages offered by locally

public information, the social capital encountered in communities or ad-hoc coalitions, continuity of social relations among rural inhabitants, and the strength of social norms. This often requires costly interventions aimed at preserving and enhancing the social capital present in local institutions and organizations.

Mechanism design can be used in devising contracts to link the local institutions with global institutions that have the comparative advantage of diversifying risks and accessing well-functioning markets. We have seen that this approach has been successful in designing new institutional arrangements to give poor rural households access to financial services. Many communities are, however, unable to harness this potential and some are dysfunctional to growth. An important field of intervention thus consists in reinforcing the ability of communities to engage in cooperative behavior. This requires costly investments in the circulation of information, the accumulation of social capital, and the formation of leadership. These investments must be done at the level of self-selected sub-coalitions if conditions do not hold in the community at large. External triggers and start-up funds are often needed for this purpose. Combating social exclusion by calling on intermediary NGOs with expertise in promoting entrepreneurship among the poor is needed to extend the benefits of institutional changes toward poorer households.

(3) *Endogenous local growth.* Coordination failures can maintain whole communities and regions in low-level equilibrium traps. Rural development must thus assume a geographical dimension. Coordination can be achieved through the promotion of local dialogue among potential investors. Since many markets close at the local level, making these markets work efficiently is fundamental for locally efficient resource use, most particularly the land rental and sales markets. However, to prevent massive displacement of a potential thriving rural middle class, liberalizing land markets should follow rather than precede setting the conditions that will enable smallholders to be competitive.

(4) *Administrative design.* Decentralization of governance, participatory development, and civil society-based institutional reconstruction call upon administrative designs for rural development that differ markedly from the state-based centralized approach followed in the 1970s for integrated rural development. A typical approach is one where funds are channeled to a local economic development agency in which participate representatives of local government, deconcentrated public agencies, NGOs, and community organizations [Romero (1996)]. These agencies receive demands for the funding of projects that emerge from organized groups in the community. Assistance for the formulation of these projects can be given by NGOs or by private experts if communities receive vouchers to defray the cost of these services. The local economic development agency then competitively allocates loans, subsidies, and technical assistance to the best projects according to predefined criteria. This demand-led pattern of development must confront in its design ways to reduce predation [Rausser (1982)] and to create incentives for targeting poor households.

(5) *Investment opportunities.*   Reducing poverty requires access to profitable investment opportunities that will sustain income growth. Hence, as was learned in the community development movement of the 1950s and 1960s, setting a macro-economic context that endows rural areas with opportunities for profitable projects is a precondition for rural development. Creating new investment opportunities for households requires changes in asset endowments, technology, institutions, regulations, information, infrastructure, and market demand. These *premia mobile* for growth are in part externally determined (e.g., via the progress of globalization and demands for new products and services) but are also the responsibility of governments and development agencies. Households and organized groups must then be assisted in identifying investment opportunities, formulating projects, identifying market niches, and mobilizing the necessary resources.

(6) *Expertise.*   Besides the expected demands in resource transfers, this new approach to rural development places heavy emphasis on the roles of behavioral patterns, imperfect information, transactions costs, market incompleteness, mitigating institutions, social capital, social norms of trust and reciprocity, local governance, organizations, coordination, and cooperation. The interventions needed to deal with these issues are "soft" in that they are intensive in human capital, information, hands-on expertise, and social capital as opposed to capital expenditures. However, precisely because they substitute these instruments for financial resources, they are extremely difficult to implement, particularly on a large and sustainable scale. Using them successfully will require systematic experimentation with alternative designs, and participatory monitoring and evaluation to learn from these experiences and innovate alternative practices. This is where the challenge in implementing this new approach to rural development currently lies.

References

Adelman, I. (1975), "Growth, income distribution, and equity-oriented development strategies", World Development 3:67–76.

Akerlof, G. (1976), "The economics of caste and the Rat Race and other woeful tales", The Quarterly Journal of Economics 90:599–617.

Alderman, H. (1996), "Saving and economic shocks in rural Pakistan", Journal of Development Economics 51:343–365.

Alderman, H., and C. Paxson (1992), "Do the poor insure? A synthesis of the literature on risk and consumption in developing countries", Research Program in Development Studies, Discussion Paper #164 (Princeton University).

Altieri, M. (1989), "A new research and development paradigm for world agriculture", Agriculture Ecosystems and Environment 27:37–46.

Altieri, M., and S. Hecht (1990), Agroecology and Small Farm Development (CRC Press, Boca Raton, FL).

Arnold, J.E.M. (1999), "Devolution of control of common-pool resources to local communities: Experiences in forestry", in: A. de Janvry, G. Gordillo, J.-P. Platteau, and E. Sadoulet, eds., Access to Land, Rural Poverty, and Public Action (Oxford University Press, Oxford). Forthcoming.

Aryeetey, E. (1996), "Rural finance in Africa: Institutional developments and access for the poor", in: M. Bruno and B. Pleskovic, eds., Annual World Bank Conference on Development Economics 1996 (The World Bank, Washington, D.C.).

Askari, H., and J. Cummings (1976), Agricultural Supply Response: A Survey of the Econometric Evidence (Praeger, New York).

Baland, J.-M., and J.-P. Platteau (1996), Halting Degradation of Natural Resources: Is There a Role for Rural Communities? (Oxford University Press, Oxford).

Baland, J.-M., and J.-P. Platteau (1998), "Division of the commons: A partial assessment of the new institutional economics of land rights", American Journal of Agricultural Economics 80:644–650.

Banerjee, A., and A. Newman (1993), "Occupational choice and the process of economic development", Journal of Political Economy 101:274–298.

Bardhan, P. (1993), "Analytics of the institutions of informal cooperation in rural development", World Development 21:633–640.

Basu, K. (1995), "Civil institutions and evolution", in: A. de Janvry, E. Thorbecke and E. Sadoulet, eds., State, Market, and Civil Organizations (Macmillan Press, London).

Bates, R. (1989), "The reality of structural adjustment", in: S. Commander, ed., Structural Adjustment and Agriculture (Overseas Development Institute and James Currey, London).

Bebbington, A., and J. Farrington (1993), "Governments, NGOs, and agricultural development: perspectives on changing inter-organizational relationships", Journal of Development Studies 29:199–219.

Becker, G. (1981), A Treatise on the Family (Harvard University Press, Cambridge, MA).

Behrman, J., A. Foster and M. Rosenzweig (1997), "The dynamics of agricultural production and the calorie-income relationship: Evidence from Pakistan", Journal of Econometrics 77:187–207.

Bendor, J., and D. Mookherjee (1987), "Institutional structure and the logic of ongoing collective action", American Political Science Review 81:129–154.

Berthélémy, J.-C., and C. Morrisson (1987), "Manufactured goods supply and cash crops in sub-Saharan Africa", World Development 15:1353–1367.

Besley, T. (1995), "Savings, credit and insurance", in: J. Behrman and T.N. Srinivasan, eds., Handbook of Development Economics, Vol. 3A (North-Holland, Amsterdam).

Besley, T. (1996), "Political economy of alleviating poverty: Theory and institutions", in: M. Bruno and B. Pleskovic, eds., Annual World Bank Conference on Development Economics 1996 (The World Bank, Washington, DC).

Besley, T., and S. Coate (1995), "Group lending, repayment incentives, and social collateral", Journal of Development Economics 46:1–18.

Besley, T., S. Coate and G. Loury (1993), "The economics of rotating savings and credit associations", American Economic Review 83:792–810.

Binswanger, H., and M. Rosenzweig (1993), "Wealth, weather risk and the composition and profitability of agricultural investments", Economic Journal 103:56–78.

Braverman, A., and J. Hammer (1986), "Multimarket analysis of agricultural pricing policies in Senegal", in: I. Singh, L. Squire and J. Strauss, eds., Agricultural Household Models (The Johns Hopkins University Press, Baltimore).

Bryden, J., et al. (1992), Farm Household Adjustment in Western Europe, 1987–1991. Vol. 1 (Commission of the European Communities, Brussels).

Carroll, T. (1992), Intermediary NGOs: The Supporting Link to Grassroots Development (Kumarian Press, West Hartford, CT).

Carter, M., and E. Zegarra (1995), "Reshaping class competitiveness and the trajectory of agrarian growth with well sequenced policy reform", Department of Agricultural Economics, University of Wisconsin, Madison.

Carter, M., and F. Zimmerman (1993), "Structural evolution under imperfect markets in developing country agriculture: A dynamic programming simulation", Department of Agricultural Economics, University of Wisconsin, Madison.

Carter, M., and R. Salgado (1997), "Land titling and peasant access to land through land markets", in: A. de Janvry, G. Gordillo, J.-P. Platteau and E. Sadoulet, eds., Access to Land, Rural Poverty, and Public Action (Oxford University Press, Oxford). Forthcoming.

Carter, M., and B. Barham (1996), "Level playing fields and laissez-faire: Postliberal development strategy in inegalitarian agrarian economies", World Development 24:1133–1149.

Cavallo, D., and Y. Mundlak (1982), "Agriculture and economic growth in an open economy: The case of Argentina", Research Report No. 36 (International Food Policy Research Institute, Washington, DC).

Chambers, R. (1993), Challenging the Professions: Frontiers for Rural Development (Intermediate Technology Publications, London).

Chaudhuri, S., and C. Paxson (1993), "Consumption smoothing and income seasonality in rural India", Manuscript, Research Program in Development Studies (Princeton University).

Chenery, H., M. Ahluwalia, C. Bell, J. Duloy and R. Jolly (1974), Redistribution With Growth (Oxford University Press, Cambridge, England).

Chenery, H., and L. Taylor (1968), "Development patterns among countries and over time", Review of Economics and Statistics 50:391–416.

Chenery, H., S. Robinson and M. Syrquin (1986), Industrialization and Growth: A Comparative Study (Oxford University Press, Oxford).

Ciccone, A., and K. Matsuyama (1996), "Start-up costs and pecuniary externalities as barriers to economic development", Journal of Development Economics 49:33–59.

Coleman, J. (1990), Foundations of Social Theory (The Belknap Press of Harvard University Press).

Coleman, B. (1997), "The impact of group lending in Northeast Thailand" (Department of Economics, University of California at Berkeley).

Collier, P. (1988), Women in Development: Defining the Issues (Population and Human Resources Department, The World Bank, Washington, DC).

Cossio, I. (1997), Bolivia: Descentralización, Participación Popular y Desarrollo Rural (FAO, Rome).

Coxhead, I. (1996), "Economic modeling of land degradation in developing countries", in: S. Mahendrarajah, A. Jakeman and M. MacAleer, eds., Modeling Change in Economic and Environmental Systems (John Wiley and Sons, Chichester).

Crener, M., et al. (1984), Integrated Rural Development: State of the Arts Review, 1982–83 (Canadian International Development Agency, Quebec).

Deere, C.D., and M. León (1997), "Women and land rights in the Latin American neo-liberal counter-reforms", Working Paper #264 (Women in International Development, Michigan State University, East Lansing, MI).

de Janvry, A. (1981), The Agrarian Question and Reformism in Latin America (Johns Hopkins University Press, Baltimore).

de Janvry, A., and E. Sadoulet (1994), "Structural adjustment under transactions costs", in: F. Heidhues and B. Kerr, eds., Food and Agricultural Policies Under Structural Adjustment (Peter Lang, Frankfurt).

de Janvry, A., et al. (1995), Reformas del Sector Agricola y el Campesinado en Mexico (International Fund for Agricultural Development, Rome).

de Janvry, A., G. Gordillo and E. Sadoulet (1997), "Mexico's second agrarian reform: Household and community responses" (Center for U.S.–Mexico Studies, University of California, San Diego, La Jolla).

de Janvry, A., M. Fafchamps and E. Sadoulet (1991), "Peasant household behavior with missing markets: Some paradoxes explained", Economic Journal 101:1400–1417.

de Janvry, A., M. Fafchamps, E. Sadoulet and M. Raki (1992), "Structural adjustment and the peasantry in Morocco: A computable household model approach", European Review of Agricultural Economics 19:427–453.

de la Brière, B. (1997), "Household behavior towards soil conservation and remittances in the Dominican Sierra", Ph.D. Dissertation (Department of Agricultural and Resource Economics, University of California at Berkeley).

de Tocqueville, A. (1835), Democracy in America (Saunders and Otley, London).

Deaton, A. (1992a), "Household savings in LDCs: Credit markets, insurance and welfare", Scandinavian Journal of Economics 94:253–273.

Deaton, A. (1992b), Understanding Consumption (Clarendon Press, Oxford).

Deininger, K. (1997), Making Market-Assisted Land Reform Work (The World Bank, Washington, DC).

Domar, E. (1947), "The problem of capital accumulation", American Economic Review 37:34–55.

Dorner, P. (1992), Latin American Land Reforms in Theory and Practice: A Retrospective Analysis (The University of Wisconsin Press, Madison).

Duncan, C., and A. Tickamyer (1988), "Poverty research and policy for rural America", The American Sociologist 19:243–259.

Echeverría, R. (1997), Elementos Estrategicos Para la Reducción de la Pobreza Rural en America Latina y el Caribe (Inter-American Development Bank, Washington DC).

ECLAC (Economic Commission for Latin America and the Caribbean) (1997), Social Panorama of Latin America, 1996 (United Nations, ECLAC, Santiago, Chile).

Edwards, S. (1993), "Openness, trade liberalization, and growth in developing countries", Journal of Economic Literature 31:1358–1393.

Eswaran, M., and A. Kotwal (1986), "Access to capital and agrarian production organization", Economic Journal 96:482–498.

Evans, P. (1996), "Government action, social capital and development: Reviewing the evidence on synergy", World Development 24:1119–1132.

Fafchamps, M. (1992a), "Cash crop production, food price volatility, and rural market integration in the Third World", American Journal of Agricultural Economics 74:90–99.

Fafchamps, M. (1992b), "Solidarity networks in pre-industrial societies: Rational peasants with a moral economy", Economic Development and Cultural Change 41:147–174.

Fafchamps, M., and J. Pender (1997), "Precautionary saving, credit constraints, and irreversible investment: Theory and evidence from semi-arid India", Journal of Business and Economics Statistics 15:180–194.

Fafchamps, M., C. Udry and K. Czukas (1998), "Drought and saving in West Africa: Are livestock a buffer stock?", Journal of Development Economics 55:273–305.

Fei, J., and G. Ranis (1964), Development of the Labor Surplus Economy: Theory and Policy (Irwin, Homewood, IL).

Fernandez, R., and D. Rodrik (1991), "Resistance to reform: Status quo bias in the persistence of individual-specific uncertainty", American Economic Review 81:1146–1155.

Finkelshtain, I., and J. Chalfant (1991), "Marketed surplus under risk: Do peasants agree with sandmo?" American Journal of Agricultural Economics 73:557–567.

Foster, A., and M. Rosenzweig (1996), "Technical change and human capital returns and investments: Evidence from the green revolution", American Economic Review 86:931–953.

Foster, A. (1995), "Prices, credit markets and child growth in low-income rural areas", Economic Journal 105:551–570.

Fox, J. (1996), "How does civil society thicken: The political construction of social capital in rural Mexico", World Development 24:1089–1103.

Frank, A.G. (1969), Capitalism and Underdevelopment in Latin America (Modern Reader, New York).

Galston, W., and K. Baehler (1995), Rural Development in the United States: Connecting Theory, Practice, and Possibilities (Island Press, Washington, DC).

Gardner, B. (1987), The Economics of Agricultural Policies (Macmillan, New York).

Gersovitz, M. (1988), "Saving and development", in: H. Chenery and T. N. Srinivasan, eds., Handbook of Development Economics, Vol. 1 (North-Holland, Amsterdam) 381–424.

Gertler, P., and J. Gruber (1997), "Insuring consumption against illness", Mimeo (University of California, Berkeley).

Ghatak, M. (1997), "Joint liability credit contracts and the peer selection effect", Mimeo (Department of Economics, University of Chicago).

Goetz, A.M., and R. Sen Gupta (1996), "Who takes the credit? Gender, power, and control over loan use in rural credit programs in Bangladesh", World Development 24:45–64.

Grepperud, S. (1997), "Poverty, land degradation, and climatic uncertainty", Oxford Economic Papers 49:586–608.

Haggard, S., and R. Kaufman (1989), "Economic adjustment in new democracies", in: J. Nelson, ed., Fragile Coalitions: The Politics of Economic Adjustment (Transaction Books, Oxford).

Haggblade, S., P. Hazell and J. Brown (1989), "Farm–nonfarm linkages in rural sub-Saharan Africa", World Development 17:1173–1201.

Hardin, G. (1968), "The tragedy of the Commons", Science 162:1243–1248.

Hayami, Y. (1988), "Community, market, and state", in: A. Maunder and A. Valdés, eds., Agriculture and Government in an Interdependent World (Dartmouth Publishing Co, Hants, U.K.).

Hayami, Y., and J.-P. Platteau (1997), "Resource endowment and agricultural development: Africa vs Asia" (Faculté des Sciences Economiques, Sociales, et de Getsion, Namur, Belgium).

Hayami, Y., and T. Kawagoe (1993), The Agrarian Origins of Commerce and Industry: A Study of Peasant Marketing in Indonesia (San Martin's Press, New York).

Hayami, Y., and V. Ruttan (1985), Agricultural Development: An International Perspective (Johns Hopkins University Press, Baltimore).

Hayek, F.A. (1989), The Fatal Conceit (Chicago University Press, Chicago).

Hecht, S. (1985), "Environment, development, and politics: The livestock sector in the Eastern Amazon", World Development 13:663–685.

Hirschman, A. (1958), The Strategy of Economic Development (Yale University Press, New Haven).

Hirschman, A. (1970), Exit, Voice, and Loyalty (Harvard University Press, Cambridge).

Hirschman, A. (1984), Getting Ahead Collectively: Grassroot Experiences in Latin America (Pergamon Press, New York).

Hoff, K., A. Braverman and J. Stiglitz (1993), The Economics of Rural Organization: Theory, Practice, and Policy (Oxford University Press, Oxford).

Holdcroft, L. (1978), "The rise and fall of community development in developing countries, 1950–65: A critical analysis and an annotated bibliography", Rural Development Paper No. 2 (Department of Agricultural Economics, Michigan State University).

Holt, S. (1994), "The village bank methodology: Performance and prospects", in: M. Otero and E. Rhyne, eds., The New World of Microenterprise Finance (Koumarian Press, West Hartford, CT).

IADB (Inter-American Development Bank) (1996), "Economic and Social Progress in Latin America", 1996 Report (IADB, Washington DC).

ICRAF (International Center for Research in Agroforestry) (1997), Annual Report (ICRAF, Nairobi, Kenya).

Jacoby, H. (1994), "Borrowing constraints and progress through school: Evidence from Peru", Review of Economics and Statistics 76:151–160.

Jaffee S., and J. Morton (1995), Marketing Africa's High-Value Foods (Kendall/Hunt Publishing Co, Dubuque, Iowa).

Jazairy, I., M. Alamgir and T. Panuccio (1992), The State of the World Rural Poverty: An Inquiry into its Causes and Consequences (New York University Press, New York).

Johnson, R.N., and G.D. Libecap (1982), "Contracting problems and regulation: The case of the fishery", American Economic Review 72:1005–1022.

Jorgenson, D. (1961), "The development of a dual economy", Economic Journal 71:309–334.

Key, N., E. Sadoulet and A. de Janvry (1999), "Transactions costs and agricultural household supply response", American Journal of Agricultural Economics. Forthcoming.

Klibanoff, P., and J. Morduch (1995), "Decentralization, externalities, and efficiency", Review of Economic Studies 62:223–247.

Kochar, A. (1995), "Explaining household vulnerability to idiosyncratic income shocks", American Economic Review 85:159–164.

Krahnen, J., and R. Schmidt (1994), Development Finance as Institution Building (Westview Press, Boulder, CO).

Krueger, A. (1974), "The political economy of the rent seeking society", American Economic Review 64:291–303.

Krueger, A., M. Schiff, and A. Valdés (1988), "Agricultural incentives in developing countries: Measuring the effect of sectoral and economywide policies", World Bank Economic Review 2:255–272.

LeClair, E., and H. Schneider (1968), Economic Anthropology: Readings in Theory and Analysis. Introduction (Holt, Rinehart, and Winston, New York).

Lele, U., and J. Mellor (1981), "Technological change, distributive bias, and labor transfer in a two-sector economy", Oxford Economic Papers 33:426–441.

Lewis, A. (1954), "Economic development with unlimited supplies of labor", The Manchester School of Economic and Social Studies 22:139–191.

Ligon, E., J.P. Thomas and T. Worrall (1997), "Informal insurance arrangements in village economies", Working Paper (University of California, Berkeley).

Lim, Y., and R. Townsend (1994), "Currency, transaction patterns, and consumption smoothing: Theory and Measurement in ICRISAT villages", Paper presented at the Minneapolis Federal Reserve Bank Conference, 1995 (University of Chicago).

Lipton, M. (1977), Why Poor People Stay Poor: A Study of Urban Bias in World Development (Harvard University Press, Cambridge, MA).

Lipton, M. (1990), "State compression: Friend or foe of agricultural liberalization?" (International Food Policy Research Institute, Washington, DC).

Lipton, M. (1993), "Land reform as commenced business: The evidence against stopping", World Development 21:641–658.

Lucas, R. (1983), "Optimal fiscal and monetary policy in an economy without capital", Journal of Monetary Economics 12:55–94.

Manor, J. (1997), "The promise and limitations of decentralization", Technical Consultation on Decentralization (FAO, Rome).

Mathijs, E., and J. Swinnen (1997), "The economics of agricultural decollectivization in East Central Europe and the former Soviet Union", Policy Research Group, Department of Agricultural Economics (Catholic University of Louvain, Louvain, Belgium).

McCarthy, N., E. Sadoulet and A. de Janvry (1998), "Common pool resource appropriation under costly cooperation" (Department of Agricultural and Resource Economics, University of California at Berkeley).

Meinzen-Dick, R., L. Brown, H. Feldstein and A. Quisumbing (1997), "Gender, property rights, and natural resources", World Development 25:1303–1315.

Mellor, J. (1976), The New Economics of Growth (Cornell University Press, Ithaca, NY).

Morduch, J. (1992), "Risk, production, and saving: Theory and evidence from Indian households", Mimeo (Harvard University).

Morduch, J. (1998), "Does microfinance really help the poor? Unobserved heterogeneity and average impacts of credit in Bangladesh", Mimeo (Harvard University).

Morduch, J. (1999), "The microfinance promise", Mimeo (Harvard University).

Murgai, R. (1997), "Savings response to economic shocks: An inquiry into portfolio choice and investment behavior", Ph.D. dissertation (Department of Agricultural and Resource Economics, University of California, Berkeley).

Murgai, R., P. Winters, E. Sadoulet and A. de Janvry (1998), "Localized and incomplete mutual insurance" (Department of Agricultural and Resource Economics, University of California at Berkeley).

Norgaard, R. (1994), Development Betrayed: The End of Progress and a Coevolutionary Revisioning of the Future (Routledge, London).

Nugent, J. (1993), "Between state, markets, and households: A neoinstitutional analysis of local organizations and institutions", World Development 21:623–632.

Nugent, J., and N. Sanchez (1998), "Common property rights and endogenous response to risk", American Journal of Agricultural Economics 80:651–657.

OECD (Organisation for Economic Co-operation and Development) (1993), What Future for Our Countryside? A Rural Development Policy (OECD, Paris).

Olson, M., Jr. (1965), The Logic of Collective Action: Public Goods and the Theory of Groups (Harvard University Press, Cambridge, MA).

Ostrom, E., and R. Gardner (1993), "Coping with asymmetries in the commons: Self-governing irrigation systems can work", Journal of Economic Perspectives 7:93–112.

Ostrom, E. (1990), Governing the Commons: The Evolution of Institutions for Collective Action (Cambridge University Press, Cambridge).

Ostrom, E. (1992), Crafting Institutions for Self-Governing Irrigation Systems (Institute for Contemporary Studies Press, San Francisco).

Ostrom, E. (2002), "Common-pool resources and institutions: Toward a revised theory", in: B.L. Gardner and G.C. Rausser, eds., Handbook of Agricultural Economics, Vol. 2 (Elsevier, Amsterdam) 1315–1339.

Otero, M. (1994), "The evolution of nongovernmental organizations toward financial intermediation", in: M. Otero and E. Rhyne, eds., The New World of Microenterprise Finance (Koumarian Press, West Hartford, CT).

Otero, M., and E. Rhyne (eds.) (1994), The New World of Microentreprise Finance (Koumarian Press, West Hartford, CT).

Otsuka, K., and A. Quisumbing (1997), "Land rights and natural resource management in the transition to individual ownership: Case studies from Ghana and Indonesia" (International Food Policy Research Institute, Washington, DC).

Parker, A. (1995), "Decentralization: The way forward for rural development?", Policy and Research Working Paper No. 1475 (The World Bank, Washington, DC).

Pender, J., and J. Kerr (1996), "Determinants of farmers' indigenous soil and water conservation investments in India's semi-arid tropics", EPTD Discussion Paper No. 17 (Environment and Production Technology Division, International Food Policy Research Institute, Washington, DC).

Piriou-Sall, S. (1997), Decentralization and Rural Development: A Review of Evidence (The World Bank, Washington, DC).

Pitt, M., and S. Khandker (1998), "The impact of group-based credit programs on poor households in Bangladesh: Does the gender of participants matter?", Journal of Political Economy 106:958–996.

Prebisch, R. (1962), "The economic development of Latin America and its principal problems", Economic Bulletin for Latin America 7:1–22.

Quizon, J., and H. Binswanger (1986), "Modeling the impact of agricultural growth and government policy on income distribution in India", World Bank Economic Review 1:101–148.

Rausser, G. (1982), "Political economic markets: PERTs and PESTs in food and agriculture", American Journal of Agricultural Economics 64:821–833.

Reardon, T., and J.E. Taylor (1996), "Agroclimatic shock, income inequality, and poverty: Evidence from Burkina Faso", World Development 24:901–914.

Reardon, T., and S. Vosti (1997), "Poverty-environment links in rural areas of developing countries", in: S. Vosti and T. Reardon, eds., Sustainability, Growth, and Poverty Alleviation: A Policy and Agroecological Perspective (Johns Hopkins University Press, Baltimore).

Rodrik, D. (1996), "Understanding economic policy reform", Journal of Economic Literature 34:9–41.

Rogers, E. (1983), The Diffusion of Innovations (Free Press, New York).

Romer, P. (1994), "The origins of economic growth", Journal of Economic Perspectives 8:3–22.

Romero, L. (1996), "Local development funds: Promoting decentralized, participatory planning and financing", Working Paper, Policy Series (United Nations Capital Development Fund, New York).

Rosenzweig, M., and H. Binswanger (1993), "Wealth, weather risk, and the composition and profitability of agricultural investments", Economic Journal 103:56–78.

Rosenzweig, M., and K. Wolpin (1993), "Credit market constraints, consumption smoothing, and the accumulation of durable production assets in low-income countries: Investment in bullocks in India", Journal of Political Economy 101:223–244.

Rostow, W. (1971), The Stages of Economic Growth: A Non-Communist Manifesto (Cambridge University Press, Cambridge).

Rozelle, S., et al. (1997), "The economics of land tenure and property rights in China's agricultural sector: Managing the transition" (Food Research Institute, Stanford University).

Sadoulet, E., A. de Janvry and C. Benjamin (1998), "Household behavior with imperfect labor market", Industrial Relations 37:85–108.

Sadoulet, E., A. de Janvry and S. Fukui (1997), "The meaning of kinship in sharecropping contracts", American Journal of Agricultural Economics 79:394–406.

Sadoulet, L. (1997), "The role of mutual insurance in group lending", Mimeo (Princeton University).

Schultz, T. (1964), Transforming Traditional Agriculture (Yale University Press, New Haven).

Seabright, P. (1993), "Managing the local commons: Theoretical issues in incentive design", Journal of Economic Perspectives 7:113–134.

Seabright, P. (1997), "Is cooperation habit-forming?", in: P. Dasgupta and K. Maler, eds., The Environment and Emerging Development Issues (Clarendon Press, Oxford).

Sen, A.K. (1985), Commodities and Capabilities (North-Holland, Amsterdam).

Sethi, R., and E. Somanathan (1996), "The evolution of social norms in common property resource use", American Economic Review 86:766–788.

Sharma, N., and J. Drèze (1996), "Sharecropping in a North Indian village", Journal of Development Studies 33:1–39.

Shiferaw, B. (1996), "Economic analysis of land degradation and incentives for soil conservation in smallholder farming: A theoretical development", Discussion Paper #D-30 (Department of Economics and Social Sciences, Agricultural University of Norway).

Singh, I., L. Squire, and J. Strauss (eds.) (1986), Agricultural Household Models (Johns Hopkins University Press, Baltimore, MD).

Stiglitz, J. (1990), "Peer monitoring and credit markets", World Bank Economic Review 4:351–367.

Stiglitz, J., and A. Weiss (1981), "Credit rationing in markets with imperfect information", American Economic Review 71:393–419.

Strauss, J., and D. Thomas (1995), "Human resources: Empirical modeling of household and family decisions", in: J. Behrman and T.N. Srinivasan, eds., Handbook of Development Economics, Vol. 3A (North-Holland, Amsterdam).

Streeten, P. (1979), "A basic needs approach to economic development", in: K. Jameson and C. Wilber, eds., Directions in Economic Development (University of Notre Dame Press, Notre Dame, Indiana).

Subbarao, K., et al. (1997), Safety Net Programs and Poverty Reduction: Lessons from Cross-Country Experience (The World Bank, Washington, DC).

Subramanian, S., and E. Sadoulet (1990), "The transmission of production fluctuations and technical change in a village economy: A social accounting matrix approach", Economic Development and Cultural Change 39:131–173.

Taylor, J.E., and I. Adelman (1996), Village Economies: The Design, Estimation, and Use of Villagewide Economic Models (Cambridge University Press, Cambridge).

Touraine, A. (1980), L'Après Socialisme (Grasset, Paris).

Townsend, R. (1994), "Risk and insurance in village India", Econometrica 62:539–591.

Tweeten, L., and C. Zulauf (1997), "Public policy for agriculture after commodity programs", Review of Agricultural Economics 19:263–280.

Udry, C. (1995), "Risk and saving in Northern Nigeria", American Economic Review 85:1287–1300.

Udry, C. (1996), "Gender, agricultural production, and the theory of the household", Journal of Political Economy 104:1010–1046.

United States Department of Agriculture, Economic Research Service (ERS) (1995), Understanding Rural America (USDA, ERS, Washington DC).

United States Department of Agriculture, Economic Research Service (ERS) (1997), "Growth in per capita income is widespread in rural America", Rural Conditions and Trends 7:25–31.

Valdés, A. (1996), "Surveillance of agriculture price and trade policy in Latin America during major policy reforms", World Bank Discussion Paper No. 349 (The World Bank, Washington, DC).

Van Zyl, J., J. Kirsten and H. Binswanger (1996), Agricultural Land Reform in South Africa: Policies, Markets, and Mechanisms (Oxford University Press, Cape Town).

Wade, R. (1987), Village Republics: Economic Conditions for Collective Action in South India (Cambridge University Press, Cambridge).

Wickrama, K.A.S., and P. Keith (1994), "Savings and credit: Women's informal groups as models for change in developing countries", Journal of Developing Areas 28:365–377.

Wik, M., and S. Holden (1996), "Risk and peasant adaptation: Do peasants behave according to the sandmo model?", Discussion Paper #D-24 (Department of Economics and Social Sciences, Agricultural University of Norway).

Williamson, J. (1990), Latin American Adjustment: How Much Has Happened? (Institute for International Economics, Washington, DC).

Wilson, P., and G. Thompson (1993), "Common property and uncertainty: Compensating coalitions by Mexico's pastoral ejidatarios", Economic Development and Cultural Change 41:299–318.

World Bank (1997), Rural Development: From Vision to Action, ESSD Studies and Monographs Series No. 12 (The World Bank, Washington, DC).

Zeller, M., G. Schreider, J. von Braun and F. Heidhues (1997), "Rural finance for food security for the poor", Food Policy Review No. 4 (International Food Policy Research Institute, Washington, DC).

Zilberman, D., M. Khanna, and L. Lipper (1997), "Economics of new technologies for sustainable agriculture", Australian Journal of Agricultural and Resource Economics 41:63–80.

Zimmerman, F., and M.R. Carter (1996), "Dynamic portfolio management under risk and subsistence constraints in developing countries", Manuscript (University of Wisconsin, Department of Agricultural Economics, Madison).

Chapter 32

AGRICULTURE IN THE MACROECONOMY: THEORY AND MEASUREMENT

PHILIP ABBOTT

Department of Agricultural Economics, Purdue University, West Lafayette, IN

ALEX McCALLA

Department of Agricultural and Resource Economics, University of California, Davis, CA

Contents

Handbook of Agricultural Economics, Volume 2, Edited by B. Gardner and G. Rausser
© *2002 Elsevier Science B.V. All rights reserved*

Abstract

Macroeconomic events and policies strongly influence agricultural sector outcomes. Chapters synthesized here delineate both feed-forward and feedback linkages between agriculture and the macroeconomy, examining how relationships change as countries develop and undergo structural transformation. Historically, most aggregate work by agricultural economists follows a neo-classical paradigm, and the micro-foundations approach to macroeconomics. More microeconomic approaches and some recent aggregate efforts address institutional issues and market imperfections that lie behind alternative approaches to macroeconomics. Controversies on macroeconomic theory and data limitations have constrained the extent to which macroeconomic issues have been incorporated into agricultural economics research.

Keywords

structural transformation, macroeconomic policy, exchange rates, CGE models, agricultural policy

JEL classification: Q10

1. Introduction

Although agricultural economists have chosen to deal mostly in the realm of micro-economics, they must also be concerned with the macroeconomic environment and the agricultural sector's linkages to it. Misunderstanding of the relationship between macro-economics and the agricultural sector was, according to Paarlberg (1999) and Schultz (1953), a major force behind the development of U.S. farm policy during the Great Depression, with its emphasis on supply control. Both recognized the importance of aggregate demand variability from business cycles, and the futility of supply control measures applied to combat the results after the fact. While we now better understand the roots of farm problems, this misunderstanding has supported emphasis on sectoral and commodity issues, which still condition the political debate.

Changes in macroeconomic conditions throughout the world are now blamed for major transitions in the fortunes of the agricultural sector. Turning points, such as the recent Asian financial crisis, which coincided with turning points in macroeconomic policies, have been accompanied by changes in the evolution of farm income and prices. Watershed events in international agricultural trade, macroeconomics, and farm income and prices include the 1973–74 world food crisis, the 1981–82 LDC (less developed country) debt crisis and Russian grain embargo, the 1986 G6 Exchange Rate Accord, and the 1997–98 Asian financial crisis. The Asian crisis, for example, is being seen as a fundamental cause of the current downturn in U.S. agriculture due to the reduced demand for exports to that region [Summers (1999)]. The International Agricultural Trade Research Consortium's trade embargo study singled out macroeconomic changes among the many events in 1981 that ended the rapid increase of agricultural exports and farm income of the late 1970s. The 1973–74 world food crisis was created in part by crop failures and stocks disposal, but also significantly by macroeconomic policies of the time that inflated away oil price increases, putting upward pressure on commodity prices. The high prices of that period stimulated a supply response that, coupled with cheap credit in inflationary times, allowed imports to grow at unprecedented rates. The macroeconomic shifts of the early 1980s reversed those trends. These events may contribute more to the long-term variability of farm income than do stochastic events within the agricultural sector (such as climate) or the policy errors made while trying to cope with these events. These macroeconomic events also led Schuh (1988) to assert that unstable monetary policy was more important than agricultural policies in determining farm income.

The role of agriculture in the macroeconomy, and how the extent and nature of feedback and feed-forward linkages change as economies develop, are fundamental to understanding the relationships examined in this chapter. These linkages are (1) the impact of agricultural sector performance on macroeconomic outcomes, and (2) the impact of macroeconomic events on agricultural performance. The nature of the development process is such that the importance of the former decreases as the latter increases (see Table 1). Economies at very early stages of development are characterized by high levels of employment in agriculture (80 percent or more) and generally by more than half of GDP originating in that sector. The economic performance of

Table 1
Agricultural sector linkages to the macroeconomy

	Importance of	
Income level (per capita GDP)	Agricultural sector on macroeconomic performance	Macroeconomic events on agriculture
Low	High	Medium
Middle	Medium to low	Medium to high
High	Low to zero	High

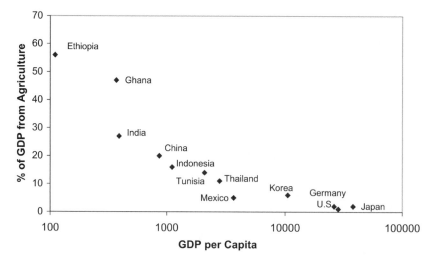

Figure 1. The structural transformation of agriculture in economic development.

the agricultural sector dominates macroeconomic performance in terms of growth, employment, fiscal revenue and expenditures, and frequently in terms of foreign exchange earnings. The development process involves a broadening of economic activity and a relative decline in the importance of agriculture in terms of all these macroeconomic variables. The process of agricultural modernization, which releases labor, involves increasing input and output market linkages with the rest of the economy. Mature economies are characterized by production agriculture contributing less than 5 percent to either employment or GDP (see Figure 1).

It depends very much on which stage of development one studies as to which linkages – agriculture on the macroeconomy or the macroeconomy on agriculture – are of critical importance. The chapters synthesized here examine how agriculture's linkages to the macroeconomy evolve at various points along the range of per capita income levels and development. Each of the chapters reviewed here looks at a point (or several points) along this development spectrum as it reviews some of the key

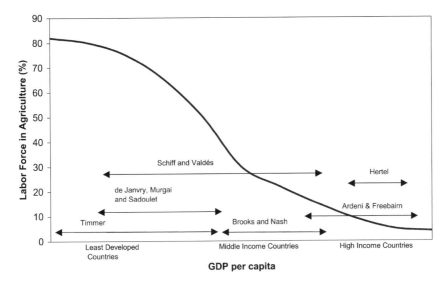

Figure 2. Handbook chapters by GDPs of countries covered.

issues that emerge from the process of structural transformation. Timmer considers the poorest countries, in which agriculture contributes a substantial portion of GDP and employment. Schiff and Valdés, and then de Janvry, Sadoulet and Murgai, examine developing countries as they pursue policies to move along this transition. Brooks and Nash look at the former Soviet Union, Eastern Europe, and centrally planned Asia, where the transition is further along, and transition from socialist to capitalist institutions is also relevant. Ardeni and Freebairn look at developed countries, where the importance of agriculture in GDP and employment has declined, but macroeconomic events can still dominate sectoral outcomes. Then Hertel considers what is becoming the predominant methodology for looking at aggregate issues, the computable general equilibrium (CGE) model, especially at the developed country end of this spectrum. Figure 2 stylistically positions the six chapters along this transition path. We will examine what these chapters tell us about the structural transformation, and just how well understood the various pieces of this story now are.

The structural transformation that drives this evolution also gives rise to a number of the key agricultural policy issues. The most basic policy concern of agriculture – how to cope with demand growth rates which decline while capital-intensive technical change frees rural labor, resulting in rising productivity but real declines in prices and incomes – is fundamentally driven by this transition. The increased importance of trade, and its links to income growth and foreign exchange positions, lies behind the importance of the 1981 LDC debt crisis, the 1997–98 Asian crisis, and their effects on agriculture. Structural adjustment policies, and the policy misalignments they seek to correct, have been key to recent evolution of agricultural policy in the Third World (Timmer, Schiff and Valdés).

The theoretical basis of this analysis is largely borrowed from the larger economics literature, which has itself undergone a substantial evolution. Contributions of agricultural economists have been largely empirical, and have drawn heavily from the school of macroeconomic thought based on establishing rigorous microeconomic foundations – consistent with the microeconomic focus of most agricultural economists. While much of what agricultural economists have done in this domain is empirical, the empirical basis for this type of research remains weak. Thompson's (1981) critique of this body of research, and what imposes these limitations, is also considered. Our review closes with suggestions for future research agendas.

2. Agriculture's structural transformation

The process of transformation from an agrarian society to an industrial/service economy unleashes a number of forces that help to explain the evolution of agricultural policy, and which are important in understanding potential future trends in agricultural production, demand, and trade. Declining employment in agriculture and generation of surpluses in the face of slowly growing demand give rise to downward trends in farm prices and income as well as increased sensitivity to variations in demand and production. Stabilization policy only slows this transformation. These forces continue as an economy develops, and as agriculture declines in importance relative to industry and services. The critical behaviors behind these trends and the policy motives they induce are well understood, even if parameters to capture them in empirical models are imprecisely known.

Engel's law is a primary force behind this transformation. It is well known that income elasticities of demand for food are typically less than one, so that the share of food in expenditure declines as income grows. Moreover, as per capita income grows, these elasticities decline, further slowing the rate of demand growth. Low price elasticities of demand mute any expansionary effects of lower prices. Agricultural economists have devoted much effort to documenting the magnitudes of these elasticities, and while they may not be known with precision, that they are quite low is well accepted.

Two additional aspects of demand patterns complicate our understanding of the transition, and are relevant to any projections or simulations of how demand, both in a country and worldwide, evolve. First, there is a dietary transition. At low income levels, while the demand elasticities for low quality cereals (subsistence goods) are low, income elasticities of demand for higher quality cereals and meats are much larger, and can even exceed one for meat in low income countries subsisting on cereals. These latter elasticities may increase with income in the very poorest countries, but then begin to decline as income grows further. Thus, as a country begins its structural transformation, the demand share of income for food (specifically meat) can increase as diets improve, but that trend will reverse as income continues to increase. This also holds implications for the growth of agricultural processing and distribution industries, and the role of trade in meeting demand for food, especially higher-value and processed foods. In some countries imports of meat may rise as income begins to grow and to bring improved diets, but this also encourages development of a domestic livestock industry, which may subsequently replace imports.

Second, as income grows consumer food purchases embody greater service. The role and size of the processing and distribution sectors increase dramatically. In the U.S., for example, while primary agriculture may account for less than 2 percent of GDP, the food system accounts for a much greater share, at over 10 percent by USDA estimates [United States Department of Agriculture, Economic Research Service (ERS) (1996)]. This same trend toward a larger role for processing and distribution is seen in international trade as well [Handy and Henderson (1994)]. High-value and processed food products (including meats) since 1992 have accounted for over half of the value of U.S. agricultural exports, and this share was achieved much earlier in Europe. Impacts of agriculture on the macroeconomy now depend strongly on what is happening in these value-added sectors.

Another force, working counter to the demand trends, is technical change in agriculture. That agricultural productivity rises faster than demand is another well-documented empirical regularity, leading to Cochrane's "treadmill". Much work in agricultural economics has pointed to the success of agricultural research in increasing productivity [Evenson (2001), Evenson and Kislev (1975)]. Throughout most of the world, productivity has grown faster than population, permitting improvements in diets and nutritional status of populations [IFPRI (1995)]. The problem with this technical change is that, according to the treadmill concept, as production increases faster than demand, prices are driven down, and farmers are driven to seek even greater improvements in productivity and cost reductions to maintain income. With demand trends and prices working against them, income trends downward, employment declines, and the sector is continually adjusting to excess production potential. The empirical facts on this can be difficult to sort out, as long-term downward trends in agricultural prices, followed by brief periods of substantial increases in prices, seem evident.

The implications of Cochrane's treadmill can be moderated by entering international markets, where demand may be more elastic. But many international agricultural markets can best be described as thin, since so many countries are largely self-sufficient in agricultural commodities. Globally, trade represents only 10 percent of cereals consumption, and only 5 percent of meat and dairy product consumption. Thus, small changes in domestic supply-demand balances for some larger countries (e.g., China) can mean large changes in international markets. When state enterprises in large countries manage changes by entering world markets sometimes as exporters and other times as importers, the effects of these changes can be both large and unpredictable. This contributes to greater variability in international markets, which impacts the developed country export markets, and counters the benefits to slowing long-run price decreases with increased instability.

Since long-run production is also known to be price-responsive, cycles can and do ensue from supply response. In certain periods, such as the 1973–74 world food crisis, and more recently during the 1995–96 cereals price run-up, demand races ahead of supply, and the focus of discussion changes to whether there will be adequate food to meet world requirements [Brown (1995), Avery (1996)]. Evidently, in each case the high prices brought forth both production and policy responses, which led to a reappearance of surpluses.

The extent of price adjustment is another empirical regularity of agriculture, which is reasonably well understood if imprecisely measured. Demand price elasticities for agricultural commodities are believed to generally be low, like the income elasticities. Supply elasticities are believed to be quite small in the short run, but production responds according to a lagged adjustment mechanism, so these supply elasticities are much larger in the longer run [Askari and Cummings (1976), Mundlak (2001)]. Since climate variability makes production uncertain, large short-run price changes are induced, which can lead to longer-run supply adjustments.

These forces have generated a perceived need for policy intervention in both developed and developing economies. However, the nature of the policy response changes during the course of development [Anderson and Hayami (1986)]. In the poorer countries, consumer subsidization and agricultural taxation are more common. This arises in part because of the perception that development is equivalent to industrialization, with the agricultural sector being largely ignored in the process, and often taxed to facilitate industrialization by keeping prices of wage goods (food) low. Some economists still see a need to emphasize industrialization over agriculture to foster development [Sachs and Warner (1997)], a typical stance of development economists in the 1960s and 1970s. Consumer subsidies can also lead to substantial fiscal costs at the macroeconomic scale, as was observed both in many developing countries that subsequently faced structural adjustment reforms in the early 1980s, and in Eastern Europe and the Soviet Union prior to the transition period of the early 1990s (Brooks and Nash).

As countries develop, the focus of policy shifts to producer support, as unemployment and underemployment emerge in rural areas, and rural incomes fall relative to urban incomes [Bates (1983)]. Today in many developing countries, producer support rather than consumer subsidies is found, because the attempt to subsidize both consumers and producers simultaneously was unsustainable. A considerable body of literature explores the political economy basis for agricultural policy evolution [Binswanger and Deininger (1997), de Gorter and Swinnen (2002), this Handbook].

The trends of declining farm income and employment are complicated by the cycles experienced in agriculture, driven in large part by cycles in the macroeconomy. As noted by Paarlberg (1999), Schultz (1953), the IATRC (1986), and others, the stabilization policies that arise to protect producers can be driven more by macroeconomic forces than by sectoral outcomes, including climate-induced variability in production. They are a reaction to both the long-run trends, and short-run events exacerbating those trends. Thus, the feed-forward mechanisms from the macroeconomy to agriculture outlined by Ardeni and Freebairn remain strong.

The role of exchange rates has received particular attention [Schuh (1974), Schiff and Valdés (2002)]. Exchange rates as a determinant of agricultural sector outcomes are seen as important in all stages of development. Early understanding of structural adjustment was that those economic problems could be corrected simply by appropriate exchange rate devaluations. After all, the problems were largely seen as trade imbalances and consequent accumulations of foreign debt due to misaligned (overvalued) exchange rates. Interactions between exchange rate policy and sectoral policy have highlighted the need to incorporate agricultural policy reform in any structural adjustment program, as is seen in some recent literature [Rodrik (1996)]. A key finding by Schiff and Valdés is that the net impacts of the constellation of policies applied to agriculture depend strongly on the extent of exchange rate overvaluation. Their finding that agriculture is generally taxed, in spite of apparent producer subsidies, due to exchange rate overvaluation, is highlighted in several of the chapters in this section.

Agricultural policy costs can contribute significantly to government deficits, so are reflected in current account deficits as governments borrow abroad to finance their debt. The macroeconomic costs of agricultural policy, especially for developing countries and economies in transition, have also been highlighted in several earlier chapters. Costs of agricultural policy are also seen as a driving force for reform in the U.S. and EU, and can become part of macroeconomic budget debates. Fiscal costs may also be key to policy reform in poorer countries. Structural adjustment programs, which demand greater fiscal discipline, often require reforms of agricultural policy, in part because of their costs. Budgetary concerns have also been cited as a key force behind the instability in China's attempts at agricultural policy reform since 1980.

Several critical policy issues emerge from conflicting views on the consequences of this structural transformation and how it might be managed. One key question, especially for agricultural economists, concerns the role of agriculture in economic development. While economists have argued for emphasis on industrialization, agricultural economists have argued that a more balanced development strategy is necessary, and that investment in agriculture has been key to development success. Timmer reviews the history of economic development, showing why the bias against agriculture arose, and why that was a mistake. He follows the framework of Johnson and Mellor (1960), according to which agriculture not only produces the food supply, and releases labor for industrialization; it also provides a market for output from the industrial sector, generates savings, and earns foreign exchange. Thus, agriculture is important not only in the trade and savings-investment balance equations, but can also play a Keynesian role in generating demand and providing a sufficiently large local market for economic output. When the agricultural sector suffers, demand, savings, and foreign exchange earnings are all constrained.

Where the role of agriculture in development becomes critical to policy is in the government's role in directing investment. According to the traditional economists' view, investment in agriculture should be a low priority. Agricultural economists have shown that returns to investment in agriculture can be high, especially in research where public funding plays a crucial role. When agricultural investment is neglected, forces can work against economic development and growth as well. De Janvry, Sadoulet, and Murgai emphasize the rural capital market imperfections that policy must overcome both for sufficient capital to be brought to agriculture, and for that capital to be placed efficiently.

Agricultural policy issues have also moved to the forefront of the structural adjustment debate. One lesson has been that macroeconomic adjustments are not sufficient to achieve a structural transformation – sectoral policy can remain problematic if not corrected. Not only must exchange rates be realigned, and government budgets balanced, but sectoral policies must also be reformed to eliminate misplaced incentives preventing the sorts of adjustment the macro policies hope to stimulate. When nominal prices are fixed (subsidized) by domestic policy, implicit taxes discourage production, and trade policies are adjusted to maintain domestic price incentives, exchange rate realignment will not correct the imbalances created by these sectoral policies. This position is not without controversy, however, as some cross-sectional evidence argues that macroeconomic policy is more important to successful economic growth than are sectoral policies [Collier and Gunning (1999)]. Evidently, correcting sectoral distortions but leaving inappropriate macro policies in place is unlikely to be very successful, while some success may be achieved by macroeconomic reforms even when sectoral disincentives remain.

An important issue not receiving much attention in the chapters of this section is the question of whether in the longer term agricultural production will continue to keep ahead of demand and allow diets worldwide to improve as economic development broadens. The process of structural transformation as described above suggests this concern is not great, and the focus of debate has been more often on surplus disposal and export promotion rather than inadequacy of supply. However, over each of the last three decades the excess of production growth rates over population growth rates has declined [IFPRI (1995)]. Yet each time shortages appeared on world markets and prices soared, supply responses in agricultural production quickly brought surpluses back. While most regions of the world continue to experience production growth faster than population growth, differences in those rates of growth are smaller, even as population growth slows. In a world where surpluses are the key concern of agricultural policy, the observed declines in investment in agriculture should not be a surprise. Whether this is sound and sustainable policy for the longer term is a concern to some, however. Issues have been raised again recently concerning the capacity of world agriculture to generate enough food for increasing populations with rising income levels. Limitation of water availability, degradation of natural resources, competition for agricultural resources from non-agricultural uses, and the slowing in the growth rates of crop yields, all bring into question sustainability of trends in agricultural production relative to demand growth.

The policy issues that received the most attention are the traditional concerns driven by structural transformation. Consumer subsidization in lower income countries nowadays gives way to producer subsidization more and more often, as income and employment problems in rural areas emerge. In spite of limitations imposed on producer subsidization in the Uruguay Round of GATT, these issues remain active in agricultural policies. Stabilization issues, due to the cycles imposed in large part by macroeconomic forces, bring attention back to these traditional support policies, in part because the process of structural transformation continues even in highly developed economies, and in part because of the wide swings in world market conditions encountered over relatively short periods of time. In addition, there remains the temptation to use policies intended for stabilization to support prices even though trying to support producer prices in the face of long-run secular declines in market prices is increasingly expensive.

3. Agriculture in the macroeconomy

The chapters we are synthesizing look at the process of structural transformation from differing perspectives, both along the development process, and to the extent that macroeconomic or microeconomic forces and tools are considered. In this section we review the contributions of each of those chapters, moving along the development spectrum.

One task undertaken in Timmer's chapter is to examine the case for investment in agriculture as a component of successful development. He first reviews Johnson and Mellor's (1960) paradigm, and why it countered the economists' conventional wisdom of ignoring agriculture. He also examines the findings from new growth theory [Barro and Sala-i-Martin (1995)] and from the debate on convergence in economic growth rates. That literature, and the examination of development determinants in general, has recently experienced a resurgence due to the availability of the Heston–Summers data (Penn world tables), which offers purchasing power parity corrected real per capita income measures across countries and time. While this work has been more on the agenda of general economists [Temple (1999)], agricultural issues arise, and Timmer highlights three broad findings of Chai, Fogel, and Dawe. Chai's (1995) work emphasizes the key role of human capital, and especially the importance of rural human capital, differentiated from urban human capital. Fogel (1994) emphasizes the importance of the nutritional status of workers as another key development determinant, while Dawe (1996) examines the relationship between price stability and growth. All of this is driven by an observed empirical correlation between successful growth in agriculture and growth in the general economy, despite the fact that theoretical underpinnings are not well established. It is also based on our evolving understanding of the Asian miracle, and the positive role agricultural development has played in the success of that region [World Bank (1998)].

Another theme emphasized by Timmer, which is a key issue in macroeconomic policy debates, is the role of stability as a policy goal per se. He notes that stabilization is often a key objective of agricultural policy, and relates food price instability to savings behavior as well as to investment inefficiency. The macroeconomic implications of these linkages decline as agriculture's shares in consumption expenditure and investment also decline, but agricultural stabilization goals persist. Schultz's analysis of macroeconomic forces behind agricultural instability is cited by Timmer, especially his observation that microeconomic interventions have failed to cope.

Schultz's paradigm emphasizes the role of market imperfections. Key issues include wage setting in urban areas, urban-rural migration, distance, and failures in land, labor, and credit markets. The relationship between migration, unemployment, and wages was an issue once at the top of the agenda for development economists, and was driven largely by the structural transformation process as labor is freed while agriculture develops. At least one recent examination of the consequences of the recent Asian crisis on agriculture resorts to these models and mechanisms – highlighting the importance of labor market adjustments with migration [Coxhead and Plangpraphan (1999)].

Timmer finds that the macroeconomic environment is critical to agricultural development. Components of appropriate macro policy include balanced internal and external accounts, price stability, an undistorted exchange rate, and transparent and unbiased trade regimes. While his policy prescription is based on the observed high returns to investment in agricultural research and technology, and the failure of the private sector to provide public goods such as irrigation, controversy persists over the appropriate role of extension services to disseminate technology. Timmer notes that there is now a recognized need for policy that gets prices right, and the need for government to intervene where public goods, economies of scale or market imperfections dictate that role. The debate continues about when goods and services, especially extension, should be treated as public goods and when they are more effectively supplied by the market.

Schiff and Valdés focus on exchange rate linkages to agriculture, an area of research they pioneered. They emphasize that distorted exchange rates have constituted a policy bias against agriculture and that macroeconomic imbalances have retarded economic development, especially in agriculture. They also note the importance of foreign capital, which can be critical to advancing technology, and of interest rates in determining agricultural investment. They also recognize the importance of removing rural capital market imperfections.

The approach of Schiff and Valdés has been to compare nominal or effective rates of protection, correcting for real exchange rate overvaluation. Recent general equilibrium model based approaches question their treatment of agricultural goods as necessarily tradable. If some agricultural goods are non-tradable, this linkage may be less pronounced than is believed in this literature [Bautista et al. (2001)]. Sorting out non-tradability due to product characteristics versus border policy is problematic in evaluating this analysis, however.

Schiff and Valdés also examine the role of agriculture in development. They raise the persistent debate in economics on the preferability of export-oriented growth strategies over import substitution strategies. But they note that economic development has seldom been built successfully on agricultural exports alone. An unresolved issue here is whether the success stories have been countries that promoted exports, or whether trade regimes in successful countries were simply closer to free trade. The recent Asian financial crisis has brought even more attention to the (possible) fragility of the "Asian miracle" and the economic forces that lie behind it.

The consequences for development of "Dutch disease" are also considered. Dutch disease occurs when earnings from a single export sector, such as an agricultural commodity, quickly expand and send signals through the exchange rate that retard growth in other critical sectors. A related issue is the increasing volatility of foreign capital flows, which can send similarly distorting signals to an economy and create irreversible investment trends, including in agriculture. Long-term capital inflows are essential for rapid development, but short-term capital flows can generate inflation, real exchange rate appreciation beyond equilibrium levels, abrupt capital outflows, and inappropriate investments in agriculture relative to resource endowments. Structural adjustment as a cure is considered, with the resulting prescription of increased public spending on agriculture, agricultural price and policy reform, and privatization, in addition to exchange rate realignment.

Price stabilization objectives are highlighted in Schiff and Valdés, as they were in Timmer. Schiff and Valdés add as an issue the "overshooting" concern: prices in agriculture are more flexible and market-responsive than in industry, so exchange rate adjustments or other external shocks drive them beyond long-run equilibrium levels for a time. This issue is covered more in the chapter on developed economies (Ardeni and Freebairn), where large-country effects make impacts of overshooting greater.

De Janvry, Sadoulet, and Murgai also present a version of the role of agriculture in economic development, while broadening coverage to include rural development issues more generally. They argue that the role of the rural sector in the growth process is not well understood, and that growth is a precondition for poverty elimination. They also highlight recent findings from new growth theory, examining policies to achieve growth with equity and emphasizing the role of human capital – a finding also prominent in Timmer's review. The income distribution issue they raise has also received a good bit of attention in recent critiques of structural adjustment programs. In addition, they develop microeconomic models of rural households, providing theoretical underpinnings to the aggregate perspective offered. That perspective draws heavily on new institutional economics, focusing on market imperfections and market organization issues – issues that may well lie behind key macroeconomic behavior. They argue that our aggregate models are weak in that they do not allow for marketing and institutional failures, for externalities, and for economies of scale.

While their focus is largely microeconomic, de Janvry, Sadoulet, and Murgai touch upon macroeconomic concerns as well. They note, for example, the findings from empirical work in the new growth theory area examining determinants of cross-country differences in per capita income [e.g., Collier and Gunning (1999)] that effects of macroeconomic policy in fostering growth are more evident than microeconomic, agricultural sector specific policies. Budget deficits limiting investments in rural development are raised as a concern. They explore the role of the state in rural development, emphasizing its role in fostering technical change. They argue that rural policy must go beyond exchange rate policy, or pricing and subsidies, and take into account institutional features of rural households and markets.

Brooks and Nash, like de Janvry, Sadoulet and Murgai, focus on microeconomic underpinnings of agricultural sector wide issues and agricultural development, while relating those findings to their macroeconomic consequences. Brooks and Nash examine economies in transition – the former Soviet Union, China, and Eastern Europe – where central planning, large, unwieldy farms, distorted incentives, and inefficient investment policies are key features. Agriculture is seen as one of the failings of the Communist model, but agriculture remains in steep decline even after the transition. They note one success: in the Chinese case substantial productivity gains were realized when institutional constraints were relaxed. The role of institutional reform in increasing Chinese agricultural productivity remains a debated point, however. In Eastern Europe and the former Soviet Union (FSU), too many resources remained in agriculture after state farms were dismantled. Productivity gains comparable to those in China have therefore not occurred in those regions.

A key empirical debate, touched upon also by Hertel, concerns whether economies of scale are important in farming. Brooks and Nash observe that the Western literature has found that small farms can be efficient, but an intellectual consensus has not yet been reached in the transition countries, where many still believe in the economies-of-scale argument behind state farming. The findings from the development literature contrast somewhat with Hertel's review of developed country agriculture, where he found that, at least in processing and some higher-value products, economies of scale may matter.

Incentives also changed after the transition. In China, prices improved for producers, accounting in part for productivity gains. In FSU and Eastern Europe, budget limits meant subsidies to producers declined. Distortions leading to very high meat consumption (given the region's per capita income) also disappeared, further reducing incentives to agriculture. Administrative control of prices also meant trade had to be managed by state agencies. The macroeconomic crisis has made it difficult for anything approaching free trade to emerge. As a result, trade barriers imposed on the West by the FSU and Eastern Europe have not declined substantially.

Institutional constraints and market failures are also highlighted by Brooks and Nash. Prior to the transition of the early 1990s there were not well-organized markets for inputs and outputs. Institutions have needed to develop after the transition. There also were not institutions to insure against risk. Managerial shortcomings were also critical to sectoral outcomes. Land tenure and establishment of private property were also important institutional concerns, as privatization has seen varying degrees of effectiveness in this region. Brooks and Nash observe that speed may have been more important than technique in effecting real institutional change. Countries that succeeded may not have put effective institutions in place at the time of reform. Delay of reforms while waiting for better institutional change was more likely to lead to economic stagnation than to effective reform begun later, however.

Macroeconomic concerns are raised in Brooks and Nash's review. They observe that national macroeconomic crises have dampened food demand, limited resources for adjustment, and introduced considerable instability into the economy. Agricultural subsidies also contributed importantly to budget deficits, trade outcomes, and so macroeconomic imbalance. Also, since transfer of technology has largely come via imported inputs and foreign capital inflows, problems with trade and macroeconomic balance continue to retard growth.

Ardeni and Freebairn cover in more depth macroeconomic issues important to agriculture in developed-country settings. They first lay out the linkages between agriculture and the general economy, noting how these evolve from the case of a developing country. Forward linkages from the general economy to agriculture are seen as much stronger than the reverse linkages in later stages of development. Those forward linkages are critical to the evolution of agriculture as well as to the importance of macroeconomic policy to agriculture. Reflecting this literature, exchange rate impacts are prominently addressed, and fiscal, monetary, and industrial policy consequences are also examined.

Macroeconomic issues highlighted by Ardeni and Freebairn include the importance of technical change in influencing productivity in agriculture, the release of labor as the sector evolves, cost-push inflationary pressure from macroeconomic events, the volatility of the sector due to climatic variations, balance of trade implications of agricultural surpluses, and budgetary implications of agricultural policy. The force of these relationships is almost always stronger from the general economy to agriculture, rather than vice versa, but situations do arise in developed countries where agricultural issues can affect macroeconomic outcomes. Certainly in the U.S. agricultural trade is significant in trade balance outcomes, and budgetary considerations are especially important in the EU, where Common Agricultural Policy (CAP) costs remain a significant fraction of the EU budget.

Ardeni and Freebairn's chapter also reviews attempts by agricultural economists to combine macroeconomic and commodity models [e.g., Shei and Thompson (1988)]. The fixed price-flex price overshooting models of Rausser and his colleagues [Rausser et al. (1986), Stamoulis and Rausser (1988)], mentioned above, are probably among the most successful in this class. They have been criticized, however, for making structural and empirical assumptions that lead to their implications, without being able to econometrically demonstrate the relevance of those assumptions. In general, these models have been difficult to empirically implement and are quite sensitive to assumptions on macroeconomic closure. This concern carries over to the computable general equilibrium (CGE) models, which now take on the task of examining agricultural issues from a more aggregate perspective. CGE model results can also be sensitive to assumptions on model closure, and the assumed paradigm is generally the neoclassical approach, leaving aside important issues from macroeconomics. Thus, while Ardeni and Freebairn lay out linkages between agriculture and the general economy consistent with theory, their relative magnitudes and influence are speculative at best.

One approach to coping with empirical difficulties, similar to a strategy employed in the macroeconomics literature, is to use time series econometric methods rather than structural models to test for the existence and magnitude of macroeconomic linkages. Schuh's (1988) hypothesis on the importance of monetary policy in determining agricultural prices has received special attention [Orden and Fackler (1989)]. Market integration and the law of one price, critical to price formation and the relevance of macroeconomic price stickiness, have also been examined extensively with time series methods. Results have been quite sensitive to judgments applied on variable inclusion, definitions of time periods, and other modeling choices. They are consistent with the critical role of macroeconomic policy in determining prices, as suggested above. The results on market integration have been inconsistent, and methods are now under attack [Barrett (1996), Baulch (1997), Fackler and Goodwin (2001) this Handbook] .

The other approach has been to adopt CGE models, in which the underlying economic theory is almost always neoclassical, and in which key parameters are set based on modeler judgments rather than on econometric results. This method has become the most often used methodology for aggregate, economy- or sector-wide issues. Hertel reviews experience and issues with this class of models.

Hertel limits his review to the most commonly applied general equilibrium models. He considers only comparative static models, not dynamic extensions (of which there are few). Models reviewed also deal with developed-country issues – he notes that an extensive literature on developing country applications exists, written mostly by general and development economists. Structural issues and market imperfections are also not emphasized, an issue which he states may be of relevance to future directions of that literature. He notes in closing that most CGE models to date are "general purpose", but future models may need to adapt more to the special circumstances of particular markets.

Advantages of this approach are more theoretically consistent measures of welfare impacts stemming from a strong underlying theoretical framework, accounting consistency, complete representation of intersectoral linkages, and an economy-wide perspective. This approach serves as a vehicle for analyzing second-best outcomes and policies. Hertel identifies problems remaining to be addressed, including effects of stockpiling, factor mobility, the heterogeneity of land, and water policy. Hertel also notes problems with aggregation choices and the adequacy of ad valorem equivalents as representations of complex agricultural policy institutions. De Janvry and Sadoulet (1987) have investigated approaches to incorporating more complex and realistic policy specifications into CGE models, and Robinson (1991) also notes the sensitivity of results to the form of policy specification.

From a macroeconomic perspective, these models focus on real-sector issues and mostly ignore monetary phenomena, financing issues, and investment behavior highlighted by Schuh (1988). The macroeconomic framework is almost always neoclassical, with perfect capital mobility in some newer models. Work on the relevance of alternative macroeconomic closures by Robinson (1991), Kilkenny and Robinson (1990), and Dewatripont and Michel (1987) is cited, however. Generally this closure involves whether trade balance is required (zero) as a constraint, or foreign capital inflows are treated in some simple manner. Capital flows are seldom related to interest rates in agricultural models. Most work by agricultural economists has also not tackled income distribution, although there are CGE formulations that examine this important macroeconomic concern.

A contribution which has emerged from this literature is the specification of demand systems that exhibit the peculiar characteristics known to exist for food demand and which lie behind the structural transformation – low and declining elasticities [Rimmer and Powell (1996)]. Specifications of profit functions also lead to better estimates of supply elasticities. Nevertheless, most models are stylized representations incorporating guessed parameters, causing Hertel to call for more systematic sensitivity analysis, using methods which facilitate that process of examining parameter alternatives for larger models. Both come from the CGE tradition of casting specifications in the framework of optimizing agents solving constrained optimization problems, hence the perfect market paradigm.

CGE models also incorporate certain assumptions that are a compromise between theory and observation. The most notable is frequent use of Armington specifications, for which substitution elasticities are not well known. The use of Armington specifications is partly due to product differentiation, but is more often a compromise to cope with the high level of aggregation causing product mixes to differ across countries, and goods to often be both imports and exports. Moreover, as Brown (1987) noted, this specification exaggerates the extent of market power, since an Armington function makes a market differentiated and so necessarily bestows market power on anyone serving that market. Given the level of aggregation required by these models, an alternative to the Armington approach is not easily found, but it does complicate welfare analysis, one of the hoped-for advantages of this approach. Hertel argues that a promising new approach is the effort to differentiate products by brand rather than country of origin.

While most CGE models adhere to the neoclassical framework, a few address market imperfections, including some of macroeconomic concern. We agree with Hertel that more of these variations on the CGE theme are needed in the future.

4. Missing issues

Given the focus and organization of the chapters synthesized here, a few key issues relevant to the relationship between agriculture and the macroeconomy were not touched upon, or pieces of literature relevant to this discussion on the relationship of agriculture to the macroeconomy were not reviewed. Some of those omissions are noted here.

While the endogenous growth literature and work based on the Heston–Summers data on purchasing power parity adjusted per capita real GDP was cited in three chapters, much more has been done, largely by general economists, than was considered here. That work has generated renewed interest in the sources of economic growth, the process of economic development, and to a lesser extent the role of agriculture in that process. Collier and Gunning's (1999) review of that literature suggests a significant role for agriculture in that research. Agricultural economists should be contributing more to this debate, given their technical expertise in the sector.

General economists in early development theory ascribed a special role to foreign exchange [Chenery and Strout (1980)]. Abbott (1984) and Shane and Stallings (1984) each looked at this issue and specifically its impact on agricultural trade after the 1981 LDC debt crisis. Weakly understood effects of foreign exchange shortages were believed to be a significant factor behind the subsequent downturn in agricultural import growth of developing countries. Foreign financial issues were at the heart of the structural adjustment debates that followed, but they also received relatively little attention in these chapters. Yet agricultural policy reform emerged at the end of that debate as a key concern. Current debates on reform of the World Bank and IMF [Kreuger (1998)] could also have profound impacts on the availability of investment resources for agriculture. The trade impacts of the recent Asian crisis may need to be understood along the same lines. Speculative bubbles leading to devaluations were influenced by foreign capital flows, and measures taken by governments to cope with them surely influenced agricultural trade and investment decisions.

While Ardeni and Freebairn are relatively complete in laying out potential linkages between agriculture and the macroeconomy, they do not assess our state of knowledge on the magnitude or relative importance of those effects. Exchange rate linkages have clearly gotten the most attention in our literature, because they directly relate to prices, and can more easily be incorporated into microeconomic models. While Thompson (1988) has ascribed a key role to interest rate linkages, these have received far less attention, probably because these linkages are not supported by econometric work. Inflation is routinely dealt with simply by deflating prices, but price transmission work often suggests more may be going on. Only a few of the works examined here come to grips with issues related to unemployment, yet much of agricultural policy is driven by what are effectively labor market issues. There was a period in the 1980s when labor market issues were at the top of the agenda for several agricultural economists, but marrying these macroeconomic concerns to largely microeconomic commodity models proved difficult empirically.

There has been work on pricing to market by agricultural economists [Pick and Park (1991), Baulch (1997), Barrett (1996)], but the border effects on price linkages that deviate from our simple, standard assumptions, emphasized by Goldberg and Knetter (1997), have not been incorporated into our macroeconomic perspective. The work of Pick and Park, however, does find some pricing to market, especially where government intervention stabilizes domestic markets or where processing is involved. Miljkovic (1999) looks more broadly at the relationship of the law of one price to agricultural work. He finds several arguments for wage and price stickiness that weaken the price linkages that are key drivers in most agricultural models. Price relationships are subject to market power, exchange rate risk, transactions costs, regionalization, policy, and institutional factors. Incorporating these price rigidities from macroeconomics into more microeconomic approaches is problematic, especially where the microeconomic foundations of the rigidities are uncertain.

Productivity concerns, a key issue in macroeconomic debates, have also been extensively examined by agricultural economists assessing relative productivity of agriculture as compared to other sectors, and in our debate on the concept of agricultural competitiveness. Measurement of total factor productivity growth was pioneered by agricultural economists, and is crucial to measuring the extent and nature of technical change. The competitiveness debate also brings concerns with the relevance of theory in explaining trade patterns and growth in the realm of both New Trade Theory and New Growth Theory. Economies of scale were occasionally relevant in the literature reviewed here, but little attention was given to either product differentiation or imperfect competition. The work of business economists on competitiveness is becoming important in the development literature [Porter (1990)], and has received little attention from agricultural economists. Institutional issues on what are necessary conditions for development and what determines investment are raised by Porter.

Most aggregate and macroeconomic approaches in this literature have followed a neoclassical paradigm. A few studies have taken a more structuralist approach, investigating the consequences of market imperfections and institutional constraints. De Janvry and Sadoulet (1987) investigated incorporating more realistic specifications of agricultural policy regimes into a CGE framework. Stoeckel and Breckling (1989) incorporated unemployment into their CGE investigation of European Union CAP reform. Coxhead and Plangpraphan (1999) included migration and foreign capital flow issues in their examination of effects on Asian agriculture of the recent financial crisis. A group in India has utilized the structuralist macroeconomics approach due to Taylor (1990), incorporating an essentially Keynesian approach into a CGE model, in investigation of agricultural policy impacts there. They emphasize the demand effects of the linkages between agriculture and the economy that were emphasized much earlier by Johnson and Mellor [Das (1989), Rakshit (1989)]. That same paradigm lies behind the work by Delgado et al. (1998) on regional multipliers from investment in agriculture. The more institutional approaches, which incorporate structural adjustment mechanisms quite different from those of a typical CGE model, can find devaluations working against agriculture, and find a more positive role for certain agricultural policy distortions as employment and demand-generation mechanisms.

Income distribution was emphasized only by de Janvry, Sadoulet, and Murgai, who looked at that from a microeconomic and rural development perspective. Income distribution is likely to be critical, however, to how growth in Asian economies, for example, translates into demand growth and rural poverty alleviation.

Stabilization issues and unemployment are key concerns behind agricultural policy, and yet are often not addressed in aggregate analyses of agricultural economists. Several of the contributors to this Handbook have cited stabilization as a key concern driving agricultural policy, especially in developing countries. An extensive literature explicitly addresses commodity price stabilization, from a more microeconomic perspective. That literature, however, seldom accepts stabilization as a legitimate objective in itself, and looks carefully at welfare impacts on separate interest groups. In macroeconomics, stabilization of economic outcomes is often seen as one key objective of policy, and this can also be seen in the agricultural policy positions of governments.

Macroeconomic linkages are also especially important to the long-range forecasting and short-run outlook work at USDA, as well as similar efforts by the Food and Agriculture Organization of the UN, the World Bank, and the International Food Policy

Research Institute (IFPRI). In those efforts a macroeconomic forecast is typically borrowed from general economists, but key variables determining projected outcomes are macroeconomic. CGE model simulations also often borrow macroeconomic projections from economists. Only feedback linkages from the general economy to agriculture are captured in that work. Given the importance of developing economies as import markets, that may become a serious oversight.

5. Theoretical basis for examining agriculture's role/methodologies employed

Much of the aggregate, macroeconomic-related work of agricultural economists is empirical rather than theoretical. The theoretical underpinnings of most of the literature synthesized here have been borrowed from the general economics literature. Agricultural economists have documented the nature and extent of linkages between agriculture and the general economy rather than contributing new theories or methods. Their work is also strongly based on microeconomic foundations and draws most heavily from the neoclassical tradition. Agricultural economists have been especially comfortable with the macroeconomic paradigm where microeconomic foundations of any admitted macroeconomic phenomenon are clearly established. Much of the modeling and empirical policy analysis work also draws largely on mainstream theory, and ignores the emerging literatures on institutions, market imperfections, and applications of game theory. There are contributions that incorporate these newer ideas, but the lag in introducing those approaches to bread-and-butter policy and staff work, and thinking about issues as related to structural transformation, is long.

The dichotomy between application of the neoclassical paradigm versus incorporation of market imperfections is clearly seen in the several chapters synthesized here. The now most common approach to aggregate or macroeconomic-related issues is the CGE model. Hertel fairly characterizes that work as focusing largely on the perfect markets case, with an underlying macroeconomic framework strongly rooted in microeconomic traditions. Some recent work by Robinson (1991) has addressed macroeconomic linkages, to some extent examining capital flows and so investment issues. Generally that is limited to deciding whether the exchange rate or current account balance is fixed. In some CGE formulations, however, perfect capital mobility is assumed when investment crosses borders in the long run to achieve the highest return worldwide. The observed imperfections in asset substitutability are just now being introduced into some models, and the effects of speculative bubbles and irrational expectations hampering predictions of exchange rate models have yet to be addressed.

The next most common approach, after the CGE models, is the commodity model. These are typically multi-product implementations of the supply-demand framework, with specifications, for agricultural production especially, which reflect a technical understanding of agriculture. They are built around supply-utilization balances, for which good data on quantity is readily available. Academic contributions extend these models in various ways. The more microeconomic approaches address more of the institutional arrangements and market imperfections inherent in agricultural markets, but policy staff work and much empirical work remains largely rooted in the perfect market approach. The weak link in using these models for countries outside the U.S. is the lack of good domestic price data. One lacuna in the chapters synthesized here is a failure to examine to any great extent the contributions of more institutional and imperfect market approaches to examining aggregate agricultural sector behavior.

In contrast to these models, macroeconomics contains much about market imperfections and how they impact behavior on an aggregate level [Krugman (1995)]. While economists have struggled to develop microeconomic foundations of those perspectives, some have declared the micro foundations project a failure, while those who are less pessimistic state that the processes identified behind such a phenomenon as the Phillips curve, while likely relevant, are insufficient as a full explanation. It should not be surprising, however, that when one looks at the economy at a macroeconomic level, several competing forces may underlie the observed aggregate behavior, and sorting that out empirically is challenging. For example, price stickiness may be due to labor unions, contracting, menu and catalog pricing, or numerous other forces, all of which relate to unemployment in different ways. There is considerable uncertainty in the macroeconomics profession as to the appropriate modeling approach and the empirical relevance of certain key assumptions, and how they relate to observed market performance [Basu and Taylor (1999)]. Non-neutrality of money – that monetary policy can affect real outcomes in the economy – is accepted by many but is still controversial. Debate rages over whether wages and/or prices are sticky, and how one can construct rigorous disequilibrium models based on rational, optimizing agents that admit these outcomes and are consistent with observed data. Exchange rate determination models fail to explain short-run movements, and whether purchasing power parity is even relevant in the longer term [Dornbusch (1989), Kenen (1985)]. While globalization clearly means markets are more integrated, borders still matter in poorly understood ways, especially for price and interest rate linkages, and capital and labor flows. Therefore, several schools of macroeconomic thought persist that propose competing models to explain business cycles, price adjustments, inflation, interest rates, exchange rates, investment, capital flows, and employment. All these variables are critical to the economic environment in which the agricultural sector operates.

The chapters in this Handbook that deal on a more microeconomic level, and that seek to understand the structural transformation process and agriculture's role in it, address market imperfections much more directly than do the chapters on method. The chapters on economic development, economies in transition, and rural development clearly raise these concerns in their critique of policy and economic performance. The market imperfections addressed are more often market-specific, however, and not the macroeconomic issues cited above.

In fairness to the work of agricultural economists, theoretical and, more importantly, empirical issues on macroeconomics (e.g., exchange rate determination, a key concern behind agricultural economics issues) remain unresolved, so modeling choices are problematic. More importantly, while there may be an understanding of relevant issues and forces, empirical magnitudes of linkages are much less well known. Data limitations and difficulties in working on aggregate behaviors frustrate work in both agricultural economics and macroeconomics.

6. Empirical issues and limitations

Agricultural economics is a largely empirical discipline. In order for neglected macroeconomic variables discussed above to be integrated into its models and analysis, empirical estimations of macroeconomic linkages are required. Unfortunately, both in macroeconomics and in the work in the 1980s trying to blend macroeconomics with commodity models, such empirical results are not always forthcoming or successful. A great deal of uncertainty as to the magnitude and often nature of relationships exists, as evidenced by the unresolved controversies in macroeconomics. Work by agricultural economists was frustrated by problems of empirically implementing models and distinguishing between competing hypotheses.

In 1981 Thompson cited empirical content as one of the key limiting factors in analysis of aggregate agricultural policy issues, especially where trade was involved. He cited limited data and prior econometric results as contributing to this limitation. While the economy is more global, and data is now more easily shared worldwide, some key data he indicated was missing – such as domestic price data of many countries, especially in wholesale and retail markets – is still not collected. Since the early 1980s more resources have been devoted to data distribution, but (probably) less effort has been spent on primary data collection, and the list of variables collected has not expanded greatly. Good data remains a challenge for those examining global agriculture from a macroeconomic perspective. Recent trends also make that data at times more expensive to the end user, as fees to obtain data are increased to help support data collection efforts, especially when data with an international dimension is required.

In the 1980s, there was a flurry of activity seeking to marry commodity models to macroeconomic models. That literature, which is reviewed by Ardeni and Freebairn, sought to explicitly address the relevance of macroeconomics concerns in agricultural policy issues. The marriage proved difficult, especially on an empirical level, in part because the underlying paradigms on market functioning are different, and in part because of poor empirical estimation results to establish the relevant linkages. Many published works emerged as synthesized rather than estimated models, using best-guess parameters in order to illustrate the consequences of the ideas under examination. Agricultural economists also resorted to time series methods to seek to determine whether such issues as the effects of monetary policy on sectoral outcomes, especially prices, were important specifically in the agricultural sector. In the process, empirical evidence on linkages emerged for some but not all relevant macroeconomic variables. This suggests that, at least in developed countries, the agricultural sector was small, so feedback to the general economy could be ignored and it was plausible to treat macroeconomic outcomes as exogenous.

While many of the stylized facts cited in the chapters reviewed here are reasonably well understood, evidence is weaker where behavioral parameters for a structural model are required. Gardiner and Dixit (1986) review of net trade elasticities in agricultural models highlights one problematic area. Cross-price elasticities and Armington elasticities required of CGE models are another area where intuition on parameter magnitudes is weak and econometric evidence is inconclusive. Evidence is better where commodities are well defined and theoretical structures of models are simple, and on firm ground. Aggregation required of a macroeconomic perspective often clouds estimation, where competing forces shape a relationship. Sometimes parameter uncertainty means that even the direction of policy impacts remains unknown, and the relative influences of competing forces cannot be sorted out.

Two approaches have been adopted by agricultural economists to cope with weak empirical evidence and poor estimates of needed behavioral parameters. Synthetic models, in which parameters are guessed based on review of the literature and the modelers' judgment, are becoming even more common. Time series econometrics, where no structural model is assumed, is also increasingly prevalent, especially where aggregate analysis is concerned. The time series approach has seen extensive application by macroeconomists, as well.

7. Conclusion

Linkages between the macroeconomy and the agricultural sector remain important and challenging concerns for agricultural economists. We need to better understand what drives economic development and what role the agricultural sector plays in that process. We also need to better understand how linkages to the macroeconomy continue to evolve once a country is developed. The structural transformation underlying changes in those linkages is critical to both effective policy formation and forecasting future market trends. A good general understanding of this process has been described in the chapters synthesized here, but our knowledge of the magnitude of linkages and our ability to model this process still exhibit weaknesses.

Better understanding of empirical linkages in part awaits collection and wide availability of better data. Data limitations still constrain empirical work, especially work with international dimensions. Better data sets in some key areas have emerged, however, and need to be more effectively exploited by agricultural economists. For example, the Heston–Summers data set on purchasing power parity adjusted income across countries has brought a resurgence of interest in economic development among general economists. While it offers an opportunity for agricultural economists to explore empirically the role of agriculture and agricultural policy in economic growth, only a limited amount of work on that has yet been done. Income distribution is another macroeconomic concern receiving renewed attention, especially in light of adjustment problems following the Asian financial crisis. A new data set on consumption and income distribution has also recently been made available from the World Bank, which should allow more empirical work on this issue, as well. Foreign price data availability remains a serious constraint to work in this area, however, as noted by those doing work on price relationships.

Work on economy-wide issues needs to address both long-run market trends and forces underlying the instability in markets as those trends unfold. In the recent GATT negotiations, for example, most work focused on static, current, one-time gains from trade liberalization. Recent market events highlight the role of stabilization policies, which remain critical concerns of most countries in spite of the apparent success of GATT. Long-run trends also remain uncertain in light of those same market events. Work in both areas needs to take better advantage of the institutional knowledge agricultural economists have gained, and should employ lessons emerging from the more sophisticated methods addressing those institutions and market imperfections. Those ideas should help to provide a better understanding of the forces at work, and how they influence underlying trends.

The chapters synthesized in this section also highlight this dichotomy in the work of agricultural economists. Microeconomic work is rich in its use of structure, institutions, detailed policy specifications, and market imperfections. The economy- and sector-wide work, especially policy evaluation and forecasting, needs to better incorporate the lessons of that microeconomic work. The perspective of macroeconomics, that aggregate market behaviors may be driven by poorly understood market imperfections, needs to be addressed in the ways in which we examine key policy issues such as trade liberalization and structural adjustment. Much of the recent work in economics, employing game theory to better understand imperfect markets, is due to this same concern. The challenge in aggregate work is finding methods to capture in more than an ad hoc manner the conflicts and compromises that exist in the imperfect world we seek to model. The structuralist approach as employed by Das (1989) and Rakshit (1989) on Indian agricultural policy, and by Taylor (1990), demonstrates that modifications to the standard methodology based on imperfect markets are possible, but that different lessons on policy or exchange rate impacts may emerge. We also need to better incorporate the lessons of new trade theory into that work. These lessons were recognized by Johnson and Mellor decades ago in their conceptual model of agriculture's role in a developing economy. Modern treatment of agriculture's role in the economy needs to more fully incorporate their insights into the role of demand on agricultural sector outcomes.

Many of these concerns have been highlighted in the chapters synthesized here. Those authors have recognized the need to better understand how agriculture and the economy interact, and to modify models and analysis to incorporate those lessons. Instances where that has started have also been frequently cited. Renewed interest in these aggregate issues is called for, since recent market events only underscore the importance ascribed to macroeconomics by Schuh and Thompson in the 1970s and '80s.

References

Abbott, P.C. (1984), "Foreign exchange constraints to trade and development", FAER 209 (ERS, USDA, Washington, DC).

Abbott, P. (1988), "Estimating U.S. agricultural export demand elasticities: Econometric and economic issues", in: C. Carter and W. Gardiner, eds., Elasticities in International Agricultural Trade (Westview Press, Boulder, CO) 53–86.

Anderson, K., and Y. Hayami (1986), The Political Economy of Agricultural Protection: East Asia in International Perspective (Allen & Unwin, London).

Ardeni, P.G., and J. Freebairn (2002), "The macroeconomics of agriculture", in: B.L. Gardner and G.C. Rausser, eds., Handbook of Agricultural Economics, Vol. 2 (Elsevier, Amsterdam) 1455–1485.

Askari, H., and J. Cummings (1976), Agricultural Supply Response: A Survey of the Econometric Evidence (Praeger, New York).

Avery, D. (1996), "Toughest rome food summit challenge is not how to end famine – but preserving wildlife", Global Food Quarterly (Hudson Institute, Indianapolis, IN).

Barrett, C.B. (1996), "Market analysis methods: Are our toolkits well suited to enlivened markets?", American Journal of Agricultural Economics 78:825–829.

Barro, R., and X. Sala-i-Martin (1995), Economic Growth (McGraw-Hill, New York).

Basu, S., and A. Taylor (1999), "Business cycles in international historical perspective", Journal of Economic Perspectives 13(1):45–68.

Bates, R. (1983), "Patterns of market intervention in agrarian agriculture", Food Policy 8:139–161.

Baulch, R.J. (1997), "Transfer costs, spatial arbitrage and testing for food market integration", American Journal of Agricultural Economics 79:477–487.

Bautista, R., S. Robinson, F. Tarp and P. Wobst (2001), "Policy bias and agriculture: Partial and general equilibrium measures", Review of Development Economics 5:89–104.

Belognia, M.T., and R. King (1983), "A monetary analysis of food price determination", American Journal of Agricultural Economics 65:131–135.

Binswanger, H., and K. Deininger (1997), "Explaining agricultural and agrarian policies in developing countries", Journal of Economic Literature 35:1958–2005.

Brooks, K., and J. Nash (2002), "The rural sector in transition economies", in: B.L. Gardner and G.C. Rausser, eds., Handbook of Agricultural Economics, Vol. 2 (Elsevier, Amsterdam) 1547–1592.

Brown, D.K. (1987), "Tariffs, the terms of trade and national product differentiation", Journal of Policy Modeling 9:503–526.

Brown, L. (1995), Who Will Feed China? (W.W. Norton and Company, New York).

Carter, C., R. Gray and W.H. Furtan (1990), "Exchange rate effects on inputs and outputs in Canadian agriculture", American Journal of Agricultural Economics 72(3):738–743.

Chai, C. (1995), "Rural human capital and economic growth in developing countries", Senior Honors Thesis (Harvard University, Cambridge, MA).

Chambers, R.G. (1988), "An overview of exchange rates and macroeconomic effects on agriculture", in: P. Paarlberg and R. Chambers, eds., Macroeconomic, Agriculture and Exchange Rates (Westview Press, Boulder, CO) 1–22.

Chambers, R., and R. Just (1979), "A critique of exchange rate treatment in agricultural trade models", American Journal of Agricultural Economics 61:249–257.

Chambers, R., and R. Just (1982), "Investigation of monetary factors on U.S. agriculture", Journal of Monetary Economics 9:235–247.

Chenery, H.B., and A. Strout (1980), "Foreign assistance and economic development", American Economic Review 70:679–733.

Collier, P., and J. Gunning (1999), "Explaining African economic performance", Journal of Economic Literature 37:64–111.

Coxhead, I., and J. Plangpraphan (1999), "Economic boom, financial bust and the decline of Thai agriculture: Was growth in the 1990s too fast?", Chulalongkorn Journal of Economics 11(1).

Das, C. (1989), "Food policy in a dual economy", in: M. Rakshit, ed., Studies in Macroeconomics of Developing Countries (Oxford University Press, Delhi) 66–93.

Dawe, D. (1996), "A new look at the effects of export instability on investment and growth", World Development.

de Gorter, H., and J. Swinnen (2002), "Political economy of agricultural policy", in: B.L. Gardner and G.C. Rausser, eds., Handbook of Agricultural Economics, Vol. 2 (Elsevier, Amsterdam) 1893–1943.

de Janvry, A., and E. Sadoulet (1987), "Agricultural price policy in general equilibrium: Results and comparisons", American Journal of Agricultural Economics 69:230–246.

de Janvry, A., E. Sadoulet and R. Murgai (2002), "Rural development and rural policy", in: B.L. Gardner and G.C. Rausser, eds., Handbook of Agricultural Economics, Vol. 2 (Elsevier, Amsterdam) 1593–1658.

Delgado, C., J. Hopkins and V. Kelly (1998), "Agricultural growth linkages in sub-Saharan Africa", IFPRI Research Report 107 (IFPRI, Washington, DC).

Dewatripont, M., and G. Michel (1987), "On closure rules, homogeneity and dynamics in applied general equilibrium models", Journal of Development Economics 26:65–76.

Dornbusch, R. (1989), "Real exchange rates and macroeconomics: A selective survey", Scandinavian Journal of Economics 91(2):401–432.

Evenson, R.E. (2001), "Economic impacts of agricultural research and extension", in: B.L. Gardner and G.C. Rausser, eds., Handbook of Agricultural Economics, Vol. 1 (Elsevier, Amsterdam) 573–628.

Evenson, R.E., and Y. Kislev (1975), "Investment in agricultural research and extension: An international survey", Economic Development and Cultural Change 23:507–521.

Fackler, P.L., and B.K. Goodwin (2001), "Spatial price analysis", in: B.L. Gardner and G.C. Rausser, eds., Handbook of Agricultural Economics, Vol. 1 (Elsevier, Amsterdam) 971–1024.

Fogel, R. (1994), "Economic growth, population theory and physiology: The bearing of long term processes on the making of economic policy", American Economic Review 84:369–395.

Francois, J., B. McDonald and H. Nordstrom (1997), "Capital accumulation in applied trade models", in: Francois and Reinert, eds., Applied Methods for Trade Policy Analysis (Cambridge University Press, Cambridge) 364–382.

Gardiner, W.H., and P.M. Dixit (1986), "Price elasticity of export demand: Concepts and estimates", Staff Report AGES860408 (Economic Research Service, USDA, Washington, DC).

Goldberg, P., and M. Knetter (1997), "Goods prices and exchange rates: What have we learned?", Journal of Economic Literature 35(3):1243–1272.

Handy, C., and D. Henderson (1994), "Assessing the role of foreign direct investment in the food manufacturing industry", in: M. Bredahl, P. Abbott and M. Reid, eds., Competitiveness in International Food Markets (Westview Press, Boulder, CO).

Hertel, T. (2002), "Applied general equilibrium analysis of agricultural and resource policies", in: B.L. Gardner and G.C. Rausser, eds., Handbook of Agricultural Economics, Vol. 2 (Elsevier, Amsterdam) 1373–1419.

Heston, A., and R. Summers (1996), "International price and quantity comparisons: Potentials and pitfalls", American Economic Review 86:20–24.

Hubbard, R.G. (1998), "Capital market imperfections and investment", Journal of Economic Literature 36(1):193–225.

International Agricultural Trade Research Consortium (IATRC) (1986), "Embargoes, surplus disposal and U.S. agriculture", AER No. 564 (Economic Research Service, USDA, Washington, DC).

International Food Policy Research Institute (IFPRI) (1995), "A 2020 vision for food agriculture and the environment" (IFPRI, Washington, DC).

Johnson, B., and J. Mellor (1960), "The nature of agriculture's contribution to economic development", Food Research Studies 1:335–356.

Kaminsky, G., and C. Reinhart (1999), "The twin crises: The causes of banking and balance of payments problems", American Economic Review 89(3):473–500.

Kenen, P. (1985), "Macroeconomic theory and policy: How the closed economy was opened", in: R. Jones and P. Kenen, eds., Handbook of International Economics, Vol. II (Elsevier, Amsterdam) 626–677.

Kilkenny, M., and S. Robinson (1990), "AGE analysis of agricultural liberalization: Factor mobility and model closure", Journal of Policy Modeling 12(3):527–556.

Kreuger, A. (1998), "Whither the World Bank and the IMF?" Journal of Economic Literature 36(4):1983–2020.

Krugman, P. (1995), "Adjustment in the world economy", in: P. Krugman, ed., Currencies and Crises (MIT Press, Cambridge, MA) 3–32.

Londono de la Cuesta, J.L. (1990), "IS-FM macroeconomics: General equilibrium linkages of the food market in Columbia", in: L. Taylor, ed., Socially Relevant Policy Analysis (MIT Press, Cambridge, MA) 85–113.

Lustig, N., and L. Taylor (1990), "Mexican food consumption policies in a structuralist CGE model", in: L. Taylor, ed., Socially Relevant Policy Analysis (MIT Press, Cambridge, MA) 71–84.

Miljkovic, D. (1999), "The law of one price in international trade: A critical review", Review of Agricultural Economics 21(1):126–139.

Mundlak, Y. (2001), "Production and supply", in: B.L. Gardner and G.C. Rausser, eds., Handbook of Agricultural Economics, Vol. 1 (Elsevier, Amsterdam) 3–85.

Obstfeld, M. (1998), "The global capital market: Benefactor or menace", Journal of Economic Perspectives 12(4):9–30.

Orden, D. (1999), "Exchange rate effects on agricultural trade and trade relations", Presented to Fifth Mexico/Canada/U.S. Conference on Policy Harmonization and Adjustment in North American Agricultural and Food Industry, March.

Orden, D., and P. Fackler (1989), "Identifying monetary impacts on agricultural prices in VAR models", American Journal of Agricultural Economics 71(2):495–502.

Orden, D., and L. Fisher (1991), "Macroeconomic policy and agricultural economics research", American Journal of Agricultural Economics 73(5):1348–1354.

Paarlberg, D. (1999), "Obituary for a farm program", Choices, 33–36.

Pick, D., and T.A. Park (1991), "The competitive structure of U.S. agricultural exports", American Journal of Agricultural Economics 73:134–141.

Porter, M. (1990), The Competitive Advantage of Nations (The Free Press, New York).

Rakshit, M. (1989), "Underdevelopment of commodity, credit and land markets: Some macroeconomic implications", in: M. Rakshit, ed., Studies in Macroeconomics of Developing Countries (Oxford University Press, Delhi) 148–182.

Rausser, G., J. Chalfant, H.A. Love and K. Stamoulis (1986), "Macroeconomic linkages, taxes and subsidies in the U.S. agricultural sector", American Journal of Agricultural Economics 68(2):399–412.

Rimmer, M.T., and A.A. Powell (1996), "An implicitly additive demand system", Applied Economics 28:1613–1622.

Robinson, S. (1991), "Macroeconomics, financial variables and computable general equilibrium models", World Development 19(11):1509–1525.

Rodrik, D. (1996), "Understanding economic policy reform", Journal of Economic Literature 34(1):9–41.

Sachs, J., and A. Warner (1997), "Fundamentals of long run growth", American Economic Review 87:184–188.

Schiff, M., and A. Valdés (2002), "Agriculture and the macroeconomy, with emphasis on developing countries", in: B.L. Gardner and G.C. Rausser, eds., Handbook of Agricultural Economics, Vol. 2 (Elsevier, Amsterdam) 1421–1454.

Schuh, G.E. (1974), "The exchange rate and US agriculture", American Journal of Agricultural Economics 56(1):1–13.

Schuh, G.E. (1988), "Some issues associated with exchange rate realignments in developing countries", in: P. Paarlberg and R. Chambers, eds., Macroeconomic, Agriculture and Exchange Rates (Westview Press, Boulder, CO).

Schultz, T.W. (1953), "Organization for price stability", in: The Economic Organization of Agriculture (McGraw-Hill, New York) Chapter 20, 335–366.

Schultz, T.W. (1964), Transforming Traditional Agriculture (Yale University Press, New Haven).

Shane, M., and D. Stallings (1984), "Trade and growth of developing countries under financial constraints", AGES840519 (Economic Research Service, USDA, Washington, DC).

Shei, S., and R.L. Thompson (1988), "Inflation and agriculture: A monetarist structuralist synthesis", in: P. Paarlberg and R. Chambers, eds., Macroeconomic, Agriculture and Exchange Rates (Westview Press, Boulder, CO) 123–161.

Stamoulis, K., and G. Rausser (1988), "Overshooting of agricultural prices", in: P. Paarlberg and R. Chambers, eds., Macroeconomic, Agriculture and Exchange Rates (Westview Press, Boulder, CO) 163–217.

Stoeckel, A., and J. Breckling (1989), "Some economy wide effects of agricultural policy in the European Union", in: Stoeckel, Vincent and Cuthbertson, eds., Macroeconomic Consequences of Farm Support Policies (Duke University Press, Durham) 94–124.

Summers, L. (1999), "American farmers: Their stake in Asia, their stake in the IMF", Treasury News RR-2241 (Office of Public Affairs, Dept. of Treasury, Washington, DC).

Taylor, L. (1979), Macro Models for Developing Countries (McGraw-Hill, New York).

Taylor, L. (1983), "Two sector models: The economy with an important food sector", in: Structuralist Macroeconomics (Basic Books, New York) 1–85.

Taylor, L. (1990), "Structuralist CGE models", in: L. Taylor, ed., Socially Relevant Policy Analysis (MIT Press, Cambridge, MA) 1–70.

Temple, J. (1999), "The new growth evidence", Journal of Economic Literature 37:112–156.

Thompson, R.L. (1981), "A survey of recent U.S. developments in international agricultural trade models", Bibliographies and Literature of Agriculture No. 21 (ERS, USDA, Washington, DC).

Thompson, R.L. (1988), "U.S. macroeconomic policy and agriculture", in: P. Paarlberg and R. Chambers, eds., Macroeconomic, Agriculture and Exchange Rates (Westview Press, Boulder, CO) 219–226.

Timmer, C.P. (2002), "Agriculture and economic development", in: B.L. Gardner and G.C. Rausser, eds., Handbook of Agricultural Economics, Vol. 2 (Elsevier, Amsterdam) 1487–1546.

United States Department of Agriculture, Economic Research Service (ERS) (1996), "Food marketing review, 1994–95", AER 743 (USDA, Washington, DC).

von Braun, J., R. Hopkins, D. Puetz and R. Pandya-Lorch (1993), "Aid to agriculture: Reversing the decline" (International Food Policy Research Institute, Washington, DC).

World Bank (1998), East Asia: The Road to Recovery (World Bank, Washington, DC).

World Bank (1999), World Development Report 1998/99 (Oxford University Press, New York).

AUTHOR INDEX

n indicates citation in footnote.

Gemmill, G. 1471
George, P.S. 1391
Gerken, A. 2024
Gerken, E., *see* Dicke, H. 1449
Gerpacio, R.V., *see* Pingali, P.L. 2205
Gerrard, C. 1915
Gersovitz, M. 1622, 1623n
Gertler, P. 1644
Getches, D.H. 2069
Ghassemi, H., *see* Beaton, G.H. 2140, 2153, 2155, 2158, 2163
Ghatak, M. 1635
Ghura, D. 1440
Giannakas, K. 1732, 1732n, 1734
Gibson, C. 1330
Gichuki, F., *see* Tiffen, M. 1230
Gielen, A. 1405
Gilbert, C.L. 1963, 1985, 2244
Gilles, J.L. 1329
Gilles, J.L., *see* Bromley, D.W. 1323
Gintis, H., *see* Bowles, S. 2076, 2077n
Gisser, M. 1699, 1715, 1718, 1920
Gittinger, J.P. 2163
Gjertsen, H. 1367
Glaeser, E.L. 1579
Glantz, M.H. 2146
Glewwe, P. 2162, 2162n
Glomm, G. 2109, 2116n, 2154
Goetz, A.M. 1638
Gohin, A.H. 1400
Golan, A.A. 2085
Goldberg, I. 1578
Goldberg, P.K. 1676, 2025
Goldin, I. 1445, 2035, 2037, 2038, 2210
Goldman, G., *see* Berck, P. 1391
Goldstein, J. 1925
Goldstein, M. 1957
Goletti, F., *see* Minot, N. 1384
Goodhue, R. 2090
Goodwin, B.K. 1820, 1959
Goodwin, B.K., *see* Fackler, P.L. 1674
Goodwin, B.K., *see* Smith, V.H. 1285, 1299
Gopinath, M. 1897
Gordillo, G., *see* de Janvry, A. 1610
Gordon, A.R. 2158
Gordon, H.S. 1318
Gordon, J., *see* Scrimshaw, N. 2107
Gordon, R.J. 1477
Gotsch, N. 1286
Gotsch, N., *see* Regev, U. 1286
Gould, B.W. 1256

Graap, E., *see* Pimentel, D. 1295
Graham, C. 2137
Graham-Tomasi, T., *see* Coggins, J.S. 1904
Granger, C.W.J. 1474n, 1475, 1475n, 1478, 1479
Granger, C.W.J., *see* Andersen, E. 1220
Granger, C.W.J., *see* Engle, R.F. 1475n, 1479n
Grasso, M., *see* Costanza, R. 1359
Graveland, C., *see* Oskam, A.J. 1269
Gray, D., *see* Tsigas, M.E. 1404
Gray, R.S., *see* Alston, J.M. 1699, 1707, 2022, 2026, 2042
Gray, R.S., *see* Carter, C.A. 1462
Gray, R.S., *see* Foster, W.E. 2081, 2087
Gray, R.S., *see* Schmitz, A. 1963
Green, D.P., *see* Krasno, J.S. 1916n
Green, G. 1260
Green, R., *see* Alston, J.M. 1405n, 1959n
Green, R., *see* Konandreas, P. 1958
Greenaway, D. 1473
Greenfield, J., *see* Konandreas, P. 2031
Greenfield, J., *see* Sharma, R. 2035–2038
Greenshields, B.L. 1958
Greer, J., *see* Foster, J. 2131n
Gregory, R. 1461
Grennes, T., *see* Dutton, J. 1959
Grennes, T., *see* Ghura, D. 1440
Grennes, T., *see* Goodwin, B.K. 1959
Grennes, T., *see* Johnson, P.R. 1471, 1958
Grepperud, S. 1225n, 1300, 1631n
Griffin, R.C. 1269, 1273
Griliches, Z. 1397, 1519
Grilli, E.R. 2130
Grimm, S.S. 1294
Grootaert, C. 2130
Gros, D. 1572
Grosh, M. 2165, 2171
Grossman, G., *see* Helpman, E. 2231
Grossman, G.M. 1911, 1922, 1926, 1970
Grossman, S. 1814
Gruber, J., *see* Gertler, P. 1644
Gruen, F.H. 1379
Guba, W., *see* Safin, M. 1573
Guesnerie, R. 1277, 1753, 1758, 1762, 1771, 1783, 1785, 1788
Guesnerie, R., *see* Caillaud, B. 1753
Gugerty, M.K., *see* Roemer, M. 1524, 1527
Guichaona, A., *see* Gaude, J. 2142
Guimard, H., *see* Caillavet, F. 1215
Gulati, S., *see* Chopra, K. 1231
Gunderson, C., *see* Rose, D. 2156
Gunning, J., *see* Collier, P. 1668, 1671, 1675

SUBJECT INDEX

HANDBOOKS IN ECONOMICS

1. HANDBOOK OF MATHEMATICAL ECONOMICS (in 4 volumes)
    Volumes 1, 2 and 3 edited by Kenneth J. Arrow and Michael D. Intriligator
    Volume 4 edited by Werner Hildenbrand and Hugo Sonnenschein

2. HANDBOOK OF ECONOMETRICS (in 6 volumes)
    Volumes 1, 2 and 3 edited by Zvi Griliches and Michael D. Intriligator
    Volume 4 edited by Robert F. Engle and Daniel L. McFadden
    Volume 5 edited by James J. Heckman and Edward Leamer
    Volume 6 is in preparation (editors James J. Heckman and Edward Leamer)

3. HANDBOOK OF INTERNATIONAL ECONOMICS (in 3 volumes)
    Volumes 1 and 2 edited by Ronald W. Jones and Peter B. Kenen
    Volume 3 edited by Gene M. Grossman and Kenneth Rogoff

4. HANDBOOK OF PUBLIC ECONOMICS (in 4 volumes)
    Volumes 1, 2 and 3 edited by Alan J. Auerbach and Martin Feldstein
    Volume 4 is in preparation (editors Alan J. Auerbach and Martin Feldstein)

5. HANDBOOK OF LABOR ECONOMICS (in 5 volumes)
    Volumes 1 and 2 edited by Orley C. Ashenfelter and Richard Layard
    Volumes 3A, 3B and 3C edited by Orley C. Ashenfelter and David Card

6. HANDBOOK OF NATURAL RESOURCE AND ENERGY ECONOMICS
    (in 3 volumes). Edited by Allen V. Kneese and James L. Sweeney

7. HANDBOOK OF REGIONAL AND URBAN ECONOMICS (in 4 volumes)
    Volume 1 edited by Peter Nijkamp
    Volume 2 edited by Edwin S. Mills
    Volume 3 edited by Paul C. Cheshire and Edwin S. Mills
    Volume 4 is in preparation (editors J. Vernon Henderson and Jacques-François Thisse)

8. HANDBOOK OF MONETARY ECONOMICS (in 2 volumes)
    Edited by Benjamin Friedman and Frank Hahn

9. HANDBOOK OF DEVELOPMENT ECONOMICS (in 4 volumes)
    Volumes 1 and 2 edited by Hollis B. Chenery and T.N. Srinivasan
    Volumes 3A and 3B edited by Jere Behrman and T.N. Srinivasan

10. HANDBOOK OF INDUSTRIAL ORGANIZATION (in 3 volumes)
    Volumes 1 and 2 edited by Richard Schmalensee and Robert R. Willig
    Volume 3 is in preparation (editors Mark Armstrong and Robert H. Porter)

FORTHCOMING TITLES

HANDBOOK OF LAW AND ECONOMICS
Editors A. Mitchell Polinsky and Steven Shavell

All published volumes available